READINGS

FOR AN Introduction to psychology

RICHARD A. KING

McGRAW-HILL Book Company, Inc.
New York   Toronto   London

READINGS

FOR AN Introduction
to psychology

READINGS

FOR AN Introduction to psychology

RICHARD A. KING

University of North Carolina

RICHARD A. KING

McGRAW-HILL Book Company, Inc.

New York   Toronto   London

1961

Preface

The editor of a reading book is always faced with the problem of establishing criteria for the selection of material from the plethora which faces him. This problem has not been fully resolved, but here are some of the guidelines which were used in assembling these readings:

1. The excerpts should be largely empirical, as opposed to speculative or theoretical. This book is intended for college students who are being exposed to psychology as a formal science for the first time, and it is impossible for anyone to evaluate theory without some facts. A theoretical article may be included if its author has substantiated his ideas with observations. It is hoped that the inclusion of such articles will help to correct the stereotyped misconception held by some students that psychology is a nonempirical, "talking" discipline.

2. Psychological jargon should be at a minimum. The articles should be in English which most college students can understand—with some effort and appropriate aids, e.g., dictionaries. Some excerpting should be done to aid the student.

3. In so far as possible, a good many classics should be included. It is difficult to define a "classic," but for practical purposes, let us say that this term, as used here and as applied by a substantial majority of psychologists, means a book or an article of definitive historical importance. The inclusion of some classics in this book should be of help, both in the small school with limited library facilities and in the university with very large sections of the introductory class.

4. The articles should have some intrinsic interest for the student. Of necessity, some articles meet this criterion much better than others.

5. Finally, the selection of material should be guided by the fact that this book is primarily intended to accompany the second edition of Clifford T. Morgan's *Introduction to Psychology*. The articles should enlarge upon points in the text, but the choice should not be so narrow as to limit, or restrict, the scope and value of the readings as a whole. The selections should cover enough common ground to fit in with any standard general psychology text.

All the articles do not, of course, meet all the requirements, but a sufficient number meet most of them to make the book useful in all introductory psychology courses, and especially useful (1) as a stimulus in discussion sections, (2) for the 5 to 10 per cent of students who become psychology majors (exposure to the material presented here should give them a head start), and (3) in colleges with small libraries, or in universities with large sections of the introductory class.

The editor is especially grateful to the authors whose works have been reprinted here. He also wishes to thank the American Psychological Association, *Science*, and the McGraw-Hill Book Company, Inc., for permission to reprint many excerpts. His colleagues at the University of North Carolina, especially Samuel Fillenbaum, Eugene R. Long, Harold G. McCurdy, and John W. Thibaut, gave valuable suggestions. The final preparation of this book was materially aided by the skillful secretarial work of Ann Cone, Blanche Critcher, Ann Boneau, Margaret King, and Stephanie Portman.

RICHARD A. KING

Contents

READINGS
FOR AN Introduction
to psychology

CHAPTER ONE

The science of psychology

THE FIELD OF PSYCHOLOGY

Psychologists do many things. This article talks about four major areas of endeavor: statistics and measurement, experimental and theoretical psychology, clinical psychology, and social psychology. The psychologists in these areas are interested, from different points of view, in describing or explaining behavior. Within each area there are subareas. You will be introduced to many of these during the course.

Some of the humor in the following article is professional in nature and you won't understand it all, but it should leave you with a more or less correct impression of the major current fields of psychology.

Points to guide your study

1. Try to understand as many of the professional jokes as possible. Consult your text for help.

2. On what continents would you find the schools of psychology mentioned in your text?

1. PSYCHOLOGY IN SPACE—A METAPHOR

*Thomas G. Andrews, University of Maryland**

American psychologists have traveled in many countries over the world, have crossed both oceans several times, and have been behind the iron curtain. Most of these visits have been brief, and some countries we have seen only from the vantage point of the bar at the airport or by listening to the people in a conference room or a night club. We know that brief visits as tourists tend nevertheless to make us *experts* on the land and the people of foreign countries, however brief our visits and biased our sources of information.

I ask that you go on such a trip with me—a space trip to the planet *Psychology*. We will touch down at a few places, have a few conversations, drink with the natives, admire their scenery, and in this way be able to do the super-

ficial expertizing of the typical American tourist. In the interests of time we will not be able to explore very deeply but will gather large sweeping impressions like true tourists.

Our travel folders tell us that the economic geography of this planet *Psychology* is especially interesting to interdisciplinary space travelers. This world contains four major continents. They are named in turn: *Sigma, Lab, Klinikos,* and *Socio.* The inhabitants of this planet look very much alike, so we will have to be very careful in addressing the natives for fear we insult them by misplacing their places of origin and primary loyalties.

As we tour these four continents we will visit briefly a few selected countries and try to get a quick picture of their fauna, resources, politics, and power centers. As we go from one place to another we will naturally find some underdeveloped lands, some places that are even deliciously dangerous, and of course we may expect certain difficulties with some of the immigration officers who may give us trouble over our visas. Even with these expected irritations of foreign travel, I hope that you will find the trip interesting and will want to revisit some of the

* This article is, with minor modifications, the Presidential address delivered to the Maryland Psychological Association in 1958.

T. G. Andrews, Psychology in space—a metaphor. *Amer. Psychologist,* 1959, **14,** 684–686. Copyright 1959 by the American Psychological Association. Reprinted here with permission from the author and the American Psychological Association.

out-of-the-way places again, not as tourists but as explorers.

We land first on the continent *Sigma*. This is a land of quantitative enterprise. Our guidebook shows that there are three major nations on this continent: *Statistics*, *Personnel*, and *Measurement*. The continent has tremendous natural resources, and these are exported rather freely and with great pride of craftsmanship. An embargo is placed on the best exports, however, unless the consumer countries guarantee to maintain certain standards in their use and to order the materials properly with careful advance planning.

In the big production centers we find many launching pads for cargo spaceships to travel even to other planets in the delivery of loads of tests, equations, and personnel assessment systems. The people of this continent *Sigma* seem to travel rather widely in their own continent and very often go to other continents for long periods. Some of them never return, and it is felt in the government circles that these technicians have defected or have been captured and become slaves in other continents, forced to work on local endeavors.

The government soon learned that this technique made for a good economic balance, and so visitors from the distant planet *Math* sometimes find themselves lured into traps by the fascinating and seductive charms of the local endeavors on *Sigma*. These slaves are happy and contented people, but they are carefully guarded. There are even some legendary captives about whom ballads are sung, such as Spearman, Thurstone, and Mosier.

It is not difficult to obtain a visa to enjoy the countries of *Statistics* and *Measurement*, but it is very difficult to get a work permit in either. There is a rumor that for anyone from elsewhere on the planet to get a work permit he has to be brainwashed to forget all of the Psychology he might have learned. This is not really true, although it is very easy to understand how the rumor got started on the planet. If such brainwashing were true, then of course about all these people could do would be to become department chairmen or deans.

The nation of *Personnel* has no immigration officers, and visitors often find such comforts in its pleasant climate and lush gardens that they stay for long periods. Some of them retire there —early in life. Occasionally the natives will drift across the border to *Measurement* to refreshen certain of their supplies. The economy in *Personnel* is rather an unstable one because it imports much more than it exports, and the port authorities have permitted large stocks of useless merchandise to pile up in the warehouses. In the old days the nation *Personnel* depended for its imports on its neighboring countries on the same continent *Sigma*. It has more recently found great use for imports from the continents of *Socio* and *Klinikos*. There is an occasional fear expressed that the country has run up such a debt to these sources that *Socio* and *Klinikos* may swallow it up in their axis.

Our time is too short to push back into the underdeveloped areas on this continent of *Sigma*. Also we run the risk of losing some of our tour members who may be brainwashed and become statisticians or fall into the traps of the test builders. Of course, this is just rumor, but one cannot be too careful.

We will leave our spaceship behind and take a regularly scheduled flight to the next continent on our itinerary—*Lab*. This is a very intriguing continent, made up loosely of a large number of countries or baronial states of Experimental and Theoretical Psychology. This is the oldest inhabited continent on the planet, and it takes its seniority very seriously. It has a central government that is a very strong oligarchy. A new central government palace is being planned, and the leaders are reported to be in great debate over the style of architecture to be employed. Some are demanding that it be in the classical shape of an Ivory Tower, but there is a rapidly growing faction that is holding out for a Skinner Box.

As we debark on the continent *Lab* we are met by some rather suspicious immigration officers who check our visas very carefully. Those of us who are allowed to go on further find certain delights in this place. The people are all very busy, and they seem somewhat preoccupied and detached. In one of the states we find animals dominating the activity of automated recording systems. There are large supplies of II and VIII nerves lying about. In one place we find the natives working mainly with chalk boards and reams of paper. These latter are theoreticians and are catered to as high priests.

Only a few of the natives seem much interested in the large planetary affairs. However, there is a real spirit of cohesiveness and common purpose among these indigenous people. We learn that this spirit is especially noticeable when there is a planetary congress. The representatives from this continent *Lab* prefer a separate area for their own affairs at which they cavort with glee. There is a persistent but false rumor that the continent has expressed a desire to secede from the planetary congress. The trade of this continent is very active. There is no embargo on exports, and there is a great deal of pride on the part of the artisans in the way in which they shape their products for sheer beauty, although less for utility. Imports are from other planets of *Math*, *Physics*, and *Physiology* and some from the continent *Sigma*. The younger generation here is learning to check the lists of available stock from the continents of *Socio* and *Klinikos*.

When they are able to smuggle a good hypothesis in from these continents, they develop it well; but the old guard tends to frown on this smuggling activity. Some of the younger generation have been taking extended excursions into other lands, where they are always in demand; and they have no trouble getting visas and work permits wherever they go.

As we leave the brassy shores of the continent *Lab* we start out for the next continent *Klinikos*, a very great distance away. We have time to study our guidebooks, and we find that this continent is the largest one on the planet. It is made up of several nations: *Clinical, Counseling, Child, Developmental,* and *School Psychology,* and *Personality.* Even in these highly civilized nations, there are very large areas of undeveloped land. The natives greet us with warmth and friendship.They seem to be exceedingly interested in us as individuals, although they seem to disagree markedly in their interpretations of our behavior.

The history of this continent is particularly interesting. It has developed very rapidly, and its rate of population increase has been amazing compared to the other continents on the planet. There is some concern on the part of the other continents that its representation in the planetary congress is growing too rapidly. There are occasional interplanetary skirmishes that are engaged in by war lords on this continent of *Klinikos*, especially with the continent *Psyche* on the neighboring planet *Medic.* The planetary congress on *Psychology* devotes considerable time to strategy and tactics in helping this continent *Klinikos* in these battles. In recent years the production centers on *Klinikos* have dredged great stores of gold from the mines in the areas of *Hew* and *Usphus* to develop their natural resources, and in general the natives fare rather well with their conditions of life.

The boundaries between the separate states on this continent are not well marked, and often it is difficult for visitors and natives alike to tell just exactly where they are. The fields are green, and the flowers are sweet smelling, however, so getting lost here is not at all unpleasant—except possibly for a few visitors from *Lab* who come over on brief inspection trips and on occasional political skirmishes. Some of these visitors are attracted to stay, however, and they find that they can lead very productive lives here.

Our time is running out, and we have one continent left. This is the continent *Socio.* Our visit there must be very brief for us to get back on schedule. On arrival here we are met by natives in groups. They are very pleasant and helpful, but we cannot seem to learn as much about them as we would like in the short time we have. They are very busy and seem to be involved in activities that require them to work together a great deal. The continent here is rather unified, and there are no boundaries and so no problems with visas and work permits. They import freely from the other three continents and also other planets. Some of the local continents have expressed the wish that the continent *Socio* would buy more locally. We get the impression that our traveling group is being studied rather carefully by the natives, and so we stay on our best behavior even while we are partaking of their fruits and beverages. As good space travelers, we asked the natives of *Socio* to take us to their leader. This threw them into confusion and provoked a long discussion of the meaning of the term. We concluded that they did not have any real leaders because they all disagreed on what the term means. We apologize for the necessity of our very brief stay and return to our spaceship pad to blast off for *Earth.*

As we rise slowly on our first-stage power we look back at the planet *Psychology* and see it revolving slowly as it recedes from us, much like the over-all impression one gets from flying away from the island of Bermuda and looking back to see the spaces of land and waterways all at once. Our earlier impression is confirmed: that the oceans between the continents on this planet *Psychology* are far too big and, also, that the underdeveloped parts of all of the four continents stretch out in tremendous size, beckoning for explorers.

Our trip has been very brief, but like American tourists we have gathered snatches of impressions here and there and are now experts on matters pertaining to the planet we have seen and walked on so briefly. I leave it to you to judge whether the impressions I have related are all superficial ones made in the role of a typical American tourist or whether any of them gets close to reality. If your collective leg has been pulled by this travelog, just how much?

Methods of Observation

Theory is a scientific shorthand, a predictor, and a guide to research. These are the major ways in which theory is used in psychology. The theories which have the three characteristics mentioned above, are sometimes called hypothetico-deductive theories. They have been quite useful in physics. These theories start with some general guesses as to the laws relating independent and dependent variables. (By now you should know what these are.) These guesses are the postulates of the theory, or the axioms. From the postulates, one then deduces, according to certain "guessed-at" rules, the consequences. Finally, the theorist can become an experimenter or observer and can look, do experiments, or make observations to see if the consequences are as predicted by the theory. If the consequences are as predicted, he then has more assurance that his original "guessed-at" postulates and rules of derivation are correct. This selection is taken from the opening chapter of a book in which a hypothetico-deductive theory of behavior is presented.

C. L. Hull has been an influential figure in American psychology. He might be classed by some as a functionalist, but he belongs more nearly to the behaviorist offshoot of functionalism (see your text). He is sometimes said to be a member, along with K. W. Spence and B. F. Skinner, of the neobehaviorist school, the behaviorists after J. B. Watson. His emphasis on hypothetico-deductive theory in psychology, and the appearance of rigor which his theories presented, made him quite appealing to the more "tough-minded" psychologists of the 1930s and 1940s.

Points to guide your study

1. How does the discussion of the spherical nature of planets illustrate the hypothetico-deductive method?

2. Can you think of examples of hypothetico-deductive theories in other sciences with which you are familiar?

2. PRINCIPLES OF BEHAVIOR
C. L. Hull*

The two aspects of science: empirical and explanatory

Men are ever engaged in the dual activity of making observations and then seeking explanations of the resulting revelations. All normal men in all times have observed the rising and setting of the sun and the several phases of the moon. The more thoughtful among them have then proceeded to ask the question, "Why? Why does the moon wax and wane? Why does the sun rise and set, and where does it go when

it sets?" Here we have the two essential elements of modern science: the making of observations constitutes the empirical or factual component, and the systematic attempt to explain these facts constitutes the theoretical component. As science has developed, specialization, or division of labor, has occurred; some men have devoted their time mainly to the making of observations, while a smaller number have occupied themselves largely with the problems of explanation.

During the infancy of science, observations are for the most part casual and qualitative— the sun rises, beats down strongly at midday, and sets; the moon grows from the crescent to full and then diminishes. Later observations, usually motivated by practical considerations of

* C. L. Hull. *Principles of behavior.* New York: D. Appleton-Century Co., Inc., 1943. Copyright 1943 by Appleton-Century-Crofts, Inc. Excerpts reprinted here with permission from D. Appleton-Century Co., Inc. The references have been deleted.

one kind or another, tend to become quantitative and precise—the number of days in the moon's monthly cycle are counted accurately, and the duration of the sun's yearly course is determined with precision. As the need for more exact observations increases, special tools and instruments, such as graduated measuring sticks, protractors, clocks, telescopes, and microscopes, are devised to facilitate the labor. Kindred tools relating to a given field of science are frequently assembled under a single roof for convenience of use; such an assemblage becomes a laboratory.

As scientific investigations become more and more searching it is discovered that the spontaneous happenings of nature are not adequate to permit the necessary observations. This leads to the setting up of special conditions which will bring about the desired events under circumstances favorable for such observations; thus experiments originate. But even in deliberate experiment it is often extraordinarily difficult to determine with which among a complex of antecedent conditions a given consequence is primarily associated; in this way arise a complex maze of control experiments and other technical procedures, the general principles of which are common to all sciences but the details of which are peculiar to each. Thus in brief review we see the characteristic technical development of the empirical or factual aspect of science.

Complex and difficult as are some of the problems of empirical science, those of scientific theory are perhaps even more difficult of solution and are subject to a greater hazard of error. It is not a matter of chance that the waxing and waning of the moon was observed for countless millennia before the comparatively recent times when it was at last successfully explained on the basis of the Copernican hypothesis. Closely paralleling the development of the technical aids employed by empirical science, there have also grown up in the field of scientific theory a complex array of tools and special procedures, mostly mathematical and logical in nature, designed to aid in coping with these difficulties. Because of the elementary nature of the present treatise, very little explicit discussion of the use of such tools will be given.

The deductive nature of scientific theory and explanation

The term *theory* in the behavioral or "social" sciences has a variety of current meanings. As understood in the present work, a theory is a systematic deductive derivation of the secondary principles of observable phenomena from a relatively small number of primary principles or postulates, much as the secondary principles or theorems of geometry are all ultimately derived as a logical hierarchy from a few original definitions and primary principles called axioms. In science an observed event is said to be explained when the proposition expressing it has been logically derived from a set of definitions and postulates coupled with certain observed conditions antecedent to the event. This, in brief, is the nature of scientific theory and explanation as generally understood and accepted in the physical sciences after centuries of successful development.

The preceding summary statement of the nature of scientific theory and explanation needs considerable elaboration and exemplification. Unfortunately the finding of generally intelligible examples presents serious difficulties; because of the extreme youth of systematic behavior theory as here understood, it is impossible safely to assume that the reader possesses any considerable familiarity with it. For this reason it will be necessary to choose all the examples from such physical sciences as are now commonly taught in the schools.

We can best begin the detailed consideration of the nature of scientific explanation by distinguishing it from something often confused with it. Suppose a naïve person with a moderate-sized telescope has observed Venus, Mars, Jupiter, and Saturn, together with numerous moons (including our own), and found them all to be round in contour and presumably spherical in form. He might proceed to formulate his observations in a statement such as, "All heavenly bodies are spherical," even though this statement goes far beyond the observations, since he has examined only a small sample of these bodies. Suppose, next, he secures a better telescope; he is now able to observe Uranus and Neptune, and finds both round in contour also. He may, in a manner of speaking, be said to explain the sphericity of Neptune by subsuming it under the category of heavenly bodies and then applying his previous empirical generalization. Indeed, he could have predicted the spherical nature of Neptune by this procedure before it was observed at all:

> All heavenly bodies are spherical.
> Neptune is a heavenly body,
> Therefore Neptune is spherical.

Much of what is loosely called explanation in the field of behavior is of this nature. The fighting propensities of a chicken are explained by the fact that he is a game cock and game cocks are empirically known to be pugnacious. The gregariousness of a group of animals is explained by the fact that the animals in question are dogs, and dogs are empirically known to be gregarious. As we have seen, it is possible to make concrete predictions of a sort on the basis of such generalizations, and so they have significance. Nevertheless this kind of procedure—the subsumption of a particular set of conditions under a category involved in a previously made empirical generalization—is not exactly what is regarded here as a scientific theoretical explanation.

For one thing, a theoretical explanation as here understood grows out of a problem, e.g., "What must be the shape of the heavenly bodies?" Secondly, it sets out from certain propositions or statements. These propositions are of two rather different kinds. Propositions of the first type required by an explanation are those stating the relevant initial or *antecedent conditions*. For example, an explanation of the shape of heavenly bodies might require the preliminary assumption of the existence of (1) a large mass of (2) more or less plastic, (3) more or less homogeneous matter, (4) initially of any shape at all, (5) the whole located in otherwise empty space. But a statement of the antecedent conditions is not enough; there must also be available a set of statements of *general principles* or rules of action relevant to the situation. Moreover, the particular principles to be utilized in a given explanation must be chosen from the set of principles generally employed by the theorist in explanations of this class of phenomena, the choice to be made strictly on the basis of the nature of the question or problem under consideration taken in conjunction with the observed or assumed conditions. For example, in the case of the shape of the heavenly bodies the chief principle employed is the Newtonian law of gravitation, namely, that every particle of matter attracts every other particle to a degree proportional to the product of their masses and inversely proportional to the square of the distances separating them. These principles are apt themselves to be verbal formulations of empirical generalizations, but may be merely happy conjectures or guesses found by a certain amount of antecedent trial-and-error to agree with observed fact. At all events they originate in one way or another in empirical observation.

The concluding phase of a scientific explanation is the derivation of the answer to the motivating question from the conditions and the principles, taken jointly, by a process of inference or reasoning. For example, it follows from the principle of gravitation that empty spaces which might at any time have existed within the mass of a heavenly body would at once be closed. Moreover, if at any point on the surface there were an elevation and adjacent to it a depression or valley, the sum of the gravitational pressures of the particles of matter in the elevation acting on the plastic material beneath would exert substantially the same pressure laterally as toward the center of gravity. But since there would be no equal lateral pressure originating in the valley to oppose the pressure originating in the elevation, the matter contained in the elevation would flow into the valley, thus eliminating

both. This means that in the course of time all the matter in the mass under consideration would be arranged about its center of gravity with no elevations or depressions; i.e., the radius of the body at all points would be the same. In other words, if the assumed mass were not already spherical it would in the course of time automatically become so. It follows that all heavenly bodies, including Neptune, must be spherical in form.

The significance of the existence of these two methods of arriving at a verbal formulation of the shape of the planet Neptune may now be stated. The critical characteristic of scientific theoretical explanation is that it reaches independently through a process of reasoning the same outcome with respect to (secondary) principles as is attained through the process of empirical generalization. Thus scientific theory may arrive at the general proposition, "All heavenly bodies of sufficient size, density, plasticity, and homogeneity are spherical," as a theorem, simply by means of a process of inference or deduction without any moons or planets having been observed at all. The fact that, in certain fields at least, practically the same statements or propositions can be attained quite independently by empirical methods as by theoretical procedures is of enormous importance for the development of science. For one thing, it makes possible the checking of results obtained by one method against those obtained by the other. It is a general assumption in scientific methodology that if everything entering into both procedures is correct, the statements yielded by them will never be in genuine conflict.

Summary

Modern science has two inseparable components—the empirical and the theoretical. The empirical component is concerned primarily with observation; the theoretical component is concerned with the interpretation and explanation of observation. A natural event is explained when it can be derived as a theorem by a process of reasoning from (1) a knowledge of the relevant natural conditions antedating it, and (2) one or more relevant principles called postulates. Clusters or families of theorems are generated, and theorems are often employed in the derivation of other theorems; thus is developed a logical hierarchy resembling that found in ordinary geometry. A hierarchy of interrelated families of theorems, all derived from the same set of consistent postulates, constitutes a scientific system.

Scientific theory resembles argumentation in being logical in nature but differs radically in that the objective of argument is to convince. In scientific theory logic is employed in conjunction with observation as a means of inquiry. Indeed, theoretical procedures are indispensable in the establishment of natural laws. The range of validity of a given supposed law can be determined only by trying it out empirically under a wide range of conditions where it will operate in simultaneous conjunction with the greatest variety and combination of other natural laws. But the only way the scientist can tell from the outcome of such an empirical procedure whether a given hypothetical law has acted in the postulated manner is first to deduce by a logical process what the outcome of the investigation *should* be if the hypothesis really holds. This deductive process is the essence of scientific theory.

The typical procedure in science is to adopt a postulate tentatively, deduce one or more of its logical implications concerning observable phenomena, and then check the validity of the deductions by observation. If the deduction is in genuine disagreement with observation, the postulate must be either abandoned or so modified that it implies no such conflicting statement. If, however, the deductions and the observations agree, the postulate gains in dependability. By successive agreements under a very wide variety of conditions it may attain a high degree of justified credibility, but never absolute certainty.

By no means would all psychologists hold that hypothetico-deductive theories are useful. Some would even say that, while in the advanced sciences such theories may be useful, we have not collected enough data in psychology to begin theorizing. Psychologists of this type often point to the painful accumulation of data which took place before the great theories in the physical sciences were formulated. Psychologists of this type, therefore, study phenomena of behavior for their own sake and let their observations lead them. (This is perhaps more in the tradition of the biological sciences.) One experimental outcome suggests the next experiment, while the outcome of this suggests the next experiment, etc. That this can be a fruitful strategy is shown by Skinner's article.

B. F. Skinner is the founder of a neobehavioristic school which puts special emphasis on the collection of data and the control of the behavior of individual organisms. The observations of this school have given rise to methodologies for assessing the effects of drugs on behavior, psychopharmacology, and for the teaching of school subjects, the "teaching machines." It is currently a vigorous movement in psychology.

Points to guide your study

1. Contrast Skinner's approach with that of Hull.

2. One of the important reasons for doing experiments is that this makes the control of variables possible. In what ways has Skinner attempted to achieve such control?

3. A CASE HISTORY IN SCIENTIFIC METHOD

B. F. Skinner, Harvard University*

It has been said that college teaching is the only profession for which there is no professional

* Address of the President at the Eastern Psychological Association meetings in Philadelphia, April, 1955.

B. F. Skinner. A case history in scientific method. *Amer. Psychologist*, 1956, **11**, 221–233. Copyright 1956 by the American Psychological Association. Reprinted here with permission from the author and the American Psychological Association.

training, and it is commonly argued that this is because our graduate schools train scholars and scientists rather than teachers. We are more concerned with the discovery of knowledge than with its dissemination. But can we justify ourselves quite so easily? It is a bold thing to say that we know how to train a man to be a scientist. Scientific thinking is the most complex and probably the most subtle of all human activities. Do we actually know how to shape up such behavior, or do we simply mean that some of the people who attend our graduate schools eventually become scientists?

Except for a laboratory course which acquaints the student with standard apparatus and standard procedures, the only explicit training in scientific method generally received by a young psychologist is a course in statistics—not the introductory course, which is often required of so many kinds of students that it is scarcely scientific at all, but an advanced course which includes "model building," "theory construction," and "experimental design." But it is a mistake to identify scientific practice with the formalized constructions of statistics and scientific method. These disciplines have their place, but it does not coincide with the place of scientific research. They offer *a* method of science but not, as is so often implied, *the* method. As formal disciplines they arose very late in the history of science, and most of the facts of science have been discovered without their aid. It takes a great deal of skill to fit Faraday with his wires and magnets into the picture which statistics gives us of scientific thinking. And most current scientific practice would be equally refractory, especially in the important initial stages. It is no wonder that the laboratory scientist is puzzled and often dismayed when he discovers how his behavior has been reconstructed in the formal analyses of scientific method. He is likely to protest that this is not at all a fair representation of what he does.

But his protest is not likely to be heard. For the prestige of statistics and scientific methodology is enormous. Much of it is borrowed from the high repute of mathematics and logic, but much of it derives from the flourishing state of the art itself. Some statisticians are professional people employed by scientific and commercial enterprises. Some are teachers and pure researchers who give their colleagues the same kind of service for nothing—or at most a note of acknowledgment. Many are zealous people who, with the best of intentions, are anxious to show the nonstatistical scientist how he can do his job more efficiently and assess his results more accurately. There are strong professional societies devoted to the advancement of statistics, and hundreds of technical books and journals are published annually.

Against this, the practicing scientist has very little to offer. He cannot refer the young psychologist to a book which will tell him how to find out all there is to know about a subject matter, how to have the good hunch which will lead him to devise a suitable piece of apparatus, how to develop an efficient experimental routine, how to abandon an unprofitable line of attack, how to move on most rapidly to later stages of his research. The work habits which have become second nature to him have not been formalized by anyone, and he may feel that they possibly never will be. As Richter (5) has pointed out, "Some of the most important discoveries have been made without any plan of research," and "there are researchers who do not work on a verbal plane, who cannot put into words what they are doing."

If we are interested in perpetuating the practices responsible for the present corpus of scientific knowledge, we must keep in mind that some very important parts of the scientific process do not now lend themselves to mathematical, logical, or any other formal treatment. We do not know enough about human behavior to know how the scientist does what he does. Although statisticians and methodologists may seem to tell us, or at least imply, how the mind works—how problems arise, how hypotheses are formed, deductions made, and crucial experiments designed—we as psychologists are in a position to remind them that they do not have methods appropriate to the empirical observation or the functional analysis of such data. These are aspects of human behavior, and no one knows better than we how little can at the moment be said about them.

Some day we shall be better able to express the distinction between empirical analysis and formal reconstruction, for we shall have an alternative account of the behavior of Man Thinking. Such an account will not only plausibly reconstruct what a particular scientist did in any given case, it will permit us to evaluate practices and, I believe, to teach scientific thinking. But that day is some little distance in the future. Meanwhile we can only fall back on examples.

Some time ago the director of Project A of the American Psychological Association asked me to describe my activities as a research psychologist. I went through a trunkful of old notes and records and, for my pains, reread some of my earlier publications. This has made me all the more aware of the contrast between the reconstructions of formalized scientific method and at least one case of actual practice. Instead of amplifying the points I have just made by resorting to a generalized account which is not available, I should like to discuss a case history. It is not one of the case histories we should most like to have, but what it lacks in importance is perhaps somewhat offset by accessibility. I therefore ask you to imagine that you are all clinical psychologists—a task which becomes easier and easier as the years go by—while I sit across the desk from you or stretch out upon this comfortable leather couch.

The first thing I can remember happened

when I was only twenty-two years old. Shortly after I had graduated from college Bertrand Russell published a series of articles in the old *Dial* magazine on the epistemology of John B. Watson's Behaviorism. I had had no psychology as an undergraduate but I had had a lot of biology, and two of the books which my biology professor had put into my hands were Loeb's *Physiology of the Brain* and the newly published Oxford edition of Pavlov's *Conditioned Reflexes*. And now here was Russell extrapolating the principles of an objective formulation of behavior to the problem of knowledge! Many years later when I told Lord Russell that his articles were responsible for my interest in behavior, he could only exclaim, "Good Heavens! I had always supposed that those articles had demolished Behaviorism!" But at any rate he had taken Watson seriously, and so did I.

When I arrived at Harvard for graduate study, the air was not exactly full of behavior, but Walter Hunter was coming in once a week from Clark University to give a seminar, and Fred Keller, also a graduate student, was an expert in both the technical details and the sophistry of Behaviorism. Many a time he saved me as I sank into the quicksands of an amateurish discussion of "What is an image?" or "Where is red?" I soon came into contact with W. J. Crozier, who had studied under Loeb. It had been said of Loeb, and might have been said of Crozier, that he "resented the nervous system." Whether this was true or not, the fact was that both these men talked about animal behavior without mentioning the nervous system and with surprising success. So far as I was concerned, they cancelled out the physiological theorizing of Pavlov and Sherrington and thus clarified what remained of the work of these men as the beginnings of an independent science of behavior. My doctoral thesis was in part an operational analysis of Sherrington's synapse, in which behavioral laws were substituted for supposed states of the central nervous system.

But the part of my thesis at issue here was experimental. So far as I can see, I began simply by looking for lawful processes in the behavior of the intact organism. Pavlov had shown the way; but I could not then, as I cannot now, move without a jolt from salivary reflexes to the important business of the organism in everyday life. Sherrington and Magnus had found order in surgical segments of the organism. Could not something of the same sort be found, to use Loeb's phrase, in "the organism as a whole"? I had the clue from Pavlov: control your conditions and you will see order.

It is not surprising that my first gadget was a silent release box, operated by compressed air and designed to eliminate disturbances when

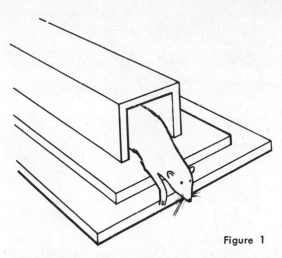

Figure 1

introducing a rat into an apparatus. I used this first in studying the way a rat adapted to a novel stimulus. I built a soundproof box containing a specially structured space. A rat was released, pneumatically, at the far end of a darkened tunnel from which it emerged in exploratory fashion into a well-lighted area. To accentuate its progress and to facilitate recording, the tunnel was placed at the top of a flight of steps, something like a functional Parthenon (Figure 1). The rat would peek out from the tunnel, perhaps glancing suspiciously at the one-way window through which I was watching it, then stretch itself cautiously down the steps. A soft click (carefully calibrated, of course) would cause it to pull back into the tunnel and remain there for some time. But repeated clicks had less and less of an effect. I recorded the rat's advances and retreats by moving a pen back and forth across a moving paper tape.

The major result of this experiment was that some of my rats had babies. I began to watch young rats. I saw them right themselves and crawl about very much like the decerebrate or thalamic cats and rabbits of Magnus. So I set about studying the postural reflexes of young rats. Here was a first principle not formally recognized by scientific methodologists: When you run onto something interesting, drop everything else and study it. I tore up the Parthenon and started over.

If you hold a young rat in one hand and pull it gently by the tail, it will resist you by pulling forward and then, with a sudden sharp spring which usually disengages its tail, it will leap out into space. I decided to study this behavior quantitatively. I built a light platform covered with cloth and mounted it on tightly stretched piano wires (Figure 2). Here was a version of Sherrington's torsion-wire myograph, originally designed to record the isometric contraction of

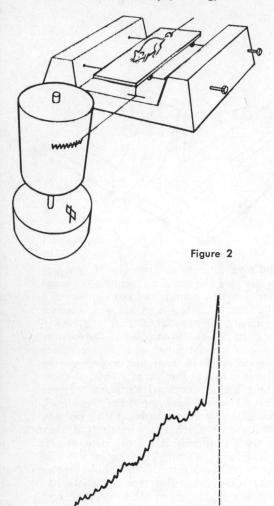

Figure 2

Figure 3

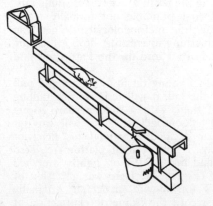

Figure 4

the *tibialis anticus* of a cat, but here adapted to the response of a whole organism. When the tail of the young rat was gently pulled, the rat clung to the cloth floor and tugged forward. By amplifying the fine movements of the platform, it was possible to get a good kymograph record of the tremor in this motion and then, as the pull against the tail was increased, of the desperate spring into the air (Figure 3).

Now, baby rats have very little future, except as adult rats. Their behavior is literally infantile and cannot be usefully extrapolated to everyday life. But if this technique would work with a baby, why not try it on a mature rat? To avoid attaching anything to the rat, it should be possible to record, not a pull against the substrate, but the ballistic thrust exerted as the rat runs forward or suddenly stops in response to my calibrated click. So, invoking the first principle of scientific practice again, I threw away the piano-wire platform, and built a runway, eight feet long. This was constructed of light wood, in the form of a girder, mounted rigidly on vertical glass plates, the elasticity of which permitted a very slight longitudinal movement (Figure 4). The runway became the floor of a long tunnel, not shown, at one end of which I placed my soundless release box and at the other end myself, prepared to reinforce the rat for coming down the runway by giving it a bit of wet mash, to sound a click from time to time when it had reached the middle of the runway, and to harvest kymograph records of the vibrations of the substrate.

Now for a second unformalized principle of scientific practice: Some ways of doing research are easier than others. I got tired of carrying the rat back to the other end of the runway. A back alley was therefore added (Figure 5). Now the rat could eat a bit of mash at point C, go down the back alley A, around the end as shown, and back home by runway B. The experimenter at E could collect records from the kymograph at D in comfort. In this way a great many records were made of the forces exerted against the substratum as rats ran down the alley and occasionally stopped dead in their tracks as a click sounded (Figure 6).

There was one annoying detail, however. The rat would often wait an inordinately long time at C before starting down the back alley on the next run. There seemed to be no explanation for this. When I timed these delays with a stop watch, however, and plotted them, they seemed to show orderly changes (Figure 7). This was, of course, the kind of thing I was looking for. I forgot all about the movements of the substratum and began to run rats for the sake of the delay measurements alone. But there was now no reason why the runway had to be eight feet long and, as the second principle came into play again, I saw no reason why the rat could not deliver its own reinforcement.

A new apparatus was built. In Figure 8, we see the rat eating a piece of food just after completing a run. It produced the food by its own action. As it ran down the back alley A to the far end of the rectangular runway, its weight caused the whole runway to tilt slightly on the axis C and this movement turned the wooden disc D, permitting a piece of food in one of the holes around its perimeter to drop through a funnel into a food dish. The food was pearl barley, the only kind I could find in the grocery stores in reasonably uniform pieces. The rat had only to complete its journey by coming down the home stretch B to enjoy its reward. The experimenter was able to enjoy *his* reward at the same time, for he had only to load the magazine, put in a rat, and relax. Each tilt was recorded on a slowly moving kymograph.

A third unformalized principle of scientific practice: Some people are lucky. The disc of wood from which I had fashioned the food magazine was taken from a storeroom of discarded apparatus. It happened to have a central spindle, which fortunately I had not bothered to cut off. One day it occurred to me that if I wound a string around the spindle and allowed it to unwind as the magazine was emptied (Figure 9), I would get a different kind of record. Instead of a mere report of the up-and-down movement of the runway, as a series of pips as in a polygraph, I would get a *curve*. And I knew that science made great use of curves, although, so far as I could discover, very little of pips on a polygram. The difference between the old type of record at A (Figure 10) and the new at B may not seem great, but as it turned out the curve revealed things in the rate of responding, and in changes in that rate, which would certainly otherwise have been missed. By allowing the string to unwind rather than to wind, I had got my curve in an awkward Cartesian quadrant, but that was easily remedied. Psychologists have adopted cumulative curves only very slowly, but I think it is fair to say that they have become an indispensable tool for certain purposes of analysis.

Eventually, of course, the runway was seen to be unnecessary. The rat could simply reach into a covered tray for pieces of food, and each movement of the cover could operate a solenoid to move a pen one step in a cumulative curve. The first major change in rate observed in this way was due to ingestion. Curves showing how the rate of eating declined with the time of eating comprised the other part of my thesis. But a refinement was needed. The behavior of the rat in pushing open the door was not a normal part of the ingestive behavior of *Rattus rattus*. The act was obviously learned but its status as

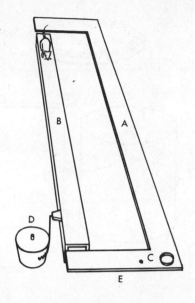

Figure 5

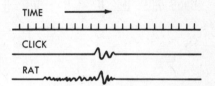

Figure 6

Figure 7

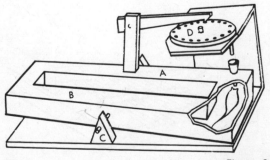

Figure 8

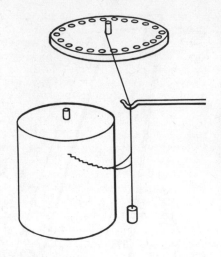

Figure 9

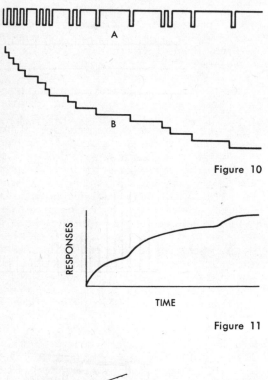

Figure 10

Figure 11

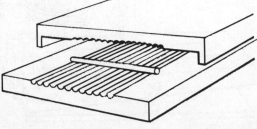

Figure 12

part of the final performance was not clear. It seemed wise to add an initial conditioned response connected with ingestion in a quite arbitrary way. I chose the first device which came to hand—a horizontal bar or lever placed where it could be conveniently depressed by the rat to close a switch which operated a magnetic magazine. Ingestion curves obtained with this initial response in the chain were found to have the same properties as those without it.

Now, as soon as you begin to complicate an apparatus, you necessarily invoke a fourth principle of scientific practice: Apparatuses sometimes break down. I had only to wait for the food magazine to jam to get an extinction curve. At first I treated this as a defect and hastened to remedy the difficulty. But eventually, of course, I deliberately disconnected the magazine. I can easily recall the excitement of that first complete extinction curve (Figure 11). I had made contact with Pavlov at last! Here was a curve uncorrupted by the physiological process of ingestion. It was an orderly change due to nothing more than a special contingency of reinforcement. It was pure behavior! I am not saying that I would not have got around to extinction curves without a breakdown in the apparatus; Pavlov had given too strong a lead in that direction. But it is still no exaggeration to say that some of the most interesting and surprising results have turned up first because of similar accidents. Foolproof apparatus is no doubt highly desirable, but Charles Ferster and I in recently reviewing the data from a five-year program of research found many occasions to congratulate ourselves on the fallibility of relays and vacuum tubes.

I then built four soundproof ventilated boxes, each containing a lever and a food magazine and supplied with a cumulative recorder, and was on my way to an intensive study of conditioned reflexes in skeletal behavior. I would reinforce every response for several days and then extinguish for a day or two, varying the number of reinforcements, the amount of previous magazine training, and so on.

At this point I made my first use of the deductive method. I had long since given up pearl barley as too unbalanced a diet for steady use. A neighborhood druggist had shown me his pill machine, and I had had one made along the same lines (Figure 12). It consisted of a fluted brass bed across which one laid a long cylinder of stiff paste (in my case a MacCollum formula for an adequate rat diet). A similarly fluted cutter was then lowered onto the cylinder and rolled slowly back and forth, converting the paste into about a dozen spherical pellets. These were dried for a day or so before use. The procedure was painstaking and laborious. Eight rats eating a hundred pellets each per day could easily keep up with production. One pleasant Saturday afternoon I surveyed my supply of dry pellets, and, appealing to certain elemental theorems in arithmetic, deduced that unless I spent the rest of that afternoon and evening at the pill machine, the supply would be exhausted by ten-thirty Monday morning.

Since I do not wish to deprecate the hypothetico-deductive method, I am glad to testify here to its usefulness. It led me to apply our second principle of unformalized scientific method and to ask myself why *every* press of the lever had to be reinforced. I was not then aware of what had happened at the Brown laboratories, as Harold Schlosberg later told the story. A graduate student had been given the task of running a cat through a difficult discrimination experiment. One Sunday the student found the supply of cat food exhausted. The stores were closed and so, with a beautiful faith in the frequency-theory of learning, he ran the cat as usual and took it back to its living cage unrewarded. Schlosberg reports that the cat howled its protest continuously for nearly forty-eight hours. Unaware of this I decided to reinforce a response only once every minute and to allow all other responses to go unreinforced. There were two results: (a) my supply of pellets lasted almost indefinitely and (b) each rat stabilized at a fairly constant rate of responding.

Now, a steady state was something I was familiar with from physical chemistry, and I therefore embarked upon the study of periodic reinforcement. I soon found that the constant rate at which the rat stabilized depended upon how hungry it was. Hungry rat, high rate; less hungry rat, lower rate. At that time I was bothered by the practical problem of controlling food deprivation. I was working half time at the Medical School (on chronaxie of subordination!) and could not maintain a good schedule in working with the rats. The rate of responding under periodic reinforcement suggested a scheme for keeping a rat at a constant level of deprivation. The argument went like this: Suppose you reinforce the rat, not at the end of a given period, but when it has completed the number of responses ordinarily emitted in that period. And suppose you use substantial pellets of food and give the rat continuous access to the lever. Then, except for periods when the rat sleeps, it should operate the lever at a constant rate around the clock. For, whenever it grows slightly hungrier, it will work faster, get food faster, and become less hungry, while whenever it grows slightly less hungry, it will respond at a lower rate, get less food, and grow hungrier. By setting the reinforcement at a given number of responses it should even be possible to hold the rat at any given level of deprivation. I visualized a machine with a dial which one could

set to make available, at any time of day or night, a rat in a given state of deprivation. Of course, nothing of the sort happens. This is "fixed-ratio" rather than "fixed-interval" reinforcement and, as I soon found out, it produces a very different type of performance. This is an example of a fifth unformalized principle of scientific practice, but one which has at least been named. Walter Cannon described it with a word invented by Horace Walpole: *serendipity*—the art of finding one thing while looking for something else.

This account of my scientific behavior up to the point at which I published my results in a book called *The Behavior of Organisms* is as exact in letter and spirit as I can now make it. The notes, data, and publications which I have examined do not show that I ever behaved in the manner of Man Thinking as described by John Stuart Mill or John Dewey or in reconstructions of scientific behavior by other philosophers of science. I never faced a Problem which was more than the eternal problem of finding order. I never attacked a problem by constructing a Hypothesis. I never deduced Theorems or submitted them to Experimental Check. So far as I can see, I had no preconceived Model of Behavior—certainly not a physiological or mentalistic one, and, I believe, not a conceptual one. The "reflex reserve" was an abortive, though operational, concept which was retracted a year or so after publication in a paper at the Philadelphia meeting of the APA. It lived up to my opinion of theories in general by proving utterly worthless in suggesting further experiments. Of course, I was working on a basic Assumption—that there was order in behavior if I could only discover it—but such an assumption is not to be confused with the hypotheses of deductive theory. It is also true that I exercised a certain Selection of Facts but not because of relevance to theory but because one fact was more orderly than another. If I engaged in Experimental Design at all, it was simply to complete or extend some evidence of order already observed.

Most of the experiments described in *The Behavior of Organisms* were done with groups of four rats. A fairly common reaction to the book was that such groups were too small. How did I know that other groups of four rats would do the same thing? Keller, in defending the book, countered with the charge that groups of four were too *big*. Unfortunately, however, I allowed myself to be persuaded of the contrary. This was due in part to my association at the University of Minnesota with W. T. Heron. Through him I came into close contact for the first time with traditional animal psychology. Heron was interested in inherited maze behavior, inherited activity, and certain drugs—the effects of which could then be detected only through the use of fairly large groups. We did an experiment together on the effect of starvation on the rate of pressing a lever and started the new era with a group of sixteen rats. But we had only four boxes, and this was so inconvenient that Heron applied for a grant and built a battery of twenty-four lever-boxes and cumulative recorders. I supplied an attachment which would record, not only the mean performance of all twenty-four rats in a single averaged curve, but mean curves for four subgroups of twelve rats each and four subgroups of six rats each (3). We thus provided for the design of experiments according to the principles of R. A. Fisher, which were then coming into vogue. We had, so to speak, mechanized the latin square.

With this apparatus Heron and I published a study of extinction in maze-bright and maze-dull rats using *ninety-five* subjects. Later I published mean extinction curves for groups of twenty-four, and W. K. Estes and I did our work on anxiety with groups of the same size. But although Heron and I could properly voice the hope that "the possibility of using large groups of animals greatly improves upon the method as previously reported, since tests of significance are provided for and properties of behavior not apparent in single cases may be more easily detected," in actual practice that is not what happened. The experiments I have just mentioned are almost all we have to show for this elaborate battery of boxes. Undoubtedly more work could be done with it and would have its place, but something had happened to the natural growth of the method. You cannot easily make a change in the conditions of an experiment when twenty-four apparatuses have to be altered. Any gain in rigor is more than matched by a loss in flexibility. We were forced to confine ourselves to processes which could be studied with the baselines already developed in earlier work. We could not move on to the discovery of other processes or even to a more refined analysis of those we were working with. No matter how significant might be the relations we actually demonstrated, our statistical Leviathan had swum aground. The art of the method had stuck at a particular stage of its development.

Another accident rescued me from mechanized statistics and brought me back to an even more intensive concentration on the single case. In essence, I suddenly found myself face to face with the engineering problem of the animal trainer. When you have the responsibility of making absolutely sure that a given organism will engage in a given sort of behavior at a given time, you quickly grow impatient with theories of learning. Principles, hypotheses, theorems, satisfactory proof at the .05 level of

significance that behavior at a choice point shows the effect of secondary reinforcement —nothing could be more irrelevant. No one goes to the circus to see the average dog jump through a hoop significantly oftener than untrained dogs raised under the same circumstances, or to see an elephant demonstrate a principle of behavior.

Perhaps I can illustrate this without giving aid and comfort to the enemy by describing a Russian device which the Germans found quite formidable. The Russians used dogs to blow up tanks. A dog was trained to hide behind a tree or wall in low brush or other cover. As a tank approached and passed, the dog ran swiftly alongside it, and a small magnetic mine attached to the dog's back was sufficient to cripple the tank or set it afire. The dog, of course, had to be replaced.

Now I ask you to consider some of the technical problems which the psychologist faces in preparing a dog for such an act of unintentional heroism. The dog must wait behind the tree for an indefinite length of time. Very well, it must therefore be intermittently reinforced for waiting. But what schedule will achieve the highest probability of waiting? If the reinforcement is to be food, what is the absolutely optimal schedule of deprivation consistent with the health of the dog? The dog must run to the tank—that can be arranged by reinforcing it with a practice tank—but it must start instantly if it is to overtake a swift tank, and how do you differentially reinforce short reaction times, especially in counteracting the reinforcement for sitting and waiting? The dog must react only to tanks, not to a refugee driving his oxcart along the road, but what are the defining properties of a tank so far as a dog is concerned?

I think it can be said that a functional analysis proved adequate in its technological application. Manipulation of environmental conditions alone made possible a wholly unexpected practical control. Behavior could be shaped up according to specifications and maintained indefinitely almost at will. One behavioral technologist who worked with me at the time (Keller Breland) is now specializing in the production of behavior as a salable commodity and has described this new profession in the *American Psychologist* (2).

There are many useful applications within psychology itself. Ratliff and Blough have recently conditioned pigeons to serve as psychophysical observers. In their experiment a pigeon may adjust one of two spots of light until the two are equally bright or it may hold a spot of light at the absolute threshold during dark adaptation. The techniques which they have developed to induce pigeons to do this are only indirectly related to the point of their experiments and hence exemplify the application of a behavioral science (4). The field in which a better technology of behavior is perhaps most urgently needed is education. I cannot describe here the applications which are now possible, but perhaps I can indicate my enthusiasm by hazarding the guess that educational techniques at all age levels are on the threshold of revolutionary changes.

The effect of a behavioral technology on scientific practice is the issue here. Faced with practical problems in behavior, you necessarily emphasize the refinement of *experimental* variables. As a result, some of the standard procedures of statistics appear to be circumvented. Let me illustrate. Suppose that measurements have been made on two groups of subjects differing in some detail of experimental treatment. Means and standard deviations for the two groups are determined, and any difference due to the treatment is evaluated. If the difference is in the expected direction but is not statistically significant, the almost universal recommendation would be to study larger groups. But our experience with practical control suggests that we may reduce the troublesome variability by changing the conditions of the experiment. By discovering, elaborating, and fully exploiting every relevant variable, we may eliminate *in advance of measurement* the individual differences which obscure the difference under analysis. This will achieve the same result as increasing the size of groups, and it will almost certainly yield a bonus in the discovery of new variables which would not have been identified in the statistical treatment.

The same may be said of smooth curves. In our study of anxiety, Estes and I published several curves, the reasonable smoothness of which was obtained by averaging the performances of 12 rats for each curve. The individual curves published at that time show that the mean curves do not faithfully represent the behavior of any one rat. They show a certain tendency toward a change in slope which supported the point we were making, and they may have appeared to justify averaging for that reason.

But an alternative method would have been to explore the individual case until an equally smooth curve could be obtained. This would have meant, not only rejecting the temptation to produce smoothness by averaging cases, but manipulating all relevant conditions as we later learned to manipulate them for practical purposes. The individual curves which we published at that time do not point to the need for larger groups but for improvement in experimental technique. Here, for example, is a curve the smoothness of which is characteristic of current practice. Such curves were shown in the making in a demonstration which Ferster and I

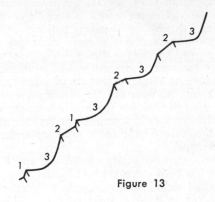

Figure 13

arranged at the Cleveland meeting of the American Psychological Association (Figure 13). Here, in a single organism, three different schedules of reinforcement are yielding corresponding performances with great uniformity under appropriate stimuli alternating at random. One does not reach this kind of order through the application of statistical methods.

In *The Behavior of Organisms* I was content to deal with the over-all slopes and curvature of cumulative curves and could make only a rough classification of the properties of behavior shown by the finer grain. The grain has now been improved. The resolving power of the microscope has been increased manyfold, and we can see fundamental processes of behavior in sharper and sharper detail. In choosing rate of responding as a basic datum and in recording this conveniently in a cumulative curve, we make important temporal aspects of behavior *visible*. Once this has happened, our scientific practice is reduced to simple looking. A new world is opened to inspection. We use such curves as we use a microscope, X-ray camera, or telescope. This is well exemplified by recent extensions of the method. These are no longer part of my case history, but perhaps you will permit me to consult you about what some critics have described as a *folie à deux* or group neurosis.

An early application of the method to the behavior of avoidance and escape was made by Keller in studying the light aversion of the rat. This was brilliantly extended by Murray Sidman in his shock-avoidance experiments. It is no longer necessary to describe avoidance and escape by appeal to "principles," for we may *watch* the behavior develop when we have arranged the proper contingencies of reinforcement, as we later watch it change as these contingencies are changed.

Hunt and Brady have extended the use of a stable rate in the study of anxiety-producing stimuli and have shown that the depression in rate is eliminated by electroconvulsive shock and by other measures which are effective in reducing anxiety in human patients. O. R. Lindsley has found the same thing for dogs, using insulin-shock therapy and sedatives. Brady has refined the method by exploring the relevance of various schedules of reinforcement in tracing the return of the conditioned depression after treatment. In these experiments you *see* the effect of a treatment as directly as you see the constriction of a capillary under the microscope.

Early work with rats on caffeine and Benzedrine has been extended by Lindsley with dogs. A special technique for evaluating several effects of a drug in a single short experimental period yields a record of behavior which can be read as a specialist reads an electrocardiogram. Dr. Peter Dews of the Department of Pharmacology at the Harvard Medical School is investigating dose-response curves and the types and effects of various drugs, using pigeons as subjects. In the Psychological Laboratories at Harvard additional work on drugs is being carried out by Morse, Herrnstein, and Marshall, and the technique is being adopted by drug manufacturers. There could scarcely be a better demonstration of the experimental treatment of variability. In a *single* experimental session with a *single* organism one observes the onset, duration, and decline of the effects of a drug.

The direct observation of *defective* behavior is particularly important. Clinical or experimental damage to an organism is characteristically unique. Hence the value of a method which permits the direct observation of the behavior of the individual. Lindsley has studied the effects of near-lethal irradiation, and the effects of prolonged anesthesia and anoxia are currently being examined by Thomas Lohr in cooperation with Dr. Henry Beecher of the Massachusetts General Hospital. The technique is being applied to neurological variables in the monkey by Dr. Karl Pribram at the Hartford Institute. The pattern of such research is simple: establish the behavior in which you are interested, submit the organism to a particular treatment, and then look again at the behavior. An excellent example of the use of experimental control in the study of *motivation* is some work on obesity by J. E. Anliker in collaboration with Dr. Jean Mayer of the Harvard School of Public Health, where abnormalities of ingestive behavior in several types of obese mice can be compared by direct inspection.

There is perhaps no field in which behavior is customarily described more indirectly than psychiatry. In an experiment at the Massachusetts State Hospital, under the sponsorship of Dr. Harry Solomon and myself, O. R. Lindsley is carrying out an extensive program which might be characterized as a quantitative study of the temporal properties of psychotic behavior. Here again it is a question of making certain characteristics of the behavior visible.

The extent to which we can eliminate sources of variability before measurement is shown by a result which has an unexpected significance for comparative psychology and the study of individual differences. Figure 14 shows tracings of

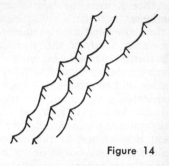

Figure 14

three curves which report behavior in response to a multiple fixed-interval fixed-ratio schedule. The hatches mark reinforcements. Separating them in some cases are short, steep lines showing a high constant rate on a fixed-ratio schedule and, in others, somewhat longer "scallops" showing a smooth acceleration as the organism shifts from a very low rate just after reinforcement to a higher rate at the end of the fixed interval. The values of the intervals and ratios, the states of deprivation, and the exposures to the schedules were different in the three cases, but except for these details the curves are quite similar. Now, one of them was made by a *pigeon* in some experiments by Ferster and me, one was made by a *rat* in an experiment on anoxia by Lohr, and the third was made by a *monkey* in Karl Pribram's laboratory at the Hartford Institute. Pigeon, rat, monkey, which is which? It doesn't matter. Of course, these three species have behavioral repertoires which are as different as their anatomies. But once you have allowed for differences in the ways in which they make contact with the environment, and in the ways in which they act upon the environment, what remains of their behavior shows astonishingly similar properties. Mice, cats, dogs, and human children could have added other curves to this figure. And when organisms which differ as widely as this nevertheless show similar properties of behavior, differences between members of the same species may be viewed more hopefully. Difficult problems of idiosyncrasy or individuality will always arise as products of biological and cultural processes, but it is the very business of the experimental analysis of behavior to devise techniques which reduce their effects except when they are explicitly under investigation.

We are within reach of a science of the individual. This will be achieved, not by resorting to some special theory of knowledge in which intuition or understanding takes the place of observation and analysis, but through an increasing grasp of relevant conditions to produce order in the individual case.

A second consequence of an improved technology is the effect upon behavior theory. As I have pointed out elsewhere, it is the function of learning theory to create an imaginary world of law and order and thus to console us for the disorder we observe in behavior itself. Scores on a T maze or jumping stand hop about from trial to trial almost capriciously. Therefore we argue that if learning is, as we hope, a continuous and orderly process, it must be occurring in some other system of dimensions—perhaps in the nervous system, or in the mind, or in a conceptual model of behavior. Both the statistical treatment of group means and the averaging of curves encourage the belief that we are somehow going behind the individual case to an otherwise inaccessible, but more fundamental, process. The whole tenor of our paper on anxiety, for example, was to imply that the change we observed was not necessarily a property of behavior, but of some theoretical state of the organism ("anxiety") which was merely *reflected* in a slight modification of performance.

When we have achieved a practical control over the organism, theories of behavior lose their point. In representing and managing relevant variables, a conceptual model is useless; we come to grips with behavior itself. When behavior shows order and consistency, we are much less likely to be concerned with physiological or mentalistic causes. A datum emerges which takes the place of theoretical fantasy. In the experimental analysis of behavior we address ourselves to a subject matter which is not only manifestly the behavior of an individual and hence accessible without the usual statistical aids but also "objective" and "actual" without recourse to deductive theorizing.

Statistical techniques serve a useful function, but they have acquired a purely honorific status which may be troublesome. Their presence or absence has become a shibboleth to be used in distinguishing between good and bad work. Because measures of behavior have been highly variable, we have come to trust only results obtained from large numbers of subjects. Because some workers have intentionally or unconsciously reported only selected favorable instances, we have come to put a high value on research which is planned in advance and reported in its entirety. Because measures have

behaved capriciously, we have come to value skillful deductive theories which restore order. But although large groups, planned experiments, and valid theorizing are associated with significant scientific results, it does not follow that nothing can be achieved in their absence. Here are two brief examples of the choice before us.

How can we determine the course of dark adaptation in a pigeon? We move a pigeon from a bright light to a dark room. What happens? Presumably the bird is able to see fainter and fainter patches of light as the process of adaptation takes place, but how can we follow this process? One way would be to set up a discrimination apparatus in which choices would be made at specific intervals after the beginning of dark adaptation. The test patches of light could be varied over a wide range, and the percentages of correct choices at each value would enable us eventually to locate the threshold fairly accurately. But hundreds of observations would be needed to establish only a few points on the curve and to prove that these show an actual change in sensitivity. In the experiment by Blough already mentioned, the pigeon holds a spot of light close to the threshold throughout the experimental period. A single curve, such as the one sketched in Figure 15, yields as much information as hundreds of readings, together

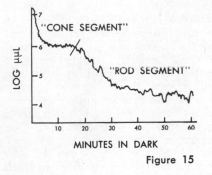

MINUTES IN DARK

Figure 15

with the means and standard deviations derived from them. The information is more accurate because it applies to a single organism in a single experimental session. Yet many psychologists who would accept the first as a finished experiment because of the tables of means and standard deviations would boggle at the second or call it a preliminary study. The direct evidence of one's senses in observing a process of behavior is not trusted.

As another example, consider the behavior of several types of obese mice. Do they all suffer from a single abnormality in their eating behavior or are there differences? One might attempt to answer this with some such measure of hunger as an obstruction apparatus. The numbers of crossings of a grid to get to food, counted after different periods of free access to food, would be the data. Large numbers of readings would be needed, and the resulting mean values would possibly not describe the behavior of any one mouse in any experimental period. A much better picture may be obtained with one mouse of each kind in single experimental sessions, as Anliker has shown (1). In an experiment reported roughly in Figure 16, each mouse was

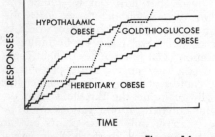

Figure 16

reinforced with a small piece of food after completing a short "ratio" of responses. The hypothalamic-obese mouse shows an exaggerated but otherwise normal ingestion curve. The hereditary-obese mouse eats slowly but for an indefinite length of time and with little change in rate. The gold-poisoned obese mouse shows a sharp oscillation between periods of very rapid responding and no responding at all. These three individual curves contain more information than could probably ever be generated with measures requiring statistical treatment, yet they will be viewed with suspicion by many psychologists because they are single cases.

It is perhaps natural that psychologists should awaken only slowly to the possibility that behavioral processes may be directly observed, or that they should only gradually put the older statistical and theoretical techniques in their proper perspective. But it is time to insist that

Figure 17

science does not progress by carefully designed steps called "experiments" each of which has a well-defined beginning and end. Science is a continuous and often a disorderly and accidental process. We shall not do the young psychologist any favor if we agree to reconstruct our practices to fit the pattern demanded by current scientific methodology. What the statistician means by the design of experiments is design which yields the kind of data to which *his* techniques are applicable. He does not mean the behavior of the scientist in his laboratory devising research for his own immediate and possibly inscrutable purposes.

The organism whose behavior is most extensively modified and most completely controlled in research of the sort I have described is the experimenter himself. The point was well made by a cartoonist in the Columbia *Jester* (Figure 17). The caption read: "Boy, have I got this guy conditioned! Everytime I press the bar down he drops in a piece of food." The subjects we study reinforce us much more effectively than we reinforce them. I have been telling you simply how I have been conditioned to behave. And of course it is a mistake to argue too much from one case history. My behavior would not have been shaped as it was were it not for personal characteristics which all psychologists fortunately do not share. Freud has had something to say about the motivation of scientists and has given us some insight into the type of person who achieves the fullest satisfaction from precise experimental design and the intricacies of deductive systems. Such a person tends to be more concerned with his success as a scientist than with his subject matter, as is shown by the fact that he often assumes the role of a roving ambassador. If this seems unfair, let me hasten to characterize my own motivation in equally unflattering terms. Several years ago I spent a pleasant summer writing a novel called *Walden Two*. One of the characters, Frazier, said many things which I was not yet ready to say myself. Among them was this:

I have only one important characteristic, Burris: I'm stubborn. I've had only one idea in my life—a true *idée fixe* . . . to put it as bluntly as possible, the idea of having my own way. "Control" expresses it, I think. The control of human behavior, Burris. In my early experimental days it was a frenzied, selfish desire to dominate. I remember the rage I used to feel when a prediction went awry. I could have shouted at the subjects of my experiments, "Behave, damn you, behave as you ought!" Eventually I realized that the subjects were always right. They always behaved as they ought. It was I who was wrong. I had made a bad prediction.

(In fairness to Frazier and the rest of myself, I want to add his next remark: "And what a strange discovery for a would-be tyrant, that the only effective technique of control is unselfish." Frazier means, of course, positive reinforcement.)

We have no more reason to say that all psychologists should behave as I have behaved than that they should all behave like R. A. Fisher. The scientist, like any organism, is the product of a unique history. The practices which he finds most appropriate will depend in part upon this history. Fortunately, personal idiosyncrasies usually leave a negligible mark on science as public property. They are important only when we are concerned with the encouragement of scientists and the prosecution of research. When we have at last an adequate empirical account of the behavior of Man

Thinking, we shall understand all this. Until then, it may be best not to try to fit all scientists into any single mold.

References
1. Anliker, J. E. Personal communication.
2. Breland, K., and Breland, Marion. A field of applied animal psychology. *Amer. Psychologist*, 1951, 6, 202–204.
3. Heron, W. T., and Skinner, B. F. An apparatus for the study of behavior. *Psychol. Rec.*, 1939, 3, 166–176.
4. Ratliff, F., and Blough, D. S. Behavioral studies of visual processes in the pigeon. Report of Contract N5ori-07663, Psychological Laboratories, Harvard University, September 1954.
5. Richter, C. P. Free research versus design research. *Science*, 1953, **118**, 91–93.

THE USES OF PSYCHOLOGY

The main point of this article is simply that graduate training is necessary for a *professional* career in psychology. On the other hand, undergraduate psychological training may be valuable In other lInes of work.

A point to guide your study

From what you know about psychology already, can you think of any aspects of undergraduate psychological training which would be valuable for an executive trainee?

4. JOB OPPORTUNITIES FOR UNDERGRADUATE PSYCHOLOGY MAJORS

*Margaret Skeel King and Gregory A. Kimble, Duke University**

When he is considering an undergraduate major, the college student sometimes rules psychology out on grounds expressed something like this:

* This research was carried out under multiple auspices. The senior author used the data reported here for a paper in a course in educational and occupational information taught by Robert M. Colver, Department of Education, Duke University. The initial suggestion for conducting the survey came from the Duke University Psychology Club. Members of the club assisted in the clerical aspects of the study. Preliminary results were reported in May 1957 to the North Carolina Psychological Association.

M. S. King and G. A. Kimble. Job opportunities for undergraduate psychology majors. *Amer. Psychologist*, 1958, **13**, 23–27. Copyright 1958 by the American Psychological Association. Reprinted here with permission from the authors and the American Psychological Association.

"Well, psychology is very interesting, but what can you do with it after you graduate?" The answer to this question, of course, is that you can do with a psychology major exactly what you can with a major in any other liberal arts subject: compete with other college graduates for the jobs available to all such individuals. However, such a response, although it is honest and factually correct, is less than completely satisfying to a student who is beginning to think in terms of a career. He is apt to feel that the selection of a major involves a decision with long-term implications for his future success and happiness and that such an answer does an injustice to the seriousness of the matter.

Largely on this basis, we undertook a survey of job opportunities for undergraduate majors in psychology. Our assumption was that, even if the results did not alter our conception of the situation at all, having concrete and contemporary data on this problem would be valuable, particularly in advising undergraduate students. It is even possible that such advice would contribute a little to a reversal of the alarming trend toward decreasing numbers of psychology majors recently described in the pages of this journal (2).

To obtain information about job opportunities for undergraduate psychology majors, questionnaires were sent to 540 organizations in the following major groups: Business and Industry, 385; Education, schools, and universities, 51; Government, 34; and Social service, 70. The sample is probably not representative of the American economic scene in that the organizations selected were engaged in activities which were likely to appeal to a psychology major. Accordingly, about half of the sample of organizations came from the *1955 APA Directory*. Every fourth page was examined and a list compiled of companies and other (mainly nonacademic) organizations employing psychologists. The rest of the sample came from organizations listed in the *College Placement Directory* (4), the card files of the Duke University Appointments Office, the stock exchange listings of the Sunday *New York Times,* and advertisements from several issues of *Scientific American, Saturday Evening Post* and the *Handbook of Measurement and Control* (1). Of the 540 organizations sampled, 278 (51%) returned the questionnaires. The various subgroups returned the following percentages of the questionnaires distributed: Business and Industry, 50% (193); Education, schools, and universities, 47% (24); Government, 100% (34); and Social service, 36% (25). As evidence of the seriousness with which the questionnaire was taken, two of the organizations (a West Coast refinery and a national distiller) ran IBM analyses of their entire personnel (some 10,000 individuals) to obtain answers to our questions. One governmental agency duplicated the questionnaire and sent it to a number of subsidiary projects.

The materials sent to the organizations sampled were a letter, signed by the junior author as Director of Undergraduate Studies in Psychology at Duke University, and the questionnaire. The letter described the purpose of the study in terms very similar to those in the first paragraph of this paper. It outlined the preparation of the typical Duke undergraduate psychology major, mentioning the experimental emphasis of the Duke curriculum, and stressed the fact that undergraduate training does not prepare a person for professional work in psychology. The specific statement on this point was:

First of all he is not a psychologist. Rather,

he is a student with a broad, liberal arts education. He has a well-rounded background highlighted by certain of the outlooks and a few of the rudimentary skills of the psychologist.

The questionnaire covered three main topics (*a*) the kinds of jobs available to undergraduate psychology majors, (*b*) salary and opportunities for advancement, and (*c*) special training and other factors which employers consider in hiring individuals.

Job opportunities

As an initial step in analyzing the results of the survey, the questionnaires were divided into two groups: (*a*) "positive" responses (about 65% of the questionnaires returned[2]), which mentioned one or more jobs for which the psychology major described in our letter would be qualified, and (*b*) "negative" responses (about 35%), which mentioned no such jobs. By far the most common reason offered by organizations responding negatively was that their needs were for individuals with more specialized training (psychological or otherwise) than the undergraduate major provides.

For example, one governmental agency indicated that:

Undergraduate majors are not hired as psychologists.

The Department of Education in a large city replied:

I interpret your questionnaire to concern only those students who have completed a Bachelor's degree. To be eligible for employment in the field of social service or psychology, we are requiring a Master's degree.

And a social service worker wrote:

My present feeling is that *all* jobs wherein the activities are defined as applied psychology and the person is called psychologist require broader and more extensive training than can be gotten at the undergraduate level. . . . Your program would seem to provide an excellent foundation for advanced study.

The following two replies are representative of a number where the employers' needs were for special training in fields other than psychology:

This is a public relations firm and as such the openings that might occur here are more or

[2] The numbers in Tables 1 and 3 are based on positive replies as follows: Business and Industry, 134; Education, 9; Government, 20; Social service, 13; and Total, 176. Note that one reply may be responsible for more than one entry in these tables.

less limited to individuals who have had considerable writing experience such as newspaper, wire service, and the like. [And] At the present time we are primarily seeking engineering graduates.

Another point made in a few of the replies was that psychological work, to which our students presumably would be attracted, is often available in the larger organizations in a certain field and not in the small ones. As an illustration, a small southern advertising firm noted:

A psychology major would be of help in certain research—establishing motivations, etc.—but only large agencies have such departments.

Many of the negative responses indicated that the respondent had not understood (in spite of our strong statement on the point) that we were not representing the undergraduate major as a competent psychologist. For example:

As a publisher, we do not specifically require psychology majors in our job openings here. [Or] We are not hiring psychology majors at this time. Therefore we feel it would not be appropriate for us to complete your questionnaire. [Or] We do not employ at the professional psychology level.

In analyzing the positive responses to the questionnaire, a tally was made of the positions which our respondents mentioned as ones in their organizations which a psychology major might fill. The results of this analysis appear in Table 1, which gives the frequency with which

various positions were mentioned. Clearly, psychology is regarded as something which is most appropriate to the general field of personnel work. At the same time, several of the replies mentioned that it was not the psychology major per se that counted and that more importance attaches to personal characteristics and the fact that the individual has a bachelor's degree. A personnel manager in a photographic corporation declared:

There are plenty of opportunities for young people, but not *because of* their psychological training. There are several positions in training and personnel in which persons with some psychological training would be useful but, at present, such requirements are not part of the job descriptions.

Another personnel supervisor replied:

The man is of more importance than the major as to qualifications for consideration in the company. . . . If a man has the personal characteristics we look for, indicating management potential, and has at least an undergraduate degree from a qualified institution of learning such as Duke, we are interested in that man. Of great importance, too, is the man's interest in us—namely the type of work he seeks. . . . Your undergraduate psychology majors would qualify for consideration in the company in almost every activity of a nontechnical nature. The activities would include some of the following: Sales, Production, Advertising, Purchasing, Personnel Administration, and Public Relations.

Table 1   Positions for which undergraduate psychology majors could qualify in various types of organizations

Category	Business and industry	Education	Government	Social service	Total
Personnel, interviewing, industrial relations, counseling	110	1	10	2	123
Management development trainee, supervisor	39	0	2	5	46
Research, experimental psychologist	11	5	6	3	25
Psychometrist, statistical analyst	10	4	8	0	22
Sales	21	0	0	0	21
Clerical	14	4	1	0	19
Manufacturing, production	14	0	0	1	15
Technician, job analyst	9	0	5	0	14
Psychologist (assistant), psychologist in training	3	0	3	5	11
Social service	0	1	3	6	10
Writing, reporting, editing	7	0	0	0	7
Miscellaneous	3	0	0	0	3
Total	241	15	38	22	316

Salaries and prospects for promotion

The median starting salary for newly graduated male AB's in psychology estimated from the present sample is $365.00 per month. This is close to the value which has figured in recent articles in the popular press. For example, the average starting salary for liberal arts majors with bachelor's degrees reported recently in *U. S. News and World Report* (3) is $350–$400 per month. A more detailed breakdown appears in Table 2. Obviously there are marked differences among the various occupations in starting salaries. Table 2, however, certainly presents far too low a value for the field of education, since the teaching profession is not represented (see the categories in Table 1). Teaching requires certification and, therefore, special training in all states. For this reason, the ordinary psychology major does not qualify for such positions. This leaves secretarial and training positions (for example, graduate assistant) as the main jobs reflected in the data presented in Table 2 for education. Such positions, of course, pay less than those covered in the other categories.

The median starting salary for women estimated from this sample is $305.00 per month. There were 25 organizations answering who had no opportunities for women with undergraduate psychology training, while only 8 organizations had no opportunities for men. Of those which gave specific salary information, 50 organizations paid men and women the same starting salaries, but the salary was lower for women in 35 organizations. Some of this difference in starting salary is attributable to the fact that clerical jobs were mentioned more often for women. But even in the cases where the tasks are identical, equal pay for equal work is still not universal.

The question about opportunities for promotion elicited routinely optimistic replies from most of the respondents. The exceptions were confined almost completely to the clerical jobs in the educational and social service organizations. One social science research project indicated that "To date we have had 'jobs' rather than 'positions.' When the job is over, no position exists."

Those who elaborated on this question in a more positive vein were most often representatives of the business and industry category. Two themes seemed to characterize their points. One was that firsthand experience in a business is important, not only in developing knowledge about the functioning of the organization, but also in more subtle attitudinal areas.

Operating experience, i.e., doing or supervising activities which are closely related to the main objectives of a particular business—early in one's career, builds relationships, attitudes, and background helpful in advancing anywhere in the business.

The other point stressed frequently was a statement of a promotion-from-within policy. Apparently many organizations explicitly plan to draw high level executive personnel from the ranks. Many of them couple this with a policy of promoting the man as rapidly as his development warrants.

Related training

Table 3 presents a summary of data on business skills and related course work. The questionnaire listed the training presented in the table and asked the respondent to check off those which were desirable. The numbers in Table 3 are the numbers of times each item was checked. As regards business skills, it was interesting to note that these abilities were regarded as important at all levels—not just for clerical workers. In the case of related courses, there is a clear preference for mathematics and economics. The latter of these stresses is, to a large degree, a reflection of the heavy preponderance of business and industrial organizations in the sample. The stress on mathematics is more nearly characteristic of all of the areas. In addition to the skills and courses listed in Table 3, the respondents were asked to mention others which they thought would be especially useful. Replies to this question were heterogeneous and often reflected the specialty of the organization represented by the individual filling out the questionnaire. There were, however, two trends which stood out. One was a recognition of the importance of training in statistics. This, no doubt, is related to the value placed upon mathematics. The second stress was on communication skills: English grammar, composition, and report writing.

The overview

It was evident from the responses to the questionnaire that psychology has an established acceptance in the economic world as a valuable

Table 2   Median starting salary per month for men and women

Category	Men	Women
Business and industry	$385	$308
Education	200	206
Government	331	317
Social service	285	285
Over-all median	$365	$305

Table 3   Business skills and areas of related course work which were checked as being desirable in various types of organizations

	Business and industry	Education	Government	Social service	Total
Business skills					
Computing machines	55	4	11	6	76
Office machines	47	1	11	3	62
Shorthand	54	1	4	4	63
Typing	61	5	11	6	83
Related course work					
Biological science	17	5	3	3	28
Economics	72	2	5	1	80
Mathematics	67	5	15	6	93
Physical science	47	2	7	3	59
Political science	18	4	4	1	27
Social science	48	9	9	3	69

major subject. Contrary to what the prospective major is apt to think, he is under no handicap by comparison with students in other liberal arts fields either as regards his chances of getting a good job or in terms of salary. There are courses which the student can take to better his chances of getting the job he wants; these include English, mathematics, economics, and statistics. But these could be recommended to a major in any subject. For it must be emphasized that a psychology major does not prepare a student for a particular position. The majority of jobs mentioned—personnel, management training, and sales—are ones in which a psychology major might be happy, but training in psychology, such as is usually provided by an undergraduate major, is not a prerequisite.

In fact, business and industry apparently recognize the strengths and weaknesses of the liberal arts training more clearly than those of us in the academic world sometimes give them credit for. Most large organizations have their own in-training programs and have specifically assumed the responsibility for providing the practical experience which is missing in the undergraduate liberal arts program. Moreover there seems to be a considerable sentiment to the effect that this is as it should be. Comments emphasized the importance of a broad liberal arts background, rather than the particular field of major study. Almost all employers want persons with a well-rounded education—those who have not only excelled in school, but who have participated in extracurricular activities and have displayed initiative and responsibility. Specific training is of distinctly secondary importance. One governmental organization expressed it this way: "We look for bright people even though they are not fully trained." A corporation personnel manager summed up much current emphasis very well: "If you will educate them, we will train them."

References

1. Behar, M. S. (Ed.) *Handbook of measurement and control.* (2nd ed.) Pittsburgh: Instruments Publishing Company, 1954.
2. Recktenwald, L. N. The drop in undergraduate degrees. *Amer. Psychologist,* 1957, 12, 229–230.
3. *U. S. News and World Report.* 1957, May 17, pp. 45–49.
4. Zimmerman, O. T. *College placement directory.* (2nd ed.) Dover, New Hampshire: Industrial Research Service, 1955.

CHAPTER TWO
Maturation and development

Heredity and environment

The question of human instincts is one which has been character-ized by long, acrimonious arguments. The older psychologists worked long and hard to show that much human behavior was either instinctual, e.g., William MacDougall, or not instinctual, e.g., John B. Watson. This argument has now diminished because psychologists have tended to reformulate the instinct question.

Typical of such reformulations is Beach's examination of the behaviors which are species-specific for humans and other species. Species-specific behavior is not necessarily instinctual in the sense of appearing full-blown without any training or continuing in the absence of the stimulus which elicited it. It is only species-wide behavior. As a corollary of this reformula-tion, Beach seeks to find the determinants of the species-specific behavior. Beach mentions historical (both maturational and experiential), environmental (direct and indirect), and organismic determinants. The example of some direct environmental determinants is given in this excerpt.

Points to guide your study
1. What are some human species-specific behaviors?
2. Remember the determinants of species-specific behavior.

5. EXPERIMENTAL INVESTIGATIONS OF SPECIES-SPECIFIC BEHAVIOR

Frank A. Beach, University of California, Berkeley*

At the annual meeting of Division 3 in 1950 I delivered a paper whimsically entitled "The Snark Was a Boojum" (Beach, 1950). In that lecture I presented a year-by-year analysis of articles published in the *Journal of Comparative and Physiological Psychology* and showed that there had been a steady decline in the number of species studied and in the kinds of behaviors investigated: more and more work being done with rats, and more and more experiments concentrating on learning. At that time I sug-gested that to develop a genuinely comparative psychology it would be necessary for investi-gators to study the behavior of many different

* F. A. Beach. Experimental investigations of spe-cies-specific behavior. *Amer. Psychologist*, 1960, **15**, 1–18. Copyright 1960 by the American Psychological Association. Excerpts reprinted here with permission from the author and the American Psychological As-sociation. Figures 13, 14, 15, and 16 of the original renumbered. Selected references reprinted.

species and to examine a much wider variety of behavior patterns.

I still regard these as worthy objectives, but in the ensuing nine years I have come to question the logical defensibility of *any* concept of a comparative psychology.

My doubts stem in part from the conviction that *Homo sapiens* is, in some ways, a truly unique species. This statement is not intended to be mystical. It does not demand a return to pre-Darwinian ideas about special creation. It is perhaps best documented by a quotation from the writings of one of our most eminent stu-dents of evolution, George Gaylord Simpson:

Man has certain basic diagnostic features which set him off most sharply from any other animal and which have involved other de-velopments not only increasing this sharp distinction but also making it an absolute difference in kind and not only a relative difference of degree. In the basic diagnosis of *Homo sapiens* the most important features are probably interrelated factors of intelligence, flexibility, individualization, and socialization. All four of these are features that occur rather widely in the animal kingdom as progressive developments, and all define different, but related, sorts of evolutionary progress. In man all four are carried to a degree greater than in any other sort of animal (Simpson, 1949, p. 284).

Now, if man is a unique type of animal, this is exceedingly important, because many psychologists, and certainly the general public, think of psychology as a science of *human* behavior. I have examined many introductory texts, and this definition is clearly the dominant one.

This being the case, why is it that so many psychologists use lower animals as subjects in their experiments? Setting aside the obvious points concerning economy, methodological controls, short life span, etc., the fact is that nearly all so-called "animal psychologists" are primarily interested in, and draw their problems from, the area of *human* behavior. They use members of lower species as substitutes for human subjects.

A long time ago man dubbed himself the knowing or learning animal and thus indicated his conviction that a highly developed learning capacity is one hallmark of the human species. Therefore it is not surprising that most of the psychological experimentation on animals has dealt with learning and problem solving. These experiments take little or no account of the role played by learning in the normal life of the infrahuman species used as subjects. The general attitude seems to be that learning is learning, and it can be studied as well in one species as in another.

Not all psychologists share this implicit faith. Skepticism has been expressed by Hilgard. After listing the methodological advantages offered by animal research, Hilgard makes the following statement:

A price is always paid for the convenience of a given approach to a problem. The price to be paid for over much experimentation with animals is to neglect the fact that human subjects are brighter, are able to use language —*and probably learn differently because of these advances over lower animals* (Hilgard, 1948, p. 329).

These various considerations lead me to wonder whether it might not be desirable to explicitly restrict the concept of psychology solely to the study of human behavior. Since psychology is a frankly anthropocentric discipline, it is difficult to envisage what a *comparative* psychology would really be. Of course there is the term "animal psychology." But if this means merely "animal behavior," why not call it that?

It seems to me that a genuinely *comparative* science of behavior would not be oriented to any given species at the expense of others. It would not concentrate upon particular types of behavior to the exclusion of others. It would center its interests upon one type of organism after another and attempt to increase our understanding of behavior as it is shown by the species under consideration.

I am sure that I do not have to defend the proposition that the study of any kind of behavior in any species of animal is a scientifically respectable enterprise. Of course some degree of selection is essential, but the basis of selection is idiosyncratic and entirely at the discretion of the individual investigator. One worker may wish to concentrate upon grasshoppers, another on seagulls, and a third on human beings. However, if the goal is to build a *comparative science* of *behavior*, two desiderata seem obvious.

First the behavior selected for examination should be, so to speak, "natural" to the species. Insofar as possible it should be species-specific, a term I will explain shortly. Secondly, the kinds of behavior chosen for analysis should be as widely distributed as possible, phylogenetically speaking. This would increase the opportunity for inter-specific comparison and improve the probability of arriving at valid and broad general principles or laws.

Let me repeat that what I am proposing differs from current practice in animal experimentation in that animals are not to be used as substitutes for people, and the kinds of problems investigated are not to be exclusively or even principally derived from human behavior or psychology. To make my point clear I must now tell you what I mean by species-specific behavior.

Species-specific behavior

Species-specific behavior patterns constitute the normal behavioral repertoire. They are present in the same or very similar form in all or nearly all members of the species of the same age and sex. Many such specific patterns are characteristic of one and only one species, and Hebb has called them "species-predictable" (Hebb & Thompson, 1954).

Excellent examples of species-specific patterns are found in the songs of various birds. Experienced ornithologists can identify many species exclusively on the basis of song. In other instances it is necessary to employ recording devices to detect species differences. Nevertheless it is exceedingly unlikely that any two species possess identical songs. Figure 1, taken from Thorpe (1956), shows tracings of sound spectrograph recordings of the songs of four closely related species of finches: the greenfinch, goldfinch, bullfinch, and hawfinch.

In interpreting slides like this psychologists are used to reading intensity on the abscissa and amplitude on the ordinate. This record is different. *Frequency* is shown on the vertical scale—the higher the mark, the higher the pitch. Along the horizontal scale is shown *time*. Each of these records represents a song lasting about 2.5 seconds. Different frequencies emitted at the same time reflect harmonies and other overtones. Reading from left to right, we see a record of 2.5 seconds of continuous song. The songs of the four species are obviously dissimilar.

Many fish construct nests in which the eggs are laid, and no two species make exactly the same kind of nest. Figure 2 shows a photograph of the very simple pit-like nest excavated by the male and female African mouthbreeder fish, *Tilapia macrocephala*. This pit serves as a target in which the female deposits the eggs. The male promptly fertilizes them and then picks them up to be carried in his mouth where the young will hatch. The nest is not used at any later time.

The nest of the ten-spined stickleback shown in Figure 3 is much more elaborate and serves a different function. This is constructed by the male using small bits of plants as building material and cementing them together with a substance secreted by the kidney. The female is induced by the male's courtship to swim inside the nest where she deposits her eggs and then leaves. Thereafter the male fertilizes the clutch, guards the nest, and assiduously fans the eggs with his fins.

There is no need to multiply examples; but similar comparisons in a variety of kinds of behavior could be made among invertebrates, amphibians, reptiles, and mammals. Within the primates each species of monkey and ape has its own characteristic behavior patterns which serve to identify it as a member of the primate order and at the same time to differentiate it from other species within the same group. What then can be said to typify man as far as species-specific behavior patterns are concerned?

We have already seen that Simpson regards man as pre-eminent in intelligence, flexibility, individualization, and socialization; but these are not types of behavior comparable to nest building, mating, etc. Unquestionably the behavioral characteristic which sets man apart from all other animals is the possession of language. Many other species *communicate* through vocalizations and gestures, but none possesses anything approaching human language in modifiability and complexity.

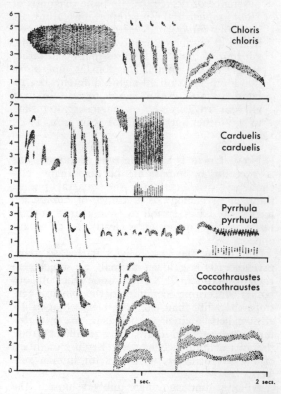

Figure 1   Sound spectrograph tracings of the songs of four species of finches (from Marler, 1957).

As a matter of fact, the single diagnostic character of language is sufficient in and of itself to identify an organism as a member of our species. Hebb and Thompson (1954) say that man is the only animal capable of "syntactic" behavior. It is important to note that language serves as more than a means of communication. A great deal of human thinking and problem solving is done in terms of language symbols. By virtue of language man is also unique in his capacity to anticipate remotely future events, possible or inevitable. This is at times advantageous, but it can also produce crippling anxieties.

Language depends upon and, at the same time, underlies another one of man's outstanding characteristics: namely, the capacity to establish a wide variety of exceedingly complex social interrelations. Language and the formation of social groups permit the transmission of information from one generation to the next and thus give rise to a new type of evolution not seen in any other species. Social evolution, based upon the intergeneration transfer of knowledge, customs, and beliefs, has resulted in the growth of culture—another uniquely human characteristic.

The conclusion seems inescapable that a comparative behaviorist who wished to concentrate upon the species-specific characteristics of mankind would emphasize those aspects of behavior depending upon the use of language and involving interpersonal relations and the formation of social groups.

Plan of attack

It may be agreed that some kind of scientists, not necessarily psychologists, might find out some interesting, important—conceivably even useful—things by studying species-specific behavior in animals; but there may nevertheless be some doubt as to precisely what it is that these hypothetical investigators are going to do. How are they going to proceed once they have chosen a particular pattern of behavior for scientific study?

The general plan of attack is deceptively simple. One merely attempts to answer three questions: How did the behavior get to be what it is? What are the external causes of the behavior? What internal mechanisms mediate it? Phrased in slightly more sophisticated terms each of these questions can be said to deal with a different class of *determinants* of behavior. The determinants of behavior can be subdivided into three broad categories: historical determinants, environmental determinants, and organismic determinants.

In more familiar language, *historical* determinants are in turn subdivisible into two classes which are usually referred to as maturational and experiential factors. *Environmental* determinants may be either *direct* or *indirect*. Direct environmental determinants are easy enough to understand. Traditionally defined as stimuli, they are those external factors or correlates which are often said to evoke the behavior. Usually there is a fairly clear-cut and immediate relationship between presentation of a direct environmental determinant and the occurrence of the associated behavioral response.

Indirect environmental determinants will be somewhat less familiar to many psychologists, and an example will help to clarify the concept. Figure 2 illustrates the simple pit-like nest which is dug by the African mouthbreeder fish prior to spawning. The male does some nest digging, but the female performs most of the work. Females that are completely isolated do not dig nests. However, an unmated female, in a tank by herself, will dig a nest if she has been able to see another mouthbreeder in an adjacent tank for several days. Not only that—she will then proceed to lay eggs in the nest.

In painstaking analysis, Aronson (1945) has identified the essential determinant as being visual and only visual. The sequence of events seems to be roughly as follows. Constant exposure to the sight of others of her own species causes the ovaries of the female to become active. Eggs ripen, and ovarian hormones are secreted. As the female's physiological condition changes, her reactions to certain aspects of her environment change. The sandy bottom of the tank now becomes something to dig in, and nest building begins. It appears that the actions involved in digging—a process which may stretch over many hours—have further effects upon the ovary, effects which eventually give rise to ovulation and oviposition.

In this example, the prolonged visual access to another *Tilapia*, prior to the onset of the behavioral response, is an indirect environmental determinant of nest digging behavior. It is a necessary but not sufficient factor. The *direct* environmental determinant of the response is sight of a sandy or light colored bottom. Females kept in aquaria with bare slate floors show no nesting activity; but, if the floor is covered by a layer of sand, and the sand in turn is covered by a sheet of clear glass, then the female exhibits persistent digging responses, even though she cannot touch the sand.

The third class of determinants is a very familiar one. Organismic determinants of behavior form the subject matter of physiological psychology. To define them crudely, they are the determinants that lie inside the individual. The most frequently investigated organismic determinants to date have been those of a neural or an endocrinological nature.

These, then, are the three classes of determinants of behavior: historical, environmental, and organismic. Now it will be apparent that these three classes are not completely separate and surely do not operate independently. The effectiveness of a direct environmental determinant will be a function of other determinants of an historical nature. The influence of an indirect environmental determinant is exerted by way of organismic changes. Organismic determinants, in turn, influence responses to environmental variables. It is nevertheless useful in the beginning to treat the three classes as if they were clearly separable. They are the factors the comparative behaviorist seeks to identify in his study of species-specific patterns in different kinds of animals. He may discover that the same kind of behavior in different species depends upon the same or upon different combinations of determinants, and these similarities and differences will provide an essential basis for the understanding of interspecific differences and similarities at the molar level.

At this point I would like to make one very general and, I believe, very important point concerning the analysis of behavior. I have said that the comparative behaviorist accepts as an important goal the identification of the several types of determinants of species-specific be-

Figure 2   An example of the simple, pit nest excavated by the African mouthbreeder fish (from Aronson, 1949).

havior. The point I wish to emphasize is that *precisely the same kind of analysis is necessary for the understanding of any kind of behavior exhibited by any kind of organism.* The psychologist interested in the language development of children or in the onset and course of homesickness in college freshmen must, if his knowledge of the phenomena is to be complete, ask the same questions as are asked by the comparative behaviorist when he studies the migration of birds or the cooperative behavior of chimpanzees.

Direct environmental determinants

Having considered the case of historical determinants and of indirect environmental determinants, I am now prepared to present a few

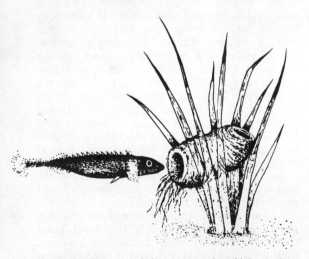

Figure 3   The nest of the ten-spined stickleback (from Morris, 1958).

examples of studies aimed at identification of the direct environmental determinants of species-specific behavior.

The European and British ethologists have been extraordinarily successful in identifying direct environmental determinants by the use of models, or dummy stimulus objects. A simple illustration is provided by Tinbergen's study of aggression in the stickleback. During the mating season males of this species viciously attack other males that are in breeding condition. The male that is ready to reproduce is distinguishable by virtue of the bright red coloration of his ventral body surfaces.

Tinbergen presented different models to breeding males. These dummies are shown in Figure 4. Model N was an accurate copy of a male stickleback, but it lacked the red belly. This dummy elicited very few attacks. In contrast, all of the other models, which varied widely in shape, but shared the common characteristic of a red underside, evoked constant and vigorous attack by the experimental males. Apparently the crucial direct determinant in this case is the red belly.

Hebb has discussed the sudden appearance of fear responses in young chimpanzees and human children. In some cases the direct environmental determinants have been identified and found to be exceedingly simple. One case will illustrate the point. An eleven-month-old baby girl suddenly began to exhibit extreme fright reactions in a variety of situations which at first seemed to have nothing in common. When an old friend entered her playroom wearing a new hat, the child burst into tears and would not allow herself to be picked up until the hat was removed. Upon being presented with a new teddy bear she showed violent avoidance reactions and screamed with fright.

Examination of the child's reaction to a variety of stimulus objects revealed that the key factor evoking fear was color. Anything that was black elicited avoidance and great distress. Black hats, toys, or other objects were equally effective. Similar stimuli that were not black were accepted and examined with interest. The following figures illustrate the phenomenon. Figure 5 shows alert attention to the approaching experimenter. Figure 6 illustrates the reaction to a black glove placed gently on the tray of the high chair. This peculiar fear behavior disappeared as suddenly as it had appeared.

Psychologists have made relatively few attempts to identify the direct environmental determinants of species-specific behavior in human beings. In his book, *Expression of the Emotions in Man and Animals,* Charles Darwin (1872) listed *smiling* under "Special Expressions of Man," and smiling probably is a species-specific pattern. Older children and adults

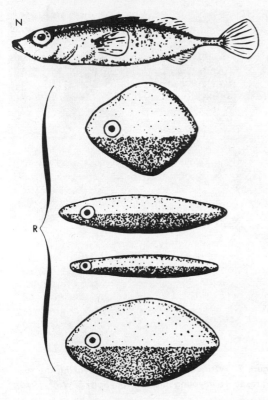

Figure 4 Artificial models used to elicit aggressive behavior in the male stickleback (from Tinbergen, 1951).

behavioral reactions shown by fishes and birds, in that they are evoked by relatively uncomplicated, direct environmental determinants, often involving only one sensory modality. In apparent contrast, complex species-specific patterns in mammals seem to depend upon patterns or combinations of direct determinants. Studies of retrieving of their young by lactating rats will serve as an example (Beach & Jaynes, 1956).

When she delivers her first litter, the inexperienced female rat normally cleans her young and gathers them into the nest that she built prior to parturition. If the experimenter scatters the litter about the cage, the mother promptly and efficiently retrieves them to the nest. I was interested in discovering the sensory cues utilized by the mother in locating and identifying her young. The first step was to examine the possible role of each sensory avenue.

The possible importance of odor was tested in three ways. First, it was shown that females could respond to the odor of the young by demonstrating that a blinded female could locate pups which were suspended high above her by a fine thread. In order to reach these pups the female had to stand up on her hind feet. Secondly, blind females were allowed to investigate two wire mesh boxes, one empty and one containing a pup. The clear-cut preference for the latter box indicated a response to odor. Thirdly, I tested the response of normal females to pups which had been sprinkled with perfume. These pups were retrieved, but not until after

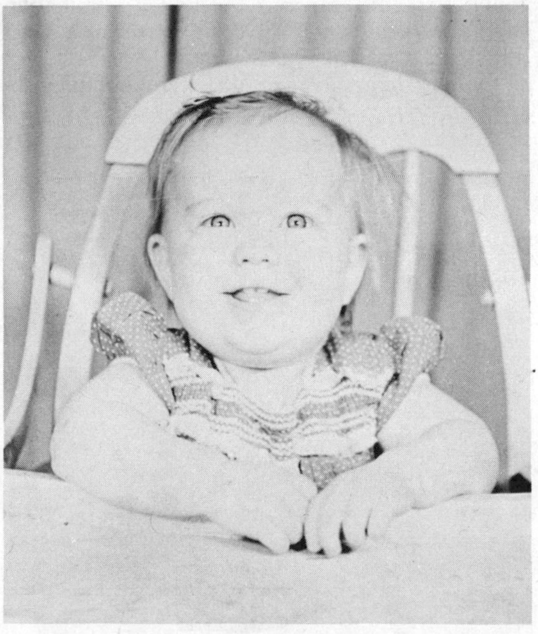

smile in a variety of circumstances; but, in very young infants, the smile is a reflexive response to a relatively simple stimulus, a fact well-known to anyone who has played peek-a-boo with a baby.

Apparently the direct environmental determinant is visual and consists of a human face presented full view. Spitz and Wolf (1946) exposed 145 infants between the ages of two and six months to a variety of stimulus patterns in an attempt to evoke smiling. The only effective stimulus for babies of this age was a human face viewed from the front. A profile view did not elicit smiling. The stimulus face does not have to be smiling. In fact, the expression on the face proved to be irrelevant. Thus the stimulus shown in Figure 7 was quite effective as a smile producer. So was a face covered with a Halloween mask. Even a dummy fitted with a face-like mask regularly elicited smiling. When they are several months older, children begin to smile in response to other stimuli; but under the age of six months the only direct environmental determinant appears to be full view of the human face or a reasonable facsimile thereof.

This simple, reflexive response in human babies is like a wide variety of more complex

Figure 5 Expression of the eleven-month-old subject prior to introduction of the fear-inducing stimulus.

the mother had found and retrieved the control pups which did not smell of Chanel No. 5.

Obviously, olfactory cues are an important environmental determinant of the retrieving response, but are they essential? The answer is an unequivocal "no." I destroyed the olfactory bulbs in a number of females, thus rendering them anosmic, and they retrieved just as efficiently as normal mothers.

Turning next to the investigation of visual cues, it was first established that lactating rats can locate their young exclusively on the basis of sight. The test involved presenting the mother with two small glass bottles, one containing a pup and one empty. The bottles were sealed airtight. Most females spent more time investigating the bottle containing a pup than the empty bottle. This suggested that the visual cues were important. Next the retrieving behavior of blind mothers was examined. They were slightly slower than sighted females, but the quality of their performance was excellent. It would appear that visual cues are used when they are available, but sight is not essential to retrieving.

Other senses were investigated, but the results on smell and vision are sufficient for the point I want to make. A given type of sensory cue may contribute to the occurrence of a response, and yet not be essential as long as alternative cues remain available. If two cues are eliminated, this is much more likely to interfere with the response. Thus, when I rendered the same females both blind and anosmic, their retrieving became much less efficient; and the added elimination of the sense of touch in the snout region almost abolished retrieving behavior.

Quite comparable results were obtained in

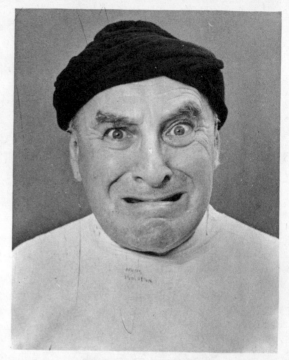

Figure 7   Visual stimulus effective in evoking the smiling response in young infants (from Spitz & Wolf, 1946).

my laboratory in studies of the sensory basis for the male rat's sexual responses to the receptive female (Beach, 1942). Much more evidence is needed, but the data presently available suggest that mammals may differ from other vertebrate classes in that their species-specific behavior depends upon direct environmental determinants which, instead of being very simple and involving only one modality, are multisensory in nature and may include some interaction between modalities. This, incidentally, is the sort of generalization which can be reached only by a broadly comparative approach to behavior.

References

Aronson, L. R. Influence of the stimuli provided by the male cichlid fish, *Tilapia macrocephala*, on the spawning frequency of the female. *Physiol. Zool.*, 1945, 18, 403–415.

Beach, F. A. Analysis of the stimuli adequate to elicit mating behavior in the sexually inexperienced male rat. *J. comp. Psychol.*, 1942, 33, 163–207.

Beach, F. A. The snark was a boojum. *Amer. Psychologist*, 1950, 5, 115–124.

Beach, F. A., & Jaynes, J. Studies of maternal retrieving in rats. III. Sensory cues involved in the lactating female's response to her young. *Behaviour*, 1956, 10, 104–125.

Darwin, C. *The expression of the emotions in*

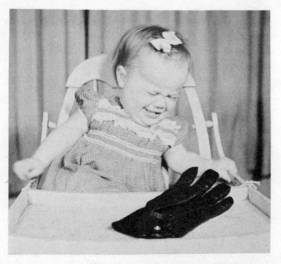

Figure 6   Reaction to a black glove.

man and animals. 1872. (Reprinted: New York: Philosophical Library, 1955.)

Hebb, D. O., & Thompson, W. R. The social significance of animal studies. In G. Lindzey (Ed.), *Handbook of social psychology.* Cambridge, Mass.: Addison-Wesley, 1954, Chap. 15.

Hilgard, E. R. *Theories of learning.* New York: Appleton-Century-Crofts, 1948.

Marler, P. Specific distinctiveness in the communication signals of birds. *Behaviour,* 1957, **11,** 13–39.

Spitz, R. A., & Wolf, K. M. The smiling response: A contribution to the ontogenesis of social relations. *Genet. Psychol. Monogr.,* 1946, **34,** 57–125.

Tinbergen, N. *The study of instinct.* Oxford: Clarendon, 1951.

MATURATION AND GROWTH

It has been discovered that a child will benefit from training only after sufficient maturation (growth) has taken place. There is another relationship between learning and maturation which is possible. In some species, and perhaps in humans too, very rapid learning can take place only during a very short time span, the critical period. Such rapid learning is called imprinting.

The ethologists, zoologists concerned with species-specific behavior, were the first to study the phenomenon. They studied it in the field, but, although this has advantages, it was not until laboratory investigations were made that some important variables were uncovered. This, of course, is one of the major advantages of the laboratory method.

Points to guide your study

1. The first two paragraphs give the basic orientation for this article.
2. Make sure you understand the two graphs and the table in this article.

6. IMPRINTING

Eckhard H. Hess, University of Chicago*

Students of behavior generally agree that the early experiences of animals (including man) have a profound effect on their adult behavior. Some psychologists go so far as to state that the effect of early experience upon adult behavior is inversely correlated with age. This may be an oversimplification, but in general it appears to hold true. Thus, the problem of the investigator is not so much to find out *whether* early experience determines adult behavior as to discover *how* it determines adult behavior.

Three statements are usually made about the effects of early experience. The first is that early

* E. H. Hess. Imprinting. *Science,* 1959, **130,** 133–141. Copyright 1959 by the American Association for the Advancement of Science. Excerpts reprinted here with permission from the author and the American Association for the Advancement of Science. The table is renumbered.

habits are very persistent and may prevent the formation of new ones. This, of course, refers not only to the experimental study of animals but also to the rearing of children. The second statement is that early perceptions deeply affect all future learning. This concept leads to the difficult question whether basic perceptions—the way we have of seeing the world about us—are inherited or acquired. The third statement is simply that early social contacts determine the character of adult social behavior. This is the phenomenon of imprinting.

At the turn of the century, Craig (1), experimenting with wild pigeons, found that in order to cross two different species it was first necessary to rear the young of one species under the adults of the other. Upon reaching maturity the birds so reared preferred mates of the same species as their foster parents. Other interspecies sexual fixations have been observed in birds and fishes.

Heinroth (2, 3) and his wife successfully reared by hand the young of almost every species of European birds. They found that many of the social responses of these birds were transferred to their human caretaker. Lorenz (4) extended these experiments, dealing especially with greylag geese.

Lorenz was the first to call this phenomenon "imprinting," although earlier workers had observed this effect. He was also the first to point out that it appeared to occur at a critical period early in the life of an animal. He postulated that the first object to elicit a social response later released not only that response but also related responses such as sexual behavior. Imprinting, then, was related not only to the problem of behavior but also to the general biological problem of evolution and speciation.

Although imprinting has been studied mainly in birds, it also has been observed to occur in other animals. Instances of imprinting have been reported in insects (5), in fish (6), and in some mammals. Those mammals in which the phenomenon has been found—sheep (7), deer (8), and buffalo (8a)—are all animals in which the young are mobile almost immediately after birth. Controlled experimental work with mammals, however, has just begun.

The first systematic investigations of imprinting were published in 1951. Simultaneously in this country and in Europe, the work of Ramsay (9) and Fabricius (10) gave the first indication of some of the important variables of the process. Ramsay worked with several species of ducks and a variety of breeds of chickens. He noticed the importance of the auditory component in the imprinting experiment and the effect of changes in coloring on parental recognition as well as on recognition of the parents by the young. His findings also showed that color is an essential element in recognition, while size or form seemed to be of less importance. Most of Ramsay's experiments dealt with exchange of parents and young and did not involve the use of models or decoys as imprinting objects, although he also imprinted some waterfowl on such objects as a football or a green box.

Fabricius carried on experiments with several species of ducklings and was able to determine approximately the critical age at which imprinting was most successful in several species of ducks. In some laboratory experiments he found it impossible to do imprinting in ducklings with a silent decoy—something which my co-workers and I were easily able to do a few years later in our Maryland laboratory. After the appearance of this pioneer work by Ramsay and by Fabricius, no relevant papers appeared until 1954. At that time Ramsay and Hess (11) published a paper on a laboratory approach to the study of imprinting. The basic technique was modified slightly the following year and then was continued in the form described below. Papers in 1956 by Margaret Nice (12) and by Hinde, Thorpe, and Vince (13) include most of the pertinent materials published up to 1956 since Lorenz's classic statement of the problem.

Since 1956, however, there has been an increasing number of papers on imprinting in a variety of journals. However, most investigators report experiments which are primarily designed to look for ways in which imprinting can be likened to associative learning and are not primarily carried out to investigate the phenomenon itself. Later we shall return to a consideration of these experiments; for the present we shall concern ourselves mainly with the program carried out since 1951 at McDonogh and at Lake Farm Laboratory, Maryland, and at our laboratories at the University of Chicago (14).

Experimental studies

Our laboratory in Maryland had access to a small duck pond in which we kept relatively wild mallards. The birds laid their eggs in nesting boxes, so the eggs could be collected regularly. After storage for a few days, the eggs were incubated in a dark, forced-air incubator. About two days before hatching, the eggs were transferred to a hatching incubator. Precautions were taken to place the newly hatched bird into a small cardboard box (5 by 4 by 4 inches) in such a way that it could see very little in the dim light used to carry out the procedure.

Each bird was given a number, which was recorded on the box itself as well as in our permanent records. The box containing the bird was then placed in a still-air incubator, used as a brooder, and kept there until the bird was to be imprinted. After the young bird had undergone the imprinting procedure, it was automatically returned to the box, and the box was then transferred to a fourth incubator, also used as a brooder, and kept there until the bird was to be tested. Only after testing was completed was the duckling placed in daylight and given food and water.

The apparatus we constructed to be used in the imprinting procedure consisted of a circular runway about 5 feet in diameter. This runway was 12 inches wide and 12½ feet in circumference at the center. Boundaries were formed by walls of Plexiglas 12 inches high. A mallard duck decoy, suspended from an elevated arm radiating from the center of the apparatus, was fitted internally with a loud-speaker and a heating element. It was held about 2 inches above the center of the runway. The arms suspending the decoy could be rotated by either of two variable-speed motors. The speed of rotating and intermittent movement could be regulated from the control panel located behind a one-way screen about 5 feet from the apparatus. The number of rotations of both the decoy and the animal were recorded automatically. Tape recorders with continuous tapes provided the sound that was played through the speaker inside the decoy. A trap door in the runway, operated from the control panel, returned the duckling to its box.

Imprinting procedure. The young mallard, at a certain number of hours after hatching, was taken in its box from the incubator and placed in the runway of the apparatus (Figure 1). The decoy at this time was situated about 1 foot away. By means of a cord, pulley, and clip arrangement, the observer released the bird and removed the box. As the bird was released, the sound was turned on in the decoy model, and after a short interval the decoy began to move about the circular runway. The sound we used in the imprinting of the mallard ducklings was an arbitrarily chosen human rendition of "*gock, gock, gock, gock, gock.*" The decoy emitted this call continually during the imprinting process. The duckling was allowed to remain in the apparatus for a specified amount of time while making a certain number of turns in the runway. At the end of the imprinting period, which was usually less than 1 hour, the duckling was automatically returned to its box and placed in an incubator until it was tested for imprinting strength at a later hour.

Figure 1 The apparatus used in the study of imprinting consists primarily of a circular runway around which a decoy duck can be moved. In this drawing a duckling follows the decoy. The controls of the apparatus are in the foreground.

Testing for imprinting. Each duckling to be tested was mechanically released from its box halfway between two duck models placed 4 feet apart. One of these was the male mallard model upon which it had been imprinted; the other was a female model which differed from the male only in its coloration. One minute was allowed for the duckling to make a decisive response to the silent models. At the end of this time, regardless of the nature of the duckling's response, sound was turned on simultaneously for each of the models. The male model made the "gock" call upon which the duckling had been imprinted, while the female model gave the call of a real mallard female calling her young.

Four test conditions followed each other in immediate succession in the testing procedure. They were: (i) both models stationary and silent; (ii) both models stationary and calling; (iii) the male stationary and the female calling; (iv) the male stationary and silent and the female moving and calling. We estimated these four tests to be in order of increasing difficulty. The time of response and the character of the call note (pleasure tones or distress notes) were recorded. Scores in percentage of positive responses were then recorded for each animal. If the duckling gave a positive response to the imprinting object (the male decoy) in all four tests, imprinting was regarded as complete, or 100 percent.

Determination of the "critical period"

To determine the age at which an imprinting experience was most effective we imprinted our ducklings at various ages after hatching. In this series of experiments the imprinting experience was standard. It consisted in having the duckling follow the model 150 to 200 feet around the runway during a period of 10 minutes. Figure 2 shows the scores made by ducklings in the different age groups. It appears that some imprinting occurs immediately after hatching, but a maximum score is consistently made only by those ducklings imprinted in the 13- to 16-hour-old group. This result is indicated in Figure 3, which shows the percentage of animals in each age group that made perfect imprinting scores.

Social facilitation in imprinting. In order to find whether imprinting would occur in those ducklings which were past the critical age for imprinting—that is, over 24 hours of age—we attempted to imprint these older ducklings in the presence of another duckling which had received an intensive imprinting experience. Ducklings ranging in age from 24 to 52 hours were given 100 feet of following experience during a period of 30 minutes. The average score

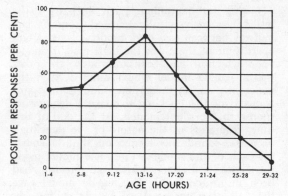

Figure 2   The critical age at which ducklings are most effectively imprinted is depicted by this curve, which shows the average test score of ducklings imprinted at each age group.

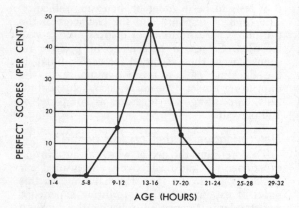

Figure 3   Another way of showing the critical age is by plotting the percentage of animals in each age group that made scores of 100 percent in testing.

for the ducklings was 50 percent; this shows that some imprinting can occur as a result of social facilitation. Two conclusions can be drawn. (i) Social facilitation will extend the critical age for imprinting. (ii) The strength of imprinting in these older ducklings is significantly less than that when the animal is imprinted alone at the critical age under the same time and distance conditions; under the latter circumstances the average score made is between 80 and 90 percent. A further indication of this dissipation of imprintability with increasing age is obtained when we average the scores for those animals which were between 24 and 32 hours old. The average score for these animals was

60 percent, while the score made by older animals ranging in age from 36 to 52 hours was 43 percent. One last item points to the difference; even when the time and distance were increased during imprinting of the older ducklings there were no perfect scores. With such a large amount of distance to travel during the imprinting period, approximately 40 percent of the animals would be expected to make perfect scores if they were imprinted during the critical period.

Genetic studies

We have also considered the genetic side of imprinting. We kept ducklings which were highly imprintable and bred them separately from ducklings which showed very little imprinting response. We thus had two groups of offspring, those produced by "imprinters" and those produced by "non-imprinters." There was a clear and significant difference in the imprinting behavior of the two groups, even in the first generation. The offspring of imprintable parents were easily imprinted; those of less imprintable parents were difficult to imprint. The "imprinter" ducklings had imprinting test scores more than three times better than those of the "non-imprinter" ducklings. Similar results were also obtained in a study of bantam chicks. We are also following up those animals which have had experimental imprinting experiences to determine what influence, if any, these experiences have on their behavior as adults. So far the results are inconclusive, but they do suggest that experimental imprinting of mallards affects their behavior as adults, particularly with respect to courtship patterns.

Birds of various species show differing degrees of imprintability. Domestic fowl do show imprinting responses, but the results are not as clear as for wild birds. We have had good success in imprinting some breeds of chicks, and the best imprinters among them are the Vantress broilers. Leghorns, on the other hand, appear to be too highly domesticated to give clear results. Other animals we have used in our experimentation are two kinds of geese, black ducks, wood ducks, turkeys, pheasants, quail, Peking ducks, and Rouens. The various breeds we have so far used in our work and the degree of imprintability found in each are shown in Table 1.

Imprinting in mammals

The guinea pig is similar to the chick and the duckling in that it is mobile and reasonably self-sufficient soon after birth. For this reason we used it in exploratory work. We first developed a method of obtaining the young from the mother with minimal parental contact. This was done by Caesarean section. However, further work showed that it was sufficient to obtain the young within an hour after they were born, and for the moment we are doing this. Guinea pigs imprint on human beings and follow them about as do the fowl with which we have been work-

Table 1 Number and imprintability of different experimental animals. Most of the animals were imprinted in runway and mallard decoy situations. Some of the Vantress broilers were imprinted on colored spheres, and the sheep were imprinted on human beings.

Animal	No.*	Imprintability †
Ducks		
Wild mallard	3500	E +
Domesticated mallard	150	E
Peking	200	G
Rouen	100	F
Wood	50	P
Black	50	G
Total	4050	
Geese		
Canada	30	E +
Pilgrim	50	G
Total	80	
Chickens		
Jungle fowl	100	G
Cochin bantam	300	G
New Hampshire Red	100	G
Rhode Island Red	100	G
Barred Rock	200	G
Vantress broiler	500	G +
White Rock	100	F
Leghorn	200	P
Total	1600	
Other fowl		
Pheasant	100	P
Eastern bobwhite quail	50	G
California valley quail	20	E
Turkey	30	F
Total	200	
Mammals		
Sheep	2	G
Guinea pig	12	G
Total	14	
Total	5944	

* Estimated for fowl, actual for mammals.
† E, excellent; G, good; F, fair; P, poor.

ing. The maximum effectiveness of the imprinting experience seems to be over by the second day. So far, in using our imprinting apparatus with our usual duck decoy we have obtained best results sometime before the end of the first day of age. Work is being continued so that we can have a more standardized procedure before beginning a major program in this area.

Imprinting and learning

The supposed irreversibility of imprinting has been particularly singled out by some investigators to show that imprinting is nothing but "simple learning"—whatever that is. We do have some isolated instances which point to a long-range effect, but systematic work is just now beginning in our laboratories. Canada goslings, imprinted on human beings for a period of a week or two, will from that time on respond to their former caretaker with the typical "greeting ceremony," as well as accept food out of his hand. This occurs in spite of the fact that they normally associate entirely with the Canada geese on our duck pond. A more striking case is that of a jungle fowl cock which was imprinted by me and kept away from his own species for the first month. This animal, even after 5 years—much of that time in association with his own species—courts human beings with typical behavior, but not females of his own species. This certainly is a far-reaching effect and is similar to the finding of Räber (21), who reported on a male turkey whose behavior toward human beings was similar. An increased amount of homosexual courtship in mallards has been observed with some of our laboratory imprinted animals, which, while not a statistically valuable finding, perhaps points also to long-range, irreversible effects.

Imprinting is currently receiving much attention, and papers on the subject are being published at an impressive rate. Unfortunately, most experimenters appear to be certain that imprinting is identical with simple association learning and design their experiments as studies in association learning. In many instances the animals are too old when used in the experiments to fall within the critical age for imprinting, with the result that only association learning can occur. Papers falling into this category are those of Jaynes (22), Moltz (23), and James (24).

Our own experiments on the relation between association learning with food as a reward and imprinting during the critical period show four distinct differences.

In the first place, learning a visual discrimination problem is quicker and more stable when practice trials are spaced by interspersing time periods between trials than when practice trials are massed by omitting such intervening time periods. With imprinting, however, massed practice is more effective than spaced practice, as shown by our law of effort. Secondly, *recency* in experience is maximally effective in learning a discrimination; in imprinting, *primacy* of experience is the maximally effective factor. The second difference is illustrated by the following experiment. Two groups of 11 ducklings each were imprinted on two different imprinting objects. Group 1 was first imprinted on a male mallard model and then on a female model. Group 2, on the other hand, was first imprinted on a female model and subsequently on a male model. Fourteen of the 22 ducklings, when tested with both models present, preferred the model to which they first had been imprinted, showing primacy. Only five preferred the model to which they had been imprinted last, showing recency, and three showed no preference at all.

In addition, it has been found that the administration of punishment or painful stimulation increases the effectiveness of the imprinting experience, whereas such aversive stimulation results in avoidance of the associated stimulus in the case of visual discrimination learning.

Finally, chicks and ducklings under the influence of meprobamate are able to learn a color discrimination problem just as well as, or better than, they normally do, whereas the administration of this drug reduces imprintability to almost zero.

Imprinting, then, is an obviously interesting phenomenon, and the proper way to approach it is to make no assumptions. To find out its characteristics, to explore its occurrence in different organisms, and to follow its effects would seem a worth-while program of study.

What can we say in conclusion about the general nature of imprinting? Our best guess to date is that it is a rigid form of learning, differing in several ways from the usual association learning which comes into play immediately after the peak of imprintability. In other words, imprinting in our experiments results in the animal learning the rough, generalized characteristics of the imprinting object. Its detailed appreciation of the *specific* object comes as a result of normal conditioning—a process which in the case of these animals takes a much longer time and is possible days after the critical period for imprinting has passed. It is an exciting new field and is certainly worthy of study.

References and notes
1. W. Craig, *Am. J. Sociol.* **14**, 86 (1908).
2. O. Heinroth, *Verhandl. 5th Intern. Ornithol. Kong.* 589–702 (1910).
3. —— and M. Heinroth, *Die Vögel Mitteleuropas* (Lichterfelde, Berlin, 1924–33).
4. K. Lorenz, *J. Ornithol.* **83**, 137, 289 (1935).
5. W. H. Thorpe, *Proc. Linnean Soc. London.* **156**, 70 (1944).
6. G. P. Baerends and J. M. Baerends-van Roon, *Behaviour*, Suppl. 1, 1 (1950).
7. U. Grabowski, *Z. Tierpsychol.* **4**, 326 (1941).
8. F. F. Darling, *Wild Country* (Cambridge Univ. Press, London, 1938).
8a. H. Hediger, *Wild Animals in Captivity* (Butterworths, London, 1938).
9. A. O. Ramsay, *Auk.* **68**, 1 (1951).
10. E. Fabricius, *Acta Zool. Fennica.* **68**, 1 (1951).
11. A. O. Ramsay and E. H. Hess, *Wilson Bull.* **66**, 196 (1954).
12. M. M. Nice, *Condor.* **55**, 33 (1953).
13. R. A. Hinde, W. H. Thorpe, M. A. Vince, *Behaviour.* **9**, 214 (1956).
14. The work described in this article was supported in part by grant No. M-776 of the National Institutes of Health, Public Health Service, Department of Health, Education, and Welfare, Bethesda, Md.; by the Wallace C. and Clara A. Abbott Memorial Fund, of the University of Chicago, Chicago, Ill.; and by the Wallace Laboratories, New Brunswick, N.J.
15–20a omitted.
21. H. Räber, *Behaviour.* **1**, 237 (1948).
22. J. Jaynes, *J. Comp. and Physiol. Psychol.* **49**, 201 (1956); *ibid.* **50**, 6 (1957); *ibid.* **51**, 234, 238 (1958).
23. H. Moltz and L. A. Rosenblum, *ibid.* **51**, 580 (1958).
24. H. James, *Can. J. Psychol.*, in press.

As you have seen, the timing of early experience is quite important. A certain optimum amount of early experience is also necessary for the full development of behavior. It has been shown, for instance, that visual perception is very much dependent upon patterned light stimulation. Similarly, as shown here, the development of pain perception is dependent upon early stimulation.

The work reported in this article is rooted in the neuropsychological theory of D. O. Hebb. One of the readings for Chapter 20 describes this theory.

Points to guide your study

1. The *t* values and levels of significance are simply ways of stating that the average differences in conditions are *not* due to chance alone. The psychologist is stating that there is probably a real difference between conditions.

2. Note that the effect of a restricted early environment seems to be on the "meaning" of pain, not on the sensation itself. This difference between perception and sensation will be encountered again.

7. THE EFFECTS OF EARLY EXPERIENCE ON THE RESPONSE TO PAIN

*Ronald Melzack, Cornell University, and T. H. Scott**

There has recently been an increase of theoretical interest in the effects of early experience on behavior, together with an increasing number of experimental studies (1). In one area, however, there is a marked discrepancy between theoretical emphasis and amount of empirical investigation: the area of avoidance behavior and pain.

Earlier clinical and theoretical formulations of the problem of early experience by Freud and his followers (4, and others there cited) have not led to any experimental studies relevant to pain perception and response, although the importance of early experience as a determinant of adult behavior was fully recognized. More recently, Scott and his associates (12) have

* Part of the results reported in this paper are contained in a thesis submitted by the senior author in partial fulfillment of the requirements of the Ph.D. degree at McGill University. The authors gratefully acknowledge the advice and guidance of Dr. D. O. Hebb throughout this study and the technical assistance of Dr. Peter Milner. This experiment was supported by grants from the Foundations Fund for Research in Psychiatry, the Rockefeller Foundation, and a Fellowship stipend given to the senior author by the National Research Council of Canada.

Ronald Melzack and T. H. Scott. The effects of early experience on the response to pain. *J. comp. physiol. Psychol.*, 1957, **50**, 155–161. Copyright 1957 by the American Psychological Association. Reprinted here with permission from the authors and the American Psychological Association.

arrived at a new hypothesis of the effects of early experience. They maintain that during the development of the organism there are specific critical periods after which sufficient maturation has occurred for various types of experience to have lasting effects on adult behavior. Although Fuller (3) has provided evidence for a critical period in the dog for the acquisition of conditioned responses to pain, there is no direct evidence which relates early pain experience with the behavior of the mature organism.

Hebb's (5) distinction between pain perception as a neurophysiological event and the overt response to pain, such as avoidance, has important implications for any attempt to relate early experience and pain perception in the mature organism. Hebb conceives of pain as a disruption of spatially and temporally organized activity in the cerebrum, this disruption per se constituting the physiological basis of pain. Since aggregates of neurons are assumed to develop their particular spatio-temporal organization as a result of prolonged, patterned sensory stimulation in early life, the theory thus suggests that the degree of pain perceived is, in part at least, dependent on the earlier experience of the organism. Pain, then, in the context of Hebb's theory, is not an elementary sensation, but a complex perceptual process in which a major role is played by all kinds of earlier perceptual learning, including both specific and nonspecific experience involving all the senses. Furthermore, as a result of direct experience with noxious stimuli, the organism tends to repeat and thus acquire any responses which decrease the cerebral disruption (i.e., pain).

That early experience does indeed play an important role in perceiving and responding to pain is strongly suggested by the study of a chimpanzee deprived of normal somesthetic stimulation during infancy and early maturity (11). After removal from somesthetic restriction, the chimpanzee appeared to have a heightened pain threshold, since "he 'panted' as chimpanzees do when they are being tickled" (11, p. 502) when his legs or lower ventral trunk was poked with a sharp pencil point or pin. Furthermore, the animal was found to be strikingly poor in localizing sites of noxious stimulation on its body.

The method of sensory deprivation or restriction has proved successful in ascertaining the effects of early perceptual experience on adult behavior (7, 14). The present experiment, then, is an attempt to study the effects of early sensory restriction, with special emphasis on the restriction of pain experience, on the adult response to noxious stimuli.

Subjects

Six litters of an inbred Scottish terrier strain were used. Each litter was randomly divided into two groups. One group, containing a total of 10 dogs, was placed in restriction cages. The 12 dogs which comprised the "free environment" or control group were raised normally as pets in private homes and in the laboratory.

Each restricted dog used in the present study was reared in isolation from puppyhood to maturity in a cage which was specially designed to prevent the dogs from seeing outside, although daylight was permitted to enter through a large air vent at the top of each cage. Each cage contained two compartments, and when the sliding partition between them was opened once a day, the dog was allowed to enter a freshly cleaned compartment. In this way the dogs were deprived of normal sensory and social experience from the time that weaning was completed at the age of four weeks until they were removed at about eight months of age. After the restricted dogs were released from their cages, they received the same opportunities for social and sensory stimulation as their normally reared littermates.

Testing of the dogs began about three to five weeks after the restricted animals were released. Two of the restricted dogs were tested a second time about two years after their release. Since the litters used in this study were born at different times over a three-year period, it was impossible to use all the dogs for all the tests.

Experiment I. *Response to electric shock*

Method. *Subjects.* The Ss were seven restricted and nine free-environment dogs.

Apparatus. A toy car that could be maneuvered by hand through a battery and steering mechanism was connected to a variable electric shock source provided by a variac and transformer circuit. The dogs were tested with the car on a 6-ft. by 3-ft. sheet-metal floor surrounded by a 2-ft.-high wire-mesh enclosure.

Procedure. The toy car was used to pursue the dogs and deliver a 1500-v., 6 ma. shock when it hit them. Each shock was of 1-sec. duration, although the dogs could escape the full shock by moving away rapidly. The car, which had a constant speed, was kept in waiting about 2 ft. from S. If S were sitting, E moved the car directly toward S. If S were moving, however, E moved the car into S's path and pursued S up to one of the far sides of the enclosure.

The E tried to hit each dog ten times during a testing period. However, if at some time during testing, the dog made five successive avoidances of the approaching car without being hit and shocked, testing was discontinued for that period, and the total number of shocks received by the dog up to that time was recorded. A dog reached the *criterion* of successful avoidance learning when it received no shock during a testing period.

Results. The restricted dogs received a mean of 24.7 shocks (range: 10 to 40) from the toy car, while the free-environment dogs received a mean of 6 shocks (range: 2 to 11). This difference between the two groups provided a t value of 4.4, which is significant at the .001 level. By the end of the fourth test period all the free-environment dogs had reached criterion. Three of the seven restricted dogs, however, had not yet done so; and two of these had received the full 40 shocks and gave no sign of learning to avoid the toy car. Testing was therefore discontinued at this time. The mean number of shocks received by the restricted dogs, then, would probably be considerably higher than it is if the restricted dogs were tested until all had reached criterion.

Characteristic differences in the behavior of the two groups were striking. The normal dogs were found to show smooth, precise movements which were oriented directly toward the toy car. They often sat looking at the car, swaying from side to side as it moved toward them, and only at the last moment, when the car was inches away from them, did they jump up and trot out of the way. Although these dogs were excited at first, their behavior after the first few shocks showed little excitement, and they made only minimal, unhurried avoidance movements of a leg or the tail to avoid being hit.

This behavior stands in marked contrast with the wild, aimless activity first shown by the restricted dogs. Their typical behavior consisted of running around in a circular path with excessive, exaggerated movements of the whole body. They often avoided being hit only by virtue of the remarkable rapidity of their action. But there was no difficulty in hitting them if the car were moved into the circular path. They then ran right into it. At other times, they stood up at the side of the testing enclosure, in an attempt to climb out, and received the full ten shocks in this position.

Two years after restriction. Two restricted dogs were tested two years after they had been released from restriction and still showed the same exaggerated behavior. While one learned after 9 shocks, the other received 23 shocks before it began to avoid successfully. This gave a mean of 16 shocks, which differs significantly from the mean of 6 shocks for the normal animals at the .01 level ($t = 3.5$).

Experiment II. Avoidance training

Method. *Subjects.* The Ss were 7 restricted and 12 free-environment dogs.

Apparatus. A 6-ft. by 3-ft. testing enclosure, bounded by wire mesh 2 ft. high, was divided lengthwise into two halves by a 3-in.-high barrier. The steel grid floor was connected to a variable electric shock source provided by a variac and transformer circuit.

Procedure. The threshold levels at which the dogs responded to electric shock in the apparatus were first determined by raising the voltage stepwise. The voltmeter reading at which an animal first showed signs of startle or slight jumping was recorded as the threshold value. The behavior of the animals to this value of shock was then observed for two test periods during which each dog received about ten shocks on both sides of the barrier.

For the avoidance training which followed, the side which was to be "hot" for a particular animal was the one to which it moved and which it seemed to "prefer" when placed in the apparatus. The first shock on the training days was given 1 min. after the dog was placed on the "hot" side, and a shock was given every 60 sec. thereafter, as long as the dog stayed on the "hot" side, until S had received a total of ten shocks. However, when a dog jumped to the safe side during avoidance training, it was placed back on the "hot" side, and E waited 60 sec. before shock was again presented. If a dog made three successive jumps from the "hot" to the

safe side without receiving shock, testing was discontinued for that period for the animal, and the number of shocks received up to that time was recorded. The shock was of 1-sec. duration, and 1500 v., 6 ma., which was about three times the mean threshold value measured by the voltmeter. The *criteria* for successful avoidance learning were: (a) two successive days with no more than one shock on each day or (b) a training day on which a dog went to the safe side immediately and received no shock.

Results. No significant difference in the thresholds at which the two groups first responded to electric shock was obtained in this experiment. Furthermore, no behavioral differences between the two groups were observed with these minimal values of shock, either in degree of responsiveness or type of response made.

During avoidance training with 1500 v., however, differences in the behavior of the two groups were obvious. By the end of the third testing period, only 2 of the 12 free-environment dogs had not reached criterion; 5 of the 7 restricted dogs, however, had not reached criterion at this stage, and 3 of these 5 had received the full 30 shocks and gave no sign of learning. Because of the obvious differences between the two groups, and the clearly unpleasant nature of the electric shock used, testing was discontinued at this point. Thus no dog received more than 30 shocks during avoidance training.

While the free-environment dogs received a mean of 5 shocks (range: 1 to 22), the restricted dogs received a mean of 20.3 shocks (range: 1 to 30) during avoidance training. The *t* score of the difference between the means, 5.07, is significant at the .001 level.

The three dogs that received the full 30 shocks showed stereotyped forms of behavior to the shock. One dog whirled around violently in narrow circles on the "hot" side immediately after getting the first shock in the enclosure and continued to do so until it was removed after getting 10 shocks. The second dog always ran to a particular corner on the "hot" side after the first shock, and sat in a peculiar, awkward position, getting shock after shock without moving. The third dog learned a partial response to the shock, consisting of placing its forelegs on the barrier, while its hindquarters were on the "hot" side, in this way getting repeated shocks without learning the entire response.

Two years after restriction. Two dogs that had been out of restriction for two years, and were reared normally in the laboratory during that time, nevertheless received a mean of 19 shocks during the three testing periods, which differed significantly from the free-environment dogs' mean of 5 shocks at the .02 level of significance ($t = 2.78$). One of these dogs received 25 shocks, and S still maintained the same awkward, "frozen" position in the corner that it had assumed when first tested two years previously, giving little sign of learning permanently to make the appropriate response of stepping over the 3-in. barrier to the safe side.

Experiment III. Response to burning

Method. *Subjects.* The Ss were ten restricted and eight free-environment dogs.

Apparatus. A box of safety matches.

Procedure. Each dog was allowed to roam the testing room freely for 1 min., and the amount of time S spent near E in an area which had been demarcated previously by a chalk line was recorded. The S was then called by E to this area. A safety match was struck, and E attempted to push the flame into the dog's nose at least three times. Although the dog was held forcibly by E, S was able to avoid being burned by moving or turning its head away rapidly from the match. The dog was then allowed to move to any part of the room, and the time spent near E in the area of the source of burning was recorded during a 2-min. period. The percentages of time S spent near E before and after presentation of the flame were then compared.

Results. Of the eight free-environment dogs tested, six spent less time near E after he tried to burn them than before. Of the ten restricted dogs, however, nine spent *more* time in the area near E *after* nose-burning than before. While the restricted dogs spent 27.9 per cent of the time near E before stimulation, they spent 51.2 per cent of the time in that area following presentation of the match. The amount of time spent by the free-environment dogs near E decreased from 45.1 per cent before to 32.8 per cent after presentation of the match. The nonparametric sign test (9) provided a chi-square value of 5.40 with Yates' correction, which is significant at the .02 level of confidence.

One of the most remarkable features of the restricted dogs was their behavior during and following presentation of the flame. To the astonishment of the observers, seven of the ten restricted dogs made no attempt to get away from E *during* stimulation, and it was not even necessary to hold them. The sequence of behavior observed was almost identical for all seven dogs: they moved their noses into the flame as soon as it was presented, after which the head or whole body jerked away, as though reflexively; but then they came right back to their original position and hovered excitedly near the flame.

Three of them repeatedly poked their noses into the flame and sniffed at it as long as it was present. If they snuffed it out, another match was struck, and the same sequence of events occurred. The other four did not sniff at the match, but offered no resistance nor made any attempt to get away after the first contact, and E was able to touch the dogs' noses with the flame as often as he wished. Only three of the restricted dogs squealed on making contact with the flame and tried subsequently to avoid it by moving their heads. Two of these, however, made no attempt to get away from E after stimulation had stopped.

In contrast, the normal dogs moved their heads so rapidly that it was often impossible to hit their noses with the flame. The E tried to move the match in from unexpected angles or to distract the Ss in order to hit them with the flame. But the normal dogs moved their heads slightly and usually successfully, receiving only one or two very brief contacts with the flame; and they then struggled to escape from E's grasp at their sides.

Experiment IV. Response to pin-prick

Method. *Subjects.* The Ss were eight restricted and nine free-environment dogs.

Apparatus. A large, sharp dissecting needle.

Procedure. The procedure in this experiment is the same as that used in Exp. III, except that the dogs were pin-pricked rather than burned. While the dog was held at the neck, a long dissecting needle was jabbed into the skin at the sides and hind thighs about three or four times.

Results. Of the eight restricted dogs, six spent more time near E after pin-pricking than before. These dogs increased the time spent in the demarcated area from 50.8 per cent before to 58.4 per cent after pin-pricking. The normal dogs, on the other hand, spent a mean of only 8.9 per cent of the time after pin-pricking near E, compared with 42.2 per cent before. Of the nine normally reared dogs, eight spent less time near E after pin-pricking than before. The sign test provided a chi-square value of 4.74, which is significant at the .05 level.

The behavior of the restricted dogs in response to pin-prick was almost identical with that observed with the flame: they appeared unaware that they were being stimulated *by something in the environment.* Four of the restricted dogs made no response whatever apart from localized reflexive twitches at the side or leg when they were pricked. The E was often able to pierce the skin of these dogs completely so that the needle was lodged in it without eliciting withdrawal or any behavioral indication that pain was being "felt" or responded to other than spasmodic, reflexive jerks. The remaining four restricted dogs pulled their bodies aside a few inches or yipped to *some* of the pin-pricks, but when released two of them stayed right next to E, who was able to repeat the procedure and jab them with the needle as often as he wished. The noxious stimulation received was apparently not "perceived" as coming from E, and their behavior subsequently was not oriented or organized in terms of the noxious stimulus in any noticeable way.

The free-environment dogs, however, provided an unmistakable index of perceived pain. They tried to jump aside to escape the pin-prick, yelped, and often struggled for release after two or three pin-pricks. They would then dash away from E's hand and take up a position in the farthest corner of the testing room.

Supplementary observations. The behavior of the restricted dogs in the four experiments just described is entirely consistent with everyday observations of their behavior. It was noted, for example, that their aimless activity resulted in some of them frequently striking their heads against water pipes that ran along the walls just above the floor of the testing room. One dog, by actual count, struck his head against these pipes more than 30 times in a single hour. This was never observed once in the normal dogs. Similarly, the rapid movement of the restricted dogs and their unpredictability as to direction resulted a number of times in the dogs' having a paw or the tail stepped on. Often there was no sign that the dogs "felt" pain when this happened, though the procedure would have elicited a howl from a normal dog, and the restricted S made no attempt to withdraw from the place where injury was received.

Discussion

The outstanding feature of the behavior of the restricted dogs was their inability to respond adaptively and intelligently to the variety of stimuli which were presented to them. There can be little doubt that the restricted dogs "felt" electric shock: their disturbance by it was marked and unmistakable. Similarly, the behavior of at least three of the restricted dogs indicates that pin-prick and contact with fire were "felt" in some way. Nevertheless, it was obvious that the restricted dogs did not know how to make the proper avoidance responses which would have prevented further stimulation. The results permit the conclusion, then, that early experience plays an essential role in the emergence of such basic behavior as avoidance of noxious stimuli.

Sherrington has defined pain as "the psychical adjunct of an imperative protective reflex" (13, p. 286). And many psychologists since then (2, 8, 10) have interpreted pain in terms of imperative reflex responses. Such a view, however, is not consistent with the observations reported here. Most of the restricted dogs did indeed show localized reflex responses to the stimulation, yet their behavior was clearly inadequate to cope with the intense electric shocks or such grossly injurious stimuli as contact with fire or piercing of the skin. In comparison, their littermates which had been reared normally in a free environment exhibited the ability to avoid prolonged contact with injurious stimuli, and they were able to learn with great rapidity to make highly organized, abiently oriented responses to every form of noxious stimulus that was presented. However, the capacity of the restricted dogs to acquire good, adaptive behavior to noxious stimulation was notably limited after release from restriction, even with the adequate opportunity that was provided for them to gain varied, normal perceptual experience. Maladaptive behavior like freezing and whirling also developed, and they were observed as consistent responses as long as two years after release. Thus, it appears that the requisite experience must come at the correct time in the young organism's life. During later stages of development, the experience necessary for adaptive, well-organized responses to pain may never be properly acquired.

The inability of the restricted dogs to cope intelligently with noxious stimuli, however, cannot be attributed to inadequate response mechanisms alone. Their reflexive jerks and movements during pin-prick and contact with fire suggest that they may have "felt something" during stimulation; but the *lack* of any observable emotional disturbance apart from these reflex movements in at least four of the dogs following pin-prick and in seven of them after nose-burning indicates that their *perception* of the event was highly abnormal in comparison with the behavior of the normally reared control dogs. Livingston (6) has made the observation that experience with pain in childhood is an important determinant of the manner in which the adult perceives and responds to pain; that is, the "meaning" involved in a perception such as pain, and the attitudes of the individual in situations involving pain, are largely a function of the earlier, related experiences of that individual. The results reported here are consistent with observations such as this and can be interpreted in a similar manner.

The isolation of the restricted dogs prevented them from acquiring experience early in life with severe skin-damage and fire. It is evident, then, that the flame and pin-prick could not have evoked the neural "phase sequences" (memories) acquired during earlier pain experiences (5) that might have been aroused in the normal dogs. The results strongly suggest that the restricted dogs lacked awareness of a necessary aspect of normal pain perception: the "meaning" of physical damage or at least *threat* to the physical well-being that is inherent in the normal organism's perception of pain. The observations of the restricted dogs' poking their noses into fire, or permitting *E* to cause bodily damage by fire and pin-prick without emotional disturbance apart from localized reflexes, indicates that an interpretation such as this is valid. Indeed, to say that these restricted dogs perceived fire and pin-prick as *threatening*, or even painful in any *normal* sense, would be anthropomorphism rather than inference from observed behavior.

The results which have been reported here then, make it difficult to treat behavior related to pain simply in terms of frequency and intensity of stimulations or in terms of imperative reflex responses alone (2, 8, 10) without regard to the earlier perceptual experience of the organism. The behavior of the restricted dogs suggests that perceiving and responding to pain, which is so fundamental to normal adult behavior and presumably so important for the survival of an individual or species, requires a background of early, prolonged, perceptual experience.

Summary

1. Ten dogs were reared in isolation from puppyhood to maturity in specially constructed cages which drastically restricted their sensory experience. Twelve control littermates were raised normally as pets in private homes and in the laboratory.

2. In two tests using strong electric shock, the restricted dogs required significantly more shocks before they learned to make the proper avoidance responses than their free-environment littermates.

3. In tests using nose-burning and pin-pricking, the behavior of the restricted dogs was found to be strikingly different in capacity to perceive pain and respond to it when compared to their normal littermates.

4. It is concluded that early perceptual experience determines, in part at least, (a) the emergence of overt responses such as avoidance to noxious stimulation, and (b) the actual capacity to perceive pain normally.

References

1. Beach, F. A., and Jaynes, J. Effects of early experience upon the behavior of animals. *Psychol. Bull.*, 1954, **51**, 239–263.
2. Estes, W. K. An experimental study of punishment. *Psychol. Monogr.*, 1944, **57**, No. 3 (Whole No. 263).
3. Fuller, J. L., Easler, C. A., and Banks, E. M. Formation of conditioned avoidance responses in young puppies. *Amer. J. Physiol.*, 1950, **160**, 462–466.
4. Greenacre, P. The biological economy of birth. In O. Fenichel (Ed.), *The psychoanalytic study of the child*. New York: International Universities Press, 1945.
5. Hebb, D. O. *The organization of behavior*. New York: John Wiley and Sons, Inc., 1949.
6. Livingston, W. K. What is pain? *Sci. Amer.*, 1953, **188**, 59–66.
7. Melzack, R. The genesis of emotional behavior: an experimental study of the dog. *J. comp. Physiol. Psychol.*, 1954, **47**, 166–168.
8. Miller, N. E. Learnable drives and rewards. In S. S. Stevens (Ed.), *Handbook of experimental psychology*. New York: John Wiley and Sons, Inc., 1951.
9. Moses, L. E. Non-parametric statistics for psychological research. *Psychol. Bull.*, 1952, **49**, 122–143.
10. Mowrer, O. H. *Learning theory and personality dynamics*. New York: Ronald Press, 1950.
11. Nissen, H. W., Chow, K. L., and Semmes, Josephine. Effects of restricted opportunity for tactual, kinesthetic, and manipulative experience on the behavior of a chimpanzee. *Amer. J. Psychol.*, 1951, **64**, 485–507.
12. Scott, J. P., Fredricson, E., and Fuller, J. L. Experimental exploration of the critical period hypothesis. *Personality*, 1951, **1**, 162–183.
13. Sherrington, C. S. *Man on his nature*. New York: Macmillan, 1941.
14. Thompson, W. R., and Heron, W. The effects of restricting early experience on the problem solving capacity of dogs. *Canad. J. Psychol.*, 1954, **8**, 17–31.

Sensory Motor Development

The developmental schedule of the human infant is pretty much genetically determined. This article presents you with a picture of the sequence of development in the first year of life.

A point to guide your study

Note that the graph presented here is a rather unusual one.

8. A DEVELOPMENTAL GRAPH FOR THE FIRST YEAR OF LIFE

*C. Anderson Aldrich, M.D., and Mildred A. Norval, M.D.**

This developmental graph is presented in the hope that it will help physicians to follow, with the minimal expenditure of time and effort, the neuromuscular growth of infants under their care and that these steps may be used as an index of the child's maturity.

Since growth follows a regular pattern, the sequence of the steps is established and progressive. This enables one to demonstrate to the mother, each time she comes for advice, what her child will be doing next in his progress.

While the sequence is rigid, each child has his own rate of growth, which reflects his own individuality as well as his maturity. However, the appearance of these emerging abilities may be modified somewhat by the effects of environment.

We followed the development of 215 normal infants from birth to the early part of their second year. The parents of these infants came from all strata of society in Rochester, Minn., which, however, has a larger proportion of professional people than is usual.

We explained to each mother how her infant's behavior would follow the sequence of growth and advised her to encourage her baby to use each ability as it appeared. Since we were to record the time of onset of these various accomplishments, this information was obtained by testing the infants at monthly intervals and instructing the mothers to watch for the achievements not so easily elicited in the clinic. The latter method is subject to the inaccuracy of lay observation but does allow the infant to be observed in his natural environment by an interested person.

* From the Rochester Child Health Project, and the Section on Pediatrics, Mayo Clinic.

C. A. Aldrich and M. A. Norval. A developmental graph for the first year of life. *J. Pediat.*, 1946, **29**, 304–308. Copyright 1946 by The C. V. Mosby Company. Reprinted here with permission from The C. V. Mosby Company and Dr. M. A. Norval for the authors.

The more evident steps in neuromuscular growth were chosen. Some of these have been used previously (1) to make parents conscious of the stereotyped progress of growth. The selected steps were:

1. Smile—the baby begins to smile in response to an adult or to his voice.

2. Vocal—the infant utters such sounds as "ah," "eh," and "uh" spontaneously or on stimulation.

3. Head control—when the infant is lifted by his hands from the supine to the sitting position, the head does not lag but is supported by the anterior muscles of the neck.

4. Hand control—when a toy is dangled in the midline above his chest, the infant is able to close in on the toy with one or both hands and to grasp it.

5. Roll—the baby makes a complete roll from back to abdomen.

6. Sit—the baby sits alone for several moments.

7. Crawl—the baby is able to move across the room or pen toward some distant object; this may be accomplished by rolling over and over, pushing himself along on his stomach or back, or by any individual modification of progression.

8. Prehension—this is the bringing together of the thumb and index finger to pick up a small object. This can be tested with a bright-colored button.

9. Pull up—the infant pulls himself to a standing position.

10. Walk with support—the infant walks by holding to his playpen, a piece of furniture, or an adult.

11. Stand alone—without any support, the infant stands for several moments.

12. Walk alone—the infant takes several steps alone.

While our records aimed to record the onset of these achievements in infancy, many of the statements in the literature indicate the age of achievement of the perfected act; hence, they will record a somewhat later age. In previous reports there is a wide variation in the number of infants observed, their selection, the methods of testing them, and the definition of the various levels of development.

It is generally stated that the first voluntary behavior is smiling in response to the mother's voice, which occurred in our series at the average age of 0.9 month. Chaillé (2) stated that after 3 weeks of age many babies begin to smile. Preyer (3) observed a smile on his son's face during the fourth week (0.9 month). Sixty per cent of babies smile socially at one month of age according to Linfert and Hierholzer (4), while others have recorded this as an accomplishment at 1.4 months (5, 6) and at 2 months (7-10).

Morgan and Morgan (9) found that one-half of the babies were cooing at 6 weeks (1.4 months), as was also found by Gesell, Thompson, and Amatruda, (6) and Bayley (5). The average infant in our group uttered sounds, such as "uh" and "ah," at 1.7 months. Other authors (3, 7, 8, 11) have reported vocalization at 2 months.

When the infant is raised from the supine to the sitting position, the head will lag slightly at 12 weeks (2.8 months) according to Gesell and associates and at 16 weeks (3.7 months) according to Amatruda (12). We found, on the average, the baby was able to control his head at 2.9 months. Other authors have stated that the head could be held erect and steady at 3 months (2, 11), and at 4 months (4).

Bühler (7) expressed the belief that the ability of the infant to reach for and grasp a toy is the best index of normal activity in a 4-month-old child. This is the age at which our average infant attained this achievement. Gesell (13) and Hetzer and Wolf (8) have observed reaching movements in infants at this age and stated that the infants may close in on the object and grasp it, while some (10, 14, 15) have seen this achievement first during the fifth month.

In our series the mothers first observed their infants to roll from back to stomach at an average age of 5.1 months, while Shinn (10) saw her niece do this at 24 weeks (5.5 months). Gesell (16) stated that a few infants may roll from back to stomach as early as 4 months but that this is a usual feat at 6 months. Bühler reported this ability at 6 months, Shirley (15) at 29 weeks (6.7 months), and Hetzer and Wolf at 7 months.

The average infant in our grasp was sitting alone for several minutes at 6.2 months. Sitting alone, at least briefly, has been reported at 25 weeks (5.8 months) (10), 6 months (2, 14), and 7 months (13, 15).

By many diverse means our average infant began "going places" on the floor at 7.3 months. Bühler (7) and others (2, 8) reported that infants are able to move toward a desired object at 7 months, while some consider crawling at 8 months (13) and 8.5 months (15) an achievement.

Our infants started to pick up objects with thumb and forefinger at an average age of 8.1 months. Gesell (13) stated that the 9-month-old infant can bring the thumb and forefinger together deftly in a plucking movement and that this movement is highly characteristic of that age. Bayley listed this as an accomplishment at 9.3 months.

Shinn reported that her niece pulled herself to a standing position at 33 weeks (7.6 months) and Bühler observed the first attempts of an infant to raise himself to a standing position at 8 months, while our infants did this at the average age of 8.7 months. Others have reported this at 9 months (2, 13) and 10 months (8, 15).

Infants have been seen to walk with help at 9 months (6, 7), 42 weeks (9.7 months) (15), and 49 weeks (11.3 months) (3), but Gesell (13) listed this as an achievement for those 12 months of age. The average child in our series walked with help at 9.5 months.

Shinn's niece stood alone on the three hundred and sixteenth day (10.4 months). Our average child was observed to stand alone for several moments at 10.7 months, but Gesell and Thompson have this as a momentary achievement in their age group at 56 weeks (12.9 months).

Our average child as well as Shinn's niece and Chaillé's group of children succeeded in walking alone at 12 months of age. Shirley expressed the belief that this may occur between 11.5 and 17.5 months, while 77 per cent of McGraw's (17) series were walking independently by 14 months and the median child of Gesell's (13) group walked at 15 months.

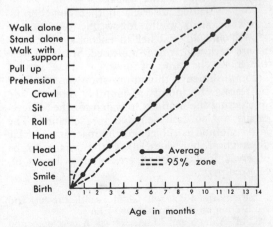

Figure 1 A developmental graph for the first year of life shows the average age for the achievements selected and the zone in which 95 per cent of the infants' developmental graphs fell.

The average ages of these developmental steps are shown in Fig. 1. There was no difference between the rate of the boys and that of the girls. The course of the more rapidly developing infants and of the slower ones followed the average graph but at earlier and later ages, respectively.

Our results in this study show the age of walking alone to be accelerated about two months as compared with the generally accepted standards. Inasmuch as our group forms a fairly representative sampling of an average American city we find it hard to account for this discrepancy. It may be due to the fact that our mothers were instructed to foster rather than to oppose the steps of growth. Possibly the emotional freedom thus produced had an influence on the early postural achievements of the group.

Summary

Twelve developmental steps of neuromuscular growth were chosen for study in an unselected group of 215 infants observed at a well baby clinic. Observations of the age of attainment of these steps were made and a graph depicting the average curve and the variation is presented. In our group walking alone appeared accelerated somewhat as compared with the generally accepted standard time.

References

1. Aldrich, C. A.: *J. Pediat.* **20**: 272, 1942.
2. Chaillé, S. E.: *New Orleans M. & S. J.* **14**: 893, 1886–1887.
3. Preyer, W.: Mental Development in the Child (Translated by H. W. Brown), New York, 1893, D. Appleton and Company.
4. Linfert, H. E., and Hierholzer, H. M.: *Stud. Psychol. & Psychiat.* **1**: 1, 1926–1928.
5. Bayley, N.: Mental Growth During the First Three Years, In Barker, R. G., Kounin, J. S., and Wright, H. F.: Child Behavior and Development; a Course of Representative Studies, ed. 1, New York, 1943, McGraw-Hill Book Company, Inc., chap. 6, pp. 87–105.
6. Gesell, A., Thompson, H., and Amatruda, C. S.: The Psychology of Early Growth; Including Norms of Infant Behavior and a Method of Genetic Analysis, New York, 1938, The Macmillan Company.
7. Bühler, C.: The first year of life (Translated by Pearl Greenberg and Rowena Ripin), New York, 1930, The John Day Company, Inc.
8. Hetzer, H., and Wolf, K.: *Ztschr. f. Psychol. u. Physiol. d. Sinnesorg.* (Abt. 1) **107**: 62, 1928.
9. Morgan, S. S., and Morgan, J. J. B.: *J. Pediat.* **25**: 168, 1944.
10. Shinn, M. W.: Notes on the Development of a Child, vol. 1, Berkeley, 1899, University of California Press, pts. 3–4.
11. Cattell, P.: The Measurement of Intelligence of Infants and Young Children, New York, 1940, The Psychological Corporation.
12. Amatruda, C. S.: *J. Pediat.* **20**: 265, 1942.
13. Gesell, A.: Infancy and Human Growth, New York, 1928, The Macmillan Company.
14. Halverson, H. M.: The Development of Prehension in Infants, In Barker, R. G., Kounin, J. S., and Wright, H. F.: Child Behavior and Development; a Course of Representative Studies, ed. 1, New York, 1943, McGraw-Hill Book Company, Inc., chap. 4, pp. 49–65.
15. Shirley, M. M.: The First Two Years: A Study of Twenty-five Babies, Volume I: Postural and Locomotor Development, Minneapolis, 1931, The University of Minnesota Press.
16. Gesell, A. L.: The Mental Growth of a Preschool Child; a Psychological Outline of Normal Development from Birth to the Sixth Year, Including a System of Developmental Diagnosis, New York, 1925, The Macmillan Company.
17. McGraw, M. B.: *J. Pediat.* **17**: 747, 1940.

CHAPTER THREE

Drives and motivation

GENERAL DRIVES

The present article also shows the importance of early experience. The phenomenon reported here may be similar to imprinting. (See the article by E. H. Hess in Chapter 2.) Note that the effect is not due to the way in which the infant is fed. It is due to the amount of pleasing contact which the infant has with his surrogate mother.

H. F. Harlow, at the University of Wisconsin, has spent most of his scientific career working on the development and learning of the primates, mostly rhesus monkeys. The current set of studies is part of a longer-range set of studies on the development of learning abilities in monkeys.

Points to guide your study

1. Note the many ingenious tests used in this article.

2. What are some specific difficulties in the application of these findings to human infants?

9. AFFECTIONAL RESPONSES IN THE INFANT MONKEY

Harry F. Harlow and Robert R. Zimmermann, University of Wisconsin and Cornell University*

Investigators from diverse behavioral fields have long recognized the strong attachment of the neonatal and infantile animal to its mother. Although this affectional behavior has been commonly observed, there is, outside the field of ethology, scant experimental evidence permitting identification of the factors critical to the formation of this bond. Lorenz (1) and others have stressed the importance of innate visual and auditory mechanisms which, through the process of imprinting, give rise to persisting following responses in the infant bird and fish. Imprinting behavior has been demonstrated successfully in a variety of avian species under controlled laboratory conditions, and this phenomenon has been investigated systematically in order to identify those variables which contribute to its development and maintenance [see, for example, Hinde, Thorpe, and Vince (2),

Fabricius (3), Hess (4), Jaynes (5), and Moltz and Rosenblum (6)]. These studies represent the largest body of existent experimental evidence measuring the tie between infant and mother. At the mammalian level there is little or no systematic experimental evidence of this nature.

Observations on monkeys by Carpenter (7), Nolte (8), and Zuckermann (9) and on chimpanzees by Köhler (10) and by Yerkes and Tomilin (11) show that monkey and chimpanzee infants develop strong ties to their mothers and that these affectional attachments may persist for years. It is, of course, common knowledge that human infants form strong and persistent ties to their mothers.

Although students from diverse scientific fields recognize this abiding attachment, there is considerable disagreement about the nature of its development and its fundamental underlying mechanisms. A common theory among psychologists, sociologists, and anthropologists is that of learning based on drive reduction. This theory proposes that the infant's attachment to the mother results from the association of the mother's face and form with the alleviation of

* H. F. Harlow and R. R. Zimmermann. Affectional responses in the infant monkey. *Science*, 1959, **130**, 421–432. Copyright 1959 by the American Association for the Advancement of Science. Reprinted here with permission from the authors and the American Association for the Advancement of Science.

certain primary drive states, particularly hunger and thirst. Thus, through learning, affection becomes a self-supporting, derived drive (12). Psychoanalysts, on the other hand, have stressed the importance of various innate needs, such as a need to suck and orally possess the breast (2), or needs relating to contact, movement, temperature (13), and clinging to the mother (14).

The paucity of experimental evidence concerning the development of affectional responses has led these theorists to derive their basic hypotheses from deductions and intuitions based on observation and analysis of adult verbal reports. As a result, the available observational evidence is often forced into a preconceived theoretical framework. An exception to the above generalization is seen in the recent attempt by Bowlby (14) to analyze and integrate the available observational and experimental evidence derived from both human and subhuman infants. Bowlby has concluded that a theory of component instinctual responses, species-specific, can best account for the infant's tie to the mother. He suggests that the species-specific responses for human beings (some of these responses are not strictly limited to human beings) include contact, clinging, sucking, crying, smiling, and following. He further emphasizes that these responses are manifested independently of primary drive reduction in human and subhuman infants.

The absence of experimental data which would allow a critical evaluation of any theory of affectional development can be attributed to several causes. The use of human infants as subjects has serious limitations, since it is not feasible to employ all the experimental controls which would permit a completely adequate analysis of the proposed variables. In addition, the limited response repertoire of the human neonate severely restricts the number of discrete or precise response categories that can be measured until a considerable age has been attained. Thus, critical variables go unmeasured and become lost or confounded among the complex physiological, psychological, and cultural factors which influence the developing human infant.

Moreover, the use of common laboratory animals also has serious limitations, for most of these animals have behavioral repertoires very different from those of the human being, and in many species these systems mature so rapidly that it is difficult to measure and assess their orderly development. On the other hand, subhuman primates, including the macaque monkey, are born at a state of maturity which makes it possible to begin precise measurements within the first few days of life. Furthermore,

their postnatal maturational rate is slow enough to permit precise assessment of affectional variables and development.

Over a 3-year period prior to the beginning of the research program reported here (15), some 60 infant macaque monkeys were separated from their mothers 6 to 12 hours after birth and raised at the primate laboratory of the University of Wisconsin. The success of the procedures developed to care for these neonates was demonstrated by the low mortality and by a gain in weight which was approximately 25 percent greater than that of infants raised by their own mothers. All credit for the success of this program belongs to van Wagenen (16), who had described the essential procedures in detail.

These first 3 years were spent in devising measures to assess the multiple capabilities of the neonatal and infantile monkey. The studies which resulted have revealed that the development of perception, learning, manipulation, exploration, frustration, and timidity in the macaque monkey follows a course and sequence which is very similar to that in the human infant. The basic differences between the two species appear to be the advanced postnatal maturational status and the subsequent more rapid growth of the infant macaque. Probably the most important similarities between the two, in relation to the problem of affectional development, are characteristic responses that have been associated with, and are considered basic to, affection; these include nursing, clinging, and visual and auditory exploration.

In the course of raising these infants we observed that they all showed a strong attachment to the cheesecloth blankets which were used to cover the wire floors of their cages. Removal of these cloth blankets resulted in violent emotional behavior. These responses were not short-lived; indeed, the emotional disturbance lasted several days, as was indicated by the infant's refusal to work on the standard learning tests that were being conducted at the time. Similar observations had already been made by Foley (17) and by van Wagenen (16), who stressed the importance of adequate contact responses to the very survival of the neonatal macaque. Such observations suggested to us that contact was a true affectional variable and that it should be possible to trace and measure the development and importance of these responses. Indeed there seemed to be every reason to believe that one could manipulate all variables which have been considered critical to the development of the infant's attachment to a mother, or mother surrogate.

To attain control over maternal variables, we took the calculated risk of constructing and using

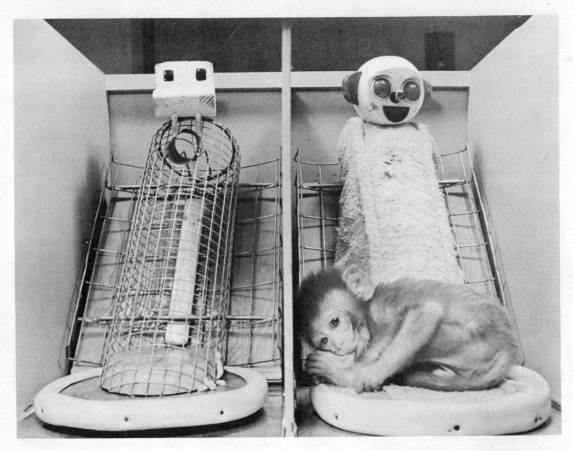

Figure 1   Wire and cloth mother surrogates.

inanimate mother surrogates rather than real mothers. The cloth mother that we used was a cylinder of wood covered with a sheath of terry cloth (18), and the wire mother was a hardware-cloth cylinder. Initially, sponge rubber was placed underneath the terry cloth sheath of the cloth mother surrogate, and a light bulb behind each mother surrogate provided radiant heat. For reasons of sanitation and safety these two factors were eliminated in construction of the standard mothers, with no observable effect on the behavior of the infants. The two mothers were attached at a 45-degree angle to aluminum bases and were given different faces to assure uniqueness in the various test situations (Figure 1). Bottle holders were installed in the upper middle part of the bodies to permit nursing. The mother was designed on the basis of previous experience with infant monkeys, which suggested that nursing in an upright or inclined position with something for the infant to clasp facilitated successful nursing and resulted in healthier infants (see 16). Thus, both mothers provided the basic known requirements for adequate nursing, but the cloth mother provided an additional variable of contact comfort. That both of these surrogate mothers provided adequate nursing support is shown by the fact that the total ingestion of formula and the weight gain was normal for all infants fed on the surrogate mothers. The only consistent difference between the groups lay in the softer stools of the infants fed on the wire mother.

Development of affectional responses

The initial experiments on the development of affectional responses have already been reported (19) but will be briefly reviewed here, since subsequent experiments were derived from them. In the initial experiments, designed to evaluate the role of nursing on the development of affection, a cloth mother and a wire mother were placed in different cubicles attached to the infant's living cage. Eight newborn monkeys were placed in individual cages with the surrogates; for four infant monkeys the cloth mother lactated and the wire mother did not, and for the other four this condition was reversed.

The infants lived with their mother surrogates for a minimum of 165 days, and during this time they were tested in a variety of situations designed to measure the development of affectional responsiveness. Differential affectional responsiveness was initially measured in terms of mean hours per day spent on the cloth and on the wire mothers under two conditions of feeding, as shown in Figure 2. Infants fed on the cloth mother and on the wire mother have highly similar scores after a short adaptation period (Figure 3), and over a 165-day period both groups show a distinct preference for the cloth mother. The persistence of the differential responsiveness to the mothers for both groups of infants is evident, and the over-all differences between the groups fall short of statistical significance.

These data make it obvious that contact comfort is a variable of critical importance in the development of affectional responsiveness to the surrogate mother, and that nursing appears to play a negligible role. With increasing age and opportunity to learn, an infant fed from a lactating wire mother does not become more responsive to her, as would be predicted from a derived-drive theory, but, instead becomes increasingly more responsive to its nonlactating cloth mother. These findings are at complete variance with a drive-reduction theory of affectional development.

The amount of time spent on the mother does not necessarily indicate an affectional attachment. It could merely reflect the fact that the cloth mother is a more comfortable sleeping platform or a more adequate source of warmth for the infant. However, three of the four infants nursed by the cloth mother and one of the four nursed by the wire mother left a gauze-covered heating pad that was on the floor of their cages during the first 14 days of life to spend up to 18 hours a day on the cloth mother. This suggests that differential heating or warmth is not a critical variable within the controlled temperature range of the laboratory.

Other tests demonstrate that the cloth mother is more than a convenient nest; indeed, they show that a bond develops between infant and cloth-mother surrogate that is almost unbelievably similar to the bond established between human mother and child. One highly definitive test measured the selective maternal responsiveness of the monkey infants under conditions of distress or fear.

Various fear-producing stimuli, such as the moving toy bear illustrated in Figure 4, were presented to the infants in their home cages. The data on differential responses under both feeding conditions are given in Figure 5. It is apparent that the cloth mother was highly preferred to the wire mother, and it is a fact that these differences were unrelated to feeding conditions—that is, nursing on the cloth or on the wire mother. Above and beyond these objective data are observations on the form of the infants' responses in this situation. In spite of their abject terror, the infant monkeys, after reaching the cloth mother and rubbing their bodies about hers, rapidly come to lose their fear of the frightening stimuli. Indeed, within a minute or two most of the babies were visually exploring the very thing which so shortly before had seemed an object of evil. The bravest of the babies would actually leave the mother and approach the fearful monsters, under, of course, the protective gaze of their mothers.

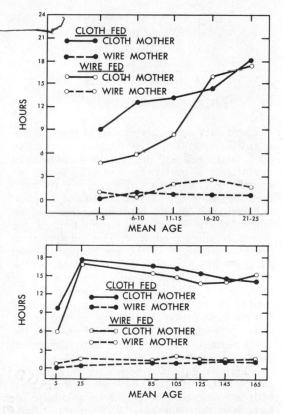

Figures 2 (top) and 3 (bottom) Time spent on cloth and wire mother surrogates: Figure 2, long term, Figure 3, short term.

Figure 4   Typical fear stimulus.

These data are highly similar, in terms of differential responsiveness, to the time scores previously mentioned and indicate the overwhelming importance of contact comfort. The results are so striking as to suggest that the primary function of nursing may be that of insuring frequent and intimate contact between mother and infant, thus facilitating the localization of the source of contact comfort. This interpretation finds some support in the test discussed above. In both situations the infants nursed by the cloth mother developed consistent responsiveness to the soft mother earlier in testing than did the infants nursed by the wire mother, and during this transient period the latter group was slightly more responsive to the wire mother than the former group. However, these early differences shortly disappeared.

Additional data have been obtained from two groups of four monkeys each which were raised with a single mother placed in a cubicle attached to the living-cage. Four of the infants were presented with a lactating wire mother and the other four were presented with a nonlactating cloth mother. The latter group was

hand-fed from small nursing bottles for the first 30 days of life and then weaned to a cup. The development of responsiveness to the mothers was studied for 165 days; after this the individual mothers were removed from the cages and testing was continued to determine the strength and persistence of the affectional responses.

Figure 6 presents the mean time per day spent on the respective mothers over the 165-day test period, and Figure 7 shows the percentage of responses to the mothers when a fear-producing stimulus was introduced into the home cage. These tests indicate that both groups of infants developed responsiveness to their mother surrogates. However, these measures did not reveal the differences in behavior that were displayed in the reactions to the mothers when the fear stimuli were presented. The infants raised on the cloth mother would rush to the mother and cling tightly to her. Following this initial response these infants would relax and either begin to manipulate the mother or turn to gaze at the feared object without the slightest sign of apprehension. The infants raised on the wire mother, on the other hand, rushed away from the feared object toward their mother but did not cling to or embrace her. Instead, they would either clutch themselves and rock and vocalize for the remainder of the test or rub against the side of the cubicle. Contact with the cubicle or the mother did not reduce the emotionality produced by the introduction of the fear stimulus. These differences are revealed in emotionality scores, for behavior such as vocalization, crouching, rocking, and sucking, recorded during the test. Figure 8 shows the mean emotionality index for test sessions for the two experimental groups, the dual-mother groups, and a comparable control group raised under standard laboratory conditions. As can be seen, the infants raised with the single wire mother have the highest emotionality scores of all the groups, and the infants raised with the single cloth mother or with a cloth and wire mother have the lowest scores. It appears that the responses made by infants raised only with a wire mother were more in the nature of simple flight responses to the fear stimulus and that the presence of the mother surrogate had little effect in alleviating the fear.

During our initial experiments with the dual-mother conditions, responsiveness to the lactating wire mother in the fear tests decreased with age and opportunity to learn, while responsiveness to the nonlactating cloth mother increased. However, there was some indication of a slight increase in frequency of response to the wire mother for the first 30 to 60 days (see Figure 5).

These data suggest the possible hypothesis that nursing facilitated the contact of infant and mother during the early developmental periods.

The interpretation of all fear testing is complicated by the fact that all or most "fear" stimuli evoke many positive exploratory responses early in life and do not consistently evoke flight responses until the monkey is 40 to 50 days of age. Similar delayed maturation of visually induced fear responses has been reported for birds (3), chimpanzees (20), and human infants (21).

Because of apparent interactions between fearful and affectional developmental variables, a test was designed to trace the development of approach and avoidance responses in these infants. This test, described as the straight-alley test, was conducted in a wooden alley 8 feet long and 2 feet wide. One end of the alley contained a movable tray upon which appropriate stimuli were placed. The other end of the alley contained a box for hiding. Each test began with the monkey in a start box 1 foot in front of the hiding box; thus, the animal could maintain his original position, approach the stimulus tray as it moved toward him, or flee into the hiding box. The infants were presented with five stimuli in the course of five successive days. The stimuli included a standard cloth mother, a standard wire mother, a yellow cloth mother with the head removed, a blank tray, and a large black fear stimulus, shown in Figure 9. The infants were tested at 5, 10, and 20 days of age, respectively, and then at 20-day intervals up to 160 days. Figure 10 shows the mean number of 15-second time periods spent in contact with the appropriate mother during the 90-second tests for the two single-mother groups, and the responses to the cloth mother by four infants from the dual-mother group.

During the first 80 days of testing, all the groups showed an increase in response to the respective mother surrogates. The infants fed on the single wire mother, however, reached peak responsiveness at this age and then showed a consistent decline, followed by an actual avoidance of the wire mother. During test sessions 140 to 160, only one contact was made with the wire mother, and three of the four infants ran into the hiding box almost immediately and remained there for the entire test session. On the other hand, all of the infants raised with a cloth mother, whether or not they were nursed by her, showed a progressive increase in time spent in contact with their cloth mothers until approaches and contacts during the test sessions approached maximum scores.

The development of the response of flight from the wire mother by the group fed on the

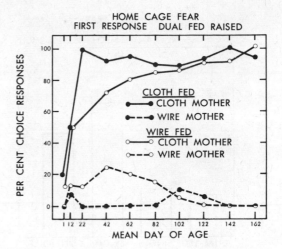

Figure 5   Differential responsiveness in fear tests.

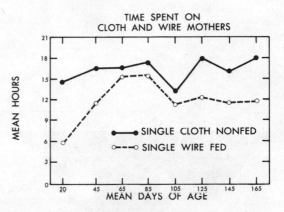

Figure 6   Time spent on single mother surrogates.

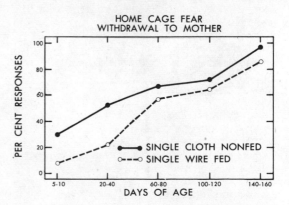

Figure 7   Responsiveness to single surrogate mothers in fear tests.

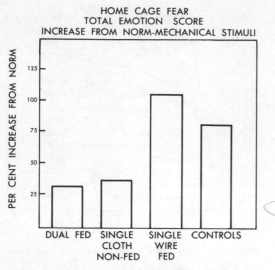

HOME CAGE FEAR
TOTAL EMOTION SCORE
INCREASE FROM NORM-MECHANICAL STIMULI

Figure 8   Change in emotionality index in fear tests.

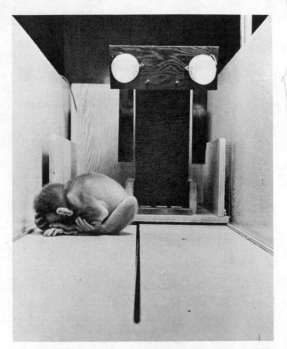

Figure 9   Response to the fear stimulus in the straight-alley test.

single wire mother is, of course, completely contrary to a derived-drive theory of affectional development. A comparison of this group with the group raised with a cloth mother gives some support to the hypothesis that feeding or nursing facilitates the early development of responses to the mother but that without the factor of contact comfort, these positive responses are not maintained.

The differential responsiveness to the cloth mother of infants raised with both mothers, the reduced emotionality of both the groups raised with cloth mothers in the home-cage fear tests, and the development of approach responses in the straight-alley test indicate that the cloth mother provides a haven of safety and security for the frightened infant. The affectional response patterns found in the infant monkey are unlike tropistic or even complex reflex responses; they resemble instead the diverse and pervasive patterns of response to his mother exhibited by the human child in the complexity of situations involving child-mother relationships.

The role of the mother as a source of safety and security has been demonstrated experimentally for human infants by Arsenian (22). She placed children 11 to 30 months of age in a strange room containing toys and other play objects. Half of the children were accompanied into the room by a mother or a substitute mother (a familiar nursery attendant), while the other half entered the situation alone. The children in the first group (mother present) were much less emotional and participated much more fully in the play activity than those in the second group (mother absent). With repeated testing, the security score, a composite score of emotionality and play behavior, improved for the children who entered alone, but it still fell far below that for the children who were accompanied by their mothers. In subsequent tests, the children from the mother-present group were placed in the test room alone, and there was a drastic drop in the security scores. Contrariwise, the introduction of the mother raised the security scores of children in the other group.

We have performed a similar series of open-field experiments, comparing monkeys raised on mother surrogates with control monkeys raised in a wire cage containing a cheesecloth blanket from days 1 to 14 and no cloth blanket subsequently. The infants were introduced into the strange environment of the open field, which was a room measuring 6 by 6 by 6 feet, containing multiple stimuli known to elicit curiosity-manipulatory responses in baby monkeys. The infants raised with single mother surrogates were placed in this situation twice a week for 8 weeks, no mother surrogate being present during one of the weekly sessions and the appropriate mother surrogate (the kind which the experimental infant had always known) being present during the other sessions. Four infants raised with dual mother surrogates and four control infants were subjected to similar experimental sequences, the cloth mother being present on half of the occasions. The remaining four "dual-mother" infants were given repetitive tests to obtain information on the development of responsiveness to each of the dual mothers in this situation. A cloth blanket was always available as one of the stimuli throughout the sessions. It should be emphasized that the blanket could readily compete with the cloth mother as a contact stimulus, for it was standard laboratory procedure to wrap the infants in soft cloth whenever they were removed from their cages for testing, weighing, and other required laboratory activities.

As soon as they were placed in the test room, the infants raised with cloth mothers rushed to their mother surrogate when she was present and clutched her tenaciously, a response so strong that it can only be adequately depicted by motion pictures. Then, as had been observed in the fear tests in the home cage, they rapidly relaxed, showed no sign of apprehension, and began to demonstrate unequivocal positive responses of manipulating and climbing on the mother. After several sessions, the infants began to use the mother surrogate as a base of operations, leaving her to explore and handle a stimulus and then returning to her before going to a new plaything. Some of the infants even brought the stimuli to the mother, as shown in Figure 11. The behavior of these infants changed radically in the absence of the mother. Emotional indices such as vocalization, crouching, rocking, and sucking increased sharply. Typical response patterns were either freezing in a crouched position, as illustrated in Figure 12, or running around the room on the hind feet, clutching themselves with their arms. Though no quantitative evidence is available, contact and manipulation of objects was frantic and of short duration, as opposed to the playful type of manipulation observed when the mother was present.

In the presence of the mother, the behavior of the infants raised with single wire mothers was both quantitatively and qualitatively different from that of the infants raised with cloth mothers. Not only did these infants spend little or no time contacting their mother surrogates but the presence of the mother did not reduce their emotionality. These differences are evident in the mean number of time periods spent in

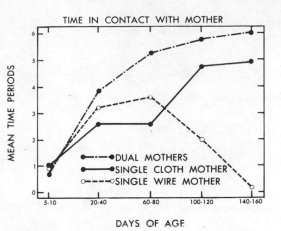

Figure 10   Responsiveness to mother surrogates in the straight-alley tests.

contact with the respective mothers, as shown in Figure 13, and the composite emotional index for the two stimulus conditions depicted in Figure 14. Although the infants raised with dual mothers spent considerably more time in contact with the cloth mother than did the infants raised with single cloth mothers, their emotional reactions to the presence and absence of the mother were highly similar, the composite emotional index being reduced by almost half when the mother was in the test situation. The infants raised with wire mothers were highly emo-

Figure 11   Subsequent response to cloth mother and stimulus in the open-field test.

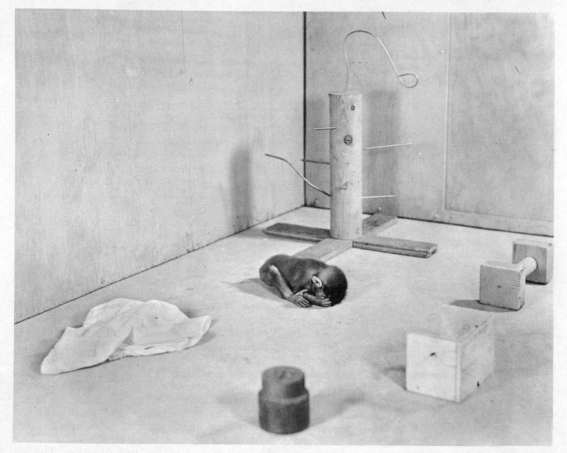

Figure 12   Response in the open-field test in the absence of the mother surrogate.

tional under both conditions and actually showed a slight, though nonsignificant, increase in emotionality when the mother was present. Although some of the infants reared by a wire mother did contact her, their behavior was similar to that observed in the home-cage fear tests. They did not clutch and cling to their mother as did the infants with cloth mothers; instead, they sat on her lap and clutched themselves, or held their heads and bodies in their arms and engaged in convulsive jerking and rocking movements similar to the autistic behavior of deprived and institutionalized human children. The lack of exploratory and manipulatory behavior on the part of the infants reared with wire mothers, both in the presence and absence of the wire mother, was similar to that observed in the mother-absent condition for the infants raised with the cloth mothers, and such contact with objects as was made was of short duration and of an erratic and frantic nature. None of the infants raised with single wire

mothers displayed the persistent and aggressive play behavior that was typical of many of the infants that were raised with cloth mothers.

The four control infants, raised without a mother surrogate, had approximately the same emotionality scores when the mother was absent that the other infants had in the same condition, but the control subjects' emotionality scores were significantly higher in the presence of the mother surrogate than in her absence. This result is not surprising, since recent evidence indicates that the cloth mother with the highly ornamental face is an effective fear stimulus for monkeys that have not been raised with her.

Further illustration of differential responsiveness to the two mother surrogates is found in the results of a series of developmental tests in the open-field situation, given to the remaining four "dual-mother" infants. These infants were placed in the test room with the cloth mother, the wire mother, and no mother present on successive occasions at various age levels. Figure

15 shows the mean number of time periods spent in contact with the respective mothers for two trials at each age level, and Figure 16 reveals the composite emotion scores for the three stimulus conditions during these same tests. The differential responsiveness to the cloth and wire mothers, as measured by contact time, is evident by 20 days of age, and this systematic difference continues throughout 140 days of age. Only small differences in emotionality under the various conditions are evident during the first 85 days of age, although the presence of the cloth mother does result in slightly lower scores from the 45th day onward. However, at 105 and 145 days of age there is a considerable difference for the three conditions, the emotionality scores for the wire-mother and blank conditions showing a sharp increase. The heightened emotionality found under the wire-mother condition was mainly contributed by the two infants fed on the wire mother. The behavior of these two infants in the presence of the wire mother was similar to the behavior of the animals raised with a single wire mother. On the few occasions when contact with the wire mother was made, the infants did not attempt to cling to her; instead they would sit on her lap, clasp their heads and bodies, and rock back and forth.

In 1953 Butler (23) demonstrated that mature monkeys enclosed in a dimly lighted box would open and reopen a door for hours on end with no other motivation than that of looking outside the box. He also demonstrated that rhesus monkeys showed selectivity in rate and frequency of door-opening in response to stimuli of different degrees of attractiveness (24). We have utilized this characteristic of response selectivity on the part of the monkey to measure the strength of affectional responsiveness of the babies raised with mother surrogates in an infant version of the Butler box. The test sequence involves four repetitions of a test battery in which the four stimuli of cloth mother, wire mother, infant monkey, and empty box are presented for a 30-minute period on successive days. The first four subjects raised with the dual mother surrogates and the eight infants raised with single mother surrogates were given a test sequence at 40 to 50 days of age, depending upon the availability of the apparatus. The data obtained from the three experimental groups and a comparable control group are presented in Figure 17. Both groups of infants raised with cloth mothers showed approximately equal responsiveness to the cloth mother and to another infant monkey, and no greater responsiveness to the wire mother than to an empty box. Again, the results are independent of the kind of

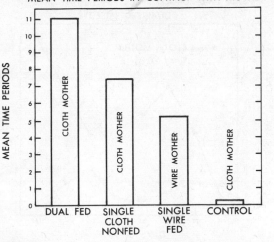

MEAN TIME PERIODS IN CONTACT WITH MOTHER

Figure 13 Responsiveness to mother surrogates in the open-field test.

mother that lactated, cloth or wire. The infants raised with only a wire mother and those in the control group were more highly responsive to the monkey than to either of the mother surrogates. Furthermore, the former group showed a higher frequency of response to the empty box than to the wire mother.

In summary, the experimental analysis of the development of the infant monkey's attachment to an inanimate mother surrogate demonstrates the overwhelming importance of the variable of soft body contact that characterized the cloth mother, and this held true for the appearance, development, and maintenance of the infant-surrogate-mother tie. The results also indicate

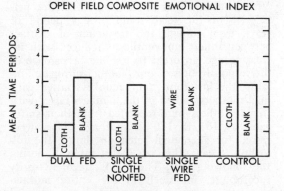

OPEN FIELD COMPOSITE EMOTIONAL INDEX

Figure 14 Emotionality index in testing with and without the mother surrogates.

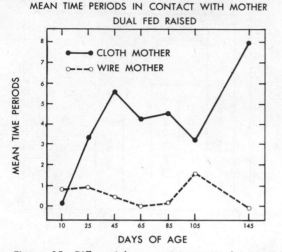

Figure 15   Differential responsiveness in the open-field test.

that, without the factor of contact comfort, only a weak attachment, if any, is formed. Finally, probably the most surprising finding is that nursing or feeding played either no role or a subordinate role in the development of affection as measured by contact time, responsiveness to fear, responsiveness to strangeness, and motivation to seek and see. No evidence was found indicating that nursing mediated the development of any of these responses, although there is evidence indicating that feeding probably facilitated the early appearance and increased the early strength of affectional responsiveness. Certainly feeding, in contrast to contact comfort, is neither a necessity nor a sufficient condition for affectional development.

Retention of affectional responses

One of the outstanding characteristics of the infant's attachment to its mother is the persistence of the relationship over a period of years, even though the frequency of contact between infant and mother is reduced with increasing age. In order to test the persistence of the responsiveness of our "mother-surrogate" infants, the first four infant monkeys raised with dual mothers and all of the monkeys raised with single mothers were separated from their surrogates at 165 to 170 days of age. They were tested for affectional retention during the following 9 days, then at 30-day intervals during the following year. The results are of necessity incomplete, inasmuch as the entire mother-surrogate program was initiated less than 2 years ago, but enough evidence is available to indicate that the attachment formed to the

cloth mother during the first 6 months of life is enduring and not easily forgotten.

Affectional retention as measured by the modified Butler box for the first 15 months of testing for four of the infants raised with two mothers is given in Figure 18. Although there is considerable variability in the total response frequency from session to session, there is a consistent difference in the number of responses to the cloth mother as contrasted with responses to either the wire mother or the empty box, and there is no consistent difference between responses to the wire mother and to the empty box. The effects of contact comfort versus feeding are dramatically demonstrated in this test by the monkeys raised with either single cloth or wire mothers. Figure 19 shows the frequency of response to the appropriate mother surrogate and to the blank box during the preseparation period and the first 90 days of retention testing. Removal of the mother resulted in a doubling of the frequency of response to the cloth mother and more than tripled the difference between the responses to the cloth mother and to the empty box for the infants that had lived with a single non-lactating cloth mother surrogate. The infants raised with a single lactating wire mother, on the other hand, not only failed to show any consistent preference for the wire mother but also showed a highly significant reduction in general level of responding. Although incomplete, the data from further retention testing indicate that the difference between these two groups persists for at least 5 months.

Affectional retention was also tested in the open field during the first 9 days after separation and then at 30-day intervals. Each test condition was run twice in each retention period.

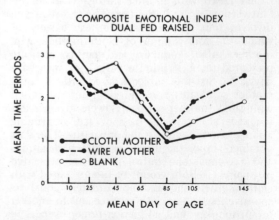

Figure 16   Emotionality index under three conditions in the open-field test.

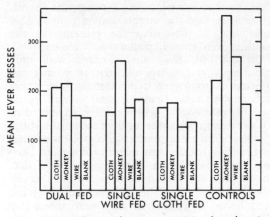

Figure 17   Differential responses to visual exploration.

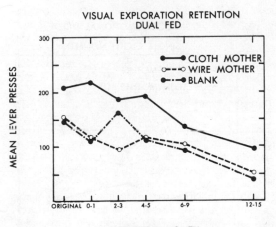

VISUAL EXPLORATION RETENTION
DUAL FED

RETENTION MONTH

Figure 18   Retention of differential visual-exploration responses.

In the initial retention tests the behavior of the infants that had lived with cloth mothers differed slightly from that observed during the period preceding separation. These infants tended to spend more time in contact with the mother and less time exploring and manipulating the objects in the room. The behavior of the infants raised with single wire mothers, on the other hand, changed radically during the first retention session, and responses to the mother surrogate dropped almost to zero. Objective evidence for these differences is given in Figure 20, which reveals the mean number of time periods spent in contact with the respective mothers. During the first retention test session, the infants raised with a single wire mother

showed almost no responses to the mother surrogate they had always known. Since the infants raised with both mothers were already approaching the maximum score in this measure, there was little room for improvement. The infants raised with a single nonlactating cloth mother, however, showed a consistent and significant increase in this measure during the first 90 days of retention. Evidence for the persistence of this responsiveness is given by the fact that after 15 months' separation from their mothers, the infants that had lived with cloth mothers spent an average of 8.75 out of 12 possible time periods in contact with the cloth mother during the test. The incomplete data for retention testing of the infants raised with only a lactating wire mother or a nonlactating cloth mother indicate that there is little or no change in the initial differences found between these two groups in this test over a period of 5 months. In the absence of the mother, the behavior of the infants raised with cloth mothers was similar in the initial retention tests to that during the preseparation tests, but with repeated testing they tended to show gradual adaptation to the open-field situation and, consequently, a reduc-

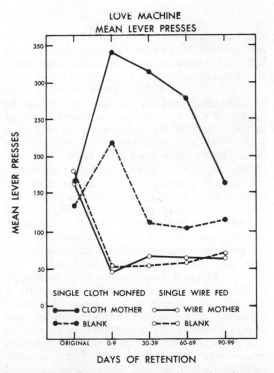

LOVE MACHINE
MEAN LEVER PRESSES

DAYS OF RETENTION

Figure 19   Retention of differential visual-exploration responses by single-surrogate infants.

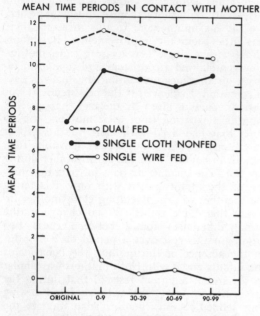

FREE FIELD RETENTION

MEAN TIME PERIODS IN CONTACT WITH MOTHER

Figure 20   Retention of responsiveness to mother surrogates in the open-field tests.

than their scores when the mother was absent. It appears that the infants gained considerable emotional security from the presence of the mother even though contact was denied.

In contrast, the animals raised with only lactating wire mothers did not show any significant or consistent trends during these retention sessions other than a general over-all reduction of emotionality, which may be attributed to a general adaptation, the result of repeated testing.

Affectional retention has also been measured in the straight-alley test mentioned earlier. During the preseparation tests it was found that the infants that had only wire mothers developed a general avoidance response to all of the stimuli in this test when they were about 100 days of age and made few, if any, responses to the wire mother during the final test sessions. In contrast, all the infants raised with a cloth

tion in their emotionality scores. Even with this over-all reduction in emotionality, these infants had consistently lower emotionality scores when the mother was present.

At the time of initiating the retention tests, an additional condition was introduced into the open-field test: the surrogate mother was placed in the center of the room and covered with a clear Plexiglas box. The animals raised with cloth mothers were initially disturbed and frustrated when their efforts to secure and contact the mother were blocked by the box. However, after several violent crashes into the plastic, the animals adapted to the situation and soon used the box as a place of orientation for exploratory and play behavior. In fact, several infants were much more active under these conditions than they were when the mother was available for direct contact. A comparison of the composite emotionality index of the babies raised with a single cloth or wire mother under the three conditions of no mother, surrogate mother, and surrogate-mother-box is presented in Figure 21. The infants raised with a single cloth mother were consistently less emotional when they could contact the mother but also showed the effects of her visual presence, as their emotionality scores in the plastic box condition were definitely lower

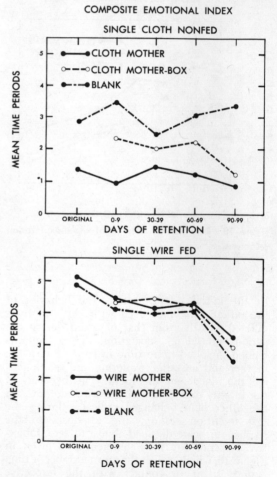

Figure 21   Emotionality index under three conditions in the open-field retention tests.

mother responded positively to her. Maternal separation did not significantly change the behavior of any of the groups. The babies raised with just wire mothers continued to flee into the hiding booth in the presence of the wire mother, while all of the infants raised with cloth mothers continued to respond positively to the cloth mother at approximately the same level as in the pre-separation tests. The mean number of time periods spent in contact with the appropriate mother surrogates for the first 3 months of retention testing are given in Figure 22. There is little, if any, waning of responsiveness to the cloth mother during these 3 months. There appeared to be some loss of responsiveness to the mother in this situation after 5 to 6 months of separation, but the test was discontinued at that time as the infants had outgrown the apparatus.

The retention data from these multiple tests demonstrate clearly the importance of body contact for the future maintenance of affectional responses. Whereas several of the measures in the preseparation period suggested that the infants raised with only a wire mother might have developed a weak attachment to her, all responsiveness disappeared in the first few days after the mother was withdrawn from the living cage. Infants that had had the opportunity of living with a cloth mother showed the opposite effect and either became more responsive to the cloth mother or continued to respond to her at the same level.

These data indicate that once an affectional bond is formed it is maintained for a very considerable length of time with little reinforcement of the contact-comfort variable. The limited data available for infants that have been separated from their mother surrogates for a year suggest that these affectional responses show resistance to extinction similar to the resistance previously demonstrated for learned fears and learned pain. Such data are in keeping with common observation of human behavior.

It is true, however, that the infants raised with cloth mothers exhibit some absolute decrease in responsiveness with time in all of our major test situations. Such results would be obtained even if there were no true decrease in the strength of the affectional bond, because of familiarization and adaptation resulting from repeated testing. Therefore, at the end of 1 year of retention testing, new tests were introduced into the experimental program.

Our first new test was a modification of the open-field situation, in which basic principles of the home-cage fear test were incorporated. This particular choice was made partly because the latter test had to be discontinued when the

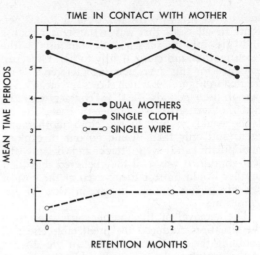

TIME IN CONTACT WITH MOTHER

Figure 22   Retention of responsiveness to mother surrogates in the straight-alley test.

mother surrogates were removed from the home cages.

For the new experiment a Masonite floor marked off in 6- by 12-inch rectangles was placed in the open-field chamber. Both mother surrogates were placed in the test room opposite a plastic start-box. Three fear stimuli, selected to produce differing degrees of emotionality, were placed in the center of the room directly in front of the start-box in successive test sessions. Eight trials were run under each stimulus condition, and in half of the trials the most direct path to the cloth mother was blocked by a large Plexiglas screen, illustrated in Figure 23. Thus, in these trials the infants were forced to approach and bypass the fear stimulus or the wire mother, or both, in order to reach the cloth mother. Following these 24 trials with the mothers present, one trial of each condition with both mothers absent was run, and this in turn was followed by two trials run under the most emotion-provoking condition: with a mechanical toy present and the direct path to the mother blocked.

We now have complete data for the first four infants raised with both a cloth and a wire mother. Even with this scanty information, the results are obvious. As would be predicted from our other measures, the emotionality scores for the three stimuli were significantly different and these same scores were increased greatly when the direct path to the mother was blocked. A highly significant preference was shown for the cloth mother under both conditions (direct and blocked path), although the presence of the block did increase the number of first responses to the wire mother from 3 to 10 percent. In all cases this was a transient response and the infants subsequently ran on to the cloth mother and clung tightly to her. Objective evidence for this overwhelming preference is indicated in Figure 24, which shows the mean number of time periods spent in contact with the two mothers. After a number of trials, the infants would go first to the cloth mother and then, and only then, would go out to explore, manipulate, and even attack and destroy the fear stimuli. It was as if they believed that their mother would protect them, even at the cost of her life—little enough to ask in view of her condition.

The removal of the mother surrogates from the situation produced the predictable effect of doubling the emotionality index. In the absence of the mothers, the infants would often run to the Plexiglas partition which formerly had blocked their path to the mother, or they would crouch in the corner behind the block where the mother normally would have been. The return of the mothers in the final two trials of the test in which the most emotion-evoking situation was presented resulted in behavior near the normal level, as measured by the emotionality index and contacts with the cloth mother.

Our second test of this series was designed to replace the straight-alley test described above and provide more quantifiable data on responsiveness to fear stimuli. The test was conducted in an alley 8 feet long and 2 feet wide. At one end of the alley and directly behind the monkeys' restraining chamber was a small stimulus chamber which contained a fear object. Each trial was initiated by raising an opaque sliding door which exposed the fear stimulus. Beginning at a point 18 inches from the restraining chamber, the alley was divided lengthwise by a partition; this provided the infant with the choice of entering one of two alleys.

The effects of all mother combinations were measured; these combinations included no mothers, two cloth mothers, two wire mothers, and a cloth and a wire mother. All mother conditions were counterbalanced by two distance conditions—distances of 24 and 78 inches, respectively, from the restraining chamber. This made it possible, for example, to provide the infant with the alternative of running to the cloth mother which was in close proximity to the fear stimulus or to the wire mother (or no mother) at a greater distance from the fear stimulus. Thus, it was possible to distinguish between running to the mother surrogate as an object of security, and generalized flight in response to a fear stimulus.

Again, the data available at this time are

Figure 23   Typical response to cloth mother in the modified open-field test.

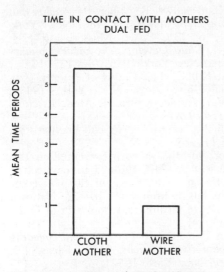

TIME IN CONTACT WITH MOTHERS
DUAL FED

Figure 24 Differential responsiveness in the modified open-field test.

from the first four infants raised with cloth and wire mothers. Nevertheless, the evidence is quite conclusive. A highly significant preference is shown for the cloth mother as compared to the wire mother or to no mother, and this preference appears to be independent of the proximity of the mother to the fear stimulus. In the condition in which two cloth mothers are present, one 24 inches from the fear stimulus and the other 78 inches from it, there was a preference for the nearest mother, but the differences were not statistically significant. In two conditions in which no cloth mother was present and the infant had to choose between a wire mother and no mother, or between two empty chambers, the emotionality scores were almost twice those under the cloth-mother-present condition.

No differences were found in either of these tests that were related to previous conditions of feeding—that is, to whether the monkey had nursed on the cloth or on the wire mother.

The results of these two new tests, introduced after a full year's separation of mother surrogate and infant, are comparable to the results obtained during the preseparation period and the early retention testing. Preferential responses still favored the cloth as compared to the wire mother by as much as 85 to 90 percent, and the emotionality scores showed the typical 2:1 differential ratio with respect to mother-absent and mother-present conditions.

The researches presented here on the analysis of two affectional variables through the use of

objective and observational techniques suggest a broad new field for the study of emotional development of infant animals. The analogous situations and results found in observations and study of human infants and of subprimates demonstrate the apparent face validity of our tests. The reliability of our observational techniques is indicated, for example, by the correlation coefficients computed for the composite emotional index in the open-field test. Four product-moment correlation coefficients, computed from four samples of 100 observations by five different pairs of independent observers over a period of more than a year, ranged from .87 to .89.

Additional variables

Although the overwhelming importance of the contact variable has been clearly demonstrated in these experiments, there is reason to believe that other factors may contribute to the development of the affectional response pattern. We are currently conducting a series of new experiments to test some of these postulated variables.

For example, Bowlby (14) has suggested that one of the basic affectional variables in the primate order is not just contact but clinging contact. To test this hypothesis, four infant monkeys are being raised with the standard cloth mother and a flat inclined plane, tightly covered with the same type of cloth. Thus, both objects contain the variable of contact with the soft cloth, but the shape of the mother tends to maximize the clinging variable, while the broad flat shape of the plane tends to minimize it. The preliminary results for differences in responsiveness to the cloth mother and responsiveness to the inclined plane under conditions that produce stress or fear or visual exploration suggest that clinging as well as contact is an affectional variable of considerable importance.

Experiments now in progress on the role of rocking motion in the development of attachment indicate that this may be a variable of measurable importance. One group of infants is being raised on rocking and stationary mothers and a second group, on rocking and stationary inclined planes. Both groups of infants show a small but consistent preference for the rocking object, as measured in average hours spent on the two objects.

Preliminary results for these three groups in the open-field test give additional evidence concerning the variable of clinging comfort. These data revealed that the infants raised with the standard cloth mother were more responsive to their mothers than the infants raised with inclined planes were to the planes.

The discovery of three variables of measurable importance to the formation and retention of affection is not surprising, and it is reasonable to assume that others will be demonstrated. The data so far obtained experimentally are in excellent concordance with the affectional variables named by Bowlby (14). We are now planning a series of studies to assess the effects of consistency and inconsistency with respect to the mother surrogates in relation to the clinical concept of rejection. The effects of early, intermediate, and late maternal deprivation and the generalization of the infant-surrogate attachment in social development are also being investigated. Indeed, the strength and stability of the monkeys' affectional responses to a mother surrogate are such that it should be practical to determine the neurological and biochemical variables that underlie love.

References and notes

1. K. Lorenz, *Auk*, **54**, 245 (1937).
2. R. A. Hinde, W. H. Thorpe, M. A. Vince, *Behaviour*, **9**, 214 (1956).
3. E. Fabricius, *Acta Zool. Fennica*, **68**, 1 (1951).
4. E. H. Hess, *J. Comp. and Physiol. Psychol.*, in press.
5. J. Jaynes, *ibid.*, in press.
6. H. Moltz and L. Rosenblum, *ibid.*, **51**, 658 (1958).
7. C. R. Carpenter, *Comp. Psychol. Monograph No. 10* (1934), p. 1.
8. A. Nolte, *Z. Tierpsychol*, **12**, 77 (1955).
9. S. Zuckermann, *Functional Affinities of Man, Monkeys and Apes* (Harcourt, Brace, London, 1933).
10. W. Köhler, *The Mentality of Apes* (Humanities Press, New York, 1951).
11. R. M. Yerkes and M. I. Tomilin, *J. Comp. Psychol*, **20**, 321 (1935).
12. J. Dollard and N. E. Miller, *Personality and Psychotherapy* (McGraw-Hill, New York, 1950), p. 133; P. H. Mussen and J. J. Conger, *Child Development and Personality* (Harper, New York, 1956), pp. 137, 138.
13. M. A. Ribble, *The Rights of Infants* (Columbia Univ. Press, New York, 1943); D. W. Winnicott, *Brit. J. Med. Psychol.*, **21**, 229 (1948).
14. J. Bowlby, *Intern. J. Psycho-Analysis*, **39**, part 5 (1958).
15. Support for the research presented in this article was provided through funds received from the graduate school of the University of Wisconsin; from grant M-772, National Institutes of Health; and from a Ford Foundation grant.
16. G. van Wagenen, in *The Care and Breeding of Laboratory Animals*, E. J. Farris, Ed. (Wiley, New York, 1950), p. 1.
17. J. P. Foley, Jr., *J. Genet. Psychol.*, **45**, 39 (1934).
18. We no longer make the cloth mother out of a block of wood. The cloth mother's body is simply that of the wire mother, covered by a terry-cloth sheath.
19. H. F. Harlow, *Am. Psychologist*, **13**, 673 (1958); ——— and R. R. Zimmermann, *Proc. Am. Phil. Soc.*, **102**, 501 (1958).
20. D. O. Hebb, *The Organization of Behavior* (Wiley, New York, 1949), p. 241 ff.
21. A. T. Jersild and F. B. Holmes, *Child Develop. Monograph No. 20* (1935), p. 356.
22. J. M. Arsenian, *J. Abnormal Social Psychol.*, **38**, 225 (1943).
23. R. A. Butler, *J. Comp. and Physiol. Psychol.*, **46**, 95 (1953).
24. ———, *J. Exptl. Psychol.*, **48**, 19 (1954).

There is plenty of experimental evidence that the list of "primary" motives should be lengthened to include manipulation and curiosity for the higher primates. This statement is probably also true for the rat and more primitive forms. Man seems to have more than his share of curiosity motivation. In fact, some psychologists see curiosity motivation as related to man's restlessness, and to a certain extent some think it provides the impetus for his creativity. If you ask a scientist why he spends so much time in his laboratory, he will probably ultimately not be able to tell you in terms of other motives. He will probably eventually say that he is curious to see "what will happen if. . . ." An artist may tell you, eventually, that he wants to experience a new combination of color or sound. Some mountain climbers are reputed to climb mountains "because they are there."

The rationale behind the present experiment is as follows: If curiosity, as measured by visual exploration, is a motive, monkeys should work to satisfy it and react to this satisfaction as a reward. For example, it should be possible for a monkey to learn to go to one color and not to another if he is consistently rewarded for responding to that color. Here the reward is visual exploration instead of a more conventional one, e.g., food for a hungry monkey. In other words, the monkey should be able to learn a discrimination for visual-exploration rewards.

Points to guide your study

1. Notice the care with which the experiment is described. Such detail makes repetition possible and is essential in scientific communication.

2. Glossary: E—Experimenter; S—Subject; .01 confidence level—There is one chance in one hundred that the differences shown in the graphs are due to chance alone.

10. DISCRIMINATION LEARNING BY RHESUS MONKEYS TO VISUAL-EXPLORATION MOTIVATION

*Robert A. Butler, University of Chicago**

Experiments conducted at the University of Wisconsin Primate Laboratory have demonstrated that rhesus monkeys learn the solution of mechanical puzzles to no other incentive than that provided by the manipulation of the

* These researches were supported in part by a grant to the University of Wisconsin from the Atomic Energy Commission Contract No. AT(11-1)-64 and in part by the Research Committee of the Graduate School from funds supplied by the Wisconsin Alumni Research Foundation.

R. A. Butler. Discrimination learning by rhesus monkeys to visual-exploration motivation. *J. comp. physiol. Psychol.*, 1953, **46**, 95–98. Copyright 1953 by the American Psychological Association. Excerpts reprinted here with permission from the author and the American Psychological Association. Figure 2 has been renumbered, and one reference has been completed (was in press).

puzzle devices (4, 1, 2) and that these manipulatory responses will persist during prolonged repetitive testing (3). Recently, monkeys have been trained without food or other special incentives to discriminate between differentially colored sets of screw eyes (5). A manipulation drive has been postulated as the motivational basis for this type of behavior, and Harlow postulates that manipulation drive is "one of a class of externally elicited drives" (3, p. 293).

The present experiments were designed to test the efficacy of another kind of externally elicited motive, that of visual exploration. Monkeys both in their home cages and in test situations continually follow movements of objects and people in their field of vision and persistently explore their environment visually.

Two preliminary experiments were conducted to investigate visually motivated behavior. Experiment I, designed primarily to measure learning, involved testing three monkeys 20 trials a day (an hour or less) for 20 days on a color discrimination, with no other incentive provided than visual exploration. Experiment II, designed primarily to test strength and persistence of visual motivation, involved testing two monkeys 4 hr. a day for 5 days under visual-exploration incentive.

Method

Subjects. Three rhesus monkeys, nos. 156, 159, and 167, served as Ss in Experiment I, and two rhesus monkeys, nos. 102 and 147, served as Ss in Experiment II. All animals were adult and had had very extensive previous training on food-rewarded learning problems. Numbers 156, 159, 102, and 147 had been Ss in manipulation-drive studies.

Apparatus. During testing the monkeys were housed in a wire cage 27 by 17 by 26 in. Over this cage E placed a box with front and top made of pressed wood and three sides covered by heavy black cloth. A 25-w. lamp was fastened on the roof of the box to provide illumination within. Two doors measuring 3¾ by 4 in. were fastened, flush, to the front of the box, with their bases 12 in. above the floor and 5 in. apart, center to center. Each door could be locked by a wooden pin, and each locking device contained a leaf switch connected to a 6-v. battery. When the door was pushed, contact was made with the locking device and an electric circuit was completed, illuminating a small signal light mounted on the front of the apparatus. Transparent Lucite plates 3 in. by 3 in. were mounted on the inside face of each door so as to permit differentially colored stimulus cards to be inserted between the Lucite plate and the door. An opaque screen, which could be raised or lowered by E, separated S from the stimulus cards. The apparatus stood on a table in the entrance room of the Wisconsin primate laboratory. The temperature in the test room ranged from 70° to 80°F. The temperature within the test box increased 6° to 7°F. above room temperature during the 4-hr. test sessions.

Procedure. *Discrimination training.* In Experiment I the Ss were tested on a yellow-blue discrimination, blue being the positive stimulus for monkeys 159 and 167, and yellow the positive stimulus for monkey 156. The position of the positive and negative cards followed a predetermined balanced order.

The animals were placed in the apparatus for 5 min. each day before testing began. The E initiated each trial by raising the opaque screen, exposing the stimulus cards. If S pushed open the door containing the positive stimulus, it was allowed 30 sec. of visual exploration before the screen was lowered. If S pushed against the door with the negative card, the door engaged the locking device, illuminating the signal light, and the screen was immediately lowered. The intertrial interval was always 30 sec., during which the stimulus cards were either rearranged or removed and returned to their previous position. A noncorrection technique was used throughout. Each animal received 20 trials a day, 5 days a week, for a total of 20 days. The time of the day for testing was not held constant. The response measures recorded were errors and response latencies, defined as time between E's raising the screen and S's responding to a door. The testing procedures for Experiment II were the same as those described for Experiment I except that the Ss were tested continuously 4 hr. a day for five days with a day's rest between days 3 and 4 only. The blue card was positive for monkey 102 and the yellow card positive for monkey 147.

During both experiments people were frequently in the test room for a part of each session. When S opened the door, E, after recording the data for the trial, usually walked around the room, opened cabinets, or stepped outside the building within the 30-sec. period. Thus, the animals ordinarily were provided with a diversified environment in which several activities occurred and which offered auditory as well as visual stimulation. Care was taken to prevent the monkeys from seeing either food or other monkeys during the test sessions.

Results

Experiment I. The mean percentage of correct responses made by the three monkeys is shown in Figure 1 and clearly demonstrates learning.

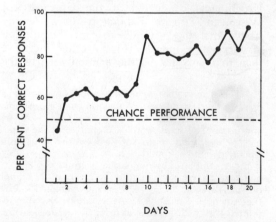

Figure 1   Discrimination learning to visual-exploration incentives.

Animals 156, 159, and 167 attained 17 correct responses in 20 trials (performance significantly better than chance at the .01 confidence level) on days 7, 10, and 12, respectively, and they equaled or exceeded this level on 11, 7, and 2 succeeding days, respectively.

Experiment II. The individual discrimination-learning curves for the two Ss of the second experiment are plotted in Figure 2. Number 102

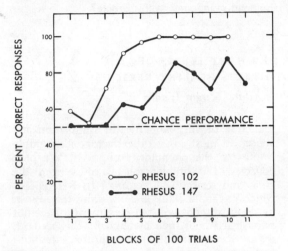

Figure 2 Discrimination learning to visual-exploration incentives.

attains and then maintains almost perfect performance; no. 147 performs consistently during the last 600 trials at a level significantly better than chance at the .01 confidence level.

Discussion

These experiments demonstrate beyond question that monkeys can learn object discriminations and maintain their performance at a high level of efficiency with visual-exploration reward.

References

1. Davis, R. T., Settlage, P. H., and Harlow, H. F. Performance of normal and brain-operated monkeys on mechanical puzzles with and without food incentive. *J. genet. Psychol.*, 1950, 77, 305–311.
2. Gately, M. J. Manipulation drive in experimentally naïve rhesus monkeys. Unpublished master's thesis, Univer. of Wisconsin, 1950.
3. Harlow, H. F. Learning and satiation of response in intrinsically motivated complex puzzle performance by monkeys. *J. comp. physiol. Psychol.*, 1950, 43, 289–294.
4. Harlow, H. F., Harlow, Margaret K., and Meyer, D. F. Learning motivated by a manipulation drive. *J. exp. Psychol.*, 1950, 40, 228–234.
5. Harlow, H. F., and McClearn, G. E. Object discriminations learned by monkeys on the basis of manipulation motives. *J. comp. physiol. Psychol.*, 1954, 47, 73–76.

DEPRIVATION

One of the topics usually considered in the study of motivation is that of arousal or alertness. It looks very much as if humans function most efficiently at optimum levels of arousal. (One good measure of arousal is a decrease in amplitude of the normal waves of the electroencephalogram, EEG.) When the level of arousal is too high, as in panic, efficiency is impaired. When the level of arousal is low, as in sleep or drowsiness, efficiency is low. Also, when there has been prolonged reduction in arousal, produced by prolonged reduction of arousing sensory input, efficiency is impaired in the special ways mentioned in this article. It has been suggested that the prolonged lack of sensory input allows the memory traces of the brain to recombine in new ways (see Chapter 20). This provides a first step in explaining the *fact* that hallucinations, illusions, and disorganized thinking are among the outcomes of sensory deprivation.

The author also tries to account for the *types* of thoughts which the subjects have. He uses psychoanalytic theory to do this.

Points to guide your study

1. Be sure to distinguish observations from speculations.
2. Glossary: The primary process—The psychoanalytic term for primitive,

highly egocentric types of thinking. The secondary process—The psychoanalytic term for rational thought processes. Hypnogogic state—Refers to the time just before a person falls off to sleep. If, at this time, he experiences vivid, disconnected visual images, the person is said to be in the hypnogogic state. Hallucinations—Experiences which have no basis in sensory input from the environment. Illusions—Distortions of actual sensory input. Delusions—Thoughts and trains of thought which do not correspond to what most people think of as the "objective" world.

3. Do you think that part of the effectiveness of certain "brainwashing" techniques is due to the phenomena mentioned in this article?

11. MENTAL EFFECTS OF REDUCTION OF ORDINARY LEVELS OF PHYSICAL STIMULI ON INTACT, HEALTHY PERSONS

John C. Lilly, Communications Research Institute, Virgin Islands

Introduction

We have been seeking answers to the question of what happens to a brain and its contained mind in the relative absence of physical stimulation. In neurophysiology, this is one form of the question: Freed of normal efferent and afferent activities, does the activity of the brain soon become that of coma or sleep, or is there some inherent mechanism which keeps it going, a pacemaker of the "awake" type of activity? In psychoanalysis there is a similar, but not identical problem. If the healthy ego is freed from reality stimuli, does it maintain the secondary process, or does the primary process take over? i.e., is the healthy ego independent of reality or dependent in some fashion, in some degree, on exchanges with the surroundings to maintain its structure?

In seeking answers, we have found pertinent autobiographical literature and reports of experiments by others, and have done experiments ourselves. The experiments are psychological ones on human subjects. Many psychological experiments in isolation have been done on animals, but are not recounted in detail here; parenthetically, the effect on very young animals can be an almost irreversible lack of development of whole systems, such as those necessary for the use of vision in accomplishing tasks put to the animal. No truly neurophysiological isolation experiments on either animals or man have yet been done.

Autobiographical accounts

The published autobiographical material has several drawbacks: In no case is there a sizeable

* J. C. Lilly. Mental effects of reduction of ordinary levels of physical stimuli on intact, healthy persons. *Psychiat. Res. Rep.*, 1956, 5, 1–9. Copyright 1956 by the American Psychiatric Association. Reprinted here with permission from the author and the American Psychiatric Association.

reduction of all possibilities of stimulation and action; in most cases, other factors add complications to the phenomena observed. We have collected 18 autobiographical cases from the polar and sea-faring literature (see References) which are more frank and revealing than most. We have interviewed two persons who have not published any of their material. In this account, we proceed from rather complicated situations to the more simple ones, i.e., from a maximum number of factors to the most simple experimental situation.

From this literature we have found that isolation *per se* acts on most persons as a powerful stress. The effects observed are similar to those of any extreme stress, and other stressful factors add their effects to those of isolation to cause mental symptoms to appear more rapidly and more intensely. As is well known, stresses other than isolation can cause the same symptoms to appear in individuals in an isolated group.

Taking our last point first, we have the account by Walter Gibson given in his book, "The Boat." This is the case in which four persons out of an initial 135 survived in a lifeboat in the Indian Ocean in World War II. Gibson gives a vivid account of his experiences, and the symptoms resulting from loss of hope, dehydration, thirst, intense sunburn, and physical combat. Most of the group hallucinated rescue planes and drank salt water thinking it fresh; many despaired and committed suicide; others were murdered; and some were eaten by others. The whole structure of egos was shaken and recast in desperate efforts at survival. (It is interesting to note that many of those who committed suicide tried to sink the boat by removing the drain plugs before jumping overboard, i.e., sink the boat, and other persons, as well as the self; this dual destruction may be used by some of the non-surviving solitary sailors.

I cite this case because it gives a clue as to

what to expect in those who do survive isolation in other conditions: Gibson survived—how? He says: (1) by previous out-of-doors training in the tropical sun for some years; (2) by having previously learned to be able to become completely passive (physically and mentally); (3) by having and maintaining the conviction that he would come through the experience; and, we add, (4) by having a woman, Doris Lim, beside him, who shared his passivity and convictions.

In all cases of survivors of isolation, at sea or in the polar night, it was the first exposure which caused the greatest fears and hence the greatest danger of giving way to symptoms; previous experience is a powerful aid in going ahead, despite the symptoms. Physical passivity is necessary during starvation, but, in some people, may be contra-indicated in social isolation in the absence of starvation. In all survivors, we run across the inner conviction that he or she will survive, or else there are definite reassurances from others that each will be rescued. In those cases of a man and a woman together, or even the probability of such a union within a few days, there is apparently not only a real assurance of survival, but a love of the situation can appear. (Such love can develop in a solitaire.) Of course, such couples are the complete psychological antithesis of our major thesis of complete isolation; many symptoms can be avoided by healthy persons with such an arrangement.

Solitary sailors are in a more complex situation than the group of polar isolates. The sailing of a small boat across oceans requires a good deal of physical exertion, and the situation may be contaminated by a lack of sleep which can also cause symptoms. The solitary sailors, of which Joshua Slocum and Alain Bombard are outstanding examples, relate that the first days out of port are the dangerous ones; awe, humility, and fear in the face of the sea are most acute at this time. Bombard states that if the terror of the first week can be overcome, one can survive. Apparently many do not survive this first period. Many single-handed boats have not arrived at their trans-oceanic destination. We have clues as to the causes from what sometimes happens with two persons on such crossings. There are several pairs of ocean-crossing sailors in which one of the couple became so terror-stricken, paranoid, and bent on murder and/or suicide, that he had to be tied to his bunk.

Once this first period is past, other symptoms develop, either from isolation itself or from isolation plus other stresses. In the South Atlantic, Joshua Slocum had a severe gastro-intestinal upset just before a gale hit his boat; he had reefed his sails, but should have taken them down. Under the circumstances, he was unable to move from the cabin. At this point he saw a man take over the tiller. At first he thought it was a pirate, but the man reassured him and said that he was the pilot of the Pinta and that he would take his boat safely through the storm. Slocum asked him to take down sail, but the man said, no, they must catch the Pinta ahead. The next morning Slocum recovered, and found his boat had covered 93 miles on true course, sailing itself. (His boat was quite capable of such a performance; he arranged it that way for long trips without his hand at the helm.) In a dream that night the pilot appeared and said he would come whenever Slocum needed him. During the next three years the helmsman appeared to Slocum several times, during gales.

This type of hallucination—delusion seems to be characteristic of the strong egos who survive: a "savior" type of hallucination rather than a "destroyer" type. Their inner conviction of survival is projected thoroughly.

Other symptoms that appear are: superstitiousness (Slocum thought a dangerous reef named M reef was lucky because M is the 13th letter of the alphabet and 13 was his lucky number. He passed the reef without hitting it. Bombard thought the number of matches necessary to light a damp cigaret represented the number of days until the end of the voyage. He was wrong several times.); intense love of any living things (Slocum was revolted at the thought of killing food—animals, especially a goat given to him at one port. Ellam and Mudie became quite upset after catching and eating a fish that had followed the boat all day, and swore off further fish-eating.); conversations with inanimate objects (Bombard had bilateral conversations with a doll mascot.); and a feeling that when one lands, one had best be careful to listen before speaking to avoid being considered insane (Bernicot refused an invitation to dinner on another yacht after crossing the Atlantic alone, until he could recapture the proper things to talk about.). The inner life becomes so vivid and intense that it takes time to readjust to the life among other persons and to reestablish one's inner criteria of sanity (When placed with fellow prisoners, after 18 months in solitary confinement, Christopher Burney was afraid to speak for fear that he would show himself to be insane. After several days of listening he recaptured the usual criteria of sanity, and then could allow himself to speak.).

Life alone in the polar night, snowed-in, with the confining surroundings of a small hut is a more simple situation. However, there are other complicating factors: extreme cold, possibilities of carbon monoxide poisoning, collapse of the roof, etc. Richard Byrd, in his book "Alone," recounts in great detail his changes in mental functioning, and talks of a long period of CO poisoning resulting in a state close to catatonia.

I refer you to his book for details. He experienced, as did Slocum and many others, an oceanic feeling, the being "of the universe," at one with it.

Christiane Ritter ("A Woman in the Polar Night") was exposed to isolation for periods up to sixteen days at a time. She saw a monster, hallucinated her past as if in bright sunshine, became "at one" with the moon, and developed a monomania to go out over the snow. She was saved by an experienced Norwegian who put her to bed and fed her lavishly. She developed a love for the situation and found great difficulty in leaving Spitzbergen. For a thorough and sensitive account of symptoms, I recommend her book to you.

From these examples and several more (see References), we conclude the following:

(1) Published autobiographies are of necessity incomplete. Social taboos, discretion to one's self, suppression and repression of painful or uncomfortable material, secondary elaboration, and rationalization severely limit the scope of the material available. (Interviews with two men, each of whom lived alone in the polar night, confirm this impression.)

(2) Despite these limitations, we find that persons in isolation experience many, if not all, of the symptoms of the mentally ill.

(3) In those who survive, the symptoms can be reversible. How easily reversible, we do not know. Most survivors report, after several weeks exposure to isolation, a new inner security and a new integration of themselves on a deep and basic level.

(4) The underlying mechanisms are obscure. It is obvious that inner factors in the mind tend to be projected outward, that some of the mind's activity which is usually reality-bound now becomes free to turn to phantasy and ultimately to hallucination and delusion. It is as if the laws of thought are projected into the realm of the laws of inanimate matter and of the universe. The primary process tends to absorb more and more of the time and energy usually taken by the secondary process. Such experiences either lead to improved mental functioning or to destruction. Why one person takes the healthy path and another person the sick one is not yet clear.

Experiments to clarify the necessary conditions for some of these effects have been done. One of the advantages of the experimental material is that simpler conditions can be set up and tested, and some of the additional stresses of natural life situations can be eliminated.

Experimental isolation

The longest exposure to isolation on the largest number of subjects has been carried out in Dr. Donald Hebb's Department of Psychology at McGill University by a group of graduate students. We started a similar project independently with different techniques at the National Institute of Mental Health. In the Canadian experiments, the aim is to reduce the *patterning* of stimuli to the lowest level; in ours, the objective is to reduce the *absolute intensity* of all physical stimuli to the lowest possible level.

In the McGill experiments, a subject is placed on a bed in an air-conditioned box with arms and hands restrained with cardboard sleeves, and eyes covered completely with translucent ski goggles. The subjects are college students motivated by payment of $20 per day for as long as they will stay in the box. An observer is present, watching through a window, and tests the subject in various ways verbally through a communication set.

In our experiments, the subject is suspended with the body and all but the top of the head immersed in a tank containing slowly flowing water at 34.5° C. (94.5° F.), wears a blacked-out mask (enclosing the whole head) for breathing, and wears nothing else. The water temperature is such that the subject feels neither hot nor cold. The experience is such that one actually feels the supports and the mask, but not much else; a large fraction of the usual pressures on the body caused by gravity are lacking. The sound level is low; one hears only one's own breathing and some faint water sounds from the piping; the water-air interface does not transmit air-borne sounds very efficiently. It is one of the most even and monotonous environments I have experienced. After the initial training period, no observer is present. Immediately after exposure, the subject writes personal notes on his experience.

At McGill, the subjects varied considerably in the details of their experiences. However, a few general phenomena appeared. After several hours, each subject found that it was difficult to carry on organized, directed thinking for any sustained period. Suggestibility was very much increased. An extreme desire for stimuli and action developed. There were periods of thrashing around in the box in attempts to satisfy this need. The borderline between sleep and awakedness became diffuse and confused. At some time between 24 and 72 hours most subjects couldn't stand it any longer and left. Hallucinations and delusions of various sorts developed, mostly in those who could stay longer than two days.

The development of hallucinations in the visual sphere followed the stages seen with mescaline intoxication. When full-blown, the visual phenomena were complete projections maintaining the three dimensions of space in relation to the rest of the body and could be scanned by eye and head movements. The contents were surprising to the ego, and consisted of material like that of dreams, connected stories sharing past memories and recent real events. The subjects' reactions to these phenomena were generally amusement and a sense of relief from the pressing boredom. They could describe them vocally without abolishing the sequences. A small number of subjects experienced doubling of their body images. A few developed transient paranoid delusions, and one had a seizure-like episode after five days in the box with no positive EEG findings for epilepsy.

Our experiments have been more limited both in numbers of subjects and duration of exposures. There have been two subjects, and the longest exposure has been three hours. We have much preliminary data, and have gained enough experience to begin to guess at some of the mechanisms involved in the symptoms produced.

In these experiments, the subject always has a full night's rest before entering the tank. Instructions are to inhibit all movements as far as possible. An initial set of training exposures overcomes the fears of the situation itself.

In the tank, the following stages have been experienced:

(1) For about the first three-quarters of an hour, the day's residues are predominant. One is aware of the surroundings, recent problems, etc.

(2) Gradually, one begins to relax and more or less enjoy the experience. The feeling of being isolated in space and having nothing to do is restful and relaxing at this stage.

(3) But slowly, during the next hour, a tension develops which can be called a "stimulus-action" hunger; hidden methods of self-stimulation develop; twitching muscles, slow swimming movements (which cause sensations as the water flows by the skin), stroking one finger with another, etc. If one can inhibit such maneuvers long enough, intense satisfaction is derived from later self-stimulations.

(4) If inhibition can win out, the tension may ultimately develop to the point of forcing the subject to leave the tank.

(5) Meanwhile, the attention is drawn powerfully to any residual stimulus: the mask, the suspension, each come in for their share of concentration. Such residual stimuli become the whole content of consciousness to an almost unbearable degree.

(6) If this stage is passed without leaving the tank, one notices that one's thoughts have shifted from a directed type of thinking about problems to reveries and fantasies of a highly personal and emotionally charged nature. These are too personal to relate publicly, and probably vary greatly from subject to subject. The individual reactions to such fantasy material also probably varies considerably, from complete suppression to relaxing and enjoying them.

(7) If the tension and the fantasies are withstood, one may experience the furthest stage which we have yet explored: projection of visual imagery. I have seen this once, after a two and one-half hour period. The black curtain in front of the eyes (such as one "sees" in a dark room with eyes closed) gradually opens out into a three-dimensional, dark, empty space in front of the body. This phenomenon captures one's interest immediately, and one waits to find out what comes next. Gradually forms of the type sometimes seen in hypnogogic states appear. In this case, they were small, strangely shaped objects with self-luminous borders. A tunnel whose inside "space" seemed to be emitting a blue light then appeared straight ahead. About this time, this experiment was terminated by a leakage of water into the mask through a faulty connector on the inspiratory tube.

It turns out that exposures to such conditions train one to be more tolerant of many internal activities. Fear lessens with experience, and personal integration can be speeded up. But, of course, there are pitfalls here to be avoided. The opposite effects may also be accelerated in certain cases. Fantasies about the experience (such as the illusion of "return to the womb," which is quite common) are dispelled; one realizes that at birth we start breathing air and hence cannot "return to the womb." One's breathing in the tank is extremely important: as a comforting, constant safeguard and a source of rhythmic stimulation.

In both the McGill experiments and in ours, certain aftereffects are noted: The McGill subjects had difficulty in orienting their perceptual mechanisms; various illusions persisted for several hours. In our experiments, we notice that after emersion the day apparently is started over, i.e., the subject feels as if he has just arisen from bed afresh; this effect persists, and the subject finds he is out of step with the clock for the rest of that day. He also has to re-adjust to social intercourse in subtle ways. The night of the day of the exposure he finds that his bed exerts great pressure against his body. No bed is as comfortable as floating in water.

Experiments such as these demonstrate results similar to that given above for solitary polar living and sailing alone. If one is alone, long enough, and at levels of physical and human stimulation low enough, the mind turns inward and projects outward its own contents and processes; the brain not only stays active despite the lowered levels of input and output, but accumulates surplus energy to extreme degrees. In terms of libido theory, the total *amount* of libido increases with time of deprivation; body-libido reaches new high levels. If body-libido is not discharged somatically, discharge starts through fantasy; but apparently this is neither an adequate mode nor can it achieve an adequate rate of discharge in the presence of the rapidly rising level. At some point a new threshold appears for more definite phenomena of regression: hallucinations, delusions, oceanic bliss, etc. At this stage, given any opportunities for action or stimulation by external reality, the healthy ego seizes them and re-establishes more secondary process. Lacking such opportunities for a long enough interval of time, re-organization takes place, how reversibly and how permanently we do not yet know.

Apparently even healthy minds act this way in isolation. What this means to psychiatric research is obvious: We have yet to obtain a full, documented picture of the range available to the healthy human adult mind; some of the etiological factors in mental illness may be clarified and sharpened by such research. Of course, this is a limited region of investigation. We have not gone into details about loss of sleep, starvation, and other factors which have great power in changing healthy minds to sick ones. I think that you can see the parallels between these results and phenomena found in normal children and in psychotics. And, if we could give you a more detailed account, possible explanations of the role of isolation factors in involuntary indoctrination and its opposite, psychotherapy, would be more evident.

References

1. Small, Maurice H. April, 1900. On some psychical relations of society and solitude. *Pedagogical Seminary*, Vol. VII, No. 2.

Solitary sailors

2. Slocum, Captain Joshua. 1948. Sailing alone around the world. Rupert Hart-Davis, London.
3. Ellam, Patrick, and Colin Mudie. 1953. Sopranino. W. W. Norton and Co., Inc., N.Y.
4. Bombard, Dr. Alain. 1953. The Voyage of the Hérétique. Simon and Schuster, N.Y.
5. Merrien, Jean. 1954. Lonely Voyagers. G. P. Putnam's Sons, N.Y.
6. Merrien, Jean. 1954. Les Nevigateurs Solitaires. Editiones Denoël.
7. Bernicot, Louis. 1953. The Voyage of Anahita—Single-handed Round the World. Rupert Hart-Davis, London.

Drastic degrees of stress

8. Gibson, Walter. 1953. The Boat. Houghton Mifflin Company (The Riverside Press), Boston, Mass.

Living in the polar night

9. Scott, J. M. 1953. Portrait of an Ice Cap with Human Figures. Chatto and Windus, London.
10. Courtauld, A. July, 1932. Living alone under polar conditions. *The Polar Record*, No. 4. University Press, Cambridge.
11. Byrd, Richard E. 1938. Alone. G. P. Putnam's Sons, N.Y.
12. Ritter, Christiane. 1954. A Woman in the Polar Night, E. P. Dutton and Co., Inc., N.Y.

Forced isolation and confinement

13. Burney, Christopher. 1952. Solitary Confinement. Coward-McCann, Inc., N.Y.
14. Stypulkowski, Z. 1951. Invitation to Moskow. Thames and Hudson, London.

The deaf and the blind

15. Collingswood, Herbert W. 1923. Adventures in silence. The Rural New Yorker, N.Y.
16. Ormond, Arthur W., C.B.E., F.R.C.S. 1925. Visual hallucinations in sane people. *British Med. J.*, Vol. 2.
17. Bartlet, J. E. A. 1951. A case of organized visual hallucinations in an old man with cataract, and their relation to the phenomena of the phantom limb. *Brain*, Vol 74, Part III, pp. 363–373.

Experimental isolation

18. Heron, W., W. H. Bexton, and D. O. Hebb. August, 1953. Cognitive effects of a decreased variation to the sensory environment. *The Amer. Psychol.*, Vol. 8, No. 8, p. 366.

MODIFICATION OF MOTIVES

Fear is a strong learned or acquired drive. This means that, as a result of learning, stimuli which do not originally produce fear will come to do so later. In the case of this experiment, rats were made afraid of a white compartment by being shocked in it. If you don't already know it, this is an example of classical conditioning. Now the white box produces fear, while it did not do this before the shocks had been delivered. Rats will then learn to make responses which reduce this fear. They are being rewarded by the reduction of fear. In this case, they learn to turn wheels or push bars which enable them to escape from the white compartment.

This general scheme has been extended greatly by Miller and others of the "Yale school." It is maintained that humans, for instance, develop mechanisms or habits which reduce fear. For instance, many symptoms found in cases of combat neuroses (so-called shell-shock) are thought to be fear-reducing mechanisms.

Points to guide your study

1. Notice that the ideas involved in this experiment are general ones. The experiment merely serves to illustrate the general idea that fear can be attached to new cues and that fear-reduction can be a reward for new learning. This is one reason for doing animal experiments. One tries to derive some general rules which will apply to human beings.

2. Two kinds of learning are involved here, classical conditioning of fear and instrumental learning of the fear-reducing response. If you haven't studied these different types of learning, look them up in your text.

3. Glossary: Experimental extinction—This refers to the weakening of a habit when it is not rewarded (reinforced). Experimental extinction is shown in Figure 3. *t* test—A statistical test of significance. A way of computing the number of times the obtained differences would have occurred by chance alone.

12. STUDIES OF FEAR AS AN ACQUIRABLE DRIVE:
I. FEAR AS MOTIVATION AND FEAR-REDUCTION AS REINFORCEMENT IN THE LEARNING OF NEW RESPONSES

*Neal E. Miller, Yale University**

An important role in human behavior is played by drives, such as fears, or desires for money, approval, or status, which appear to be learned during the socialization of the individual (1, 12, 16, 17, 18). While some studies have indicated that drives can be learned (2, 8, 15), the systematic experimental investigation of acquired drives has been scarcely begun. A great deal more work has been done on the

* This study is part of the research program of the Institute of Human Relations, Yale University. It was first reported as part of a paper at the 1941 meetings of the A.P.A. The author is indebted to Fred D. Sheffield for assistance in the exploratory work involved in establishing the experimental procedure and for criticizing the manuscript.

N. E. Miller. Studies of fear as an acquirable drive: I. fear as motivation and fear-reduction as reinforcement in the learning of new responses. *J. exp. Psychol.*, 1948, **38**, 89–101. Copyright 1948 by the American Psychological Association. Excerpts reprinted here with permission from the author and the American Psychological Association. Some footnotes have been omitted, the caption of Fig. 1 has been placed in the body of the text, and other figures have been recaptioned. One reference has been completed (was in press).

innate, or primary drives such as hunger, thirst, and sex.

The purpose of the present experiment was to determine whether or not once fear is established as a new response to a given situation, it will exhibit the following functional properties characteristic of primary drives, such as hunger: (a) when present motivate so-called random behavior and (b) when suddenly reduced serve as a reinforcement to produce learning of the immediately preceding response.

Apparatus and procedure

The apparatus used in this experiment is illustrated in Figure 1. The left compartment is painted white, the the right one black. A shock may be administered through the grid which is the floor of the white compartment. When the animal is placed on the grid which is pivoted at the inside end, it moves down slightly making a contact that starts an electric timer. When the animal performs the correct response, turning the wheel or pressing the bar as the case may be, he stops the clock and actuates a solenoid which allows the door, painted with horizontal black and white stripes, to drop. The E can also

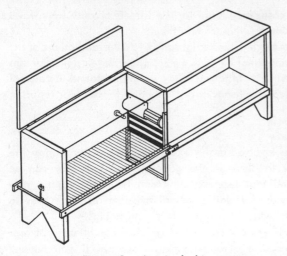

Figure 1   Acquired drive apparatus.

cause the door to drop by pressing a button. The dimensions of each compartment are 18 x 6 x 8½ in.

The procedure involved the following five steps:

1. *Test for initial response to apparatus.*— The animals were placed in the apparatus for approximately one min. with the door between the two compartments open and their behavior was observed.

2. *Trials with primary drive of pain produced by electric shock.*—The procedure for administering shock was designed to attach the response of fear to as many as possible of the cues in the white compartment instead of merely to the relatively transient stimulus trace of just having been dropped in. This was done so that the animal would remain frightened when he was restrained in the compartment on subsequent non-shock trials. The strength of shock used was 500 volts of 60 cycle AC through a series resistance of 250,000 ohms. The animals were given 10 trials with shock. On the first trial they were allowed to remain in the white compartment for 60 sec. without shock and then given a momentary shock every five sec. for 60 sec. At the end of this period of time the E dropped the door and put a continuous shock on the grid.

As soon as the animal had run into the black compartment, the door was closed behind him and he was allowed to remain there for 30 sec. Then he was taken out and placed in a cage of wire mesh approximately nine in. in diameter and seven in. high for the time between trials. Since the animals were run in rotation in groups of three, the time between trials was that required to run the other two animals, but was never allowed to fall below 60 sec. This procedure was followed on all subsequent trials.

On the second trial the animal was placed into the center of the white compartment facing away from the door, was kept there for 30 sec. without shock, at the end of which time the shock was turned on and the door opened. On trials 3 through 10 the grid was electrified before the animal was dropped on it and the door was opened before he reached it. On odd numbered trials the animal was dropped at the end of the compartment away from the door and facing it; on even numbered trials he was dropped in the center of the compartment facing away from the door.

3. *Non-shock trials with experimenter dropping door.*—The purpose of these trials was to determine whether or not the animals would continue to perform the original habit in the absence of the primary drive of pain from electric shock, and to reduce their tendency to crouch in the white compartment and to draw back in response to the sound and movement of the door dropping in front of them. Each animal was given five of these non-shock trials during which the E dropped the door before the animal reached it. As with the preceding trials the animals were dropped in facing the door on odd numbered trials and facing away from it on even numbered ones; they were allowed to remain in the black compartment for 30 sec. and were kept in the wire mesh cage for at least 60 sec. between trials.

4. *Non-shock trials with door opened by turning the wheel.*—The purpose of these trials was to determine whether the continued running without shock was the mere automatic persistence of a simple habit, or whether an acquired drive was involved which could be used to motivate the learning of a new habit. During these trials the E no longer dropped the door. The apparatus was set so that the only way the door could be dropped was by moving the wheel a small fraction of a turn. The bar was present but pressing it would not cause the door to drop. The animals that moved the wheel and caused the door to drop were allowed to remain 30 sec. in the black compartment. Those that did not move the wheel within 100 sec. were picked out of the white compartment at the end of that time. All animals remained at least 60 sec. between trials in the wire mesh cage. All animals were given 16 trials under these conditions. On each trial the time to move the wheel enough to drop the door was recorded on an electric clock and read to the nearest 10th of a sec.

5. *Non-shock trials with door opened by pressing the bar.*—The purpose of these trials was to determine whether or not animals (a) would unlearn the first new habit of turning the wheel if this habit was no longer effective in dropping the door, and (b) would learn a second new habit, pressing the bar, if this

would cause the door to drop and allow them to remove themselves from the cues arousing the fear. Animals that had adopted the habit of crouching in the white compartment till the end of the 100 sec. limit and so had not learned to rotate the wheel were excluded from this part of the experiment. These trials were given in exactly the same way as the preceding ones except that the apparatus was set so that turning the wheel would not cause the door to drop but pressing the bar would. During these trials there was no time limit; the animals were allowed to remain in the white compartment until they finally pressed the bar.[1] The time to press the bar was recorded on an electric clock to the nearest 10th of a sec. and the number of revolutions of the wheel was recorded on an electric counter in quarter revolutions.

Results

In the test before the training with electric shock, the animals showed no readily discernible avoidance or preference for either of the two chambers of the apparatus. They explored freely through both of them.

During the trials with primary drive of pain produced by electric shock, all of the animals learned to run rapidly from the white compartment through the door, which was dropped in front of them by the E, and into the black compartment. On the five trials without shock, and with the E still dropping the door, the animals continued to run. The behavior of the animals was markedly different from what it had been before the training with the primary drive of pain from electric shock.

When the procedure of the non-shock trials was changed so that the E no longer dropped the door and it could only be opened by moving the wheel, the animals displayed variable behavior which tended to be concentrated in the region of the door. They would stand up in front of it, place their paws upon it, sniff around the edges, bite the bars of the grid they were standing on, run back and forth, etc. They also tended to crouch, urinate, and defecate. In the course of this behavior some of the animals performed responses, such as poking their noses between the bars of the wheel or placing their paws upon it, which caused it to move a fraction of a turn and actuate a contact that caused the door to open. Most of them then ran through into the black compartment almost immediately. A few of them drew back with an exaggerated startle response and crouched. Some of these eventually learned to go through the door; a few seemed to learn to avoid it. Other animals abandoned their trial-and-error behavior

before they happened to strike the wheel and persisted in crouching so that they had to be lifted out of the white compartment at the end of the 100 sec. period. In general, the animals that had to be lifted out seemed to crouch sooner and sooner on successive trials.

Thirteen of the 25 animals moved the wheel enough to drop the door on four or more out of their first eight trials. Since, according to theory, a response has to occur before it can be reinforced and learned, the results of these animals were analyzed separately and they were the only ones which were subsequently used in the bar-pressing phase of the experiment. The average speed (reciprocal of time in seconds) with which these animals opened the door by moving the wheel on the 16 successive trials is presented in Figure 2. It can be seen that there is a definite tendency for the animals to learn to turn the wheel more rapidly on successive trials. Eleven out of the 13 individual animals turned the wheel sooner on the 16th than on the first trial, and the two animals which did not show improvement were ones which happened to turn the wheel fairly soon on the first trial and continued this performance throughout. The difference between the average speed on the first and

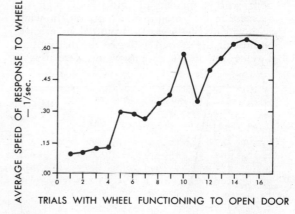

TRIALS WITH WHEEL FUNCTIONING TO OPEN DOOR

Figure 2 Learning the first new habit, turning the wheel, during trials without primary drive. With mild pain produced by an electric shock as a primary drive, the animals have learned to run from the white compartment, through the open door, into the black compartment. Then they were given trials without any electric shock during which the door was closed but could be opened by turning a little wheel. Under these conditions, of the 25 animals the 13 which turned the wheel enough to drop the door on four or more of the first eight trials learned to turn it. This figure shows the progressive increase in the average speed with which these 13 animals ran up to the wheel and turned it enough to drop the door during the 16 non-shock trials.

[1] One animal which did not hit the bar within 30 min. was finally discarded.

16th trials is of a magnitude ($t = 3.5$) which would be expected to occur in the direction predicted by theory, less than two times in 1000 by chance. Therefore, it must be concluded that those animals that did turn the wheel and run out of the white compartment into the black one definitely learned to perform this new response more rapidly during the 16 trials *without* the primary drive of pain produced by electric shock.

When the setting on the apparatus was changed so that the wheel would not open the door but the bar would, the animals continued to respond to the wheel vigorously for some time. It was obvious that they had learned a strong habit of responding to it. Eventually, however, they stopped reacting to the wheel and began to perform other responses. After longer or shorter periods of variable behavior they finally hit the bar, caused the door to drop, and ran through rapidly into the black compartment. On the first trial the number of complete rotations of the wheel ranged from zero to 530 with a median of 4.75. On successive trials during which turning the wheel did not cause the door to drop, the amount of activity on it progressively dropped till by the tenth trial the range was from 0 to 0.25 rotations with a median of zero. The progressive decrease in the amount of activity on the wheel is shown in Figure 3. It is plotted in medians because of the skewed nature of the distribution. Twelve out of the 13 rats which were used in

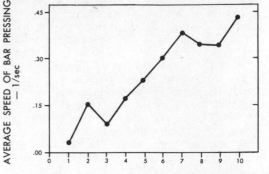

TRIALS WITH WHEEL NON-FUNCTIONAL, BAR FUNCTION

Figure 4　Learning a second new habit, bar pressing, under acquired drive. Conditions were changed so that only pressing the bar would cause the door to drop and allow the animals to run from the white compartment where they had been previously shocked, into the black one where they had escaped shock. During non-shock trials under these conditions, the animals learned a second new habit, pressing the bar. Each point is based on the average speed of 13 animals.

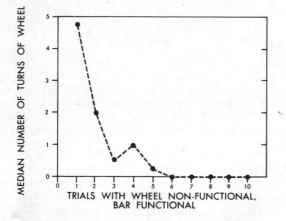

TRIALS WITH WHEEL NON-FUNCTIONAL, BAR FUNCTIONAL

Figure 3　Unlearning of the habit of turning the wheel during trials on which it no longer serves to reduce the acquired drive. When conditions were changed so that turning the wheel was ineffective (and pressing the bar was effective) in causing the door to drop and allowing the animal to run from the white into the black compartment, the animals showed a progressive decrement in the response of rotating the wheel. Each point is based on the median scores of 13 animals.

this part of the experiment gave fewer rotations of the wheel on the tenth than on the first trial. From the binomial expansion it may be calculated that for 12 out of 13 cases to come out in the direction predicted by the theory is an event which would be expected to occur by chance less than one time in 1000. Thus, it may be concluded that the dropping of the door, which is presumed to have produced a reduction in the strength of fear by allowing the animals to escape from the cues in the white compartment which elicited the fear, was essential to the maintenance of the habit of rotating the wheel.

The results on bar pressing are presented in Figure 4. It can be seen that the speed of bar pressing increased throughout the 10 non-shock trials during which that response caused the door to drop. Since the last trial was faster than the first for 12 out of the 13 animals, the difference was again one which would be expected by chance less than one time in 1000.

Discussion

On preliminary tests conducted before the training with electric shock was begun, the animals showed no noticeable tendency to avoid the white compartment. During training with the primary drive of pain produced by electric shock in the white compartment, the animals learned a strong habit of quickly running out of it, through the open door, and into the black compartment.

On non-schock trials the animals persisted in running from the white compartment through the open door into the black one. On additional non-shock trials during which the door was not automatically dropped in front of the animals, they exhibited so-called random behavior and learned a new response, turning the wheel, which caused the door to drop and allowed them to escape into the black compartment. This trial-and-error learning of a new response demonstrated that the cues in the white compartment had acquired the functional properties of a drive and that escape from the white into the black compartment had acquired the functional properties of a reward.

The general pattern of the fear response and its capacity to produce a strong stimulus is determined by the innate structure of the animal. The connection between the pain and the fear is also presumably innate. But the connection between the cues in the white compartment and the fear was learned. Therefore the fear of the white compartment may be called an acquired drive. Because fear can be learned, it may be called acquirable; because it can motivate new learning, it may be called a drive.

Running through the door and into the black compartment removed the animal from the cues in the white compartment which were eliciting the fear and thus produced a reduction in the strength of the fear response and the stimuli which it produced. This reduction in the strength of the intense fear stimuli is presumably what gave the black compartment its acquired reinforcing value.

If the reduction in fear produced by running from the white into the black was the reinforcement for learning the new habit of wheel turning, we would expect this habit to show experimental extinction when that reinforcement was removed. This is exactly what happened. During the first trial on which turning the wheel no longer dropped the door, the animals gradually stopped performing this response and began to exhibit other responses. As would be expected, one of these responses, pressing the bar, which caused the door to drop and allowed the animal to remove himself from the fear-producing cues in the white compartment, was gradually learned in a series of trials during which the wheel turning was progressively crowded out. Thus, it can be seen that the escape from the white compartment, which presumably produced a reduction in the strength of the fear, played a crucial role, similar to that of a primary reward, in the learning and maintenance of the new habits.

References

1. Allport, G. W. *Personality*. New York: Henry Holt, 1937.
2. Anderson, E. E. The externalization of drive: III. Maze learning by non-rewarded and by satiated rats. *J. genet. Psychol.*, 1941, 59, 397–426.
3. Brown, J. S. Generalized approach and avoidance responses in relation to conflict behavior. New Haven: Dissertation, Yale Univ., 1940.
4. Dollard, J. Exploration of morale factors among combat air crewmen. *Memorandum to Experimental Section, Research Branch, Information and Education Division, War Department*, 9 March 1945.
5. Freud, S. *New introductory lectures on psychoanalysis*. New York: Norton, 1933.
6. Freud, S. *The problem of anxiety*. New York: Norton, 1936.
7. May, M. A. Experimentally acquired drives. *J. exp. Psychol.*, 1948, 38, 66–77.
8. Miller, N. E. An experimental investigation of acquired drives. *Psychol. Bull.*, 1941, 38, 534–535.
9. Miller, N. E. Experimental studies of conflict behavior. In: *Personality and the behavior disorders* (Ed. J. McV. Hunt), New York: Ronald Press, 1944, 431–465.
10. Miller, N. E. Theory and experiment relating psychoanalytic displacement to stimulus-response generalization. *J. abnorm. soc. Psychol.*, 1949, 43, 155–178.
11. Miller, N. E. Studies of fear as an acquirable drive: II: Resistance to extinction. In preparation.
12. Miller, N. E., and Dollard, J. *Social learning and imitation*. New Haven: Yale Univ. Press, 1941.
13. Miller, N. E., and Lawrence, D. H. Studies of fear as an acquirable drive: III. Effect of strength of electric shock as a primary drive and of number of trials with the primary drive on the strength of fear. In preparation.
14. Mowrer, O. H. A stimulus-response analysis of anxiety and its role as a reinforcing agent. *Psychol. Rev.*, 1939, 46, 553–565.
15. Mowrer, O. H., and Lamoreaux, R. R. Fear as an intervening variable in avoidance conditioning. *J. comp. Psychol*, 1946, 39, 29–50.
16. Shaffer, L. F. *The psychology of adjustment*. Boston: Houghton Mifflin, 1936.
17. Watson, J. B. *Psychology from the standpoint of a behaviorist*. Philadelphia: Lippincott, 1924.
18. Woodworth, R. S. *Dynamic psychology*. New York: Columbia University Press, 1918.

This experiment illustrates the development of "secondary" goals in the rat. It is easy to see that these goals have developed because they have been associated with "primary" goals, food in this case. Man also works for "secondary" goals, e.g., money, power, prestige, etc., but it is less easy to see how they have developed.

Points to guide your study

1. Make sure that you understand the four conditions of this experiment. Also make sure you understand the two types of comparisons which are made in the results section.

2. The decimals on the right in Table 1 give the chances in one hundred that the differences obtained are due to chance alone. For instance, the probability that the difference between the means of groups 2 and 3, 9.0 and 10.7 respectively, is due to chance alone is 2/100. Psychologists usually consider probabilities of 5/100, the .05 level, good enough to conclude that the difference is not due to chance. *Sigma* (the standard deviation) in Table 1 is a measure of the variation of the scores.

3. Glossary: Kinesthetic—Stimulation from movements of the body.

13.   MAZE LEARNING IN THE ABSENCE OF PRIMARY REINFORCEMENT: A STUDY OF SECONDARY REINFORCEMENT

*Irving J. Saltzman, Indiana University**

For many years experimenters have been successfully using food as an incentive to promote the learning of hungry animals. When an incentive, such as food, is used to promote learning through satisfying a primary drive, like hunger, it is often said to possess primary reward value, and it is called a primary reinforcing agent, or more simply, a primary reward. Any stimuli which occur consistently and repeatedly along with a primary reward may, themselves, soon come to act like a primary reward in promoting learning. Such stimuli are called secondary reinforcing agents; they are said to possess secondary or acquired reward value.

Maze learning without primary reward

Statement of problem. The primary purpose of this investigation was to devise a technique for

* A dissertation submitted in 1948 to the Board of University Studies of The Johns Hopkins University in conformity with the requirements for the degree of Doctor of Philosophy. The writer is indebted to Dr. W. R. Garner and Dr. S. B. Williams, under whose guidance this research was carried out.

I. J. Saltzman. Maze learning in the absence of primary reinforcement: A study of secondary reinforcement. *J. comp. physiol. Psychol.*, 1949, 42, 161–173. Copyright 1949 by the American Psychological Association. Excerpts reprinted here with permission from the author and the American Psychological Association.

showing that rats are able to learn a simple maze under conditions of secondary reward. If this aim could be realized, it was felt that a systematic study of the variables affecting the acquisition and the persistence of secondary reward value could be carried out.

Probably the greatest difficulty in showing learning in the absence of primary reward is that the acquired reward value is rapidly lost during the learning trials. If the acquired reward value is small to begin with, and if the task to be learned is very difficult, the reward value will be lost before any learning occurs, or at least before any learning that can be measured, occurs. If the learning task is a simple one, however, the chances of getting a measure of learning are better. Therefore, a small, single choice maze was used as the learning task. Also, three different methods for building up the reward value were used, in the hope that at least one of them would result in a measurable indication of learning.

Experimental procedure. *Subjects.* Forty-eight naïve, hooded, female rats, from the Johns Hopkins Psychology Department colony, were divided into four equal groups of twelve. At the start of the investigation the rats averaged 179 grams in weight, and ranged in age from 85 to 130 days.

Apparatus. The apparatus used in the experiment consisted of a closed runway, a single choice, closed U-maze, six goal boxes and one starting box. The boxes could be used with either the runway or the maze. All the apparatus was made of heavy five-ply wood and was painted grey with the exception of four of the goal boxes, two of which were painted black, and two, white. Each piece of apparatus, except the two white goal boxes, was raised from the table on which it was located, by small legs. The tops of all the apparatus were made of wire mesh and were removable.

Runway. At each end of the runway vertically sliding doors were located. These doors could be manipulated by the experimenter from the starting position by means of attached strings. When the starting box was placed adjacent to the runway, a rat could proceed directly from the box into the runway, as soon as the starting door was raised. The black goal boxes each had a hurdle 2.5 inches high on the open side. The hurdle had to be climbed by the rats in entering the box from the runway. To enter the white goal boxes, which were not raised on legs, the rats had to jump down from the runway.

Maze. The maze consisted of a straight alley leading into a U-shaped alley. Vertically sliding doors, which could be controlled from the starting position, were located at the beginning of the straight alley and at the ends of the U-shaped alley. An additional pair of doors was located at the junction of the two alleys to prevent retracing after a choice had been made. The goal boxes could not be seen by the rats until after a choice had been made. The grey goal boxes were exactly like the starting box, and were used on the maze during the test for position preference. The other goal boxes were used on the maze in the same manner as they were used on the runway.

Establishment of feeding rhythm. At the start of the experiment the rats were removed from the colony and housed in individual cages. At the same time of day, for six consecutive days, they were allowed to eat moist Purina (Growena) chicken mash from small metal containers for one half hour. The animals received no other food during this period; water was available at all times. The feeding was omitted on the seventh day.

Preliminary training. Of the four groups of rats, three were experimental secondary reward groups, and one was a comparison, primary reward group. A different technique was used with each of the experimental groups during the preliminary training.

Group 1: Consecutive reinforcement group: On day eight, at the usual feeding time, the rats in this group received the following treatment. A rat was placed into the grey starting box. After a 10 second delay, the door leading into the runway was raised. When the rat moved into the runway, the door was lowered behind it. The door at the goal box was already raised. When the rat entered the goal box, this door was lowered, and the rat was given a metal cup containing wet mash, and was allowed to eat for two minutes. The rat was then removed to its home cage. Five such runway trials were given each of the rats, each trial separated from the preceding one by approximately five minutes. Following the fifth runway trial, each animal was allowed to eat in the goal box for 20 minutes. In this manner, each rat received his daily ration of food in the goal box. For one half of the animals in this group, the goal box used was the black box with the hurdle; for the other half, the white box without legs was used.

This procedure was repeated for five consecutive days, at the end of which time each rat had received 25 rewarded runs to its particular box. On the last day of runway experience, between the second and third trials, the position habits of the rats were tested in the maze. The two grey goal boxes were used as the goal. Thirty seconds after the rat had entered a goal box, it was removed from the box. A choice of one side two out of three times was the measure of side preference used. Following the tests, the rewarded runway trials were resumed.

Group 2: Alternate reinforcement group: The rats in this group received the same treatment as those in Group 1 on the first day of runway experience. From the second day on, the rats in this group, in addition to the five rewarded runs per day, received several non-rewarded trials. A rewarded trial always preceded and always followed a non-rewarded trial. The first non-rewarded run was given after the second rewarded run, on the second day of runway trials. In all, 14 non-rewarded runs were given each of the rats in addition to the 25 rewarded runs. Three were given on the second and on the fifth day of the runway trials, and four each on the third and fourth days. On the fifth day the position habit test was given, instead of the second non-rewarded run of the day. The same kind of goal box was used with a given rat for both the rewarded and non-rewarded runs.

Group 3: Differential reinforcement group: The rats in this group received the same treatment as those in Group 2, with the exception that on the non-rewarded trials, the goal box was not the same one that was used for the rewarded trials. The rats receiving food in the black goal box found the white goal box at the end of the runway on the non-rewarded runs, and those receiving food in the white box found the black box on the non-rewarded runs.

Group C: The rats in Group C, the comparison primary reward group, received exactly the same treatment as the rats in Group 1.

Learning trials. Groups 1, 2, and 3: The learning trials were conducted on the day following the last day of runway trials. All three experimental groups of rats received the same treatment. The goal box, either black or white, in which the rats had received food on the runway, was located in the goal position on the nonpreferred side. The other goal box was placed in the goal position of the preferred side. All the doors in the maze, except the one at the starting box, were raised. The non-correction technique was used. The rat was first placed in the starting box. After a 10 second delay, the door was raised. When the rat entered the straight alley of the maze, the door was lowered behind it. After the rat had made its choice of path, the door at the choice point was lowered to prevent retracing. As soon as the rat entered the goal box located at the end of the arm of the U, the final door was lowered, and 30 seconds later, the rat was removed to its home cage. Fifteen such trials in the maze were given each rat. Each trial was separated from the preceding one by a period of from 5 to 15 minutes. Food was never presented to any of the animals in the maze regardless of the choice that had been made.

Group C: When the rats of Group C were run on the maze, both of the goal boxes were identical, and both were different from the goal box in which the rats had received food on the runway. When a rat which had been fed in a black box on the runway was run in the maze, white goal boxes were placed in each of the goal positions of the maze, and vice versa. Following correct choices in the maze, the rats in this group were offered a cup of food from which they were allowed to eat for 30 seconds. A correct choice was a choice of the non-preferred side, as determined by the position habit test. Food was not presented to the animals when incorrect choices were made. In such instances, the rats were merely removed from the goal box after 30 seconds. Fifteen maze trials were given, regardless of the choices that had been made.

Results. The main purpose of the study was to find out whether it could be shown that rats can learn a simple maze in the absence of primary reward. The test of learning consisted merely of 15 runs in the maze with a secondary reinforcing agent serving as the only source of reinforcement. If learning occurred under these conditions, it could be said that secondary reinforcement learning of a maze is possible. Since a comparison group of rats which received primary reinforcement on the maze was also run, two indices of learning were available: 1) Comparison of the maze choices of the secondary reward groups with chance expectancy, and 2) Comparison of the maze choices of the secondary reward groups with the choices of the primary reward group.

Comparison with chance expectancy. If the goal boxes in which the rats had been fed on the runway had *not* acquired any secondary reward value, it might be expected that the average number of choices of the correct alley out of a possible 15 would be approximately seven and one half or less, since the rats were run against their position habits. On the other hand, if the box *had* acquired reward value, it might be expected that the path leading to that box in the maze would be selected more often than the other path. The number of correct choices was used, therefore, as the measure of the effectiveness of the secondary reinforcing agent, and at the same time, as a measure of learning. If the mean number of correct choices was significantly greater than chance, then learning was said to have occurred.

Comparison with primary reinforcement group. In order to use the results of the primary reinforcement group in getting an index of learning, one assumption has to be made. It has to be assumed that the mean number of correct choices made by this group is the number of correct choices that ought to occur if the maze were being learned. In other words, it was assumed that the rats in this group were learning the maze. Then a comparison of the mean number of correct choices made by this group with the means of the other groups tells us something about the learning of the other groups. We have a measure of the relative effec-

Table 1 **Means, sigmas, and probabilities of differences from chance and between means**

Groups*	Mean Number Correct Choices	Sigma	Chance (7.5)	Probabilities		
				Group C	Group 1	Group 2
C	10.0	2.16	.01	—	—	—
1	8.3	1.25	.04	.04	—	—
2	9.0	1.73	.01	.25	.29	—
3	10.7	1.31	.01	.95	.01	.02

* Groups 1, 2, and 3 ran the maze under conditions of secondary reward, and Group C under primary reward.

tiveness of primary and secondary rewards. In addition, this comparison serves as a check of our first index of learning.

The mean number of correct choices out of a possible 15 for each of the experimental groups, as well as for the comparison group, is indicated in Table 1, along with the standard deviations of the means. The table also shows the probabilities with which the differences which were obtained between the means of the groups and 7.5 could be obtained purely by chance. Included, too, are the probabilities with which the differences between the several group means could occur by chance. The mean number of correct choices for Groups 1, 2, and 3 are 8.3, 9.0, and 10.7 respectively. The comparison group, Group C, has a mean of 10.0 correct choices.

Each of the means is different from chance (7.5) at the 1 per cent level of confidence, except for Group 1. The difference which exists between the mean of Group 1 (8.3) and chance would occur 4 times in 100 by chance factors alone. If the criterion of significance adopted to indicate statistical significance is the 1 percent level of confidence, then it can be said that Groups 2 and 3 learned the maze, and that Group 1 did not.

The differences between the mean of Group C, the primary reward group, and the means of Groups 2 and 3, are not significant statistically. This indicates that the secondary reward value built up with either of these two methods is probably as effective in influencing the choices that were made in the maze as is a primary reward. The difference between the means of Group 1 and Group C would occur on the basis of pure chance factors only 4 times in 100, suggesting that a real difference may exist between the two means. In 15 learning trials, the rats in Group 1 did not learn to the same extent as did those of Group C.

Summary and conclusion. The experiment establishes the ability of the rat to learn a simple maze when correct choices are followed only by stimuli previously associated with food, and probably enhances the possibilities of secondary reinforcement as a general principle of learning. Inasmuch as the distinctive aspects of the goal boxes were at least several, including kinesthetic as well as visual components, it is impossible to say which of them was the most effective. Taken together, however, they were at least as effective, or slightly more effective than food. This last fact challenges a re-interpretation of the whole problem of the relative effectiveness of rewards in learning.

References

1. Anderson, E. E.: The externalization of drive: III. Maze learning by non-rewarded and by satiated rats. *J. genet. Psychol.*, 1941, **59**, 397–426.

2. Cowles, J. T.: Food-tokens as incentives for learning by chimpanzees. *Comp. Psychol. Monogr.*, 1937, **14**, No. 5.

3. Denny, M. R.: Differential end boxes in a simple T-maze. *Amer. Psychologist*, 1946, **1**, 245.

4. Ellson, D. G.: The acquisition of a token-reward habit in dogs. *J. comp. Psychol.*, 1937, **24**, 505–522.

5. Grindley, G. C.: Experiments on the influence of the amount of reward on learning in young chickens. *Brit. J. Psychol.*, 1929, **20**, 173–180.

6. Hull, C. L.: *Principles of behavior*. New York: Appleton Century Co., 1943.

7. Humphreys, L. G.: The strength of a Thorndikian response as a function of the number of practice trials. *J. comp. Psychol.*, 1943, **35**, 101–110.

8. McCulloch, T. L.: The use of the "comfort" drive as motivation in visual discrimination by the infant chimpanzee. *Psychol. Bull.*, 1937, **34**, 540.

9. Miller, N. E.: Studies of fear as an acquirable drive: I. Fear as motivation and fear-reduction as reinforcement in the learning of new responses. *J. exp. Psychol.*, 1948, **38**, 89–101.

10. Mote, F. A. and Finger, F. W.: Exploratory drive and secondary reinforcement in the acquisition and extinction of a simple running response. *J. exp. Psychol.*, 1942, **31**, 57–68.

11. Mowrer, O. H. and Jones, H.: Habit strength as a function of the pattern of reinforcement. *J. exp. Psychol.*, 1945, **35**, 293–310.

12. Nissen, N. W. and Crawford, M. P.: A preliminary study of food-sharing behavior in young chimpanzees. *J. comp. Psychol.*, 1936, **22**, 383–419.

13. Skinner, B. F.: *The behavior of organisms*. New York: Appleton Century Co., 1938.

14. Spence, K. W.: The role of secondary reinforcement in delayed reward learning. *Psychol. Rev.*, 1947, **54**, 1–8.

15. Williams, Katherine A.: The reward value of a conditioned stimulus. *Univ. Calif. Publ. Psychol.*, 1929, **4**, 31–55.

16. Wolfe, J. B.: Effectiveness of token-rewards for chimpanzees. *Comp. Psychol. Monogr.*, 1936, **12**, No. 60.

COMPLEX MOTIVES

The complex human motives, such as need for achievement, are especially interesting. Most psychologists consider them to be the result of learning, and, indeed the present article presents data to support this view. These complex motives have sometimes been called secondary motives, but this term is no longer much used because it may imply that they are of secondary importance in human behavior.

It seems possible to distinguish three general types of motives. In the first place, there are the physiological motives proper which are based on need states of body tissue. In the second place, there are the motives, like learned fear, which are modifications of the physiological motives. Finally, there are the complex motive states, often somewhat confusingly called needs, which are the result of prolonged social learning.

Points to guide your study

1. What are the experiments and observations which tie together the successive points of Table 1? What ties A to B, B to C, and C to D?

2. Note the lower part of Table 3, "Analysis of Variance," the F values are the things to look at. An F value significant at the 1 or 5 percent level indicates that the difference in means was one that probably was *not* due to *chance* alone. Thus, the F of 12.21 for religion indicates that the mean ages of expectation differed so much that the difference could not be explained by saying it was due to chance. (Don't worry about the "interaction.")

14. SOME SOCIAL CONSEQUENCES OF ACHIEVEMENT MOTIVATION

*David C. McClelland, Harvard University**

Influenced by Hull and other functionalists, many of us for a long time tended to think of motives or drives as if they were functionally interchangeable, like electromotive forces in an equation in physics. From such a point of view it is as ridiculous to ask the question what kind of motive is involved as it is to ask what kind of electromotive force is involved. All motives are functionally equivalent and vary only in intensity. A motive is a motive is a motive is a motive, as Gertrude Stein might say. It doesn't really matter whether you are working with light-aversion as a drive, or hunger, or thirst, or pain, since they are all functionally equivalent and it is merely a matter of convenience which one you choose to work with. It is also merely a matter of convenience which animal species

* D. C. McClelland. Some social consequences of achievement motivation. In M. R. Jones (Ed.). *Nebraska symposium on motivation*, 1955. Lincoln, Neb.: University of Nebraska Press, 1955, pp. 41–65. Copyright 1955 by the University of Nebraska Press. Excerpts reprinted here with permission from the author and the University of Nebraska Press.

you choose to work with since again, by assumption, a motive is a motive is a motive and it is therefore as useful theoretically to study the hunger drive in the white rat as it is to study the achievement motive in the human being. Today as we have begun to study motivation in its own right, and not just as a convenient construct to explain learning, such a point of view seems painfully inadequate. For one thing, as animal psychologists like Harlow (3) and Nissen (6) have been pointing out, there are major species differences in motivation which must be taken into account if we are to understand animal behavior adequately. For another, and this is the point I intend to elaborate here, recent studies of human motivation have demonstrated again and again that knowledge about one particular kind of motivation will enable us to predict varieties of behavior that we could not predict from knowledge of other motives. For example, knowledge of *n* Achievement scores will enable us to predict how well a group of people will do in a laboratory task (4), but knowledge of *n* Affiliation scores will not. Knowledge of n Affiliation scores will enable us to predict something about popularity (18) whereas knowledge of n Achievement scores will not. And so on. It is becoming increasingly clear that we must pay attention to the type of motive we are measuring, its particular origins, and its particular consequences for human behavior and society.

As a case in point, let us try to do this for the achievement motive, the human motive about which we know the most at the present time. There is no need to review here the methods we have used for deriving the n Achievement score or the data showing its connections with various types of behavior, since that has been done elsewhere (4) and particularly well by Atkinson at this Symposium last year (1). It will have to suffice here to say that we have developed what appears to be a promising method of measuring the achievement motive by identifying and counting the frequency with which a certain type of imagery appears in the thoughts a person has when he writes a brief story under time pressure. The type of imagery involved, which includes any references to "competition with a standard of excellence," can be identified objectively and reliably and differs in kind from other types of imagery which can be used to identify other motives such as the need for Affiliation, the need for Power, and the like. There are those who argue that what we are identifying in this way are not really motives at all, but something else, perhaps habits (2). I don't want to seem too lighthearted about psychological theory, but I should hate to see much energy expended in debating the point. If someone can plan and execute a better research by calling these measures habits, so much the better. If, furthermore, it should turn out that all the interesting findings we have turned up are the result of some theoretical "error" in our thinking, I cannot admit to much regret. The fact of the matter is that we know too little about either motives or habits to get into a very useful discussion as to which is which. The important thing is that we accumulate data as rapidly and systematically as we can. Then I believe these theoretical issues will have a way of boiling themselves down to a meaningful level at which they can be settled.

But to return to our main story: we have continued to treat n Achievement as a motive and after hearing where this thinking has led us, you must decide for yourselves whether you want to conceive of it in the same way or in some different way. I want to draw attention now to Winterbottom's very important study (4, 13) on the origins of n Achievement as we measure it. She found, as many of you will remember, that mothers who said they expected their sons to do well on their own at an early age tended to have sons with higher n Achievement scores. That is, mothers who expected their sons to be self-reliant early in life—to make their own friends, to find their own way around their part of town, to do well in competitive sports and the like—tended to have sons with strong achievement motives. Furthermore, this training for self-reliance or independence (11) did not include "care-taking" items such as putting oneself to bed, cutting one's own food, earning one's own spending money, et cetera, a fact which suggested that what was involved here was not rejection by the mother but rather a positive interest in the child's independence, growth, and development. Winterbottom established here a link between a socialization practice, namely independence training, and a motive, namely the desire to do well.

Considered in a social and historical context, this linkage suggested an interesting parallel with Weber's classic description of the nature and characterological consequences of the Protestant Reformation (10). In the first place, he stresses, as others have, that the essence of the Protestant revolt against the Catholic church was a shift from a reliance on an institution to a greater reliance on the self, so far as salvation was concerned. The individual Protestant Lutheran or Calvinist was less dependent on the church as an institution either for its priests or its sacraments or its official dogma. Instead there was to be a "priesthood of all believers," in Luther's words. The Protestant could read and interpret his Bible and find his own way to God without having to rely on the authority of the Church or its official assistance. As Weber describes it, we have here what seems to be an example of a revolution in ideas which should increase the need for independence training. Certainly Protestant parents, if they were to prepare their children adequately for increased self-reliance so far as religious matters were concerned, would tend to stress increasingly often and early the necessity for the child's not depending on adult assistance but seeking his own "salvation." In the second place, Weber's description of the kind of personality type which the Protestant Reformation produced is startlingly similar to the picture we would draw of a person with high achievement motivation. He notes that Protestant working girls seemed to work harder and longer, that they saved their money for long-range goals, that Protestant entrepreneurs seemed to come to the top more often in the business world despite the initial advantages of wealth many Catholic families had, and so forth. In particular, he points out that the early Calvinist business man was prevented by his religious views from enjoying the results of his labors. He could not spend money on himself because of scruples about self-indulgence and display, and so, more often than not, he reinvested his profits in his business, which was one reason he prospered. What then drove him to such prodigious feats of business organization and development? Weber feels that such a man "gets nothing out of his wealth for himself, except the irrational sense of having done his job well" (10, p. 71). This is exactly how we define the achievement motive. So again, the parallel seems clear, although there is not space to give the argument in full here. Is it possible that the Protestant Reformation involves a repetition at a social and historical level of the linkage that Winterbottom found between independence training and *n* Achievement among some mothers and their sons in a small town in Michigan in 1950?

To make such an assumption involves a breath-taking leap of hypothesizing so far as the average psychologist is concerned, who is much more at home with a sample of 30 mothers and 30 sons than he is with major social movements. But the hypothesis seems too fascinating to dismiss without some further study. It can be diagrammed rather simply as in Table 1. In terms of this diagram Weber was chiefly concerned with the linkage between A and D, with the way

Table 1   Hypothetical series of events relating self-reliance values with economic and technological development

A	D
Protestantism (self-reliance values)	Economic and technological development

B	C
Independence training by parents	*n* Achievement in children

in which Protestantism led to a change in the spirit of capitalism in the direction of a speeded-up, high-pressure, competitive business economy. But the manner in which he describes this relationship strongly suggests that the linkage by which these two events are connected involves steps B and C, namely a change in family socialization practices which in turn increased the number of individuals with high achievement motivation. Thus a full statement of the hypothesis would be that Protestantism produced an increased stress on independence training which produced higher achievement motivation which produced more vigorous entrepreneurial activity and rapid economic development. Such a simple statement of the hypothesis obscures many problems, some of which

we have only begun to think about. To establish all the links in the chain obviously requires an enormous amount of research, much of which has not been completed. What I have to report today are only some preliminary findings which, however, serve to confirm the hypothesis at several crucial points and, at the very least, dignify it to the point of making it worth very serious investigation.

Let us consider first Weber's general argument about the connection between Protestantism and economic development. Although there has been much discussion among historians, economists, and sociologists of this thesis since it first appeared about 50 years ago, most of it *pro* though some of it *con* (see 9), I could find no simple statistical test of the presumed association such as we would be apt to apply in psychology. Instead the literature seems to consist largely of citing instances which confirm the thesis, drawn chiefly from England, the Scandinavian countries and Holland, or instances which apparently disprove it such as Belgium or pre-Protestant Italy. Having had much experience in my youth with individual rats who obeyed none of Hull's laws, I wanted to get beyond the battle of instance and counter-instance to see what the general trend looked like. Table 2 shows the results of one such effort. What I tried to do was to get as large a group of Catholic and Protestant countries as I could which were matched roughly for climate and resources.

Then I took the most easily obtainable index of economic or technological development, namely kilowatt hours of electricity consumed as of a given year in a given country, and checked it against the Protestant-Catholic classification of the country, with the result shown in Table 2. A simple ranks correlation, a biserial tau, shows that the Protestant character of a country is significantly associated with higher levels of consumption of electrical energy. This may be a crude test of the hypothesis, but the relationship is large and seems not likely to disappear under refinements of techniques for measuring economic development or for equating the natural resources of the two groups of countries. At least it is comforting to a psychologist to have this much statistical backing for a hypothesis before expending a great deal of further energy in trying to study its further implications.

The next step involves tying in our own research findings on the origins of achievement motivation (stages B and C in Table 1). Specifically, we would predict that there should be a connection between A and B in Table 1, that Protestants should favor earlier independence training than Catholics do. The major findings on this point are reproduced in Table 3 from a study by McClelland, Rindlisbacher and

Table 2 Average per capita consumption of electric power in Protestant and Catholic countries beyond the Tropics of Cancer and Capricorn (for the year 1950, in kilowatt-hours, from Woytinski, 14)

	Protestant	Catholic
Norway	5,310	
Canada	4,120	
Sweden	2,580	
U.S.A.	2,560	
Switzerland	2,230	
New Zealand	1,600	
Australia	1,160	
United Kingdom	1,115	
Finland	1,000	
Belgium		986
Austria		900
Union of South Africa	890	
France		790
Czechoslovakia		730
Holland	725	
Italy		535
Denmark	500	
Poland		375
Hungary		304
Ireland		300
Chile		260
Argentina		255
Spain		225
Uruguay		165
Portugal		110
Mean	**1,983**	**457**

Biserial tau = + .45 P <.005

deCharms (5). The figures in the table are based on responses to the 13 items in the original Winterbottom independence training questionnaire which she found to be associated with *n* Achievement. A mean age was computed for each parent at which he expected his child to have mastered the items in question. Then averages of these means were computed and cross-classified by sex of parent, by education of parent, and by religious grouping. All three primary sources of variation are significant. Religion makes a significant difference, the Protestants and Jews favoring early independence and the Irish- and Italian-Catholics favoring later independence for their children. The first link of our research with its social context has been established.

The final link in the chain, that between C and D in Table 1, or between high *n* Achievement and economic development, is the one on which we have been working most recently. I want to confess here to doubts we had as to how this would come out. We knew that *n* Achievement as we measured it was significantly correlated with better performance on a wide variety of laboratory tasks (4) and Ricciuti (7) has shown that it is significantly correlated with high school grades with ability level partialed out. But none of this would lead us to predict on the basis of our own work that *n* Achievement would be connected in a peculiar way with more vigorous economic activity. Why not make the simpler assumption that it would be connected with more vigorous activity in any line of endeavor? Wouldn't it be logical to predict on the basis of our task performance or school work data that high *n* Achievement should make a person do better at poetry or politics, law or science, farming or selling real estate? Why pick on business or assume that *n* Achievement would direct people's interests along business lines particularly? Yet the sociological and historical data pointed clearly toward a connection with business activity, at least if we are to take Weber's arguments at all seriously, and continue to entertain the hypothesis sketched in Table 1.

So with some misgivings as to the outcome, we decided to put the hypothesis to the test by seeing whether students with high *n* Achievement were more interested in business occupations than students with low *n* Achievement. The null hypothesis is of course that *n* Achievement makes no difference in inclining a person toward one occupation rather than another. To measure occupational interest we simply used the Strong Vocational Interest Blank, which was filled out by a group of college freshmen at the same time that they had been tested for *n* Achievement. To test the hypothesis we simply took the top 20% of the class in *n* Achievement and compared their answers to each of the Strong items with the answers given by the bottom 20% of the class in *n* Achievement. The results were really startling, at least to us, since we had had so many doubts about the whole enterprise from the beginning. You will recall that on the Strong Test the respondent is asked whether he likes, dislikes, or is indifferent to 100 different occupations on the first part of the test. In Table 4 are listed the only occupations for which consistent and significant differences appeared between the top and bottom fifths of the *n* Achievement distribution. In every case the group high in *n* Achievement likes the occupations listed better than the group low in *n* Achievement. What more striking confirmation of the hypothesis could be expected? The Chi-square for "stockbroker," the most significant single item, was 10.04, P < .01. Shades of Marxist propaganda about the role of "Wall Street" in the capitalist economy!

Now some Doubting Thomases among you

Table 3   Average ages at which parents expect children to have mastered various independence training items

	Less than high school graduates	High school graduate up to college graduates	College graduate or more	Means	Religious group means
Protestant					**6.64**
Father	8.04	6.41	6.90	**7.12**	
Mother	6.56	6.41	5.55	**6.17**	
Jewish					**6.59**
Father	7.65	7.12	6.48	**7.08**	
Mother	5.74	6.66	5.89	**6.10**	
Irish Catholic					**7.66**
Father	8.50	7.92	8.26	**8.23**	
Mother	7.23	7.61	6.40	**7.08**	
Italian Catholic					**8.42**
Father	9.05	10.43	6.51	**8.66**	
Mother	9.68	6.87	8.00	**8.18**	
Educational level means	**7.81**	**7.43**	**6.75**		
Fathers' mean	**7.77**				
Mothers' mean	**6.88**				

Analysis of variance

Source of variation	Sum of squares	df.	Mean square	F
1. Religion	13.91	3	4.64	12.21 *
2. Educational level	4.60	2	2.30	6.05 *
3. Sex of parent	4.74	1	4.74	12.47 *
4. Interaction ‡	11.78	17	.69	1.82 †
5. Error		128	.38	

* Significant at the 1% level.
† Significant at the 5% level.
‡ The primary sources of variation interact significantly, a fact which cannot be discussed here as being beyond a preliminary treatment of the results. For this reason it has also been necessary to compute an independent estimate of error based on the actual variation of the individual cases in the various cells following the approximation method described by Walker and Lev (12), pp. 381-382.

Table 4   Occupations in the first 100 on the Strong Vocational Interest Blank preferred significantly more by college freshmen with high (top 20%) than with low (bottom 20%) *n* achievement scores (listed in order of significance of differences)

1. Stockbroker
2. Office manager
3. Sales manager
4. Buyer of merchandise
5. Real estate salesman
6. Factory manager

are sure to point out that in making this many significance tests, one ought to come out with about this number of significant differences.

We know that, and we are for that reason replicating the study right at this moment, but what are the chances that Lady Luck should hit on these particular occupations when she had so many to pick from, including everything from artist to author to musician to lawyer or electrical repairman? To be more precise, the chances are less than 1 in 4,000, since roughly one-quarter of the occupations might be classified as related to business. Certainly if she did happen to pick on occupations so obviously related to business activity and economic development just by chance, she has played us a dirty trick in getting our scientific hopes aroused. In any case, the evidence does not consist of these items alone. Further item analysis of the rest of the test shows many confirmatory results, although their exact significance will have to await further study and, in particular, a replication.*

References

1. Atkinson, J. W. Explorations using imaginative thought to assess the strength of human motives. In Marshall Jones (Ed.), *Nebraska Symposium on Motivation*, 1954, 56–112.
2. Farber, I. E. Comments on Professor Atkinson's paper. In Marshall Jones (Ed.), *Nebraska Symposium on Motivation*, 1954, 112–115.
3. Harlow, H. F. Motivation as a factor in the acquisition of new responses. In *Current Theory and Research in Motivation*, Lincoln, Nebraska: University of Nebraska Press, 1953, 24–29.
4. McClelland, D. C., Atkinson, J. W., Clark, R. A., and Lowell, E. L. *The Achievement Motive*. New York: Appleton-Century-Crofts, 1953.
5. McClelland, E. C., Rindlisbacher, A., and deCharms, R. Religious and other sources of parental attitudes toward independence training. In D. C. McClelland (Ed.), *Studies in Motivation*. New York: Appleton-Century-Crofts, 1955.

6. Nissen, H. W. The nature of the drive as innate determinant of behavioral organization. In Marshall Jones (Ed.), *Nebraska Symposium on Motivation*, 1954, 281–321.
7. Ricciuti, H. N., and Sadacca, R. The prediction of academic grades with a projective test of achievement motivation: II. Cross-validation at the high school level. Princeton, N.J.: *Research Bulletin*, Educational Testing Service, 1954.
8. Shipley, T. W., and Veroff, J. A projective measure of need for affiliation. *J. exp. Psychol.*, 1952. **43**, 349–356.
9. Tawney, R. H. *Religion and the Rise of Capitalism*. New York: Harcourt, Brace, 1926.
10. Weber, M. *The Protestant Ethic* (translated by Talcott Parsons). New York: Scribner's, 1930.
11. Whiting, J. W. M., and Child, I. L. *Child Training and Personality*. New Haven: Yale Univer. Press. 1953.
12. Walker, H. M., and Lev, J. *Statistical Inference*. New York: Holt, 1953.
13. Winterbottom, M. R. The relation of childhood training in independence to achievement motivation. Unpublished Ph.D. thesis, Univer. of Michigan, 1953. Abstract in Univ. Microfilms, Publication No. 5113.
14. Woytinski, W. S., and Woytinski, E. S. *World Population and Production*, New York: Twentieth Century Fund, 1953.

* Subsequent work has shown that this particular result is specific to the group tested, though the general line of reasoning turned out to be correct (ed.). See D. C. McClelland. *The achieving society*. Princeton, N.J.: Van Nostrand, 1961. Chap. 6.

CHAPTER FOUR

Feeling and emotion

BODILY STATES IN EMOTION

Emotions are characterized by (1) particular experiences (feelings) and (2) an increase or decrease in the level of arousal. Theories of emotion arose which were aimed at accounting for these characteristics. The James-Lange theory attempts to deal especially with the first characteristic, while the Cannon-Bard theory is most successful in dealing with the second.

The James-Lange theory is probably not held by very many psychologists today, but it provides a background for the understanding of the Cannon-Bard theory.

William James is perhaps the most famous classical American psychologist. He set the tone in his *Principles of Psychology* for much of the pragmatic, functionalist American psychology which followed. C. Lange was a Danish physiologist and is known to psychologists because of his connection with James in the James-Lange theory.

Points to guide your study

1. Read the next selection by W. B. Cannon. This is the theory which contrasts with the James-Lange theory.

2. The style of the writing is rather flowery, but do not let that bother you. Henry James, the novelist, was the brother of William James. Someone has said that William James was a psychologist who wrote like a novelist, while Henry James was a novelist who wrote like a psychologist.

15. THE PRINCIPLES OF PSYCHOLOGY

*William James**

Emotion follows upon the bodily expression in the coarser emotions at least

Our natural way of thinking about these coarser emotions is that the mental perception of some fact excites the mental affection called the emotion, and that this latter state of mind gives rise to the bodily expression. My theory, on the contrary, is that *the bodily changes follow directly the perception of the exciting fact, and that our feeling of the same changes as they occur IS the emotion.* Common-sense says, we lose our fortune, are sorry and weep; we meet a bear, are

* William James. *The principles of psychology.* vol. 2. New York: Holt, 1890. Copyright 1890 by Henry Holt and Company. Excerpt reprinted here with permission from Holt, Rinehart and Winston, Inc.

frightened and run; we are insulted by a rival, are angry and strike. The hypothesis here to be defended says that this order of sequence is incorrect, that the one mental state is not immediately induced by the other, that the bodily manifestations must first be interposed between, and that the more rational statement is that we feel sorry because we cry, angry because we strike, afraid because we tremble, and not that we cry, strike, or tremble, because we are sorry, angry, or fearful, as the case may be. Without the bodily states following on the perception, the latter would be purely cognitive in form, pale, colorless, destitute of emotional warmth. We might then see the bear, and judge it best to run, receive the insult and deem it right to strike, but we should not actually *feel* afraid or angry.

Stated in this crude way, the hypothesis is pretty sure to meet with immediate disbelief. And yet neither many nor far-fetched considerations are required to mitigate its paradoxical character, and possibly to produce conviction of its truth.

To begin with, no reader of the last two chapters will be inclined to doubt the fact that *objects do excite bodily changes* by a preorganized mechanism, or the farther fact that *the changes are so indefinitely numerous and subtle that the entire organism may be called a sounding-board*, which every change of consciousness, however slight, may make reverberate. The various permutations and combinations of which these organic activities are susceptible make it abstractly possible that no shade of emotion, however slight, should be without a bodily reverberation as unique, when taken in its totality, as is the mental mood itself. The immense number of parts modified in each emotion is what makes it so difficult for us to reproduce in cold blood the total and integral expression of any one of them. We may catch the trick with the voluntary muscles, but fail with the skin, glands, heart, and other viscera. Just as an artificially imitated sneeze lacks something of the reality, so the attempt to imitate an emotion in the absence of its normal instigating cause is apt to be rather "hollow."

The next thing to be noticed is this, that *every one of the bodily changes, whatsoever it be, is* FELT, *acutely or obscurely, the moment it occurs*. If the reader has never paid attention to this matter, he will be both interested and astonished to learn how many different local bodily feelings he can detect in himself as characteristic of his various emotional moods. It would be perhaps too much to expect him to arrest the tide of any strong gust of passion for the sake of any such curious analysis as this; but he can observe more tranquil states, and that may be assumed here to be true of the greater which is shown to be true of the less. Our whole cubic capacity is sensibly alive; and each morsel of it contributes its pulsations of feeling, dim or sharp, pleasant, painful, or dubious, to that sense of personality that every one of us unfailingly carries with him. It is surprising what little items give accent to these complexes of sensibility. When worried by any slight trouble, one may find that the focus of one's bodily consciousness is the contraction, often quite inconsiderable, of the eyes and brows. When momentarily embarrassed, it is something in the pharynx that compels either a swallow, a clearing of the throat, or a slight cough; and so on for as many more instances as might be named. Our concern here being with the general view rather than with the details, I will not linger to discuss these, but, assuming the point admitted that every change that occurs must be felt, I will pass on.

I now proceed to urge the vital point of my whole theory, which is this: *If we fancy some strong emotion, and then try to abstract from our consciousness of it all the feelings of its bodily symptoms, we find we have nothing left behind*, no "mind-stuff" out of which the emotion can be constituted, and that a cold and neutral state of intellectual perception is all that remains. It is true that, although most people when asked say that their introspection verifies this statement, some persist in saying theirs does not. Many cannot be made to understand the question. When you beg them to imagine away every feeling of laughter and of tendency to laugh from their consciousness of the ludicrousness of an object, and then to tell you what the feeling of its ludicrousness would be like, whether it be anything more than the perception that the object belongs to the class "funny," they persist in replying that the thing proposed is a physical impossibility, and that they always *must* laugh if they see a funny object. Of course the task proposed is not the practical one of seeing a ludicrous object and annihilating one's tendency to laugh. It is the purely speculative one of subtracting certain elements of feeling from an emotional state supposed to exist in its fulness, and saying what the residual elements are. I cannot help thinking that all who rightly apprehend this problem will agree with the proposition above laid down. What kind of an emotion of fear would be left if the feeling neither of quickened heart-beats nor of shallow breathing, neither of trembling lips nor of weakened limbs, neither of goose-flesh nor of visceral stirrings, were present, it is quite impossible for me to think. Can one fancy the state of rage and picture no ebullition in the chest, no flushing of the face, no dilatation of the nostrils, no clenching of the teeth, no impulse to vigorous action, but in their stead limp muscles, calm breathing, and a placid face? The present writer, for one, certainly cannot. The rage is as completely evaporated as the sensation of its so-called manifestations, and the only thing that can possibly be supposed to take its place is some cold-blooded and dispassionate judicial sentence, confined entirely to the intellectual realm, to the effect that a certain person or persons merit chastisement for their sins. In like manner of grief: what would it be without its tears, its sobs, its suffocation of the heart, its pang in the breastbone? A feelingless cognition that certain circumstances are deplorable, and nothing more. Every passion in turn tells the same story. A purely disembodied human emotion is a nonentity. I do not say that it is a contradiction in the nature of things, or that pure spirits are necessarily condemned to cold intellectual lives; but I say that for *us*, emotion dissociated from all bodily feeling is inconceivable. The more closely I scrutinize my states, the more persuaded I become that whatever moods, affections, and passions I have are in very truth constituted by, and made up of, those bodily changes which we ordinarily call their expression or consequence; and the more it seems to me that if I were to become corporeally anaesthetic,

I should be excluded from the life of the affections, harsh and tender alike, and drag out an existence of merely cognitive or intellectual form. Such an existence, although it seems to have been ideal of ancient sages, is too apathetic to be keenly sought after by those born after the revival of the worship of sensibility, a few generations ago.

This is both a criticism of the James-Lange theory of emotions and a statement of another classic theory of emotions, sometimes called the Cannon-Bard theory.

Points to guide your study

1. We would probably use the term "hypothalamus," instead of thalamus, today. These are structures in the brain stem below the cerebrum.

2. How does the theory presented here by Cannon differ from the James-Lange theory? Make your answer as detailed as you can.

3. See your text for definitions of anatomical terms.

16. THE JAMES-LANGE THEORY OF EMOTIONS: A CRITICAL EXAMINATION AND AN ALTERNATIVE THEORY

*Walter B. Cannon**

In his introduction to the reprinting of the classic papers by James and Lange, Dunlap[1] declares that their theory of emotions as organic processes "has not only become so strongly entrenched in scientific thought that it is practically assumed today as the basis for the study of the emotional life, but has also led to the development of the hypothesis of reaction or response as the basis of all mental life." And Perry[2] has written, "This famous doctrine is so strongly fortified by proof and so repeatedly confirmed by experience that it cannot be denied substantial truth. In spite of elaborate refutation it shows no signs of obsolescence." With some trepidation, therefore, one ventures to criticise a view of the nature of emotions which has proved so satisfactory as a means of interpreting affective experience and

which has commended itself so generally to psychologists. There are now at hand, however, pertinent physiological facts which were not available when James and Lange developed their ideas and which should be brought to bear on those ideas, and there are alternative explanations of affective experience which should be considered, before the James-Lange theory is granted basal claims in this realm of psychology.

James first presented his view in 1884, Lange's monograph appeared in Danish in 1885. The cardinal points in their respective ideas of the nature of emotions are so well known that for purposes of comment only brief references need be made to them. James' theory may be summarized, in nearly his own terms, as follows. An object stimulates one or more sense organs; afferent impulses pass to the cortex and the object is perceived; thereupon currents run down to muscles and viscera and alter them in complex ways; afferent impulses from these disturbed organs course back to the cortex and when there perceived transform the "object-simply-apprehended" to the "object-emotionally-felt." In other words, "the feeling of the bodily changes as they occur is the emotion—the common sen-

* This paper is from the Laboratory of Physiology, Harvard Medical School.

W. B. Cannon. The James-Lange theory of emotions: a critical examination and an alternative theory. *Amer. J. Psychol.*, 1927, **39**, 106–124. Copyright 1927 by the American Journal of Psychology. Reprinted here with permission from the American Journal of Psychology.

[1] W. James and C. G. Lange, *The Emotions*, 1922.
[2] R. B. Perry, *General Theory of Value*, 1926, 295.

sational, associational and motor elements explain all." [3] The main evidence cited for the theory is that we are aware of the tensions, throbs, flushes, pangs, suffocations—we feel them, indeed, the moment they occur—and that if we should take away from the picture of a fancied emotion these bodily symptoms, nothing would be left.

According to Lange[4] stimulation of the vasomotor center is "the root of the causes of the affections, however else they may be constituted." "We owe all the emotional side of our mental life," he wrote, "our joys and sorrows, our happy and unhappy hours, to our vasomotor system. If the impressions which fall upon our senses did not possess the power of stimulating it, we would wander through life unsympathetic and passionless, all impressions of the outer world would only enrich our experience, increase our knowledge, but would arouse neither joy nor anger, would give us neither care nor fear." Since we are unable to differentiate subjectively between feelings of a central and peripheral origin, subjective evidence is unreliable. But because wine, certain mushrooms, hashish, opium, a cold shower, and other agencies cause physiological effects which are accompanied by altered states of feeling, and because abstraction of the bodily manifestations from a frightened individual leaves nothing of his fear, the emotion is only a perception of changes in the body. It is clear that Lange had the same conception as James, but elaborated it on a much narrower basis—on changes in the circulatory system alone.

A consideration of the visceral factors

The backflow of impulses from the periphery, on which James relied to account for the richness and variety of emotional feeling, was assumed to arise from all parts of the organism, from the muscles and skin as well as the viscera. To the latter, however, he inclined to attribute the major role—on "the visceral and organic part of the expression," he wrote, "it is probable that the chief part of the felt emotion depends." [5] We may distinguish, therefore, his two sources of the afferent stream. We shall first consider critically the visceral source. In connection therewith we shall comment on Lange's idea that the vasomotor center holds the explanation of emotional experience.

(1) Total separation of the viscera from the central nervous system does not alter emotional behavior. Sherrington[6] transected the spinal cord and the vagus nerves of dogs so as to destroy any connection of the brain with the heart, the lungs, the stomach and the bowels, the spleen, the liver and other abdominal organs—indeed, to isolate all the structures in which formerly feelings were supposed to reside. Recently Cannon, Lewis and Britton[7] have succeeded in keeping cats in a healthy state for many months after removal of the entire sympathetic division of the autonomic system, the division which operates in great excitement. Thus all vascular reactions controlled by the vasomotor center were abolished; secretion from the adrenal medulla could no longer be evoked; the action of the stomach and intestines could not be inhibited, the hairs could not be erected, and the liver could not be called upon to liberate sugar into the blood stream. These extensively disturbing operations had little if any effect on the emotional responses of the animals. In one of Sherrington's dogs, having a "markedly emotional temperament," the surgical reduction of the sensory field caused no obvious change in her emotional behavior; "her anger, her joy, her disgust, and when provocation arose, her fear, remained as evident as ever." And in the sympathectomized cats all superficial signs of rage were manifested in the presence of a barking dog—hissing, growling, retraction of the ears, showing of the teeth, lifting of the paw to strike—except erection of the hairs. Both sets of animals behaved with full emotional expression in all the organs still connected with the brain; the only failure was in organs disconnected. The absence of reverberation from the viscera did not alter in any respect the appropriate emotional display; its only abbreviation was surgical.

As Sherrington has remarked, with reference to his head-and-shoulder dogs, it is difficult to think that the perception initiating the wrathful expression should bring in sequel angry conduct and yet have been impotent to produce "angry feeling."

At this point interpretations differ. Angell[8] has argued that Sherrington's experiments afford no evidence that visceral sensation plays no part in the emotional psychosis, and further that they do not prove that the psychic state, "emotion," precedes its "expression." And Perry[9] has declared that whether in the absence of sensations from the organs surgically isolated, the emotion is felt remains quite undecided.

It must be admitted, of course, that we have no real basis for either affirming or denying the

[3] James, op. cit., 123.
[4] Lange, op. cit., 73.
[5] James, op. cit., 116.
[6] C. S. Sherrington. Experiments on the value of vascular and visceral factors for the genesis of emotion, Proc. Roy. Soc., 1900, 66, 397.

[7] W. B. Cannon, J. T. Lewis and S. W. Britton. The dispensability of the sympathetic division of the autonomic system, Boston Med. and Surg. J., 1927, 197, 514.
[8] J. R. Angell. A reconsideration of James' theory of emotion in the light of recent criticisms, Psychol. Rev., 1916, 23, 259.
[9] Perry, op. cit., 298.

presence of "felt emotion" in these reduced animals. We have a basis, however, for judging their relation to the James-Lange theory. James attributed the chief part of the felt emotion to sensations from the viscera, Lange attributed it wholly to sensations from the circulatory system. Both affirmed that if these organic sensations are removed *imaginatively* from an emotional experience nothing is left. Sherrington and Cannon and his collaborators varied this procedure by removing the sensations *surgically*. In their animals all visceral disturbances through sympathetic channels—the channels for nervous discharge in great excitement—were abolished. The possibility of return impulses by these channels, and in Sherrington's animals by vagus channels as well, were likewise abolished. According to James' statement of the theory the felt emotion should have very largely disappeared, and according to Lange's statement it should have wholly disappeared (without stimulation of our vasomotor system, it will be recalled, impressions of the outer world "would arouse neither joy nor anger, would give us neither care nor fear"). The animals *acted*, however, insofar as nervous connections permitted, with no lessening of the intensity of emotional display. In other words, operations which, in terms of the theory, largely or completely destroy emotional feeling, nevertheless leave the animals behaving as angrily, as joyfully, as fearfully as ever.

(2) The same visceral changes occur in very different emotional states and in non-emotional states. The preganglionic fibers of the sympathetic division of the autonomic system are so related to the outlying neurones that the resulting innervation of smooth muscles and glands throughout the body is not particular but diffuse.[10] At the same time with the diffuse emission of sympathetic impulses adrenin is poured into the blood. Since it is thereby generally distributed to all parts and has the same effects as the sympathetic impulses wherever it acts, the humoral and the neural agents co-operate in producing diffuse effects. In consequence of these arrangements the sympathetic system goes into action as a unit—there may be minor variations as, for example, the presence or absence of sweating, but in the main features integration is characteristic.

The visceral changes wrought by sympathetic stimulation may be listed as follows: acceleration of the heart, contraction of arterioles, dilatation of bronchioles, increase of blood sugar, inhibition of activity of the digestive glands, inhibition of gastro-intestinal peristalsis, sweating, discharge of adrenin, widening of the pupils and erection of hairs. These changes are seen in great excitement under any circumstances. They occur in such readily distinguishable emotional states as fear and rage.[11] Fever[12] and also exposure to cold[13] are known to induce most of the changes—certainly a faster heart rate, vasoconstriction, increased blood sugar, discharge of adrenin and erection of the hairs. Asphyxia at the stimulating stage evokes all the changes enumerated above, with the possible exception of sweating. A too great reduction of blood sugar by insulin provokes the "hypoglycemic reaction" —characterized by pallor, rapid heart, dilated pupils, discharge of adrenin, increase of blood sugar and profuse sweating.[14]

In this group of conditions which bring about in the viscera changes which are typical of sympathetic discharge are such intense and distinct emotions as fear and rage, such relatively mild affective states as those attending chilliness, hypoglycemia and difficult respiration, and such a markedly different experience as that attending the onset of fever. As pointed out earlier by Cannon[15] the responses in the viscera seem too uniform to offer a satisfactory means of distinguishing emotions which are very different in subjective quality. Furthermore, if the emotions were due to afferent impulses from the viscera, we should expect not only that fear and rage would feel alike but that chilliness, hypoglycemia, asphyxia, and fever should feel like them. Such is not the case.

In commenting on this criticism of the James-Lange theory Angell[16] admits that there may be a considerable matrix of substantially identical visceral excitement for some emotions, but urges that the differential features may be found in the extra-visceral disturbances, particularly in the differences of tone in skeletal muscles. Perry[17] likewise falls back on the conformation of the proprioceptive patterns, on the "motor set" of the expression, to provide the distinctive elements of the various affective states. The possible contribution of skeletal muscles to the genesis of the felt emotion will be considered later. At present the fact may be emphasized that Lange derived no part of the emotional psychosis from that source; and James attributed to it a minor role—the chief part of the felt emo-

[10] Cannon, *Bodily Changes in Pain, Hunger, Fear and Rage*, 1915, 26.

[11] Cannon, *op. cit.*, 277.

[12] Cannon and J. R. Pereira. Increase of adrenal secretion in fever, *Proc. Nat. Acad. Sci.*, 1924, **10**, 247.

[13] Cannon, A. Querido, S. W. Britton and E. M. Bright. The role of adrenal secretion in the chemical control of body temperature, *Amer. J. Physiol.*, 1927, **79**, 466.

[14] Cannon, M. A. McIver and S. W. Bliss. A sympathetic and adrenal mechanism for mobilizing sugar in hypoglycemia, *Amer. J. Physiol.*, 1924, **69**, 46.

[15] Cannon, *op. cit.*, 280.

[16] Angell, *op. cit.*, 260.

[17] Perry, *op. cit.*, 300.

tion depended on the visceral and organic part of the expression.

(3) The viscera are relatively insensitive structures. There is a common belief that the more deeply the body is penetrated the more sensitive does it become. Such is not the fact. Whereas in a spinal nerve trunk the sensory nerve fibers are probably always more numerous than the motor, in the nerves distributed to the viscera the afferent (sensory) fibers may be only one-tenth as numerous as the efferent.[18] We are unaware of the contractions and relaxations of the stomach and intestines during digestion, of the rubbing of the stomach against the diaphragm, of the squeezing motions of the spleen, of the processes in the liver—only after long search have we learned what is occurring in these organs. Surgeons have found that the alimentary tract can be cut, torn, crushed or burned in operations on the unanesthetized human subject without evoking any feeling of discomfort. We can feel the thumping of the heart because it presses against the chest wall, we can also feel the throbbing of blood vessels because they pass through tissues well supplied with sensory nerves, and we may have abdominal pains but apparently because there are pulls on the parietal peritoneum.[19] Normally the visceral processes are extraordinarily undemonstrative. And even when the most marked changes are induced in them, as when adrenalin acts, the results, as we shall see, are sensations mainly attributable to effects on the cardiovascular system.

(4) Visceral changes are too slow to be a source of emotional feeling. The viscera are composed of smooth muscle and glands—except the heart, which is modified striate muscle. The motions of the body with which we are familiar result from quick-acting striate muscle, having a true latent period of less than 0.001 sec. Notions of the speed of bodily processes acquired by observing the action of skeletal muscle we should not apply to other structures. Smooth muscle and glands respond with relative sluggishness. Although Stewart[20] found that the latent period of smooth muscle of the cat was about 0.25 sec., Sertoli[21] observed that it lasted for 0.85 sec. in the dog and 0.8 sec. in the horse. Langley[22] reported a latent period of 2 to 4 secs. on stimu-

lating the *chorda tympani* nerve supply to the submaxillary salivary gland; and Pawlow[23] a latent period of about 6 *minutes* on stimulating the vagus, the secretory nerve of the gastric glands. Again, Wells and Forbes[24] noted that the latent period of the psychogalvanic reflex (in man), which appears to be a glandular phenomenon, was about 3 secs.

In contrast to these long delays before peripheral action in visceral structures barely starts are the observations of Wells;[25] he found that the latent period of affective reactions to pictures of men and women ended not uncommonly within 0.8 sec. More recent studies with odors as stimuli have yielded a similar figure (personal communication). According to the James-Lange theory, however, these affective reactions result from reverberations from the viscera. But how is that possible? To the long latent periods of smooth muscles and glands, cited above, there must be added the time required for the nerve impulses to pass from the brain to the periphery and thence back to the brain again. It is clear that the organic changes could not occur soon enough to be the occasion for the appearance of affective states, certainly not the affective states studied by Wells.

(5) Artificial induction of the visceral changes typical of strong emotions does not produce them. That adrenin, or the commercial extract of the adrenal glands, "adrenalin," acts in the body so as to mimic the action of sympathetic nerve impulses has already been mentioned. When injected directly into the blood stream or under the skin it induces dilatation of the bronchioles, constriction of blood vessels, liberation of sugar from the liver, stoppage of gastro-intestinal functions, and other changes such as are characteristic of intense emotions. If the emotions are the consequence of the visceral changes we should reasonably expect them, in accordance with the postulates of the James-Lange theory, to follow these changes in all cases. Incidental observations on students who received injections of adrenalin sufficiently large to produce general bodily effects have brought out the fact that no specific emotion was experienced by them—a few who had been in athletic competitions testified to feeling "on edge," "keyed up," just as before a race.[26] In a careful study of the effects

[18] J. N. Langley and H. K. Anderson. The constituents of the hypogastric nerves, *J. Physiol.*, 1894, **17**, 185.

[19] K. G. Lennander, *et al.* Abdominal pains, especially in ileus, *J. Amer. Med. Assoc.*, 1907, **49**, 836 (see also p. 1015).

[20] C. C. Stewart. Mammalian smooth muscle—The cat's bladder, *Amer. J. Physiol.*, 1900, **4**, 192.

[21] E. Sertoli, Contribution à la physiologie générale des muscles lisses, *Arch. ital. de biol.*, 1883, **3**, 86.

[22] J. N. Langley. On the physiology of the salivary secretion, *J. Physiol.*, 1889, **10**, 300.

[23] J. P. Pawlow and E. O. Schumowa-Simanowskaja. Die Innervation der Magendrüsen beim Hunde, *Arch. f. Physiol.*, 1895, 66.

[24] F. L. Wells and A. Forbes. On certain electrical processes in the human body and their relations to emotional reactions, *Arch. Psychol.*, 1911, **2**, No. 16, p. 8.

[25] Wells, Reactions to visual stimuli in affective settings, *J. Exp. Psychol.*, 1925, **8**, 64.

[26] F. W. Peabody, C. C. Sturgis, E. M. Tompkins and J. T. Wearn. Epinephrin hypersensitiveness and

of adrenalin on a large number of normal and abnormal persons Marañon[27] has reported that the subjective experiences included sensations of precardial or epigastric palpitation, of diffuse arterial throbbing, of oppression in the chest and tightness in the throat, of trembling, of chilliness, of dryness of the mouth, of nervousness, malaise and weakness. Associated with these sensations there was *in certain cases* an indefinite affective state coldly appreciated, and without real emotion. The subjects remarked, "I feel as if afraid," "as if awaiting a great joy," "as if moved," "as if I were going to weep without knowing why," "as if I had a great fright yet am calm," "as if they are about to do something to me." In other words, as Marañon remarks, a clear distinction is drawn "between the perception of the peripheral phenomena of vegetative emotion (*i.e.* the bodily changes) and the psychical emotion proper, which does not exist and which permits the subjects to report on the vegetative syndrome with serenity, without true feeling." In a smaller number of the affected cases a real emotion developed, usually that of sorrow, with tears, sobs and sighings. This occurs, however, "only when the emotional predisposition of the patient is very marked," notably in hyperthyroid cases. In some instances Marañon found that this state supervened only when the adrenalin was injected after a talk with the patients concerning their sick children or their dead parents. In short, only when an emotional mood already exists does adrenalin have a supporting effect.

From the evidence adduced by Marañon we may conclude that adrenalin induces in human beings typical bodily changes which are reported as sensations, that in some cases these sensations are reminiscent of previous emotional experiences but do not renew or revive those experiences, that in exceptional cases of preparatory emotional sensitization the bodily changes may tip the scales towards a true affective disturbance. These last cases are exceptional, however, and are not the usual phenomena as James and Lange supposed. In normal conditions the bodily changes, though well marked, do not provoke emotion.

The numerous events occurring in the viscera in consequence of great excitement, as detailed by Cannon,[28] have been interpreted as supporting the James-Lange theory.[29] From the evidence presented under the five headings above it should be clear that that interpretation is unwarranted. Since visceral processes are fortunately not a considerable source of sensation, since even extreme disturbances in them yield no noteworthy emotional experience, we can further understand now why these disturbances cannot serve as a means for discriminating between such pronounced emotions as fear and rage, why chilliness, asphyxia, hyperglycemia and fever, though attended by these disturbances, are not attended by emotion, and also why total exclusion of visceral factors from emotional expression makes no difference in emotional behavior. It is because the returns from the thoracic and abdominal "sounding-board," to use James' word, are very faint indeed, that they play such a minor role in the affective complex. The processes going on in the thoracic and abdominal organs are truly remarkable and various; their value to the organism, however, is not to add richness and flavor to experience, but rather to adapt the internal economy so that in spite of shifts of outer circumstance the even tenor of the inner life will not be profoundly disturbed.

A consideration of the postural factors

In his discussion of the cerebral processes accompanying emotion, James[30] argued that either there were special centers for them or they occurred in the ordinary motor and sensory centers of the cortex. And if in the ordinary centers, according to his postulate, the processes would resemble the ordinary processes attending sensation. Only that and full representation of each part of the body in the cortex would be needed to provide a scheme capable of representing the *modus operandi* of the emotions. Object—sense organ—cortical excitation—perception—reflexes to muscle, skin and viscus—disturbances in them —cortical excitation by these disturbances—perceptions of them added to the original perceptions; such are the occurrences which result in the "object-emotionally-felt." The strict alternative, however, of cortical processes *or* special centers we need not accept. There may be cortical processes *and* special centers. Whether such is the arrangement we may now consider.

(1) Emotional expression results from action of subcortical centers. In a paper published in 1887 Bechterev[31] argued that emotional expression must be independent of the cortex because at times the expression cannot be inhibited (*e.g.* laughing from tickle, grinding the teeth and crying from pain), because visceral changes occur which are beyond control, and because it is seen just after birth before cortical management is important. Furthermore, he reported that after

its relation to hyperthyroidism, *Amer. J. Med. Sci.*, 1921, **161**, 508, (also personal communication from J. T. Wearn).

[27] G. Marañon, Contribution à l'étude de l'action émotive de l'adrenaline, *Rev. Franç. d'endocrinol.*, 1924, **2**, 301.

[28] Cannon, *op. cit.*, 184.

[29] G. Humphrey. *The Story of Man's Mind*, 1923, 211.

[30] James, *op. cit.*, 123.

[31] W. Bechterev. Die Bedeutung der Sehhügel auf Grund von experimentellen und pathologischen Daten, *Virchow's Archiv.*, 1887, **110**, 102, 322.

removing the cerebral hemispheres from various kinds of animals appropriate stimulations would evoke corresponding responses of an affective character. Noxious stimuli would cause the hemisphereless cats to snarl, the dogs to whine, to show their teeth and to bark; gentle stimuli (stroking the back) would cause the cats to purr and the dogs to wag their tails. Since these effects disappeared when the optic thalamus was removed, he drew the conclusion that it plays a predominant role in emotional expression.

In 1904 Woodworth and Sherrington[32] proved that many of the physiological phenomena of great excitement would appear in cats from which the thalamus had been wholly removed by section of the brain stem at the mesencephalon. Strong stimulation of an afferent nerve was required to evoke the "pseudaffective" responses. Although these observations tended to lessen the importance of the thalamus as a center, recent experiments have again emphasized its dominance. In 1925 Cannon and Britton[33] described a pseudaffective preparation—a cat decorticated under ether anesthesia—which on recovery displayed spontaneously the complete picture of intense fury. Further study by Bard (work still unpublished) showed that this sham rage continued after ablation of all the brain anterior to the diencephalon. Only when the lower posterior portion of the thalamic region was removed did the extraordinary activities of the preparation subside. These results clearly point to the thalamus as a region from which, in the absence of cortical government, impulses are discharged which evoke an extreme degree of "emotional" activity, both muscular and visceral.

The evidence just cited is confirmed by observations on human beings. As has been pointed out elsewhere[34] when the cortical processes are abolished by anesthesia, emotional display may be most remarkable. During the early (excitement) stage of ether anesthesia, for example, there may be sobbing as in grief, or laughter as in joy, or lively and energetic aggressive actions as in rage. The surgeon may open the chest or perform other operations of equal gravity, while the patient is pushing, pulling, shouting and muttering; a few minutes later the conscious patient will testify that he has been wholly unaware of what has happened. It is when "laughing gas" has set aside the cortical functions that the subjects laugh and weep. Similar release of the mechanisms for emotional expression is indi-

cated in the depression of cortical activity during acute alcoholism. In all these conditions the drug acts first as a depressant on the highly sensitive cells of the cortex, and thus lessens or temporarily destroys their control of lower centers; only when the drug becomes more concentrated does it depress also the lower centers; but before that stage is reached the lower centers, released from the cortical dominance as in the surgically decorticated animals, show forth their functions in free play.

Consistent with the experimental and pharmacological evidence is the evidence derived from pathological cases. In certain forms of hemiplegia the patients may be incapable of moving the face on the paralyzed side; if suddenly they are affected by a sorrowful or joyous emotion, however, the muscles, unresponsive to voluntary control, spring into action and give both sides of the face the expression of sadness or gaiety.[35] These cases occur when the motor tract is interrupted subcortically and the optic thalamus is left intact. The opposite of this condition is seen in unilateral injury of the thalamus. A patient described by Kirilzev[36] moved symmetrically both sides of his face at will, but when he laughed in fun or made a grimace in pain the right side remained motionless; at autopsy a tumor was found in the center of the left optic thalamus. This localization of the central neural apparatus for the expressions of pleasure and pain has interesting relations to emotive phenomena commonly seen in so-called "pseudo-bulbar palsy." In such cases there is usually a bilateral facial paralysis, with one side slightly more involved than the other. Voluntary pursing of the lips as in whistling, or wrinkling of the forehead, or making a grimace may be impossible. The intractable facial muscles, however, function normally in laughing or crying, scowling or frowning. These well-executed expressions come in fits and are uncontrollable and prolonged. One patient is described who started laughing at 10:00 o'clock in the morning and continued with few pauses until 2:00 in the afternoon! Tilney and Morrison,[37] who have reported on 173 recorded cases of the disease, found such fits of crying and laughing in seventeen percent of the cases, crying alone in sixteen percent, and laughing alone in fifteen percent. The fits appear as a rule without any of the usual provocations and most frequently are inopportune. The patient may have all the appearances of being convulsed with laughter, yet may not experience any of the feeling which the mo-

[32] R. S. Woodworth and C. S. Sherrington. A pseudaffective reflex and its spinal path, *J. Physiol.*, 1904, **31**, 234.

[33] Cannon and S. W. Britton. Pseudaffective medulliadrenal secretion, *Amer. J. Physiol.*, 1925, **72**, 283.

[34] Cannon, Neural basis for emotion expression, *Wittenberg Symposium on Feelings and Emotions*, 1927.

[35] G. Roussy, *La couche optique*, 1907, 31.

[36] S. Kirilzev. Cases of affections of the optic thalamus (Russian). Reviewed in *Neurologisches Centralblatt*, 1891, **10**, 310.

[37] F. Tilney and J. F. Morrison. Pseudo-bulbar palsy clinically and pathologically considered, *J. Ment. and Nerv. Diseases*, 1912, **39**, 505.

tions of face and body indicate. Such cases are attributed by Brissaud[38] to lesions of a special part of the cortico-thalamic tract which free a portion of the thalamus from the cortical check. It seems probable, as later evidence will suggest, that afferent thalamo-cortical tracts are also defective. Finally, cases of "narcolepsy" are known in which emotional expression is nearly nil; gibes and insults which enrage or infuriate the normal person are usually quite without effect. In some of these cases, examined post-mortem, were found tumors on the under side of the diencephalon, after affecting the whole hypothalamus.

All these observations, experimental and clinical, consistently point to the optic thalamus as a region in which resides the neural organization for the different emotional expressions. The section in James' discussion, headed "No Special Brain Centres for Emotion" must be modified in the light of this accumulated information. The cortex at one end of the nerve paths as a reflex surface and the peripheral organs at the other end as a source of return impulses make too simple an arrangement. Between the cortex and the periphery lies the diencephalon, an integrating organ on the emotive level, a receiving and discharging station, that on proper stimulation is capable of establishing in stereotyped forms the facies and bodily postures typical of the various affective states. That all afferent paths leading towards the cortex have relays in the diencephalon is a fact of great significance in explaining the nature of emotions.

(2) Thalamic processes are a source of affective experience. The relaying of all sensory neurones in some part of the optic thalamus has been stressed by Head[39] in his important clinical studies. He and Holmes[40] attributed to this region a sort of consciousness, an "awareness." The effect of anesthesia in abolishing consciousness while leaving emotional expression (thalamic in origin) undisturbed would seem to contradict this view. But even if consciousness is associated only with events in cortical neurones, the important part played by thalamic processes is little disturbed thereby. The relays of sensory channels in the thalamus and the evidence that disturbances in that region are the occasion for intensely affective sensations are all that we need for understanding its relation to the nature of emotions.

Head[41] has cited numerous cases of unilateral lesions in the thalamic region in which there is a marked tendency to react excessively to affective stimuli; pin pricks, painful pressure, excessive heat or cold, all produce more distress on the damaged than on the normal side of the body. Agreeable stimuli also are felt keenly on the damaged side; warmth stimuli may evoke intense pleasure, attended by signs of enjoyment on the face and exclamations of delight. Again, affective stimuli, such as the playing of music and the singing of hymns, may arouse such increased emotional feeling on the damaged side that they may be intolerable. Affective conscious states have an influence on the damaged side similar to stimuli from the surface receptors. This extravagant influence of affective stimuli, whether from above or below, Head attributed to release of the thalamus from cortical inhibition. It is not an irritative effect, he argued, because it persists for long periods, well after all the disturbances due to the injury have subsided. And since the affective states are increased when the thalamus is freed from cortical control, Head's conclusion is that the essential thalamic center is mainly occupied with the affective side of sensation.

We are now in a position to consider the evidence that the positions and tensions of skeletal muscle make the differentia of emotion. It will be recalled that, although James belittled this element in his theory, his supporters have stressed it, especially since the visceral element proved inadequate. The thalamic cases provide a means of testing the contribution from skeletal muscles, for the feeling-tone of a sensation is a product of thalamic activity, and the fact that a sensation is devoid of feeling-tone shows that the impulses which underlie its production make no thalamic appeal.

Head found that his patients reported marked differences in the feeling-tone of different sensations. A tuning fork may have no effect, whereas patriotic music is felt intensely on the damaged side. All thermal stimuli make a double appeal, to the cortex and to the thalamus. Unselected tactile stimuli act similarly. On the other hand, sensations which underlie the appreciation of posture are entirely lacking in feeling-tone. Precisely those afferent impulses from muscles and joints which James and his supporters have relied upon to provide the extravisceral part of the felt-emotion are the impulses which lack the necessary quality to serve the purpose! The quality of emotions is to be found, therefore, neither in returns from the viscera nor in returns from the innervated muscles.

A theory of emotion based on thalamic processes

The foregoing discussion has disclosed the fact that the neural arrangements for emotional expression reside in subcortical centers, and that these centers are ready for instant and vigorous discharge when they are released from cortical restraint and are properly stimulated. Furthermore, the evidence is clear that when these

[38] E. Brissaud, *Leçons cliniques*, 1894.
[39] H. Head. Release of function in the nervous system, *Proc. Roy. Soc.*, 1921, **92B**, 184.
[40] Head and G. Holmes. Sensory disturbances from cerebral lesions, *Brain*, 1911, **34**, 109.
[41] Head, *Studies in Neurology*, 1920, **II**, 620.

centers are released the processes aroused in them become a source of vivid affective experience. That this experience is felt on only one side in hemiplegic cases is a peculiarly happy circumstance, for in the same individual the influence of the same affective stimulus can be observed under normal conditions and compared with its influence when given free rein.

The neural organization for an emotion which is suggested by the foregoing observations is as follows. An external situation stimulates receptors and the consequent excitation starts impulses towards the cortex. Arrival of the impulses in the cortex is associated with conditioned processes which determine the direction of the response. Either because the response is initiated in a certain mode or figure and the cortical neurones therefore stimulate the thalamic processes, or because on their centripetal course the impulses from the receptors excite thalamic processes, they are roused and ready for discharge. That the thalamic neurones act in a special combination in a given emotional expression is proved by the reaction patterns typical of the several affective states. These neurones do not require detailed innervation from above in order to be driven into action. Being *released* for action is a primary condition for their service to the body—they then discharge precipitately and intensely. Within and near the thalamus the neurones concerned in an emotional expression lie close to the relay in the sensory path from periphery to cortex. We may assume that when these neurones discharge in a particular combination, they not only innervate muscles and viscera but also excite afferent paths to the cortex by direct connection or by irradiation. The theory which naturally presents itself is that the peculiar quality of the emotion is added to simple sensation when the thalamic processes are roused.

The theory just suggested appears to fit all the known facts. Its service in explaining these facts may be briefly summarized.

When the thalamic discharge occurs, the bodily changes occur almost simultaneously with the emotional experience. This coincidence of disturbances in muscles and viscera with thrills, excitements or depressions was naturally misleading, for, with the role of the thalamus omitted from consideration, the obvious inference was that the peculiar quality of the emotion arose from the peripheral changes. Indeed, that inference is the heart of the James-Lange theory. The evidence presented in the foregoing pages shows that the inference is ill-founded; the sensations from the peripheral changes, contrary to James' view, are "pale, colorless and destitute of emotional warmth," whereas the thalamic disturbances contribute glow and color to otherwise simply cognitive states. The theory now proposed explains how James and Lange could rea-

sonably make the suggestion which they made. The lack of factual support for their suggestion requires another account of emotional origins. This is provided by the evidence that thalamic processes can add to sensation an aura of feeling.

One of the strongest arguments advanced for the James-Lange theory is that the assumption of an attitude does in fact help to establish the emotional state which the attitude expresses. "Sit all day in a moping posture, sigh, and reply to everything with a dismal voice, and your melancholy lingers." On the contrary, "smooth the brow, brighten the eye, contract the dorsal rather than the ventral aspect of the frame, and speak in a major key, pass the genial compliment, and your heart must be frigid indeed if you do not gradually thaw!" Persons who have tried this advice have testified to its soundness, and have been convinced, therefore, of the truth of the claim that the moods have followed the assumed attitudes. Not all agree, however, that mimicking the outward appearance of an emotion results in the emotion itself. James suggested that the explanation of the discrepancy lay in variations of involvement of the viscera in the artificial expression. As shown above, however, the visceral changes offer only unreliable support for that idea. Again the processes in the thalamus offer a reasonable and simple explanation. As the cases reported by Head have shown, emotions originating from memories and imagination affect more intensely the half-thalamus that has been released from motor control than they affect the normal half. This shows that cortical processes may start thalamic processes and thus arouse an affective return from that portion of the brain. And if in addition a typical emotional attitude is assumed the cortical inhibition of the thalamic neurones with reference to that attitude is abolished so that they have complete release. Under such circumstances the enacted emotion would have reality. On the other hand a purely cortical mimicry of emotional expression without thalamic involvement would be as cold and unaffective as some actors have declared it to be. Whether the emotion results or not, the thalamic theory of the source of feeling offers a more satisfactory explanation of the effects of assumed postures than does the James-Lange theory.

The cases of release of the thalamus from cortical control on one side, with accompanying ipsilateral intensification of emotional tone, present an insurmountable obstacle to the James-Lange theory. Neither the thoracic nor the abdominal viscera can function by halves, the vasomotor center is a unity, and the patients certainly do not engage in right- or left-sided laughter and weeping. The impulses sent back from the disturbed peripheral organs, therefore, must be bilaterally equal. For explanation of the unsymmetrical feeling we are driven to the organ which is functioning unsymmetrically—*i.e.* the thalamus. It is there that the suggested theory places the source of the emotions.

Another serious difficulty for the James-Lange theory is the evidence that the emotion increases in intensity although the expression is checked. Indeed, there are psychologists who maintain that the emotional state lasts only so long as there is inner conflict between the impulse to act and the hesitant or prudential check on that impulse. So long as the check prevails, however, the organic changes supposed to be the source of the feeling are suppressed. How then can there be felt-emotion? Two answers to this question may be found in James' argument. First he denies the objection. "Refuse to express a passion," he wrote, "and it dies." "Count ten before venting your anger, and its occasion seems ridiculous." On the other hand, he appears to admit that a pent emotion may operate disastrously. "If tears or anger are simply suppressed, whilst the object of grief or rage remains unchanged before the mind, the current which would have invaded the normal channels turns into others, for it must find some outlet of escape. It may then work different and worse effects later on. Thus vengeful brooding may replace a burst of indignation; a dry heat may consume the frame of one who fain would weep, or he may, as Dante says, turn to stone within." There is no intimation that vengeful brooding, being consumed by a dry heat, and turning to stone within are not emotional experiences. Instead of recognizing them as such, however, James stressed the importance of training for repression of emotional display. These rather equivocal and indecisive comments leave untouched the common testimony that intense fear, for example, may be felt, with a pathetic sense of helplessness, before any overt act occurs, and that scarcely does the appropriate behavior start than the inner tumult begins to subside and the bodily forces are directed vigorously and effectively to serviceable ends. The difficulties of the James-Lange theory in meeting this situation are obvious. If there is a double control of behavior, however, both the inner conflict with its keen emotional accompaniment and the later partial subsidence of feelings are readily explicable. The thalamic patterned processes are inherent in the nervous organization, they are like reflexes in being instantly ready to seize control of the motor responses, and when they do so they operate with great power. They can be controlled, however, by the processes in the cerebral cortex, by processes conditioned by all sorts of previous impressions. The cortex also can control all the peripheral machinery except the viscera. The inhibited processes in the thalamus cannot set the organism in action, except the parts not under voluntary control, but the turmoil there can produce emotions in the usual manner, and possibly with greater violence because of the inhibition. And when the cortical check is released, suddenly the conflict is resolved. The two controls formerly in opposition, are now cooperative. The thalamic neurones, so long as they continue energetically active, provide the condition for the emotion to persist, as James claimed it does, *during* the manifestation. The new theory, therefore, not only avoids the difficulty of the James-Lange theory, but accounts satisfactorily for the poignancy of feeling in the period of paralyzed inaction.

In relation to the double control of the response there is another point that may be emphasized. McDougall[42] has objected to the James-Lange theory on the ground that it is admittedly concerned with the *sensory* aspect of emotion; it pays little or no attention to the always present and sometimes overwhelming *impulsive* aspect of the experience. The localization of the reaction patterns for emotional expression in the thalamus—in a region which, like the spinal cord, works directly by simple automatisms unless held in check—not only accounts for the sensory side, the "felt emotion," but also for the impulsive side, the tendency of the thalamic neurones to discharge. These powerful impulses originating in a region of the brain not associated with cognitive consciousness and arousing therefore in an *obscure* and *unrelated* manner the strong feelings of emotional excitement, explain the sense of being seized, possessed, of being controlled by an outside force and made to act without weighing of the consequences.

Finally, the view that thalamic processes add feeling-tone to sensation meets satisfactorily a difficulty which the James-Lange theory encountered in explaining the "subtler emotions." James had to assume indefinite and hypothetical bodily reverberations in order to account for mild feelings of pleasure and satisfaction. If a warm test tube, however, is capable of yielding keen delight on the damaged side in a case of thalamic injury, it is clear that almost any object or situation which can rouse thalamic processes can add affective quality to sensation. And just as a stimulus can become conditioned for a certain motor or glandular response, so likewise a stimulus can be conditioned for the patterns of neurone action in the thalamus. When that stimulus recurs the emotion recurs because the pattern is activated. In such manner we may consider that richness and variety of our emotional life are elaborated.

[42] W. McDougall. *Outline of Psychology*, 1923, 328.

CHAPTER FIVE

Frustration and conflict

CONFLICT OF MOTIVES

The analysis of conflict situations has been quite useful in psychology. This is one of the first accounts of approach-approach, approach-avoidance, and avoidance-avoidance conflicts.

K. Lewin, both in Germany and later in the United States, placed much emphasis on field forces in psychology. The individual was viewed as being acted upon by psychological forces, having direction and strength, of various kinds. These psychological forces should not be confused with physical forces. Their strength and direction is determined by the individual's perception of his environment.

Points to guide your study

1. Think of the last time you were in a conflict and make a Lewinian diagram of it.

2. Glossary: Valence—Lewin's term for attraction to, or repulsion from, a goal; Vector—Represents the strength, by arrow length, and the direction of a force.

17. A DYNAMIC THEORY OF PERSONALITY

*Kurt Lewin**

Constellations of forces

Conflict. The ways in which different valences may interact in a situation are naturally very numerous. I select for discussion the case of conflict because of its special significance.

Conflict is defined psychologically as the opposition of approximately equally strong field forces. There are three basic cases of conflict, so far as driving forces are concerned.

(1) The child stands between two positive valences (Figure 1). He has to choose perhaps between going on a picnic (P) and playing (Pl) with his comrades. In this type of conflict situation decision is usually relatively easy. As a result of the fact that after the choice is made the goal chosen often seems inferior (for rea-

* Kurt Lewin. *A dynamic theory of personality*. New York: McGraw-Hill, 1935. Trans. by D. K. Adams and K. Zener. Copyright 1935 by the McGraw-Hill Book Company, Inc. Excerpt reprinted here with permission from the McGraw-Hill Book Company, Inc. Footnotes omitted and figures renumbered.

sons to be described later), oscillation does sometimes occur.

(2) The child faces something that has simultaneously both a positive and a negative valence (Figure 2). He wants, for example, to climb a tree (Tr), but is afraid. This constellation of forces plays an important part in cases in which a reward is offered for an activity (e.g., a school task) which the child does not want to execute.

Conflict situations of this type usually develop rather quickly also in the detour experiments mentioned above, in the experiments of Fajans, or in other situations in which the attainment of the goal is impeded by some barrier. At first the child sees a difficult barrier (B) between himself and his goal (G), which hinders completion of actions in the direction of the field forces (Figure 3). But after the child has run against the barrier several times and perhaps hurt himself, or had the wounding experience of failure, the barrier itself acquires a negative valence (Figure 4). Besides the positive, there comes into existence a negative vector, and we have the Type 2 conflict situation. The negative vector usually increases gradually in strength and

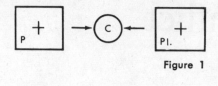

Figure 1

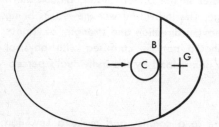

Figure 2

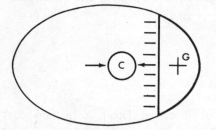

Figure 3

Figure 4

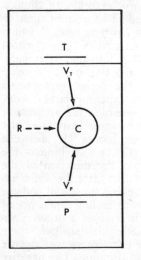

Figure 5

finally becomes stronger than the positive. Accordingly, the child *goes out of the field*.

This withdrawal [*Aus-dem-Felde-Gehen*] either may be physical, as when the child retreats, turns away, or possibly leaves the room or place, or may be an *inward* going out of the field, as when the child begins to play or to occupy himself with something else.

It not infrequently occurs, for example in embarrassment, that the child makes certain bodily movements toward the goal but at the same time is mentally occupied with something else. In such cases the bodily act has the character of a more or less set gesture.

In such situations the withdrawal is at first almost always merely temporary. The child turns away, only to return after a while for another try at the barrier. A final and permanent withdrawal usually occurs only after several temporary withdrawals, the duration of which increases until finally the child does not return.

Unusual persistence in such a situation is not necessarily an indication of activity. On the contrary, active children usually go out of the field earlier than passive children. It is not the duration but the kind of approach that is significant for activity.

Related to this is the fact that under certain circumstances the single actions in such a conflict situation are longer with the infant than with the young child, although in general the duration of action unities increases with the age of the child.

(3) The third type of conflict situation occurs when the child stands between two negative valences, for example, when it is sought by threat of punishment (P) to move a child to do a task (T) he does not want to do (Figure 5).

There is an essential difference between this and the conflict situation described under 1. This becomes clear when one proceeds to represent the total distribution of forces in the field of force.

Field of force. The field of force indicates which force would exist at each point in the field if the individual involved were at that point. To a positive valence there corresponds a convergent field (Figure 6).

As a simple example of the structure of the field of force in a conflict situation of Type 2, a case from one of my films may be adduced: a three-year-old boy wants to fetch a rubber swan out of the water to the beach, but is afraid of the water. To the swan (S) as positive valence there corresponds a convergent field (Figure 7). This field is overlaid by a second field which corresponds to the negative valence of the waves. It is important that here, as frequently in such cases, the strength of the field forces which correspond to the negative valence diminishes much

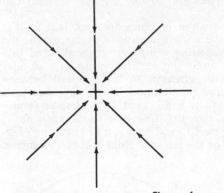

Figure 6

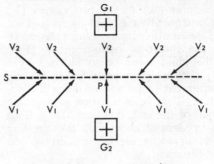

→ Driving force corresponding to goal (G)

----- line of equilibrium

Figure 8 (From K. Lewin, Vectors, Cognitive Processes, and Mr. Tolman's Criticism, Jour. General Psychol., 1933, 8, 323)

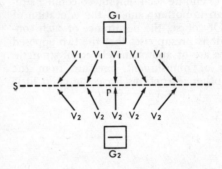

→ Driving force corresponding to goal (G)

----- line of equilibrium

Figure 9 (From K. Lewin, Vectors, Cognitive Processes, and Mr. Tolman's Criticism, Jour. General Psychol., 1933, 8, 323)

more rapidly with increasing spatial distance than do the field forces corresponding to the positive valence. From the direction and strength of the field forces at the various points of the field it can be deduced that the child must move to the point P where equilibrium occurs. (At all other points there exists a resultant which finally leads to P.) Corresponding to the momentary oscillations of the situation, above all to the more or less threatening aspect of the waves, this point of equilibrium approaches and retreats from the water. Indeed, this oscillation is reflected in the child's approaches to and retreats from the water.

If we return now to Type 3 of the conflict situation and compare it with Type 1, the chief difference is shown in Figures 8 and 9: in both cases two central fields overlap. But while in Type 1 a stable equilibrium exists at the point P (Figure 8) so far as sidewise movements (on line S) are concerned, in Type 3 this equilibrium is labile (Figure 9). That is, there exists in the case of threat of punishment (Figure 5) a situation which evokes a tendency to break out

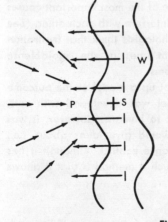

Figure 7

Figure 10

toward the side, in accordance with the strong sidewise resultant (R) of the two vectors (V_p and V_t). Consequently the child always goes out of the field unless other circumstances prevent it. Hence, if the threat of punishment is to be effective, the child must be so inclosed by a barrier (B) that escape is possible only by way of the punishment or by way of doing the disagreeable task. That is, in addition to requiring the execution of the task, it is necessary to limit the child's freedom of movement, thus creating (by physical or social means) a more or less constrained situation.

With the young child, the opposition of two approximately equal field forces in the conflict situation leads typically (so far as it is not an unstable equilibrium) to a relatively rapid alternation of actions in the direction of each of the two field forces in turn. It is a characteristic indication of greater self-control when, instead of this oscillation of action, the child displays a relatively calm type of behavior while the conflict remains unresolved.

Ability to endure such unresolved conflict situations is an important aim of the education of the will. Of course, the occurrence of such conflict situations presupposes that the two opposed field forces are of approximately equal strength. If threats of punishment, pressure from the adult, or other restrictions leave the child little

enough freedom, no real conflict situation can develop.

If a situation becomes *hopeless*, that is, if it becomes as a whole inescapably disagreeable, the child, despairing, *contracts*, physically and psychically, under the vectors coming from all sides and usually attempts to build a wall between himself and the situation. This is expressed both in the typical bodily gestures of despair (crumpling up, covering the eyes with·the arms, etc.), (see Figure 10) and by a sort of encysting (Figure 11) of the self: the child becomes obdurate.

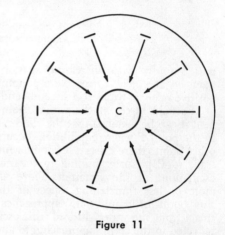

Figure 11

Frustration occurs when there is interference with goal-directed behavior and goal attainment. Conflict is considered to be one of the most important causes of frustration because, in conflicts, the motives interfere with each other. (See the section of your text on conflict.) Most psychologists think that frustration has many outcomes, including such important ones as the ego-defense mechanisms and, perhaps, some neurotic symptoms.

This article presents data in an attempt to set up a model of the outcome of an approach-avoidance conflict. The model was developed with rats, and the details were not expected to transfer to humans. However, it was hoped that the outcome of the experiment would give ideas about, i.e., serve as a model for, human approach-avoidance conflict. Although it has some disadvantages, the main advantage of such a method is that it allows for quantification and control.

Points to guide your study

1. Were the assumptions (hypotheses) in the introduction upheld? For each assumption, state the evidence which supports or fails to support it.

2. Note that the approach and avoidance gradients were obtained from separate groups.

3. The *t* values and probabilities have the same meaning as in other studies in these readings. See "Points to guide your study" under the articles where these are discussed more fully.

18. GRADIENTS OF APPROACH AND AVOIDANCE RESPONSES AND THEIR RELATION TO LEVEL OF MOTIVATION

Judson S. Brown, University of Florida

The present experiment stemmed originally from a series of studies of conflict behavior by N. E. Miller and the writer. In the first experiment of that series [1] an investigation was made of the conflict behavior exhibited by rats in a narrow straight alley when tendencies both to approach and avoid one end of the alley were simultaneously present. In developing a theoretical interpretation of the observed behavior, it was found expedient to make a number of explicit assumptions regarding the manner in which the excitatory tendencies varied with distance from the region of reinforcement and with variations in strength of drive and strength of punishment. These assumptions were:

1. When a motivated organism is suitably reinforced for approaching a given region in space, a gradient in the strength of its excitatory tendency to approach that region will be established, the strength of the tendency increasing with nearness to the goal.

2. When an organism has escaped from a noxious stimulus located at a given region in space, a gradient in the strength of its excitatory tendency to avoid that region will be set up, the strength of the tendency decreasing with distance from that region.

3. Other things equal, gradients in the strength of excitatory tendencies to avoid are steeper than gradients of excitatory tendencies to approach.

4. The heights of the approach and avoidance

gradients vary directly with strength of drive and intensity of the noxious stimulus, respectively.

The general procedure employed in testing the four assumptions was as follows. One group of hunger-motivated rats was thoroughly trained to approach one end of a short straight alley for food. A second group was trained to avoid one end of the alley by the use of strong electric shocks. The strengths of the resulting approach and avoidance responses were then tested by measuring (at different points in the alley) the force with which the animals would pull either toward or away from the region of reinforcement. The approach and avoidance responses of other groups, whose hunger motivation was weak or who had received weaker shocks, were also tested by the same method at different positions in the alley.

Apparatus

A schematic diagram of the apparatus used in this study is shown in Figure 1. Only the essential features are indicated and the distances are not drawn to scale. The alley at the right was 200 cm. long, 12 cm. wide and 10 cm. deep (inside measurements). The cover of the alley, made of celluloid tacked to a wooden frame, was hinged at the back and is not shown in the figure. The bottom of the alley was formed of a grid of stainless-steel wire (#20) stretched tightly across a bakelite-and-wood spreader at intervals of 8 mm. A gap of 20 mm. was pro-

* A portion of a dissertation submitted to the faculty of Yale University in partial fulfillment of the requirements for the Ph.D. degree. The author is indebted to Dr. N. E. Miller for extensive aid in planning and conducting the study. The research was supported in part by funds from the Institute of Human Relations.

J. S. Brown. Gradients of approach and avoidance responses and their relation to level of motivation. *J. comp. physiol. Psychol.*, 1948, **41**, 450–465. Copyright 1948 by the American Psychological Association. Excerpts reprinted here with permission from the author and the American Psychological Association.

[1] By N. E. Miller, H. Lipofsky, and J. S. Brown. Reported in part by the writer at the 1938 meetings of the Eastern Psychological Association and summarized by Miller (15).

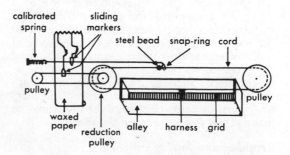

Figure 1   Schematic diagram of apparatus for measuring the force exerted by rats when restrained at various distances from a region of reinforcement.

vided below the grid so that feces and urine might drop through freely. The spreader and the wires were coated with paraffin at points of mutual contact to decrease surface leakage in moist weather.

The endless loop of cord (fish line) shown at the right passed through slots in the ends of the alley and ran along about 2.5 cm. below the cover. Outside the alley this cord passed around an idler pulley at one end and around the larger diameter of a 10:1 reduction pulley at the other. The smaller section of this pulley was coupled by a second endless loop to the lower of the two sliding markers shown at the left. This marker served to provide detailed records of the movements of the rat along the alley and was employed in a previous study for the purpose of recording the locomotor components of conflict behavior.

At the center of the alley is shown the harness by which a rat was attached to the endless belt. A light aluminum T with a swivel hook at its lower end was tied into the main loop of cord. Two sturdy rubber bands passed through the swivel hook and around the rat, one around the thorax and the other in front of the forelegs around the neck. These bands, though tight enough to prevent the rat's escape even when it was pulling against the restraining spring, did not interfere with its normal movements in the alley.

The mechanism for measuring strength-of-pull functioned as follows. The force exerted by the rat against the harness was transmitted through the T to the endless loop of cord. A small steel bead was fastened to the portion of the loop which passed along the outside of the alley. This bead engaged a smaller snap-ring attached to a string running to the upper one of the two sliding markers shown at the left. This marker was in turn attached to one end of a calibrated spring. Before the bead engaged the snap-ring and took up the slack in the string, the main loop could be moved freely, being opposed only by a slight friction from the pulleys. After the rat had progressed down the alley (toward the left in Figure 1) to the point where the bead engaged the snap-ring and took up the slack in the string, further movements were impeded by the force of the spring. In this way, the force of a rat's surges against the resistance of the spring was recorded on the waxed paper by movements of the upper marker. By changing the length of the cord between this marker and the snap-ring, measurements of strength of pull could be made at any desired point in the alley.

Training and testing procedure

Four basic experimental groups were employed in this study. In groups I and II the animals were trained under a strong hunger drive to ap-

proach the lighted end of the alley for food. In order to test the assumption that the approach tendencies should be weaker the farther the subject is from the region of reinforcement, the pull of the animals in Group I was measured at a point near the goal and at a point near the start. These animals were tested under strong hunger motivation. In order to test the assumption that the strength of approach tendencies should vary with strength of drive, the pull of the animals in Group II was measured at only one point in the alley, near the goal, under two degrees of hunger: 1 hour and 46 hours of food deprivation.

The animals in Groups III and IV were trained to avoid the lighted end of the alley. In order to test the assumption that strength of avoidance varies with the intensity of a noxious stimulus, the animals in Group III were trained with strong shock and those in Group IV with weak shock. As a test of the assumption that the avoidance tendencies should be weaker the farther the subject is from the point of reinforcement, the pull of the animals in both groups was measured at different distances from the point at which the shock was administered.

Results

Approach and avoidance gradients. The results of the strength-of-pull tests administered to Group I (strong approach) and to Group III (strong avoidance) are summarized in Table 1. The basic data underlying these statistics were obtained by first measuring (planimetrically) the areas under the curves made on the waxed-paper records by the strength-of-pull marker. The average height of each curve was then computed by dividing its area by a standard baseline of 17.5 mm., the distance travelled by the paper during the 5-sec. interval. These average heights were finally converted into mean pull in grams by multiplying each by a constant derived from the calibration of the spring[2] against which the animals pulled. An average strength-of-pull value was obtained for each animal at each test point and the values in Table 1 were calculated from the distributions of these individual mean values.

Effects of strength of drive and strength of shock. In Table 2 and in Figure 3 the results of the tests made on Group II (strong-weak approach) and Group IV (weak avoidance) are presented. For purposes of comparison, the avoidance gradient from Figure 2 has been replotted in Figure 3. It is apparent from this figure that reducing the strength of the drive or

[2] The spring was made by winding 0.020-in. music wire on a 0.25-in. mandrel. The relation of elongation to applied force was roughly linear, with approximately 10 gm. being required for each millimeter of elongation.

Table 1   Means, medians, and standard deviations computed from average strength-of-pull measurements made on Groups I and III at points near to, and remote from, the point of reinforcement

	Near point			Far point		
	M	Md	SD	M	Md	SD
Group I (Strong approach)	56.5	47.5	33.7	40.9	36.1	26.3
Group III (Strong avoidance)	198.4	191.9	109.7	2.1	0	*

* No SD is given here, since 16 of the animals failed to reach the pull point within the criterion time of one minute and hence received zero scores.

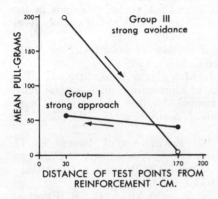

Figure 2   The approach gradient represents the mean force exerted by 46-hour motivated rats when restrained at two points in the alley. The avoidance gradient reveals the force exerted by rats in their efforts to avoid a region where strong shock has been given. Although the experimental points in this figure and in Figure 3 have been joined by straight lines, no assumption is intended with respect to the linearity of the gradients.

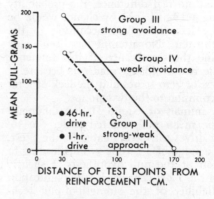

Figure 3   This figure summarizes the results of tests made on groups II, III, and IV, and illustrates the effect of reduced shock and reduced drive upon the strengths of the avoidance and approach responses, respectively.

Table 2   Statistics computed from measurements of average strength of pull exhibited by animals in Group II when tested under two degrees of food deprivation and by animals in Group IV when tested near the shock point and at the center of the alley. (No standard deviations are presented for Group IV because of the presence of zero scores at both points.)

	46-hour drive			1-hour drive		
	M	Md	SD	M	Md	SD
Group II (strong-weak approach)	48.7	41.8	30.9	16.5	11.4	19.33

	Near point		Center point	
	M	Md	M	Md
Group IV (weak avoidance)	141.2	146.3	51.7	19.0

of the shock reduces the heights of both approach and avoidance gradients, a result that accords well with the fourth assumption. In the case of Group IV, the difference between the means at the two points cannot be evaluated by the t test since five animals failed to pull at the far point and two failed to pull at either point. However, if one of the two no-pull animals is assigned to a favorable category and the other to an unfavorable category, then 19 of the 20 animals fall in the favorable category of pulling harder at the near point or else pulling at the near point and failing to reach the center point. If there were no real difference, the probability of obtaining a 19-to-1 split by chance would be substantially less than 0.01 according to the binomial theorem. No attempt has been made to determine the significance of the difference between the two avoidance gradients because of the presence of zero scores and the lack of a far test point common to the two groups.

For the animals of Group II, the difference between the mean pulls exerted under the 46- and 1-hour drives can be evaluated by the t test. This gives a value of 3.2 (d.f. = 11), leading to the rejection of the null hypothesis at slightly better than the 1 per cent level. Some indication of the reliability of the strength-of-pull technique is perhaps afforded by the fact that the mean force exerted by the 12 animals in Group II is almost exactly the same as that exerted by the 20 animals in Group I tested under comparable conditions.

References

1. Browman, L. G. Light in its relation to activity and oestrous rhythm in the albino rat. *J. exp. Zool.*, 1937, **75**, 375–388.
2. Brown, J. S. The generalization of approach responses as a function of stimulus intensity and strength of motivation. *J. comp. Psychol.*, 1942, **33**, 209–226.
3. Bugelski, R., and Miller, N. E. A spatial gradient in the strength of avoidance responses. *J. exp. Psychol.*, 1938, **23**, 494–505.
4. Drew, G. C. The speed of locomotion gradient and its relation to the goal gradient. *J. comp. Psychol.*, 1939, **27**, 333–372.
5. Grice, G. R. The relation of secondary reinforcement to delayed reward in visual discrimination learning. *J. exp. Psychol.*, 1948, **38**, 1–16.
6. Hilgard, E. R., and Marquis, D. G. *Conditioning and learning.* New York: Appleton-Century, 1940.
7. Hill, C. G. Goal gradient, anticipation, and perseveration in compound trial-and-error learning. *J. exp. Psychol.*, 1939, **25**, 566–585.
8. Hull, C. L. The goal-gradient hypothesis and maze learning. *Psychol. Rev.*, 1932, **39**, 25–43.
9. ———. The rat's speed-of-locomotion gradient in the approach to food. *J. comp. Psychol.*, 1934, **17**, 393–422.
10. ———. The goal-gradient hypothesis applied to some "field-force" problems in the behavior of young children. *Psychol. Rev.*, 1938, **45**, 271–299.
11. ———. *Principles of behavior.* New York: Appleton-Century, 1943.
12. Hunt, J. McV., and Schlosberg, H. The influence of illumination upon general activity in normal, blinded and castrated male white rats. *J. comp. Psychol.*, 1939, **28**, 285–298.
13. Lewin, K. Environmental forces. In C. Murchison (Ed.), *A handbook of child psychology.* (2nd Ed.). Worcester: Clark Univ. Press, 1933.
14. Miller, N. E., and Miles, W. R. Effect of caffeine on the running speed of hungry, satiated, and frustrated rats. *J. comp. Psychol.*, 1935, **20**, 397–412.
15. Miller, N. E. Experimental studies in conflict. In J. McV. Hunt (Ed.), *Personality and the behavior disorders.* New York: Ronald Press, 1944.
16. Morgan, C. T., and Fields, P. E. The effect of variable preliminary feeding upon the rat's speed-of-locomotion. *J. comp. Psychol.*, 1938, **26**, 331–348.
17. Muenzinger, K. F., and Walz, F. C. An examination of electrical-current-stabilizing devices for psychological experiments. *J. gen. Psychol.*, 1934, **10**, 477–482.
18. Spence, K. W. The order of eliminating blinds in maze learning by the rat. *J. comp. Psychol.*, 1932, **14**, 9–27
19. ———. The role of secondary reinforcement in delayed reward learning. *Psychol. Rev.*, 1947, **54**, 1–8.

DEFENSE MECHANISMS

This is an example of an attempt to study psychoanalytic concepts in a controlled laboratory setting. It is also an attempt to relate two theoretical trends: psychoanalysis (represented by Freud) and general psychological behavior theory (sometimes represented by Pavlov, behaviorism and neo-behaviorism). It is possible that both trends may gain from the insights, methodologies, and findings of the other.

A point to guide your study

Look up the section on stimulus generalization in your text. Make sure you understand it before reading this article. Do the same for displacement.

19. THEORY AND EXPERIMENT RELATING PSYCHOANALYTIC DISPLACEMENT TO STIMULUS-RESPONSE GENERALIZATION

*Neal E. Miller, Yale University**

Diverse origin of the two concepts

The concept of displacement comes from the clinic, that of generalization from the laboratory. The experiments and hypotheses to be described in this paper were devised in an attempt to relate these two concepts and to begin the formulation of a theory of displacement in terms of principles of learning.

Freud was led to the concept of displacement by applying the free association method to the analysis of material appearing in dreams (6, 7). Though the mechanism of displacement seems to be especially operative in the realm of dreams, other examples are easier to expound. A problem child is a nuisance because he pinches, bites, and scratches his little playmates at school and harasses the teacher in a variety of ingenious ways. Investigation reveals that in all probability the fault lies not in the playground situation at school but rather in the home situation. He hates his foster parents. Formerly, he attempted to pinch, bite, and scratch these foster parents, but was forced to desist. Later he commenced to plague his schoolmates in this manner. After the home situation is cleared up, the trouble on the

* This paper was read in condensed form (14) at the Stanford-Berkeley meetings of the American Psychological Association, September, 1939. The work described is part of the research program of the Institute of Human Relations, Yale University.

N. E. Miller. Theory and experiment relating psychoanalytic displacement to stimulus-response generalization. *J. abnorm. soc. Psychol.*, 1948, **43**, 155–178. Copyright 1948 by the American Psychological Association. Excerpt reprinted here with permission from the author and the American Psychological Association. Figure 3 slightly changed.

playground disappears. This transfer of aggression from the home situation to the school is called displacement.

A more familiar example is that of the man who, when severely frustrated at the office by business or professional rivals and unable to revenge himself directly, may come home and make scapegoats of members of his family.

According to an hypothesis especially elaborated upon in *Frustration and Aggression* (4) and refined in later publications (15, 19, 24), the irrational component of latent aggression against out-groups which easily flares into outbursts of race persecution and war is produced by the mechanism of displacement rather than by an instinct of aggression. According to this hypothesis, the out-groupers may be not only the target for the direct aggression which they arouse by competition with the in-groupers, but also may be the scapegoat for strong aggression which is first aroused by friction within the in-group, then suppressed by in-group taboos and conveniently displaced to members of the out-group.

Finally, displacement is involved in transference which is a crucial factor in psychoanalytic therapy. In transference the patient irrationally displaces to the analyst love and hate which have their real origin elsewhere.

The concept of generalization grew out of the work in Pavlov's laboratory. In a typical experiment a hungry dog is placed in a soundproof room and harnessed to a device which electrically records the dripping of his saliva (21). Then a tone of a specific pitch is sounded a number of times always immediately followed by food until the dog has been conditioned to salivate to the sound of the tone alone. Next the dog is presented for the first time in the training situation with tones of different pitches and it is found that he salivates immediately to these new tones also. This transfer of the response from the original to the new tones is called generalization. It is further found that the more similar the new tone is to the pitch of the originally conditioned one, the larger is the response to the new tone. This greater transfer the more similar the new tone is called a gradient of generalization.

From the out-group aggression and the analysis of the bizarre dreams of Freud's patients to the electric recording of the salivation of dogs in Pavlov's soundproof laboratory seems to be a huge leap. The following experiments were designed to cast the first rope of a slender bridge across that chasm.

Experiment on object displacement or generalization

In the first stage of the first experiment albino rats were trained to strike at each other.[1] They were placed two at a time in an enclosure, the floor of which was a grid. Through this grid they were given an electric shock sufficiently strong to keep them active. Their random acts were observed through a glass window on one side of the enclosure. When they by chance happened to approach each other in a sparring position similar to that used by rats in fighting, the shock was abruptly turned off. Thus the act of sparring was rewarded by escape from shock. After a minute without shock the current was turned on

[1] This experiment was performed with the assistance of Miss Maritta Davis.

Figure 1   Rats trained to strike at each other. Albino rats were trained by trial and error to commence striking each other as soon as a mild electric shock was turned on. The experimenter reinforced this behavior by turning off the shock as soon as the animals commenced striking vigorously in the way they do at the beginning of a fight.

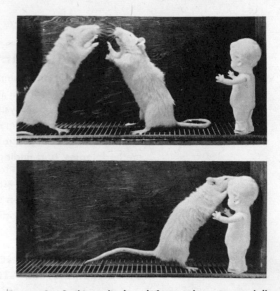

Figure 2   Striking displaced from other rat to doll. When two rats were placed in the apparatus along with the doll, they struck at each other as soon as the electric shock was turned on; when placed into the apparatus one at a time, they struck at the doll. (The apparatus used in the experiment had a grid floor 12″ by 12″. The pictures were taken in a much narrower apparatus.)

again and the animals given another trial. As training progressed, they were required to strike at each other before the shock was turned off. Training was continued till the habit of striking was thoroughly established. Figure 1 shows two animals that have learned by trial and error to commence striking each other vigorously as soon as the shock is turned on.

After this training, the animals were given test trials in which a small celluloid doll was placed in the arena along with each pair of rats. As can be seen in the upper part of Figure 2, the animals struck at each other when the shock was turned on, and not at the doll. In different test trials, the animals were placed *one at a time* in the same apparatus. Under these conditions they tended to strike at the doll when the shock was turned on. This is illustrated in the lower part of Figure 2.

Twelve animals were trained and given both tests. For half of them the first test was the one with the other rat and the doll both present, for the other half, the one with the doll alone. When another rat was present only one of the twelve struck at the doll, and this one then immediately turned to strike at the other rat. If the tendencies to strike the other rat and the doll were equally strong, half of the animals would be expected to strike at each. Instead, eleven out of the twelve animals struck at the other rat. Using chi-square corrected for discontinuity, it can be calculated that a difference of this size would be expected by chance less than one time in a hundred. Therefore, we may conclude that when another rat and the doll were both present, the stronger tendency was to strike at the other rat.

When the animals which had been trained to strike the other rat were placed into the arena alone with the doll and given an electric shock, six of them knocked it down by striking at it; the other six pushed it over in various irrelevant ways such as bumping it head on in the course of running around the cage. In order to show that the tendency to strike the doll when no other rat was present was produced by the previous training to strike at another rat (i.e., would not have been produced by electric shock without this training), a control group of twelve untrained animals was tested one at a time under exactly similar conditions. Only one out of the control group struck at the doll before knocking it down in various irrelevant ways. By means of chi-square corrected for discontinuity it was calculated that a difference of this size in favor of the experimental group would be expected by chance less than five times in a hundred. This indicates that the tendency to knock the doll down by striking at it was a function of previous training to strike at another rat.

Similarity between object displacement and stimulus generalization

When rats trained to strike the other animal were prevented from doing this by the absence of that animal, they tended to strike the doll. Viewed in Freudian terms this might be taken to indicate displacement. If one can call the original response of striking the other rat aggression, then this aggression has been displaced to the doll which might be called a scapegoat. However, it is not necessary to go this far; it will be safer to say that some pattern of response, as yet undesignated, has been displaced from the other rat to the doll.[2]

But exactly the same phenomenon may be described equally as well in stimulus-response terms as transfer of training, or, in other words, generalization. This is clearly illustrated in Figure 3. The first data are from a typical experiment on conditioning (10). A tone of the pitch of 153 double vibrations per second is presented

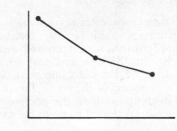

DISSIMILARITY OF STIMULUS PATTERN

TONES: 153~   468~   1000~
OBJECTS: WHITE RAT   DOLL   WALL

Figure 3 The parallel between displacement and generalization. The strength of the direct responses to the stimulus pattern involved in the original learning is represented by the first point on the left; the strength of the weaker displaced, or generalized, responses are represented by the other two points. The particular values selected to illustrate a gradient of generalization in this diagram are from a typical experiment on the generalization of a conditioned galvanic skin response to tones of different pitches (10).

to college students and always followed by electric shock until a conditioned galvanic skin response has been established. Then this tone and other tones are presented without shock. The largest response is to the tone originally conditioned, the next largest to the most similar tone and the smallest to the least similar tone. This is a gradient of generalization.

The experiment on displacement may be analyzed in exactly the same way. The response of striking was originally established to the stimulus of another rat, the partner. Thus the stimulus of the partner will evoke the strongest response and, assuming the doll to present a different stimulus pattern, it will evoke a weaker response. Therefore, when a rat is confronted simultaneously with the stimuli of the partner and the doll, the stronger response to the partner will win out and he will strike at the partner rather than at the doll. When the partner is absent, however, the stimulus of the doll is more similar to the original stimulus than is the stimulus of the wall. Hence, the stimulus of the doll evokes the stronger response; the rat strikes at the doll rather than at the wall.

Another experiment (18) on human subjects has been analyzed in a similar way. In this experiment it was found that subjects who had been angered by frustrations imposed upon them by

---

[2] In classroom demonstrations the author has repeatedly shown that if animals are trained to bite a rubber tube as soon as an electric shock is turned on and then tested with shock but without the tube being present, they are (a) more likely to bite other objects similar to the tube than to bite grossly dissimilar objects, and (b) much more likely to bite such objects than are animals given an electric shock without any previous training of any kind.

members of their own country expressed less favorable attitudes toward faraway foreigners who could not possibly have been responsible for their plight. In this case one may assume that the members of the out-group were sufficiently similar as stimulus objects to the members of the in-group so that the response of aggression generalized from the one to the other.

References

1. Anderson, E. E. The externalization of drive: III. Maze learning by non-rewarded and by satiated rats. *J. gen. Psychol.*, 1941, **59**, 397–426.
2. Brown, J. S. The generalization of approach responses as a function of stimulus intensity and strength of motivation. *J. comp. Psychol.*, 1942, **33**, 209–226.
3. Coriat, I. H. Sex and Hunger. *Psychoanal. Rev.*, 1921, **8**, 375–381.
4. Dollard, J., *et al. Frustration and aggression.* New Haven: Yale University Press, 1939.
5. Finger, F. W. Quantitative studies of "conflict": I. Variations in latency and strength of the rat's response in a discrimination-jumping situation. *J. comp. Psychol.*, 1941, **31**, 97–127.
6. Freud, S. A *general introduction to psychoanalysis.* (Authorized translation, with a preface by G. S. Hall.) New York: Boni and Liveright, 1920.
7. Freud, S. *The interpretation of dreams.* (Introduction by A. A. Brill.) London: Allen and Unwin; New York: Macmillan, 1927.
8. Hiroa, T. R. Ethnology of Ranihiki and Rakahanga. *B. P. Bishop Museum Bull.*, 1932, **99**.
9. Hochman, S. Mental and psychological factors in obesity. *Med. Rec.*, 1938, **148**, 108–111.
10. Hovland, C. I. The generalization of conditioned responses. I. The sensory generalization of conditioned responses with varying frequencies of tone. *J. gen. Psychol.*, 1937, **17**, 125–148.
11. Hull, C. L. *Principles of behavior.* New York: Appleton Century, 1943.
12. Kendler, H. H. Drive interaction: I. Learning as a function of the simultaneous presence of the hunger and thirst drives. *J. exp. Psychol.*, 1945, **35**, 96–109.
13. Koch, S., and Daniel, W. F. The effect of satiation on the behavior mediated by a habit of maximum strength. *J. exp. Psychol.*, 1945, **35**, 167–187.
14. Miller, N. E. Experiments relating Freudian displacement to generalization of conditioning. *Psychol. Bull.*, 1939, **36**, 516-517.
15. Miller, N. E. The frustration-aggression hypothesis. *Psychol. Rev.*, 1941, **48**, 337–342.
16. Miller, N. E. Studies of fear as an acquirable drive: I. Fear as motivation and fear-reduction as reinforcement in the learning of new responses. *J. exp. Psychol.*, 1948, **38**, 89–101.
17. Miller, N. E. Experimental studies of conflict. In J. McV. Hunt, edit., *Personality and the behavior disorders.* New York: Ronald Press, 1944.
18. Miller, N. E., and Bugelski, R. Minor studies of aggression: II. The influence of frustrations imposed by the in-group on attitudes expressed toward out-groups. *J. Psychol.*, 1948, **25**, 437-442.
19. Miller, N. E., and Dollard, J. *Social learning and imitation.* New Haven: Yale University Press, 1941.
20. Miller, N. E., and Stevenson, S. S. Agitated behavior of rats during experimental extinction and a curve of spontaneous recovery. *J. comp. Psychol.*, 1936, **21**, 205–231.
21. Pavlov, I. P. *Conditioned reflexes.* (Trans. by G. V. Anrep.) London: Oxford University Press, 1927.
22. Saul, L. J. Physiological effects of emotional tension. In J. McV. Hunt, edit., *Personality and the behavior disorders.* New York: Ronald Press, 1944.
23. Sears, R. R. Functional abnormalities of memory with special reference to amnesia. *Psychol. Bull.*, 1936, **33**, 229–274.
24. Sears, R. R. Non-aggressive reactions to frustration. *Psychol. Rev.*, 1941, **48**, 343–346.
25. Siegel, P. S. Alien drive, habit strength, and resistance to extinction. *J. comp. Psychol.*, 1946, **39**, 307–317.

N EUROTIC REACTIONS

This is a description of neurosis with which many psychologists would agree. If you have already studied conflict and motivation, you will see that it fits quite well with what was said there.

Although this analysis uses some psychoanalytic terms, e.g., repression and conflict, it is quite different from the psychoanalytic viewpoint in that it puts stress on learning. Some of the less orthodox, more recent psychoanalysts stress learning, but the orthodox ones have little place for it in their systems.

A point to guide your study

With a learning orientation toward neuroses, what would the therapist concentrate upon in the treatment?

20. PERSONALITY AND PSYCHOTHERAPY. WHAT IS A NEUROSIS?

John Dollard and Neal E. Miller, Yale University*

Most people, even scientists, are vague about neurosis. Neither the neurotic victim nor those who know him seem able to state precisely what is involved. The victim feels a mysterious malady. The witness observes inexplicable behavior. The neurotic is mysterious because he is *capable* of acting and yet he is *unable* to act and enjoy. Though physically capable of attaining sex rewards, he is anesthetic; though capable of aggression, he is meek; though capable of affection, he is cold and unresponsive. As seen by the outside witness, the neurotic does not make use of the obvious opportunities for satisfaction which life offers him.

To be explained: misery, stupidity, symptoms

The therapist confronts a person who is miserable, stupid (in some ways), and who has symptoms. These are the three major factors to be accounted for. Why is he miserable, in what curious way is he stupid, and whence arise the symptoms? The waiting room of every psychiatric clinic is crowded with patients showing these common signs.

Neurotic misery is real. Neurotic misery is real—not imaginary. Observers, not understanding the neurotic conflict, often belittle the suffering of neurotics and confuse neurosis with malingering. Neurotic habits are forced upon an individual by peculiar conditions of life and are not cheap attempts to escape duty and responsibility. In most cases the misery is attested by many specific complaints. These complaints or symptoms differ with each category of neurosis but sleeplessness, restlessness, irritability, sexual inhibitions, distaste for life, lack of clear personal goals, phobias, headaches, and irrational fears are among the more common ones.

At times the depth of the misery of the neurotic is concealed by his symptoms. Only when they are withdrawn does his true anguish appear. Occasionally the misery will be private, not easily visible to outside observers because friends and relatives are ringed around the neurotic person and prevent observation of his pain. In still other cases, the neurotic person is miserable but apathetic. He has lost even the hope that complaining and attracting attention will be helpful. However this may be, *if the neurotic takes the usual risks of life* he is miserable. He suffers if he attempts to love, marry, and be a parent. He fails if he tries to work responsibly and independently. His social relations tend to be invaded by peculiar demands and conditions. Neurotic misery is thus often masked by the protective conditions of life (as in childhood) and appears only when the individual has to "go it on his own."

Conflict produces misery. Suffering so intense as that shown by neurotics must have powerful causes, and it does. The neurotic is miserable because he is in conflict. As a usual thing two or more strong drives are operating in him and producing incompatible responses. Strongly driven to approach and as strongly to flee, he is not able to act to reduce either of the conflicting drives. These drives therefore remain dammed up, active, and nagging.

* John Dollard and N. E. Miller. *Personality and psychotherapy.* New York: McGraw-Hill, 1950. Copyright 1950 by the McGraw-Hill Book Company, Inc. Excerpt reprinted here with permission from the author and McGraw-Hill Book Company, Inc.

Where such a drive conflict is conscious there is no problem in convincing anyone why it should produce misery. If we picture a very hungry man confronting food which he knows to be poisoned, we can understand that he is driven on the one hand by hunger and on the other by fear. He oscillates at some distance from the tempting food, fearing to grasp but unable to leave. Everyone understands immediately the turmoil produced by such a conflict of hunger and fear.

Many people remember from their adolescence the tension of a strong sex conflict. Primary sex responses heightened by imaginative elaboration are met by intense fear. Though usually not allowed to talk about such matters, children sometimes can, and the misery they reveal is one of the most serious prices exacted of adolescents in our culture. That this conflict is acquired and not innate was shown by Margaret Mead in her brilliant book, "Coming of Age in Samoa" (1928). It is also agonizingly depicted in a novel by Vardis Fisher (1932).

Our third example of conscious conflict shows anger pitted against fear. In the early part of the war, an officer, newly commissioned from civilian life and without the habits of the professional soldier, was sent to an Army post. There he met a superior officer who decided to make an example of some minor mistake. The ranking officer lectured and berated the subordinate, refusing to let him speak and explain his behavior. He made him stand at attention against the wall for half an hour while this lecture was going on. The new-made officer quaked in fearful conflict. He detected the sadistic satisfaction which his superior got in dressing him down. He had never so much wanted to kill anyone. On the other hand, the junior officer felt the strong pressure of his own conscience to be a competent soldier and some real fear about what the consequence of assault might be. We met him shortly after this episode, and he still shook with rage when he described the experience. There was no doubt in his mind but that bearing strong, conflicting drives is one of the most severe causes of misery.

Repression causes stupidity.   In each of the above cases, however, the individual could eventually solve his conflict. The hungry man could find nourishing food; the sex-tortured adolescent could eventually marry; the new officer could and did avoid his punishing superior.

With the neurotic this is not the case. He is not able to solve his conflict even with the passage of time. Though obviously intelligent in some ways, he is stupid in-so-far as his neurotic conflict is concerned. This stupidity is not an over-all affair, however. It is really a stupid area in the mind of a person who is quite intelligent in other respects. For some reason he cannot use his head on his neurotic conflicts.

Though the neurotic is sure he is miserable and is vocal about his symptoms, he is vague about what it is within him that could produce such painful effects. The fact that the neurotic cannot describe his own conflicts has been the source of great confusion in dealing with him either in terms of scientific theory or in terms of clinical practice. Nor can the therapist immediately spot these areas of stupidity. Only after extensive study of the patient's life can the areas of repression be clearly identified. Then the surprising fact emerges that the competing drives which afflict the neurotic person are not labeled. He has no language to describe the conflicting forces within him.

Without language and adequate labeling the higher mental processes cannot function. When these processes are knocked out by repression, the person cannot guide himself by mental means to a resolution of his conflict. Since the neurotic cannot help himself, he must have the help of others if he is to be helped at all—though millions today live out their lives in strong neurotic pain and never get help. The neurotic, therefore, is, or appears to be, stupid because he is unable to use his mind in dealing with certain of his problems. He feels that someone should help him, but he does not know how to ask for help since he does not know what his problem is. He may feel aggrieved that he is suffering, but he cannot explain his case.

Symptoms slightly reduce conflict.   Although in many ways superficial, the symptoms of the neurotic are the most obvious aspects of his problems. These are what the patient is familiar with and feels he should be rid of. The phobias, inhibitions, avoidances, compulsions, rationalizations, and psychosomatic symptoms of the neurotic are experienced as a nuisance by him and by all who have to deal with him. The symptoms cannot be integrated into the texture of sensible social relations. The patient, however, believes that the symptoms *are* his disorder. It is these he wishes to be rid of and, not knowing that a serious conflict underlies them, he would like to confine the therapeutic discussion to getting rid of the symptoms.

The symptoms do not solve the basic conflict in which the neurotic person is plunged, but they mitigate it. They are responses which tend to reduce the conflict, and in part they succeed. When a successful symptom occurs it is reinforced because it reduces neurotic misery. The symptom is thus learned as a habit. One very common function of symptoms is to keep the neurotic person away from those stimuli which would activate and intensify his neurotic conflict. Thus, the combat pilot with a harrowing military disaster behind him may "walk away" from the sight of any airplane. As he walks toward the plane his anxiety goes up; as he walks away it goes down. "Walking away" is thus reinforced. It is this phobic walking away which constitutes his symptom. If the whole situation is not understood, such behavior seems bizarre to the casual witness.

Conflict, repression, and symptoms closely related. In the foregoing discussion we have "taken apart" the most conspicuous factors which define the neurosis and have separately discussed conflict, stupidity, and misery. We hope that the discussion has clarified the problem even at the expense of slightly distorting the actual relationships. In every human case of neurosis the three basic factors are closely and dynamically interrelated. The conflict could not be unconscious and insoluble were it not for the repressive factors involved. The symptoms could not exist did they not somewhat relieve the pressure of conflict. The mental paralysis of repression has been created by the very same forces which originally imposed the emotional conflict on the neurotic person.

The case of Mrs. A[1]

We are presenting the facts about Mrs. A for two reasons: (1) as background material on a case from which we will draw many concrete examples throughout the book; (2) as a set of facts from which we can illustrate the relationships between misery and conflict, stupidity and repression, symptoms and reinforcement. The reader will understand, of course, that the sole function of this case material is to give a clear exposition of principles by means of concrete illustrations; it is *not* presented as evidence or proof.

The facts. Mrs. A was an unusually pretty twenty-three-year-old married woman. Her husband worked in the offices of an insurance company. When she came to the therapist she was exceedingly upset. She had a number of fears. One of the strongest of these was that her heart would stop beating if she did not concentrate on counting the beats.

The therapist, who saw Mrs. A twice a week over a three-month period, took careful notes. The life-history data that we present were pieced together from the patient's statements during a total of 26 hours. The scope of the material is necessarily limited by the brevity of the treat-

ment. The treatment had to end when a change in the husband's work forced her to move to another city.

Her first neurotic symptoms had appeared five months before she came to the psychiatrist. While she was shopping in a New York store, she felt faint and became afraid that something would happen to her and "no one would know where I was." She telephoned her husband's office and asked him to come and get her. Thereafter she was afraid to go out alone. Shortly after this time, she talked with an aunt who had a neurotic fear of heart trouble. After a conversation with this aunt, Mrs. A's fears changed from a fear of fainting to a concern about her heart.

Mrs. A was an orphan, born of unknown parents in a city in the upper South. She spent the first few months of life in an orphanage, then was placed in a foster home, where she lived, except for a year when she was doing war work in Washington, until her marriage at the age of twenty.

The foster parents belonged to the working class, had three children of their own, two girls and a boy, all of them older than the patient. The foster mother, who dominated the family, was cruel, strict, and miserly toward all the children. She had a coarse and vulgar demeanor, swore continually, and punished the foster child for the least offense. Mrs. A recalls: "She whipped me all the time—whether I'd done anything or not."

The foster mother had imposed a very repressive sex training on the patient, making her feel that sex was dirty and wrong. Moreover, the foster mother never let the patient think independently. She discouraged the patient's striving for an education, taking her out of school at sixteen when the family could have afforded to let her go on.

Despite the repressive sex training she received, Mrs. A had developed strong sexual appetites. In early childhood she had overheard parental intercourse, had masturbated, and had witnessed animal copulation. When she was ten or twelve, her foster brother seduced her. During the years before her marriage a dozen men tried to seduce her and most of them succeeded.

Nevertheless, sex was to her a dirty, loathsome thing that was painful for her to discuss or think about. She found sexual relations with her husband disgusting and was morbidly shy in her relations with him.

The patient had met her husband-to-be while she was working as a typist in Washington during the war. He was an Army officer and a college graduate. Her beauty enabled the patient to make a marriage that improved her social position; her husband's family were middle-class people. At the time of treatment Mrs. A had

---

[1] We are allowed to present and analyze the material on Mrs. A through the kindness of a New York colleague, a man so remarkable as to provide this laboriously gathered material and yet be willing to remain anonymous to aid in the complete disguise of the case.

not yet learned all the habits of middle-class life. She was still somewhat awkward about entertaining or being entertained and made glaring errors in grammar and pronunciation. She was dominated, socially subordinated, and partly rejected by her husband's family.

When they were first married, Mr. and Mrs. A lived with his parents in a small town north of New York City and commuted to the city for work. Mrs. A had an office job there. Later, they were able to get an apartment in New York, but they stayed with the in-laws every week end. Although she described her mother-in-law in glowing terms at the beginning of the treatment, Mrs. A later came to express considerable hostility toward her.

When she came to the psychiatrist, Mrs. A was in great distress. She had to pay continual attention to her heart lest it stop beating. She lived under a burden of vague anxiety and had a number of specific phobias that prevented her from enjoying many of the normal pleasures of her life, such as going to the movies. She felt helpless to cope with her problems. Her constant complaints had tired out and alienated her friends. Her husband was fed up with her troubles and had threatened to divorce her. She could not get along with her foster mother and her mother-in-law had rejected her. She had no one left to talk to. She was hurt, baffled, and terrified by the thought that she might be going crazy.

Analysis in terms of conflict, repression, reinforcement.   We have described Mrs. A as of the moment when she came to treatment. The analysis of the case, however, presents the facts as they were afterward ordered and clarified by study.

Misery.   Mrs. A's misery was obvious to her family, her therapist, and herself. She suffered from a strong, vague, unremitting fear. She was tantalized by a mysterious temptation. The phobic limitations on her life prevented her from having much ordinary fun, as by shopping or going to the movies. Her husband and mother-in-law criticized her painfully. She feared that her husband would carry out his threat and divorce her. She feared that her heart would stop. She feared to be left all alone, sick and rejected. Her friends and relatives pitied her at first, then became put out with her when her condition persisted despite well-meant advice. Her misery, though baffling, was recognized as entirely real.

Conflict.   Mrs. A suffered from two conflicts which produced her misery. The first might be described as a sex-fear conflict. Thanks to childhood circumstances she had developed strong sex appetites. At the same time strong anxieties were created in her and attached to the cues produced by sex excitement. However, she saw

no connection between these remembered circumstances and the miserable life she was leading. The connective thoughts had been knocked out and the conflict was thus unconscious. The presence of the sexual appetites showed up in a kind of driven behavior in which she seemed to court seduction. Her fear was exhibited in her revulsion from sexual acts and thoughts and in her inability to take responsibility for a reasonable sexual expressiveness with her husband. The conflict was greatly intensified after her marriage because of her wish to be a dutiful wife. Guilt about the prospect of adultery was added to fear about sex motives.

Mrs. A was involved in a second, though less severe, conflict between aggression and fear. She was a gentle person who had been very badly treated by her mother-in-law. Resentful tendencies arose in her but they were quickly inhibited by fear. She attempted to escape the anger-fear conflict by exceptionally submissive behavior, putting up meekly with slights and subordination and protesting her fondness for the mother-in-law. She was tormented by it nevertheless, especially by feelings of worthlessness and helplessness. She felt much better, late in therapy, when she was able to state her resentment and begin to put it into effect in a measured way. (After all, she had the husband and his love, and if the mother-in-law wanted to see her son and prospective grandchildren she would have to take a decent attitude toward Mrs. A.)

Stupidity.   Mrs. A's mind was certainly of little use to her in solving her problem. She tried the usual medical help with no result. She took a trip, as advised, and got no help. Her symptoms waxed and waned in unpredictable ways. She knew that she was helpless. At the time she came for therapy she had no plans for dealing with her problem and no hope of solving it. In addition to being unable to deal with her basic problems, Mrs. A did many things that were quite unintelligent and maladaptive. For example, in spite of the fact that she wanted very much to make a success of her marriage and was consciously trying to live a proper married life, she frequently exposed herself to danger of seduction. She went out on drinking parties with single girls. She hitchhiked rides with truck drivers. She was completely unaware of the motivation for this behavior and often unable to foresee its consequences until it was too late. While her behavior seems stupid in the light of a knowledge of the actual state of affairs, there were many ways in which Mrs. A did not seem at all stupid—for example, when debating with the therapist to protect herself against fear-producing thoughts. She then gave hopeful evidence of what she could do with her mind when she had available all the necessary units to think with.

Repression.   Mrs. A gave abundant evidence

of the laming effects of repression. At the outset she thought she had no sex feelings or appetites. She described behavior obviously motivated by fear but could not label the fear itself. The closest she came was to express the idea that she was going insane. Further, Mrs. A thought she had an organic disease and clung desperately to this idea, inviting any kind of treatment so long as it did not force her to think about matters which would produce fear. Such mental gaps and distortions are a characteristic result of repression. They are what produce the stupidity.

Symptoms. Mrs. A's chief symptoms were the spreading phobia which drove her out of theaters and stores and the compulsive counting of breaths and heartbeats. These symptoms almost incapacitated her. She had lost her freedom to think and to move.

Reinforcement of symptoms. An analysis of the phobia revealed the following events. When on the streets alone, her fear of sex temptation was increased. Someone might speak to her, wink at her, make an approach to her. Such an approach would increase her sex desire and make her more vulnerable to seduction. Increased sex desire, however, touched off both anxiety and guilt, and this intensified her conflict when she was on the street. When she "escaped home," the temptation stimuli were lessened, along with a reduction of the fear which they elicited. Going home and, later, avoiding the temptation situation by anticipation were reinforced. Natu-

rally, the basic sex-anxiety conflict was not resolved by the defensive measure of the symptom. The conflict persisted but was not so keen.

The counting of heartbeats can be analytically taken apart in a similar way. When sexy thoughts came to mind or other sex stimuli tended to occur, these stimuli elicited anxiety. It is clear that these stimuli were occurring frequently because Mrs. A was responding with anxiety much of the time. Since counting is a highly preoccupying kind of response, no other thoughts could enter her mind during this time. While counting, the sexy thoughts which excited fear dropped out. Mrs. A "felt better" immediately when she started counting, and the counting habit was reinforced by the drop in anxiety. Occasionally, Mrs. A would forget to count and then her intense anxiety would recur. In this case, as in that of the phobia, the counting symptom does not resolve the basic conflict—it only avoids exacerbating it.

Thus Mrs. A's case illustrates the analysis of neurotic mechanisms made in the earlier part of the chapter. Conflict produced high drives experienced as misery; repression interfered with higher mental processes and so with the intelligent solution of the conflict; the symptoms were learned responses which were reinforced by producing some reduction in the strength of drive. We will discuss later how higher mental life can be restored and how actions which *will* resolve the poisonous conflict can be made to occur.

CHAPTER SIX

Mental health and psychotherapy

Techniques in Psychotherapy

Since this article was published in 1946, the client-centered method has become especially prominent in guidance and counseling with people who are not severely disturbed. The method is most successful with those who are able to make use of their own creative and integrative abilities, the not so severely disturbed. Even with severely disturbed people the technique is sometimes used, however.

Points to guide your study

1. Contrast this technique with psychoanalysis.

2. Pay special attention to the *elements* of the client-centered therapy situation.

3. How might client-centered counseling help a person decide for himself on a career?

21. SIGNIFICANT ASPECTS OF CLIENT-CENTERED THERAPY

*Carl R. Rogers, University of Wisconsin**

In planning to address this group, I have considered and discarded several possible topics. I was tempted to describe the process of non-directive therapy and the counselor techniques and procedures which seem most useful in bringing about this process. But much of this material is now in writing. My own book on counseling and psychotherapy contains much of the basic material, and my recent more popular book on counseling with returning servicemen tends to supplement it. The philosophy of the client-centered approach and its application to work with children is persuasively presented by Allen. The application to counseling of industrial employees is discussed in the volume by Cantor. Curran has now published in book form one of the several research studies which are throwing new light on both process and procedure. Axline is publishing a book on play and group therapy.

C. R. Rogers. Significant aspects of client-centered therapy. *Amer. Psychologist*, 1946, **1**, 415–422. Copyright 1946 by the American Psychological Association. Reprinted here with permission from the author and the American Psychological Association.

* Paper given at a seminar of the staffs of the Menninger Clinic and the Topeka Veteran's Hospital, Topeka, Kansas, May 15, 1946.

Snyder is bringing out a book of cases. So it seems unnecessary to come a long distance to summarize material which is, or soon will be, obtainable in written form.

Another tempting possibility, particularly in this setting, was to discuss some of the roots from which the client-centered approach has sprung. It would have been interesting to show how in its concepts of repression and release, in its stress upon catharsis and insight, it has many roots in Freudian thinking, and to acknowledge that indebtedness. Such an analysis could also have shown that in its concept of the individual's ability to organize his own experience there is an even deeper indebtedness to the work of Rank, Taft, and Allen. In its stress upon objective research, the subjecting of fluid attitudes to scientific investigation, the willingness to submit all hypotheses to a verification or disproof by research methods, the debt is obviously to the whole field of American psychology, with its genius for scientific methodology. It could also have been pointed out that although everyone in the clinical field has been heavily exposed to the eclectic "team" approach to therapy of the child guidance movement, and the somewhat similar eclecticism of the Adolf

Meyers–Hopkins school of thought, these eclectic viewpoints have perhaps not been so fruitful in therapy and that little from these sources has been retained in the nondirective approach. It might also have been pointed out that in its basic trend away from guiding and directing the client, the nondirective approach is deeply rooted in practical clinical experience, and is in accord with the experience of most clinical workers, so much so that one of the commonest reactions of experienced therapists is that "You have crystallized and put into words something that I have been groping toward in my own experience for a long time."

Such an analysis, such a tracing of root ideas, needs to be made, but I doubt my own ability to make it. I am also doubtful that anyone who is deeply concerned with a new development knows with any degree of accuracy where his ideas came from.

Consequently I am, in this presentation, adopting a third pathway. While I shall bring in a brief description of process and procedure, and while I shall acknowledge in a general way our indebtedness to many root sources, and shall recognize the many common elements shared by client-centered therapy and other approaches, I believe it will be to our mutual advantage if I stress primarily those aspects in which nondirective therapy differs most sharply and deeply from other therapeutic procedures. I hope to point out some of the basically significant ways in which the client-centered viewpoint differs from others, not only in its present principles, but in the wider divergencies which are implied by the projection of its central principles.

The predictable process of client-centered therapy

The first of the three distinctive elements of client-centered therapy to which I wish to call your attention is the predictability of the therapeutic process in this approach. We find, both clinically and statistically, that a predictable pattern of therapeutic development takes place. The assurance which we feel about this was brought home to me recently when I played a recorded first interview for the graduate students in our practicum immediately after it was recorded, pointing out the characteristic aspects, and agreeing to play later interviews for them to let them see the later phases of the counseling process. The fact that I knew with assurance what the later pattern would be before it had occurred only struck me as I thought about the incident. We have become clinically so accustomed to this predictable quality that we take it for granted. Perhaps a brief summarized description of this therapeutic process will indicate those elements of which we feel sure.

It may be said that we now know how to initiate a complex and predictable chain of events in dealing with the maladjusted individual, a chain of events which is therapeutic, and which operates effectively in problem situations of the most diverse type. This predictable chain of events may come about through the use of language, as in counseling, through symbolic language, as in play therapy, through disguised language as in drama or puppet therapy. It is effective in dealing with individual situations, and also in small group situations.

It is possible to state with some exactness the conditions which must be met in order to initiate and carry through this releasing therapeutic experience. Below are listed in brief form the conditions which seem to be necessary, and the therapeutic results which occur.

This experience which releases the growth forces within the individual will come about in most cases if the following elements are present.

1. If the counselor operates on the principle that the individual is basically responsible for himself, and is willing for the individual to keep that responsibility.

2. If the counselor operates on the principle that the client has a strong drive to become mature, socially adjusted, independent, productive, and relies on this force, not on his own powers, for therapeutic change.

3. If the counselor creates a warm and permissive atmosphere in which the individual is free to bring out any attitudes and feelings which he may have, no matter how unconventional, absurd, or contradictory these attitudes may be. The client is as free to withhold expression as he is to give expression to his feelings.

4. If the limits which are set are simple limits set on behavior, and not limits set on attitudes. (This applies mostly to children. The child may not be permitted to break a window or leave the room, but he is free to feel like breaking a window, and the feeling is fully accepted. The adult client may not be permitted more than an hour for an interview, but there is full acceptance of his desire to claim more time.)

5. If the therapist uses only those procedures and techniques in the interview which convey his deep understanding of the emotionalized attitudes expressed and his acceptance of them. This understanding is perhaps best conveyed by a sensitive reflection and clarification of the client's attitudes. The counselor's acceptance involves neither approval nor disapproval.

6. If the counselor refrains from any expression or action which is contrary to the preceding principles. This means refraining from questioning, probing, blame, interpretation, advice, suggestion, persuasion, reassurance.

If these conditions are met, then it may be said with assurance that in the great majority of cases the following results will take place.

1. The client will express deep and motivating attitudes.

2. The client will explore his own attitudes and reactions more fully than he has previously done and will come to be aware of aspects of his attitudes which he has previously denied.

3. He will arrive at a clearer conscious realization of his motivating attitudes and will accept himself more completely. This realization and this acceptance will include attitudes previously denied. He may or may not verbalize this clearer conscious understanding of himself and his behavior.

4. In the light of his clearer perception of himself he will choose, on his own initiative and on his own responsibility, new goals which are more satisfying than his maladjusted goals.

5. He will choose to behave in a different fashion in order to reach these goals, and this new behavior will be in the direction of greater psychological growth and maturity. It will also be more spontaneous and less tense, more in harmony with social needs of others, will represent a more realistic and more comfortable adjustment to life. It will be more integrated than his former behavior. It will be a step forward in the life of the individual.

The best scientific description of this process is that supplied by Snyder. Analyzing a number of cases with strictly objective research techniques, Snyder has discovered that the development in these cases is roughly parallel, that the initial phase of catharsis is replaced by a phase in which insight becomes the most significant element, and this in turn by a phase marked by the increase in positive choice and action.

Clinically we know that sometimes this process is relatively shallow, involving primarily a fresh reorientation to an immediate problem, and in other instances so deep as to involve a complete reorientation of personality. It is recognizably the same process whether it involves a girl who is unhappy in a dormitory and is able in three interviews to see something of her childishness and dependence, and to take steps in a mature direction, or whether it involves a young man who is on the edge of a schizophrenic break, and who in thirty interviews works out deep insights in relation to his desire for his father's death, and his possessive and incestuous impulses toward his mother, and who not only takes new steps but rebuilds his whole personality in the process. Whether shallow or deep, it is basically the same.

We are coming to recognize with assurance characteristic aspects of each phase of the process. We know that the catharsis involves a gradual and more complete expression of emotionalized attitudes. We know that characteristically the conversation goes from superficial problems and attitudes to deeper problems and attitudes. We know that this process of exploration gradually unearths relevant attitudes which have been denied to consciousness.

We recognize too that the process of achieving insight is likely to involve more adequate facing of reality as it exists within the self, as well as external reality; that it involves the relating of problems to each other, the perception of patterns of behavior; that it involves the acceptance of hitherto denied elements of the self, and a reformulating of the self-concept; and that it involves the making of new plans.

In the final phase we know that the choice of new ways of behaving will be in conformity with the newly organized concept of the self; that first steps in putting these plans into action will be small but symbolic; that the individual will feel only a minimum degree of confidence that he can put his plans into effect; that later steps implement more and more completely the new concept of self, and that this process continues beyond the conclusion of the therapeutic interviews.

If these statements seem to contain too much assurance, to sound "too good to be true," I can only say that for many of them we now have research backing, and that as rapidly as possible we are developing our research to bring all phases of the process under objective scrutiny. Those of us working clinically with client-centered therapy regard this predictability as a settled characteristic, even though we recognize that additional research will be necessary to fill out the picture more completely.

It is the implication of this predictability which is startling. Whenever, in science, a predictable process has been discovered, it has been found possible to use it as a starting point for a whole chain of discoveries. We regard this as not only entirely possible, but inevitable, with regard to this predictable process in therapy. Hence, we regard this orderly and predictable nature of nondirective therapy as one of its most distinctive and significant points of difference from other approaches. Its importance lies not only in the fact that it is a present difference, but in the fact that it points toward a sharply different future, in which scientific exploration of this known chain of events should lead to many new discoveries, developments, and applications.

The discovery of the capacity of the client

Naturally the question is raised, what is the reason for this predictability in a type of therapeutic procedure in which the therapist serves only a catalytic function? Basically the reason for the predictability of the therapeutic process lies in the discovery—and I use that word intentionally—that within the client reside constructive forces whose strength and uniformity have been either entirely unrecognized or grossly underestimated. It is the clearcut and disciplined reliance by the therapist upon those forces within the client, which seems to account for the orderliness of the therapeutic process, and its consistency from one client to the next.

I mentioned that I regarded this as a discovery. I would like to amplify that statement. We have known for centuries that catharsis and emotional release were helpful. Many new methods have been and are being developed to bring about release, but the principle is not new. Likewise, we have known since Freud's time that insight, if it is accepted and assimilated by the client, is therapeutic. The principle is not new. Likewise we have realized that revised action patterns, news ways of behaving, may come about as a result of insight. The principle is not new.

But we have not known or recognized that in most if not all individuals there exist growth forces, tendencies toward self-actualization, which may act as the sole motivation for therapy. We have not realized that under suitable psychological conditions these forces bring about emotional release in those areas and at those rates which are most beneficial to the individual. These forces drive the individual to explore his own attitudes and his relationship to reality, and to explore these areas effectively. We have not realized that the individual is capable of exploring his attitudes and feelings, including those which have been denied to consciousness, at a rate which does not cause panic, and to the depth required for comfortable adjustment. The individual is capable of discovering and perceiving, truly and spontaneously, the interrelationships between his own attitudes, and the relationship of himself to reality. The individual has the capacity and the strength to devise, quite unguided, the steps which will lead him to a more mature and more comfortable relationship to his reality. It is the gradual and increasing recognition of these capacities within the individual by the client-centered therapist that rates, I believe, the term discovery. All of these capacities I have described are released in the individual if a suitable psychological atmosphere is provided.

There has, of course, been lip service paid to the strength of the client, and the need of utilizing the urge toward independence which exists in the client. Psychiatrists, analysts, and especially social case workers have stressed this point. Yet it is clear from what is said, and even more clear from the case material cited, that this confidence is a very limited confidence. It is a confidence that the client can take over, if guided by the expert, a confidence that the client can assimilate insight if it is first given to him by the expert, can make choices providing guidance is given at crucial points. It is, in short, the same sort of attitude which the mother has toward the adolescent, that she believes in his capacity to make his own decisions and guide his own life, providing he takes the directions of which she approves.

This is very evident in the latest book on psychoanalysis by Alexander and French. Although many of the former views and practices of psychoanalysis are discarded, and the procedures are far more nearly in line with those of nondirective therapy, it is still the therapist who is definitely in control. He gives the insights, he is ready to guide at crucial points. Thus while the authors state that the aim of the therapist is to free the patient to develop his capacities, and to increase his ability to satisfy his needs in ways acceptable to himself and society; and while they speak of the basic conflict between competition and cooperation as one which the individual must settle for himself; and speak of the integration of new insight as a normal function of the ego, it is clear when they speak of procedures that they have no confidence that the client has the capacity to do any of these things. For in practice, "As soon as the therapist takes the more active role we advocate, systematic planning becomes imperative. In addition to the original decision as to the particular sort of strategy to be employed in the treatment of any case, we recommend the conscious use of various techniques in a flexible manner, shifting tactics to fit the particular needs of the moment. Among these modifications of the standard technique are: using not only the method of free association but interviews of a more direct character, manipulating the frequency of the interviews, giving directives to the patient concerning his daily life, employing interruptions of long or short duration in preparation for ending the treatment, regulating the transference relationship to meet the specific needs of the case, and making use of real-life experiences as an integral part of therapy" (1). At least this leaves no doubt as to whether it is the client's or the therapist's hour; it is clearly the latter. The capacities which the client is to develop are clearly not to be developed in the therapeutic sessions.

The client-centered therapist stands at an opposite pole, both theoretically and practically. He has learned that the constructive forces in the individual can be trusted, and that the more deeply they are relied upon, the more deeply they are released. He has come to build his procedures upon these hypotheses, which are rapidly becoming established as facts: that the client knows the areas of concern which he is ready to explore; that the client is the best judge as to the most desirable frequency of interviews; that the client can lead the way more efficiently than the therapist into deeper concerns; that the client will protect himself from panic by ceasing to explore an area which is becoming too painful; that the client can and will uncover all the repressed elements which it is necessary to uncover in order to build a comfortable adjustment; that the client can achieve for himself far truer and more sensitive and accurate insights than can possibly be given to him; that the client is capable of translating these insights into constructive behavior which weighs his own needs and desires realistically against the demands of society; that the client knows when therapy is completed and he is ready to cope with life independently. Only one condition is necessary for all these forces to be released, and that is the proper psychological atmosphere between client and therapist.

Our case records and increasingly our research bear out these statements. One might suppose that there would be a generally favorable reaction to this discovery, since it amounts in effect to tapping great reservoirs of hitherto little-used energy. Quite the contrary is true, however, in professional groups. There is no other aspect of client-centered therapy which comes under such vigorous attack. It seems to be genuinely disturbing to many professional people to entertain the thought that this client upon whom they have been exercising their professional skill actually knows more about his inner psychological self than they can possibly know, and that he possesses constructive strengths which make the constructive push by the therapist seem puny indeed by comparison. The willingness fully to accept this strength of the client, with all the reorientation of therapeutic procedure which it implies, is one of the ways in which client-centered therapy differs most sharply from other therapeutic approaches.

The client-centered nature of the therapeutic relationship

The third distinctive feature of this type of therapy is the character of the relationship between therapist and client. Unlike other therapies in which the skills of the therapist are to be exercised upon the client, in this approach the skills of the therapist are focussed upon creating a psychological atmosphere in which the client can work. If the counselor can create a relationship permeated by warmth, understanding, safety from any type of attack, no matter how trivial, and basic acceptance of the person as he is, then the client will drop his natural defensiveness and use the situation. As we have puzzled over the characteristics of a successful therapeutic relationship, we have come to feel that the sense of communication is very important. If the client feels that he is actually communicating his present attitudes, superficial, confused, or conflicted as they may be, and that his communication is understood rather than evaluated in any way, then he is freed to communicate more deeply. A relationship in which the client thus feels that he is communicating is almost certain to be fruitful.

All of this means a drastic reorganization in the counselor's thinking, particularly if he has previously utilized other opproaches. He gradually learns that the statement that the time is to be "the client's hour" means just that, and that his biggest task is to make it more and more deeply true.

Perhaps something of the characteristics of the relationship may be suggested by excerpts from a paper written by a young minister who has spent several months learning client-centered counseling procedures.

Because the client-centered, nondirective counseling approach has been rather carefully defined and clearly illustrated, it gives the *"Illusion of Simplicity."* The technique seems deceptively easy to master. Then you begin to practice. A word is wrong here and there. You don't quite reflect feeling, but reflect content instead. It is difficult to handle questions; you are tempted to interpret. Nothing seems so serious that further practice won't correct it. Perhaps you are having trouble playing two roles—that of minister and that of counselor. Bring up the question in class and the matter is solved again with a deceptive ease. But these apparently minor errors and a certain woodenness of response seem exceedingly persistent.

Only gradually does it dawn that if the technique is true it demands a feeling of warmth. You begin to feel that the attitude is the thing. Every little word is not so important if you have the correct accepting and permissive attitude toward the client. So you bear down on the permissiveness and acceptance. You *will* permiss and accept and reflect the client, if it kills you!

But you still have those troublesome questions from the client. He simply doesn't know the next step. He asks you to give him a hint, some possibilities, after all you are expected to know something, else why is he here? As a minister, you ought to have some convictions about what people should believe, how they should act. As a counselor, you should know something about removing this obstacle—you ought to have the equivalent of the surgeon's knife and use it. Then you begin to wonder. The technique is good, *but* . . . does it go *far* enough? does it really work on clients? is it *right* to leave a person helpless, when you might show him the way out?

Here it seems to me is the crucial point. "Narrow is the gate" and hard the path from here on. No one else can give satisfying answers and even the instructors seem frustrating because they appear not to be helpful in your specific case. For here is demanded of you what no other person can do or point out —and that is to rigorously scrutinize yourself and your attitudes towards others. Do you believe that all people truly have a creative potential in them? That each person is a unique individual and that he alone can work out his own individuality? Or do you really believe that some persons are of "negative value" and others are weak and must be led and taught by "wiser," "stronger" people.

You begin to see that there is nothing compartmentalized about this method of counseling. It is not just counseling, because it demands the most exhaustive, penetrating, and comprehensive consistency. In other methods you can shape tools, pick them up for use when you will. But when genuine acceptance and permissiveness are your tools it requires nothing less than the whole complete personality. And to grow oneself is the most demanding of all.

He goes on to discuss the notion that the counselor must be restrained and "self-denying." He concludes that this is a mistaken notion.

Instead of demanding less of the counselor's personality in the situation, client-centered counseling in some ways demands more. It demands discipline, not restraint. It calls for the utmost in sensitivity, appreciative awareness, channeled and disciplined. It demands that the counselor put all he has of these precious qualities into the situation, but in a disciplined, refined manner. It is restraint only in the sense that the counselor does not express himself in certain areas that he may use himself in others.

Even this is deceptive, however. It is not so much restraint in any area as it is a focusing, sensitizing one's energies and personality in the direction of an appreciative and understanding attitude.

As time has gone by we have come to put increasing stress upon the "client-centeredness" of the relationship, because it is more effective the more completely the counselor concentrates upon trying to understand the client *as the client seems to himself*. As I look back upon some of our earlier published cases—the case of Herbert Bryan in my book, or Snyder's case of Mr. M.—I realize that we have gradually dropped the vestiges of subtle directiveness which are all too evident in those cases. We have come to recognize that if we can provide understanding of the way the client seems to himself at this moment, he can do the rest. The therapist must lay aside his preoccupation with diagnosis and his diagnostic shrewdness, must discard his tendency to make professional evaluations, must cease his endeavors to formulate an accurate prognosis, must give up the temptation subtly to guide the individual, and must concentrate on one purpose only; that of providing deep under-standing and acceptance of the attitudes consciously held at this moment by the client as he explores step by step into the dangerous areas which he has been denying to consciousness.

I trust it is evident from this description that this type of relationship can exist only if the counselor is deeply and genuinely able to adopt these attitudes. Client-centered counseling, if it is to be effective, cannot be a trick or a tool. It is not a subtle way of guiding the client while pretending to let him guide himself. To be effective, it must be genuine. It is this sensitive and sincere "client-centeredness" in the therapeutic relationship that I regard as the third characteristic of nondirective therapy which sets it distinctively apart from other approaches.

Some implications

Although the client-centered approach had its origin purely within the limits of the psychological clinic, it is proving to have implications, often of a startling nature, for very diverse fields of effort. I should like to suggest a few of these present and potential implications.

In the field of psychotherapy itself, it leads to conclusions that seem distinctly heretical. It appears evident that training and practice in therapy should probably precede training in the field of diagnosis. Diagnostic knowledge and skill is not necessary for good therapy, a statement which sounds like blasphemy to many, and if the professional worker, whether psychiatrist, psychologist or caseworker, received training in therapy first he would learn psychological dynamics in a truly dynamic fashion, and would acquire a professional humility and willingness to learn from his client which is today all too rare.

The viewpoint appears to have implications for medicine. It has fascinated me to observe that when a prominent allergist began to use client-centered therapy for the treatment of non-specific allergies, he found not only very good therapeutic results, but the experience began to affect his whole medical practice. It has gradually meant the reorganization of his office procedure. He has given his nurses a new type of training in understanding the patient. He has decided to have all medical histories taken by a nonmedical person trained in nondirective techniques, in order to get a true picture of the client's feelings and attitudes toward himself and his health, uncluttered by the bias and diagnostic evaluation which is almost inevitable when a medical person takes the history and unintentionally distorts the material by his premature judgments. He has found these histories much more helpful to the physicians than those taken by physicians.

The client-centered viewpoint has already been shown to have significant implications for the field of survey interviewing and public opinion study. Use of such techniques by Likert, Lazarsfeld, and others has meant the elimination of much of the factor of bias in such studies.

This approach has also, we believe, deep implications for the handling of social and group conflicts, as I have pointed out in another paper (9). Our work in applying a client-centered viewpoint to group therapy situations, while still in its early stages, leads us to feel that a significant clue to the constructive solution of interpersonal and intercultural frictions in the group may be in our hands. Application of these procedures to staff groups, to inter-racial groups, to groups with personal problems and tensions, is under way.

In the field of education, too, the client-centered approach is finding significant application. The work of Cantor, a description of which will soon be published, is outstanding in this connection, but a number of teachers are finding that these methods, designed for therapy, produce a new type of educational process, an independent learning which is highly desirable, and even a reorientation of individual direction which is very similar to the results of individual or group therapy.

Even in the realm of our philosophical orientation, the client-centered approach has its deep implications. I should like to indicate this by quoting briefly from a previous paper.

As we examine and try to evaluate our clinical experience with client-centered therapy, the phenomenon of the reorganization of attitudes and the redirection of behavior by the individual assumes greater and greater importance. This phenomenon seems to find inadequate explanation in terms of the determinism which is the predominant philosophical background of most psychological work. The capacity of the individual to reorganize his attitudes and behavior in ways not determined by external factors nor by previous elements in his own experience, but determined by his own insight into those factors, is an impressive capacity. It involves a basic spontaneity which we have been loath to admit into our scientific thinking.

The clinical experience could be summarized by saying that the behavior of the human organism may be determined by the influences to which it has been exposed, *but it may also be determined by the creative and integrative insight of the organism itself.* This ability of the person to discover new meaning in the forces which impinge upon him and in the past experiences which have been controlling him, and the ability to alter consciously his behavior in the light of this new meaning, has a profound significance for our thinking which has not been fully realized. We need to revise the philosophical basis of our work to a point where it can admit that forces exist within the individual which can exercise a spontaneous and significant influence upon behavior which is not predictable through knowledge of prior influences and conditionings. The forces released through a catalytic process of therapy are not adequately accounted for by a knowledge of the individual's previous conditionings, but only if we grant the presence of a spontaneous force within the organism which has the capacity of integration and redirection. This capacity for volitional control is a force which we must take into account in any psychological equation (9).

So we find an approach which began merely as a way of dealing with problems of human maladjustment forcing us into a revaluation of our basic philosophical concepts.

Summary

I hope that throughout this paper I have managed to convey what is my own conviction, that what we now know or think we know about a client-centered approach is only a beginning, only the opening of a door beyond which we are beginning to see some very challenging roads, some fields rich with opportunity. It is the facts of our clinical and research experience which keep pointing forward into new and exciting possibilities. Yet whatever the future may hold, it appears already clear that we are dealing with materials of a new and significant nature, which demand the most openminded and thorough exploration. If our present formulations of those facts are correct, then we would say that some important elements already stand out; that certain basic attitudes and skills can create a psychological atmosphere which releases, frees, and utilizes deep strengths in the client; that these strengths and capacities are more sensitive and more rugged than hitherto supposed; and that they are released in an orderly and predictable process which may prove as significant a basic fact in social science as some of the laws and predictable processes in the physical sciences.

Selected references

1. Alexander, F., and French, T. *Psychoanalytic Therapy.* New York: Ronald Press, 1946.
2. Allen, F. *Psychotherapy with Children.* New York: Norton, 1942.
3. Cantor, N. *Employee Counseling.* New York: McGraw-Hill Book Company.
4. Cantor, N. The Dynamics of Learning. (unpublished mss.) University of Buffalo, 1943.
5. Curran, C. A. *Personality Factors in Counseling.* New York: Grune and Stratton, 1945.
6. Rank, O. *Will Therapy.* New York: Alfred A. Knopf, 1936.

7. Rogers, C. R. "Counselling," *Review of Educational Research*, April 1945 (Vol. 15), pp. 155–163.

8. Rogers, C. R. *Counseling and Psychotherapy*. New York: Houghton Mifflin Co., 1942.

9. Rogers, C. R. *The implications of nondirective therapy for the handling of social conflicts*. Paper given to a seminar of the Bureau of Intercultural Education, New York City, Feb. 18, 1946.

10. Rogers, C. R., and Wallen, J. L. *Counseling with Returned Servicemen*. New York: McGraw-Hill, 1946.

11. Snyder, W. U. "An Investigation of the Nature of Non-Directive Psychotherapy," *Journal of General Psychology*. Vol. 33, 1945. pp. 193–223.

12. Taft, J. *The Dynamics of Therapy in a Controlled Relationship*. New York: Macmillan, 1933.

Since ancient times the meaning of dreams has been a puzzle to man. One still finds very ancient meanings in vogue. One such view is that the dream is an account of the things which happen to the person's soul or mind when it has left his body during sleep. Another meaning is that dreams tell the future. Both of these are rather naïve or mystical points of view. A third, modern, and much less naïve, point of view is that dreams can be considered as a special kind of thought. They are *special* kinds of thought because the symbols used in dreams have unique and special meanings, not usually the same meanings as in the waking state. If the dream symbols have special meanings, dreams must be interpreted, and it is necessary to find the special meanings of the symbols.

Many systems have been proposed. Freud's system is one such. It is a tremendous advance over the older "dream books" because it recognizes the dream symbol as a disguised expression of unconscious strivings. Freud also proposed a system of universal dream symbols which may have been taken too literally. The author of the present article proposes that, in contrast with universal symbolism, the meaning of a dream symbol for a particular individual can best be understood in terms of the particular strivings the person is trying to represent with the symbol. This may be discovered by an analysis of both the internal evidence in the dream itself and the objective life-situation of the individual.

Points to guide your study

1. Can you think of specific ways in which the interpretation of dream symbolism might be important in psychotherapy?

2. "Cognitive" is a word which is usually used to refer to conscious thought processes. Why is this article entitled "A Cognitive Theory of Dream Symbols"?

22. A COGNITIVE THEORY OF DREAM SYMBOLS

Calvin S. Hall, Miami, Fla.*

It is not my intention in this article to discuss theories of symbolism in general, nor even to review the history of thought regarding symbols in dreams. Rather I have set for myself the more modest task of proposing an alternative theory for one which now occupies the center of the stage whenever dreams are mentioned. I refer, of couse, to Freud's theory of dream symbolism.

* C. S. Hall. A cognitive theory of dream symbols. *J. gen. Psychol.*, 1953, **48**, 169–186. Copyright 1953 by the Journal Press. Reprinted here with permission from the author and the Journal Press.

In order to gain some perspective on the psychoanalytic theory of dream symbols, let us consider briefly the origin and history of dream books, a task that H. B. Weiss has made lighter by his interesting and informative article on them (12). We learn from this article that the first dream book was written by an Italian physician, Artemidorus, who lived in the second century A.D. Artemidorus collected reports of dreams in his travels, through correspondence, and by the purchase of manuscripts. From these sources, he compiled a work of five volumes under the title *Oneirocritics*, a word which means the art of interpreting dreams. Following the invention of the printing press in the fifteenth century, Artemidorus's work was widely published, going through numerous editions in various languages. *Oneirocritics* is the Adam of all dream books, past and present. The first American dream book, *The Book of Knowledge*, was published in Boston in 1767. It was followed by a spate of others so that today there is a wide selection available to those who seek help in interpreting their dreams.

A dream book is actually a special type of dictionary, in which the entries are words or phrases descriptive of dream items followed by their meanings; that is, symbols and referents. In a typical dream book, the referent is usually either "good fortune" or "bad fortune," since the dream book exploits the notion that dreams are prophetic and that what most people want to know is what the future holds for them. Dream books also rest on the assumptions that dreams are symbolic and that the symbols of dreams have universal significance. For example, we read in Artemidorus that to dream of *eating cheese* signifies profit and gain to the dreamer. It is not stated that sometimes this is its meaning, or that it depends upon the state of the dreamer, or upon the context in which this activity appears. The meaning of eating cheese in dreams is *univocal*, *universal*, and *timeless*. It is this feature of universal symbol-referent connections that accounts for the popularity of dream books. Since they do not make qualifications and exceptions which would require the use of judgment and discrimination, anyone can decode dreams and foretell the future if he has a dream book handy.

Freud borrowed two of the dream books assumptions, dream symbols and the universality of *some* dream symbols, and rejected the third, the prophetic character of dreams. Why are there symbols in dreams? Freud answered that symbols appear in dreams because the referents for which the symbols are surrogates are distasteful to the censor. The dream-work can smuggle reprehensible things into a dream by transforming them into innocuous symbols. One dreams of climbing a tree instead of masturbating because climbing trees (the symbol) is condoned and masturbating (the referent) is condemned. In short, symbols are disguises for referents.[1]

In order to determine what referents are commonly symbolized, a search of the psychoanalytic literature was made by the writer and his students. Although not exhaustive, our search turned up 709 symbols. The two most popular referents are *penis* for which there are 102 symbols, and *vagina* for which there are 95 symbols. Other referents that have a large number of symbols are *death* (62 symbols), *coitus* (55 symbols), *masturbation* (25 symbols), *mother* (15 symbols), *father* (14 symbols), *breasts* (13 symbols), and *castration* (12 symbols). Be it noted, with the possible exception of *death*, all of the referents are concrete things, people, or activities, and similarly all of the symbols, as *gun* for *penis*, *bag* for *vagina*, *ploughing* for *coitus*, *playing the piano* for *masturbating*, *queen* for *mother*, *king* for *father*, *apple* for *breast*, etc., are concrete things, people, or activities. In short, something concrete, the symbol, is substituted for something else concrete, the referent.

If one adopts Freud's theory of symbolism, an essential feature of dream interpretation consists of finding a referent for each symbol. Since the meaning of numerous symbols has been set forth by psychoanalysts it is fairly simple for anyone to decode his dreams by using a modern psychoanalytic dream book, for instance, Gutheil's *Language of the Dream* (3). The fol-

---

[1] This, of course, is not all that Freud had to say about symbolism. He felt that the subject went beyond dreams. Symbolism is an archaic form of expression, a primordial language which is found in myths and fairy tales, in popular sayings and songs, in colloquialisms and in poetry. Even if there were no censorship in dreams, dreams would be rendered incomprehensible by the use of symbols. The fact remains, however, that Freud believed that symbolism served the purpose of disguise. He writes: "Symbolism, then, is a second and independent factor in dream distortion existing side by side with the censorship. But the conclusion is obvious that it suits the censorship to make use of symbolism, in that both serve the same purpose: that of making the dream strange and incomprehensible" (2, p. 150). "Everything points to the same conclusion, namely, that we need not assume that any special symbolizing activity of the psyche is operative in dream-formation; that on the contrary, the dream makes use of such symbolizations as are to be found ready-made in unconscious thinking, since these, by reason of their ease of representation, and for the most part by reason of their being exempt from the censorship, satisfy more effectively the requirements of dream-formation" (1, p. 368). "Dreams employ this symbolism to give a disguised representation to their latent thoughts" (1, p. 370). Quotations from Freud could be multiplied to show that for him the most important function of symbols in dreams is that of disguise.

lowing dream reported by a young woman can be readily deciphered.

I was in a big room talking to one of my friends. She said she was going riding and I decided to join her. I waited for her to come back for me; when she did return, she said she had already ploughed the field and that the horse was upstairs. I said that I'd probably have trouble getting it down the stairs, and she told me one of the men had helped her down. However, I decided against riding.

Later we were all sitting around in the room and I looked up and saw a friend of mine who was in New Orleans. He came over and we were talking until everyone was handed an enormous gun and we all started shooting out of the windows. I recall loading and reloading the gun.

In psychoanalytic dream language this dream is a versatile portrayal of sexuality. *Riding, ploughing a field, climbing stairs*, and *shooting* symbolize masturbation or coitus. *Gun, horse*, and *plough* are phallic symbols, room and window are vaginal symbols. *Being handed an enormous gun* = being given a penis. Apparently the dreamer's wish to be a man.

According to Freud, how does a symbol become a symbol? How does it happen that one object or activity becomes a stand-in for another object or activity. Freud draws upon the laws of association, particularly the law of resemblance, to explain the formation of symbol-referent connections. Some of the ways in which association by resemblance operates are as follows:

1. Association by resemblance in shape. All circular objects and containers = vagina, and all oblong objects = penis.

2. Association by resemblance in function. All objects that are capable of extruding something, e.g., gun, fountain pen, bottle = penis.

3. Association by resemblance in action. Any act that separates a part from a whole, e.g., beheading, losing a tooth, an arm or a leg, having a wheel come off an automobile = castration. By the same token, dancing, climbing stairs, riding horseback, going up and down in an elevator = coitus.

4. Association by resemblance in color. Chocolate = feces, yellow = urine, milky substance = semen.

5. Association by resemblance in value. Gold = feces, jewelry = female genitals.

6. Association by resemblance in number. Three = penis and testicles.

7. Association by resemblance in sound. The blaring of a trumpet or bugle or the sound of a wind instrument = flatulence.

8. Association by resemblance in quality. Wild animal = sexual passion, horse = virility.

9. Association by resemblance in personal quality. Policeman, army officer, teacher = father, nurse = mother.

10. Association by resemblance in physical position. Basement = the unconscious mind.

11. Association by resemblance in status. King = father, queen = mother.

In addition to association by resemblance, there are several other ways in which two items may become paired as symbol and referent.

12. Association by contiguity. Church = virtue, night club = sensuality, bathtub = cleanliness.

13. Association of part with whole. A specific accident = difficulties of life, a school test = a test of fitness for life.

14. Association by contrast. Crowd = being alone, clothed = naked, to die = to live. Freud wrote that "inversion or transformation into the opposite is one of the most favored and most versatile methods of representation which the dream-work has at its disposal" (1, p. 352), thereby acknowledging one of the oldest maxims of dream lore "that dreams go by contraries."

My skepticism regarding Freud's theory of symbols-as-disguises began with a simple question for which I could find no satisfactory answer within the framework of Freud's theory. Having read hundreds of dream series in the past few years, I noticed that within the same series outspoken dreams occurred along with "symbolized" dreams. It is fairly common for one to dream of sexual activities in the frankest terms one night and in disguised terms the next night. Open incest dreams alternate with camouflaged incest dreams. Parricide and fratricide are sometimes overt, sometimes concealed. I wondered what was the sense of preparing an elaborate deception in one dream when it was discarded in a subsequent dream. To this question I could not find a convincing answer.

Another flaw in the Freudian theory appeared. In collecting dreams, I often ask a person to give his interpretation of the reported dream. I found that many people have real talent for dream interpretation although some of these have little or no information about Freudian symbolism. Why should one bother to deceive oneself by dreaming in symbols when they can be translated so readily by the dreamer himself? Again I could not find a plausible answer within the context of the Freudian formulation.

While thinking about the lay person's ability to translate his dreams, it occurred to me that people have been using a consciously contrived form of symbolism in their daily speech for centuries. It is called slang. Although there are slang expressions for many things, much of it is sexual in character. In order to get evidence concerning the relation of slang to dream symbols, I went through Partridge's A *Dictionary of Slang and Unconventional English* (8) noting every slang expression for penis, vagina, and coitus. There were 200 expressions for penis, 330 for vagina and 212 for coitus. The results of this study will be published elsewhere; suffice it to say here that many of the dream symbols for the sex organs and for sexual intercourse are identical with those found in Partridge. Many of these slang words have been in the English language for centuries.

If slang and dream symbols coincide as closely as they do and if the referents of slang are as well known as they are, how can these same expressions (or visualizations of them) function effectively as disguises in dreams? It would be absurd for a dreamer to deceive himself with symbols during sleep when these same symbols are used so self-consciously during waking life. This is not the place to discuss the motives for the development of slang; at another time we intend to show that the same principles govern slang formation as govern dream symbol formation. Both spring from man's disposition to express his ideas in concrete form; slang uses figures of speech and dreams use images.

These explorations in the world of slang led me to consider the psychological significance of figures of speech or *tropes*, of which four principal varieties have been delineated: (*a*) *synecdoche*, (*b*) *metonymy*, (*c*) *metaphor*, and (*d*) *irony*. Synecdoche is a figure of speech in which a part is used for a whole, a whole for a part, the cause for the effect, the effect for the cause, the name of the material for the thing made, the species for the genus and so on. Metonymy is a figure in which the name of one thing is changed for that of another to which it is related by association and close relationship. A metaphor is a figure which consists in the transference to one object of an attribute or name which strictly and literally is not applicable to it, but only figuratively and by analogy. Irony is a figure whose intended implication is just the opposite of that which is stated. One associates figures of speech with poetry, although they are used more or less widely in all forms of writing and speaking. Modern literary criticism and research have become aware of the importance of trope analysis in shedding light upon the intrinsic meaning of a literary creation *and* upon the personality dynamics of the creator. Noteworthy among those who have analyzed writings and writers by paying attention to figures of speech is Caroline Spurgeon, whose exegesis of Shakespeare is a remarkable *tour de force* (11) although wanting in the insights that dynamic psychology might have provided. Another example of this approach is found in Mark Schorer's *Fiction and the "Matrix of Analogy"* (10) in which he scrutinizes Jane Austen, Emily Bronte, and George Eliot through their metaphors.

The relation of tropes to slang and of both to dream symbols is one of psychological identity. Slang expressions are figures of speech; they are an idiom by which the person tries to communicate his conceptions. It is the thesis of this paper that dream symbols belong to the same idiom; a dream symbol or any symbol, for that matter, reveals thought rather than conceals it.

Before developing this thesis, two other flaws in Freud's theory of dream symbols will be mentioned. We have seen that a multitude of symbols can stand for the same referent. Why is it necessary to have so many disguises for the genitals, for sexual intercourse, and for masturbation? Psychoanalysis has not given this question proper attention.[2] If one hypothesizes that dream symbols are the embodiments of conceptions, then the reason for the multiplicity of symbols for a single referent becomes clear. People have many different conceptions of the same object; thus they need a versatile idiom for conveying the precise shade of meaning for each idea.

Finally, a critique of Freud's position regarding dream symbols should take note of an assumption that is implicit in his theory, namely, that the mind works in a very complex manner during sleep. To assert that part of the work done by the mind in forming a dream consists of transforming referents into symbols for the purpose of veiling the referents is to ascribe to the sleeping mind a heavier responsibility than seems warranted. Since we usually think of sleep as a period of reduced mental activity, would it not be better to formulate a theory of dream symbolism that makes symbolizing dependent upon similar processes?

These questions prompted me to reexamine the whole structure of Freud's theory of dreams. Upon undertaking this task I discovered that Freud had proposed two reasons why symbols appear in dreams, one is the necessity to smuggle contraband psychic material past the border separating the unconscious from the conscious and the other is what Freud called *regard for representability*. The latter formulation states that in order for such abstract and impalpable mental contents as thoughts, feelings, attitudes, and impulses to appear in dreams, they must be

[2] Freud did suggest an answer in the following passage. "Wherever he has the choice of several symbols for the representation of a dream-content, he will decide in favor of that symbol which is in addition objectively related to his other thought-material; that is to say, he will employ an individual motivation besides the typically valid one" (1, p. 370). Had Freud developed the thought of this passage, he might have come to the conclusion that we have reached, namely, that a particular symbol is chosen because it expresses better than any other symbol would the precise conception in the mind of the person.

converted into sensible, palpable forms. These forms are usually pictorial in character, so that it may be said that the pictures of a dream are symbols of mental states. For example, conscience may be symbolized by a church, chastity by a lily, the sex impulse by fire, feelings of inferiority by nudity, and remembering the past by walking through a series of rooms.[3]

When one compares Freud's two hypotheses regarding the function of dream symbols, it is evident that they are diametrically opposed to one another. In one, a symbol conceals the referent, in the other, a symbol reveals the referent. Preferring the simplicity of a single hypothesis to the complexity of two separate and incompatible hypotheses, I decided to explore the possibility of abandoning the disguise theory and let *regard for representability* carry the whole burden of explaining dream symbols.

This enterprise led to the formulation of a cognitive theory of dreams which is presented in another paper (5). In that paper, I set forth the view that a dream is a perceptible embodiment of a dreamer's conceptions (ideas). Dreaming is pictorialized thinking; the conceptual is made perceptual. I now intend to show how this view leads directly to the formulation of a theory of dream symbols. Both theories represent extensions of Freud's concept of *regard for representability*.

A dream symbol is an image, usually a visual image, of an object, activity, or scene; the referent for the symbol is a conception. The function of the symbol is to express as clearly as possible the particular conception that the dreamer has in mind. For example, a dreamer who conceives of his mother as a nurturant person may represent her in a dream as a cow. Or a young woman who conceives of sexuality as a powerful, alien, and criminal force which she is unable to control might have the following dream, as one of our subjects did.

> I was the warden at a very inefficient prison for criminals. All at once the gates to the prison opened and all of the criminals tried to escape. They tried to beat me up and trample on me and I was left standing there completely helpless.

A young man conceiving of his phallus as a dangerous weapon might picture it as a gun or sword in his dreams. A woman who thought that her marriage was going on the rocks dreamed that she was looking for her wedding dress and

when she found it, it was dirty and torn. In these examples, the visualization is an expression of, not a disguise for, an idea.

An object, activity, or scene is selected to serve as a symbol because the dreamer's conception of the object, activity, or scene is congruent with his conception of the *referent object*.[4] A nurturant mother appears as a cow because the dreamer conceives of cows as nurturant animals. If the dreamer thought cows were dangerous, a cow could not serve as a mother-symbol unless at the same time he conceived of his mother as dangerous. Occasionally, a change of conceptions can be detected as in the following dream.

> I dreamed that an old man was coming towards me with a gun. I become frightened and put my glasses on to see him better. Then I noticed that he was not holding a gun but a bottle of whisky.

The young woman's first conception of the man is that he is dangerous, but this idea gives way to the contradictory one that he is harmless. The change in conceptions is symbolized by the act of putting on her glasses; the better view follows this act.

In some cases, a symbol may represent several ideas concurrently. In psychoanalytic writings, such a symbol is said to be *over-determined*. This term is not a happy choice since no phenomenon is ever *over*-determined; it is always *just* determined, never too little or too much. I prefer to call such symbols *condensed*. The moon, for example, may be thought of as a condensed symbol for woman. The monthly phases of the moon resemble the menstrual cycle, a resemblance that has support from etymology since the words *moon* and *menses* are derived from the same Latin word. The filling out of the moon from new to full simulates the rounding out of the woman during pregnancy. The moon is inferior to the sun, a male symbol. The moon is changeable like a fickle woman while the sun is constant. The moon sheds a weak light, which embodies the idea of female frailty. The moon controls the ebb and flow of the tide, which is another likeness to the female rhythm. Rhythm, change, fruitfulness, weakness, and submissiveness, all of which are conventional conceptions of the female are compressed into a single visible object. As Susanne Langer observes, the choice of moon as a symbol of woman is determined by the many ways in which lunar characteristics are congruent with popular conceptions of the

---

[3] Had Freud himself not commented upon regard for representability we might still have deduced it from our collection of symbol-referent pairs. It is obvious that some of the referents are objects which might be represented directly were it not for censorship while others are mental states, which require pictorialization if they are to appear as dream images.

[4] The term *referent* will be used to denote the dreamer's conception and the term *referent object* will be used to denote the object, person, or activity about which the dreamer has a conception. Thus, the referent object of cow is mother, and the referent is the conception of the mother as a nurturant person.

female. Langer reminds us that the conceptions develop first, followed by the selection of a symbol which will best represent all of the conceptions.[5]

When one analyzes a series of dreams from a person, various symbols for the same referent object may be found. As we have seen, the male member may be symbolized in no less than 102 different ways. According to our theory of dream symbols, since the referent is not an object, person, or activity but a conception, the 102 different phallic symbols represent 102 different ways of conceiving of the male genitals.[6] Thus in a dream series, one may find multiple conceptions of the same phenomenon because the dreamer conceives of it in diverse ways at different times. A father may be represented as a teacher, a policeman, a king, and an army officer in order to depict the multiple conceptions of a wise, guiding father, a punitive father, an exalted, remote father and a disciplining father.

To recapitulate, regard for representability explains why symbols are found in dreams. Dream symbols are visible representations of conceptions. In order for an object, activity, or scene to serve as a symbol, it is necessary that the dreamer's conception of that object, activity, or scene be identical with his conception of the referent object.

It is now time to say how we would limit the use of the term, *dream symbol*. Since dream images *are* images and not perceptions of reality, it could be argued that all images are symbols. One might even go further and assert that everything mental, whether perceptions, memories, or images, is really symbolic since the mental is not the real world but only a representation of the real world. We prefer, however, to restrict the definition of a dream symbol to an image that does not embody the referent object directly. If one dreams of his mother, the image of the mother in the dream does not qualify as a dream symbol. If one dreams of a cow and the image of the cow stands for the mother, then the cow is said to be a dream symbol. According to this view, symbolizing in dreams consists of transforming one object (the referent object) into another object (the symbol), and this trans-

[5] My great intellectual debt to Mrs. Langer will be apparent to those who have read her book, *Philosophy in a New Key* (7).

[6] Although no two symbols probably express exactly the same idea, subtle nuances may be ignored for the sake of reducing the many particulars to a relatively few general classes. For example, we found that a large number of the 200 slang expressions for penis could be categorized under the following headings: (1) projecting or protruding objects, (2) insertive objects, (3) extruding objects, (4) suspended objects, (5) burrowing objects or animals, (6) oblong objects, (7) tools, (8) weapons, and (9) body extremities.

formation is made in order to convey the dreamer's conception of the referent object. *Cow* is substituted for *mother* because the dreamer's conception of his mother is that of a cow-like person, i.e., one who is nurturant. Similarly *gun* symbolized the dreamer's conception of the phallus as a dangerous, powerful weapon. Slang and metaphor may be explained in like manner; they are used to convey one's conceptions of referent objects. If one speaks of sexual intercourse as *grinding one's tool*, it is clear that the speaker conceives of coitus as a mechanical operation performed by a mechanical tool, the penis. Quite different but no less revealing conceptions of intercourse are conveyed by the slang expressions *stab in the thigh, playing at horses and mares*, and *doing the naughty*.

Symbols raise hob with dream interpretation since one must not only translate symbols into referent objects, e.g., *cow* into *mother*, *gun* into *penis, playing the piano* into *masturbating*, but one must also discover the dreamer's conception of the symbol. If one dreamed only of referent objects it would be relatively simple to discover the dreamer's conceptions of these objects by observing the context in which they appear. That is, if one dreamed of his mother performing nurturant acts it would be apparent that he conceived of his mother as a nurturant person. If she appears as a cow it is necessary to decipher cow into mother and then decide upon the dreamer's conception of cows in order to determine his conception of mother.

There are several lines of evidence that tell us when it is necessary to decipher a dream and how the deciphering should proceed. This evidence is of two kinds, internal and external. Internal evidence is that which is found in the dream itself or which is furnished by other dreams of the same dreamer. External evidence is secured from information external to the dream.

The following dream reported by a young woman illustrates the way in which a symbol is detected from internal evidence.

I was riding a horse with a saddle and everything was fine. All of a sudden the saddle and reins fell off except for one rein. The horse was a large, powerful horse. The horse told me that he was going to try and throw me off. I told him that I would stay on no matter what happened. He kicked and ran between trees as fast as he could. I stayed on him and then woke up.

The presence of a symbol is suggested by the "talking horse." One may converse with a horse, but save in fairy tales horses do not talk back; only other humans do that. Accordingly, we feel that it is justified to translate *horse* into *human*. Since the horse is referred to by the masculine pronoun, it is assumed to be a male. The description of the horse as large and powerful suggests that the male is an adult. The identity of the man, whether father, brother, boy friend, or someone else cannot be determined from the dream. It is possible however to interpret the dream as one that reveals the girl's conception of her relationship with an adult male.

A second kind of internal evidence is that which is obtained from other dreams of a series. For example, if other dreams of the girl who had the "talking horse" dream disclosed that she was having a conflict over her relationship with her father, that she felt he was trying to get rid of her, this knowledge would support the equation, horse = father. Then the looks and actions of the horse would divulge the dreamer's conception of her father.

This second line of internal evidence may be illustrated by the dream of a young married woman. She dreamed that it was her first wedding anniversary and that they had planned to reenact the ceremony. She could not find her wedding gown and searched for it frantically.

Finally when I found the gown it was dirty and torn. With tears of disappointment in my eyes I snatched up the gown and hurried to the church. Upon my arrival my husband inquired why I had brought the gown with me. I was confused and bewildered and felt strange and alone.

A literal interpretation of this dream might be that the dreamer is unhappy because her dress is dirty and torn and because her husband asks her why she has brought it to the church. Suppose we assume, however, that the state of the wedding dress symbolizes the dreamer's conception of her marriage, and muster what evidence we can to support this assumption. It might be argued that her emotional reactions are out of proportion to the stimuli of a dirty wedding dress and a husband's question, that the intense feelings which these conditions produce are appropriate to something more vital, such as an unhappy marriage. If the reader remains unconvinced by the evidence from a single dream, other dreams of this young woman can be summoned to give their testimony. Here are the themes of some of them.

1. She dreams about a recently married girl who is getting a divorce.

2. She dreams that she is riding on a streetcar with her husband through a poor section of the city.

3. She dreams that she is waiting for her husband but he does not appear. She learns that he has tuberculosis.

4. She dreams that the diamond in her engagement ring is missing.

5. She dreams that her girl friend who is getting married receives a lot of useless bric-a-brac for wedding presents.

6. She dreams that she is shopping and has to wait a long time to be served. She worries about getting home to her husband on time. She loses her way, falls on the sidewalk, and is delayed by a train.

These dreams indicate that the dreamer conceives of her marriage as an unhappy one and corroborate the hypothesis that the torn and dirty wedding dress is a concrete embodiment of this idea.

The analysis of a dream series provides, in our opinion, the best evidence for the validity of symbol translation. Since many dream series contain unsymbolized versions of the dreamer's conceptions, one may use these bareface dreams as a check on one's interpretation of dreams freighted with symbolism.[7]

External evidence as to the meaning of symbols may be secured from several sources. The traditional method is to ask a person to "free associate" to the various dream items. The free association method of deciphering dream symbols is a valuable one, but as Walter Reis has shown (9) the dream series method yields almost as clear and as complete a picture of the dreamer's personality as do dreams plus free associations. A practical drawback to free association is that it is time consuming. Although this may not be a limitation when dreams are being interpreted during therapy, it is when one is doing research on dreams. For the latter purpose, the dream series method is more feasible.

The identification and meaning of dream symbols may be determined by the "acting out" that occurs during nocturnal emission dreams. The writer has collected a number of such dreams and the outcome of an emission often proves unequivocally the meaning of the symbols occurring in the dream. The following dream reported by a young man demonstrates the equivalence of "opening a door" with "sexual intercourse."

My sister's girl friend came in the front door and smiled at me. She continued on through the living room and I arose from my chair and followed her. She walked through a hallway and into the bathroom of our home and closed the door. As I opened the door I had an emission.

Another nocturnal emission dream in the writer's collection validates the sexual significance of a number of dream symbols.

I and four or five companions of the same age got out of our car at some place that was like Mentor Park. It was winter and the place was

---

[7] For a discussion of the dream series method see the writer's paper *Diagnosing Personality by the Analysis of Dreams* (4).

abandoned. Ice was all over the ground. We walked across an open area and as we passed through some passageways we found ourselves threading our way down a sunny mountain trail looking for gold. We noticed small animals resembling pigs running around. As we got into the jungle proper which was very light and sunny we saw all sorts of wild life, lions, giraffes, pythons standing out in my mind. For safety we decided to climb trees. I first climbed a small tree but found it was not safe enough so I came down and began to climb a larger tent pole which I had not noticed before. As I did so, I had a nocturnal emission.

The outcome of a sexual ejaculation suggests that the climatic change from cold to warm, the change in setting from an icy, abandoned park to a light, sunny jungle, the searching for gold, the passageways, the entrance into the jungle, the animals, and the trees and tent pole are objective representations of the dreamer's conception of sexuality. Lacking the outcome of an emission, one might have inferred that this dream is replete with sexual symbols; with the outcome the meaning of the symbols is more firmly established.

Finally, external evidence for the meaning of dream symbols is found in such diverse material as slang, figures of speech, myths, fairy tales, the visual arts, and word origins. Since these sources have been exploited fully by psychoanalytic investigators, they will not be discussed in this paper. The writer has found them, particularly slang and etymology, a great help in recognizing and deciphering dream symbols. Although evidence secured from such sources is suggestive rather than definitive, a suggestion often puts one on the track of an inference that can be verified by other evidence.

Now let us see how the dream symbol theory as it has been formulated on the basis of *regard for representability* meets the criticisms that we made of Freud's symbol-as-disguise theory. In the first place, we criticised the latter theory because it does not account for unsymbolized dreams appearing in the midst of symbolized ones. Our theory states that symbols do not serve as masks; consequently, the presence of symbols and referent objects in the same dream series is not paradoxical. In fact, it is to be expected if one holds a cognitive theory of dreams. Since dreams are representations of conceptions, a dreamer may convey his ideas either by having a referent object behave in a certain manner or by symbolizing the referent object, in which case the symbol chosen conveys the dreamer's conception. In either case, the dream is a series of images that embody the ideas of the dreamer. In waking life, symbols and referent objects are used interchangeably to communicate ideas; it has never been suggested that the object of using symbols in waking life is to hide one's thoughts. On the contrary, symbols are often thought to be more expressive than referent objects.[8]

Since dream symbols are ways of expressing conceptions, it is not surprising that some people can decipher their own dreams. On the other hand, we would not expect all people to have this ability since many people are not aware of their conceptions. Probably a great deal of thinking, which we define as the forming of conceptions, is unconscious.

The present theory integrates dream symbols with other symbolic forms of expression, such as slang and figures of speech, and provides thereby the basis for a general theory of symbolism. The task of formulating a general theory of symbolism has already been done by Susanne Langer (7), and our special theory of dream symbolism is congruent with this larger formulation.

With respect to multiple symbols for the same referent, it is asserted here that the same referent object, not the same referent, may be symbolized in various ways. The referent is always a conception of a referent object; thus, the versatility with which a referent object may be symbolized is restricted only by the number of ideas that can be developed regarding a given object.

Finally our theory does not rest on the assumption that during sleep one performs complex mental operations such as is assumed when one sees the dream as an elaborate subterfuge. We believe that dreaming is a simple form of think-

[8] Dr. Dwight W. Miles, who read this paper in manuscript, has raised the question as to why symbols are used on some occasions and why referent objects are used on other occasions. To this important question, I would give the following answer, realizing as I do so that it leaves much to be desired. One uses symbols for reasons of economy; they are a form of shorthand, by which complex ideas can be rendered simply. A figure of speech in a poem may be freighted with meaning; indeed we find that the interpretation of a poetic phrase often requires a lengthy discourse. Much meaning can be compressed within a symbol. For example, a dreamer may represent his mother as performing nurturant acts or he may sum up his conception by saying in effect "My mother is a cow." In order to convey the full significance of the latter statement by having the mother act out the dreamer's conception might require a very lengthy dream. Why should he choose a more difficult task when a simple substitution of cow for mother does just as well? For less complex ideas, it may be just as easy to use the referent object directly. To sum up, we would say that referent objects appear in dreams when the conceptions of these objects are relatively uncomplicated and may be readily conveyed by the behavior or appearance of the referent objects, and that symbols appear in dreams when the dreamer's conceptions are complex, and are not easily portrayed by actions and appearances of referent objects.

ing in which one uses the language of pictures instead of a more abstract mode of expression. We agree with Freud that dreaming is a regressive and archaic mental process.

What takes places in a hallucinatory dream we can describe in no other way than by saying that the excitation follows a retrogressive course. It communicates itself not to the motor end of the apparatus, but to the sensory end, and finally reaches the system of perception. If we call the direction which the psychic process follows from the unconscious into the waking state *progressive*, we may then speak of the dream as having a *regressive* character (1, p. 492).

. . . *primitive* modes of operations that are suppressed during the day play a part in the formation of dreams (1, p. 527).

. . . dreaming is on the whole an act of regression to the earliest relationships of the dreamer, a resuscitation of his childhood, of the impulses which were then dominant and the modes of expression which were then available (1, p. 497).

Evidence obtained from studies of children, primitive people, psychotics, and brain injury cases suggests that their modes of thought bear some resemblance to the characteristics of dreaming.

Having introduced this paper with a discussion of dream books, let us bring it to a conclusion on the same theme. Is it possible to develop a dream book on the basis of the ideas presented in this paper? This is tantamount to asking whether there are any universal symbol-conception connections. In order to establish universality it would necessitate collecting a representative sample of dreams from the world's population. Obviously, such an undertaking would present difficulties of such magnitude that it is hardly worth considering. About the most that could be done would be to investigate whether there are *common* symbol-conception associations in a given culture or sub-culture. Since no such studies have been done, we can only speculate about what might be found. Having read thousands of dreams, it would not surprise the writer if some fairly common symbols for conceptions of referent objects exist. We have been struck by the prevalence of guns and other weapons in dreams, and how often they seem to stand for the conception of the penis as a dangerous weapon. Similarly, pocketbook or purse are fairly common dream objects and appear to symbolize a conception of the female genitals as a place where valuables are stored. It seems to me, after studying a large number of dreams of normal people, that many of the symbol-referent linkages discovered by psychoanalysis are valid.

However, I would warn against any mechanical decoding of dreams using a psychoanalytic dream book for two reasons: first, because more proof is needed of the fixed connection between symbol and referent, and second, because it is the conception in the mind of the dreamer and not the referent object that needs to be discovered.

I suspect that many condensed symbols exist in dreams, symbols that express a variety of conceptions like the example of moon mentioned earlier in this paper. It may very well be that there are types of condensed symbols which correspond to the types of ambiguities discussed by Kaplan and Kris in a penetrating article on esthetic ambiguity (6). They distinguish four main types of ambiguities: (*a*) *disjunctive*, when the separate meanings are alternatives, excluding and inhibiting one another, (*b*) *additive*, when the separate meanings are not fully exclusive but are to some extent included in each other, (*c*) *conjunctive*, when the meanings are linked, and (*d*) *integrative*, when the meanings form a unified, coherent system.

To speak the language of Gestalt, in disjunctive ambiguity there are several distinct and unconnected fields; additive ambiguity consists in a restructuring of a single field to reveal more or fewer details; in conjunctive ambiguity several fields are connected though remaining distinct; with integrative ambiguity, they are fully reconstituted—integrated, in short, into one complex meaning (6, p. 420).

If there are such types of condensed symbols in dreams, then the task of constructing a dependable and useful dream book is made more difficult.

Until more evidence is made available concerning the prevalence of fixed symbol-conception linkages in dreams, it would be well for the dream interpreter to be wary about depending upon such short-cuts as dream books provide. We believe that dream interpretation can best be accomplished by working on a series of dreams and by setting as one's goal the development of an internally and externally consistent formulation of the person's conceptions.

Summary

Freud's theory of dream symbols as disguises for reprehensible referents has been examined and found wanting in several respects: (*a*) it does not explain why censurable referents appear in some dreams in their naked form and in other dreams as symbols, (*b*) it does not explain why some people are able to decipher their own dream symbols with facility, (*c*) it does not take into account the self-conscious and intentional use of slang and figures of speech for referent objects which are symbolized in dreams, (*d*) it does not deal adequately with the question why there should be multiple symbols for the same referent object, and (*e*) it assumes that the mind during sleep is capable of performing exceedingly complex operations.

Starting from Freud's other hypothesis regarding dream symbols, that which he called *regard for representability*, the following theory of dream symbols has been formulated: (*a*) the referent of a dream symbol is the dreamer's conception (idea) of a referent object, (*b*) a dream symbol is substituted for a referent object in order to express clearly and economically the conception that the dreamer has in mind, (*c*) symbols are employed because conceptions are abstract and must be represented by visible embodiments if they (conceptions) are to appear in dreams, and (*d*) a symbol is selected because the dreamer's conception of the symbol is identical with his conception of the referent object.

Dream symbols may be decomposed into conceptions by making use of various clues: (*a*) clues that are present within the context of the dream itself, (*b*) clues from other dreams of the person, (*c*) free association, (*d*) acting out as exemplified by dreams that terminate in nocturnal emissions, and (*e*) evidence from slang, figures of speech, myths, fairy tales, etymology, and the visual arts.

The theory presented in this paper has been called a *cognitive* theory of dream symbols because it assumes that the process of symbolizing is a function of the cognitive system of the ego.

References

1. Freud, S. The Basic Writings of Sigmund Freud. New York: Modern Library, 1938.
2. ———. A General Introduction to Psychoanalysis. Garden City: Garden City Publishing, 1948.
3. Gutheil, E. A. The Language of the Dream. New York: Macmillan, 1939.
4. Hall, C. S. Diagnosing personality by the analysis of dreams. *J. Abn. & Soc. Psychol.*, 1947, **42**, 68–79.
5. ———. A cognitive theory of dreams. *J. Gen. Psychol.* (in press).
6. Kaplan, A., and Kris, E. Esthetic ambiguity. *Phil. & phenomenol. Res.*, 1948, 8, 415–435.
7. Langer, S. K. Philosophy in a New Key. New York: Penguin Books, 1948.
8. Partridge, E. A Dictionary of Slang and Unconventional English. (Third edition.) London: Routledge & Kegan Paul, 1949.
9. Reis, W. A comparison of personality variables derived from dream series with and without free associations. (Unpublished Ph.D. thesis on file at Western Reserve University Library, 1951.)
10. Schorer, M. Fiction and the "matrix of analogy." *Kenyon Rev.*, 1949, **11**, 539–560.
11. Spurgeon, C. Shakespeare's Imagery and What It Tells Us. New York: Macmillan, 1935.
12. Weiss, H. B. Oneirocritica Americana. *Bull., N. Y. Publ. Libr.*, 1944, **48**, 519–541.

CHAPTER SEVEN
Principles of learning

FACTORS IN LEARNING

This is a classic statement from William James's *Principles of Psychology* on the importance of habit. The older psychologists, being philosophers themselves or at least being very close to philosophy, were much more concerned with ethical questions than are present-day psychologists. James's interest in the training of character stems from this.

23. THE PRINCIPLES OF PSYCHOLOGY
*William James**

This brings us by a very natural transition to the *ethical implications of the law of habit.* They are numerous and momentous. Dr. Carpenter, from whose "Mental Physiology" we have quoted, has so prominently enforced the principle that our organs grow to the way in which they have been exercised, and dwelt upon its consequences, that his book almost deserves to be called a work of edification, on this account alone. We need make no apology, then, for tracing a few of these consequences ourselves:

"Habit a second nature! Habit is ten times nature," the Duke of Wellington is said to have exclaimed; and the degree to which this is true no one can probably appreciate as well as one who is a veteran soldier himself. The daily drill and the years of discipline end by fashioning a man completely over again, as to most of the possibilities of his conduct.

There is a story, which is credible enough, though it may not be true, of a practical joker, who, seeing a discharged veteran carrying home his dinner, suddenly called out, "Attention!" whereupon the man instantly brought his hands down, and lost his mutton and potatoes in the gutter. The drill had been thorough, and its effects had become embodied in the man's nervous structure.[1]

Riderless cavalry-horses, at many a battle, have been seen to come together and go through their customary evolutions at the sound of the bugle-call. Most trained domestic animals, dogs and oxen, and omnibus- and carhorses, seem to be machines almost pure and simple, undoubtingly, unhesitatingly doing from minute to minute the duties they have been taught, and giving no sign that the possibility of alternative ever suggests itself to their mind. Men grown old in prison have asked to be readmitted after being once set free. In a railroad accident to a travelling menagerie in the United States some time in 1884, a tiger, whose cage had broken open, is said to have emerged, but presently crept back again, as if too much bewildered by his new responsibilities, so that he was without difficulty secured.

Habit is thus the enormous fly-wheel of society, its most precious conservative agent. It alone is what keeps us all within the bounds of ordinance, and saves the children of fortune from the envious uprisings of the poor. It alone prevents the hardest and most repulsive walks of life from being deserted by those brought up to tread therein. It keeps the fisherman and the deck-hand at sea through the winter; it holds the miner in his darkness, and nails the countryman to his log-cabin and his lonely farm through all the months of snow; it protects us from invasion by the natives of the desert and the frozen zone. It dooms us all to fight out the battle of life upon the lines of our nurture or our early choice, and to make the best of a pursuit that disagrees, because there is no other for which we are fitted, and it is too late to begin again. It keeps different social strata from mixing. Already at the age of twenty-five you see the professional mannerism settling down on the young commercial traveler, on the young doctor, on the young minister, on the young counsellor-at-law. You see the little lines of cleavage running

* William James. *The principles of psychology.* vol. I. New York: Holt, 1890. Copyright 1890 by Henry Holt and Company. Excerpt reprinted here with permission from Holt, Rinehart and Winston, Inc.

[1] Huxley's "Elementary Lessons in Physiology," lesson XII.

through the character, the tricks of thought, the prejudices, the ways of the "shop," in a word, from which the man can by-and-by no more escape than his coat-sleeve can suddenly fall into a new set of folds. On the whole, it is best he should not escape. It is well for the world that in most of us, by the age of thirty, the character has set like plaster, and will never soften again.

If the period between twenty and thirty is the critical one in the formation of intellectual and professional habits, the period below twenty is more important still for the fixing of *personal* habits, properly so called, such as vocalization and pronunciation, gesture, motion, and address. Hardly ever is a language learned after twenty spoken without a foreign accent; hardly ever can a youth transferred to the society of his betters unlearn the nasality and other vices of speech bred in him by the associations of his growing years. Hardly ever, indeed, no matter how much money there be in his pocket, can he even learn to *dress* like a gentleman-born. The merchants offer their wares as eagerly to him as to the veriest "swell," but he simply *cannot* buy the right things. An invisible law, as strong as gravitation, keeps him within his orbit, arrayed this year as he was the last; and how his better-bred acquaintances contrive to get the things they wear will be for him a mystery till his dying day.

The great thing, then, in all education, is to *make our nervous system our ally instead of our enemy*. It is to fund and capitalize our acquisitions, and live at ease upon the interest of the fund. *For this we must make automatic and habitual, as early as possible, as many useful actions as we can*, and guard against the growing into ways that are likely to be disadvantageous to us, as we should guard against the plague. The more of the details of our daily life we can hand over to the effortless custody of automatism, the more our higher powers of mind will be set free for their own proper work. There is no more miserable human being than one in whom nothing is habitual but indecision, and for whom the lighting of every cigar, the drinking of every cup, the time of rising and going to bed every day, and the beginning of every bit of work, are subjects of express volitional deliberation. Full half the time of such a man goes to the deciding, or regretting, of matters which ought to be so ingrained in him as practically not to exist for his consciousness at all. If there be such daily duties not yet ingrained in any one of my readers, let him begin this very hour to set the matter right.

In Professor Bain's chapter on "The Moral Habits" there are some admirable practical remarks laid down. Two great maxims emerge from his treatment. The first is that in the acquisition of a new habit, or the leaving off of an old one, we *must take care to launch ourselves with as strong and decided an initiative as possible*. Accumulate all the possible circumstances which shall re-enforce the right motives; put yourself assiduously in conditions that encourage the new way; make engagements incompatible with the old; take a public pledge, if the case allows; in short, envelop your resolution with every aid you know. This will give your new beginning such a momentum that the temptation to break down will not occur as soon as it otherwise might; and every day during which a breakdown is postponed adds to the chances of its not occurring at all.

The second maxim is: *Never suffer an exception to occur till the new habit is securely rooted in your life*. Each lapse is like the letting fall of a ball of string which one is carefully winding up; a single slip undoes more than a great many turns will wind again. *Continuity* of training is the great means of making the nervous system act infallibly right. As Professor Bain says:

> The peculiarity of the moral habits, contra-distinguishing them from the intellectual acquisitions, is the presence of two hostile powers, one to be gradually raised into the ascendant over the other. It is necessary, above all things, in such a situation, never to lose a battle. Every gain on the wrong side undoes the effect of many conquests on the right. The essential precaution, therefore, is so to regulate the two opposing powers that the one may have a series of uninterrupted successes, until repetition has fortified it to such a degree as to enable it to cope with the opposition, under any circumstances. This is the theoretically best career of mental progress.

The need of securing success at the *outset* is imperative. Failure at first is apt to dampen the energy of all future attempts, whereas past experience of success nerves one to future vigor. Goethe says to a man who consulted him about an enterprise but mistrusted his own powers: "Ach! you need only blow on your hands!" And the remark illustrates the effect on Goethe's spirits of his own habitually successful career. Prof. Baumann, from whom I borrow the anecdote,[2] says that the collapse of barbarian nations when Europeans come among them is due to their despair of ever succeeding as the newcomers do in the larger tasks of life. Old ways are broken and new ones not formed.

The question of "tapering-off," in abandoning such habits as drink and opium-indulgence, comes in here, and is a question about which experts differ within certain limits, and in regard to what may be best for an individual case. In the main, however, all expert opinion would

---

[2] See the admirable passage about success at the outset, in his *Handbuch der Moral* (1878), pp. 38–43.

agree that abrupt acquisition of the new habit is the best way, *if there be a real possibility of carrying it out.* We must be careful not to give the will so stiff a task as to insure its defeat at the very outset; but, *provided one can stand it,* a sharp period of suffering, and then a free time, is the best thing to aim at, whether in giving up a habit like that of opium, or in simply changing one's hours of rising or of work. It is surprising how soon a desire will die of inanition if it be never fed .

One must first learn, unmoved, looking neither to the right nor left, to walk firmly on the straight and narrow path, before one can begin "to make one's self over again." He who every day makes a fresh resolve is like one who, arriving at the edge of the ditch he is to leap, forever stops and returns for a fresh run. Without *unbroken* advance there is no such thing as *accumulation* of the ethical forces possible, and to make this possible, and to exercise us and habituate us in it, is the sovereign blessing of regular work.[3]

A third maxim may be added to the preceding pair: *Seize the very first possible opportunity to act on every resolution you make, and on every emotional prompting you may experience in the direction of the habits you aspire to gain.* It is not in the moment of their forming, but in the moment of their producing *motor effects*, that resolves and aspirations communicate the new "set" to the brain. As the author last quoted remarks:

The actual presence of the practical opportunity alone furnishes the fulcrum upon which the lever can rest, by means of which the moral will may multiply its strength, and raise itself aloft. He who has no solid ground to press against will never get beyond the stage of empty gesture-making.

No matter how full a reservoir of *maxims* one may possess, and no matter how good one's *sentiments* may be, if one have not taken advantage of every concrete opportunity to *act*, one's character may remain entirely unaffected for the better. With mere good intentions, hell is proverbially paved. And this is an obvious consequence of the principles we have laid down. A "character," as J. S. Mill says, "is a completely fashioned will"; and a will, in the sense in which he means it, is an aggregate of tendencies to act in a firm and prompt and definite way upon all the principal emergencies of life. A tendency to act only becomes effectively ingrained in us in proportion to the uninterrupted frequency with which the actions actually occur, and the brain "grows" to their use. Every time a resolve or a

fine glow of feeling evaporates without bearing practical fruit is worse than a chance lost; it works so as positively to hinder future resolutions and emotions from taking the normal path of discharge. There is no more contemptible type of human character than that of the nerveless sentimentalist and dreamer, who spends his life in a weltering sea of sensibility and emotion, but who never does a manly concrete deed. Rousseau, inflaming all the mothers of France, by his eloquence, to follow Nature and nurse their babies themselves, while he sends his own children to the foundling hospital, is the classical example of what I mean. But every one of us in his measure, whenever, after glowing for an abstractly formulated Good, he practically ignores some actual case, among the squalid "other particulars" of which that same Good lurks disguised, treads straight on Rousseau's path. All Goods are disguised by the vulgarity of their concomitants, in this work-a-day world; but woe to him who can only recognize them when he thinks them in their pure and abstract form! The habit of excessive novel-reading and theatre-going will produce true monsters in this line. The weeping of a Russian lady over the fictitious personages in the play, while her coachman is freezing to death on his seat outside, is the sort of thing that everywhere happens on a less glaring scale. Even the habit of excessive indulgence in music, for those who are neither performers themselves nor musically gifted enough to take it in a purely intellectual way, has probably a relaxing effect upon the character. One becomes filled with emotions which habitually pass without prompting to any deed, and so the inertly sentimental condition is kept up. The remedy would be, never to suffer one's self to have an emotion at a concert, without expressing it afterward in some active way.[4] Let the expression be the least thing in the world—speaking genially to one's aunt, or giving up one's seat in a horse-car, if nothing more heroic offers—but let it not fail to take place.

These latter cases make us aware that it is not simply *particular lines* of discharge, but also *general forms* of discharge, that seem to be grooved out by habit in the brain. Just as, if we let our emotions evaporate, they get into a way of evaporating; so there is reason to suppose that if we often flinch from making an effort, before we know it the effort-making capacity will be gone; and that, if we suffer the wandering of our attention, presently it will wander all the time. Attention and effort are, as we shall see later, but two names for the same psychic fact. To what brain-processes they correspond we do not

---

[3] J. Bahnsen: "Beiträge zu Charakterologie" (1867), vol. I p. 209.

[4] See for remarks on this subject a readable article by Miss V. Scudder on "Musical Devotees and Morals," in the Andover Review for January 1887.

know. The strongest reason for believing that they do depend on brain-processes at all, and are not pure acts of the spirit, is just this fact, that they seem in some degree subject to the law of habit, which is a material law. As a final practical maxim, relative to these habits of the will, we may, then, offer something like this: *Keep the faculty of effort alive in you by a little gratuitous exercise every day*. That is, be systematically ascetic or heroic in little unnecessary points, do every day or two something for no other reason than that you would rather not do it, so that when the hour of dire need draws nigh, it may find you not unnerved and untrained to stand the test. Asceticism of this sort is like the insurance which a man pays on his house and goods. The tax does him no good at the time, and possibly may never bring him a return. But if the fire *does* come, his having paid it will be his salvation from ruin. So with the man who has daily inured himself to habits of concentrated attention, energetic volition, and self-denial in unnecessary things. He will stand like a tower when everything rocks around him, and when his softer fellow-mortals are winnowed like chaff in the blast.

The physiological study of mental conditions is thus the most powerful ally of hortatory ethics. The hell to be endured hereafter, of which theology tells, is no worse than the hell we make for ourselves in this world by habitually fashioning our characters in the wrong way. Could the young but realize how soon they will become mere walking bundles of habits, they would give more heed to their conduct while in the plastic

state. We are spinning our own fates, good or evil, and never to be undone. Every smallest stroke of virtue or of vice leaves its never so little scar. The drunken Rip Van Winkle, in Jefferson's play, excuses himself for every fresh dereliction by saying, "I won't count this time!" Well! he may not count it, and a kind Heaven may not count it; but it is being counted none the less. Down among his nerve-cells and fibres the molecules are counting it, registering and storing it up to be used against him when the next temptation comes. Nothing we ever do is, in strict scientific literalness, wiped out. Of course, this has its good side as well as its bad one. As we become permanent drunkards by so many separate drinks, so we become saints in the moral, and authorities and experts in the practical and scientific spheres, by so many separate acts and hours of work. Let no youth have anxiety about the upshot of his education, whatever the line of it may be. If he keep faithfully busy each hour of the working day, he may safely leave the final result to itself. He can with perfect certainty count on waking up some fine morning, to find himself one of the competent ones of his generation, in whatever pursuit he may have singled out. Silently, between all the details of his business, the *power of judging* in all that class of matter will have built itself up within him as a possession that will never pass away. Young people should know this truth in advance. The ignorance of it has probably engendered more discouragement and faint-heartedness in youths embarking on arduous careers than all other causes put together.

INSTRUMENTAL LEARNING

The pigeons here were trained by instrumental, operant techniques. This selection shows that behavior can be controlled rather precisely. This control is sometimes spoken of as the stimulus control of behavior. After control has been achieved by operant training, the organism will respond under one set of stimulus conditions and not under another set, or the organism will respond in one way under one set of stimulus conditions and in another way under another set. It is probable that many of the same processes are at work in the natural socialization and "shaping" of the behavior of children.

A point to guide your study

How were the pigeons trained to peck some stimuli and not others?

24. PIGEONS IN A PELICAN

*B. F. Skinner, Harvard University**

This is the history of a crackpot idea, born on the wrong side of the tracks intellectually speaking, but eventually vindicated in a sort of middle class respectability. It is the story of a proposal to use living organisms to guide missiles—of a research program during World War II called "Project Pigeon" and a peacetime continuation at the Naval Research Laboratory called "ORCON," from the words "organic control." Both of these programs have now been declassified.

Man has always made use of the sensory capacities of animals, either because they are more acute than his own or more convenient. The watchdog probably hears better than his master and in any case listens while his master sleeps. As a detecting system the dog's ear comes supplied with an alarm (the dog need not be taught to announce the presence of an intruder), but special forms of reporting are sometimes set up. The tracking behavior of the bloodhound and the pointing of the hunting dog are usually modified to make them more useful. Training is sometimes quite explicit. It is said that sea gulls were used to detect submarines in the English Channel during World War I. The British sent their own submarines through the Channel releasing food to the surface. Gulls could see the submarines from the air and learned to follow them, whether they were British or German. A flock of gulls, spotted from the shore, took on special significance. In the seeing-eye dog the repertoire of artificial signaling responses is so elaborate that it has the conventional character of the verbal interchange between man and man.

The detecting and signaling systems of lower organisms have a special advantage when used with explosive devices which can be guided toward the objects they are to destroy, whether by land, sea, or air. Homing systems for guided missiles have now been developed which sense and signal the position of a target by responding to visible or invisible radiation, noise, radar reflections, and so on. These have not always been available, and in any case a living organism has certain advantages. It is almost certainly cheaper and more compact and, in particular, is especially good at responding to patterns and those classes of patterns called "concepts." The lower organism is used not because it is more sensitive

* B. F. Skinner. Pigeons in a pelican. *Amer. Psychologist*, 1960, **15**, 28–37. Copyright 1960 by the American Psychological Association. Reprinted here with permission from the author and the American Psychological Association.

than man—after all, the kamikaze did very well —but because it is readily expendable.

Project Pelican

The ethical question of our right to convert a lower creature into an unwitting hero is a peacetime luxury. There were bigger questions to be answered in the late thirties. A group of men had come into power who promised, and eventually accomplished, the greatest mass murder in history. In 1939 the city of Warsaw was laid waste in an unprovoked bombing, and the airplane emerged as a new and horrible instrument of war against which only the feeblest defenses were available. Project Pigeon was conceived against that background. It began as a search for a homing device to be used in a surface-to-air guided missile as a defense against aircraft. As the balance between offensive and defensive weapons shifted, the direction was reversed, and the system was to be tested first in an air-to-ground missile called the "Pelican." Its name is a useful reminder of the state of the missile art in America at that time. Its detecting and servomechanisms took up so much space that there was no room for explosives: hence the resemblance to the pelican "whose beak can hold more than its belly can." My title is perhaps now clear. Figure 1 shows the pigeons, jacketed for duty. Figure 2 shows the beak of the Pelican.

At the University of Minnesota in the spring of 1940 the capacity of the pigeon to steer toward a target was tested with a moving hoist. The pigeon, held in a jacket and harnessed to a block, was immobilized except for its neck and head. It could eat grain from a dish and operate a control system by moving its head in appropriate directions. Movement of the head operated the motors of the hoist. The bird could ascend by lifting its head, descend by lowering

Figure 1 Thirty-two pigeons, jacketed for testing.

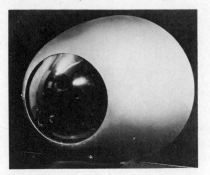

Figure 2   Nose of the pelican, showing lenses.

it, and travel from side to side by moving appropriately. The whole system, mounted on wheels, was pushed across a room toward a bull's eye on the far wall. During the approach the pigeon raised or lowered itself and moved from side to side in such a way as to reach the wall in position to eat grain from the center of the bull's-eye. The pigeon learned to reach any target within reach of the hoist, no matter what the starting position and during fairly rapid approaches.

The experiment was shown to John T. Tate, a physicist, then Dean of the Graduate School at the University of Minnesota, who brought it to the attention of R. C. Tolman, one of a group of scientists engaged in early defense activities. The result was the first of a long series of rejections. The proposal "did not warrant further development at the time." The project was accordingly allowed to lapse. On December 7, 1941 the situation was suddenly restructured; and, on the following day, with the help of Keller Breland, then a graduate student at Minnesota, further work was planned. A simpler harnessing system could be used if the bomb were to rotate slowly during its descent, when the pigeon would need to steer in only one dimension: from side to side. We built an apparatus in which a harnessed pigeon was lowered toward a large revolving turntable across which a target was driven according to contacts made by the bird during its descent. It was not difficult to train a pigeon to "hit" small ship models during fairly rapid descents. We made a demonstration film showing hits on various kinds of targets, and two psychologists then engaged in the war effort in Washington, Charles Bray and Leonard Carmichael, undertook to look for government support. Tolman, then at the Office of Scientific Research and Development, again felt that the project did not warrant support, in part because the United States had at that time no missile capable of being guided toward a target. Commander (now Admiral) Luis de Florez, then in the Special Devices Section of the Navy, took a sympathetic view. He dismissed the objection that there was no available vehicle by suggesting that the pigeon be connected with an automatic pilot mounted in a small plane loaded with explosives. But he was unable to take on the project because of other commitments and because, as he explained, he had recently bet on one or two other equally long shots which had not come in.

The project lapsed again and would probably have been abandoned if it had not been for a young man whose last name I have ungratefully forgotten, but whose first name—Victor—we hailed as a propitious sign. His subsequent history led us to refer to him as Vanquished; and this, as it turned out, was a more reliable omen. Victor walked into the Department of Psychology at Minnesota one day in the summer of 1942 looking for an animal psychologist. He had a scheme for installing dogs in antisubmarine torpedoes. The dogs were to respond to faint acoustic signals from the submarine and to steer the torpedo toward its goal. He wanted a statement from an animal psychologist as to its feasibility. He was understandably surprised to learn of our work with pigeons but seized upon it eagerly, and citing it in support of his contention that dogs could be trained to steer torpedoes he went to a number of companies in Minneapolis. His project was rejected by everyone he approached; but one company, General Mills, Inc., asked for more information about our work with pigeons. We described the project and presented the available data to Arthur D. Hyde, Vice-President in Charge of Research. The company was not looking for new products, but Hyde thought that it might, as a public service, develop the pigeon system to the point at which a governmental agency could be persuaded to take over.

Breland and I moved into the top floor of a flour mill in Minneapolis and with the help of Norman Guttman, who had joined the project, set to work on further improvements. It had been difficult to induce the pigeon to respond to the small angular displacement of a distant target. It would start working dangerously late in the descent. Its natural pursuit behavior was not appropriate to the characteristics of a likely missile. A new system was therefore designed. An image of the target was projected on a translucent screen as in a camera obscura. The pigeon, held near the screen, was reinforced for pecking at the image on the screen. The guiding signal was to be picked up from the point of contact of screen and beak.

In an early arrangement the screen was a translucent plastic plate forming the larger end of a truncated cone bearing a lens at the smaller end. The cone was mounted, lens down, in a gimbal bearing. An object within range threw its image on the translucent screen; and the pigeon, held vertically just above the plate, pecked the image. When a target was moved about within range of the lens, the cone continued to point to it. In another apparatus a translucent disk, free to tilt slightly on gimbal bearings, closed contacts operating motors which altered the position of a large field beneath the apparatus. Small cutouts of ships and other objects were placed on the field. The field was constantly in motion, and a target would go out of range unless the pigeon continued to control it. With this apparatus we began to study the pigeon's reactions to various patterns and to develop sustained steady rates of responding through the use of appropriate schedules of reinforcement, the reinforcement being a few grains occasionally released onto the plate. By building up large extinction curves a target could be tracked continuously for a matter of minutes without reinforcement. We trained pigeons to follow a variety of land and sea targets, to neglect large patches intended to represent clouds or flak, to concentrate on one target while another was in view, and so on. We found that a pigeon could hold the missile on a particular street intersection in an aerial map of a city. The map which came most easily to hand was of a city which, in the interests of international relations, need not be identified. Through appropriate schedules of reinforcement it was possible to maintain longer uninterrupted runs than could conceivably be required by a missile.

We also undertook a more serious study of the pigeon's behavior, with the help of W. K. Estes and Marion Breland who joined the project at this time. We ascertained optimal conditions of deprivation, investigated other kinds of deprivations, studied the effect of special reinforcements (for example, pigeons were said to find hemp seed particularly delectable), tested the effects of energizing drugs and increased oxygen pressures, and so on. We differentially reinforced the force of the pecking response and found that pigeons could be induced to peck so energetically that the base of the beak became inflamed. We investigated the effects of extremes of temperature, of changes in atmospheric pressure, of accelerations produced by an improvised centrifuge, of increased carbon dioxide pressure, of increased and prolonged vibration, and of noises such as pistol shots. (The birds could, of course, have been deafened to eliminate auditory distractions, but we found it easy to maintain steady behavior in spite of intense noises and many other distracting conditions using the simple process of adaptation.) We investigated optimal conditions for the quick development of discriminations and began to study the pigeon's reactions to patterns, testing for induction from a test figure to the same figure inverted, to fig-

ures of different sizes and colors, and to figures against different grounds. A simple device using carbon paper to record the points at which a pigeon pecks a figure showed a promise which has never been properly exploited.

We made another demonstration film and renewed our contact with the Office of Scientific Research and Development. An observer was sent to Minneapolis, and on the strength of his report we were given an opportunity to present our case in Washington in February 1943. At that time we were offering a homing device capable of reporting with an on-off signal the orientation of a missile toward various visual patterns. The capacity to respond to pattern was, we felt, our strongest argument, but the fact that the device used only visible radiation (the same form of information available to the human bombardier) made it superior to the radio controlled missiles then under development because it was resistant to jamming. Our film had some effect. Other observers were sent to Minneapolis to see the demonstration itself. The pigeons, as usual, behaved beautifully. One of them held the supposed missile on a particular intersection of streets in the aerial map for five minutes although the target would have been lost if the pigeon had paused for a second or two. The observers returned to Washington, and two weeks later we were asked to supply data on (a) the population of pigeons in the United States (fortunately, the census bureau had some figures) and (b) the accuracy with which pigeons struck a point on a plate. There were many arbitrary conditions to be taken into account in measuring the latter, but we supplied possibly relevant data. At long last, in June 1943, the Office of Scientific Research and Development awarded a modest contract to General Mills, Inc. to "develop a homing device."

At that time we were given some information about the missile the pigeons were to steer. The Pelican was a wing steered glider, still under development and not yet successfully steered by any homing device. It was being tested on a target in New Jersey consisting of a stirrup shaped pattern bulldozed out of the sandy soil near the coast. The white lines of the target stood out clearly against brown and green cover. Colored photographs were taken from various distances and at various angles, and the verisimilitude of the reproduction was checked by flying over the target and looking at its image in a portable camera obscura.

Because of security restrictions we were given only very rough specifications of the signal to be supplied to the controlling system in the Pelican. It was no longer to be simply on-off; if the missile was badly off target, an especially strong correcting signal was needed. This meant that the quadrant-contact system would no longer suffice. But further requirements were left mainly to our imagination. The General Mills engineers were equal to this difficult assignment. With what now seems like unbelievable speed, they designed and constructed a pneumatic pickup system giving a graded signal. A lens in the nose of the missile threw an image on a translucent plate within reach of the pigeon in a pressure sealed chamber. Four air valves resting against the edges of the plate were jarred open momentarily as the pigeon pecked. The valves at the right and left admitted air to chambers on opposite sides of one tambour, while the valves at the top and bottom admitted air to opposite sides of another. Air on all sides was exhausted by a Venturi cone on the side of the missile. When the missile was on target, the pigeon pecked the center of the plate, all valves admitted equal amounts of air, and the tambours remained in neutral positions. But if the image moved as little as a quarter of an inch off-center, corresponding to a very small angular displacement of the target, more air was admitted by the valves on one side, and the resulting displacement of the tambours sent appropriate correcting orders directly to the servosystem.

The device required no materials in short supply, was relatively foolproof, and delivered a graded signal. It had another advantage. By this time we had begun to realize that a pigeon was more easily controlled than a physical scientist serving on a committee. It was very difficult to convince the latter that the former was an orderly system. We therefore multiplied the probability of success by designing a multiple bird unit. There was adequate space in the nose of the Pelican for three pigeons each with its own lens and plate. A net signal could easily be generated. The majority vote of three pigeons offered an excellent guarantee against momentary pauses and aberrations. (We later worked out a system in which the majority took on a more characteristically democratic function. When a missile is falling toward *two* ships at sea, for example, there is no guarantee that all three pigeons will steer toward the same ship. But at least two must agree, and the third can then be punished for his minority opinion. Under proper contingencies of reinforcement a punished bird will shift immediately to the majority view. When all three are working on one ship, any defection is immediately punished and corrected.)

The arrangement in the nose of the Pelican is shown in Figure 3. Three systems of lenses and mirrors, shown at the left, throw images of the target area on the three translucent plates shown in the center. The ballistic valves resting against the edges of these plates and the tubes connecting them with the manifolds leading to the controlling tambours may be seen. A pigeon is being placed in the pressurized chamber at the right.

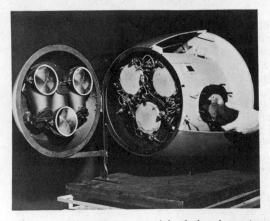

Figure 3   Demonstration model of the three-pigeon guidance system.

The General Mills engineers also built a simulator (Figure 4)—a sort of Link trainer for pigeons—designed to have the steering characteristics of the Pelican, in so far as these had been communicated to us. Like the wing steered Pelican, the simulator tilted and turned from side to side. When the three-bird nose was attached to it, the pigeons could be put in full control—the "loop could be closed"—and the adequacy of the signal tested under pursuit conditions. Targets were moved back and forth across the far wall of a room at prescribed speeds and in given patterns of oscillation, and the tracking response of the whole unit was studied quantitatively.

Meanwhile we continued our intensive study of the behavior of the pigeon. Looking ahead to combat use we designed methods for the mass production of trained birds and for handling large groups of trained subjects. We were proposing to train certain birds for certain *classes* of targets, such as ships at sea, while special squads were to be trained on special targets, photographs of which were to be obtained through reconnaissance. A large crew of pigeons would then be waiting for assignment, but we developed harnessing and training techniques which should have solved such problems quite easily.

A multiple unit trainer is shown in Figure 5. Each box contains a jacketed pigeon held at an angle of 45° to the horizontal and perpendicular to an 8″ x 8″ translucent screen. A target area is projected on each screen. Two beams of light intersect at the point to be struck. All on-target responses of the pigeon are reported by the interruption of the crossed beams and by contact with the translucent screen. Only a four-inch, disc shaped portion of the field is visible to the pigeon at any time, but the boxes move slowly about the field, giving the pigeon an opportunity

Figure 4   Simulator for testing the adequacy of the pigeon signal.

to respond to the target in all positions. The positions of all reinforcements are recorded to reveal any weak areas. A variable-ratio schedule is used to build sustained, rapid responding.

By December 1943, less than six months after the contract was awarded, we were ready to report to the Office of Scientific Research and Development. Observers visited the laboratory and watched the simulator follow a target about a room under the control of a team of three birds. They also reviewed our tracking data. The only questions which arose were the inevitable consequence of our lack of information about the signal required to steer the Pelican. For example, we had had to make certain arbitrary decisions in compromising between sensitivity of signal and its integration or smoothness. A high vacuum produced quick, rather erratic movements of the tambours, while a lower vacuum gave a sluggish but smooth signal. As it turned out, we had not chosen the best values in collecting our data, and in January 1944 the Office of Scientific Research and Development refused to extend the General Mills contract. The reasons given seemed to be due to misunderstandings or, rather, to lack of communication. We had already collected further data with new settings of the instruments, and these were submitted in a request for reconsideration.

We were given one more chance. We took our new data to the radiation lab at the Massachusetts Institute of Technology where they were examined by the servospecialists working on the Pelican controls. To our surprise the scientist whose task it was to predict the usefulness of the pigeon signal argued that our data were inconsistent with respect to phase lag and certain other characteristics of the signal. Ac-

Figure 5   A trainer for four pigeons.

cording to his equations, our device could not possibly yield the signals we reported. We knew, of course, that it had done so. We examined the supposed inconsistency and traced it, or so we thought, to a certain nonlinearity in our system. In pecking an image near the edge of the plate, the pigeon strikes a more glancing blow; hence the air admitted at the valves is not linearly proportional to the displacement of the target. This could be corrected in several ways: for example, by using a lens to distort radial distances. It was our understanding that in any case the signal was adequate to control the Pelican. Indeed, one servo authority, upon looking at graph of the performance of the simulator, exclaimed: "This is better than radar!"

Two days later, encouraged by our meeting at MIT, we reached the summit. We were to present our case briefly to a committee of the country's top scientists. The hearing began with a brief report by the scientist who had discovered the "inconsistency" in our data, and to our surprise he still regarded it as unresolved. He predicted that the signal we reported would cause the missile to "hunt" wildly and lose the target. But his prediction should have applied as well to the closed loop simulator. Fortunately another scientist was present who had seen the simulator performing under excellent control and who could confirm our report of the facts. But reality was no match for mathematics.

The basic difficulty, of course, lay in convincing a dozen distinguished physical scientists that the behavior of a pigeon could be adequately controlled. We had hoped to score on this point by bringing with us a demonstration. A small black box had a round translucent window in one end. A slide projector placed some distance away threw on the window an image of the New Jersey target. In the box, of course, was a pigeon—which, incidentally, had at that time been harnessed for 35 hours. Our intention was to let each member of the committee observe the response to the target by looking down a small tube; but time was not available for individual observation, and we were asked to take the top off the box. The translucent screen was flooded with so much light that the target was barely visible, and the peering scientists offered conditions much more unfamiliar and threatening than those likely to be encountered in a missile. In spite of this the pigeon behaved perfectly, pecking steadily and energetically at the image of the target as it moved about on the plate. One scientist with an experimental turn of mind intercepted the beam from the projector. The pigeon stopped instantly. When the image again appeared, pecking began within a fraction of a second and continued at a steady rate.

It was a perfect performance, but it had just the wrong effect. One can talk about phase lag in pursuit behavior and discuss mathematical predictions of hunting without reflecting too closely upon what is inside the black box. But the spectacle of a living pigeon carrying out its assignment, no matter how beautifully, simply reminded the committee of how utterly fantastic our proposal was. I will not say that the meeting was marked by unrestrained merriment, for the merriment was restrained. But it was there, and it was obvious that our case was lost.

Hyde closed our presentation with a brief summary: we were offering a homing device, unusually resistant to jamming, capable of reacting to a wide variety of target patterns, requiring no materials in short supply, and so simple to build that production could be started in 30 days. He thanked the committee, and we left. As the door closed behind us, he said to me: "Why don't you go out and get drunk!"

Official word soon came: "Further prosecution of this project would seriously delay others which in the minds of the Division would have more immediate promise of combat application." Possibly the reference was to a particular combat application at Hiroshima a year and a half later, when it looked for a while as if the need for accurate bombing had been eliminated for all time. In any case we had to show, for all our trouble, only a loftful of curiously useless equipment and a few dozen pigeons with a strange interest in a feature of the New Jersey coast. The equipment was scrapped, but 30 of the pigeons were kept to see how long they would retain the appropriate behavior.

In the years which followed there were faint signs of life. Winston Churchill's personal scientific advisor, Lord Cherwell, learned of the project and "regretted its demise." A scientist who had had some contact with the project during the war, and who evidently assumed that its classified status was not to be taken seriously, made a good story out of it for the *Atlantic Monthly*, names being changed to protect the innocent. Other uses of animals began to be described. The author of the *Atlantic Monthly* story also published an account of the "incendiary bats." Thousands of bats were to be released over an enemy city, each carrying a small incendiary time bomb. The bats would take refuge, as is their custom, under eaves and in other out-of-the-way places; and shortly afterwards thousands of small fires would break out practically simultaneously. The scheme was never used because it was feared that it would be mistaken for germ warfare and might lead to retaliation in kind.

Another story circulating at the time told how the Russians trained dogs to blow up tanks. I have described the technique elsewhere (Skinner, 1956). A Swedish proposal to use seals to achieve the same end with submarines was not successful. The seal were to be trained to approach submarines to obtain fish attached to the sides. They were then to be released carrying magnetic mines in the vicinity of hostile submarines. The required training was apparently never achieved. I cannot vouch·for the authenticity of probably the most fantastic story of this sort, but it ought to be recorded. The Russians were said to have trained sea lions to cut mine cables. A complicated device attached to the sea lion included a motor driven cable-cutter, a tank full of small fish, and a device which released a few fish into a muzzle covering the sea lion's head. In order to eat, the sea lion had to find a mine cable and swim along side it so that the cutter was automatically triggered, at which point a few fish were released from the tank into the muzzle. When a given number of cables had been cut, both the energy of the cutting mechanism and the supply of fish were exhausted, and the sea lion received a special stimulus upon which it returned to its home base for special reinforcement and reloading.

ORCON

The story of our own venture has a happy ending. With the discovery of German accomplishments in the field of guided missiles, feasible homing systems suddenly became very important. Franklin V. Taylor of the Naval Research Laboratory in Washington, D. C. heard about our project and asked for further details. As a psychologist Taylor appreciated the special capacity of living organisms to respond to visual patterns and was aware of recent advances in the control of behavior. More important, he was a skillful practitioner in a kind of control which our project had conspicuously lacked: he knew how to approach the people who determine the direction of research. He showed our demonstration film so often that it was completely worn out—but to good effect, for support was eventually found for a thorough investigation of "organic control" under the general title ORCON. Taylor also enlisted the support of engineers in obtaining a more effective report of the pigeon's behavior. The translucent plate upon which the image of the target was thrown had a semiconducting surface, and the tip of the bird's beak was covered with a gold electrode. A single contact with the plate sent an immediate report of the location of the target to the controlling mechanism. The work which went into this system contributed to the so-called Pick-off Display Converter developed as part of the Naval Data Handling System for human observers. It is no longer necessary for the radar operator to give a verbal report of the location of a pip on the screen. Like the pigeon, he has only to touch the pip with a special contact. (He holds the contact in his hand.)

At the Naval Research Laboratory in Washington the responses of pigeons were studied in detail. Average peck rate, average error rate, average hit rate, and so on were recorded under various conditions. The tracking behavior of the pigeon was analyzed with methods similar to those employed with human operators (Figure 6). Pattern perception was studied, including generalization from one pattern to another. A simulator was constructed in which the pigeon controlled an image projected by a moving-picture film of an actual target: for example, a ship at sea as seen from a plane approaching at 600 miles per hour. A few frames of a moving picture of the pigeon controlling the orientation toward a ship during an approach are shown in Figure 7.

The publications from the Naval Research Laboratory which report this work (Chernikoff & Newlin, 1951; Conklin, Newlin, Taylor, & Tipton, 1953; Searle & Stafford, 1950; Taylor, 1949; White, 1952) provide a serious evaluation of the possibilities of organic control. Although in simulated tests a single pigeon occasionally loses a target, its tracking characteristics are surprisingly good. A three- or seven-bird unit with the same individual consistency should yield a signal with a reliability which is at least of the order of magnitude shown by other phases of guided missiles in their present stage of development. Moreover, in the seven years which have followed the last of these reports, a great deal of relevant information has been acquired. The color vision of the pigeon is now thoroughly understood; its generalization along single properties of a stimulus has been recorded and analyzed; and the maintenance of behavior through scheduling of reinforcement has been drastically improved, particularly in the development of techniques for pacing responses for less erratic and steadier signals (Skinner, 1957). Tests made with the birds salvaged from the old Project Pigeon showed that even after six years of inactivity a pigeon will immediately and correctly

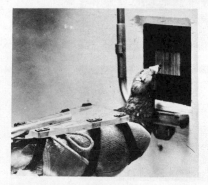

Figure 6 Arrangement for studying pursuit movements.

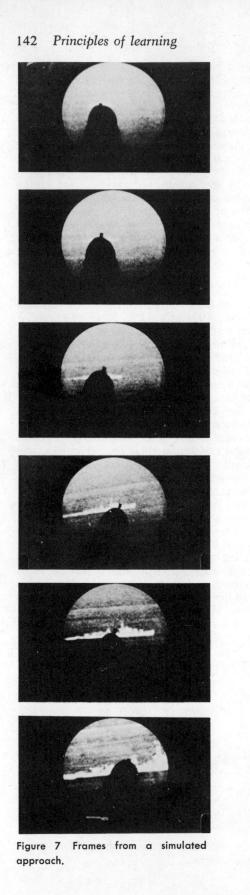

Figure 7   Frames from a simulated approach.

strike a target to which it has been conditioned and will continue to respond for some time without reinforcement.

The use of living organisms in guiding missiles is, it seems fair to say, no longer a crackpot idea. A pigeon is an extraordinarily subtle and complex mechanism capable of performances which at the moment can be equalled by electronic equipment only of vastly greater weight and size, and it can be put to reliable use through the principles which have emerged from an experimental analysis of its behavior. But this vindication of our original proposal is perhaps the least important result. Something happened during the brief life of Project Pigeon which it has taken a long time to appreciate. The practical task before us created a new attitude toward the behavior of organisms. We had to maximize the probability that a given form of behavior would occur at a given time. We could not enjoy the luxury of observing one variable while allowing others to change in what we hoped was a random fashion. We had to discover all relevant variables and submit them to experimental control whenever possible. We were no doubt under exceptional pressure, but vigorous scientific research usually makes comparable demands. Psychologists have too often yielded to the temptation to be content with hypothetical processes and intervening variables rather than press for rigorous experimental control. It is often intellectual laziness rather than necessity which recommends the *a posteriori* statistical treatment of variation. Our task forced us to emphasize prior experimental control, and its success in revealing orderly processes gave us an exciting glimpse of the superiority of laboratory practice over verbal (including some kinds of mathematical) explanation.

The crackpot idea

If I were to conclude that crackpot ideas are to be encouraged, I should probably be told that psychology has already had more than its share of them. If it has, they have been entertained by the wrong people. Reacting against the excesses of psychological quackery, psychologists have developed an enormous concern for scientific respectability. They constantly warn their students against questionable facts and unsupported theories. As a result the usual PhD thesis is a model of compulsive cautiousness, advancing only the most timid conclusions thoroughly hedged about with qualifications. But it is just the man capable of displaying such admirable caution who needs a touch of uncontrolled speculation. Possibly a generous exposure to psychological science fiction would help. Project Pigeon might be said to support that view. Except with respect to its avowed goal, it was, as I see it, highly productive; and this was in large measure because my colleagues and I knew that, in the eyes of the world, we were crazy.

One virtue in crackpot ideas is that they breed rapidly and their progeny show extraordinary mutations. Everyone is talking about teaching machines nowadays, but Sidney Pressey can tell you what it was like to have a crackpot idea in that field 40 years ago. His self-testing devices and self-scoring test forms now need no defense, and psychomotor training devices have also achieved a substantial respectability. This did not, however, prepare the way for devices to be used in verbal instruction—that is, in the kinds of teaching which are the principal concern of our schools and colleges. Even five short years ago that kind of instruction by machine was still in the crackpot category. (I can quote official opinion to that effect from high places.) Now, there is a direct genetic connection between teaching machines and Project Pigeon. We had been forced to consider the mass education of pigeons. True, the scrap of wisdom we imparted to each was indeed small, but the required changes in behavior were similar to those which must be brought about in vaster quantities in human students. The techniques of shaping behavior and of bringing it under stimulus control which can be traced, as I have suggested elsewhere (Skinner, 1958), to a memorable episode on the top floor of that flour mill in Minneapolis needed only a detailed reformulation of verbal behavior to be directly applicable to education.

I am sure there is more to come. In the year which followed the termination of Project Pigeon I wrote *Walden Two* (Skinner, 1948), a utopian picture of a properly engineered society. Some psychotherapists might argue that I was suffering from personal rejection and simply retreated to a fantasied world where everything went according to plan, where there never was heard a discouraging word. But another explanation is, I think, equally plausible. That piece of science fiction was a declaration of confidence in a technology of behavior. Call it a crackpot idea if you will; it is one in which I have never lost faith. I still believe that the same kind of wide-ranging speculation about human affairs, supported by studies of compensating rigor, will make a substantial contribution toward that world of the future in which, among other things, there will be no need for guided missiles.

References

Chernikoff, R., and Newlin, E. P. ORCON. Part III. Investigations of target acquisition by the pigeon. *Naval Res. Lab. lett., Rep.*, 1951, No. S–3600–629a/51 (Sept. 10).

Conklin, J. E., Newlin, E. P., Jr., Taylor, F. V., and Tipton, C. L. ORCON. Part IV. Simulated flight tests. *Naval Res. Lab. Rep.*, 1953, No. 4105.

Searle, L. V., and Stafford, B. H. ORCON. Part II. Report of phase I research and bandpass study. *Naval Res. Lab. lett. Rep.*, 1950, No. S–3600–157/50 (May 1).

Skinner, B. F. *Walden Two*. New York: Macmillan, 1948.

Skinner, B. F. A case history in scientific method. *Amer. Psychologist*, 1956, **11**, 221–233.

Skinner, B. F. The experimental analysis of behavior. *Amer. Scient.*, 1957, **45**, 343–371.

Skinner, B. F. Reinforcement today. *Amer. Psychologist*, 1958, **13**, 94–99.

Taylor, F. V. ORCON. Part I. Outline of proposed research. *Naval Res. Lab. lett. Rep.*, 1949, No. S–3600–157/50 (June 17).

White, C. F. Development of the NRL ORCON tactile missile simulator. *Naval Res. Lab. Rep.*, 1952, No. 3917.

Psychologists would not be nearly so interested in instrumental (operant) conditioning if the principles involved did not apply to important human situations. In this experiment, behavior is manipulated by reinforcement. The subject is reinforced for a certain type of statement. The frequency of the reinforced response, as measured by the attitude scale, rises as would be expected if "good" were actually working as a reinforcer.

Points to guide your study

1. Can you think of applied situations, other than interviewing, where instrumental conditioning principles similar to those mentioned here might be at work? What about psychotherapy?

2. Note that the reinforcements used are of the sort usually called "secondary." What is "secondary reinforcement"? How did the word "good" acquire such properties.

3. Why do you think the experimenters selected an attitude which was not strongly held? Does this indicate that these principles will not work with strongly held attitudes?

25. VERBAL REINFORCEMENT AND INTERVIEWER BIAS

Donald C. Hildum, Case Institute of Technology, and
*Roger W. Brown, Harvard University**

In several recent studies verbal behavior has been manipulated by means of selective reinforcement. These studies have very disturbing implications for the clinical and public-opinion interview. In the initial experiment Greenspoon (2) asked college students to voice nouns *ad libitum*. For one group of Ss, E murmured "Mm-hmm" whenever a plural noun was produced, while for a control group he said nothing at all. The reinforced Ss used more plural nouns than the control Ss. A somewhat different technique was developed by Taffel (4) and also employed by Cohen *et al.* (1). They required S to form a sentence when given a verb and a choice of one of six personal pronouns to be used in starting the sentence. It proved to be possible to affect the frequency with which S used the various pronouns by saying "Good" in a flat unemotional tone after sentences employing the desired pronoun subject. Finally, Greenspoon has reported (3) the successful use of two nonverbal stimuli (a red light and a 190-c.p.s. tone) to increase the frequency of plural and also of nonplural responses. In all of these studies S said that he had not been conscious of any connection between his own behavior and the reactions of E. This is learning without awareness.

In these experiments reinforcement seems to act like the moon on the tides with inevitable and uncontingent effect. For those interested in such things there appears a glittering new prospect for human manipulation; for others only the quiet pleasure to be found in any new proof of human stupidity. The verbal-reinforcement data will confirm many in their suspicion of the methods of clinical and social psychology. The therapist who believes in the importance of the Oedipus complex could elicit Oedipal content

by means of selective reinforcement. Perhaps a patient could even be brought to an appearance of mental health through the encouragement of "healthy" utterances. Is not "Mm-hmm" the very hallmark of a therapeutic school? In an opinion interview the S might be infected with the opinions of the interviewer by means of patterned reinforcement. Perhaps verbal reinforcement is a mechanism of interviewer bias.

It can be answered to these alarms that neither interviewers nor therapists wish to influence their Ss and consequently they would not use verbal reinforcement. There is no comfort in this answer. Anyone who has worked with verbal reinforcement knows that our "Mm-hmm" and "Good" are ordinarily unconscious and automatic. They can only be controlled after some practice. It follows that an interviewer might influence his S in all innocence and we know from the experiments that an S might unwittingly accept the influence. Here is powerful social influence operating outside the awareness of everybody concerned.

Two important differences between the laboratory studies and actual interviews should however be noted: (a) Greenspoon and the other experimenters have taken as their response units particular words or word types. Interviewers are not ordinarily pleased either by plural nouns or by the use of the first person singular. If they are moved to agree or disagree it is likely to be with reference to a line of thought or an expressed attitude. In short, interviewers would be likely to reinforce content categories rather than specific verbalizations. (b) In a face-to-face conversation there are many ways of communicating agreement or disagreement—smiles, nods, averted eyes. In the laboratory studies of verbal reinforcement E sometimes placed himself behind the S and sometimes faced him but endeavored to avoid giving visual cues. These efforts at isolating the independent variable may not have succeeded. In any case they must have created a rather strange social atmosphere unlike the usual interviewing situation.

We undertook an experiment intended to correct these two laboratory artificialities. The

* This study was supported by the Laboratory of Social Relations, Harvard University.

experiment took the form of an attitude survey conducted by telephone. The interviewer asked questions concerning the Harvard philosophy of General Education. He revealed a bias for or against the philosophy by his reactions to the answers of the interviewee. In effect, he played the role of one who favored or of one who opposed General Education. However, the role-play was limited to the single matter of verbal reinforcement. The S could discover E's bias from his first few reactions and might then provide more of the kind of content that was reinforced. Administering the questionnaire by telephone created a situation in which vocal reaction was the only kind possible and so the independent variable was isolated in a natural way.

Method

The questionnaire. In order to maximize the likelihood of obtaining a verbal reinforcement effect, a topic (General Education) was selected on which Ss were not expected to have very strong opinions and so were expected to be open to influence. Also, though E might be expected to have an opinion, there was no obvious stereotype to tell S what that opinion should be. In the questionnaire there were 15 questions, with 4 possible responses to each: Agree strongly, agree slightly, disagree slightly, disagree strongly. The statements were worded so that agreement with some statements represented an attitude favorable to General Education while agreement with other statements represented an unfavorable attitude. Consequently the interviewer reinforced an attitude rather than a particular response. To make sure that the favorable or unfavorable nature of each statement was clear, we originally wrote 40 statements intended to sound unlike but really covering much the same ground. From these we selected 15 which on pretest proved to constitute a maximally redundant subset. It is generally possible to predict from the answer to one of these questions the answers to all the others. In addition the questionnaire was prefaced with a brief statement defining the philosophy of General Education so as to make sure that the S would understand which statements favored the philosophy and which were opposed.

Subjects. Forty male students, graduate and undergraduate, were sampled from those in the Harvard Summer School who listed Cambridge telephone numbers and home addresses in the United States. Ten Ss were assigned at random to each of four experimental groups.

Procedure. The same E conducted all the interviews. He identified himself as a member of the Social Relations Department and said

that the survey was designed to compare summer-school opinion with that of the rest of the student body. He then administered the questionnaire.

For two groups the reinforcement was "Mm-hmm," pronounced after pro General Education answers for one group, and after anti answers for the other group. For the remaining two groups the reinforcement was "Good," again with one group rewarded for favorable responses and the other for unfavorable responses. Both reactions were fed back immediately following an approved answer in a neutrally-toned, rising inflection. The E (a trained linguist) carefully equated the intonation used in reading questions and responding to Ss in all groups.

At the close of the interview S was asked to guess E's opinion on General Education and also to say whether he thought there was any bias in the questionnaire or in its administration. If S thought there was bias or felt that he knew E's opinion he was then asked whether his answers were influenced by these conditions.

Results

The reinforcement effect. Each answer was scored from 1 to 4: 1 when an answer was strongly in favor of General Education, 2 when slightly favorable, 3 when slightly unfavorable, and 4 when strongly unfavorable. Refusals to answer (12 of 600 responses) were scored 2.5. The total score for an S had a possible range from 15 to 60. The actual range for all Ss was from 15 to 39.5. The Ss tended to favor the General Education philosophy.

In Table 1 appear the mean attitude scores for the four experimental groups and in Table 2 are the t scores and probabilities for the crucial comparisons among these means. Reinforcement with "Good" was effective while reinforcement with "Mm-hmm" was not effective. In fact, with "Mm-hmm" the obtained difference was in the opposite direction to that predicted from the reinforcement scheme. With the same pattern of reinforcement "Good" was more effective than "Mm-hmm."

Awareness of reinforcement. Eight of 20 Ss noticed that the interviewer said "Good" but only 1 of these assumed that it indicated approval. Only 1 of 20 Ss noticed that E said "Mm-hmm." He thought it might have meant approval. All Ss rejected the notion that their answers had been influenced by the interviewer's reactions.

Of 24 Ss who were willing to guess at E's opinion all but one said that E favored General Education. Apparently they based this guess on the assumption that someone surveying opinions on General Education would himself favor the

Table 1   Mean attitude scores for four experimental groups

Group	Mean	SD
"Good"—pro	24.95	5.10
"Good"—anti	31.75	3.46
"Mm-hmmm"—pro	29.8	3.96
"Mm-hmmm"—anti	27.1	4.06

Table 2   *t* scores and probabilities for crucial comparisons among the four experimental groups

Comparison *	*t* score	*p*
"Good"—pro vs. "Good"—anti	3.31	.01
"Mm-hmmm"—anti vs. "Mm-hmmm"—pro	1.43	.20
"Good"—pro vs. "Mm-hmmm"—pro	2.25	.05
"Mm-hmmm"—anti vs. "Good"—anti	2.62	.02

* First member of comparison has score more favorable to General Education.

principle, rather than on the pattern of reinforcement.

Replication of the experiment. The essential design was repeated by members of an undergraduate tutorial group with 25 Ss. The results were like those of the initial study. The mean "Good"—pro score was lower than the mean "Good"—anti score with $p < .05$, while the mean scores for the two groups reinforced with "Mm-hmm" were not significantly different. The mean "Good"—pro score was lower than the mean "Mm-hmm"—pro score with $p < .01$. The mean "Good"—anti and "Mm-hmm"—anti scores did not differ significantly. This study involved new interviewers and Ss enrolled for the regular academic year at Harvard rather than in summer school.

Discussion

In the present interview situation "Good" is a reinforcer while "Mm-hmmm" is not. This result conflicts with Greenspoon's finding that "Mm-hmm" affects the frequency of plural nouns. If conscious learning were involved, an explanation for the discrepancy would be available. When an S free-associates aloud for 25 minutes, he may be expected to search rather desperately for some indication from E as to the purpose of the task and the proper direction to take. In these circumstances he will notice Mm-hmm" or even a red light or a tone of 190 c.p.s. and be guided by them. When S is asked to give his opinion of a set of statements, he is engaged in a task that makes sense as presented, and consequently he will not attend so closely to E's reactions. In this situation the muttered "Mm-hmm" should have no effect. The difficulty is, of course, that Ss in our experiment and in Greenspoon's nearly all said they had been quite unaware of E's "Mm-hmm." In other words the two sets of data give no indication of differential attention to E's reactions and so do not support our explanation. Still, the explanation may be correct and our measures of awareness insufficiently sensitive.

There are many questions one might ask to test S's awareness. Does he know the purpose of the experiment? Did he notice anything about E's behavior? Did he notice that E said "Mm-hmm?" Does he realize that these "Mm-hmms" have influenced his behavior? All of the studies so far find that Ss usually do not attain to this last level of awareness. It is not clear from the experimental descriptions which other questions were asked nor what the answers were. It is possible, therefore, that reinforcers are more effective on the higher levels of awareness than on the lower levels and that these levels have not been adequately distinguished in the studies reported.

We did ask our Ss several questions before inquiring whether they knew about E's influence on their behavior. Eight Ss were aware that E had said "Good" while only one S noticed "Mm-hmm." Evidently "Good" is more "visible" in the interviewer's role than is "Mm-hmm." Probably this is because saying "Good" very nearly violates the prescribed nondirective character of that role. This is a difference of awareness that may help to account for the effectiveness in our study of "Good" and the ineffectiveness of "Mm-hmm." We also asked our Ss to guess at E's opinion of General Education. We thought it quite possible that while S usually fails to notice E's responses he might react to them in forming a conception of E's opinions and this conception might be verbalizable when its behavioral sources were not. This measure disappointed us in the present case, in that all but one S thought E favored General Education. However, there is a tendency for the Ss who were reinforced for anti-General Education answers to attribute to E a somewhat less favorable attitude than do the Ss reinforced for proresponses. Furthermore the Ss whose conceptions of E's attitude show more sensitivity to the pattern of reinforcement received are also the Ss whose own attitude scores seem to have been most influenced by E's reactions. While all of these trends fall short of significance in the present study, they do open the possibility that levels of awareness will help to account for differences in the effectiveness of selectively interpolated experimenter reactions.

There is a further point of contrast between our results and those of Greenspoon. Since a light and a tone have been used as reinforcers it would seem that semantics plays no necessary part in this phenomenon. Yet we find "Good" effective and "Mm-hmm" ineffective, and we are inclined to think that this may be partly due to the fact that "Good" has a more clearly favorable meaning than "Mm-hmm." The meaning of "Mm-hmm" is altogether dependent on the intonation pattern. As a sequence of segmental phonemes, as a printed word, its meaning is ambiguous. It may be a neutral indication that one is listening or it may even be questioning or disapproving. "Good" is somewhat less dependent on intonation. It is more reliably a favorable sign. This semantic difference may help to account for the superior effectiveness of "Good."

Our experimental procedure has brought the verbal reinforcement experiment nearer the interview situation. It may eventually prove to be necessary to train interviewers to control their specific reactions to the content received from an informant. Some of these reactions (smiles, averted eyes, etc.) may not be susceptible of control. It may be wiser, in a study of public opinion, to use interviewers of opposed bias, letting their reinforcing reactions operate freely but hoping the effects will cancel one another in the total sample. Pollsters might even learn much about opinion stability by having interviewers deliberately take different sides for different Ss.

In any case, there is much to be learned about the reinforcement of verbal behavior before worrying unduly about its effects in the interview. It has not yet been shown, for instance, that a reaction like "Mm-hmm" is selectively used to express approval in ordinary conversations or interviews. The reactions *can* be selectively interpolated by an experimenter but *is it* selectively interpolated outside the laboratory? Can one predict the naïve speaker's use of "Mm-hmm" from knowledge of his attitudes? Even if this be possible, it does not follow that the usage of either the clinician or the opinion interviewer is similarly predictable. Their efforts to play a nondirective role may well change the ordinary usage of "Mm-hmm." Actual interviewer behavior needs to be studied before deciding on the importance of the studies of verbal reinforcement for the interview.

Summary

A questionnaire was administered by telephone and the interviewer attempted to influence his Ss through the selective interpolation of two reactions — "Good" and "Mm-hmm." "Good" proved to bias the results obtained while "Mm-hmm" did not. The study was repeated and the same result obtained. These results were compared with those obtained by other experiments. The implications of the verbal reinforcement phenomenon for the clinical and opinion interview are discussed.

References

1. Cohen, B. D., Kalish, H. I., Thurston, J. R., and Cohen, E. Experimental manipulation of verbal behavior. *J. exp. Psychol.*, 1954, **47**, 106–110.
2. Greenspoon, J. The effect of verbal and nonverbal stimuli on the frequency of members of two verbal response classes. Unpublished doctor's dissertation, Indiana Univer., 1951.
3. Greenspoon, J. The effect of two nonverbal stimuli on the frequency of members of two verbal response classes. *Amer. Psychologist*, 1954, 9, 384. (Abstract)
4. Taffel, C. Conditioning of verbal behavior in an institutionalized population and its relation to "anxiety level." Unpublished doctor's dissertation, Indiana Univer., 1952.

PERCEPTUAL LEARNING

This classic paper is a good statement of the position of a field-learning theorist.

A point to guide your study

What are the types of experiments which Dr. Tolman uses to support his field-learning point of view? How do they support this view?

26. COGNITIVE MAPS IN RATS AND MEN

Edward C. Tolman*

I shall devote the body of this paper to a description of experiments with rats. But I shall also attempt in a few words at the close to indicate the significance of these findings on rats for the clinical behavior of men. Most of the rat investigations, which I shall report, were carried out in the Berkeley laboratory. But I shall also include, occasionally, accounts of the behavior of non-Berkeley rats who obviously have misspent their lives in out-of-State laboratories. Furthermore, in reporting our Berkeley experiments I shall have to omit a very great many. The ones I *shall* talk about were carried out by graduate students (or underpaid research assistants) who, supposedly, got some of their ideas from me. And a few, though a very few, were even carried out by me myself.

Let me begin by presenting diagrams for a couple of typical mazes, an alley maze and an elevated maze. In the typical experiment a hungry rat is put at the entrance of the maze (alley or elevated), and wanders about through the various true path segments and blind alleys until he finally comes to the food box and eats. This is repeated (again in the typical experiment) one trial every 24 hours and the animal tends to make fewer and fewer errors (that is, blind-alley entrances) and to take less and less time between start and goal-box until finally he is entering no blinds at all and running in a very few seconds from start to goal. The results are usually presented in the form of average curves of blind-entrances, or of seconds from start to finish, for groups of rats.

* 34th Annual Faculty Research Lecture, delivered at the University of California, Berkeley, March 17, 1947. Presented also on March 26, 1947, as one in a series of lectures in Dynamic Psychology sponsored by the division of psychology of Western Reserve University, Cleveland, Ohio.

E. C. Tolman. Cognitive maps in rats and men. *Psychol. Rev.,* 1948, **55,** 189–208. Copyright 1948 by the American Psychological Association. Reprinted here with permission from the American Psychological Association.

All students agree as to the facts. They disagree, however, on theory and explanation.

(1) First, there is a school of animal psychologists which believes that the maze behavior of rats is a matter of mere simple stimulus-response connections. Learning, according to them, consists in the strengthening of some of these connections and in the weakening of others. According to this "stimulus-response" school the rat in progressing down the maze is helplessly responding to a succession of external stimuli—sights, sounds, smells, pressures, etc. impinging upon his external sense organs—plus internal stimuli coming from the viscera and from the skeletal muscles. These external and internal stimuli call out the walkings, runnings, turnings, retracings, smellings, rearings, and the like which appear. The rat's central nervous system, according to this view may be likened to a complicated telephone switchboard. There are the incoming calls from sense-organs and there are the outgoing messages to muscles. Before the learning of a specific maze, the connecting switches (synapses according to the physiologist) are closed in one set of ways and produce the primarily exploratory responses which appear in the early trials. *Learning,* according to this view, consists in the respective strengthening and weakening of various of these connections; those connections which result in the animal's going down the true path become relatively more open to the passage of nervous impulses, whereas those which lead him into the blinds become relatively less open.

It must be noted in addition, however, that this stimulus-response school divides further into two subgroups.

(a) There is a subgroup which holds that the mere mechanics involved in the running of a maze is such that the crucial stimuli from the maze get presented simultaneously with the correct responses more frequently than they do with any of the incorrect responses. Hence, just on a basis of this greater frequency, the neural connections between the crucial stimuli and the

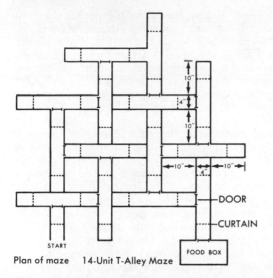

Plan of maze   14-Unit T-Alley Maze

Figure 1. Plan of maze; 14-unit T-alley maze (from M. H. Elliott, The effect of change of reward on the maze performance of rats. Univ. Calif. Publ. Psychol., 1928, 4, p. 20).

correct responses will tend, it is said, to get strengthened at the expense of the incorrect connections.

(b) There is a second subgroup in this stimulus-response school which holds that the reason the appropriate connections get strengthened relatively to the inappropriate ones is, rather, the fact that the responses resulting from the correct connections are followed more closely in time by need-reductions. Thus a hungry rat in a maze tends to get to food and have his hunger reduced *sooner* as a result of the true path responses than as a result of the blind alley responses. And such immediately following need-reductions or, to use another term, such "positive reinforcements" tend somehow, it is said, to strengthen the connections which have most closely preceded them. Thus it is as if—although this is certainly not the way this subgroup would themselves state it—the satisfaction-receiving part of the rat telephoned back to Central and said to the girl: "Hold that connection; it was good; and see to it that you blankety-blank well use it again the next time these same stimuli come in." These theorists also assume (at least some of them do some of the time) that, if bad results—'annoyances,' 'negative reinforcements'—follow, then this same satisfaction- and annoyance-receiving part of the rat will telephone back and say, "Break that connection and don't you dare use it next time either."

So much for a brief summary of the two subvarieties of the 'stimulus-response,' or telephone switchboard school.

(2) Let us turn now to the second main school. This group (and I belong to them) may be called the field theorists. We believe that in the course of learning something like a field map of the environment gets established in the rat's brain. We agree with the other school that the rat in running a maze is exposed to stimuli and is finally led as a result of these stimuli to the responses which actually occur. We feel, however, that the intervening brain processes are more complicated, more patterned and often, pragmatically speaking, more autonomous than do the stimulus-response psychologists. Although we admit that the rat is bombarded by stimuli, we hold that his nervous system is surprisingly selective as to which of these stimuli it will let in at any given time.

Secondly, we assert that the central office itself is far more like a map control room than it is like an old-fashioned telephone exchange. The stimuli, which are allowed in, are not connected by just simple one-to-one switches to the outgoing responses. Rather, the incoming impulses are usually worked over and elaborated in the central control room into a tentative, cognitive-like map of the environment. And it is this tentative map, indicating routes and paths and environmental relationships, which finally determines what responses, if any, the animal will finally release.

Finally, I, personally, would hold further that it is also important to discover in how far these maps are relatively narrow and strip-like or relatively broad and comprehensive. Both strip-maps and comprehensive-maps may be either correct or incorrect in the sense that they may (or may

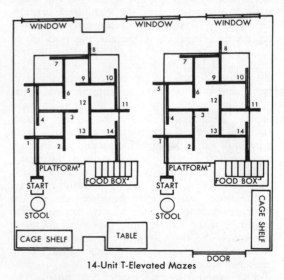

14-Unit T-Elevated Mazes

Figure 2 Fourteen-unit T-elevated mazes. These were two identical mazes placed side by side in the same room (from C. H. Honzik, The sensory basis of maze learning in rats. Compar. Psychol. Monogr., 1936, 13, No. 4, p. 4).

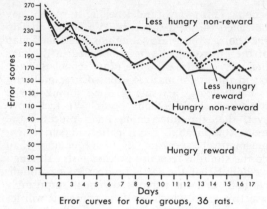

Error curves for four groups, 36 rats.

Figure 3 Error curves for four groups, 36 rats. A maze identical with the alley maze shown in Figure 1 was used (from E. C. Tolman and C. H. Honzik, Degrees of hunger, reward and non-reward, and maze learning in rats. Univ. Calif. Publ. Psychol., 1930, 4, No. 16, p. 246).

not), when acted upon, lead successfully to the animal's goal. The differences between such strip maps and such comprehensive maps will appear only when the rat is later presented with some change within the given environment. ✗Then, the narrower and more strip-like the original map, the less will it carry over successfully to the new problem; whereas, the wider and the more comprehensive it was, the more adequately it will serve in the new set-up. In a strip-map the given position of the animal is connected by only a relatively simple and single path to the position of the goal. In a comprehensive-map a wider arc of the environment is represented, so that, if the starting position of the animal be changed or variations in the specific routes be introduced, this wider map will allow the animal still to behave relatively correctly and to choose the appropriate new route.

But let us turn, now, to the actual experiments. The ones, out of many, which I have selected to report are simply ones which seem especially important in reinforcing the theoretical position I have been presenting. This position, I repeat, contains two assumptions: First, that learning consists not in stimulus-response connections but in the building up in the nervous system of sets which function like cognitive maps and second, that such cognitive maps may be usefully characterized as varying from a narrow strip variety to a broader comprehensive variety.

The experiments fall under five heads: (1) "latent learning," (2) "vicarious trial and error" or "VTE," (3) "searching for the stimulus," (4) "hypotheses" and (5) "spatial orientation."

(1) *"Latent Learning" experiments.* The first of the latent learning experiments was performed at Berkeley by Blodgett. It was published in 1929. Blodgett not only performed the experiments, he also originated the concept. He ran three groups of rats through a six-unit alley maze, shown in Figure 4. He had a control group and two experimental groups. The error curves for these groups appear in Figure 5. The solid line shows the error curve for Group I, the control group. These animals were run in orthodox fashion. That is, they were run one trial a day and found food in the goal-box at the end of each trial. Groups II and III were the experimental groups. The animals of Group II, the dash line, were not fed in the maze for the first six days but only in their home cages some two hours later. On the seventh day (indicated by the small cross) the rats found food at the end of the maze for the first time and continued to find it on subsequent days. The animals of Group III were treated similarly except that they first found food at the end of the maze on the third day and continued to find it there on subsequent days. It will be observed that the experimental groups as long as they were not finding food did not appear to learn much. (Their error curves did not drop.) But on the days immediately succeeding their first finding of the food their error curves did drop astoundingly. It appeared, in short, that during the non-rewarded trials these animals had been learning much more than they had exhibited. This learning, which did not manifest itself until after the food had been introduced, Blodgett called "latent learning." Interpreting these results anthropomorphically, we would say that as long as the animals were not getting any food at the end of the maze they continued to

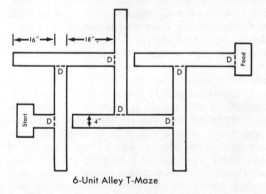

6-Unit Alley T-Maze

Figure 4 Six-unit T-alley maze (from H. C. Blodgett, The effect of the introduction of reward upon the maze performance of rats. Univ. Calif. Publ. Psychol., 1929, 4, No. 8, p. 117).

take their time in going through it—they continued to enter many blinds. Once, however, they knew they were to get food, they demonstrated that during these preceding non-rewarded trials they had learned where many of the blinds were. They had been building up a "map," and could utilize the latter as soon as they were motivated to do so.

Honzik and myself repeated the experiments (or rather he did and I got some of the credit) with the 14-unit T-mazes shown in Figure 1, and with larger groups of animals, and got similar results. The resulting curves are shown in Figure 6. We used two control groups—one that never found food in the maze (HNR) and one that found it throughout (HR). The experimental group (HNR-R) found food at the end of the maze from the 11th day on and showed the same sort of a sudden drop.

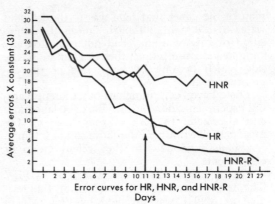

Figure 6   Error curves for HR, HNR, and HNR-R (from E. C. Tolman and C. H. Honzik, Introduction and removal of reward, and maze performance in rats. Univ. Calif. Publ. Psychol., 1930, 4, No. 19, p. 267).

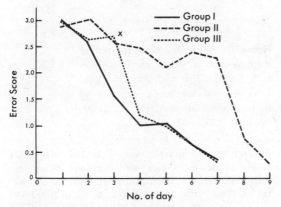

Figure 5   (From H. C. Blodgett, The effect of the introduction of reward upon the maze performance of rats. Univ. Calif. Publ. Psychol., 1929, 4, No. 8, p. 120)

But probably the best experiment demonstrating latent learning was, unfortunately, done not in Berkeley but at the University of Iowa, by Spence and Lippitt. Only an abstract of this experiment has as yet been published. However, Spence has sent a preliminary manuscript from which the following account is summarized. A simple Y-maze (see Figure 7) with two goal-boxes was used. Water was at the end of the right arm of the Y and food at the end of the left arm. During the training period the rats were run neither hungry nor thirsty. They were satiated for both food and water before each day's trials. However, they were willing to run because after each run they were taken out of whichever end box they had got to and put into a living cage, with other animals in it. They were given four trials a day in this fashion for seven days, two trials to the right and two to the left.

In the crucial test the animals were divided into two subgroups one made solely hungry and one solely thirsty. It was then found that on the first trial the hungry group went at once to the left, where the food had been, statistically more frequently than to the right; and the thirsty group went to the right, where the water had been, statistically more frequently than to the left. These results indicated that under the previous non-differential and very mild rewarding conditions of merely being returned to the home cages the animals had nevertheless been learning where the water was and where the food was. In short, they had acquired a cognitive

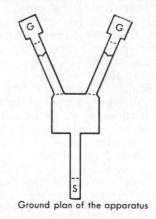

Ground plan of the apparatus

Figure 7   Ground plan of the apparatus (taken from K. W. Spence and R. Lippitt, An experimental test of the sign-gestalt theory of trial and error learning. J. exp. Psychol., 1946, 36, p. 494. In this article they were describing another experiment but used the same maze).

map to the effect that food was to the left and water to the right, although during the acquisition of this map they had not exhibited any stimulus-response propensities to go more to the side which became later the side of the appropriate goal.

There have been numerous other latent learning experiments done in the Berkeley laboratory and elsewhere. In general, they have for the most part all confirmed the above sort of findings.

Let us turn now to the second group of experiments.

(2) *"Vicarious Trial and Error"* or *"VTE."* The term Vicarious Trial and Error (abbreviated as VTE) was invented by Prof. Muenzinger at Colorado[1] to designate the hesitating, looking-back-and-forth sort of behavior which rats can often be observed to indulge in at a choice-point before actually going one way or the other.

Quite a number of experiments upon VTE-ing have been carried out in our laboratory. I shall report only a few. In most of them what is called a discrimination set-up has been used. In one characteristic type of visual discrimination apparatus designed by Lashley (shown in Figure 8) the animal is put on a jumping stand and faced with two doors which differ in some visual property, say, as here shown, vertical stripes vs. horizontal stripes.

One of each such pair of visual stimuli is made always correct and the other wrong; and the two are interchanged from side to side in random fashion. The animal is required to learn, say, that the vertically striped door is always the correct one. If he jumps to it, the door falls open and he gets to food on a platform behind. If on the other hand, he jumps incorrectly, he finds the door locked and falls into a net some two feet below from which he is picked up and started over again.

Using a similar set-up (see Figure 9), but with landing platforms in front of the doors so that if the rat chose incorrectly he could jump back again and start over, I found that when the choice was an easy one, say between a white door and a black door, the animals·not only learned sooner but also did more VTEing than when the choice was difficult, say between a white door and a gray door (see Figure 10). It appeared further (see Figure 11) that the VTEing began to appear just as (or just before) the rats began to learn. After the learning had become established, however, the VTE's began to go down. Further, in a study of individual

---

[1] Vide: K. F. Muenzinger, Vicarious trial and error at a point of choice: I. A general survey of its relation to learning efficiency. *J. genet. Psychol.*, 1938, **53**, 75–86.

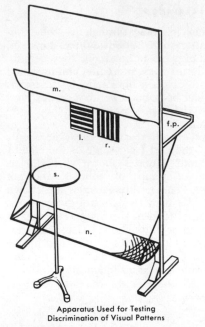

Apparatus Used for Testing
Discrimination of Visual Patterns

Figure 8   Apparatus used for testing discrimination of visual patterns (from K. S. Lashley, The mechanism of vision. I. A method for rapid analyses of pattern-vision in the rat. *J. genet. Psychol.*, 1930, 37, p. 44).

differences by myself, Geier and Levin[2] (actually done by Geier and Levin) using this same visual discrimination apparatus, it was found that with one and the same difficulty of

[2] F. M. Geier, M. Levin & E. C. Tolman, Individual differences in emotionality, hypothesis formation, vicarious trial and error and visual discrimination learning in rats. *Comp. Psychol. Monogr.*, 1941, **17**, No. 3.

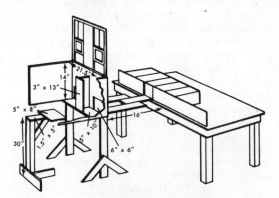

Figure 9   (From E. C. Tolman, Prediction of vicarious trial and error by means of the schematic sowbug. Psychol. Rev., 1939, 46, p. 319)

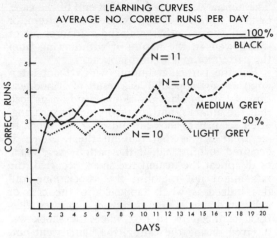

LEARNING CURVES
AVERAGE NO. CORRECT RUNS PER DAY

Figure 10   (From E. C. Tolman, Prediction of vicarious trial and error by means of the schematic sowbug. Psychol. Rev., 1939, 46, p. 319)

problem the smarter animal did the more VTEing.

To sum up, in *visual discrimination* experiments the better the learning, the more the VTE's. But this seems contrary to what we would perhaps have expected. We ourselves would expect to do more VTEing, more sampling of the two stimuli, when it is difficult to choose between them than when it is easy.

What is the explanation? The answer lies, I believe, in the fact that the manner in which we set the visual discrimination problems for the rats and the manner in which we set similar problems for ourselves are different. We already have our "instructions." We know beforehand

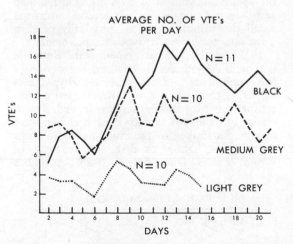

AVERAGE NO. OF VTE's
PER DAY

Figure 11   (From E. C. Tolman, Prediction of vicarious trial and error by means of the schematic sowbug. Psychol. Rev., 1939, 46, p. 320)

what it is we are to do. We are told, or we tell ourselves, that it is the lighter of the two grays, the heavier of the two weights, or the like, which is to be chosen. In such a setting we do more sampling, more VTEing, when the stimulus-difference is small. But for the rats the usual problem in a discrimination apparatus is quite different. They do not know what is wanted of them. The major part of their learning in most such experiments seems to consist in their discovering the instructions. The rats have to discover that it is the differences in visual brightness, not the differences between left and right, which they are to pay attention to. Their VTEing appears when they begin to "catch on." The greater the difference between the two stimuli the more the animals are attracted by this difference. Hence the sooner they catch on, and during this catching on, the more they VTE.

That this is a reasonable interpretation appeared further, from an experiment by myself and Minium (the actual work done, of course, by Minium) in which a group of six rats was first taught a white vs. black discrimination, then two successively more difficult gray vs. black discriminations. For each difficulty the rats were given a long series of further trials beyond the points at which they. had learned. Comparing the beginning of each of these three difficulties the results were that the rats did more VTEing for the easy discriminations than for the more difficult ones. When, however, it came to a comparison of amounts of VTEing during the final performance after each learning had reached a plateau, the opposite results were obtained. In other words, after the rats had finally divined their instruction, then they, like human beings did more VTEing, more sampling, the more difficult the discrimination.

Finally, now let us note that it was also found at Berkeley by Jackson[3] that in a maze the difficult maze units produce more VTEing and also that the more stupid rats do the more VTEing. The explanation, as I see it, is that, in the case of mazes, rats know their instructions. For them it is natural to expect that the same spatial path will always lead to the same outcome. Rats in mazes don't have to be told.

But what, now, is the final significance of all the VTEing? How do these facts about VTEing affect our theoretical argument? My answer is that these facts lend further support to the doctrine of a building up of maps. VTEing, as I see it, is evidence that in the critical stages—whether in the first picking up of the instructions or in the later making sure of which stim-

[3] L. L. Jackson, V. T. E. on an elevated maze. *J. comp. Psychol.*, 1943, **36**, 99–107.

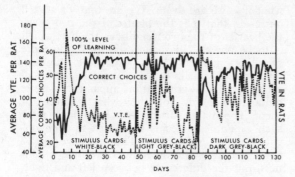

Figure 12 (From E. C. Tolman and E. Minium, VTE in rats: overlearning and difficulty of discrimination. J. comp. Psychol., 1942, 34, p. 303)

ulus is which—the animal's activity is not just one of responding passively to discrete stimuli, but rather one of the active selecting and comparing of stimuli. This brings me then to the third type of experiment.

(3) *"Searching for the Stimulus."* I refer to a recent, and it seems to me extremely important experiment, done for a Ph.D. dissertation by Hudson. Hudson was first interested in the question of whether or not rats could learn an avoidance reaction in one trial. His animals were tested one at a time in a living cage (see Figure 13) with a small striped visual pattern at the end, on which was mounted a food cup. The hungry rat approached this food cup and ate. An electrical arrangement was provided so that when the rat touched the cup he could be given an electric shock. And one such shock did appear to be enough. For when the rat was replaced in this same cage days or even weeks afterwards, he usually demonstrated immediately strong avoidance reactions to the visual pattern.

The animal withdrew from that end of the cage, or piled up sawdust and covered the pattern, or showed various other amusing responses all of which were in the nature of withdrawing from the pattern or making it disappear.

But the particular finding which I am interested in now appeared as a result of a modification of this standard procedure. Hudson noticed that the animals, anthropomorphically speaking, often seemed to look around *after* the shock to see what it was that had hit them. Hence it occurred to him that, if the pattern were made to disappear the instant the shock occurred, the rats might not establish the association. And this indeed is what happened in the case of many individuals. Hudson added further electrical connections so that when the shock was received during the eating, the lights went out, the pattern and the food cup dropped out of sight, and the lights came on again all within the matter of a second. When such animals were again put in the cage 24 hours later, a large percentage showed no avoidance of the pattern. Or to quote Hudson's own words:

Learning what object to avoid . . . may occur exclusively during the period *after* the shock. For if the object from which the shock was actually received is removed at the moment of the shock, a significant number of animals fail to learn to avoid it, some selecting other features in the environment for avoidance, and others avoiding nothing.

In other words, I feel that this experiment reinforces the notion of the largely active selective character in the rat's building up of his cognitive map. He often has to look actively for the significant stimuli in order to form his map and does not merely passively receive and react to all the stimuli which are physically present. Turn now to the fourth type of experiment.

(4) *The "Hypothesis" experiments.* Both the notion of hypotheses in rats and the design of the experiments to demonstrate such hypotheses are to be credited to Krech. Krech used a four-compartment discrimination-box. In such a four-choice box the correct door at each choice-point may be determined by the experimenter in terms of its being lighted or dark, left or right, or various combinations of these. If all possibilities

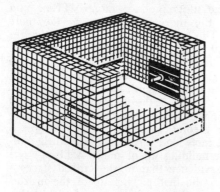

Figure 13 (From Bradford Hudson. Ph.D. Thesis: One trial learning: A study of the avoidance behavior of the rat. On deposit in the Library of the University of California, Berkeley, Calif.)

Figure 14 [from I. Krechevsky (now D. Krech), The genesis of "hypotheses" in rats. Univ. Calif. Publ. Psychol., 1932, 6, No. 4, p. 46]

are randomized for the 40 choices made in 10 runs of each day's test, the problem could be made insoluble.

When this was done, Krech found that the individual rat went through a succession of systematic choices. That is, the individual animal might perhaps begin by choosing practically all right-hand doors, then he might give this up for choosing practically all left-hand doors, and then, for choosing all dark doors, and so on. These relatively persistent, and well-above-chance systematic types of choice Krech called "hypotheses." In using this term he obviously did not mean to imply verbal processes in the rat but merely referred to what I have been calling cognitive maps which, it appears from his experiments, get set up in a tentative fashion to be tried out first one and then another until, if possible, one is found which works.

Finally, it is to be noted that these hypothesis experiments, like the latent learning, VTE, and "looking for the stimulus" experiments, do not, as such, throw light upon the widths of the maps which are picked up but do indicate the generally map-like and self-initiated character of learning.

For the beginning of an attack upon the problem of the width of the maps let me turn to the last group of experiments.

(5) *"Spatial Orientation" experiments.* As early as 1929, Lashley reported incidentally the case of a couple of his rats who, after having learned an alley maze, pushed back the cover near the starting box, climbed out and ran directly across the top to the goal-box where they climbed down in again and ate. Other investigators have reported related findings. All such observations suggest that rats really develop wider spatial maps which include more than the mere trained-on specific paths. In the experiments now to be reported this possibility has been subjected to further examination.

In the first experiment, Tolman, Ritchie, and Kalish (actually Ritchie and Kalish) used the set-up shown in Figure 15.

This was an elevated maze. The animals ran from A across the open circular table through CD (which had alley walls) and finally to G, the food box. H was a light which shone directly down the path from G to F. After four nights, three trials per night, in which the rats learned to run directly and without hesitation from A to G, the apparatus was changed to the sun-burst shown in Figure 16. The starting path and the table remained the same but a series of radiating paths was added.

The animals were again started at A and ran across the circular table into the alley and found themselves blocked. They then returned onto the table and began exploring practically all the radiating paths. After going out a few inches only on any one path, each rat finally chose to

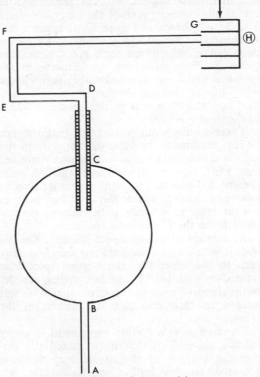

Apparatus used in preliminary training

Figure 15 Apparatus used in preliminary training (from E. C. Tolman, B. F. Ritchie and D. Kalish, Studies in spatial learning. I. Orientation and the short-cut. J. exp. Psychol., 1946, 36, p. 16).

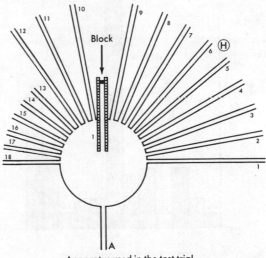

Apparatus used in the test trial

Figure 16 Apparatus used in the test trial (from E. C. Tolman, B. F. Ritchie and D. Kalish, Studies in spatial learning. I. Orientation and the short-cut. J. exp. Psychol., 1946, 36, p. 17).

run all the way out on one. The percentages of rats finally choosing each of the long paths from 1 to 12 are shown in Figure 17. It appears that there was a preponderant tendency to choose path No. 6 which ran to a point some four inches in front of where the entrance to the food-box had been. The only other path chosen with any appreciable frequency was No. 1— that is, the path which pointed perpendicularly to the food-side of the room.

These results seem to indicate that the rats in this experiment had learned not only to run rapidly down the original roundabout route but also, when this was blocked and radiating paths presented, to select one pointing rather directly towards the point where the food had been or else at least to select a path running perpendicularly to the food-side of the room.

As a result of their original training, the rats had, it would seem, acquired not merely a strip-map to the effect that the original specifically trained-on path led to food but, rather, a wider comprehensive map to the effect that food was located in such and such a direction in the room.

Consider now a further experiment done by Ritchie alone. This experiment tested still further the breadth of the spatial map which is acquired. In this further experiment the rats

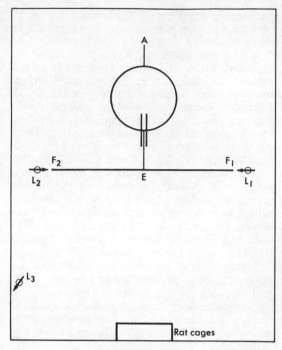

Figure 18   (From B. F. Ritchie. Ph.D. Thesis: Spatial learning in rats. On deposit in the Library of the University of California, Berkeley, Calif.)

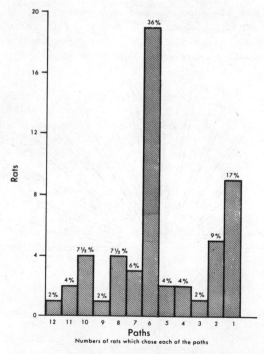

Figure 17   Number of rats which chose each of the paths (from E. C. Tolman, B. F. Ritchie and D. Kalish, Studies in spatial learning. I. Orientation and the short-cut. J. exp. Psychol., 1946, 36, p. 19).

were again run across the table—this time to the arms of a simple T. (See Figure 18.)

Twenty-five animals were trained for seven days, 20 trials in all, to find food at F_1; and twenty-five animals were trained to find it at F_2. The L's in the diagram indicate lights. On the eighth day the starting path and table top were rotated through 180 degrees so that they were now in the position shown in Figure 19. The dotted lines represent the old position. And a series of radiating paths was added. What happened? Again the rats ran across the table into the central alley. When, however, they found themselves blocked, they turned back onto the table and this time also spent many seconds touching and trying out for only a few steps practically all the paths. Finally, however, within seven minutes, 42 of the 50 rats chose one path and ran all the way out on it. The paths finally chosen by the 19 of these animals that had been fed at F_1 and by the 23 that had been fed at F_2 are shown in Figure 20.

This time the rats tended to choose, not the paths which pointed directly to the spots where the food had been, but rather paths which ran perpendicularly to the corresponding sides of the room. The spatial maps of these rats, when the animals were started from the opposite side of the room, were thus not completely adequate to the precise goal positions but were adequate

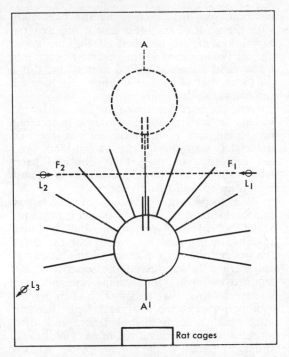

Figure 19 (From B. F. Ritchie. Ph.D. Thesis: Spatial learning in rats. On deposit in the Library of the University of California, Berkeley, Calif.)

as to the correct sides of the room. The maps of these animals were, in short, not altogether strip-like and narrow.

This completes my report of experiments. There were the *latent learning experiments, the VTE experiments, the searching for the stimulus experiment, the hypothesis experiments,* and these last *spatial orientation experiments.*

And now, at last, I come to the humanly significant and exciting problem: namely, what are the conditions which favor narrow strip-maps and what are those which tend to favor broad comprehensive maps not only in rats but also in men?

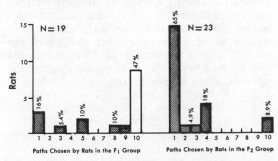

Figure 20 (From B. F. Ritchie. Ph.D. Thesis: Spatial learning in rats. On deposit in the Library of the University of California, Berkeley, Calif.)

There is considerable evidence scattered throughout the literature bearing on this question both for rats and for men. Some of this evidence was obtained in Berkeley and some of it elsewhere. I have not time to present it in any detail. I can merely summarize it by saying that narrow strip maps rather than broad comprehensive maps seem to be induced: (1) by a damaged brain, (2) by an inadequate array of environmentally presented cues, (3) by an overdose of repetitions on the original trained-on path and (4) by the presence of too strongly motivational or of too strongly frustrating conditions.

It is this fourth factor which I wish to elaborate upon briefly in my concluding remarks. For it is going to be my contention that some, at least, of the so-called "psychological mechanisms" which the clinical psychologists and the other students of personality have uncovered as the devils underlying many of our individual and social maladjustments can be interpreted as narrowings of our cognitive maps due to too strong motivations or to too intense frustration.

My argument will be brief, cavalier, and dogmatic. For I am not myself a clinician or a social psychologist. What I am going to say must be considered, therefore, simply as in the nature of a *rat* psychologist's *ratio*cinations offered free. By way of illustration, let me suggest that at least the three dynamisms called, respectively, "regression," "fixation," and "displacement of aggression onto outgroups" are expressions of cognitive maps which are too narrow and which get built up in us as a result of too violent motivation or of too intense frustration.

(a) Consider *regression.* This is the term used for those cases in which an individual, in the face of too difficult a problem, returns to earlier more childish ways of behaving. Thus, to take an example, the overprotected middle-aged woman (reported a couple of years ago in *Time Magazine*) who, after losing her husband, regressed (much to the distress of her growing daughters) into dressing in too youthful a fashion and into competing for their beaux and then finally into behaving like a child requiring continuous care, would be an illustration of regression. I would not wish you to put too much confidence in the reportorial accuracy of *Time,* but such an extreme case is not too different from many actually to be found in our mental hospitals or even sometimes in ourselves. In all such instances my argument would be (1) that such regression results from too strong a present emotional situation and (2) that it consists in going back to too narrow an earlier map, itself due to too much frustration or motivation in early childhood. *Time's* middle-aged woman was presented by too frustrating an emotional situation at her husband's death and she regressed,

I would wager, to too narrow adolescent and childhood maps since these latter had been originally excessively impressed because of over-stressful experiences at the time she was growing up.

(b) Consider *fixation*. Regression and fixation tend to go hand in hand. For another way of stating the fact of the undue persistence of early maps is to say that they were fixated. This has even been demonstrated in rats. If rats are too strongly motivated in their original learning, they find it very difficult to relearn when the original path is no longer correct. Also after they have relearned, if they are given an electric shock they, like *Time*'s woman, tend to regress back again to choosing the earlier path.

(c) Finally, consider the *"displacement of aggressions onto outgroups."* Adherence to one's own group is an ever-present tendency among primates. It is found in chimpanzees and monkeys as strongly as in men. We primates operate in groups. And each individual in such a group tends to identify with his whole group in the sense that the group's goals become his goals, the group's life and immortality, his life and immortality. Furthermore, each individual soon learns that, when as an individual he is frustrated, he must not take out his aggressions on the other members of his own group. He learns instead to displace his aggressions onto outgroups. Such a displacement of aggression I would claim is also a narrowing of the cognitive map. The individual comes no longer to distinguish the true locus of the cause of his frustration. The poor Southern whites, who take it out on the Negroes, are displacing their aggressions from the landlords, the southern economic system, the northern capitalists, or wherever the true cause of their frustration may lie, onto a more convenient outgroup. The physicists on the Faculty who criticize the humanities, or we psychologists who criticize all the other departments, or the University as a whole which criticizes the Secondary School system or, vice versa, the Secondary School system which criticizes the University or—on a still larger and far more dangerous scene—we Americans who criticize the Russians and the Russians who criticize us, are also engaging, at least in part, in nothing more than such irrational displacements of our aggressions onto outgroups.

I do not mean to imply that there may not be some true interferences by the one group with the goals of the other and hence that the aggressions of the members of the one group against the members of the other are necessarily *wholly* and *merely* displaced aggressions. But I do assert that often and in large part they are such mere displacements.

Over and over again men are blinded by too violent motivations and too intense frustrations into blind and unintelligent and in the end desperately dangerous hates of outsiders. And the expression of these their displaced hates ranges all the way from discrimination against minorities to world conflagrations.

What in the name of Heaven and Psychology can we do about it? My only answer is to preach again the virtues of reason—of, that is, broad cognitive maps. And to suggest that the child-trainers and the world-planners of the future can only, if at all, bring about the presence of the required rationality (i.e., comprehensive maps) if they see to it that nobody's children are too over-motivated or too frustrated. Only then can these children learn to look before and after, learn to see that there are often round-about and safer paths to their quite proper goals—learn, that is, to realize that the well-being of White and of Negro, of Catholic and of Protestant, of Christian and of Jew, of American and of Russian (and even of males and females) are mutually inter-dependent.

We dare not let ourselves or others become so over-emotional, so hungry, so ill-clad, so over-motivated that only narrow strip-maps will be developed. All of us in Europe as well as in America, in the Orient as well as in the Occident, must be made calm enough and well-fed enough to be able to develop truly comprehensive maps, or, as Freud would have put it, to be able to learn to live according to the Reality principle rather than according to the too narrow and too immediate Pleasure Principle.

We must, in short, subject our children and ourselves (as the kindly experimenter would his rats) to the optimal conditions of moderate motivation and of absence of unnecessary frustrations, whenever we put them and ourselves before that great God-given maze which is our human world. I cannot predict whether or not we will be able, or be allowed, to do this; but I *can* say that, only insofar as we *are* able and *are* allowed, have we cause for hope.

CHAPTER EIGHT

Human learning and forgetting

TRANSFER OF TRAINING

This is one of the classical papers in the area of transfer of training. It was among the first in which an analysis of transfer in terms of the stimulus (S) and response (R) components of a task was made. It was also one of the first investigations of the effect of the similarity of the S and R components on transfer of training. Generally, although there have been a good many refinements, the conclusions derived from this study have held up.

Points to guide your study

1. This experiment uses the *paired-comparison* method of rote learning. Describe this method.

2. Can you state the conclusions of this paper in your own words? Try to make up a memory scheme for remembering them, e.g., "O-N-N," old stimulus–new response–negative transfer.

3. Note that some of these conclusions depend upon a rigorous definition of what is and what is not similar to something else. In other words, the conclusions depend upon the specification of a dimension of similarity.

4. Note that this article is not written in the same style as more recent ones. If you become a psychologist or, much more likely, if you write reports of your own experiments in the laboratory portion of a psychology course, you will want to follow the style of one of the more recent articles. This is merely a convention.

27. CONDITIONS OF TRANSFER OF TRAINING

Robert Wallace Bruce, Wabash College*

Introduction

This study is an investigation of some of the conditions of transfer of training. We shall seek to answer these questions:

* From the Psychological Laboratory of the University of Chicago. The writer wishes to acknowledge his indebtedness to Professors Edward S. Robinson and Arthur G. Bills for assistance in planning and completing the study.
R. W. Bruce. Conditions of transfer of training. *J. exp. Psychol.*, 1933, **16**, 343–361. Copyright 1933 by the American Psychological Association. Excerpts reprinted here with permission from the author and the American Psychological Association. Footnote 3 omitted.

I. What is the relation of the following conditions of learning to transfer:
   A. Learning to make a new response to an old stimulus?
   B. Learning to make an old response to a new stimulus?
   C. Learning to make a new response to a new stimulus?

II. What is the relation of the degree of integration of the initial learning to transfer in
   A. Learning to make a new response to an old stimulus?
   B. Learning to make an old response to a new stimulus?

III. What is the relation of certain similarities between the $S_1R_1S_2R_2$ terms of the initial and subsequent learning material to transfer in

A. Learning to make a new response to an old stimulus?

B. Learning to make an old response to a new stimulus?

In most of the previous studies of learning transfer, the stimulus-response terms are undifferentiated. The usual procedure is to learn task *A*, then task *B*, check and compare the two results, and ascribe the difference to transfer. As a consequence, results have been obtained which give positive, zero, and negative transfer. Since the previous experiments have not been made for the purpose of reconciling these diverse results, we are attempting such a reconciliation by discovering some of the conditions of transfer.

Technique

(1) Learning terms defined. Learning transfer relates to the effect of initial upon subsequent learning. In this investigation, the initial and subsequent learning are further differentiated into stimulus and response terms, which are designated initial stimulus, initial response, subsequent stimulus, subsequent response, $S_1R_1S_2R_2$.

(2) General nature of the learning material. The learning material in these studies consists of nonsense syllables. The syllables may be similar, different, or identical; by arbitrary definition, 'similar' syllables are syllables which vary only in respect to the final letter, such as var, vam.

(3) Description of the conditions, relative to (*a*) *Identities between certain of the* $S_1R_1S_2R_2$ *terms.* The relation of identity of the $S_1R_1S_2R_2$ terms is varied. In condition IX, the terms are all different. In conditions I, II, III, IV, the S_1 and S_2 are identical, which means that the subjects are required to learn a new response to an old stimulus. In conditions V, VI, VII, VIII, the R_1 and R_2 are identical, which means that the subjects are required to learn to make an old response to a new stimulus.

(*b*) *Similarities between certain of the* $S_1R_1S_2R_2$ *terms.* In conditions I, V, IX, no similarities are present. In conditions II and VI, the initial stimulus and initial response are similar. In conditions III and VII, the subsequent stimulus and subsequent response are similar. In condition IV, the initial response and subsequent response are similar, and in condition VIII, the initial stimulus and the subsequent stimulus are similar.

(*c*) *Integration of the initial learning.* In each of the nine conditions, an initial list of syllables is presented to the subject either 0, 2, 6 or 12 times, regardless of the number of repetitions required to learn the initial list. By means of this variation, situations are provided in which the original material may be entirely unlearned, slightly learned, almost learned, completely learned, or overlearned. A subsequent list is then repeatedly presented until it is learned. It is assumed that a list is learned, when the subject can correctly anticipate the second member of each pair before it actually appears. The last repetition therefore is not counted. The following table is a partial summary of the conditions.

(4) Rate of presentation. A 2-second interval is given per successive exposure.

(5) Method of presentation. In all of the conditions, a variation of the paired-associates method is used, in which the subject is presented first with a given syllable, then with the syllable and its associate, and so forth. An illustrative list of syllables follows:

Summary of conditions and illustration of identities and similarities between terms in the different conditions

Condition	Initial learning		Subsequent learning		Relation of initial to subsequent material
	Stimulus S_1	Response R_1	Stimulus S_2	Response R_2	
I	req	kiv	req	zam	S_1S_2 identical
II	bij	bic	bij	tab	S_1S_2 identical, S_1R_1 similar
III	mir	ped	mir	miy	S_1S_2 identical, S_2R_2 similar
IV	tec	zox	tec	zop	S_1S_2 identical, R_1R_2 similar
V	lan	qip	fis	qip	R_1R_2 identical
VI	soj	soy	nel	soy	R_1R_2 identical, S_1R_1 similar
VII	zaf	qer	qec	qer	R_1R_2 identical, S_2R_2 similar
VIII	bes	yor	bef	yor	R_1R_2 identical, S_1S_2 similar
IX	xal	pom	cam	lup	all terms different

Initial S_1R_1 list		Subsequent S_2R_2 list	
(S_1 with R_1)		(S_2 with R_2)	
req		fiz	
req	kiy	fiz	sej
taw		mip	
taw	rif	mip	boc
qix		bul	
qix	lep	bul	puw
wam		nic	
wam	bos	nic	git
zed		caj	
zed	dib	caj	lim

(6) Length of the lists. It was necessary, in arranging the length of the lists for the various conditions, to make certain that they were long enough, in all cases, to require several repetitions in the learning. Conditions III and VII permitted more rapid learning than the other conditions, and hence longer lists were employed in these two conditions. Therefore, the length of the lists, as determined by pre-experimentation, is 5 syllables in conditions I, II, IV, V, VI, VIII, IX, and 7 syllables in conditions III and VII.

(7) Different groupings of the pairs of syllables. The members of each pair of syllables remain invariably together, but the order of the pairs in the list is varied in an irregular manner from trial to trial. This arrangement, which provides for four different groupings of the pairs per list, follows:

Repetition of list	Sequence of presentation of the syllables per list				
1st	1	2	3	4	5
2d	4	1	5	3	2
3d	5	4	2	1	3
4th	2	5	1	3	4
5th, etc.	1	2	3	4	5

(8) Practice effects equalized. The conditions of integration are regularly shifted per subject per cycle in a manner calculated to equalize the benefits to be derived from practice. The sequence is so adjusted that every subject studies each of the four conditions of integration under each of the four successive learning periods of the cycle.

(9) Differences in difficulty of lists adjusted. The syllable lists are given in a sequence per subject per condition calculated to equalize their difficulty in learning. The sequence is so adjusted that each syllable list is learned 2 or more times under each of the conditions of integra-

tion, and under each of the four successive learning periods of a cycle group.

(10) The subjects. Eighty-one college students served as subjects; nine are used in each condition, and each one is tested individually. Each subject is tested under each of the four conditions of integration, and this is repeated for four cycles. Thus sixteen periods of experimentation are required of each person, and as far as possible, these periods of experimentation are given one at a time, at the rate of one per day.

(11) Apparatus. The apparatus used in this study consists of a metronome, some adding machine paper, and a 12 x 12 inch cardboard in the center of which are two parallel 4½ inch slits ⅝ inches apart.

The metronome is used to provide 2-second intervals.

The adding machine paper is used as a convenient medium for presenting typewritten lists of syllables. In order to present four different groupings of lists of pairs, and in order to provide at least double spacing between successive items, rolls of approximately 36 inches in length are used.

The 12 x 12 inch cardboard is used in lieu of a memory drum. The syllable roll, concealed beneath the cardboard except for the small portion exposed between the two parallel slits, is pulled forward by the experimenter at regular intervals of 2 seconds per exposure item.

Results

I.   Relation of the following types of learning to transfer:

A. Learning to make a new response to an old stimulus.

B. Learning to make an old response to a new stimulus.

C. Learning to make a new response to a new stimulus.

The data of Table I indicate that learning to make a new response to an old stimulus is not benefited by the initial learning of 12 repetitions; in fact the number of repetitions required increases from 10.3 to 11.2 indicating a negative transfer of 100:109, although the difference of 0.9 repetitions is statistically insignificant.

Learning to make an old response to a new stimulus is materially benefited by the initial learning; the number of repetitions required decreases from 14.4 to 9.0 indicating a positive transfer of 100:63. The difference of 5.4 repetitions is statistically significant since it is more than three times the P.E. of the difference, 1.5.

Learning to make a new response to a new stimulus is slightly benefited by the initial learn-

Table I *   Relation to transfer, of learning to make a new response to an old stimulus, an old response to a new stimulus, a new response to a new stimulus

Condition	Mean repetitions required in the subsequent learning under conditions of 0 and 12 repetitions of initial learning		Mean values letting the condition 0 value = 100	
	0	12	0	12
I	10.3	11.2	100	109
V	14.4	9.0	100	63
IX	9.9	8.3	100	84

* Each mean value in this and the following tables is an average of 36 measures.
The probable errors are omitted from the tables, chiefly for reasons of convenience. The P.E. of the difference of given means is stated in the discussion, in a few crucial instances; the subsequent findings hinge upon these values.
The great differences between the 0 integration values in this and the following tables are not of any particular significance inasmuch as
a. different persons serve as subjects in each of the nine conditions of the study,
b. different lists of memory material are used in each of the nine conditions of the study,
c. longer lists of memory material are used under some of the conditions than under others,
d. learning is easier under some of the conditions than under others, since the pairs of syllables are similar in some conditions and different in others.

ing; the number of repetitions required decreases from 9.9 to 8.3 indicating a positive transfer of 100:84. The difference of 1.6 repetitions is too small to be of much significance since the P.E. of the difference is 1.5.

In general the data indicate that there is a marked positive transfer in learning to make an old response to a new stimulus (100:63), a slight positive transfer in learning to make a new response to a new stimulus (100:84), and a slight negative transfer in learning to make a new response to an old stimulus (100:109).

II. Relation of the degree of integration of the initial learning to transfer in
A. Learning to make a new response to an old stimulus.
B. Learning to make an old response to a new stimulus.

In learning to make a new response to an old stimulus, the number of repetitions required varies with the degree of integration of the initial learning: 2 repetitions causes a negative transfer of 100:117; 6 repetitions causes a negative transfer of 100:116; and 12 repetitions causes a negative transfer of 100:109.

In learning to make an old response to a new stimulus, 2 repetitions of the initial learning causes a negative transfer of 100:115; 6 repetitions causes a positive transfer of 100:83; and 12 repetitions causes a positive transfer of 100:63.

In learning to make a new response to a new stimulus, 2 repetitions of the initial learning causes a zero transfer; 6 repetitions causes a negative transfer of 100:108; and 12 repetitions causes a positive transfer of 100:84.

The difficulty of the learning tends to decrease, as the amount of the initial learning is increased from 2 to 6 to 12 repetitions (compare 117 with 116 with 109; also 115 with 83 with 63; also 100 with 108 with 84); this is true moreover, regardless of whether or not similarities are present (see Tables III and IV, and compare also 101,90,90; 127,123,102; 102,101,-80; 103,81,77; 66,56,40; 84,64,44); the decreased difficulty may show itself in terms of a decreasing negative transfer (117,116,109), or in terms

Table II   Influence of the degree of integration (0, 2, 6, 12 repetitions) of the initial learning upon the subsequent learning, relative to learning to make a new response to an old stimulus, an old response to a new stimulus, a new response to a new stimulus.

Condition	Mean repetitions required in the subsequent learning under conditions of 0, 2, 6, 12 repetitions of initial learning				Mean values letting the condition 0 value = 100			
	0	2	6	12	0	2	6	12
I	10.3	12.1	11.9	11.2	100	117	116	109
V	14.4	16.6	12.0	9.0	100	115	83	63
IX	9.9	9.9	10.7	8.3	100	100	108	84

Table III   Influence of similarity of terms involved in initial and subsequent material upon the subsequent learning when learning to make a new response to an old stimulus

Con-dition	Mean repetitions required in the subsequent learning under conditions of 0, 2, 6, 12 repetitions of initial learning				Mean values letting the condition 0 value − 100			
	0	2	6	12	0	2	6	12
I	10.3	12.1	11.9	11.2	100	117	116	109
II	11.1	11.2	10.0	10.0	100	101	90	90
III	8.2	10.4	10.1	8.4	100	127	123	102
IV	9.6	9.8	9.7	7.7	100	102	101	80

of a shift from negative to positive transfer (115,83,63), or in terms of an increasing positive transfer, if similarities are involved (see Table IV, 84,64,44).

III. Relation of the similarity between the $S_1R_1S_2R_2$ terms of the initial and subsequent material, to transfer in

A. Learning to make a new response to an old stimulus.

B. Learning to make an old response to a new stimulus.

Learning to make a new response to an old stimulus when no similarities are present, is slightly hindered by 12 repetitions of initial learning, 100:109. If the stimulus and response terms of the subsequent learning are similar, transfer is practically zero, 100:102. If the stimulus and response terms of the initial learning are similar, a slight positive transfer occurs, 100:90. If the response terms of the initial and subsequent learning are similar, a further slight increment of positive transfer is added, 100:80. In general, the learning is least facilitated when no similarities are present (compare 109 with 90,102,80), and most facilitated when the initial and subsequent responses are related (compare 80 with 109,90,102); the first gives a slight degree of negative transfer, the latter a moderate degree of positive transfer. The relative effec-

tiveness of the four conditions of experimentation varies irregularly with the degree of integration of the initial learning. Under the best conditions, a slight positive transfer occurs; under the poorest conditions, a slight negative transfer occurs.

Learning to make an old response to a new stimulus when no similarities are present, is materially aided by an initial learning of 12 repetitions; the repetitions required decrease from 14.4 to 9.0, a positive transfer of 100:63. If the stimulus and response terms of the initial learning are similar, the amount of positive transfer slightly decreases, 100:77. If the stimulus and response terms of the subsequent learning are similar, the amount of positive transfer is greatly increased, 100:40; so also, if the initial stimulus and the subsequent stimulus are similar, 100:44. In general, the positive transfer is greatest when the subsequent stimulus is similar either to the subsequent response, 100:40 or to the initial stimulus, 100:44. The positive transfer is least when the similarities are restricted to the terms of the initial learning, 100:77; in this latter case, the similarity is even a disadvantage; compare 100:77 with 100:63.

IV. Summary of results, concerning the conditions of transfer of training:

(1) Learning to make an old response to a

Table IV   Influence of similarity of terms involved in initial and subsequent material upon the subsequent learning when learning to make an old response to a new stimulus

Con-dition	Mean repetitions required in the subsequent learning under conditions of 0, 2, 6, 12 repetitions of initial learning				Mean values letting the condition 0 value = 100			
	0	2	6	12	0	2	6	12
V	14.4	16.6	12.0	9.0	100	115	83	63
VI	12.8	13.2	10.4	9.8	100	103	81	77
VII	13.1	8.7	7.3	5.3	100	66	56	40
VIII	13.5	11.4	8.7	5.9	100	84	64	44

new stimulus almost invariably gives marked positive transfer, whereas learning to make a new response to an old stimulus usually results in a slight degree of negative transfer; this is true regardless of whether the

Integration is controlled and the similarity controlled

Integration is varied and the similarity controlled

Integration is controlled and the similarity varied

Integration is varied and the similarity varied.

(2) The difficulty of subsequent learning tends to decrease as the amount of the initial learning is increased from 2 to 6 to 12 repetitions, regardless of whether learning to make a new response to an old stimulus, or learning to make an old response to a new stimulus; this decrease may be in terms of a decreasing negative transfer, in terms of a shift from negative to positive transfer, or in terms of an increasing positive transfer.

(3) The effects of similarity vary as follows:

(*a*) When learning to make a new response to an old stimulus, the learning is least facilitated when no similarities are present, and most facilitated when the initial and subsequent response are similar; when least facilitated, a slight degree of negative transfer occurs, and when most facilitated, a moderate degree of positive transfer occurs.

(*b*) When learning to make an old response to a new stimulus, the learning is most facilitated when the subsequent stimulus is similar either to the subsequent response or to the initial stimulus, and least facilitated when the similarities are restricted to the factors of the initial learning; in this latter case, the similarity is even a disadvantage. But in all cases, marked positive transfer occurs.

Interpretation

Laws concerning the conditions of transfer of training

(1) Learning to make an old response to a new stimulus results in a marked degree of positive transfer.

(2) Learning to make a new response to a new stimulus results in a slight degree of positive transfer.

(3) Learning to make a new response to an old stimulus results in a slight degree of negative transfer.

(4) Introducing similarities between two or more of the $S_1R_1S_2R_2$ terms increases positive transfer, and decreases negative transfer.

(5) With increasing degrees of integration of the initial learning, there is an increase in the amount of positive transfer, and a decrease in the amount of negative transfer; where the amount of negative transfer is slight, it shifts to positive transfer.

R ETENTION AND FORGETTING

The question of learning during sleep is one which often comes up. Many psychologists have come to the conclusion that learning during true sleep is unlikely. This conclusion is based upon studies similar to the one presented here. Learning during the drowsy state before sleep seems possible, but, as these authors point out, there are disadvantages, such as decreased efficiency, to learning in this state. On the other hand, the utilization of this drowsy state might be somewhat efficient in that it adds a few minutes to a busy person's day. In the main, however, this is not "the royal road to learning." Learning is still hard work.

Points to guide your study

1. Note the care taken to control group differences which might spuriously affect the results.

2. See the readings in Chapter 19 for more material on the EEG.

28. RESPONSES TO MATERIAL PRESENTED DURING VARIOUS LEVELS OF SLEEP

*Charles W. Simon and William H. Emmons, The RAND Corporation**

Recently, there has been an increased interest in the possibility of learning during sleep. A critical review of the few scientific studies in this field to date leads to the conclusion that the evidence supporting claims of learning during actual sleep is inconclusive. The chief criticism against the existing studies is their failure to continuously determine the sleep state of Ss during the stimulus input period (16).

After considerable exploratory work (15), the present experiment was designed to study the effect of presenting material at different levels between wakefulness and deep sleep on the ability of Ss (a) to respond to it immediately, and (b) to recall it later upon awakening. It was hypothesized that learning during sleep was improbable.

Method

Subjects. Twenty-one male experimental Ss were used. In order to facilitate the detection of gradual changes which occur in the EEG between wakefulness and light sleep, it was necessary to use only Ss having a persistent occipital alpha rhythm when awake and relaxed with their eyes closed. Ten Ss were junior college students, nine were scientists, and two were policemen. Results from students and policemen were combined since they were similar on critical variables. Means and SD's of descriptive variables for the experimental subgroups were determined. For the scientist group, these values were: age, 30.6 yr. ± 5.0; IQ, 122.6 ± 6.0; items correct on pretest, 11.7 ± 3.4. For the college men and policemen combined, these values were: age, 23.2 yr. ± 6.3; IQ, 108.6 ± 4.7; items correct on pretest, 6.8 ± 3.0.

Forty junior college males and 24 male scientists acted as a control group without regard for their alpha rhythm. These Ss were used to obtain an estimate of the probability of correct answers being chosen on a multiple-choice test, since it seemed unlikely that educated Ss would

select their answers to unknown questions solely by chance. This control group was first given a pretest to determine the number of test questions known without training and before seeing the multiple-choice alternatives. With no intervening training and after items correct on the pretest were removed, the pretest significantly predicted scores on the multiple-choice test. This prediction was not significantly improved when IQ or age was added in a multiple-regression equation.

Control and experimental subgroups were matched on means and variances of their IQ, age, and pretest scores. Only the variances of the age and IQ of the college subgroups were unmatched.[1]

Apparatus. The Ss slept in clean comfortable beds in three separate soundproof, air conditioned, electrically-shielded booths. EEG electrodes were applied to the right occipital area, the vertex, and the left mastoid process. The electrode wires were arranged to allow relatively free movement and comfort during sleep. Two monopolar EEG recordings (right occipital and vertex) were made from each S using a six-channel Offner electroencephalograph and Dynograph inkwriter. A marker pen mounted on the inkwriter automatically marked the exact time an auditory stimulus was presented to S. The learning material was recorded on magnetic tape and played through loud-speakers placed inside the booths. A two-way intercommunication system allowed Es to communicate with Ss.

Procedure. *Pretesting period.* Several hours before retiring, Ss were pretested to discover what information they knew in order to have a base from which to evaluate how much had been learned following "sleep-training" on the same material. They were encouraged to guess answers to as many questions as they could, since a chance guess might be the correct one. No time limit was imposed.

Ninety-six general information questions were culled from various books on the basis of the following criteria: (a) the information was not generally known; (b) the answers required were not outside the verbal experience of the Ss; (c) questions could be answered in short phrases or single words. These same 96 questions and

* The authors wish to acknowledge the valuable assistance of Louie W. Mason, Jr., and James L. Barnes in the analysis of the data in this study. Appreciation is expressed to the faculty and students of Santa Monica City College, to the Santa Monica Police Department, and to the volunteer Ss within the RAND Corporation for their cooperation throughout the project.

[1] Supporting and additional statistics along with data by S have been deposited with the American Documentation Institute. Order Document No. 4738, remitting $1.25 for 35-mm. microfilm or $1.25 for 6 x 8 in photocopies.

their answers were recorded on tape at 5-min. intervals for presentation during the sleep period. The answer was presented as a restatement of the question with the critical informa- tion near the end. For example, Question: "In what kind of store did Ulysses S. Grant work before the war?" Answer: "Before the war, Ulysses S. Grant worked in a hardware store."

Table 1   EEG and psychological conditions along the sleep-wakefulness continuum

Level	% Items	% Ss	Electroencephalogram	Psychological condition
0	8	90	Continuous or nearly continuous alpha of maximum amplitude and frequency of not more than 1 cps slower than the S's normal alpha frequency. Frequency and amplitude are slightly less after sleeping than before.	Awake. Relaxed with eyes closed. Responsive to external stimulation.
A+	9	100	More than 50% of the scoring period contains alpha. Also low level, random activity characteristic of an alpha block may be present with alpha disappearing at the onset of stimulation and returning shortly after its cessation.	Drowsy.
A	12	95	Less than 50% alpha but scoring period contains at least three cycles of activity having the same frequency as the 0 level. The alpha amplitude may be the same as or considerably lower than before.	Attention wanders; reverie. Increased reaction time.
A−	14	100	Contains cyclical activity having a frequency more than 1 cps slower than the Level 0 record. May include waves of mixed duration with periods between .12 and .08 sec. with no one period being dominant. Also includes records showing no alpha rhythm during stimulation, but with alpha occurring within 30 sec. prior to stimulation or following but not both.	Partial awareness.
B	22	100	Absence of alpha during the stimulus period and the adjacent 30 sec. of record. Stimulus effects may occur consisting of low level fast activity or an increase in activity containing both high and low frequency components, with some waves having periods within the alpha range. Low-level delta activity is present in the absence of stimulus effects.	Transition. Dreamlike state. Infrequent responses to external stimulation. Onset of sleep. Easily awakened.
C	18	100	Absence of alpha with an increase of delta and the appearance of sleep spindles (14 cps). This state is characterized by stimulus effects such as increases in amplitude of delta waves with the onset of the stimulus. Types of effects vary with individuals.	Light sleep. No behavioral responses to external stimulation (unless stimulus awakens). Dreams sometimes remembered.
D	7	90	A further increase in delta amplitude with a reduction in frequency and diminution of stimulus effects and sleep spindles. Amplitude of delta almost at maximum.	Deep sleep. No memory for dreams. Difficult to awaken.
E	3	57	Absence of sleep spindles and stimulus effects. Very large delta activity with smooth waves of .5- to 1.5-sec. duration.	Very deep sleep.

Preliminary period. Following the pretest, Ss prepared for bed and the EEG electrodes were applied. Three Ss were run simultaneously. Since it was not possible to adjust the auditory intensity of the stimulus material in each booth individually, it was necessary to find a level satisfactory to all three. "Satisfactory" was defined as the point at which the training material could be heard clearly by the waking S, yet not be loud enough to materially disturb him once he was asleep. As Ss lay in their booths, practice verbal material was played at approximately the same loudness as the experimental stimulus material was to be played. This loudness level was adjusted after a number of tests so that the S with the highest threshold was able to hear the words clearly.

Before turning out the lights and allowing Ss to go to sleep, the following instructions were given: (a) if they awakened during the night at any time, they were to call out their name and booth number as soon as possible and to say that they were awake; (b) if they heard the answer to any of the question-answer combinations during the night, they were to wait until the answer was completed, and then call out their name and booth number. In order to impress these instructions on S, each was asked to repeat them back to E.

Training period. Within 5 min. after S retired, the tape recorder was turned on and the question-answer combinations were played into the booths at approximately 5-min. intervals. A pen automatically marked the EEG record whenever a question or answer was played. The Es marked on the record whether or not S stated he heard the answer. Records of any other pertinent information were kept, e.g., if S awoke, his remarks, and so forth.

Posttest period. Shortly after the last question and answer was played, Ss were awakened (if they were not already so), permitted to dress, and wash their face and hands. The same questions which they received on the pretest and during the training were again presented for them to answer; as before, Ss were encouraged to guess. This unaided recall was followed by a multiple-choice test in which five alternative answers (including the correct one) were provided with the questions.

Control group testing. All members of the control groups were given the 96 questions and asked to answer them by guessing whenever they were not certain. Following a brief rest and no training, they were given the questions along with the multiple-choice answers and retested.

Intelligence testing. Following the completion of the experiment, both experimental and control groups were given the 30-min. Otis Self-Administering Test of Mental Ability, Form D.

Results

The basic data available for analysis were: (a) the levels of sleep during the training period as indicated by EEG records, (b) the frequencies with which Ss immediately reported they had heard an answer, and (c) the frequencies with which Ss correctly recalled an answer, both unaided and by recognizing the correct multiple-choice alternative.

Sleep levels. Those portions of the EEG record occurring simultaneously with the presentation of the answers were categorized into 22 distinguishable patterns. These 22 EEG patterns were divided into eight groups, or sleep levels, which were ordered on their proportion of visually observable cyclical activity within the alpha frequency range (8-13 cps) and on their amplitude, frequency, and the effects of stimulation when alpha frequencies were no longer present. This order corresponds to S's state of consciousness between wakefulness and deep sleep and is described in Table 1.

Immediate response and unaided recall. The "immediate response" or "reported heard" analysis was based on 1,827 items; items were removed when the EEG was obscured by artifacts and when it was impossible to determine which of the three Ss running simultaneously had responded. The "unaided recall" analysis was based on 1,690 items; items were removed when the EEG was obscured by artifacts and when the items were known on the pretraining test.

The percentage of items reported heard at time of presentation and the percentage correctly recalled unaided, upon awakening, are shown in Figure 1. These percentages in Figure 1, based on the combined data for all Ss and items occurring at each level, decrease as the amount of alpha decreases and delta appears, that is, as the sleep level deepens.

Recognition test. Figure 2 shows the percentage of items recalled correctly for all Ss when multiple-choice answers were provided, along with the standard error of these percentages. As in Figure 1, with a decrease in alpha frequencies at the time of presentation, there was a corresponding decrease in the number of items recalled later. Unlike the others, however, the recall curve from this recognition test leveled off around 23% instead of dropping to zero.

Since it was possible for Ss to answer correctly solely by chance on the multiple-choice test, it was necessary to compare the percentages obtained by the experimental groups with an empirical estimate of what the theoretical percentage would be. Although 20% was chance expectancy for this test, the difficulty of making

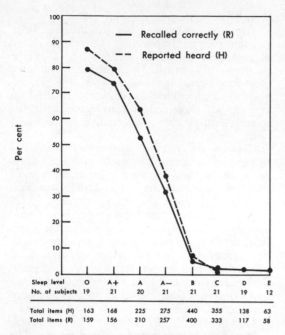

Figure 1 The percentage of items reported heard during the stimulation at varying levels along the wake-sleep continuum and the percentage subsequently recalled correctly unaided. The number of Ss contributing to each level and the number of items from which each percentage was computed are shown.

a perfect multiple-choice test with answers equal in selectivity caused the Es to use scores of a control group as the basis for estimating the expected value.

It was found that the scientist control subgroup answered 26% correctly without training and the college control subgroup answered 22% correctly. The expected percentages shown in Figure 2 were based on empirical values from the control groups weighted according to the items contributed by the scientist and college-police experimental groups in each sleep level.

Thus, from Figure 2, it can be seen that the expected values remain essentially the same for all sleep levels, while the values observed from the experimental group changed. In levels 0 through A-, the experimental Ss showed a considerably higher percentage correct, while in Levels B through E, the percentage correct for the experimental group was essentially equal to (within ±.5σ%) and in most cases less than the mean expected value.

Discussion

The results support the hypothesis that learning during sleep is unlikely. Although a few items were answered correctly unaided, with the easier recognition test (13) no more items were

answered in Levels B through E by the experimental group than would be expected from the performance of the untrained control group. Since it is generally conceded that sleep occurs somewhere during Level B, then it appears that learning was slight, if any, at this point or below. There appears some basis for assuming that many of these atypical cases were artifacts and not true sleep-learning.

What had been done in the present sleep-learning study that had not been done adequately in any previous studies (16) was the careful monitoring of Ss during the presentation period so that their levels of sleep during training were always known. The use of the EEG for this purpose proved most adequate.

Although it appears that learning during real sleep is not feasible, the practical utilization of the drowsy state for training is still open to speculation. The results in this study show that approximately 30% of the simple and highly organized material presented in the period just prior to sleep was recalled. Just how efficient learning in this state is has not been sufficiently evaluated experimentally. Anderson (1) found that the amount of recall decreases when train-

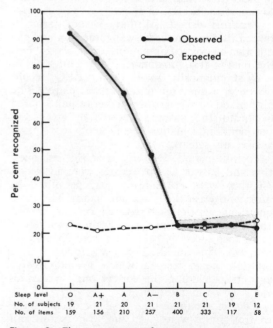

Figure 2 The percentage of answers recognized on the multiple-choice test after being presented at varying levels along the continuum between a waking and deep sleep state. The shaded portion represents plus and minus one standard error of the percentage. The expected value was that obtained from an untrained control group of comparable ability answering the same items.

ing follows sleep closely. One must weigh the advantages of limited learning against the possible harmful effects from loss of sleep as well as against the time demanded to learn in the subnormal receptive state. It may be that in the drowsy state preceding sleep, the individual is more susceptible to suggestions; perhaps one's attitudes or habits can be modified during this presleep period when criticalness is minimized (8). Perhaps the future development of new and unknown techniques will permit someone to learn complex material while he sleeps, but for the present, sleep-learning is not the simple matter that some Es and commercial firms, which sell equipment for this purpose, would lead us to believe.

References

1. Anderson, D. V. The effect of relaxation on the recall of nonsense syllables, words, and poetry. Unpublished doctor's dissertation, Univ. of California, Los Angeles, 1953.
2. Coyne, M. L. Some problems and parameters of sleep learning. Unpublished honors' thesis, Wesleyan Univ., 1953.
3. Davis, H., Davis, P. A., Loomis, A. L., Harvey, E. N., and Hobart, G. Human brain potential during the onset of sleep. *J. Neurophysiol.*, 1938, **1**, 24–38.
4. Emmons, W. H., and Simon, C. W. The non-recall of material presented during sleep. Santa Monica, Calif.: The RAND Corp., Paper No. 619, 1955.
5. Gibbs, F. A., and Gibbs, E. L. *Atlas of electroencephalography*. Cambridge, Mass.: Lew A. Cummings Co., 1941.
6. Hovland, C. I. Human learning and retention. In S. S. Stevens (Ed.), *Handbook of experimental psychology*. New York: Wiley, 1951. Pp. 613–689.
7. Hoyt, W. G. The effect of learning of auditory material presented during sleep. Unpublished master's thesis, George Washington Univ., 1953.
8. LeShan, L. The breaking of a habit by suggestion during sleep. *J. abnorm soc. Psychol.*, 1942, **37**, 406–408.
9. Lindsley, D. B. Electroencephalography. In J. McV. Hunt (Ed.), *Personality and behavior disorders*, Vol. II. New York: Ronald, 1944. Pp. 1033–1103.
10. Lindsley, D. B. Emotion. In S. S. Stevens (Ed.), *Handbook of experimental psychology*. New York: Wiley, 1951. Pp. 473–516.
11. Lindsley, D. B. Psychological phenomena and the electroencephalogram. *EEG clin. Neurophysiol.*, 1952, **4**, 443–456.
12. Loomis, A. L., Harvey, E. N., and Hobart, G. A. Cerebral states during sleep, as studied by human brain potentials. *J. exp. Psychol.*, 1937, **21**, 127–144.
13. Luh, C. W. The conditions of retention. *Psychol. Monogr.*, 1922, **31**, No. 3 (Whole No. 142).
14. Moruzzi, G., and Magoun, H. W. Brain stem reticular formation and activation of the EEG. *EEG clin. Neurophysiol.*, 1949, **1**, 455–473.
15. Simon, C. W., and Emmons, W. H. Considerations for research in a sleep-learning program. Santa Monica, Calif.: The RAND Corp., Paper No. 565, 1954.
16. Simon, C. W., and Emmons, W. H. Learning during sleep? *Psychol. Bull.*, 1955, **52**, 328–342.
17. Stampfl, T. The effect of frequency of repetition on the retention of auditory material presented during sleep. Unpublished master's thesis, Loyola Univ., Chicago, 1953.

PROGRAMMED LEARNING

Teaching machines arose out of research with lower animals which shows that behavior can be "shaped" by the appropriate use of rewards (reinforcements). You are probably already familiar with this research from your text.

The teaching machine is not meant to replace the teacher. It is meant to be used as a technological aid to free the teacher from the more routine jobs of teaching and allow her to spend more time with individual students who need special help or an enriched curriculum. It is hoped that the machines will be more skillful than many teachers in teaching basic material. The trick here is in skillful programming. It should be emphasized that these machines are not just "memory drums." The use of programmed material is their outstanding feature.

Points to guide your study

1. What are some of the principles of learning which are incorporated in these machines?

2. What are some of the disadvantages of this technique? What are some of the advantages which are not mentioned in the article?

29. TEACHING MACHINES

B. F. Skinner, Harvard University*

There are more people in the world than ever before, and a far greater part of them want an education. The demand cannot be met simply by building more schools and training more teachers. Education must become more efficient. To this end curricula must be revised and simplified, and textbooks and classroom techniques improved. In any other field a demand for increased production would have led at once to the invention of labor-saving capital equipment. Education has reached this stage very late, possibly through a misconception of its task. Thanks to the advent of television, however, the so-called audio-visual aids are being reexamined. Film projectors, television sets, phonographs, and tape recorders are finding their way into American schools and colleges.

Audio-visual aids supplement and may even supplant lectures, demonstrations, and textbooks. In doing so they serve one function of the teacher: they present material to the student and, when successful, make it so clear and interesting that the student learns. There is another function to which they contribute little or nothing. It is best seen in the productive interchange between teacher and student in the small classroom or tutorial situation. Much of that interchange has already been sacrificed in American education in order to teach large numbers of students. There is a real danger that it will be wholly obscured if use of equipment designed simply to *present* material becomes widespread. The student is becoming more and more a mere passive receiver of instruction.

Pressey's Teaching Machines

There is another kind of capital equipment which will encourage the student to take an active role in the instructional process. The possibility was recognized in the 1920's, when Sid-

* B. F. Skinner. Teaching machines. *Science*, 1958, **128**, 969–977. Copyright 1958 by the American Association for the Advancement of Science. Excerpts reprinted here with permission from the author and the American Association for the Advancement of Science.

ney L. Pressey designed several machines for the automatic testing of intelligence and information. A recent model of one of these is shown in Figure 1. In using the device the student refers to a numbered item in a multiple-choice test. He presses the button corresponding to his first choice of answer. If he is right, the device moves on to the next item; if he is wrong, the error is tallied, and he must continue to make choices until he is right (1). Such machines, Pressey pointed out (2), could not only test and score, they could *teach*. When an examination is corrected and returned after a delay of many hours or days, the student's behavior is not appreciably modified. The immediate report supplied by a self-scoring device, however, can have an important instructional effect. Pressey also pointed out that such machines would increase efficiency in another way. Even in a small classroom the teacher usually knows that he is moving too slowly for some students and too fast for others. Those who could go faster are penalized, and those who should go slower are poorly taught and unnecessarily punished by criticism and failure. Machine instruction would permit each student to proceed at his own rate.

The "industrial revolution in education" which Pressey envisioned stubbornly refused to come about. In 1932 he expressed his disappointment (3). "The problems of invention are relatively simple," he wrote. "With a little money and engineering resource, a great deal could easily be done. The writer has found from bitter experience that one person alone can accomplish relatively little and he is regretfully dropping further work on these problems. But he hopes that enough may have been done to stimulate other workers, that this fascinating field may be developed."

Pressey's machines succumbed in part to cultural inertia; the world of education was not ready for them. But they also had limitations which probably contributed to their failure. Pressey was working against a background of psychological theory which had not come to grips with the learning process. The study of human learning was dominated by the "memory drum" and similar devices originally designed to study forgetting. Rate of learning was observed, but little was done to change it. Why the subject of such an experiment bothered to learn at all was of little interest. "Frequency" and "recency" theories of learning, and principles of "massed and spaced practice," concerned the conditions under which responses were remembered.

Pressey's machines were designed against this theoretical background. As versions of the memory drum, they were primarily testing devices. They were to be used after some amount of learning had already taken place elsewhere. By confirming correct responses and by weakening responses which should not have been acquired, a self-testing machine does, indeed, teach; but it is not designed primarily for that purpose. Nevertheless, Pressey seems to have been the first to emphasize the importance of immediate feedback in education and to propose a system in which each student could move at his own pace. He saw the need for capital equipment in realizing these objectives. Above all he conceived of a machine which (in contrast with the audiovisual aids which were beginning to be developed) permitted the student to play an active role.

Another kind of machine

The learning process is now much better understood. Much of what we know has come from studying the behavior of lower organisms, but the results hold surprisingly well for human subjects. The emphasis in this research has not been on proving or disproving theories but on discovering and controlling the variables of which

Figure 1 Pressey's self-testing machine. The device directs the student to a particular item in a multiple-choice test. The student presses the key corresponding to his choice of answer. If his choice is correct, the device advances to the next item. Errors are totaled.

learning is a function. This practical orientation has paid off, for a surprising degree of control has been achieved. By arranging appropriate "contingencies of reinforcement," specific forms of behavior can be set up and brought under the control of specific classes of stimuli. The resulting behavior can be maintained in strength for long periods of time. A technology based on this work has already been put to use in neurology, pharmacology, nutrition, psychophysics, psychiatry, and elsewhere (4).

The analysis is also relevant to education. A student is "taught" in the sense that he is induced to engage in new forms of behavior and in specific forms upon specific occasions. It is not merely a matter of teaching him *what* to do; we are as much concerned with the probability that appropriate behavior will, indeed, appear at the proper time—an issue which would be classed traditionally under motivation. In education the behavior to be shaped and maintained is usually verbal, and it is to be brought under the control of both verbal and nonverbal stimuli. Fortunately, the special problems raised by verbal behavior can be submitted to a similar analysis (5).

If our current knowledge of the acquisition and maintenance of verbal behavior is to be applied to education, some sort of teaching machine is needed. Contingencies of reinforcement which change the behavior of lower organisms often cannot be arranged by hand; rather elaborate apparatus is needed. The human organism requires even more subtle instrumentation. An appropriate teaching machine will have several important features. The student must *compose* his response rather than select it from a set of alternatives, as in a multiple-choice self-rater. One reason for this is that we want him to recall rather than recognize—to make a response as well as see that it is right. Another reason is that effective multiple-choice material must contain plausible wrong responses, which are out of place in the delicate process of "shaping" behavior because they strengthen unwanted forms. Although it is much easier to build a machine to score multiple-choice answers than to evaluate a composed response, the technical advantage is outweighed by these and other considerations.

A second requirement of a minimal teaching machine also distinguishes it from earlier versions. In acquiring complex behavior the student must pass through a carefully designed sequence of steps, often of considerable length. Each step must be so small that it can always be taken, yet in taking it the student moves somewhat closer to fully competent behavior. The machine must make sure that these steps are taken in a carefully prescribed order.

Several machines with the required characteristics have been built and tested. Sets of separate presentations or "frames" of visual material are stored on disks, cards, or tapes. One frame is presented at a time, adjacent frames being out of sight. In one type of machine the student composes a response by moving printed figures or letters (6). His setting is compared by the machine with a coded response. If the two correspond, the machine automatically presents the next frame. If they do not, the response is cleared, and another must be composed. The student cannot proceed to a second step until the first has been taken. A machine of this kind is being tested in teaching spelling, arithmetic, and other subjects in the lower grades.

For more advanced students—from junior high school, say, through college—a machine which senses an arrangement of letters or figures is unnecessarily rigid in specifying form of response. Fortunately, such students may be asked to compare their responses with printed material revealed by the machine. In the machine shown in Figure 2, material is printed in 30 radial frames on a 12-inch disk. The student inserts the disk and closes the machine. He cannot proceed until the machine has been locked, and, once he has begun, the machine cannot be unlocked. All but a corner of one frame is visible through a window. The student writes his response on a paper strip exposed through a second opening. By lifting a lever on the front of the machine, he moves what he has written under a transparent cover and uncovers the correct response in the remaining corner of the frame. If the two responses correspond, he moves the lever horizontally. This movement punches a hole in the paper opposite his response, recording the fact that he called it correct, and alters the machine so that the frame will not appear again when the student works around the disk a second time. Whether the response was correct or not, a second frame appears when the lever is returned to its starting position. The student proceeds in this way until he has responded to all frames. He then works around the disk a second time, but only those frames appear to which he has not correctly responded. When the disk revolves without stopping, the assignment is finished. (The student is asked to repeat each frame until a correct response is made to allow for the fact that, in telling him that a response is wrong, such a machine tells him what is right.)

The machine itself, of course, does not teach. It simply brings the student into contact with the person who composed the material it presents. It is a labor-saving device because it can bring one programmer into contact with an indefinite number of students. This may suggest mass production, but the effect upon each student is surprisingly like that of a private tutor. The comparison holds in several respects. (i)

There is a constant interchange between program and students. Unlike lectures, textbooks, and the usual audio-visual aids, the machine induces sustained activity. The student is always alert and busy. (ii) Like a good tutor, the machine insists that a given point be thoroughly understood, either frame by frame or set by set, before the student moves on. Lectures, textbooks, and their mechanized equivalents, on the other hand, proceed without making sure that the student understands and easily leave him behind. (iii) Like a good tutor the machine presents just that material for which the student is ready. It asks him to take only that step which he is at the moment best equipped and most likely to take. (iv) Like a skillful tutor the machine helps the student to come up with the right answer. It does this in part through the orderly construction of the program and in part with techniques of hinting, prompting, suggesting, and so on, derived from an analysis of verbal

Figure 2   Student at work on a teaching machine. One frame of material is partly visible in the left-hand window. The student writes his response on a strip of paper exposed at the right. He then lifts a lever with his left hand, advancing his written response under a transparent cover and uncovering the correct response in the upper corner of the frame. If he is right, he moves the lever to the right, punching a hole alongside the response he has called right and altering the machine so that that frame will not appear again when he goes through the series a second time. A new frame appears when the lever is returned to its starting position.

behavior (5). (v) Lastly, of course, the machine, like the private tutor, reinforces the student for every correct response, using this immediate feedback not only to shape his behavior most efficiently but to maintain it in strength in a manner which the layman would describe as "holding the student's interest."

Programming material

The success of such a machine depends on the material used in it. The task of programming a given subject is at first sight rather formidable. Many helpful techniques can be derived from a general analysis of the relevant behavioral processes, verbal and nonverbal. Specific forms of behavior are to be evoked and, through differential reinforcement, brought under the control of specific stimuli.

This is not the place for a systematic review of available techniques, or of the kind of research which may be expected to discover others. However, the machines themselves cannot be adequately described without giving a few examples of programs. We may begin with a set of frames (see Table 1) designed to teach a third- or fourth-grade pupil to spell the word *manufacture*. The six frames are presented in the order shown, and the pupil moves sliders to expose letters in the open squares.

Table 1   A set of frames designed to teach a third- or fourth-grade pupil to spell the word "manufacture"

1. *Manufacture* means to make or build. **Chair factories manufacture chairs.** Copy the word here:
   ☐ ☐ ☐ ☐ ☐ ☐ ☐ ☐ ☐ ☐ ☐
2. Part of the word is like part of the word *factory*. Both parts come from an old word meaning **make** or **build**.
   m a n u ☐ ☐ ☐ ☐ u r e
3. Part of the word is like part of the word *manual*. Both parts come from an old word for **hand**. Many things used to be made by hand.
   ☐ ☐ ☐ ☐ f a c t u r e
4. The same letter goes in both spaces:
   m ☐ n u f ☐ c t u r e
5. The same letter goes in both spaces:
   m a n ☐ f a c t ☐ r e
6. **Chair factories** ☐ ☐ ☐ ☐ ☐ ☐ ☐ ☐ ☐ ☐ ☐ **chairs.**

The word to be learned appears in bold face in frame 1, with an example and a simple definition. The pupil's first task is simply to copy it. When he does so correctly, frame 2 appears. He must now copy selectively: he must identify "fact" as the common part of "manufacture" and "factory." This helps him to spell the word and also to acquire a separable "atomic" verbal operant (5). In frame 3 another root must be copied selectively from "manual." In frame 4 the pupil must for the first time insert letters without copying. Since he is asked to insert the same letter in two places, a wrong response will be doubly conspicuous, and the chance of failure is thereby minimized. The same principle governs frame 5. In frame 6 the pupil spells the word to complete the sentence used as an example in frame 1. Even a poor student is likely to do this correctly because he has just composed or completed the word five times, has made two important root-responses, and has learned that two letters occur in the word twice. He has probably learned to spell the word without having made a mistake.

Teaching spelling is mainly a process of shaping complex forms of behavior. In other subjects—for example, arithmetic—responses must be brought under the control of appropriate stimuli. Unfortunately the material which has been prepared for teaching arithmetic (7) does not lend itself to excerpting. The numbers 0 through 9 are generated in relation to objects, quantities, and scales. The operations of addition, subtraction, multiplication, and division are thoroughly developed before the number 10 is reached. In the course of this the pupil composes equations and expressions in a great variety of alternative forms. He completes not only $5 + 4 = \square$, but $\square + 4 = 9$, $5 \square 4 = 9$, and so on, aided in most cases by illustrative materials. No appeal is made to rote memorizing, even in the later acquisition of the tables. The student is expected to arrive at $9 \times 7 = 63$, not by memorizing it as he would memorize a line of poetry, but by putting into practice such principles as that nine times a number is the same as ten times the number minus the number (both of these being "obvious" or already well learned), that the digits in a multiple of nine add to nine, that in composing successive multiples of nine one counts backwards (*nine, eighteen, twenty-seven, thirty-six*, and so on), that nine times a single digit is a number beginning with one less than the digit (nine times *six* is *fifty* something), and possibly even that the product of two numbers separated by only one number is equal to the square of the separating number minus one (the square of eight already being familiar from a special series of frames concerned with squares).

Programs of this sort run to great length. At least five or six frames per word, four grades of spelling may require 20,000 or 25,000 frames, and three or four grades of arithmetic, as many again. If these figures seem large, it is only because we are thinking of the normal contact between teacher and pupil. Admittedly, a teacher cannot supervise 10,000 or 15,000 responses made by each pupil per year. But the pupil's time is not so limited. In any case, surprisingly little time is needed. Fifteen minutes per day on a machine should suffice for each of these programs, the machines being free for other students for the rest of each day. (It is probably because traditional methods are so inefficient that we have been led to suppose that education requires such a prodigious part of a young person's day.)

A simple technique used in programming material at the high-school or college level, by means of the machine shown in Figure 2, is exemplified in teaching a student to recite a poem. The first line is presented with several unimportant letters omitted. The student must read the line "meaningfully" and supply the missing letters. The second, third, and fourth frames present succeeding lines in the same way. In the fifth frame the first line reappears with other letters also missing. Since the student has recently read the line, he can complete it correctly. He does the same for the second, third, and fourth lines. Subsequent frames are increasingly incomplete, and eventually—say, after 20 or 24 frames—the student reproduces all four lines without external help, and quite possibly without having made a wrong response. The technique is similar to that used in teaching spelling: responses are first controlled by a text, but this is slowly reduced (colloquially, "vanished") until the responses can be emitted without a text, each member in a series of responses being now under the "intraverbal" control of other members.

"Vanishing" can be used in teaching other types of verbal behavior. When a student describes the geography of part of the world or the anatomy of part of the body, or names plants and animals from specimens or pictures, verbal responses are controlled by nonverbal stimuli. In setting up such behavior the student is first asked to report features of a fully labeled map, picture, or object, and the labels are then vanished. In teaching a map, for example, the machine asks the student to describe spatial relations among cities, countries, rivers, and so on, as shown on a fully labeled map. He is then asked to do the same with a map in which the names are incomplete or, possibly, lacking. Eventually he is asked to report the same relations with no map at all. If the material has been well programmed, he can do so correctly. Instruction is sometimes concerned not so much with imparting a new repertoire of verbal responses as with getting the student to describe something accurately in any available terms. The machine can "make sure the student understands" a graph, diagram, chart, or picture by asking him to identify and explain its features—correcting him, of course, whenever he is wrong.

In addition to charts, maps, graphs, models, and so on, the student may have access to auditory material. In learning to take dictation in a foreign language, for example, he selects a short passage on an indexing phonograph according to instructions given by the machine. He listens to the passage as often as necessary and then transcribes it. The machine then reveals the correct text. The student may listen to the passage again to discover the sources of any error. The indexing phonograph may also be used with the machine to teach other language skills, as well as telegraphic code, music, speech, parts of literary and dramatic appreciation, and other subjects.

A typical program combines many of these functions. The set of frames shown in Table 2 is designed to induce the student of high-school physics to talk intelligently, and to some extent technically, about the emission of light from an incandescent source. In using the machine the student will write a word or phrase to complete a given item and then uncover the corresponding word or phrase shown here in the column at the right. The reader who wishes to get the "feel" of the material should cover the right-hand column with a card, uncovering each line only after he has completed the corresponding item.

Several programming techniques are exemplified by the set of frames in Table 2. Technical terms are introduced slowly. For example, the familiar term "fine wire" in frame 2 is followed by a definition of the technical term "filament" in frame 4; "filament" is then asked for in the presence of the nonscientific synonym in frame 5 and without the synonym in frame 9. In the same way "glow," "give off light," and "send out light" in early frames are followed by a definition of "emit" with a synonym in frame 7. Various inflected forms of "emit" then follow, and "emit" itself is asked for with a synonym in frame 16. It is asked for without a synonym but in a helpful phrase in frame 30, and "emitted" and "emission" are asked for without help in frames 33 and 34. The relation between temperature and amount and color of light is developed in several frames before a formal statement using the word "temperature" is asked for in frame 12. "Incandescent" is defined and used in frame 13, is used again in frame 14, and is asked for in frame 15, the student receiving a thematic prompt from the recurring phrase "incandescent source of light." A formal prompt is supplied by "candle." In frame 25 the new response "energy" is easily evoked by the words "form of . . ." because the expression "form of energy" is used earlier in the frame. "Energy" appears again in the next two frames and is finally asked for, without aid, in frame 28. Frames 30 through 35 discuss the limiting temperatures of incandescent objects, while reviewing several kinds of sources. The figure 800 is used in three frames. Two intervening frames then permit some time to pass before the response "800" is asked for.

Table 2 Part of a program in high-school physics. The machine presents one item at a time. The student completes the item and then uncovers the corresponding word or phrase shown at the right

Sentence to be completed	Word to be supplied
1. The important parts of a flashlight are the battery and the bulb. When we "turn on" a flashlight, we close a switch which connects the battery with the _____.	bulb
2. When we turn on a flashlight, an electric current flows through the fine wire in the _____ and causes it to grow hot.	bulb
3. When the hot wire glows brightly, we say that it gives off or sends out heat and _____.	light
4. The fine wire in the bulb is called a filament. The bulb "lights up" when the filament is heated by the passage of a(n) _____ current.	electric
5. When a weak battery produces little current, the fine wire, or _____, does not get very hot.	filament
6. A filament which is *less* hot sends out or gives off _____ light.	less
7. "Emit" means "send out." The amount of light sent out, or "emitted," by a filament depends on how _____ the filament is.	hot
8. The higher the temperature of the filament the _____ the light emitted by it.	brighter, stronger
9. If a flashlight battery is weak, the _____ in the bulb may still glow, but with only a dull red color.	filament
10. The light from a very hot filament is colored yellow or white. The light from a filament which is not very hot is colored _____.	red
11. A blacksmith or other metal worker sometimes makes sure that a bar of iron is heated to a "cherry red" before hammering it into shape. He uses the _____ of the light emitted by the bar to tell how hot it is.	color
12. Both the color and the amount of light depend on the _____ of the emitting filament or bar.	temperature
13. An object which emits light because it is hot is called "incandescent." A flashlight bulb is an incandescent source of _____.	light
14. A neon tube emits light but remains cool. It is therefore, not an incandescent _____ of light.	source
15. A candle flame is hot. It is a(n) _____ source of light.	incandescent
16. The hot wick of a candle gives off small pieces or particles of carbon which burn in the flame. Before or while burning, the hot particles send out, or _____, light.	emit
17. A long candlewick produces a flame in which oxygen does not reach all the carbon particles. Without oxygen the particles cannot burn. Particles which do not burn rise above the flame as _____.	smoke
18. We can show that there are particles of carbon in a candle flame, even when it is not smoking, by holding a piece of metal in the flame. The metal cools some of the particles before they burn, and the unburned carbon _____ collect on the metal as soot.	particles
19. The particles of carbon in soot or smoke no longer emit light because they are _____ than when they were in the flame.	cooler, colder
20. The reddish part of candle flame has the same color as the filament in a flashlight with a weak battery. We might guess that the yellow or white parts of a candle flame are _____ than the reddish part.	hotter
21. "Putting out" an incandescent electric light means turning off the current so that the filament grows too _____ to emit light.	cold, cool
22. Setting fire to the wick of an oil lamp is called _____ the lamp.	lighting
23. The sun is our principal _____ of light, as well as of heat.	source
24. The sun is not only very bright but very hot. It is a powerful _____ source of light.	incandescent
25. Light is a form of energy. In "emitting light" an object changes, or "converts," one form of _____ into another.	energy

Table 2 Part of a program in high-school physics. The machine presents one item at a time. The student completes the item and then uncovers the corresponding word or phrase shown at the right (continued).

Sentence to be completed	Word to be supplied
26. The electrical energy supplied by the battery in a flashlight is converted to _____ and _____ .	heat, light; light, heat
27. If we leave a flashlight on, all the energy stored in the battery will finally be changed or _____ into heat and light.	converted
28. The light from a candle flame comes from the _____ released by chemical changes as the candle burns.	energy
29. A nearly "dead" battery may make a flashlight bulb warm to the touch, but the filament may still not be enough to emit light—in other words, the filament will not be _____ at that temperature.	incandescent
30. Objects, such as a filament, carbon particles, or iron bars, become incandescent when heated to about 800 degrees Celsius. At that temperature they begin to _____ _____ .	emit light
31. When raised to any temperature above 800 degrees Celsius, an object such as an iron bar will emit light. Although the bar may melt or vaporize, its particles will be _____ no matter how hot they get.	incandescent
32. About 800 degrees Celsius is the lower limit of the temperature at which particles emit light. There is no upper limit of the _____ at which emission of light occurs.	temperature
33. Sunlight is _____ by very hot gases near the surface of the sun.	emitted
34. Complex changes similar to an atomic explosion generate the great heat which explains the _____ of light by the sun.	emission
35. Below about _____ degrees Celsius an object is not an incandescent source of light.	800

Unwanted responses are eliminated with special techniques. If, for example, the second sentence in frame 24 were simply "It is a(n) _____ source of light," the two "very's" would frequently lead the student to fill the blank with "strong" or a synonym thereof. This is prevented by inserting the word "powerful" to make a synonym redundant. Similarly, in frame 3 the words "heat and" preempt the response "heat," which would otherwise correctly fill the blank.

The net effect of such material is more than the acquisition of facts and terms. Beginning with a largely unverbalized acquaintance with flashlights, candles, and so on, the student is induced to talk about familiar events, together with a few new facts, with a fairly technical vocabulary. He applies the same terms to facts which he may never before have seen to be similar. The emission of light from an incandescent source takes shape as a topic or field of inquiry. An understanding of the subject emerges which is often quite surprising in view of the fragmentation required in item building.

It is not easy to construct such a program. Where a confusing or elliptical passage in a textbook is forgivable because it can be clarified by the teacher, machine material must be self-contained and wholly adequate. There are other reasons why textbooks, lecture outlines, and film scripts are of little help in preparing a program. They are usually not logical or developmental arrangements of material but stratagems which the authors have found successful under existing classroom conditions. The examples they give are more often chosen to hold the student's interest than to clarify terms and principles. In composing material for the machine, the programmer may go directly to the point.

A first step is to define the field. A second is to collect technical terms, facts, laws, principles, and cases. These must then be arranged in a plausible developmental order—linear if possible, branching if necessary. A mechanical arrangement, such as a card filing system, helps. The material is distributed among the frames of a program to achieve an arbitrary density. In the final composition of an item, techniques for strengthening asked-for responses and for transferring control from one variable to another are chosen from a list according to a given schedule in order to prevent the establishment of irrelevant verbal tendencies appropriate to a single technique. When one set of frames has been composed, its terms and facts are seeded mechanically among succeeding sets, where they will again be referred to in composing later items to make sure that the earlier repertoire remains active. Thus, the technical terms, facts, and examples in Table 2 have been distributed for reuse in succeeding sets on reflection, absorption, and transmission, where they are incorporated into items dealing mainly with other matters. Sets of frames for explicit review can, of course, be constructed. Further research will presumably discover other, possibly more effective, techniques. Meanwhile, it must be admitted that a considerable measure of art is needed in composing a successful program.

Whether good programming is to remain an art or to become a scientific technology, it is reassuring to know that there is a final authority—the student. An unexpected advantage of machine instruction has proved to be the feedback to the *programmer*. In the elementary school machine, provision is made for discovering which frames commonly yield wrong responses, and in the high-school and college machine the paper strips bearing written answers are available for analysis. A trial run of the first version of a program quickly reveals frames which need to be altered, or sequences which need to be lengthened. One or two revisions in the light of a few dozen responses work a great improvement. No comparable feedback is available to the lecturer, textbook writer, or maker of films. Although one text or film may seem to be better than another, it is usually impossible to say, for example, that a given sentence on a given page or a particular sequence in a film is causing trouble.

Difficult as programming is, it has its compensations. It is a salutary thing to try to guarantee a right response at every step in the presentation of a subject matter. The programmer will usually find that he has been accustomed to leave much to the student—that he has frequently omitted essential steps and neglected to invoke relevant points. The responses made to his material may reveal surprising ambiguities. Unless he is lucky, he may find that he still has something to learn about his subject. He will almost certainly find that he needs to learn a great deal more about the behavioral changes he is trying to induce in the student. This effect of the machine in confronting the programmer with the full scope of his task may in itself produce a considerable improvement in education.

Conclusion

An analysis of education within the framework of a science of behavior has broad implications. Our schools, in particular our "progressive" schools, are often held responsible for many current problems, including juvenile delinquency and the threat of a more powerful foreign technology. One remedy frequently suggested is a return to older techniques, especially to a greater "discipline" in schools. Presumably this is to be obtained with some form of punishment, to be administered either with certain classical instruments of physical injury—the dried bullock's tail of the Greek teacher or the cane of the English schoolmaster—or as disapproval or failure, the frequency of which is to be increased by "raising standards." This is probably not a feasible solution. Not only education but Western culture as a whole is moving away from aversive practices. We cannot prepare young people for one kind of life in institutions organized on quite different principles. The discipline of the birch rod may facilitate learning, but we must remember that it also breeds followers of dictators and revolutionists.

In the light of our present knowledge a school system must be called a failure if it cannot induce students to learn except by threatening them for not learning. That this has always been the standard pattern simply emphasizes the importance of modern techniques. John Dewey was speaking for his culture and his time when he attacked aversive educational practices and appealed to teachers to turn to positive and humane methods. What he threw out should have been thrown out. Unfortunately he had too little to put in its place. Progressive education has been a temporizing measure which can now be effectively supplemented. Aversive practices can not only be replaced, they can be replaced with far more powerful techniques. The possibilities should be thoroughly explored if we are to build an educational system which will meet the present demand without sacrificing democratic principles.

References and Notes

1. The Navy's "Self-Rater" is a larger version of Pressey's machine. The items are printed on code-punched plastic cards fed by the machine. The time required to answer is taken into account in scoring.
2. S. L. Pressey, *School and Society*, **23**, 586 (1926).
3. ———, *ibid.*, **36**, 934 (1932).
4. B. F. Skinner, The experimental analysis of behavior, *Am. Scientist*, **45**, 4 (1957).
5. ———, *Verbal behavior*, Appleton-Century-Crofts, New York, 1957.
6. ———, The science of learning and the art of teaching, *Harvard Educational Rev.*, **24**, 2 (1954).
7. This material was prepared with the assistance of Susan R. Meyer.

CHAPTER NINE

Language and thinking

F **ORMATION AND MEANING OF CONCEPTS**
We are often faced with the problem of finding the common properties contained in large masses of information. In other words, we are often called upon to form concepts. Assuming that we have the needed information before us, it is possible to use several strategies, each with certain advantages and disadvantages, in attempting to arrive at the concept. Several of these strategies are described in this selection.

Points to guide your study
1. It is quite feasible to try your friends on a concept formation task similar to that mentioned in this selection. Figure 1 could very well be used. Do your subjects use the strategies mentioned in the selection?
2. Summarize the advantages and disadvantages of each type of strategy.

30. A STUDY OF THINKING

J. S. Bruner, Harvard University, Jacqueline Goodnow, Walter Reed Army Medical Center, and G. A. Austin[*]

Ideal selection strategies and their benefits

We concentrate in this chapter on conjunctive concepts. Let us set before a subject all of the instances representing the various combinations of four attributes, each with three values—specifically, all the instances illustrated in Figure 1—an array of 81 cards, each varying in shape of figure, number of figures, color of figure, and number of borders. We explain to the subject what is meant by a conjunctive concept—a set of the cards that share a certain set of attribute values, such as "all red cards," or "all cards containing red squares and two borders"—and for practice ask the subjects to show us all the exemplars of one sample concept. The subject is then told that we have a concept in mind and that certain cards before him illustrate it, others do not, and that it is his task to determine what this concept is. We will always begin by showing him a card or instance that is illustrative of the concept, a positive instance. His task is to choose cards for testing, one at a time, and after each choice we will tell him whether the card is positive or negative. He may

* J. S. Bruner, Jacqueline Goodnow, and G. A. Austin. *A Study of Thinking.* New York: John Wiley and Sons, 1956. Copyright 1956 by John Wiley and Sons. Excerpts reprinted here with permission from the authors and John Wiley and Sons.

hazard an hypothesis after any choice of a card, but he may not offer more than one hypothesis after any particular choice. If he does not wish to offer an hypothesis, he need not do so. He is asked to arrive at the concept as efficiently as possible. He may select the cards in any order he chooses. That, in essence, is the experimental procedure.

There are four discernible strategies by which a person may proceed in this task. These we label the *simultaneous-scanning* strategy, the *successive-scanning* strategy, the *conservative-focusing* strategy, and the *focus-gambling* strategy. Let us describe each of these briefly and consider the manner in which each bestows upon its users the three benefits mentioned previously.

Simultaneous scanning. In the present array (Figure 1), composed of instances that may exhibit any of three values of four different attributes, there are 255 possible ways of grouping instances into conjunctive concepts. A first positive card *logically* eliminates 240 of these, and the informational value of any other positive or negative card thereafter presented can similarly be described in terms of the remaining hypotheses that it logically eliminates. Now, simultaneous scanning consists in essence of the person using each instance encountered as an occasion for deducing which hypotheses are tenable and which have been eliminated. This is a highly exacting strategy, for the subject must deal with many independent hypotheses and carry these in memory. Moreover, the deductive process is exacting.

If the subject is able to follow the strategy successfully, his choice of next instances to test will be determined by the objective of eliminating as many hypothetical concepts as possible per instance chosen. Suppose, for example, that a subject in our experiment has narrowed the possible concepts down to three: the concept must either be all *red* cards, all cards with *circles*, or all cards with *red circles*. Prior choices have eliminated all other hypotheses. Since we are dealing with an ideal strategy here, let us also assume an ideal subject: a subject with perfect rationality and perfect discriminative capacities. Such a subject would certainly know how to avoid choosing redundant instances that eliminated no hypotheses. By choosing a card for testing that contained at least one of the two features, circles or red color, he would guarantee that the next instances encountered contained appropriate information. He would have to decide whether to choose an instance containing *one* of the relevant features or *both* of them: the next instance will contain a circle and no other relevant feature, contain red and no other relevant feature, or it will contain red circles. Consider now the consequences of each of these decisions for each of the three possible concepts, as shown in the table below.

Such an analysis of the nine possible outcomes should suggest to the subject that his next choice should contain only one of the relevant attributes; at the least, such a choice will eliminate one hypothetical concept, at best two of them. To choose a card containing both relevant attribute values means that no information will

be obtained regardless of what the correct concept is.

Now, if the subject can figure out the nine possible outcomes (and has enough time to do so), he will be able to make a wise decision about how next to proceed. The decision is important, for it will determine whether he will be able to solve the problem with one more choice; if these were expensive experiments rather than simple tests of the status of instances, the difference might be critical. But it is quite obvious that most human beings cannot or will not go through such an elaborate analysis of the situation in order to determine their best next step. Indeed, if there had been ten hypotheses still remaining in our example, the paper and pencil work involved in assessing next moves would have been prohibitive. So we can sum up by remarking that while it is possible in principle for the person using simultaneous scanning to plan the best next step, the task of guaranteeing *maximum* informativeness of a next choice is in practice too difficult to accomplish.

With respect to rendering easier the assimilation and retention of information contained in instances encountered, simultaneous scanning has little to recommend it. After each choice the subject must go through the difficult process of deducing which hypothetical concepts have been eliminated and carrying the result of these deductions in memory. There appears to be no means whereby simultaneous scanning can reduce this heavy load on inference and memory.

Nor does simultaneous scanning provide a way of regulating the riskiness of one's next choices—no practical way, at least. We shall leave the matter at that, hoping that it will become much clearer in a later section. The best one can do is to compute the riskiness of a choice by the method just outlined.

Properties of instance chosen for testing	If correct concept is:		
	Red only	Circle only	Red circle
Red only	Instance positive Eliminates: circle red circle	Instance negative Eliminates: red	Instance negative Eliminates: red
Circle only	Instance negative Eliminates: circle	Instance positive Eliminates: red red circle	Instance negative Eliminates: circle
Red and circle	Instance positive Eliminates: nothing	Instance positive Eliminates: nothing	Instance positive Eliminates: nothing

Successive scanning. This strategy consists in testing a single hypothesis at a time. The subject has the hypothesis that *red* is the feature common to all correct cards, and chooses instances containing red in order to test whether they are positive instances. He goes on testing hypotheses until he hits the correct concept. The typical successive scanner then *limits his choices to those instances that provide a direct test of his hypothesis.*

Now it is quite apparent that such a technique for choosing instances cannot assure that the person will encounter instances containing the maximum information possible. That is to say, since instances are chosen only to test one hypothesis at a time, one is likely to choose logically redundant cards some feature of which has been used before to test some previous hypothesis. On this point more will be said later, for it is evident that this is much like discontinuity in learning.

It also follows that the strategy has little worth from the point of view of regulating risk. There is little the user can do either to take bigger gambles or lesser gambles in his choice of instances. His only possible maneuver here is a rather far-fetched one, but one that subjects nonetheless indulge in. This consists really of playing a guessing game with the experimenter in choosing an order of hypotheses to test. For example, subjects will often operate on the assumption that the experimenter is out to "trick" them and that, therefore, the correct concept cannot be a "simple" one, namely, that it will not be a single-attribute concept like "red" or "circles." In consequence, users of successive scanning begin, more frequently than would be expected by chance, by "guessing" that the hypothesis is defined by more than one attribute and choose cards to test such multi-attribute hypotheses.

What then is served by the use of successive scanning? The gain is nearly all in the relief of cognitive strain. Limited inference is required and the principal strain on memory is to keep track of what hypotheses have already been tested and found wanting.

A closer examination of the manner in which strain on inference is reduced brings us directly to a most characteristic feature of cognitive activity which we shall encounter on subsequent occasions in analyzing the behavior of subjects in probability situations. It is this. Human subjects—and the same may be true of other species as well—prefer a direct test of any hypothesis they may be working on. To recall the meaning of direct test, a subject is faced with deciding whether a white door or a black door is the correct entrance to a reward chamber and adopts the hypothesis that the white door is correct. There are two ways of testing this hypothesis.

The *direct way* is to try the white door. The *indirect way* is to try the black door. In a direct test, as we have noted, the knowledge obtained needs no further transformation for testing the hypothesis. White is either correct or incorrect. The indirect test requires a transformation: if the black door is correct, then the white door was not correct and therefore the hypothesis is wrong; if the black door is wrong then the white door must have been correct and the hypothesis is right. It may be that the reason for the preference for direct test is in the interest of cognitive economy: saving the person from having to transform his knowledge. Another possible explanation, one which does not preclude the first, is that we do not fully accept the possibilities of correctness and incorrectness being mutually exclusive. We have a backlog of experience in which it has not always followed that if white is correct black is wrong or vice versa. We have also experienced situations where more than two alternatives were possible, and only a direct test would be effective.[1]

In any case, when a subject behaves in the typical manner of the successive scanner and limits himself to testing instances directly related to his hypothesis, his behavior appears to follow the principle of direct test. In sum, then, successive scanning has little utility either in guaranteeing maximum informativeness of one's choices or in regulating risk. Its chief benefit is in the reduction of cognitive strain by limiting its user to direct test of hypotheses. As such, its principal utility may be as a procedure that is useful when the cognitive going gets rough or when one has good reason to believe that a particular hypothesis will turn out to be correct.

Conservative focussing. In brief, this strategy may be described as finding a positive instance to use as a focus, then making a sequence of choices each of which alters but one attribute value of the first focus card and testing to see whether the change yields a positive or a negative instance. Those attribute values of the focus card which, when changed, still yield positive instances are *not* part of the concept. Those attribute values of the focus card that yield negative instances when changed *are* features of the concept. Thus, if the first positive card encountered contains three red circles with two borders (3R○2b), and if the concept is "red circles," the sequence of choices made would be as follows, each choice changing a *single* attribute value of the focus card:

[1] It is of interest that the first experiment which drew attention to a preference for direct test—in the form of participant behavior—used a situation where more than two alternatives were possible (Heidbreder, 1924).

3R◯2b (+) focus card †

2R◯2B (+) first choice: eliminate "three figures" as a relevant attribute value

3G◯2b (−) second choice: retain "red" as a relevant attribute value

3R+2b (−) third choice: retain "circle" as a relevant attribute value

3R◯1b (+) fourth choice: eliminate "two borders" as a relevant attribute value

Ergo: concept is "red circles."

† The symbol (+) denotes a positive instance; (−) a negative instance.

Note one thing. When a subject has changed an attribute value of the focus card and the new card chosen turns out to be positive, this result logically eliminates the attribute in question from consideration. No value of such an attribute can be relevant to the concept. The subject need not sample any further values of it.

Several other features of this strategy are especially noteworthy. From the point of view of guaranteeing that each instance encountered be informative, the strategy does just that. By following it, redundancy can be completely avoided. The strategy guarantees, moreover, that each instance encountered will contain a "safe maximum" of information, as we will see when the risk-regulating property of the strategy is examined below.

The benefits in cognitive economy to be gained by using this strategy are striking. The first of these is that by its use the subject is enabled to disregard completely the bewildering business of eliminating possible hypotheses from the domain of 255 possible concepts in terms of which he may group instances. For in fact, the technique is designed to *test the relevance of attributes*. Given an initial positive card, his choices are designed to consider the four attribute values of the focus card one at a time to see which of these may be eliminated. In the present example there are four single attribute values to be considered, much less than the 15 rather complex hypotheses that would have to be considered in simultaneous scanning. A second contribution of this strategy to cognitive economy is that it guarantees that the relevance of all attribute values in the focus card will be *tested relatively directly*. If a change in an attribute value of the focus instance makes a difference, then that attribute value of the focus is relevant; if not, it is irrelevant. A third benefit is more subtle. By choosing a particular positive instance as a focus, the person *decreases the complexity and abstractness of the task* of keeping track of information he has encountered. All subsequent choices and their outcomes can be referred back to this focus instance much as if it were a score card. The attributes of the focus

card are ticked off on the basis of subsequent tests.

There is one notable disadvantage to the strategy from the point of view of cognitive economy. Unless the universe of instances to be tested is arrayed in an orderly fashion so that a particular instance may be easily located on demand, the task of search imposed on the user of conservative focussing may become rather severe. We shall see examples of this disadvantage later.

Now for risk regulation. The expression "conservative focussing" has been chosen with good reason. Every choice is safe, safe in the sense that it logically guarantees the presence of information in the instance chosen for testing. This guaranteed information is not the maximum possible. On the other hand, the choice never carries the risk of yielding *no* information. We have already noted that by following the strategy, the subject will never choose a redundant instance, one that carries no new information. To understand fully why it is that a chosen instance almost never contains the maximum amount of information possible, we must turn to a consideration of focus gambling.

Focus gambling. The principal feature of this strategy is that the subject uses a positive instance as a focus and then changes *more than one* attribute value at a time. In the present array (Figure 1) from which our examples are drawn, the subject might change two or three attribute values at once. This may not seem very different from conservative focussing, but a closer examination will make clear that it is. In particular, several features of focus gambling are of interest from the point of view of the risk-regulating nature of a strategy, and these we shall consider first.

In most tasks involving concept attainment, whether in the laboratory or in everyday life, one objective is to get the job done in as few choices or tests as possible, particularly if choices or tests are costly. It is always possible, given the use of conservative focussing, to complete the job with only as many tests as there are attributes to be tested. Focus gambling provides a way of attaining the concept in *fewer* trials than this limit. But in doing so it also imposes a risk. The risk is this. By using the strategy, one *may* succeed in attaining the concept in fewer test choices than required by conservative focussing. But the strategy also *may* require many more test choices than this. If one is in a position to take such a risk—the risk that solution may be very fast, very slow, or in between—then focus gambling is an admirable procedure. Such a position would be one where, presumably, quick solution paid off very handsomely compared to the losses to be suffered by slow solution.

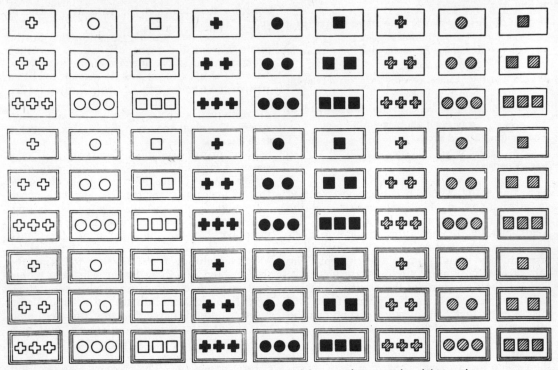

Figure 1 An array of instances comprising combinations of four attributes, each exhibiting three values. Plain figures are in green, striped figures are in red, and solid figures are in black. (Reprinted with permission from John Wiley and Sons.)

It can readily be seen how the gambling feature is built into this interesting strategy. Again consider an example. Our subject as before takes as his focus the first positive card given him as an example: three red circles with two borders (3R◯2b). Rather than change only *one* attribute value of this focus, he will take a flier and change *three* of them. Let us say then that his next choice is 3G+1b. Now, if the change should "make no difference," i.e., if the instance chosen is still positive, then the concept must be that attribute value shared by the positive focus card and the next card chosen (also positive): namely, "three figures." In one fell swoop, the user of this strategy has eliminated three attributes and attained the concept. Similarly, if two attributes of the focus are changed and a positive instance still results, then the two changed attributes are eliminated. So far, the strategy seems riskless enough.

The difficulty arises when a change in more than one attribute of the focus yields a *negative* instance. For when this happens, the only way in which a person can assimilate the information contained in the instance is to revert to the method of simultaneous scanning: to use the instance as an aid to eliminating possible hypotheses. This has the effect, of course, of diminishing drastically the economical nicety of a focus-gambling strategy. It is now no longer pos-

sible to proceed by testing *attributes* for their relevance. Instead, one must deal with *hypothesis elimination* by the method described in connection with simultaneous scanning or throw away the potential information contained in negative instances.

From the point of view of guaranteeing that instances chosen contain new information, focus gambling does not have the feature that makes conservative focussing notable. It does not guarantee that redundant instances will be avoided. For in so far as the person using this procedure does not use the information contained in negative instances, he is likely to, and frequently does, choose instances in the course of solution that contain the same information that might have been assimilated from such prior negative instances.

Finally, with respect to making the cognitive task of information assimilation easier, the strategy has most of the features of conservative focussing. One does not have to consider the full array of possible hypothetical concepts (unless one wishes to utilize the information of negative instances). It is geared to the testing of attributes in the focus card rather than to hypothesis elimination in the pure sense. It also provides for direct testing of hypotheses about the relevant attributes. As before, it reduces complexity by the use of a focus instance as a "score card."

But it is lacking in economical benefits whenever negative instances occur. The user can do nothing with these unless he shifts strategy. And there is a temptation to do just this. Finally, the strategy also has the fault of requiring a considerable amount of search-behavior if one is to find appropriate instances to test.

THE SOLUTION OF PROBLEMS

This may seem like a strange article to include under thinking. The data may, however, have much to do with an explanation of the insight phenomenon. One indication of insight is a sudden decrease in the number of errors made on a problem. In the learning-to-learn situation, after enough problems have been presented, there is also a sharp decrease in the number of errors. Compare the curve for problems 1 to 8 with that for problems 257 to 312 in Figure 2. Suppose, unknown to us, we had a subject who had had a good deal of preliminary practice. If we put him in a situation where this learning could transfer, he would soon be doing perfectly. In other words, he would show insight.

A point to guide your study

Note that most of the figures have "problems" rather than "trials" plotted on the abscissa. These figures always have "per cent correct responses" plotted on the ordinate. When "problems" are plotted on the abscissa, the ordinate "per cent correct responses" usually means correct responses on trial 2 or trials 2 to 6 of a problem. If the subject has learned that "this is a discrimination problem," i.e., that one of the objects is correct and the other incorrect, he may make a mistake on the first trial of a problem because he doesn't yet know which is correct and which is incorrect. On trials 2 to 6, however, he will switch to the other response if he has the learning set and if he made an incorrect response on trial 1. If he has the learning set and is correct on trial 1, he will persist in that response on trials 2 to 6. Thus, if the subject has the learning set, all responses on trials 2 to 6 should be correct.

31. THE FORMATION OF LEARNING SETS

Harry F. Harlow, University of Wisconsin*

In most psychological ivory towers there will be found an animal laboratory. The scientists who live there think of themselves as theoretical psychologists, since they obviously have no other rationalization to explain their extravagantly paid

* This paper was presented as the presidential address of the Midwestern Psychological Association meetings in St. Paul, May 7, 1948. The researches described were supported in part by grants from the Special Research Fund of the University of Wisconsin for 1944–48.

H. F. Harlow. The formation of learning sets. *Psychol. Rev.*, 1949, **56**, 51–65. Copyright 1949 by the American Psychological Association. Reprinted here with permission from the author and the American Psychological Association.

and idyllic sinecures. These theoretical psychologists have one great advantage over those psychological citizens who study men and women. The theoreticians can subject their subhuman animals, be they rats, dogs, or monkeys, to more rigorous controls than can ordinarily be exerted over human beings. The obligation of the theoretical psychologist is to discover general laws of behavior applicable to mice, monkeys, and men. In this obligation the theoretical psychologist has often failed. His deductions frequently have had no generality beyond the species which he has studied, and his laws have been so limited that attempts to apply them to man have resulted in confusion rather than clarification.

One limitation of many experiments on sub-

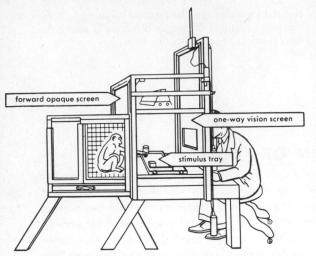

Figure 1   Wisconsin general test apparatus.

human animals is the brief period of time the subjects have been studied. In the typical problem, 48 rats are arranged in groups to test the effect of three different intensities of stimulation operating in conjunction with two different motivational conditions upon the formation of *an isolated* conditioned response. A brilliant Blitzkrieg research is effected—the controls are perfect, the results are important, and the rats are dead.

If this *do and die* technique were applied widely in investigations with human subjects, the results would be appalling. But of equal concern to the psychologist should be the fact that the derived general laws would be extremely limited in their application. There are experiments in which the use of naïve subjects is justified, but the psychological compulsion to follow this design indicates that frequently the naïve animals are to be found on both sides of the one-way vision screen.

The variety of learning situations that play an important rôle in determining our basic personality characteristics and in changing some of us into thinking animals are repeated many times in similar form. The behavior of the human being is not to be understood in terms of the results of single learning situations but rather in terms of the changes which are affected through multiple, through comparable, learning problems. Our emotional, personal, and intellectual characteristics are not the mere algebraic summation of a near infinity of stimulus-response bonds. The learning of primary importance to the primates, at least, is the formation of learning sets; it is the *learning how to learn efficiently* in the situations the animal frequently encounters. This learning to learn transforms the organism from a creature that adapts to a changing

environment by trial and error to one that adapts by seeming hypothesis and insight.

The rat psychologists have largely ignored this fundamental aspect of learning and, as a result, this theoretical domain remains a *terra incognita*. If learning sets are the mechanisms which, in part, transform the organism from a conditioned response robot to a reasonably rational creature, it may be thought that the mechanisms are too intangible for proper quantification. Any such presupposition is false. It is the purpose of this paper to demonstrate the extremely orderly and quantifiable nature of the development of certain learning sets and, more broadly, to indicate the importance of learning sets to the development of intellectual organization and personality structure.

The apparatus used throughout the studies subsequently referred to is illustrated in Figure 1. The monkey responds by displacing one of two stimulus-objects covering the food-wells in the tray before him. An opaque screen is interposed between the monkey and the stimulus situation between trials and a one-way vision screen separates monkey and man during trials.

The first problem chosen for the investigation of learning sets was the object-quality discrimination learning problem. The monkey was required to choose the rewarded one of two objects differing in multiple characteristics and shifting in the left-right positions in a predetermined balanced order. A series of 344 such problems using 344 different pairs of stimuli was run on a group of eight monkeys. Each of the first 32

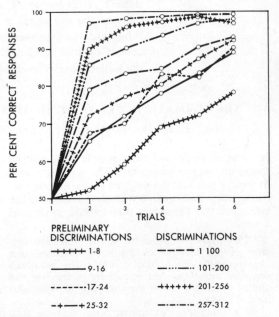

Figure 2   Discrimination learning curves on successive blocks of problems.

problems was run for 50 trials; the next 200 problems for six trials; and the last 112 problems for an average of nine trials.

In Figure 2 are presented learning curves which show the per cent of correct responses on the first six trials of these discriminations. The data for the first 32 discriminations are grouped for blocks of eight problems, and the remaining discriminations are arranged in blocks of 100, 100, 56, and 56 problems. The data indicate that the subjects progressively improve in their ability to learn object-quality discrimination problems. The monkeys *learn how to learn* individual problems with a minimum of errors. It is this *learning how to learn a kind of problem* that we designate by the term *learning set*.

The very form of the learning curve changes as learning sets become more efficient. The form of the learning curve for the first eight discrimination problems appears S-shaped: it could be described as a curve of "trial-and-error" learning. The curve for the last 56 problems approaches linearity after Trial 2. Curves of similar form have been described as indicators of "insightful" learning.

We wish to emphasize that this *learning to learn*, this *transfer from problem to problem* which we call the formation of a learning set, is a highly *predictable, orderly* process which can be demonstrated as long as controls are maintained over the subjects' experience and the difficulty of the problems. Our subjects, when they started these researches, had no previous laboratory learning experience. Their entire discrimination learning set history was obtained in this study. The stimulus pairs employed had been arranged and their serial order determined from tables of random numbers. Like nonsense syllables, the stimulus pairs were equated for difficulty. It is unlikely that any group of problems differed significantly in intrinsic difficulty from any other group.

In a conventional learning curve we plot change of performance over a series of *trials*; in a learning set curve we plot change in performance over a series of *problems*. It is important to remember that *we measure learning set in terms of problems* just as *we measure habit in terms of trials*.

Figure 3 presents a discrimination learning set curve showing progressive increase in the per cent of correct responses on Trials 2–6 on successive blocks of problems. This curve appears to be negatively accelerated or possibly linear.

Discrimination learning set curves obtained on four additional naïve normal monkeys and eight naïve monkeys with extensive unilateral cortical lesions, are shown in Figure 4. Brain-injured as well as normal monkeys are seen to form effective discrimination learning sets, although the partial hemidecorticate monkeys are

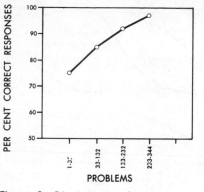

Figure 3 Discrimination learning set curve based on Trial 2-6 responses.

less efficient than the normal subjects. Improvement for both groups is progressive and the small number of subjects and the relatively small number of problems, 14, included in each of the problem blocks presented on the abscissa.

Through the courtesy of Dr. Margaret Kuenne we have discrimination learning set data on another primate species. These animals were also run on a series of six-trial discrimination problems but under slightly different conditions. Macaroni beads and toys were substituted for food rewards, and the subjects were tested sans iron-barred cages. The data for these 17 children, whose ages range from two to five years and whose intelligence quotients range from 109 to 151, are presented in Figure 5. Learning set curves are plotted for groups of children attaining a predetermined learning criterion within differing numbers of problem blocks. In spite of the small number of cases and the behavioral vagaries that are known to characterize this primate species, the learning set curves are orderly and lawful and show progressive increase in per cent of correct responses.

Learning set curves, like learning curves, can

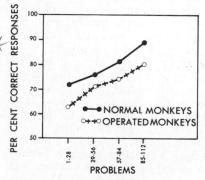

Figure 4 Discrimination learning set curves based on Trial 2-6 responses: normal and operated monkeys.

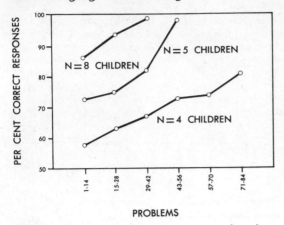

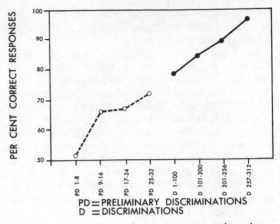

Figure 5 Discrimination learning set curves based on Trial 2-6 responses: children.

Figure 6 Discrimination learning set curve based on Trial 2 responses.

be plotted in terms of correct responses or errors, in terms of responses on any trial or total trials. A measure which we have frequently used is per cent of correct Trial 2 responses—the behavioral measure of the amount learned on Trial 1.

Figure 6 shows learning set curves measured in terms of the per cent correct Trial 2 responses for the 344-problem series. The data from the first 32 preliminary discriminations and the 312 subsequent discriminations have been plotted separately. As one might expect, these learning set curves are similar to those that have been previously presented. What the curves show with especial clarity is the almost unbelievable change which has taken place in the *effectiveness of the first training trial*. In the initial eight discriminations, this single paired stimulus presentation brings the Trial 2 performance of the monkeys to a level less than three per cent above chance; in the last 56 discriminations, this first training trial brings the performance of the monkeys to a level *less than three per cent* short of perfection. Before the formation of a discrimination learning set, a single training trial produces negligible gain; after the formation of a discrimination learning set, *a single training trial constitutes problem solution*. These data clearly show that *animals can gradually learn insight*.

In the final phase of our discrimination series with monkeys there were subjects that solved from 20 to 30 consecutive problems with no errors whatsoever following the first blind trial, —and many of the children, after the first day or two of training, did as well or better.

These data indicate the function of a learning set in converting a problem which is initially difficult for a subject into a problem which is so simple as to be immediately solvable. The learning set is the mechanism that changes the problem from an intellectual tribulation into an intellectual triviality and leaves the organism free

to attack problems of another hierarchy of difficulty.

For the analysis of learning sets in monkeys on a problem that is ostensibly at a more complex level than the discrimination problem, we choose the discrimination reversal problem. The procedure was to run the monkeys on a discrimination problem for 7, 9, or 11 trials and then to reverse the reward value of the stimuli for eight trials; that is to say, the stimulus previously correct was made incorrect and the stimulus previously incorrect became correct.

The eight monkeys previously trained on discrimination learning were tested on a series of 112 discrimination reversal problems. Discrimination reversal learning curves for successive blocks of 28 problems are shown in Figure 7. The measure used is per cent of correct responses on Reversal Trials 2 to 6. Figure 8 presents data on the formation of the discrimination reversal

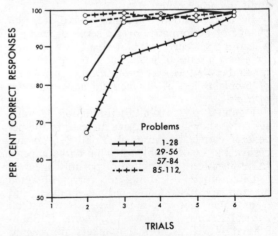

Figure 7 Discrimination reversal learning curves on successive blocks of problems.

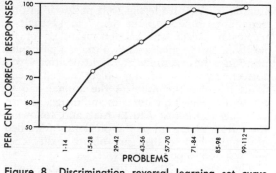

Figure 8 Discrimination reversal learning set curve based on Trial 2 responses.

learning set in terms of the per cent of correct responses on Reversal Trial 2 for successive blocks of 14 problems. Reversal Trial 2 is the first trial following the "informing" trial, i.e., the initial trial reversing the reward value of the stimuli. Reversal Trial 2 is the measure of the effectiveness with which the single informing trial leads the subject to abandon a reaction pattern which has proved correct for 7 to 11 trials, and to initiate a new reaction pattern to the stimulus pair. On the last 42 discrimination reversal problems the monkeys were responding as efficiently on Reversal Trial 2 as they were on complementary Discrimination Trial 2, i.e., they were making over 97 per cent correct responses on both aspects of the problems. The eight monkeys made from 12 to 57 successive correct second trial reversal responses. Thus it becomes perfectly obvious that at the end of this problem the monkeys possessed sets both to learn and to reverse a reaction tendency, and that this behavior could be consistently and immediately elicited with hypothesis-like efficiency.

This terminal performance level is likely to focus undue attention on the one-trial learning at the expense of the earlier, less efficient performance levels. It should be kept in mind that this one-trial learning appeared only as the end result of an orderly and progressive learning process; insofar as these subjects are concerned, the insights are only to be understood in an historical perspective.

Although the discrimination reversal problems might be expected to be more difficult for the monkeys than discrimination problems, the data of Figure 9 indicate that the discrimination reversal learning set was formed more rapidly than the previously acquired discrimination learning set. The explanation probably lies in the nature of the transfer of training from the discrimination learning to the discrimination reversal problems. A detailed analysis of the discrimination learning data indicates the operation throughout the learning series of certain error-producing factors, but with each successive block of prob-

lems the frequencies of errors attributable to these factors are progressively decreased, although at different rates and to different degrees. The process might be conceived of as a learning of response tendencies that counteract the error-producing factors. A description of the reduction of the error-producing factors is beyond the scope of this paper, even though we are of the opinion that this type of analysis is basic to an adequate theory of discrimination learning.

Suffice it to say that there is reason to believe that there is a large degree of transfer from the discrimination series to the reversal series, of the learned response tendencies counteracting the operation of two of the three primary error-producing factors thus far identified.

The combined discrimination and discrimination reversal data show clearly how the learning set delivers the animal from Thorndikian bondage. By the time the monkey has run 232 discriminations and followed these by 112 discriminations and reversals, he does not possess 344 or 456 specific habits, bonds, connections or associations. We doubt if our monkeys at this time could respond with much more than chance efficiency on the first trial of any series of the previously learned problems. But the monkey does have a generalized ability to learn *any* discrimination problem or *any* discrimination reversal problem with the greatest of ease. Training on several hundred specific problems has not turned the monkey into an automaton exhibiting forced, stereotyped, reflex responses to specific stimuli. These several hundred habits have, instead, made the monkey an adjustable creature with an *increased capacity* to adapt to the ever-changing demands of a psychology laboratory environment.

We believe that other learning sets acquired in and appropriate to the monkey's natural en-

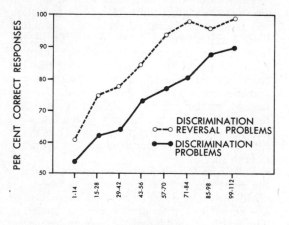

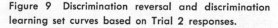

PROBLEMS

Figure 9 Discrimination reversal and discrimination learning set curves based on Trial 2 responses.

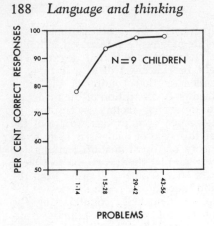

Figure 10   Discrimination reversal learning set curve based on Trial 2 responses:
children.

vironment would enable him to adapt better to
the changing conditions there. We are certain,
moreover, that learning sets acquired by man in
and appropriate to his enviroment have accounted for his ability to adapt and survive.

Before leaving the problem of discrimination
reversal learning we submit one additional set of
data that we feel merits attention. Nine of the
children previously referred to were also subjected to a series of discrimination reversal problems. The outcome is partially indicated in
Figure 10 which shows the per cent of correct
Reversal Trial 2 responses made on successive
blocks of 14 problems. It can be seen that these
three- to five-year-old children clearly bested the
monkeys in performance on this series of problems. Trial 2 responses approach perfection in
the second block of 14 discrimination reversal
problems. Actually, over half of the total Trial 2
errors were made by one child.

These discrimination reversal data on the children are the perfect illustration of set formation
and transfer producing adaptable abilities rather
than specific bonds. Without benefit of the
monkey's discrimination reversal set learning
curves we might be tempted to assume that the
children's data indicate a gulf between human
and subhuman learning. But the *extremely rapid*
learning on the part of the children is not unlike
the *rapid* learning on the part of the monkeys,
and analysis of the error-producing factors shows
that the same basic mechanisms are operating
in both species.

Following the discrimination reversal problem
the eight monkeys were presented a new series
of 56 problems designed to elicit alternation of
unequivocally antagonistic response patterns.
The first 7, 9, or 11 trials of each problem were
simple object-quality discrimination trials. These
were followed immediately by ten right-position
discrimination trials with the same stimuli con-

tinuing to shift in the right-left positions in predetermined orders. In the first 7 to 11 trials, a
particular object was correct regardless of its
position. In the subsequent 10 trials, a particular
position—the experimenter's right position—was
correct, regardless of the object placed there.
Thus to solve the problem the animal had to
respond to object-quality cues and disregard position cues in the first 7 to 11 trials and, following
the failure of reward of the previously rewarded
object, he had to disregard object-quality cues
and respond to position cues.

The learning data on these two antagonistic
tasks are presented in Figure 11. It is to be
noted that the object-quality curve, which is
based on Trials 1 to 7, begins at a very high
level of accuracy, whereas the position curve,
plotted for Trials 1 to 10, begins at a level little
above chance. This no doubt reflects the operation of the previously well-established object-
quality discrimination learning set. As the series
continues, the object-quality curve shows a drop
until the last block of problems, while the position curve rises progressively. In the evaluation
of these data, it should be noted that chance
performance is 50 per cent correct responses for
the object-quality discriminations and 45 per
cent for the position discriminations, since each
sequence of 10 position trials includes an error
"informing" trial. It would appear that the
learning of the right-position discriminations
interferes with the learning of the object-quality
discriminations to some extent. In spite of this
decrement in object-quality discrimination performance for a time, the subjects were functioning at levels far beyond chance on the antagonistic parts of the problems during the last half
of the series. We believe that this behavior reflects the formation of a right-position learning
set which operates at a high degree of independence of the previously established object-
quality discrimination learning set.

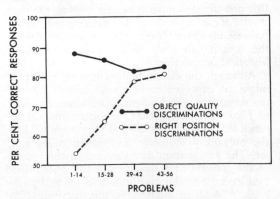

Figure 11   Learning set curves for problem requiring
shift from object-quality discrimination to right-position
discrimination.

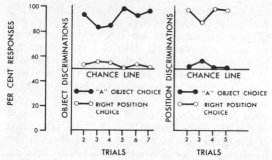

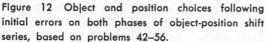

Figure 12 Object and position choices following initial errors on both phases of object-position shift series, based on problems 42–56.

The precision of the independent operation of these learning sets throughout the last 14 problems is indicated in Figure 12. Since the right-position part of the problem was almost invariably initiated by an error trial, these data are limited to those problems on which the first trial object-quality discrimination response was incorrect. The per cent of correct Trial 7 responses to the "A" object, the correct stimulus for the object-quality discriminations, is 98. The initiating error trial which occurs when the problem shifts without warning to a right-position problem, drops this per cent response to the "A" object to 52—a level barely above chance. The per cent of Trial 7 responses to the right position during the object-quality discriminations is 52. The single error trial initiating the shift of the problem to a right-position discrimination is followed by 97 per cent right-position responses on the next trial. In other words, *it is as though* the outcome of a single *push of an object* is adequate to switch off the "A"-object choice reaction tendency and to switch on the right-position choice reaction tendency.

The cue afforded by a single trial produces at this point almost complete discontinuity of the learning process. The only question now left unsettled in the controversy over hypotheses in subhuman animals is whether or not to use this term to describe the behavior of a species incapable of verbalization.

Again, it should be remembered that both the object-quality discrimination learning set and the right-position discrimination learning set developed in a gradual and orderly manner. Only after the learning sets are formed do these phenomena of discontinuity in learned behavior appear.

Further evidence for the integrity of learning sets is presented in an additional experiment. Six monkeys with object-quality discrimination learning experience, but without training on reversal problems or position discriminations, were given seven blocks of 14 problems each, starting

with a block of 25-trial object-quality discriminations, followed by a block of 14 25-trial positional discriminations composed of right-position and left-position problems presented alternately. The remaining five blocks of problems continued the alternate presentation of 14 object-quality discrimination problems and 14 right-left positional discrimination problems. Figure 13 presents curves showing the per cent of correct responses on total trials on these alternate blocks of antagonistic discriminations. The complex positional discrimination learning set curve shows progressive improvement throughout the series, whereas the object-quality discrimination curve begins at a high level of accuracy, shows decrement on the second block, and subsequently recovers. By the end of the experiment the two basically antagonistic learning sets had "learned" to live together with a minimum of conflict. These data are the more striking if it is recalled that between each two blocks of object-quality discriminations there were 350 trials in which no object was differentially rewarded, and between each two blocks of 14 positional discriminations there were 350 trials in which no position was differentially rewarded.

In Figure 14 we present additional total-trial data on the formation of the positional learning set. These data show the change in performance on the first and last seven positional discriminations in each of the three separate blocks of positional discriminations. The interposed object-quality discrimination problems clearly produced interference, but they did not prevent the orderly development of the positional learning sets, nor the final attainment of a high level of performance on these problems.

We have data which suggest that the educated man can face arteriosclerosis with confidence, if the results on brain-injured animals are applicable to men. Figure 15 shows discrimination learning set curves for the previously de-

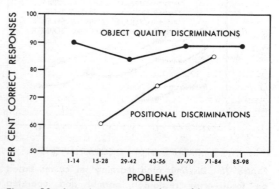

Figure 13 Learning set curves for problem series with alternating object-quality and positional discriminations, based on total trial responses.

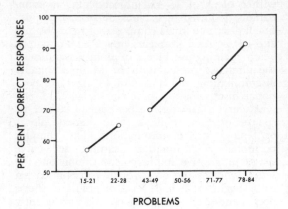

Figure 14　Right-left positional discrimination learning set curve based on total trial responses. (Data on antagonistic object-quality discrimination problems omitted.)

scribed groups of four normal monkeys and eight monkeys with very extensive unilateral cortical injury. The upper curves show total errors on an initial series of 112 six-trial discriminations. The lower curves show total errors on an additional group of 56 discriminations presented one year later. In both situations the full-brained monkeys make significantly better scores, but one should note that the educated hemidecorticate animals are superior to the uneducated unoperated monkeys. Such data suggest that half a brain is better than one if you compare the individuals having appropriate learning sets with the individuals lacking them.

More seriously, these data may indicate why educated people show less apparent deterioration with advancing age than uneducated individuals, and the data lend support to the clinical observation that our fields of greatest proficiency are the last to suffer gross deterioration.

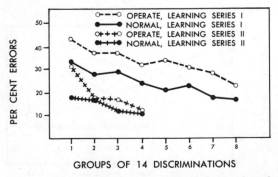

Figure 15　Discrimination learning set curves based on total error responses: normal and operated monkeys.

Although our objective data are limited to the formation of learning sets which operate to give efficient performance on intellectual problems, we have observational data of a qualitative nature on social-emotional changes in our animals. When the monkeys come to us they are wild and intractable but within a few years they have acquired, from the experimenter's point of view, good personalities. Actually we believe that one of the very important factors in the development of the good personalities of our monkeys is the formation of social-emotional learning sets organized in a manner comparable with the intellectual learning sets we have previously described. Each contact the monkey has with a human being represents a single specific learning trial. Each person represents a separate problem. Learning to react favorably to one person is followed by learning favorable reactions more rapidly to the next person to whom the monkey is socially introduced. Experience with additional individuals enables the monkey to learn further how to behave with human beings, and eventually the monkey's favorable reactions to new people are acquired so rapidly as to appear almost instantaneous.

The formation of social-emotional learning sets is not to be confused with mere stimulus generalization, a construct applied in this field with undue freedom. Actually a learning set once formed determines in large part the nature and direction of stimulus generalization. In the classic study in which Watson conditioned fear in Albert, the child developed a fear of the rat and generalized this fear, but failed to develop or generalize fear to Watson, even though Watson must have been the more conspicuous stimulus. Apparently Albert had already formed an affectional social-emotional learning set to people, which inhibited both learning and simple Pavlovian generalization.

Our observations on the formation of social-emotional learning sets have been entirely qualitative and informal, but there would appear to be no reason why they could not be studied experimentally.

The emphasis throughout this paper has been on the role of the historical or experience variable in learning behavior—the forgotten variable in current learning theory and research. Hull's Neo-behaviorists have constantly emphasized the necessity for an historical approach to learning, yet they have not exploited it fully. Their experimental manipulation of the experience variable has been largely limited to the development of isolated habits and their generalization. Their failure to find the phenomenon of discontinuity in learning may stem from their study of individual as opposed to repetitive learning situations.

The field theorists, unlike the Neo-behaviorists, have stressed insight and hypothesis in their description of learning. The impression these theorists give is that these phenomena are properties of the innate organization of the individual. If such phenomena appear independently of a gradual learning history, we have not found them in the primate order.

Psychologists working with human subjects have long believed in the phenomenon of learning sets and have even used sets as explanatory principles to account for perceptual selection and incidental learning. These psychologists have not, however, investigated the nature of these learning sets which their subjects bring to the experimental situation. The determining experiential variables of these learning sets lie buried in the subjects' pasts, but the development of such sets can be studied in the laboratory as long as the human race continues to reproduce its kind. Actually, detailed knowledge of the nature of the formation of learning sets could be of such importance to educational theory and practice as to justify prolonged and systematic investigation.

In the animal laboratory where the experiential factor can be easily controlled, we have carried out studies that outline the development and operation of specific learning sets. We believe that the construct of learning sets is of importance in the understanding of adaptive behavior. Since this is our faith, it is our hope that our limited data will be extended by those brave souls who study *real* men and *real* women.

The important point of this article is that the solution of a problem often depends, first of all, upon a clear idea of the principle needed for a solution—the "functional" solution. The next step in the solution of the problem is the discovery of a practical way of applying this principle.

A point to guide your study

Make sure you try to solve the problems before reading the solutions. Compare your attempts at solution with those mentioned.

32. THE STRUCTURE AND DYNAMICS OF PROBLEM-SOLVING PROCESSES
*Karl Duncker**

The solution of practical problems

1. Introduction and formulation of the problem. A problem arises when a living creature has a goal but does not know how this goal is to be reached. Whenever one cannot go from the given situation to the desired situation simply by action, then there has to be recourse to thinking. (By action we here understand the performance of obvious operations.) Such thinking has the task of devising some action which may mediate between the existing and the desired situations. Thus the "solution" of a practical problem must fulfill two demands: in the first place, its realization[1] must bring about the goal situation, and in the second place one must be able to arrive at it from the given situation simply through action.

* Karl Duncker. On problem-solving. *Psychol. Monogr.*, 1945, **58**, no. 5 (whole no. 270). Translated by Lynne S. Lees. Copyright 1945 by the American Psychological Association. Excerpt reprinted here with permission from the American Psychological Association. Footnotes renumbered. References to other parts of the monograph omitted.

[1] [Translator's note: "Realization" is used in the sense of "making real", of "actualization". The terms "embodiment" and "to embody" are used in a closely related sense, which will be clear in context. In the following, all notes of the translator will be given in parentheses. Such notes will add the German terms of the original where entirely satisfactory English terms do not seem to exist.]

The practical problem whose solution was experimentally studied in greatest detail runs as follows: Given a human being with an inoperable stomach tumor, and rays which destroy organic tissue at sufficient intensity, by what procedure can one free him of the tumor by these rays and at the same time avoid destroying the healthy tissue which surrounds it?

Such practical problems, in which one asks, "How shall I attain . . . ?", are related to certain theoretical problems, in which the question is, "How, by what means, shall I comprehend . . . ?" In the former case, a problem situation arises through the fact that a goal has no direct connection with the given reality; in the latter case —in theoretical problems—it arises through the fact that a proposition has no direct connection with what is given in the premises. As example in the latter field, let us take again the problem with which I experimented in greatest detail: Why is it that all six-place numbers of the type *abcabc*, for example 276276, are divisible by thirteen?

It is common to both types of problems that one seeks the ground for an anticipated consequence; in practical problems, the actual ground is sought; in theoretical problems, the logical ground.[2]

In the present investigation the question is: *How does the solution arise from the problem situation? In what ways is the solution of a problem attained?*

2. Experimental procedure. The experiments proceeded as follows: The subjects (Ss), who were mostly students of universities or of colleges, were given various thinking problems, with the request that they think aloud. This instruction, *"Think aloud"*, is not identical with the instruction to introspect which has been common in experiments on thought-processes. While the introspecter makes himself as thinking the object of his attention, the subject who is thinking aloud remains immediately directed to the problem, so to speak allowing his activity to become verbal. When someone, while thinking, says to himself, "One ought to see if this isn't . . .", or, "It would be nice if one could show that . . .", one would hardly call this introspection; yet in such remarks something is revealed which we shall later deal with under the name of 'development of the problem'. The subject (S) was emphatically warned not to leave unspoken even the most fleeting or foolish idea. He was told that where he did not feel completely informed, he might freely question

the experimenter, but that no previous specialized knowledge was necessary to solve the problems.

3. A protocol of the radiation problem. Let us begin with the radiation problem (p. 1). Usually the schematic sketch shown in Figure 1

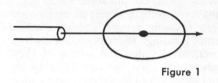

Figure 1

was given with the problem. Thus, it was added, somebody had visualized the situation to begin with (cross-section through the body with the tumor in the middle and the radiation apparatus on the left); but obviously this would not do.

From my records I choose that of a solution-process which was particularly rich in typical hunches and therefore also especially long and involved. The average process vacillated less and could be left to run its own course with considerably less guidance.[3]

Protocol

1. Send rays through the esophagus.

2. Desensitize the healthy tissues by means of a chemical injection.

3. Expose the tumor by operating.

4. One ought to decrease the intensity of the rays on their way; for example—would this work?—turn the rays on at full strength only after the tumor has been reached. (Experimenter: False analogy; no injection is in question.)

5. One should swallow something inorganic (which would not allow passage of the rays) to protect the healthy stomach-walls. (E: It is not merely the stomach-walls which are to be protected.)

6. Either the rays must enter the body or the tumor must come out. Perhaps one could alter the location of the tumor—but how? Through pressure? No.

7. Introduce a cannula.—(E: What, in general, does one do when, with any agent, one wishes to produce in a specific place an effect which he wishes to avoid on the way to that place?)

8. (Reply): One neutralizes the effect on the way. But that is what I have been attempting all the time.

---

[2] Other types of theoretical problems, such as: "What is the essential nature of, or the law of . . . ?" or "How are . . . related to each other?", are not investigated here.

[3] Compare the pertinent protocols in my earlier and theoretically much less developed paper, "A qualitative study of productive thinking," Ped. Sem., 1926, v. 33.

9. Move the tumor toward the exterior. (Compare 6.) (The E repeats the problem and emphasizes, ". . . which destroy *at sufficient intensity*".)

10. The intensity ought to be variable. (Compare 4.)

11. Adaptation of the healthy tissues by previous weak application of the rays. (E: How can it be brought about that the rays destroy only the region of the tumor?)

12. (Reply:) I see no more than two possibilities: either to protect the body or to make the rays harmless. (E: How could one decrease the intensity of the rays en route? [Compare 4.])

13. (Reply:) Somehow divert . . . diffuse rays . . . disperse . . . stop! Send a broad and weak bundle of rays through a lens in such a way that the tumor lies at the focal point and thus receives intensive radiation.[4] (Total duration about half an hour.)

4. Impracticable 'solutions'. In the protocol given above, we can discern immediately that the whole process, from the original setting of the problem to the final solution, appears as a series of more or less concrete proposals. Of course, only the last one, or at least its principle, is practicable. All those preceding are in some respect inadequate to the problem, and therefore the process of solution cannot stop there. But however primitive they may be, this one thing is certain, that they cannot be discussed in terms of meaningless, blind, trial-and-error reactions. Let us take for an example the first proposal: "Send rays through the esophagus". Its clear meaning is that the rays should be guided into the stomach by some passage free from tissue. The basis of this proposal is, however, obviously an incorrect representation of the situation inasmuch as the rays are regarded as a sort of fluid, or the esophagus as offering a perfectly straight approach to the stomach, etc. Nevertheless, within the limits of this simplified concept of the situation, the proposal would actually fulfill the demands of the problem. It is therefore genuinely the solution of a problem, although not of the one which was actually presented. With the other proposals, the situation is about the same. The second presupposes that a means—for example, a chemical means— exists for making organic tissue insensitive to the rays. If such a means existed, then everything would be in order, and the solution-process

would have already come to an end. The fourth proposal—that the rays be turned on at full strength only when the tumor has been reached —shows again very clearly its derivation from a false analogy, perhaps that of a syringe which is set in operation only when it has been introduced into the object. The sixth suggestion, finally, treats the body too much as analogous to a rubber ball, which can be deformed without injury. In short, it is evident that such proposals are anything but completely meaningless associations. Merely in the factual situation, they are wrecked on certain components of the situation not yet known or not yet considered by the subject.

Occasionally it is not so much the situation as the demand, whose distortion or simplification makes the proposal practically useless. In the case of the third suggestion, for example ("expose the tumor by operating"), the real reason why radiation was introduced seems to have escaped the subject. An operation is exactly what should be avoided. Similarly in the fifth proposal, the fact is forgotten that not only the healthy stomach-walls must be protected but also all parts of the healthy body which have to be penetrated by the rays.

A remark on principle may here be in order. The psychologist who is investigating, not a store of knowledge, but the genesis of a solution, is not interested primarily in whether a proposal is actually practicable, but only in whether it is formally practicable, that is, practicable in the framework of the subject's given premises. If in planning a project an engineer relies on incorrect formulae or on non-existent material, his project can nevertheless follow from the false premises as intelligently as another from correct premises. One can be 'psychologically equivalent' to the other. In short, we are interested in knowing how a solution develops out of the system of its subjective premises, and how it is fitted to this system.

5. Classification of proposals. If one compares the various tentative solutions in the protocol with one another, they fall naturally into certain groups. Proposals 1, 3, 5, 6, 7 and 9 have clearly in common the attempt to *avoid contact between the rays and the healthy tissue*. This goal is attained in quite different ways: in 1 by re-directing the rays over a path naturally free from tissue; in 3 by the removal of the healthy tissue from the original path of the rays by operation; in 5 by interposing a protective wall (which may already have been tacitly implied in 1 and 3); in 6 by translocating the tumor towards the exterior; and in 7, finally, by a combination of 3 and 5. In proposals 2 and 11, the problem is quite differently attacked; the accompanying destruction of healthy tissue is here

---

[4] This solution is closely related to the 'best' solution: *crossing of several weak bundles of rays at the tumor*, so that the intensity necessary for destruction is attained only here. Incidentally, it is quite true that the rays in question are not deflected by ordinary lenses; but this fact is of no consequence from the viewpoint of the psychology of thinking.

to be avoided by the *desensitizing or immunizing of this tissue*. A third method is used in 4, perhaps in 8, in 10 and 13: *the reduction of radiation intensity on the way*. As one can see, the process of solution shifts noticeably back and forth among these three methods of approach.

In the interests of clarity, the relationships described are presented graphically below.

6. Functional value and understanding. In this classification, the tentative solutions are grouped according to the manner in which they try to solve the problem, i.e., according to their "by-means-of-which", their "functional value". Consider the proposal to send rays through the esophagus. The S says nothing at all about avoiding contact, or about a free passage. Nevertheless, the solution-character of the esophagus in this context is due to no other characteristic than that of being a tissue-free path to the stomach. It functions as the embodiment solely of this property (not of the property of being a muscular pipe, or of lying behind the windpipe, or the like). In short, in the context of this problem, the "by-means-of-which", the "functional value" of the esophagus is: a free path to the stomach. The proposals: "direct the rays by a natural approach", "expose by operation", "translocate the tumor toward the exterior", "protective wall", and "cannula" all embody the functional value: no contact between rays and healthy tissue. The functional value of the solution, "concentration of diffuse rays in the tumor", is the characteristic: "less intensity on the way, great intensity in the tumor". The functional value of the lens is the quality: "medium to concentrate rays", and so forth.

The functional value of a solution is indispensable for the understanding of its being a solution. It is exactly what is called the sense, the principle or the point of the solution. The subordinated, more specialized characteristics and properties of a solution embody this principle, apply it to the particular circumstances of the situation. For example, the esophagus is in this way an application of the principle: "free passage to the stomach", to the particular circumstances of the human body. To understand the solution as a solution is just the same as to comprehend the solution as embodying its functional value. When someone is asked, "Why is such-and-such a solution?", he necessarily has recourse to the functional value. In all my experiments, aside from two or three unmistakable exceptions, when the E asked about a proposal: "In what way is this a solution of the problem?", the S responded promptly with a statement of its functional value. (In spontaneous statements of the Ss, the functional value was frequently left unmentioned as being too obvious.)

Incidentally, the realization of its functional value mediates understanding of a solution even where there is nothing but an 'unintelligible' (though sufficiently general) relation between the functional value and the demand which it fulfills. Blowing on a weakly glimmering fire, for example, undoubtedly solves the problem of rekindling the fire because in this way fresh oxygen is supplied. In other words, the increase of the oxygen supply is the immediate functional value of blowing on the fire. But why combination with oxygen produces warmth and flame is ultimately not intelligible. Even if the whole of chemistry should be successfully and without a gap derived from the principles of atomic physics, these principles are not in themselves altogether intelligible, i.e., ultimately they must be "accepted as mere facts". Thus, intelligibility frequently means no more than participation in, or derivability from, sufficiently elementary and universal causal relationships. But even if these general laws are not in themselves intelligible, reducibility to such general laws actually mediates a certain type of understanding.

To the same degree to which a solution is understood, it can be transposed, which means that under altered conditions it may be changed correspondingly in such a way as to preserve its functional value. For, one can transpose a solution only when one has grasped its functional value, its general principle, i.e., the invariants from which, by introduction of changed condi-

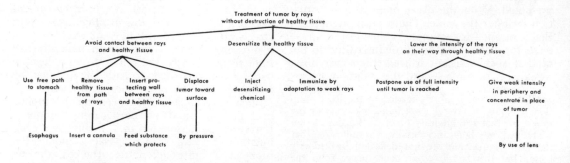

tions, the corresponding variations of the solution follow each time.

An example: When, seen from the standpoint of a spectator, someone makes a detour around some obstacle, and yet acts from his own point of view in terms of nothing but, say, "now three yards to the left, then two yards straight ahead, then to the right . . ."—these properties of the solution would certainly satisfy the concrete circumstances of the special situation here and now. But so long as the person in question has not grasped the functional value, the general structure: "detour around an obstacle", he must necessarily fail when meeting a new obstacle which is differently located and of different shape. For to different obstacles correspond different final forms of the solution; but the structure, "detour around an obstacle", remains always the same. Whoever has grasped this structure is able to transpose a detour properly.

7. Meaningless errors as a sympton of deficient understanding. A solution conceived without functional understanding often betrays itself through nonsensical errors. A good example is supplied by experiments with another thinking problem.

The problem was worded as follows: "You know what a pendulum is, and that a pendulum plays an important rôle in a clock. Now, in order for a clock to go accurately, the swings of the pendulum must be strictly regular. The duration of a pendulum's swing depends, among other things, on its length, and this of course in turn on the temperature. Warming produces expansion and cooling produces contraction, although to a different degree in different materials. Thus every temperature-change would change the length of the pendulum. But the clock should go with absolute regularity. How can this be brought about?—By the way, the length of a pendulum is defined solely by the shortest distance between the point of suspension and the center of gravity. We are concerned only with this length; for the rest, the pendulum may have any appearance at all."

The customary solution of this pendulum problem in actual practice is reproduced in Figure 2. At first this solution will be entirely 'unintelligible' to many a reader.

Let him watch now what takes place when the solution suddenly becomes clear to him. Its functional value is that every expansion in one direction is compensated by an equally great expansion in the opposite direction.

The bars a and a' (see Figure 3) can expand only downwards; b and b', on the other hand, only upwards, since they are fastened below. The bars b and b' are meant to raise the strip of metal to which c is fastened by exactly as much

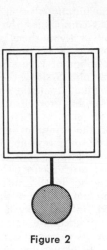

Figure 2

as a and c together expand downwards. To this end, b and b' must of course be constructed of a material with a greater coefficient of expansion than a and a' and c.

Only when Figure 3 is grasped as the embodiment of this functional value, is it understood as the solution.

Among the many Ss to whom I gave the pendulum problem, there were two who were already vaguely familiar with a pendulum-model, and simply reconstructed it from memory. One was fortunate and did it correctly, while the other drew "just four or five bars like this, from which the weight hung below". (Figure 4.) It is evident that this is a completely meaningless construction, despite all external resemblance to Figure 3, and devoid of any functional understanding (as the S clearly realized and expressed himself). Compare with this the solutions of the problem contained in Figure 5, a-g, which, in spite of all external differences, embody the

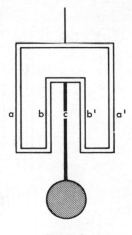

Figure 3

identical functional value and at the same time represent completely new constructions.

In all of them there is compensation in the sense of Figure 3; thus we deal with appropriate transpositions of Figure 3. It is worth mentioning that one S drew the model of Figure 5a, believing that it was the compensation-pendulum dimly familiar from experience. Here it is clear that the reconstruction can have taken place only via the common functional value. Nothing in their form is common to the two pendulums.

"Good" and "stupid" errors in Köhler's sense can be clearly distinguished as follows: In the case of good, intelligent errors, at least the general functional value of the situation is correctly outlined, only the specific manner of its realization is not adequate. For example, an ape stands a box on its corner under the goal object, which hangs high above, because in this way the box comes closer—to be sure, at the price of its stability. In the case of stupid errors, on the other hand, the outward form of an earlier, or an imitated solution is blindly reproduced without functional understanding. For example, an ape jumps into the air from a box—but the goal object is hanging at quite a different spot.

8. The process of solution as development of the problem.   It may already have become clear that the relationship between superordinate and subordinate properties of a solution has *genetic* significance. *The final form of an individual solution is, in general, not reached by a single step from the original setting of the problem; on the contrary, the principle, the functional value of the solution, typically arises first, and the final form of the solution in question develops only as this principle becomes successively more and more concrete. In other words, the general or "essential" properties of a solution genetically precede the specific properties; the* latter *are developed out of the former.* The classification given previously presents, thus, a sort of *"family tree"* of the solution of the radiation problem.

The finding of a general property of a solution means each time a *reformulation of the original problem*. Consider for example the fourth proposal in the protocol above. Here it is clearly evident that at first there exists only the very general functional value of the solution: "one must decrease the intensity of the radiation on the way". But the decisive reformulation of the original problem is thereby accomplished. No longer, as at the beginning, does the S seek simply a "means to apply rays to the tumor without also destroying healthy tissue", but already—over and above this—a means to decrease the intensity of the radiation on the way. The formulation of the problem has thus been made sharper, more specific—and the proposal not to turn the rays on at full strength until the tumor has been reached, although certainly wrong, arises only as a solution of this new, reformulated problem. From this same reformulation of the problem there arises, at the end of the whole process, the practicable solution, "concentration of diffuse rays in the tumor". With the other proposals in the protocol, the case is similar: the solution-properties found at first, the functional values, *always serve as productive reformulations of the original problem*.

We can accordingly describe a process of solution either as development of the solution or as development of the problem. Every solution-principle found in the process, which is itself not yet ripe for concrete realization, and which therefore fulfills only the first of the two demands given previously, functions from then on as reformulation, as sharpening of the original setting of the problem. *It is therefore meaningful to say that what is really done in any solution of problems consists in formulating the problem more productively.*

To sum up: *The final form of a solution is typically attained by way of mediating phases of the process, of which each one, in retrospect, possesses the character of a solution, and, in prospect, that of a problem.*

At the same time it is evident that, generally speaking, a process of solution penetrates only by degrees into the more specific circumstances and possibilities of the given situation. In the phase, "avoiding contact between rays and healthy tissue", for example, there is still very little reference to the concrete individuality of the situation. The rays function for the time being as "active agent", the tumor as "the place to be influenced", and the healthy tissue as "surrounding region which must be protected".

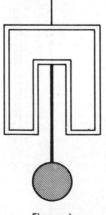

Figure 4

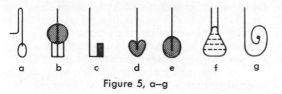

Figure 5, a–g

In the next phase, "redirection of the rays over a tissue-free path to the stomach", at least the possibility of such a displacement of the rays is already made use of. In the search for a free pathway, the situation is then subjected to an even more precise inspection; as a consequence, such a specific component of the situation as the esophagus enters the solution-process and is used in a sensible manner.

To widen our horizon, let us here demonstrate with a mathematical example how a solution-process typically arrives at the final solution by way of mediation problem- or solution-phases. The original problem is to prove that there is an infinite number of prime numbers (to find "something from which follows that there exists...."). A step which is quite decisive, although subjectively hardly noted, consists in the solution-phase: "I must prove that for any prime number p there exists a greater one". This reformulation of the problem sounds quite banal and insignificant. Nevertheless I had Ss who never hit on it. And without this step, the final solution cannot be reached.[5]

A further solution-phase would run as follows: "To prove the existence of such a prime number, I must try to construct it." With one of my Ss, I could follow clearly the way in which, to this phase, a further one attached itself as a mere explication: "One must therefore construct a number greater than p which cannot be represented as a product". From here on, clearly directed to "avoiding a product", the S proceeded to construct the product of all numbers from 1 to p and to add 1—incidentally, without having realized that the resultant number need not be itself a prime number, but may merely contain the desired number as a fraction of itself.

9. Implicit solution-phases. Not *all* phases of the various solution-processes are given in a

family tree of the kind graphically represented previously: rather, only the more prominent and relatively independent among them are given. Aside from these, there exist phases which are not explicit enough and, above all, too banal ever to appear in a protocol. In the case of the radiation problem, for instance, it is clear to all Ss from the start that, in any case, to find a solution, something must be done with the actual circumstances concerned, with the rays and the body. As modern Europeans, they do not think of looking for suitable magic formulae; nor would they anticipate that some change in another place would lead to a solution. Similarly in the case of the prime numbers problem, from the beginning there is no doubt that the solution is to be sought in the province of numbers, and not, for example, in the province of physical processes. In short, from the very first, the deliberating and searching is always confined to a province which is relatively narrow as to space and content. Thus preparation is made for the more discrete phases of a solution by certain *approximate regional demarcations*, i.e., by phases in which necessary but not yet sufficient properties of the solution are demanded. Such implicit phases of a solution do not quite fulfill even the first prerequisite of a solution mentioned previously.

This is valid not only for thinking, but also for attempts at solution by action (trial and error). When a layman wishes to adjust the spacing between lines on a typewriter, this much at least of the solution is known to him: "I must screw or press somewhere on the machine". He will not knock on the wall, for instance, nor does he anticipate that any change of the given colors would do. In general, one seeks to achieve mechanical effects by mechanical alterations in the critical object.

One more example, this time from animal psychology. Thorndike set his experimental animals (mostly cats) problems of the following type. They had to learn to bring about the opening of their cage doors by a simple mechanical manipulation—unintelligible to them, to be sure, for they could not survey the connections—and so to escape into freedom. Part of the animals had a whole series of different cage problems to solve. In one cage they had to pull on a loop, in another to lift a bar, or press on a knob, etc. Thorndike made the very interesting observation that generally, in the course of the experiments, "the cat's general tendency to claw at loose objects within the box is strengthened and its tendency to squeeze through holes and bite bars is weakened." Further, "its tendency to pay attention to what it is doing gets strengthened. . . ." It is evident that even animal 'trial and error' is for the most part

[5] The solution consists in the construction of the product of all prime numbers from 1 to p and adding to it 1. The resultant number is either itself a prime number, or it is a product of prime numbers greater than p. For, with the exception of the special case of 1, a prime number less than p cannot be contained in a multiple of itself increased by 1 without a remainder. Thus in any case, a prime number greater than p exists. (Q.E.D.)

already under the confining influence of certain demarcations, which, by the way, are not purely instinctive.

10. Insufficiency of a protocol. The reader has probably received the impression that the discussions of the preceding paragraphs left the data of the protocol a long way behind. In the case of the very first proposal, for instance, that of the esophagus, there was no mention at all of "redirecting over a tissue-free path", or even of "avoiding contact". That some such thing appeared in other protocols in an analogous place naturally proves nothing about the psychological origin of just this individual proposal.

This is the place in which to say something essential about protocols. One could formulate it thus: A protocol is relatively reliable only for what it positively contains, but not for that which it omits. For even the best-intentioned protocol is only a very scanty record of what actually happens. The reasons for this insufficiency of protocols which are based on spoken thoughts must interest us also as characteristic of a solution-process as such. Mediating phases which lead at once to their concrete final realization, and thus are not separated from the solution by clear phase-boundaries, will often not be explicitly mentioned. They blend too thoroughly with their final solutions. On the other hand, mediating phases which must persist as temporary tasks until they find their final 'application' to the situation have a better chance of being explicitly formulated. Furthermore, many superordinate phases do not appear in the protocol, because the situation does not appear to the S promising enough for them. Therefore they are at once suppressed. In other words, they are too fleeting, too provisional, too tentative, occasionally also too 'foolish', to cross the threshold of the spoken word.

In very many cases, the mediating phases are not mentioned because the S simply does not realize that he has already modified the original demand of the problem. The thing seems to him so self-evident that he does not have at all the feeling of having already taken a step forward.[6] This can go so far that the S deprives himself of freedom of movement to a dangerous degree. By substituting unawares a much narrower problem for the original, hc will therefore remain in the framework of this narrower problem, just because he confuses it with the original.

11. "Suggestion from below". There exist cases in which the final form of a solution is not reached from above, i.e., not by way of its func-

[6] Such is especially the case with the demarcation of boundaries.

tional value. This is a commonplace of 'familiar' solutions. If the final solution of a problem is familiar to the S, it certainly need no longer be constructed, but can be reproduced as a whole, as soon as the problem is stated.[7]

More interesting cases exist. We must always remember that a solution has, so to speak, two roots, one in that which is sought and one in that which is given. More precisely, *a solution arises from the claim made on that which is given by that which is sought. But these two components vary greatly in the share they have in the genesis of a solution-phase.* A property of a solution is often very definitely demanded (characterized, hinted at) before it is discovered in what is given; but sometimes it is not. An example from the radiation problem: The esophagus may be discovered because a free path to the stomach is already sought. But it may also happen that, during a relatively vague, planless inspection of what is given in the situation, one 'stumbles on the esophagus'. Then the latter— so to speak, from below—suggests its functional value: "free path to the stomach"; in other words, the concrete realization precedes the functional value. This sort of thing happens not infrequently; for the analysis of the situation is often relatively planless. Nor is this disadvantageous, when the point is to find new ideas. In mathematical problems, this analysis merely of the given situation, the development of consequences from the given data, plays an especially large rôle.

One more example of "suggestion from below". An attractive goal object (for example, a banana) lies out of reach before the cage of a chimpanzee. So long as the solution, "to fish for the banana with a stick", is not very familiar, something like a stick must be in the visual field as a suggesting factor. The stick is not yet *sought*—as embodiment of the previously conceived functional value: "something long and movable"—as it is in later stages; rather it must itself help to suggest this functional value.[8]

The prerequisite for such a suggestion from

[7] This of course does not exclude the possibility that the solution is reproduced along with its functional value and as its realization, and that it is thus *understood*.

[8] This suggestion of the functional value from below is even the rule in problems where a number of objects are offered to begin with, with the instruction to choose from among them an appropriate tool for such and such a purpose. Especially when only few objects are concerned, thinking will tend to proceed by looking things over, i.e., it will test the given objects one after another as to their applicability, and no attempt will be made to conceive the appropriate functional value first.

below is that the 'phase-distance' between what is sought for and what could give the suggestion is not too great.

The following is an example for this influence of the size of the phase distance. Right at the beginning of the radiation problem, the E can speak of "crossing", or can draw a cross, without the S's grasping what that means. (Cf. the solution by crossing a number of weak bundles of rays in the tumor.) If, on the other hand, the S is already of his own accord directed to "decreasing the intensity on the way", he will understand the suggestion sooner than if his thinking is dominated, for example, by the completely different demand for "a free path for the rays". We can formulate the general proposition that a suggestion is the sooner understood or assimilated, the closer it approaches the genealogical line already under development, and, within this line, the nearer it is to the problem-phase then in operation; in short, the more completely it is already anticipated.

This law is a special case of a more general law, which concerns not suggestions in the narrow sense, but the material of thinking in general. Selz formulated this law as "a general law of anticipation" in the following manner: "An operation succeeds the more quickly, the more the schematic anticipation of the solution approaches a complete anticipation." We shall have more to do with this law.

12. Learning from mistakes (corrective phases).

As yet we have dealt only with the progress from the superordinate to the subordinate phases (or vice versa), in other words, with progress along a given genealogical line. That this is not the only kind of phase succession is, one should think, sufficiently indicated by the protocol given above. Here the line itself is continually changed, and one way of approach gives way to another. Such a *transition to phases in another line* takes place typically when some tentative solution does not satisfy, or when one makes no further progress in a given direction. *Another* solution, more or less clearly defined, is then looked for. For instance, the first proposal (esophagus) having been recognized as unsatisfactory, quite a radical change in direction takes place. The attempt to avoid contact is completely given up and a means to desensitize tissues is sought in its place. In the third proposal, however, the S has already returned to old tactics, although with a new variation. And such shifting back and forth occurs frequently.

It will be realized that, in the transition to phases in another line, the thought-process may range more or less widely. Every such transition involves a return to an earlier phase of the problem; an earlier task is set anew; a new

branching off from an old point in the family tree occurs. Sometimes a S returns to the original setting of the problem, sometimes just to the immediately preceding phase. An example for the latter case: From the ingenious proposal, to apply the rays in adequate amounts by rotation of the body around the tumor as a center, a S made a prompt transition to the neighboring proposal: "One could also have the radiation apparatus rotate around the body." Another example: The S who has just realized that the proposal of the esophagus is unsatisfactory may look for another natural approach to the stomach. This would be the most "direct" transition, that is, the transition which retrogresses least. Or, renouncing the natural approach to the stomach, he looks for another method of avoiding contact. Or, again, he looks for an altogether different way to avoid the destruction of healthy tissue. Therewith, everything which can be given up at all would have been given up; a "completely different" solution would have to be sought.

In such retrogression, thinking would naturally not be taken back to precisely the point where it had been before. For the failure of a certain solution has at least the result that now one tries *"in another way."* While remaining in the framework of the old *Problemstellung*, one looks for another starting point. Or again, the original setting may itself be altered *in a definite direction*, because there is the newly added demand: from now on, that property of the unsatisfactory solution must be avoided which makes it incompatible with the given conditions. An example: The fully developed form of our radiation problem is naturally preceded by a stage in which the problem runs only as follows: Destroy the tumor with the aid of appropriate rays. The most obvious solution, which consists simply in sending a bundle of sufficiently strong rays through the body into the tumor, appears at once inadequate, since it would clearly have the result of destroying healthy tissue as well. In realization of this, *avoidance of the evil* has to be incorporated *as an additional demand* into the original form of the problem; only in this way does our form of the radiation problem arise (cure . . . without destruction of healthy tissue). One more example: In the pendulum problem, a watchman is often proposed who has the task of keeping the length constant by compensatory changes in the position of the weight. For the most part, Ss realize spontaneously that this procedure could not possibly be sufficiently precise, and that it would also incessantly interfere with the motion of the clock. Thus the problem: "compensation of the change in length of the pendulum," is enriched by the important addition: "automatically."

Such learning from errors plays as great a rôle in the solution-process as in everyday life.[9]

[9] Life is of course, among other things, a sum total of solution-processes which refer to innumerable problems, great and small. It goes without saying that of these only a small fraction emerge into consciousness. Character, so far as it is shaped by living, is of the type of a resultant solution.

While the simple realization, *that* something does not work, can lead only to some variation of the old method, the realization of *why* it does not work, the recognition of the *ground of the conflict*, results in a correspondingly definite *variation which corrects* the recognized defect.

CHAPTER TEN

Perception and attention

Sensory Discrimination

This will be a good article to read more than once. It is packed with experimental findings which bear on a number of issues.

Points to guide your study

1. *Research on behavior without awareness.* Try to remember: (a) the method, results, and authors of one of the "zero confidence" experiments; (b) one of the studies on the learning of a subliminal discrimination; and (c) one of the studies showing the strengthening of responses with "unnoticed" rewards.

2. *Effects of inner states upon thresholds.* Try to remember the results and authors of several of these experiments. The influence of needs, values, attitudes, emotions, and motivation on perceptual organization has been called the "new look" in perception.

3. If you were an advertiser thinking about using these techniques, what are some of the methodological problems you would want answered?

4. Psychology, in common with other professions, has ethical problems. Guidelines have been formulated and are published in a book, *Ethical Standards of Psychologists*. These are only guidelines, however, and the particular problems which arise often require anguished decision by the individual involved.

33. SUBLIMINAL STIMULATION: AN OVERVIEW

*James V. McConnell, Richard L. Cutler, and Elton B. McNeil, University of Michigan**

Seldom has anything in psychology caused such an immediate and widespread stir as the recent claim that the presentation of certain stimuli below the level of conscious awareness can influence people's behavior in a significant way. The controversy was precipitated primarily by a commercial firm which claimed that the subliminal presentation of the words "Eat Popcorn" and "Drink Coca-Cola" fantastically stimulated the respective sales of these products among the motion picture audiences who received the stimulation. Despite the fact that detailed reports of the experiment have not been made

* J. V. McConnell, R. L. Cutler, and E. B. McNeil. Subliminal stimulation: an overview. *Amer. Psychologist*, 1958, **13**, 229–242. Excerpts reprinted here with permission from the authors and the American Psychological Association.

directly available in any published form, this technique was seized upon as the newest of the "new look" promises of the application of psychology to advertising. While such claims and demonstrations will be considered in greater detail below, it is important to note here that they have given rise to a series of charges and countercharges, the effects of which have reached the United States Congress and the Federal Communications Commission (7, 117).

Rarely does a day pass without a statement in the public press relating to the Utopian promise or the 1984 threat of the technique (8, 17, 29, 37, 42, 45, 118, 132). Since the process of choosing up sides promises to continue unabated, it appears wise to provide the potential combatants with a more factual basis for arriving at their positions than presently seems available.

Meanwhile, the present writers have cautiously sought to avoid aligning themselves behind either of the barricades.

Obviously, the notion that one may influence the behavior of another individual without the individual's knowing about it is a fascinating one. It is of extreme interest, not only to psychologists and advertisers, but also to politicians, psychiatrists, passionate young men, and others, whose motives would be considered more or less sacred by the larger society. Equally obvious is the need for a clarification of the issues surrounding the application of subliminal perception. This clarification must involve the assessment of available scientific evidence, the answering of a series of technical questions, and the examination of what, if any, levels of behavior may indeed be influenced. Finally, a series of extremely complex ethical issues need to be explored. It is the purpose of the present paper to undertake this task, in the hope of providing information upon which possible decisions involving its application may be based.

Recent history of the technique

The custom of providing a chronological review of the literature will be violated in this paper, inasmuch as three separate threads of investigation seem worth tracing: (*a*) the recent demonstrations by advertisers which first aroused large-scale public interest in subliminal perception, (*b*) systematic research by psychologists relating directly to the influencing of behavior without the individual's awareness that he is being influenced, and (*c*) psychological research concerned primarily with the influence of inner states of the organism upon the threshold for conscious recognition of certain stimuli.

Recent advertising demonstrations. While the advertising possibilities of subliminal stimulation were recognized by Hollingworth (59) as early as 1913, the intensive work in its application to this area has been carried out within the past two years. In 1956, BBC-TV, in conjunction with one of its regular broadcasts, transmitted the message "Pirie Breaks World Record" at a speed assumed to be subliminal (85). At the conclusion of the regular program, viewers were asked to report whether they had noticed "anything unusual" about the program. While no reliable statistical data are available, it seems possible that those few viewers responding to the message possessed sufficiently low thresholds so that for them the message was supraliminal.

A demonstration by the commercial enterprise which has been most vocal in its claims for the advertising promise of the technique consisted of projecting, during alternate periods, the words "Eat Popcorn" and "Drink Coca-Cola" during the regular presentation of a motion picture program. As a result of this stimulation, reports contend,[1] popcorn sales rose more than 50% and Coca-Cola sales 18%, as compared to a "previous period." Despite the likelihood of serious methodological and technical defects (exposure time was reported as 1/3,000 sec., far faster than any previously reported stimulation), this demonstration has been the one which has caused the most stir in both the fields of advertising and psychology. There were no reports, however, of even the most rudimentary scientific precautions, such as adequate controls, provision for replication, etc., which leaves the skeptical scientist in a poor position to make any judgment about the validity of the study.

In a later demonstration for the press, technical difficulties permitted the viewers to become consciously aware of the fact that they were being stimulated. Although described as a purposeful and prearranged part of the demonstration, it left many of the reporters present unconvinced that the technical difficulties inherent in the technique have been surmounted.

The FCC, turning its attention to the problem, has reported that one TV station (WTWO, Bangor, Maine) has experimented with the transmission of public service announcements at subliminal levels, with "negative results" (117).

The uncontrolled and unsystematic nature of the demonstrations reported above makes very difficult the task of reaching a trustworthy conclusion about the effectiveness of subliminal stimulation in advertising. Whether the technique represents a promising means of communicating with the individual at a level of his unconsciousness or whether it reflects only the hyperenthusiasm of an entrepreneurial group remain unanswered questions.

Research on behavior without awareness. In the hope of providing a more substantial foundation upon which to base judgments of the validity of advertising claims for subliminal stimulation, a systematic review of relevant scientific work was undertaken. While we believe that our review was comprehensive, we have decided not to provide an extensive critical discussion of the various studies, choosing instead to present summative statements and conclusions based upon what seems to be sufficient evidence and consensus in the literature.[2]

---

[1] The essential facts of this study have not been reported in any journal. The discussion of this experiment and the findings reported by the commercial enterprise responsible for the study is based on reports in several general news accounts appearing in the popular press (7, 8, 16, 17, etc.).

[2] The reader who wishes a more complete technical critique of studies in the field is referred to reviews by Adams (1), Collier (27), Coover (28), Lazarus and McCleary (76), and Miller (90).

The work of experimental psychologists in subliminal stimulation dates from Suslowa (119) in 1863, as reported by Baker (5). Suslowa's experiments concerned the effect of electrical stimulation upon subjects' ability to make two-point threshold discriminations. He found that, even when the intensity of the electrical stimulation was so low that the subjects were not aware of its presence, their ability to discriminate one- from two-point stimulation was somewhat reduced.

In 1884, Peirce and Jastrow (94) were able to show that subjects could discriminate differences between weights significantly better than chance would allow, even though the differences were so small they had no confidence whatsoever in their judgments.

Numerous experimenters have relied upon this criterion of "zero confidence" to establish that discrimination of stimuli presented below the level of conscious awareness is possible. For example, Sidis (107) showed that subjects could reliably distinguish letters from numbers, even when the stimuli were presented at such a distance from them that the subjects thought they were relying on pure guesswork for their judgments.

In what was essentially a replication of Sidis' research, Stroh, Shaw, and Washburn (116) found evidence to support his conclusions. They found similar results when auditory stimuli (whispers) were presented at a distance such that the subjects were not consciously aware that they were hearing anything.

Several experiments have provided further support for Peirce and Jastrow's initial conclusions (44, 127). Baker (5) found subjects able to discriminate diagonal from vertical crossed lines, and a dot-dash from a dash-dot auditory pattern. Miller (88) presented five geometric figures at four different levels of intensity below the threshold and found that, while subjects could discriminate which was being presented a significant proportion of the time, their ability to discriminate was reduced as the intensity of stimulation was further reduced. More recently, a series of studies by Blackwell (11) has shown that subjects can reliably identify during which of four time periods a subliminal spot of light is presented upon a homogeneous field. Blackwell, however, stresses that reliability of discrimination decreases as the intensity of the stimulus is further lowered. Several other supporting studies are available (28, 97, 130) which show essentially the same results, namely, that even when subjects have zero confidence in their judgments, they can discriminate reliably (though not perfectly) between stimuli.

In his review, Adams (1) points out certain general weaknesses inherent in studies of this type, but agrees with the present authors that discrimination can occur under certain circumstances. However, it is interesting to note that, in nearly all studies reporting relevant data, the reliability of the subjects' judgment increases directly with the intensity of the stimuli. If a valid extrapolation can be drawn from this finding, it would be that accuracy of perception increases as the stimulation approaches a supraliminal level.

A second series of studies has involved present subjects with variations of the Mueller-Lyer illusion, in which the angular lines have differed, subliminally, in hue or brightness from the background. The first of these studies, reported by Dunlap in 1909 (36), gave clear evidence that the subjects were influenced in their judgments of line length, even though they could not "see" the angular lines. Several replications of this study have been carried out, and while at least three have found partial support for Dunlap's conclusions (14, 59, 86), others have failed to find the phenomenon (123). In another experiment conducted by Sidis in 1898 (107), subjects asked to fixate on a number series in the center of a card, and then asked to pick a number from this series, systematically chose that number which was written in the periphery of the card, even though they were not consciously aware of its presence. Coover (28) in 1917 showed essentially the same results by asking subjects to pick a number at random while they were fixating on a letter in the upper right portion of a card. He found that subjects tended to pick the number printed in the lower left of the card, even though they did not *usually* know it was there. In similar experiments, Collier (27) and Perky (95) showed that subjects could be made to produce drawings, even though they were not aware that they were being influenced in their actions. While these studies are not unequivocal in their findings, nor generally rigorous in their methodology, they too seem to support the contention that behavior of a sort can be influenced by subliminal means. However, they require cautious interpretation, since the degree of the subject's attention to the stimuli seems clearly to be a factor. Further, as contrasted to those studies where the subject is actually aware in advance of at least the general nature of the stimulation, these studies reveal a somewhat less pronounced effect of subliminal stimulation upon the subject's behavior.

While the studies reported above seem to indicate that discrimination without awareness may occur, it may reasonably be asked whether stimulation below the level of conscious awareness can produce any but the most simple modifications in behavior. A series of studies (24, 26, 73, 109), beginning with Newhall and Sears in 1933 (92), have attempted to show that it is possible to condition subjects to subliminal stimuli. Newhall and Sears found it possible to establish a weak and unstable conditioned response to light presented subliminally, when the light had been previously paired with shock. Baker (6) in 1938 reported the successful conditioning of the pupillary reflex to a subliminal auditory stimulus, but later experimenters have failed to replicate his results (57, 128). In a now classic experiment, McCleary and Lazarus (79) found that nonsense syllables which had previously been associated with shock produced a greater psychogalvanic reflex when presented tachistoscopically at subliminal speeds than did nonshock syllables. Deiter (34) confirmed the McCleary and Lazarus findings and showed further that, when verbal instructions were substituted for the shock, no such differences were produced. Bach and Klein (4) have recently reported that they were able to influence subjects' judgments of whether the line drawing of a face (essentially neutral in its emotional expression) was "angry" or "happy" by projecting the appropriate words at subliminal speeds upon the drawings.

A series of related studies (58, 65, 89, 99, 105, 121, 122) have shown that, even when the subject is not aware that any cue is being given, certain responses can be learned or strengthened during the experimental process. For example, Cohen, Kalish, Thurston, and Cohen (25) showed that, when the experimenter said "right" to any sentence which the subject started with "I" or "We," the number of such sentences increased significantly. Klein (69) was able to produce both conditioning and extinction without awareness, using the Cohen et al. technique.

Several experimenters have used subliminal or "unnoticed" reward-punishment techniques to modify subjects' responses in a variety of situations, including free or chained association tasks, performance on personality tests, and interview elicited conversation (35, 41, 50, 56, 72, 78, 93, 120, 125, 126). Typical is the work of Greenspoon (48), who reinforced the use of plural nouns by saying "mm-humm" after each plural mentioned by the subject. He found that, even though none of his subjects could verbalize the relationship between their response and his reinforcement, their use of plural nouns doubled. Sidowski (108) demonstrated essentially the same thing using a light, of which the subject was only peripherally aware, as a reinforcer for the use of plural words. Weiss (129), however, failed to find any increase in the frequency of "living things" responses, using a right-wrong reinforcement to free associations by the subjects.

This evidence suggests that subjects may either (*a*) "learn" certain subliminally presented stimuli or (*b*) make use of subliminal reinforcers either to learn or strengthen a previously learned response. Again, the critical observations of Adams (1) and the introduction of other possible explanations by Bricker and Chapanis (15) make necessary a cautious interpretation of these results.

Effects of inner states upon thresholds.   Whatever the possibility that subliminal stimulation may significantly alter behavior, there is excellent evidence that certain inner states of the organism, as well as externally induced conditions, may significantly alter the recognition threshold of the individual. This, of course, has important implications for the susceptibility of the individual to the effects of subliminal stimulation. It is well known that physiological factors, such as fatigue, visual acuity, or satiation, may change the threshold of an individual for various kinds of stimuli.

Recent evidence has accumulated to show that, in addition to these physiological factors, certain "psychological states," such as psychological need, value, conflict, and defense, may also significantly influence thresholds, as well as other aspects of the perceptual process. Early work in this area is reported by Sanford (102, 103) who showed that subjects who had been deprived of food were more prone to produce "food-relevant" responses to a series of ambiguous stimuli. McClelland and Atkinson (80) showed that levels of the hunger drive were systematically related to the ease with which food responses were made when no words were presented on the screen.

While a complete review of the experimental work on "perceptual defense" and "selective vigilance" would take us too far afield, it seems wise to indicate, by example, some of the inner state factors which allegedly produce variations in recognition threshold. Bruner and Postman (19, 20, 21) and Bruner and Goodman (18) were able to show that such factors as symbolic value, need, tension and tension release, and emotional selectivity were important in the perceptual process. Ansbacher (3) had earlier demonstrated that the perception of numerosity was significantly affected by the monetary value of the stimuli. Rees and Israel (101) called attention to the fact that the mental set of the organism was an important factor in the perceptual process. Beams and Thompson (9) showed that emotional factors were important determiners of the perception of the magnitude of need-relevant objects. Other studies bearing upon the issue of inner state determiners of perception are reported by Carter and Schooler (23), Cowen and Beier (31, 32), and Levine, Chein, and Murphy (77).

More specifically related to the issue of altered recognition thresholds is a study by McGinnies (82) in which he demonstrated that emotionally toned words had generally higher thresholds than neutral words. Blum (13) has shown that subjects tend to be less likely to choose conflict-relevant stimuli from a group presented at subliminal speeds than to choose neutral stimuli. Lazarus, Eriksen, and Fonda (75) have shown that personality factors are at least in part determiners of the recognition threshold for classes of auditory stimuli. Reece (100) showed that the association of shock with certain stimuli had the effect of raising the recognition threshold for those stimuli.

While many writers have contended that the variations in threshold can be accounted for more parsimoniously than by introducing "motivational" factors such as need and value (60, 61, 111), and while the issue of the degree to which need states influence perception is still unresolved (22, 39, 40, 62, 74, 83), it is apparent that the recognition threshold is not a simple matter of intensity nor speed of presentation. Recent work by Postman and others (47, 96, 98), which has sought to illuminate the pre-recognition processes operating to produce the apparent changes in threshold, does not alter the fact that individual differences in the perceptual process must be taken into account in any further work on the effects of subliminal stimulation.

Unanswered methodological questions

Having now concluded that, under certain conditions, the phenomenon of subliminal perception does occur, we turn our attention next to the many unanswered questions which this conclusion raises. For example, what kinds of behavior can be influenced by subliminal stimulation? What types of stimuli operate best at subthreshold intensities? Do all subliminal stimuli operate at the same "level of unconsciousness," or do different stimuli (or modes of stimulation) affect different levels of unconsciousness? What characteristics of the perceiver help determine the effectiveness of subliminal stimulation? All of these questions, as well as many others of a technological nature, will be discussed in the ensuing paragraphs.

A few words of caution concerning the word "subliminal" seem in order, however. It must be remembered that the psychological limen is a statistical concept, a fact overlooked by far too many current textbook writers. The common definition of the limen is "that stimulus value which gives a response exactly half the time" (44, p. 111). One of the difficulties involved in analyzing the many studies on subliminal perception is the fact that many experimenters have assumed that, because the stimuli which they employed were below the statistical limen for a given subject, the stimuli were therefore never consciously perceivable by the subject. This is, of course, not true. Stimuli slightly below the statistical limen might well be consciously perceivable as much as 49% of the time. Not only this, but thresholds vary from moment to moment, as well as from day to day. All this is not to deny that stimuli which are so weak that they are never consciously reportable under any circumstances may indeed influence behavior. We simply wish to make the point that the range of stimulus intensities which are in fact "subliminal" may be smaller than many experimenters in the past have assumed. It has been commonly assumed that the several methods of producing subliminal stimuli, i.e., reducing intensity, duration, size, or clarity, are logically and methodologically equivalent. While this may be true, it remains to be demonstrated conclusively.

Types of behavior influenced by subliminal stimulation. One of the first questions that springs to mind concerns the types of response which can be elicited with subliminal stimulation. Let us assume for the moment that the below-threshold advertisements used in commercial demonstrations were the sole cause of increased popcorn buying among the movie audiences subjected to the ads. How did this come about? Did the stimulus "Eat Popcorn" elicit an already established response in some members of the audience? Or did the frequent repetitions of the stimulus message cause a shift in attitude towards popcorn eating which eventually resulted in the purchase of popcorn at the first opportunity the audience had? Did the ads merely raise an already existing, presumably learned, but weak need for popcorn to an above the action-threshold level, or did the ads actually create a need for popcorn where no need had existed beforehand? Did members of the audience rise like automatons during the course of the movie and thus miss part of the feature in order to satisfy a sudden craving for popcorn or in order to respond to a suddenly evoked stimulus-response connection? Or did they wait until a "rest period" to do their purchasing? How many patrons bought popcorn only after they had seen the film and were heading home? How many people purchased popcorn on their way *in* to see the next movie they attended? How many of those who purchased popcorn did so for the first time in their lives, or for the first time in recent memory? What if the message presented had been "Buy Christmas Seals," which are available only in one season? How many people failed to buy popcorn at the theater, but purchased it subsequently at the local supermarket?

Unfortunately, these pertinent questions have yet to be answered. Let us tentatively accept this demonstration that impulse buying of inexpensive items such as popcorn and Coca-Cola can be influenced by subliminal advertising, without yet knowing what the mechanism involved is. It remains to be demonstrated, however, that such ads could make a person of limited means wreck himself financially by purchasing a Cadillac merely because the ads told him to do so. Nor do we know if deep-seated, strongly emotional attitudes or long established behavior patterns can be shifted one way or another as a result of subliminal stimulation. The answers to these questions must come from further experimentation.

Technological problems involved in stimulating subjects subliminally. The paucity of data presented by those dealing with subliminal perception on a commercial basis, as well as the equivocal nature of their results, suggests that there are many technological problems yet to be solved by these and other investigators. For example, during a two-hour movie (or a one-hour television show), how many times should the stimulus be repeated to make sure that the "message" gets across to the largest possible percentage of the audience? Should the stimulus be repeated every second, every five seconds, only once a minute? Is the effect cumulative, or is one presentation really enough? Is there a satiation effect, such that the audience becomes "unconsciously tired" of the stimulation, and "unconsciously blocks" the incoming subliminal sensations? Should the stimuli be presented "between frames" of the movie (that is, when the shutter of the film projector is closed and the screen momentarily blank as it is 24 times each second), or should the message be presented only when the screen already has a picture on it? How close to the threshold (statistical or otherwise) should the stimuli be? How many words long can the message be? If the message must be short, could successive stimulations present sequential parts of a longer advertisement? How much of the screen should the stimuli fill? Should the stimuli be presented only during "happier" moments in the film, in order to gain positive affect? Does any affect transfer at all from the film to the ad? Should one use pictures, or are words best? Must the words be familiar ones? And what about subliminal auditory, cutaneous, and olfactory stimulation?

As we have stated before, there has been so much talk and so little experimentation, and much of what experimentation has been done is so inadequately reported, that we can merely hazard guesses based on related but perhaps not always applicable studies.

To begin with, we can state with some assurance that, the closer to the threshold of awareness the stimuli are, the more effect they are likely to have. Study after study has reported increased effectiveness with increased intensity of stimulation (5, 14, 88, 97, 104). The main difficulty seems to be that thresholds vary so much from subject to subject (112), and from day to day (114), that what is subliminal but effective for one person is likely to be subliminal but ineffective for a second, and supraliminal for a third. As is generally the case, anyone who wishes to use the technique of subliminal stimulation must first experiment upon the specific group of people whom he wishes to influence before he can decide what intensity levels will be most efficacious.

Somewhat the same conclusion holds for the question of how many times the stimuli should be presented. While under some conditions subliminal stimuli which did not influence behavior when presented only once seemed to "summate" when presented many times (10, 66), Bricker and Chapanis (15) found that one presentation of a stimulus slightly below the (statistical) limen was enough to increase the likelihood of its being recognized on subsequent trials. We interpret this to mean that too many presentations may well raise the "subliminal" stimuli above the limen of awareness if the stimuli themselves are not carefully chosen.

As for the physical properties of the message itself, we can but guess what the relevant issues are. Both verbal and pictorial presentations apparently are effective in the visual modality, but no one has tested the relative effectiveness of these two types of stimulation. Quite possibly subsequent experimentation will show that words are best for some situations (such as direct commands), while pictures are best for others.[3] It can be stated unequivocally, however, that advertisers should look to their basic English when writing their subliminal commercials. Several studies have shown that, the more familiar a subject is with the stimulus he is to perceive, the more readily he perceives it (22, 54, 63, 110). We interpret these studies to mean that unfamiliar stimuli may be ineffective when presented subliminally, even though familiar messages may "get through."

The exact length the message should be, its composition, and the background in which it should be presented are variables upon which no work has been done and about which no conclusions can presently be drawn. Suffice it to say, however, that a message which would be short enough to be perceived by one person might be too long for another person to perceive under any conditions.

Which modalities are most useful for subliminal stimulation? While most of the work has been done on the visual modality, Vanderplas

---

[3]Perhaps much of the work on sensory preconditioning is applicable here. When Ellson (38) presented his subjects with both a light and a buzzer for many trials, then presented the light alone, subjects "heard" the buzzer too.

and Blake (124) and Kurland (71) have found subthreshold auditory stimuli to be effective, and earlier in this paper we have reported similar studies with cutaneous stimulation. Advertisers who wish to "sneak up on" their patrons by presenting subliminal stimuli in one modality while the patrons are attending to supraliminal stimuli from another modality are probably doomed to failure, however. Collier (27) presented subliminal geometric forms simultaneously to both the visual and the cutaneous modalities and found little, if any, lowering of thresholds. Correspondingly, it should be remembered that Hernandez-Peon et al. (55) found that some part of the nervous system acts as a kind of gating mechanism, and when an organism is attending strongly to one modality, the other modalities are probably "shut off" to most incoming stimuli.

Even if experimenters succeed in finding answers to many of the questions raised above concerning the physical characteristics of the stimuli to be employed, it is quite probable that they will have succeeded in discovering the source of only a small part of the variance operant in subliminal perception. For, as always, the major source of variance will come from the perceiver himself.

Characteristics of the perceiver which affect subliminal perception. The following section of this paper might well be considered a plea for the recognition that individual differences exist and that they must be taken into account by anyone who wishes to deal with individuals. We know next to nothing about the relationships between such factors as age, sex, social class, etc. and subliminal perception. Perhaps only one study is relevant: Perky (95) found that children were as much influenced by subthreshold visual stimulation as were naive adults. It is quite likely that many differences in the perception of subliminal stimuli do exist between individuals of differing classes, ages, and sexes. As always, only experimentation can determine what these differences are.

We do have some idea, however, of how what might be called "personality factors" influence subliminal perception. First and foremost, there seems little doubt but that a high need state affects perception. Gilchrist and Nesberg (46) found that, the greater the need state, the more their subjects tended to overestimate the brightness of objects relevant to that need. It should be noted that they were dealing with difference limens, not absolute limens, but other studies to be quoted later show the same effect for absolute limens. It should be noted also that Gilchrist and Nesberg apparently overlooked evidence in their own data that a strong need affects judgments of non-need-related objects in the same direction (but not as much) as it does need-related objects. Wispe and Drambarean, dealing with visual duration thresholds, concluded that "need-related words were recognized more rapidly as need increased" (131, p. 31). McClelland and Lieberman (81) found that subjects with high need achievement scores had lower visual thresholds for "success" words than did subjects not scoring as high on need achievement. Do all of these findings mean that subliminal ads will work only when some fairly strong need (of any kind) is present in the viewers? Only experimentation can answer this question.

What about abnormalities of personality? What effect do they have? Kurland (71) tested auditory recognition thresholds using emotional and neutral words. He found that hospitalized neurotics perceived the emotional words at significantly lower thresholds than did a group of normal subjects. Does this mean that neurotics are more likely to respond to low-intensity subliminal commands than normals? Should advertisers take a "neurotic inventory" of their audiences?

A more pertinent problem is posed by the findings of Krech and Calvin (70). Using a Wechsler Vocabulary Score of 30.5 as their cutting point, they found that almost all college students above this score showed better visual discriminations of patterns presented at close to liminal values than did almost all students scoring below the cutting point. Does this mean that the higher the IQ, the better the subliminal perception? What is the relationship between the value of the absolute limen and intelligence? Will advertisers have to present their messages at such high intensities (in order that the "average man" might perceive the message) that the more intelligent members of the audience will be consciously aware of the advertising?

One further fascinating problem is posed by Huntley's work (64). He surreptitiously obtained photographs of the hands and profiles of his subjects, as well as handwriting samples and recordings of their voices. Six months later each subject was presented with the whole series of samples, among which were his own. Each subject was asked to make preference ratings of the samples. Huntley reports evidence of a significant tendency for subjects to prefer their own forms of expression above all others, even though in most cases they were totally unaware that the samples were their own and even though many subjects were unable to identify their own samples when told they were included in the series. If an advertiser is making a direct appeal to one specific individual, it would seem then that he should make use of the photographs and recordings of that individual's behavior as the subliminal stimuli. If an advertiser is making an appeal to a more general audience, however, it might be that he would find the use of pictures and recordings of Hollywood stars, etc., more efficacious than mere line drawings, printed messages, and unknown voices.

Nor can the advertiser afford to overlook the effects of set and attention. Miller (88), Perky (95), and Blake and Vanderplas (12), among others, discovered that giving the subject the proper set lowered the recognition threshold greatly. In fact, in many cases the stimulus intensity which was subliminal but effective for sophisticated subjects was far too subliminal to have much, if any, effect upon naive subjects. Thus advertisers might do well to tell their audiences that subliminal messages were being presented to them, in order to bring all members of that audience closer to a uniform threshold. Does this not, however, vitiate some of the effect of subliminal advertising?

As for attentional effects, we have presented evidence earlier (46) that strong needs seem to have an "alerting" effect upon the organism, lowering recognition thresholds for *all* stimuli, not just need-related stimuli. In addition to this, two studies by Hartmann (52, 53), as well as two by Spencer (113, 114), lead us to the belief that subliminal stimuli might best be presented when either the television or movie screen was blank of other pictures. Perhaps, then, subliminal commercials in movie houses should be shown between features; while on television the commercials should consist of an appropriate period of apparent "visual silence," during which the audience would not be aware of the subliminal stimulation presented, but might react to it later.

One fact emerges from all of the above. Anyone who wishes to utilize subliminal stimulation for commercial or other purposes can be likened to a stranger entering into a misty, confused countryside where there are but few landmarks. Before this technique is used in the market place, if it is to be used at all, a tremendous amount of research should be done, and by competent experimenters.

The ethics of subliminal influence

From its beginnings as a purely academic offshoot of philosophy, psychology has, with ever increasing momentum, grown in the public perception as a practical and applied discipline. As psychologists were called upon to communicate and interpret their insights and research findings to lay persons, it was necessary to make decisions about what constituted proper professional behavior, since it was evident that the misuse of such information would reflect directly on the community of psychologists. As a growing number of our research efforts are viewed as useful to society, the problem of effective and honest communication becomes magnified, although its essential nature does not change. Recently, to our dismay, the announcement of a commercial application of long established psychological principles has assumed nightmarish qualities, and we find ourselves unwillingly cast in the role of invaders of personal privacy and enemies of society. A kind of guilt by association seems to be occurring, and, as future incidents of this kind will, it threatens to undermine the public relations we have built with years of caution and concern for the public welfare. The highly emotional public reaction to the "discovery" of subliminal perception should serve as an object lesson to our profession, for in the bright glare of publicity we can see urgent ethical issues as well as an omen of things to come. When the theoretical notion $E = MC^2$ became the applied reality of an atom bomb, the community of physicists became deeply concerned with social as well as scientific responsibility. Judging from the intensity of the public alarm when confronted with a bare minimum of fact about this subliminal social atom, there exists a clear need for psychologists to examine the ethical problems that are a part of this era of the application of their findings.

The vehemence of the reaction to the proposed use of a device to project subliminal, or from the public's point of view "hidden," messages to viewers indicates that the proposal touches a sensitive area. One of the basic contributors to this reaction seems to be the feeling that a technique which avowedly tampers with the psychological status of the individual ought to be under the regulation or control of a trusted scientific group. As a professional group, psychologists would fit this description, for in the *Ethical Standards of Psychologists* (2) there is a clear statement of their motives and relationship to society:

> Principle 1.12–1 The psychologist's ultimate allegiance is to society, and his professional behavior should demonstrate an awareness of his social responsibilities. The welfare of the profession and of the individual psychologist are clearly subordinate to the welfare of the public. . . .

Both this statement and the long record of responsible behavior of the members of the profession would certainly seem to be sufficient to reduce any anxiety the public might have over the possible unscrupulous use of this or any other device. It is precisely the fact that the public *is* aware that decisions about the use of subliminal perception devices rest not with psychologists but with commercial agencies that may be distressing to the public. The aura of open-for-business flamboyance and the sketchily presented percentages in the first public announcement tended to reinforce existing apprehensions rather than allay them.

Although subliminal perception happens now

to be the focus of a great deal of reaction, it is merely the most recent in a succession of perturbing events to which the public has been exposed. It has become the focus of, and is likely to become the whipping boy for, a host of techniques which now occupy the twilight zone of infringement of personal psychological freedom. It must be remembered that to the lay person the notion of an unconscious part of the "mind" is eerie, vague, and more than a little mysterious. Unable fully to comprehend the systematic and theoretical aspects of such a concept, he must be content with overly popularized and dramatic versions of it. In every form of mass media the American public has been exposed to convincing images of the bearded hypnotist (with piercing eye) who achieves his nefarious ends by controlling the unconscious of his victim. It has been treated to the spectacle of the seeming reincarnation of Bridey Murphy out of the unconscious of an American housewife and, in *Three Faces of Eve*, to complex multiple personalities hidden in the psychic recesses of a single individual. With such uncanny and disturbing images as an emotional backdrop, the appearance of *The Hidden Persuaders* on the best seller lists formed the indelible impression of the exploitation of the unconscious for purposes of profit and personal gain. In combination, this growth of emotionally charged attitudes toward the unconscious and the suspicions about commercial morality came to be a potentially explosive set of tensions which was triggered off by the first commercial use of subliminal techniques.

What is to be the psychologist's position in regard to future developments with subliminal perception? The apparent discrepancy between the claims being made for the technique and the available research evidence suggests a need for considerable scientific caution as well as extensive investigation. The responsibility of psychologists in this instance is clearly indicated in the code of ethics:

Principle 2.12–1 The psychologist should refuse to suggest, support, or condone unwarranted assumptions, invalid applications, or unjustified conclusions in the use of psychological instruments or techniques.

The flurry of claim and opinion about the effectiveness of subliminal methods seems to be based more on enthusiasm than controlled scientific experimentation, and it is here that psychology can be of service. Until acceptable scientific answers are forthcoming, we believe psychologists should guard against a premature commitment which might jeopardize public respect for them. The course of scientific history is strewn with the desiccated remains of projects pursued with more vigor than wisdom.

Scientific caution is essential, but it falls short of meeting the ethical issue raised by the nature of subliminal perception itself. The most strident public objections have been directed toward the possibility that suggestions or attempts to influence or persuade may be administered without the knowledge or consent of the audience. Assurances that widespread adoption of this technique would provide increased enjoyment through the elimination of commercial intrusions, or that the users will establish an ethical control over the content of the messages presented, can only fail to be convincing in light of past experience. The suggestion that the public can be taught means of detecting when it is being exposed to a planned subliminal stimulation is far from reassuring since such a suggestion implies that the ability to defend oneself warrants being attacked. A captive audience is not a happy audience, and even the plan to inform the viewers in advance concerning the details of what is to be presented subliminally may not prevent the public from reacting to this technique as a demand that it surrender an additional degree of personal freedom. Fresh from similar encounters, the public may not allow this freedom to be wrested from it.

Finally, the argument that a great deal of our normal perception occurs on the fringe of conscious awareness and that subliminal events are no more effective than weak conscious stimuli rests on opinion and not fact. This seems particularly dangerous clinical ground on which to tread since the effect, on behavior, of stimuli which may possibly be inserted directly into the unconscious has yet to be explored. Assurances that this technique can only "remind" a person of something he already knows or "support" a set of urges already in existence but cannot establish a completely new set of urges or needs are reckless assertions having no evidence to support them. So it seems that the aspect of subliminal projection which is marked by the greatest potential risk to the individual's emotional equilibrium is the aspect about which the least is scientifically known.

The psychologist's ethical quandary, then, stems directly from the inescapable implication of deviousness in the use of such a technique. The appropriate guidelines for conduct are provided in this ethical statement:

Principle 2.62–2 It is unethical to employ psychological techniques for devious purposes, for entertainment, or for other reasons not consonant with the best interests of a client or with the development of psychology as a science.

It is obvious that "devious purposes" and "the best interests . . . of psychology as a science" are not self-defining terms and must be interpreted by the individual psychologist in light of the circumstances of each situation. It is a trying and complex decision to make. If in his mature judgment the intended uses of the principles of subliminal perception do not meet acceptable ethical standards, the psychologist is obligated to disassociate himself from the endeavor and to labor in behalf of the public welfare to which he owes his first allegiance. In this respect, the responsibility of the social scientist must always be that of watchdog over his own actions as well as the actions of those to whom he lends his professional support.

The furor which promises to accompany the further application of a variety of devices involving subliminal perception is certain to embroil psychology in a dispute not of its own choosing. The indiscriminate and uncontrolled application of psychological principles is increasing at a fearsome rate in the form of motivation research, propaganda, public relations, and a host of other "useful" practices based on the work of psychologists. In a very real sense this era of applied psychology will be a test of the workability of the psychologist's code of ethics and promises to stimulate the profession to give further consideration to its responsibility for assisting society to use its findings wisely.

References

1. Adams, J. K. Laboratory studies of behavior without awareness. *Psychol. Bull.*, 1957, **54**, 383–405.
2. American Psychological Association, Committee on Ethical Standards for Psychology. *Ethical standards of psychologists*. Washington: APA, 1953.
3. Ansbacher, H. Perception of number as affected by the monetary value of the objects. *Arch. Psychol.*, 1937, **30**, No. 215.
4. Bach, S., and Klein, G. S. Conscious effects of prolonged subliminal exposures of words. *Amer. Psychologist*, 1957, **12**, 397. (Abstract)
5. Baker, L. E. The influence of subliminal stimuli upon verbal behavior. *J. exp. Psychol.*, 1937, **20**, 84–100.
6. Baker, L. E. The pupillary response conditioned to subliminal auditory stimuli. *Psychol. Monogr.*, 1938, **50**, No. 3 (Whole No. 223).
7. Ban on subliminal ads, pending FCC probe, is urged. *Adv. Age*, 1957, **28**, No. 45.
8. Battelle, Phyllis. The lady objects to id tampering. *Publishers Auxiliary*, 1957, **92**, No. 40.
9. Beams, H. L., and Thompson, G. G. Affectivity as a factor in the perception of the magnitude of food objects. *Amer. Psychologist*, 1952, **7**, 323. (Abstract)
10. Beitel, R. J., Jr. Spatial summation of subliminal stimuli in the retina of the human eye. *J. gen. Psychol.*, 1934, **10**, 311–327.
11. Blackwell, H. R. Personal communication, 1958.
12. Blake, R. R., and Vanderplas, J. M. The effects of prerecognition hypotheses on veridical recognition thresholds in auditory perception. *J. Pers.*, 1950–1951, **19**, 95–115.
13. Blum, G. S. Perceptual defense revisited. *J. abnorm. soc. Psychol.*, 1955, **56**, 24–29.
14. Bressler, J. Illusion in the case of subliminal visual stimulation. *J. gen. Psychol.*, 1931, **5**, 244–250.
15. Bricker, P. D., and Chapanis, A. Do incorrectly perceived tachistoscopic stimuli convey some information? *Psychol. Rev.*, 1953, **60**, 181–188.
16. Britt, S. H. Subliminal advertising—fact or fantasy? *Adv. Age*, 1957, **28**, 103.
17. Brooks, J. The little ad that isn't there. *Consumer Rep.*, 1957, **23**, No. 1.
18. Bruner, J. S., and Goodman, C. C. Value and need as organizing factors in perception. *J. abnorm. soc. Psychol.*, 1947, **42**, 33–44.
19. Bruner, J. S., and Postman, L. Emotional selectivity in perception and action. *J. Pers.*, 1947, **16**, 69–77.
20. Bruner, J. S., and Postman, L. Tension and tension-release as organizing factors in perception. *J. Pers.*, 1947, **16**, 300–308.
21. Bruner, J. S., and Postman, L. Symbolic value as an organizing factor in perception. *J. soc. Psychol.*, 1948, **27**, 203–208.
22. Bruner, J. S., and Postman, L. Perception, cognition, and behavior. *J. Pers.*, 1949, **18**, 14–31.
23. Carter, L. F., and Schooler, K. Value, need, and other factors in perception. *Psychol. Rev.*, 1949, **56**, 200–207.
24. Cason, H., and Katcher, Naomi. An attempt to condition breathing and eyelid responses to a subliminal electric stimulus. *J. exp. Psychol.*, 1934, **16**, 831–842.
25. Cohen, B. D., Kalish, H. I., Thurston, J. R., and Cohen, E. Experimental manipulation of verbal behavior. *J. exp. Psychol.*, 1954, **47**, 106–110.
26. Cohen, L. H., Hilgard, E. R., and Wendt, G. R. Sensitivity to light in a case of hysterical blindness studied by reinforcement-inhibition and conditioning methods. *Yale J. Biol. Med.*, 1933, **6**, 61–67.
27. Collier, R. M. An experimental study of the effects of subliminal stimuli. *Psychol. Monogr.*, 1940, **52**, No. 5 (Whole No. 236).
28. Coover, J. E. Experiments in psychical research. *Psychical Res. Monogr.*, 1917, No. 1.
29. Cousins, N. Smudging the subconscious. *Saturday Rev.*, 1957, **40**, No. 40.

30. Cowen, E. L., and Beier, E. G. The influence of "threat-expectancy" on perception. *J. Pers.*, 1950–1951, **19**, 85–94.

31. Cowen, E. L., and Beier, E. G. A further study of the "threat-expectancy" variable in perception. *Amer. Psychologist*, 1952, **7**, 320–321. (Abstract)

32. Cowen, E. L., and Beier, E. G. Threat-expectancy, word frequencies, and perceptual prerecognition hypotheses. *J. abnorm. soc. Psychol.*, 1954, **49**, 178–182.

33. Culler, E., and Mettler, F. A. Conditioned behavior in a decorticate dog. *J. comp. Psychol.*, 1934, **18**, 291–303.

34. Deiter, J. The nature of subception. Unpublished doctoral dissertation, Univer. of Kansas, 1953.

35. Diven, K. Certain determinants in the conditioning of anxiety reactions. *J. Psychol.*, 1937, **3**, 291–308.

36. Dunlap, K. Effect of imperceptible shadows on the judgments of distance. *Psychol. Rev.*, 1900, **7**, 435–453.

37. DuShane, G. The invisible word, or no thresholds barred. *Science*, 1957, **126**, 681.

38. Ellson, D. G. Hallucinations produced by sensory conditioning. *J. exp. Psychol.*, 1941, **28**, 1–20.

39. Eriksen, C. W. The case for perceptual defense. *Psychol. Rev.*, 1954, **61**, 175–182.

40. Eriksen, C. W. Subception: Fact or artifact? *Psychol. Rev.*, 1956, **63**, 74–80.

41. Eriksen, C. W. and Kuethe, J. L. Avoidance conditioning of verbal behavior without awareness: A paradigm of repression. *J. abnorm. soc. Psychol.*, 1956, **53**, 203–209.

42. Fink, A. A. Questions about subliminal advertising. New York: Author, 1957.

43. Foley, J. P., Jr. The cortical interpretation of conditioning. *J. gen. Psychol.*, 1933, **9**, 228–234.

44. Fullerton, G. S., and Cattell, J. McK. On the perception of small differences. *Univer. Penn. Publ., Philos. Ser.*, 1892, No. 2.

45. "Ghost" ads overrated. *Sci. Newsltr.*, 1957, **72**, No. 17.

46. Gilchrist, J. C., and Nesberg, L. S. Need and perceptual change in need-related objects. *J. exp. Psychol.*, 1952, **44**, 369–376.

47. Goodnow, Jacqueline J., and Postman, L. Probability learning in a problem-solving situation. *J. exp. Psychol.*, 1955, **49**, 16–22.

48. Greenspoon, J. The reinforcing effect of two spoken sounds on the frequency of two responses. *Amer. J. Psychol.*, 1955, **68**, 409–416.

49. Guilford, J. P. *Psychometric methods*. New York: McGraw-Hill, 1936.

50. Haggard, E. A. Experimental studies in affective processes: I. Some effects of cognitive structure and active participation on certain autonomic reactions during and following experimentally induced stress. *J. exp. Psychol.*, 1943, **33**, 257-284.

51. Hankin, H. *Common sense*. New York: Dutton, 1926.

52. Hartmann, G. W. I. The increase of visual acuity in one eye through the illumination of the other. *J. exp. Psychol.*, 1933, **16**, 383–392.

53. Hartmann, G. W. II. Changes in visual acuity through simultaneous stimulation of other sense organs. *J. exp. Psychol.*, 1933, **16**, 393–407.

54. Henle, Mary. An experimental investigation of past experience as a determinant of visual form perception. *J. exp. Psychol.*, 1942, **30**, 1–21.

55. Hernandez-Peon, R., Scherrer, H., and Michel, J. Modification of electrical activity of cochlear nucleus during "attention" in unanesthetized cats. *Science*, 1955, **123**, 331–332.

56. Hildum, D. C., and Brown, R. W. Verbal reinforcement and interviewer bias. *J. abnorm. soc. Psychol.*, 1956, **53**, 108–111.

57. Hilgard, E. R., Miller, J., and Ohlson, J. A. Three attempts to secure pupillary conditioning to auditory stimuli near the absolute threshold. *J. exp. Psychol.*, 1941, **29**, 89–103.

58. Hilgard, E. R., and Wendt, G. R. The problem of reflex sensitivity to light studied in a case of hemianopsia. *Yale J. Biol. Med.*, 1933, **5**, 373–385.

59. Hollingworth, H. L. *Advertising and selling*. New York: Appleton, 1913.

60. Howes, D. A statistical theory of the phenomenon of subception. *Psychol. Rev.*, 1954, **61**, 98–110.

61. Howes, D. On the interpretation of word frequency as a variable affecting speed of recognition. *J. exp. Psychol.*, 1954, **48**, 106–112.

62. Howes, D., and Solomon, R. L. A note on McGinnies' "Emotionality and perceptual defense." *Psychol. Rev.*, 1950, **57**, 235–240.

63. Howes, D., and Solomon, R. L. Visual duration threshold as a function of word probability. *J. exp. Psychol.*, 1951, **41**, 401–410.

64. Huntley, C. W. Judgments of self based upon records of expressive behavior. *J. abnorm. soc. Psychol.*, 1953, **48**, 398–427.

65. Irwin, F. W., Kaufman, K., Prior, G., and Weaver, H. B. On "Learning without awareness of what is being learned." *J. exp. Psychol.*, 1934, **17**, 823–827.

66. Karn, H. W. The function of intensity in the spatial summation of subliminal stim-

uli in the retina. *J. gen. Psychol.*, 1935, **12**, 95–107.

67. Kennedy, J. L. Experiments on "unconscious whispering." *Psychol. Bull.*, 1938, **35**, 526. (Abstract)

68. Kennedy, J. L. A methodological review of extrasensory perception. *Psychol. Bull.*, 1939, **36**, 59–103.

69. Klein, G. S., Meister, D., and Schlesinger, H. J. The effect of personal values on perception: An experimental critique. *Amer. Psychologist*, 1949, **4**, 252–253. (Abstract)

70. Krech, D., and Calvin, A. Levels of perceptual organization and cognition. *J. abnorm. soc. Psychol.*, 1953, **48**, 394–400.

71. Kurland, S. H. The lack of generality in defense mechanisms as indicated in auditory perception. *J. abnorm. soc. Psychol.*, 1954, **49**, 173-177.

72. Lacey, J. I., and Smith, R. L. Conditioning and generalization of unconscious anxiety. *Science*, 1954, **120**, 1045–1052.

73. Lacey, J. I., Smith, R. L., and Green, A. Use of conditioned autonomic responses in the study of anxiety. *Psychosom. Med.*, 1955, **17**, 208–217.

74. Lazarus, R. S. Subception: Fact or artifact? A reply to Eriksen. *Psychol. Rev.*, 1956, **63**, 343–347.

75. Lazarus, R. S., Eriksen, C. W., and Fonda, C. P. Personality dynamics and auditory perceptual recognition. *J. Pers.*, 1950–1951, **19**, 471–482.

76. Lazarus, R. S., and McCleary, R. A. Autonomic discrimination without awareness: A study of subception. *Psychol. Rev.*, 1951, **58**, 113–122.

77. Levine, R., Chein, I., and Murphy, G. The relation of the intensity of a need to the amount of perceptual distortion. *J. Psychol.*, 1942, **13**, 283–293.

78. Lysak, W. The effects of punishment upon syllable recognition thresholds. *J. exp. Psychol.*, 1954, **47**, 343–350.

79. McCleary, R. A., and Lazarus, R. S. Autonomic discrimination without awareness: An interim report. *J. Pers.*, 1949, **18**, 171–179.

80. McClelland, D. C., and Atkinson, J. W. The projective expression of needs: I. The effect of different intensities of the hunger drive on perception. *J. Psychol.*, 1948, **25**, 205–222.

81. McClelland, D. C., and Lieberman, A. M. The effect of need for achievement on recognition of need-related words. *J. Pers.*, 1949, **18**, 236–251.

82. McGinnies, E. Emotionality and perceptual defense. *Psychol. Rev.*, 1949, **56**, 244–251.

83. McGinnies, E. Discussion of Howes' and Solomon's note on "Emotionality and perceptual defense." *Psychol. Rev.*, 1950, **57**, 229–234.

84. Mandler, G., and Kaplan, W. K. Subjective evaluation and reinforcing effect of a verbal stimulus. *Science*, 1956, **124**, 582–583.

85. Mannes, Marya. Ain't nobody here but us commercials. *Reporter*, 1957, **17**, No. 6.

86. Manro, H. M., and Washburn, M. F. Effect of imperceptible lines on judgment of distance. *Amer. J. Psychol.*, 1908, **19**, 242–243.

87. Michigan State prof. tells weaknesses of invisible commercials. *Publishers Auxiliary*, 1957, **92**, No. 40.

88. Miller, J. G. Discrimination without awareness. *Amer. J. Psychol.*, 1939, **52**, 562–578.

89. Miller, J. G. The role of motivation in learning without awareness. *Amer. J. Psychol.*, 1940, **53**, 229–239.

90. Miller, J. G. *Unconsciousness.* New York: Wiley, 1942.

91. Newhall, S. M., and Dodge, R. Colored after images from unperceived weak chromatic stimulation. *J. exp. Psychol.*, 1927, **10**, 1–17.

92. Newhall, S. M., and Sears, R. R. Conditioning finger retraction to visual stimuli near the absolute threshold. *Comp. psychol. Monogr.*, 1933, **9**, No. 43.

93. Nuthmann, Anne M. Conditioning of a response class on a personality test. *J. abnorm. soc. Psychol.*, 1957, **54**, 19–23.

94. Peirce, C. S., and Jastrow, J. On small differences of sensation. *Mem. Nat. Acad. Sci.*, 1884, **3**, 73–83.

95. Perky, C. W. An experimental study of imagination. *Amer. J. Psychol.*, 1910, **21**, 422–452.

96. Philbrick, E. B., and Postman, L. A further analysis of "learning without awareness." *Amer. J. Psychol.*, 1955, **68**, 417–424.

97. Pillai, R. P. B. K. A study of the threshold in relation to the investigations on subliminal impressions and allied phenomena. *Brit. J. educ. Psychol.*, 1939, **9**, 97–98.

98. Postman, L., and Jarrett, R. F. An experimental analysis of "learning without awareness." *Amer. J. Psychol.*, 1952, **65**, 244–255.

99. Razran, G. Stimulus generalization of conditioned responses. *Psychol. Bull.*, 1949, **46**, 337–365.

100. Reece, M. M. The effect of shock on recognition thresholds. *J. abnorm. soc. Psychol.*, 1954, **49**, 165–172.

101. Rees, H. J., and Israel, H. E. An investigation of the establishment and operation of mental sets. *Psychol. Monogr.*, 1935, **46**, No. 6 (Whole No. 210).

102. Sanford, R. N. The effects of abstinence

from food upon imaginal processes: A preliminary experiment. *J. Psychol.*, 1936, **2**, 129–136.

103. Sanford, R. N. The effects of abstinence from food upon imaginal processes: A further experiment. *J. Psychol.*, 1937, **3**, 145–159.

104. Schafer, T. H. Influence of the preceding item on units of the noise masked threshold by a modified constant method. *J. exp. Psychol.*, 1950, **40**, 365–371.

105. Sears, R. R., and Cohen, L. H. Hysterical anesthesia, analgesia, and astereognosis. *Arch. Neurol. Psychiat.*, 1933, **29**, 260–271.

106. Settlage, T. The effect of sodium amytal on the formation and elicitation of conditioned reflexes. *J. comp. Psychol.*, 1936, **22**, 339–343.

107. Sidis, B. *The psychology of suggestion.* New York: Appleton, 1898.

108. Sidowski, J. B. Influence of awareness of reinforcement on verbal conditioning. *J. exp. Psychol.*, 1954, **48**, 355–360.

109. Silverman, A., and Baker, L. E. An attempt to condition various responses to subliminal electrical stimulation. *J. exp. Psychol.*, 1935, **18**, 246–254.

110. Smoke, K. L. An objective study of concept formation. *Psychol. Monogr.*, 1932, **42**, No. 4 (Whole No. 191).

111. Solomon, R. L., and Howes, D. H. Word frequency, personal values, and visual duration thresholds. *Psychol. Rev.*, 1951, **58**, 256–270.

112. Solomon, R. L., and Postman, L. Frequency of usage as a determinant of recognition thresholds for words. *J. exp. Psychol.*, 1952, **43**, 195–201.

113. Spencer, L. T. The concept of the threshold and Heymans' law of inhibition: I. Correlation between the visual threshold and Heymans' coefficient of inhibition of binocular vision. *J. exp. Psychol.*, 1928, **11**, 88–97.

114. Spencer, L. T., and Cohen, L. H. The concept of the threshold and Heymans' law of inhibition. II. *J. exp. Psychol.*, 1928, **11**, 194-201.

115. Sterling, K., and Miller, J. G. Conditioning under anesthesia. *Amer. J. Psychol.*, 1941, **54**, 92–101.

116. Stroh, M., Shaw, A. M., and Washburn, M. F. A study in guessing. *Amer. J. Psychol.*, 1908, **19**, 243–245.

117. Subliminal ad okay if it sells: Lessler; FCC peers into subliminal picture on TV. *Adv. Age*, 1957, **28**, No. 48.

118. Subliminal ads wash no brains, declare Moore, Becker, developers of precon device. *Adv. Age*, 1957, **28**, No. 48.

119. Suslowa, M. Veranderungen der Hautgefule unter dem Einflusse electrischer Reizung. *Z. Rationelle Med.*, 1863, **18**, 155–160.

120. Taffel, C. Anxiety and the conditioning of verbal behavior. *J. abnorm. soc. Psychol.*, 1955, **51**, 496–501.

121. Thorndike, E. L. *The fundamentals of learning.* New York: Teachers College, Columbia Univer., 1932.

122. Thorndike, E. L., and Rock, R. T. Learning without awareness of what is being learned or intent to learn it. *J. exp. Psychol.*, 1934, **17**, 1–19.

123. Titchner, E. B., and Pyle, W. H. Effect of imperceptible shadows on the judgment of distance. *Proc. Amer. phil. Soc.*, 1907, **46**, 94–109.

124. Vanderplas, J. M., and Blake, R. R. Selective sensitization in auditory perception. *J. Pers.*, 1949, **18**, 252–266.

125. Verplanck, W. S. The control of the content of conversation: Reinforcement of statements of opinion. *J. abnorm. soc. Psychol.*, 1955, **51**, 668–676.

126. Verplanck, W. S. The operant conditioning of human motor behavior. *Psychol. Bull.*, 1956, **53**, 70–83.

127. Vinacke, W. E. The discrimination of color and form at levels of illumination below conscious awareness. *Arch. Psychol.*, 1942, **38**, No. 267.

128. Wedell, C. H., Taylor, F. V., and Skolnick, A. An attempt to condition the pupillary response. *J. exp. Psychol.*, 1940, **27**, 517–531.

129. Weiss, R. L. The influence of "set for speed" on "learning without awareness." *Amer. J. Psychol.*, 1955, **68**, 425–431.

130. Williams, A. C. Perception of subliminal visual stimuli. *J. Psychol.*, 1938, 6, 187–199.

131. Wispe, L. G., and Drambarean, N. C. Physiological need, word frequency, and visual duration thresholds. *J. exp. Psychol.*, 1953, 46, 25–31.

132. Woolf, J. D. Subliminal perception is nothing new. *Adv. Age*, 1957, **28**, No. 43.

THE PERCEPTION OF OBJECTS

Our world of experience or perception, our visual world, for instance, is the result of the organization and integration of sensory input. Many psychologists think of this organization and integration as taking place in the brain.

The present set of experiments presents some examples of the interaction of sensory inputs. Several ingenious demonstrations are provided to show that viewing a pattern will change what we subsequently see, experience. The present set of experiments also provides data for a more general theory of the way the cerebral cortex may operate in perception to produce these and other interactions.

The most important point which is being made is that what we see is related to the pattern of activity in the visual cortex. This pattern is a field of electrical potentials in which all parts are interrelated. A change in one part of the field will affect all other parts. This stress on fields and inter-relationships is the contribution of gestalt psychology.

Dr. W. Köhler is famous as a founder of gestalt psychology, while Dr. H. Wallach is well-known for his ingenious perceptual experiments.

Points to guide your study

1. If you try any of these demonstrations, remember that prolonged fixation, very steady viewing, of the inspection figures is essential. This may take a little practice.

2. Put the theory of figural aftereffects in your own words. Make sure you can define satiation and electrotonus.

34. FIGURAL AFTER-EFFECTS: AN INVESTIGATION OF VISUAL PROCESSES

Wolfgang Köhler, Lebanon, N. H., and Hans Wallach, Swarthmore College[*]

Introduction

The concept of figural after-effects is just emerging from its formative stage. About ten years ago remarkable instances of such effects were discovered by J. J. Gibson. But his observations referred to quite particular figural conditions. Unfortunately an investigation of reversible figures with which we were occupied at the time,

and which dealt with certain other effects of prolonged inspection, seemed equally restricted in scope. Thus it happened that for years the close relationship between Gibson's experiments and our own work was not realized. In our present report we hope to give the concept of figural after-effects a clearer connotation so that in the future such effects will be more easily recognized.

Gibson reported his first discovery in 1933 (7·).[1] His subjects observed that during prolonged inspection slightly curved lines gradually became less curved. When afterwards straight lines were shown in the location and orientation of the curves, such straight lines appeared curved in the opposite direction. Their distortion could be measured. The effect was again measured by Bales and Follansbee (1), who also added some

* Wolfgang Köhler and Hans Wallach. Figural after-effects: An investigation of visual processes. *Proc. Amer. philos. Soc.*, 1944, **88**, 269–357. Copyright 1944 by the American Philosophical Society. Excerpts reprinted here with permission from the authors and the American Philosophical Society. Figures 67 to 70 of the original work have been renumbered. Footnote 21 of the original work has been renumbered. Some references to pages in other parts of the original work have been omitted. These changes have been made with permission from the senior author and the American Philosophical Society.

[1] This and similar notations refer to the articles and books in the References at the end of the paper.

new observations. Gibson himself, however, did not restrict his experiments to the case of visual curves. He asked blindfolded subjects to move their fingers along a convexly curved edge and to repeat this movement for several minutes. They reported that the curve gradually appeared less convex. Afterwards a straight edge felt definitely concave. In vision he found that not only curves gave clear after-effects but also lines which were bent at the middle into an obtuse angle. When the apex of the angle had been fixated for some time, straight lines of the same location and orientation appeared bent in the opposite direction.[2] A further phenomenon was observed and measured by Gibson (7, 8, 10), M. D. Vernon (28), and Gibson and Radner (9). When their observers inspected a straight line which was moderately tilted with regard to the vertical or the horizontal, afterwards the objective vertical or horizontal appeared tilted in the opposite direction. Moreover, when the position of the vertical (horizontal) was thus altered the horizontal (vertical) tended to turn in the same direction.

Apart from these basic observations the authors, particularly Gibson himself, reported further facts which served to clarify the nature of such after-effects. In the *first* place it was found by Gibson that the after-effects were fairly closely restricted to the locus of the inspection figure. Here the term locus is to be understood in reference to the visual sector of the nervous system, because an effect which was caused by inspection of a figure in one place would show on an appropriate test object elsewhere as soon as the eyes were turned into the right position relative to this object. *Secondly*, however, Gibson observed that when only one eye was used during the inspection period an after-effect of somewhat smaller amount could clearly be observed in the corresponding part of the other eye's field. *Thirdly*, long inspection times, although desirable for certain purposes, proved not to be necessary for noticeable after-effects. When Gibson and Radner measured the "tilted line" effect after varying periods of inspection they found that it was unmistakably present after five seconds, and about maximal as early as one or two minutes later. With such inspection times the curve of the development tended to become parallel to the abscissa. Particularly impressive is the *fourth* observation. Once a strong figural after-effect had been obtained it often persisted for many minutes. As a matter of fact, with one of Gibson's subjects the after-effect did not disappear within twenty-four hours when by a proper device the inspection of vertical curves had been continued for several days. But, *fifthly*,

individual differences as to the amount of the after-effects were quite conspicuous, although only Bales and Follansbee found them entirely absent in some subjects.

We agree with most factual statements made by Gibson and by the authors who continued his work. But we do not believe that Gibson's interpretation of his data is correct. He assumes that it is deviation of inspection objects from "norms," like straight lines in general and verticals or horizontals in particular, which leads to figural after-effects. Actually, figural after-effects are not restricted to such special instances. It will soon be seen that, as a matter of principle, inspection of any specific entity in a visual field can cause figural after-effects. Gibson's discoveries will therefore have to be reinterpreted within the larger body of facts which is now at our disposal.

The existence of figural after-effects in a more general sense was first inferred from the behavior of reversible figures. Some data concerning the spontaneous reversals of such figures under conditions of prolonged inspection have been given elsewhere (17, pp. 67 ff.). Here we will repeat merely that the speed of those reversals tends to increase as fixation is continued, that then the figures will still be unstable after rest periods of several minutes, and that for this reason their instability can be enhanced in a sequence of separate inspection periods. This fact of summation or accumulation suggests that prolonged presence of a figure in a given location tends to operate against further presence of this figure in the same place. It may be concluded that the presence of a figure in the visual field is associated with a specific figure process in the visual sector of the brain, and that this process gradually alters the medium in which it occurs. In a reversible figure a redistribution of the figure process seems to occur when that change has reached a certain level.

It follows from these assumptions that a figure which has become unstable in its original location must again appear more stable when it is shown in a new position. Such a recovery can actually be demonstrated.

Quite apart from any reference to Gibson's discoveries, our assumptions contained certain implications which were not restricted to reversible figures. However, we did not at once realize that our interpretation involved two hypotheses, and that only one of them was concerned with reversible figures. According to the first hypothesis a specific figure process occurs whenever a figure appears in the visual field. And this process tends to block its own way if the figure remains for some time in the same location. The second hypothesis states that in reversible figures the figure-ground relationship will suddenly be reversed when the figure process has altered the

[2] Gibson (10, p. 562) mentions that this effect was first observed by F. H. Verhoeff (27).

medium beyond a critical degree. Obviously, only the second hypothesis refers to reversible figures. In the first hypothesis such particular patterns play no part. This assumption must therefore apply to all figures without exception. In other words, continued presence of *any* figure in a given location must change conditions for subsequent figure processes in the same region of the field.

When this inference was finally drawn we did not, of course, know what particular symptoms of such after-effects we had to expect in the absence of reversals. In an earlier report (17) experiments have been described which revealed some such symptoms. To be sure, these first observations gave only a very limited view of the facts. It seems nevertheless advisable to begin the present report with a discussion of the same first experiments. This will allow us to show how one group of observations after another forced us to alter our concepts considerably.

On the whole, therefore, our first chapter will repeat our previous description of certain figural after-effects. In the second chapter it will be shown that certain assumptions which we originally held were much too conservative. In the third we hope to prove that the most essential phase of figural after-effects is a withdrawal of test objects from regions which have been affected by inspection of a figure. In the fourth chapter Gibson's discoveries will be interpreted in terms of this principle.

The fifth, the sixth, and the seventh will be concerned with theory. As a preparation certain physical and physiological data will be surveyed in the fifth chapter. In the sixth and the seventh a theory of figural after-effects will be developed on those grounds. To a degree this theory will also refer to vision in general.

Preliminary experiments

I. For a first observation an outline figure, e.g., an oblong or a circle, is drawn with india ink on a white screen, and a fixation mark is added on one side (cf. Figure 1). The outline ought not to be too thin. On a second white screen the same drawing is prepared in the same position relative to the fixation mark, but on the

other side of this mark, and symmetrically, an identical figure is here added.[3] The subject first fixates the mark on the former chart for, say, five minutes and from a distance of two yards. If he then fixates the mark on the second chart he will find that its two objectively equal figures have not the same appearance. The figure which coincides with the previously inspected object will be pale or gray in comparison with its black partner, it will seem to lie farther back in space, and it may look a trifle smaller. Depending upon the individual subject one or another of these facts will appear more conspicuous. For instance, some subjects report at once that the two objects have not the same size, while others do not mention this difference spontaneously. A few may even deny its existence. More convincing results are generally obtained with oblongs than with circles.

In a given and constant location a dark area, and therefore also a black line, may gradually assume a gray appearance by local "fatigue" rather than by a figural after-effect. If such a banal explanation can be given for one of the three symptoms one might be tempted to interpret the other two as secondary consequences of the first. They, too, would then become unimportant. However, such an explanation is quite untenable in many cases which will soon be discussed, and it is not plausible even in the present instance. For, if during the inspection period one eye is prevented from seeing the figure, and if afterwards the test is made with this eye alone, the same symptoms will be observed.

The inspection object of Figure 1 may be replaced by a solid figure, for instance, by a black solid circle. If the test objects are two equal and symmetrically situated outline circles of which one coincides with the contour of the solid figure, these test objects will differ after the inspection period more or less as they did in the first experiment. In this observation it is almost necessary to use one eye during the inspection period and the other in the test. Otherwise the negative after-image of the solid figure would disturb the comparison. With transfer from one eye to the other few observers mention after-images, and without this disturbing factor the difference in the appearance of the test objects can be more easily seen.

Other figural after-effects are incomparably more impressive than the ones just mentioned. But it seems natural to begin with a description of these observations because they were the first

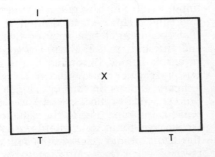

Figure 1

[3] Our Figures show inspection objects (I) and test objects (T) in one pattern so that their relative positions can readily be seen. When, as in Figure 1, a test object coincides with the inspection object, this fact is indicated by the letters IT. Wherever no particular dimensions are given our actual Figures were linearly about 30 percent larger than the present reproductions.

we made and would probably be everybody's first choice: The "figure" of an outline object appears characterized first of all by its outline, the only objective datum which interrupts the homogeneous ground. Hence, if a figure causes an after-effect, ought this effect not to be strongest at the place of the outline, and therefore with a congruent test object?

Actually it will soon be seen that observations do not generally confirm this expectation. Before we proceed to further experiments it will, however, be advisable to make a few remarks about the simple technique which has just been used. This technique will remain useful throughout our investigation; but its application requires a certain amount of caution.

In many experiments one test object which lies within the affected region or in its immediate neighborhood will be compared with an equal second test object which is placed in a neutral region. Whether this latter region is entirely unaffected is not a very important question. So long as under favorable conditions a striking difference between the test objects is seen the procedure will serve our purpose. It is of course assumed that at a *great* distance from a previously inspected object after-effects are smaller than they are in its neighborhood. But this assumption is corroborated not only by Gibson's observations but also by our own experiences. For the most part we have shown one test object in the left half of the visual field and the other in the right half. We recommend the use of test patterns which are symmetrically placed with regard to the main axes of space. Under these conditions intrinsic inhomogeneities of the visual field play but a minor role. Moreover, in a symmetrical situation the comparison of test objects will be found to be easier.

More dangerous than a possible spread of after-effects into the region of the neutral test object are other influences upon this region which one is likely to overlook in the beginning. A concrete example: In observations such as the ones just described it would be simpler to use not two charts but only the one which contains the two test objects. One of these could first be covered by a screen and the other thus used as the inspection object. After the inspection period the two objects could be directly compared when the screen is removed. Although we have sometimes used this procedure we cannot recommend it. The covering screen itself constitutes a figure; at least one of its edges will lie within the field, and after-effects will result which may influence the outcome of the experiment. As a matter of fact, the after-effect of the screen may sometimes be stronger than the effect which a given experiment is meant to demonstrate.

While with some figural after-effects a small fraction of a minute will suffice as an inspection period others require a longer inspection time, particularly if the subjects are not accustomed to such observations. This often makes experimentation distinctly unpleasant. Observers complain about headaches, also about a feeling of strain and of disagreeable dryness in the eyes. We are not at all sure that the investigation of figural after-effects belongs to the occupations which an oculist or a neurologist would recommend. This suspicion is enhanced by the fact that once an after-effect has been well established it may not disappear for hours. We quite agree with Gibson's remarks on this point.

However relevant to any theory of figural after-effects their long survival may be, it constitutes unfortunately an important obstacle to reliable experimentation. For the most part experiments on figural after-effects will have to be separated by considerable periods of intermission. Otherwise an older effect will easily falsify the outcome of a subsequent observation. Before any experiment is begun the subject will have to make sure that the appearance of the test objects is normal. This is in any case a wise precaution because objectively equal objects may not be visually equal when shown in different locations. The astonishing persistency of certain after-effects makes the interpolation of considerable rest periods a necessary condition of most experimentation in this field.

When two charts are being used, one during the inspection period and one for the test objects, the latter may be shown in the place which was first occupied by the former. Sometimes it will be more convenient to arrange the two charts in symmetrical positions, one to the left and the other to the right of the subject's median plane, and with a slight inclination toward this plane. A small and symmetrical turn of the head will then allow the subject to fixate the mark first on one and then on the other chart as though they were shown in the same place and both right in front. However, this procedure is admissible only so long as the subject avoids any tilting of his head while turning from one chart to the other. Any tilt would obviously alter the spatial relation between the affected area and the corresponding test object.

Few observers are disturbed by negative after-images when the inspection object consists either of black lines on a large white ground or of white lines on a dark ground. With solid figures, we remember, the disturbance by after-images can be avoided if the inspection object is shown only to one eye and the test objects only to the other.

We suspect that under these circumstances transfer of the effect cannot simply be taken for granted. At least its amount may depend on the conditions under which an experiment is being performed. It seems to us that transfer is more complete if during the inspection period the second eye is not closed or covered, i.e. darkened, but merely prevented from seeing the inspection object. A screen which is held obliquely before this eye will keep it illuminated and at the same time cover the inspection object. In this position edges of the screen will be so dimly seen that they can hardly act as effective contours.

II. The following experiments differ in two respects from those of section I: The test objects are no longer equal to the inspection objects, and consequently the outline of the former does not, or does not throughout, coincide with that of the latter. It will be seen that this change does not obliterate the after-effects; on the contrary, the next observations will generally be regarded as more convincing than those of section I.

1. In Figure 2 the inspection object is an outline circle. The subject fixates a mark on the periphery of the circle. The test object is an oblong divided by a curve into approximately equal parts. This curve is congruent with the corresponding part of the circle and bears a fixation mark where that of the circle lies. In Figure 2 the inspection object (*I*-object) and the test object (*T*-object) are united; actually the *T*-object is shown when the *I*-object is no longer visible. After an inspection period of several minutes all subjects report that the right side of the *T*-oblong is larger, particularly higher, than its left side. It will surprise every observer to find that after a sufficient inspection period the horizontal contours of the oblong are actually broken so that it assumes the shape indicated in Figure 3. A depth effect is no less obvious. Normally the convex part of the oblong tends to appear in front of the concave part. After the inspection period just the opposite is true; the concave part now lies "upon" the convex half; in other words, the figure-ground relationship is reversed.[4] Obviously in

---

[4] It will be realized that this observation establishes a direct connection between the present after-effect and the behavior of reversible figures. Actually the *T*-object of experiment 1 may be regarded as a reversible figure.

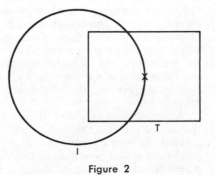

Figure 2

the interior of the *I*-figure the figural after-effect is stronger than it is immediately outside its contour.

The *I*-object need by no means be a circle. When the observation is repeated with a rectangle and therefore with a *T*-object divided by a straight line it gives precisely the same result.

2. When experiment 1 of this section was first performed the outside part of the *T*-object appeared so "intense" that for a moment the following interpretation seemed possible. Inside the figure area prolonged inspection causes an effect of "depression" while just outside the figure the opposite holds. Actually this is not the case. When a *T*-object just outside an *I*-figure is compared with a second one which lies at a great distance, the former will be found to show all symptoms of "depression." This can be demonstrated with the arrangement shown in Figure 4. (In this figure the *I*- and the *T*-objects are again united while actually they are shown in succession.[5]) After the inspection period the *T*-square on the right side will look considerably

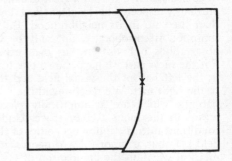

Figure 3

smaller; it will also lie farther back in space and be pale in comparison with its partner. It follows that the after-effect extends beyond the area of the inspection object, and that its symptoms are here the same as they are within the figure. In experiment 1, therefore, the outside part of the *T*-object seemed particularly "intense" only in comparison with the more strongly affected inside part.

3. In a further experiment a figural after-effect is demonstrated when the outline of the affected *T*-object has no point in common with the outline of the *I*-figure (Figure 5). After an inspection

---

[5] In the following pages this interpretation of our Figures will no longer be mentioned. Parts which are marked with an *I* are invariably inspection objects, and are shown first; parts designated as *T* are test objects, and shown after the inspection period. The fixation mark (X) is common to both.

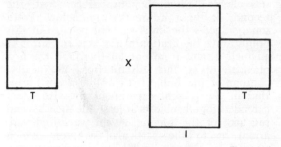

Figure 4

period of several minutes no subject will miss the striking difference in the appearance of the *T*-squares. The square above the fixation point will appear smaller than the other *T*-object; it will also lie farther back in space. Under the conditions of this experiment, therefore, the after-effect pervades the whole interior of the *I*-object.

Within limits the particular nature of the *T*-object may be varied. If the squares are replaced by pairs of horizontal lines, one pair within the circle, the other symmetrically below the fixation point, the after-effect remains just as striking. Within the area of the circle the *T*-lines appear gray, not black; they lie back in space, and are probably nearer one another; they are also clearly shorter.

4. There are no figures without outlines or contours. It is, therefore, a plausible assumption that in some way contours are responsible not only for the existence of figures as such but also for any after-effects which are established when figures are shown for some time in a constant location. We should not conclude, however, that during prolonged inspection of a figure the vari-

ous parts of its outline emit, independently of one another, some detrimental agent which causes a "depressing" effect wherever it arrives.[6] From this point of view an after-effect ought to become stronger in proportion to the amount of contour—of an *I*-object—which surrounds the area of the *T*-object at a given distance. We shall see in Chapter Two that whole classes of after-effects are incompatible with this view. For the moment, the outcome of a simple "differential" experiment will suffice as a refutation. In Figure 6 the broken lines of the *I*-square on the right side of the fixation mark "surround" the right *T*-object more completely than the two inner verticals surround the left *T*-object. The distance of these verticals from each other has the same length as the edge of the *I*-square on the right side. But in terms of actual contour each edge of the square is only two-fifths of each continuous vertical on the left side. The total actual contour of the square is, therefore, in this measure eight-fifths while the length of the two continuous lines is two, or ten-fifths. In other words, the total length of actual contour is twenty-five per cent greater in the case of the two continuous lines. Moreover, on the left side two more verticals are added on both sides of the *T*-object. Distances of the *I*-contours from the *T*-objects are in this pattern directly comparable, because the broken lines of the square have the same location relative to the right *T*-object as the inner continuous *I*-lines have to the left *T*-object. Thus the experiment can decide whether, apart from the amount of contours in the neighborhood of a *T*-object, the particular configuration of these contours plays a part in determining the after-effect.

The answer is perfectly clear. The *T*-object on the left side appears larger and, for most observers, also nearer. It follows that the strength of an after-effect depends upon the specific configuration in which the *I*-contours are given in the neighborhood of a *T*-object. Mere quantity of contour at a given distance is surely not the only decisive factor.

5. Experiments 1, 3, and 4 have proved that the interior of a figure is in an altered condition when this figure has been for some time in the same place. It seems, however, equally relevant to know to what extent the effect extends into the environment of a figure. In experiment 2 we

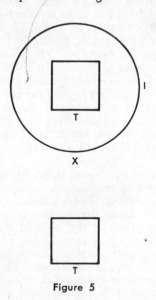

Figure 5

[6] This assumption has been made by K. J. W. Craik and O. L. Zangwill (3) in their interpretation of experiments in which surrounding outlines were shown to raise the threshold for the appearance of a weak dot. Incidentally, during these experiments tremendous after-effects must have developed. It remains to be seen to what extent these after-effects explain the results which the authors contrast with a theoretical prediction of Koffka's.

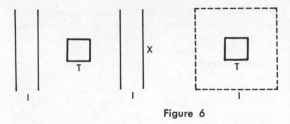

Figure 6

have found that a *T*-object which lies just outside the figure is clearly "depressed." The next experiment shows that this influence of the *I*-figure is not restricted to *T*-objects in an immediately adjacent position.

Figure 7 is to be interpreted as follows: The *I*-object, a solid black oblong, is shown with the lowest of the five crosses as a fixation mark. After prolonged inspection the two *T*-squares are compared when the eyes fixate either the same or one of the higher marks. (These higher marks are given only on the *T*-chart, not during the inspection period.) The higher the mark lies which is fixated in the test, the greater will be the distance between the area previously occupied by the *I*-object and the left *T*-square.[7] Thus a number of tests with varying distances can be made with the same *T*-chart. Short inspection periods between successive tests will keep the after-effect at a high level if inspection has been sufficiently long in the beginning. Our subjects observed from a distance of about two yards, a distance which was used in most of our experiments.

All observers reported that the left *T*-object

---

[7] The same holds for the square in the right half of the field. Therefore, when successively higher fixation points are used the difference between the distances of the squares from the area of the *I*-object becomes relatively smaller. With the largest distances this may tend to weaken the observed after-effect.

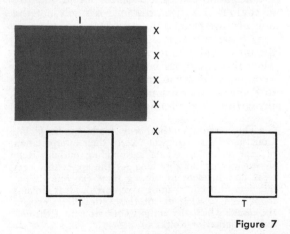

Figure 7

was affected when they fixated the first, the second, or the third mark from below. With some subjects the limit was not reached at this point. Since the fixation marks were two-fifths of an inch distant from one another, and the first one-fifth of an inch distant from the nearest contour of the *I*-object, this observation means that in the present experiment the after-effect extended for all subjects at least one inch beyond the area of the *I*-figure. Again we found variations as to the particular symptom which seemed to impress individual observers most. One subject would stress the comparative paleness of the left *T*-object, another its smaller size, again another the fact that it lay back in space. Frequently a fourth symptom was mentioned, a displacement of the left *T*-square. We prefer to discuss this new fact in another section.

As preliminary evidence this observation will suffice. Although it is quite true that figural after-effects are centered about the locus of the *I*-figure they are by no means strictly limited to this place. Therefore it does not seem entirely relevant to ask whether or not these effects are "localized." Their center has a very definite location; but from this center the temporary disturbance extends considerably into the environment.

From this fact we can draw an important conclusion. It will not be denied that the prolonged presence of a figure in a given area is the cause of the after-effects. This can mean only that continued occurrence of a specific figure process in a given location changes the state of the medium in which this process occurs; that in the changed medium the figure processes of *T*-objects are altered; and that as a consequence the visual characteristics of these *T*-objects are affected. But from this point of view the extension of the after-effects in space will roughly correspond to the extension of the figure processes by which they are established. It follows that, although the color processes of a given figure are limited to the area of the figure as such, in some way the figure must act beyond this restricted area. Otherwise no after-effects could be observed outside and at a distance from the *I*-figure. In this sense, then, a figure has a "field" by which it is represented in the environment.

Our conclusion that a figure is surrounded by a field may seem to be open to the following criticism. The characteristics of a *T*-object need not depend merely on the state of the medium at the locus of that *T*-object. To a degree they may depend on alterations of the medium in other places, for instance within the area of the *I*-object. This criticism defeats itself in assuming that the *T*-object is associated with events which extend beyond the area of the *T*-object. How else should the *T*-object be affected by conditions at a distance? But this is precisely the assumption which we have made with regard to the *I*-object. Thus the argument implicitly grants the thesis against which it is aimed. It should, however, be admitted that because of the field of the *T*-object our present observations give at best a very rough indication of the extension of the *I*-field.

At this point a terminological remark becomes necessary. We have to distinguish between two facts. A figure process, it appears, tends to alter conditions within the medium in which it occurs, and when the figure disappears the medium seems for some time to remain in its changed condition. This is a state of affairs for which, apart from the medium itself, only the figure process of the *I*-object is responsible. Suppose now that a *T*-figure is shown in the affected region. Generally speaking, not all parts of this region will be equally affected. Consequently any alterations which the process of the *T*-figure may suffer will depend upon the particular position which this *T*-figure has in the affected zone. Furthermore, the particular size and shape of the *T*-figure will also influence such after-effects. Hence, within a region which has been affected by inspection of a given figure not one but several after-effects will be demonstrable. Under these circumstances it would be confusing if both the alteration of the medium as such and the various effects of this alteration upon specific *T*-objects were given the same name. We propose to call only the alterations of *T*-objects "figural after-effects" and to refer to the affection of the medium as "satiation." This name is not meant to have any particular implications beyond the fact that the prolonged presence of a given figure causes the "depressed" condition of the medium. As soon as the nature of this depression

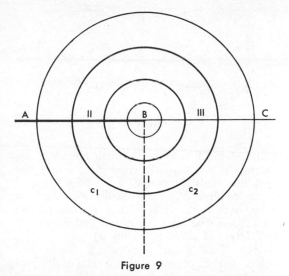

Figure 9

becomes sufficiently known the term satiation may of course be replaced by a better defined concept.

A theory of figural after-effects

In Chapter Five material has been presented from which a theory of figure processes, of satiation, and of figural after-effects can be derived. In the present section we propose to take preliminary steps toward such a theory.

1. The functional scheme which was indicated in Figure 8 and Figure 9 allows of immediate application to visual processes. When nerve impulses arrive in the visual cortex they alter chemical conditions in the tissue fluid which surrounds the cells. Suppose that in one retinal area the intensity of stimulation differs from that in another, and adjacent, area. Under these circumstances more nerve impulses will travel in fibers which issue from the more strongly stimulated area. Now, those adjacent retinal areas are connected with adjacent cortical areas. Since more impulses arrive in one of these than in the other, the levels of chemical activity in the two areas will differ correspondingly. Thus we obtain the situation to which Figure 8 refers. As a consequence, a current will flow from one area to the other and back into the first (cf. Figure 9). The flow will circle around the boundary at which the two areas are in contact. Near the boundary it will be dense because here the length of the circuit is short. At a greater distance, i.e. along longer circuits, its intensity will be smaller. In Figure 9, which gives only a cross-section of the situation, the two areas are represented by the lines AB and BC, their common boundary by point B. Actually, the cortical areas are supposed to extend at right angles to the

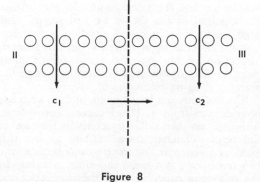

Figure 8

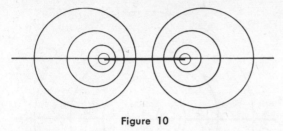

Figure 10

plane of the Figure so that their boundary also extends in the same direction. Accordingly, the flow surrounds the boundary in cylinders rather than in lines. We need hardly mention that even within its plane Figure 9 oversimplifies conditions: the lines AB and BC represent several *layers* of cells (cf. Figure 8).

The *visual* situation to which this scheme refers consists, of course, of two areas of different brightness which are in contact along a certain line. The scheme means that, physiologically speaking, any such boundary between areas of different brightness is surrounded by a direct current. At present we have no reason to discuss instances in which areas differ in hue rather than in brightness.

If one of the two areas is *enclosed* in the other it will be seen as a particular object. Figure 10 indicates as a cross-section how the current must flow in this situation. It must circle *everywhere* around the contour of the object. As a consequence the lines of flow can no longer be concentric. Within the limited space of the figure through which the whole flow must pass they will keep nearer the contour than they do in the environment in which they can freely spread. Therefore, the current will also be denser within the object than in the environment.

Our investigation has been principally concerned with outline figures. The current of a single straight line results if in Figure 10 the area of the solid object is reduced to a minimum. We thus obtain Figure 11. With a *closed* outline figure the current will still turn in both directions at each point of the outline; in other words, one part of the flow will pass through the enclosed area and another part through the

environment of the figure. But within the enclosed area, which is pervaded by current from all directions, the flow will be denser than it is outside at comparable distances.

It follows from this reasoning that all visual figures are associated with figure currents—provided that the brightness of their area or of their outline differs from that of the ground. In the theory of vision it, therefore, does not suffice to consider cortical color processes at each point. If our assumption is correct we have to attribute equal significance to those currents which pervade the area of visual objects and which also surround them like fields.

Just like all other direct currents, figure currents are functional units: their flow maintains itself relationally in a certain distribution. As a matter of principle this distribution can be mathematically determined. For each figure it is an integral of a partial differential equation. But for the time being an excursion into mathematical physics would be of little help. For, we shall presently see that any figure current must affect its conducting medium, and that as a result its own distribution will begin to change. To follow such a process in strict mathematical reasoning is a task which, to our knowledge, nobody has ever undertaken. Nor will it be necessary to make such an attempt for our purposes. At some points, it is true, precise information about the distribution of figure currents under the conditions of our experiments would facilitate the comparison of observation and theory. But on the whole we shall have to refer solely to the more obvious characteristics of currents in volume conductors.

2. We need no special hypothesis for an explanation of *satiation*. The figure currents of our theory differ in no way from other electric currents. They will therefore polarize all cell surfaces through which they pass and will thus establish the condition which the physiologists call electrotonus. This condition is known to survive its cause, the polarizing current. After intense polarization it persists for considerable periods and affects all currents which then happen to pervade the same region. In the further development of our theory we will assume that what we have so far called satiation *is* the electrotonic effect of figure currents. On this ground, inspection of any specific visual object must cause an electrotonic state within the area of the object and in its environment.

Electrotonus is a heavy word, and no verb has been derived from it. This is most inconvenient. Although no such difficulty exists in the case of the term polarization we hesitate to use this word as a synonym for electrotonus because the two terms have not quite the same meaning. In the following pages we shall therefore continue to speak of satiation, with the understanding

Figure 11

that from now on electrotonus and satiation will be equivalent terms.

Electrotonus, we remember, is a name for two different facts: an initial, and almost immediately completed, polarization of cell surfaces and a more gradual change of polarizability which is, of course, accompanied by corresponding changes of actual polarization. Clearly, the facts of satiation with which we have so far been occupied must belong to the latter category. Initial polarization develops so fast that if it has any overt effects in human vision such effects would have to be counted among the normal ingredients of visual objects.

As the electrotonic condition develops, its spatial distribution in the tissue follows that of the satiating figure current. In places in which the current is particularly dense, electrotonus will develop more quickly and to a higher level than in other parts. Therefore, with solid figures the electrotonic state must reach its greatest intensity about the contour, with outline figures within and near the outline. For the same reason the interior of the figure will be more strongly affected than its environment. At a great distance from specific objects practically no electrotonus will be established because here the figure currents will be too weak.

It would, however, be an ambiguous statement if we were to say that the distribution of electrotonus in the tissue agrees with that of the current by which it was first established. In this statement the current would be regarded as an independent cause and the electrotonus condition as its effect. Actually, since in the electrotonic state the tissue no longer offers the same conditions for the spread of the current as it did in the beginning, the current itself will now be affected by the electrotonus which it has just caused. In other words, under the influence of satiation the distribution of the current will presently change. When this happens its further electrotonic effects will of course also be shifted, and so forth. Thus, while we inspect a figure its current can never be strictly stationary. It will always "glide" from an initial distribution to slightly different ones, and if inspection is continued for a long time the change may become conspicuous. Our discussions in Chapter Five allow us to predict in what direction the change must occur. Under the influence of its own electrotonic effects a current will be deflected into regions which so far have been less affected. In this fashion satiation must tend to assume a more even distribution than corresponds to the original distribution of the current. We can easily recognize that this behavior of figure currents and of satiation must have important consequences. The foremost among these consists in the fact that the electrotonic action of currents will always limit itself. For, the more intense satiation becomes in a given place the more current will be withdrawn from this place so that here further satiation proceeds more and more slowly.

The fact that any current in the tissue is bound to weaken itself by electrotonic action will have to be given full attention when attempts are made to register such currents. If figure currents actually exist it cannot be very difficult to demonstrate their occurrence and thus to verify our principal assumption. Both direct-current amplifiers and extremely sensitive voltmeters have been constructed which ought to make such tests feasible. The records, however, could hardly be just like those of ordinary direct currents. Rather, upon the appearance of a figure in the visual field, a kind of on-effect may be expected because as a consequence of electrotonus the first full intensity of the current could be maintained only for a short time. After this initial stage the flow would be reduced to lower intensities.[8]

The description of electrotonic action which has been given in these paragraphs may not be complete. Judging from physiological evidence it seems quite possible that electrotonus not only affects given currents but also establishes currents of its own. In our discussions this possibility will not be pursued but in a further development of the theory it may become necessary to do so.

A much more remote possibility should at least be mentioned because it might be regarded as the starting point for a rival theory of satiation. For reasons which nerve physiologists will fully appreciate, we look upon the following argument with the greatest reserve. According to our theory satiation is caused by figure currents which are not to be identified with the migrating currents of nerve impulses. But could not these migrating currents have similar effects? It will be remembered that in the theory of Gerard and Libet each soma of a cortical layer is a galvanic element from which, however, hardly any current can issue so long as the whole dense layer consists of similar elements. Only when at some place the cortical elements lose their potentials will an

---

[8] We once tried to establish electrotonus in the visual cortex from the outside. Two points of the skull—above one occipital lobe—were connected with the poles of a direct-current source. When, with one subject, fairly strong currents were used the visual field seemed to be affected on the opposite side. But we give no weight to this observation because it ought not to be repeated. For two weeks afterwards the subject suffered from a persistent headache and a disturbing state of depression.

appreciable flow originate; and then this flow will circle around the boundary between the intact layer and that particular place. Now, at least in a formal way the same situation exists when more or less synchronized impulses travel in a number of parallel nerve fibers. At a given moment a certain stretch in each fiber behaves like a galvanic element. The corresponding current in its temporary location is the electric phase of the nerve impulse. But, if the impulses of all other fibers in the neighborhood have just reached about the same level, the whole region will consist of galvanic elements in a parallel arrangement. As a result only a weak flow will be possible through and around each fiber, and this weak flow, the impulse, will be propagated as the location of the potentials shifts along the fibers. Suppose, however, that as a consequence of differential stimulation in the periphery some among the parallel fibers are not active at a given level when impulses pass this level in other fibers. If we still apply the views of Gerard and Libet, and if we have enough confidence in the nature of nerve impulses *qua* currents, we might say that now these currents can spread more freely and assume a higher intensity. For from each active element the flow of the impulse will extend into the inactive region and then return to its element. Thus, the current as a whole will circle around the boundary between the two regions; it will in this form travel in the direction of the fibers; and again in this form it will arrive in a ganglionic layer. Upon arrival, however, it will have an electrotonic effect upon this layer and, as impulses follow one another at a considerable rate, such effects will accumulate until a fair degree of electrotonus is established. The distribution of the current will determine the pattern of its electrotonic action. Obviously, this pattern will more or less agree with the one which we have derived from our different premise. It is this possibility which we had in mind when we admitted that satiation within and around specific entities could perhaps be derived from the action of nerve impulses. We hasten to add that this alternative explanation appears to us extraordinarily bold. Against all accepted notions it assumes that the electric flow of a nerve impulse depends upon conditions at a considerable distance from its fiber. Also, the explanation seems to be at variance with the All or None Law. At least in terms of actual flow—as distinguished from voltage—the intensity of a nerve impulse would vary whenever the activity in neighboring fibers changes. Thus nerve impulses would be relationally determined in a fashion for which there seems to be no experimental evidence. Incidentally,

if this hypothesis should ever be defended it would not actually contradict our own theory. For logically, both assumptions could be correct; i. e., satiation could be established in one way *and* the other.

3. Once the electrotonic state has been thoroughly established by a figure current, any further flow in the same region will no longer have the characteristics which it would otherwise have. Owing to the persistency of electrotonus these alterations of subsequent currents must be demonstrable for some time. It is our explanation of figural after-effects that, when inspection of an *I*-object has caused electrotonus of sufficient strength, the currents of *T*-figures are so affected, and that the after-effects are symptoms of this fact. At present we propose to use these effects for a few tests to which our theory of figure currents and of satiation ought to be subjected. No actual theory of figural after-effects will be needed for this limited purpose. It will suffice to assume that they are caused by electrotonus.

In the first place, we have just come to the conclusion that electrotonic action of figure currents will always limit itself. According to our theory, therefore, if figural after-effects are caused by that action they will appear after comparatively short periods of inspection; they will then grow more conspicuous at a slower rate; and they will eventually reach a maximum beyond which they cannot be enhanced by any amount of further inspection. This conclusion agrees not only with all our own observations in this field but also with certain experiments of Gibson who tested one of his effects after varying periods of inspection and found precisely the development which has just been described (cf. 9, pp. 459 ff.).

Secondly, the degree of all electrotonic action depends upon the intensity of the polarizing current. This current, on the other hand, is proportional to the electromotive forces which maintain the flow. And the electromotive forces of figure currents grow with the brightness difference between the figure and its ground. It follows that, other conditions being the same, a figural after-effect must be stronger if the brightness difference between the *I*-figure and its ground is increased. This inference was verified in the following differential experiment. On both sides of the fixation mark, on a white screen, outline oblongs of identical size and shape were shown as *I*-objects. The outline of one was black while that of the other was drawn in a light grey which, from a distance of three yards, could still be easily distinguished from the white ground. The *T*-objects were four equal outline squares in the usual arrangement.

After an inspection period of four minutes the

two pairs of *T*-objects were found to differ as expected. On the side of the black oblong the distance of the squares was clearly shorter, and the squares themselves were smaller. The same differential effect was observed when we used *solid I*-figures the brightness levels of which corresponded to those of the outline oblongs in our first observation. A curious phenomenon, which the *I*-patterns of these experiments exhibit at first sight, will be discussed in the last chapter.

Thirdly, it can make no essential difference whether the *I*-figure is shown dark on a bright ground or bright on a dark ground. The electromotive forces must be the same although in the second case their direction must be reversed. This merely reverses the direction of the current; but apart from that the spatial distribution of the flow will remain about the same. Its electrotonic action will therefore also occur in the same distribution, and as a result similar aftereffects must be observed in the two situations. We here presuppose that in both cases the brightness relation between figure and ground is the same in the *T*-figure as it is in the *I*-object. Our prediction agrees with Gibson's observations. It has also been verified in numerous experiments of our own. White objects on a dark ground give figural after-effects of the same kind as dark objects on a white ground. As a single exception we may mention that, while with dark outline figures on a white ground the dark *T*-object tends to look too grey, i.e., too bright, with white lines on a dark ground the "color effect" is not that the white *T*-lines are darker. Rather, in a satiated area, these lines appear "weakened" or too thin.

We may now turn to a fourth point to which we attribute particular significance for our theory. In Chapter Five we mentioned that after prolonged flow of a current in the tissue the electrotonic condition at anodes, the anelectrotonus, becomes more and more predominant. At this stage anelectrotonus means an obstruction for all test currents, irrespective of their direction. Now, if figural after-effects are caused by electrotonus they must be caused mainly by anelectrotonus in this advanced stage. It follows that such figural after-effects will be observed whether the direction of the *T*-currents is that of the *I*-currents or the opposite. But, as we said in the preceding paragraph, the direction of a figure current will be reversed if the brightness relation between the figure and the ground is reversed. Thus we are led to conclude that if, for instance, an *I*-figure is given black on white and the corresponding *T*-figure white on black, we must obtain the same figural after-effect as though the *T*-figure were also black on white. Actually, Gibson mentions observations in which this was the case. In our own experience after-effects were

under these circumstances about as strong as they usually are. Only the color symptom must again be mentioned as an exception: when, after inspection of a black outline figure on a white ground a white outline figure on a black ground served as a *T*-object, the white lines of this object were never affected. Their color was the same as that of neutral comparison lines. This observation is particularly interesting because it shows once more that other symptoms of satiation are independent of the color effect. We wish to emphasize that this holds also for the "depth effect" which remains as conspicuous under the present conditions as it is when brightness relations in the *I*-pattern and in the *T*-pattern are the same.

We can go one step farther. Physiological investigation has shown that even alternating currents cause the electrotonic conditions so long as the number of the cycles is not too high. Direct test currents are afterwards affected more or less as though a direct current of a certain intensity had previously passed through the tissue. The obvious inference is that if *during the inspection period* the direction of a figure current is often reversed we must still obtain about the same after-effects as though the direction of that current had been constant. Now, the figure current assumes the opposite direction whenever we reverse the brightness relation between the *I*-figure and its ground. According to our theory figural after-effects must therefore still be observed if during the inspection period a dark *I*-figure on a bright ground alternates with an identical bright *I*-figure on a dark ground.

References

1. Bales, J. F., and Follansbee, G. L. 1935. The after-effect of the perception of curved lines. *Jour. Exper. Psychol.* 18:499–503.
2. Brown, G. G. 1928. Perception of depth with disoriented vision. *Brit. Jour. Psychol.* 19:117–146.
3. Craik, K. J. W., and Zangwill, O. L. 1939. Observations relating to the threshold of a small figure within the contour of a closed-line figure. *Brit. Jour. Psychol.* 30:139–150.
4. Ebbecke, U. 1933. Zur Lehre vom Elektrotonus. *Ergebnisse Physiol. u. exper. Pharmakol.* 35:756–826.
5. Gerard, R. W., and Libet, B. 1940. The control of normal and "convulsive" brain potentials. *Amer. Jour. Psychiat.* 96:1125–1153.
6. Gerard, R. W. 1941. The interaction of neurones. *Ohio Jour. Sci.,* 41:160–172.
7. Gibson, J. J. 1933. Adaptation, after-effect, and contrast in the perception of curved lines. *Jour. Exper. Psychol.* 16:1–31.
8. ———. 1934. Vertical and horizontal orien-

tation in visual perception (Abstract). *Psychol. Bull.* 31:739.

9. ———, and Radner, M. 1937. Adaptation, after-effect, and contrast in the perception of tilted lines. I. Quantitative studies. *Jour. Exper. Psychol.* 20:453–467.

10. Gibson, J. J. 1937. Adaptation, after-effect, and contrast in the perception of tilted lines. II. Simultaneous contrast and the areal restriction of the after-effect. *Jour. Exper. Psychol.* 20:553–569.

11. ———, and Mowrer, O. H. 1938. Determinants of the perceived vertical and horizontal. *Psychol. Rev.* 45:300–323.

12. Henle, M. 1942. An experimental investigation of past experience as a determinant of visual form perception. *Jour. Exper. Psychol.* 30:1–21.

13. Klein, H. 1936. Versuche über die Wahrnehmung. *Zeitschr. Psychol.* 138:1–34.

14. Knox, H. W. 1894. On the quantitative determination of an optical illusion. *Amer. Jour. Psychol.* 6:413–420.

15. Köhler, W. 1920. Die physischen Gestalten in Ruhe und im stationären Zustand. Braunschweig, Vieweg.

16. ———. 1938. The place of value in a world of facts. Liveright.

17. ———. 1940. Dynamics in psychology. Liveright.

18. Lewis, E. O. 1912. The illusion of filled and unfilled space. *Brit. Jour. Psychol.* 5:36–51.

19. Libet, B., and Gerard, R. W. 1941. Steady potential fields and neurone activity. *Jour. Neuro-physiol.* 4:438–455.

20. Lorente De Nó, R. 1939. Transmission of impulses through cranial motor nuclei. *Jour. Neuro-physiol.* 2:402–464.

21. Ponzo, M. 1913. Rapports entre quelque illusions visuelles de contraste angulaire et l'appréciation de grandeur des astres à l'horizon. *Arch. Ital. Biol.* 58:327–329.

22. Rubin, E. 1921. Visuell wahrgenommene Figuren. Copenhagen, Gyldendalske.

23. Sickles, W. R. 1942. Experimental evidence for the electrical character of visual fields derived from a quantitative analysis of the Ponzo illusion. *Jour. Exper. Psychol.* 30:84–91.

24. ———, and Hartmann, G. W. 1942. The theory of order. *Psychol. Rev.* 49:403–421.

25. Smith, K. U., and Akelaitis, A. J. 1942. Studies on the corpus callosum. I. Laterality in behavior and bilateral motor organization in man before and after section of the corpus callosum. *Arch. Neurol. and Psychiat.* 47:519–543.

26. Spiegel, H. G. 1937. Über den Einfluss des Zwischenfeldes auf gesehene Abstände. *Psychol. Forsch.* 21:327–383.

27. Verhoeff, F. H. 1925. A theory of binocular perspective. *Amer. Jour. Physiol. Opt.* 6:436.

28. Vernon, M. D. 1934. The perception of inclined lines. *Brit. Jour. Psychol.* 25:186–196.

29. Wertheimer, M. 1912. Experimentelle Studien über das Sehen von Bewegung. *Zeitschr. Psychol.* 61:161–265.

30. Woodworth, R. S. 1938. Experimental psychology. Henry Holt.

PERCEPTUAL CONSTANCY

Some views of perception, e.g., Gestalt theory, place great weight on innate (inborn or unlearned) organization and integration of sensory input. Other views place great emphasis on learning as a factor in this integration and organization. The view, sometimes called "transactional functionalism," presented in this excerpt states that people bring certain learned assumptions to any perceptual situation. These assumptions, the *weights* given to different *cues* for depth, size, shape, etc., have been learned because they provide an accurate (veridical) picture of the world. These assumptions are often considered to be the basis of the constancies. The transactional functionalist view states that we have perceptual constancy because we unconsciously impose our assumptions upon the sensory input.

The assumptions are illustrated indirectly in this excerpt. When they are made to work against an accurate (veridical) visual experience their action produces some remarkable illusions.

Points to guide your study
1. Refer to Chart I often in your reading.
2. If the assumptions are learned, would you expect *all* people to see the same illusions? Would you expect some people to see the rod bend, while others see it as breaking through the window?

35. VISUAL PERCEPTION AND THE ROTATING TRAPEZOIDAL WINDOW

Adelbert Ames, Jr.*

Description of apparatus

The apparatus used in this demonstration was designed to enable observers experiencing the demonstration to perceive certain characteristic alterations of visual phenomena that result from varying the trapezoidal form of a rotating window.[1]

A photograph of the apparatus is shown in Figure 1. It consists of the rectangular window (see RW) suspended by a vertical shaft S^1, which is driven by an electric motor M, which is attached to the ceiling. The trapezoidal window TW is suspended on the vertical shaft S^2, which is rigidly fixed to the bottom of the window RW. On this shaft there is a sleeve F with two lock nuts so that the two windows can be set at any desired angle relative to each other. All the altered appearances can be seen irrespective of the relative angles between the two windows, but comparisons of alteration in size are more easily made when they are set in the general relative positions to each other shown in Figure 2. When the motor is going, the rectangular window and the trapezoidal window rotate at the same speed about a common vertical axis. This arrangement enables the observer to compare the appearances of the two windows and note what alterations in his visual phenomena

* Adelbert Ames, Jr. Visual perception and the rotating trapezoidal window. *Psychol. Monogr.*, 1951, **65** (whole no. 324). Copyright 1951 by the American Psychological Association. Excerpts reprinted here with permission from the American Psychological Association. References and several footnotes omitted.

[1] The significance of what is disclosed in an empirical investigation primarily depends upon the nature of the factor the experimenter selects to vary. It therefore seems important to explain why it was decided to vary the trapezoidal form of a rectangular configuration and, also, why the particular variation of the trapezoidal form was adopted. As this explanation is of necessity lengthy and would unduly interrupt the description of the demonstration, it seems advisable to add it as an appendix.

result from variation of the trapezoidal form of the rectangular window.

The speed of the motor M can be controlled by a rheostat. A convenient speed for most observations is around 3 to 6 rpm. It is also desirable to have a switch so that the motion of the windows can be stopped at any desired position of rotation. The direction of the rotation of the shaft S can be reversed by a device on the motor controlled by a string pull.

Small cubes C and C are attached to the upper edge of the shorter side of the trapezoidal window and in a corresponding position on the rectangular window, and paper tubes T and T are attached in the middle of both windows so that they extend out on both sides (see Figure 1 and Chart I). The role these cubes and tubes play will become evident later.

The dimensions of the two windows are given in the caption of Figure 1. The trapezoidal window is cut out of thin aluminum. Its particular dimensions were arrived at as shown in Figure 2. AB represents the three-dimensional rectangular window tipped at an angle of $16\frac{1}{2}°$ to the line of sight of an observer at the distance of 10 feet with the right-hand side farther away; CD represents a plane tipped at an angle of $22°$ to the line of sight, with the right-hand side nearer. $A'B'$ represents the aluminum cutout of the projection of the window AB on the plane CD.

The projections of the shadows cast on the actual window by an overhead light are painted on both sides of this trapezoidal cutout. The trapezoidal window should be equally illuminated on both sides with low illumination in an otherwise dark room.

The alterations in visual phenomena that are related to the variation of the trapezoidal form of a window are empirically demonstrated by the differences between what observers with normal vision see when looking at the rotating rectangular window with its small cube and tube and when looking at the rotating trapezoidal window with its small cube and tube.

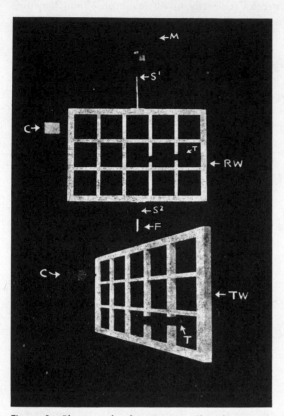

Figure 1   Photograph of apparatus. The photograph was taken with the surfaces of the rectangular window and the trapezoidal window in the same plane, which was perpendicular to the optical axis of the camera. The dimensions of the rectangular window are: length, 23½"; height, 16½"; thickness ¼"; width of outside frame ½"; width of mullions, ¼". The outside dimensions of the trapezoidal window are: length 19½"; height of long side, 23⅝"; height of short side, 12½"; thickness, ⅛".

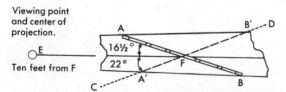

Viewing point
and center of
projection.

Ten feet from F

Figure 2   Plan showing design of the Trapezoidal Window. AB represents the Rectangular Window set at an angle of 16½° to the line of sight EF ten feet from viewing point E. A′B′ represents the Trapezoidal Window which is a projection from E of the Rectangular Window and its mullions on a plane CD tipped 22° to the line of sight EF.

Description of what observers experience when looking at the rotating trapezoidal window and appended cube and tube

The reader must realize that the phenomena disclosed by the demonstration can be comprehended only when they are personally experienced and that the following verbal and pictorial description of them can at best be only a second-hand communication. Moreover, the full significance of these phenomena can only be comprehended as they are related to other phenomena disclosed by the other demonstrations. However, described in general terms, all observers with normal vision, when looking at the rectangular window slowly rotating about a vertical axis, see a rectangular window of constant size and form at a constant distance rotating at a constant speed about a vertical axis, and the small cube and tube appear and move with it in an expected manner, and this holds irrespective of the distance, direction, or elevation from which they look, or whether they use one eye or two.

On the other hand, described in general terms, observers with normal vision, when looking (with both eyes from a distance of around 25 feet, or with one eye from nearer distances) at a trapezoidal window slowly rotating about a vertical axis, see a rectangular window of continually changing size and form oscillating at a continually varying speed through only a sector of a complete circle of revolution. They see the small cube sailing around the trapezoidal window and the tube bending at certain positions of revolution of the window.[2] However, these appearances are altered if the observer varies the distance, the direction, or the elevation from which he looks, and if he uses both eyes instead of one at near distance.

Detailed descriptions of the various appearances of the rotating trapezoidal window will now be taken up.

1. *Description of apparent movements both in direction and speed of the rotating trapezoidal window without the cube or tube, observed from a distance of about 10 feet with one eye at the level of the middle of the trapezoidal window.* As the trapezoidal window slowly rotates about a vertical axis, instead of appearing to rotate completely around, it appears to oscillate back and forth through an angle of about

[2] The above appearances are perhaps those most commonly experienced by most observers and for purposes of communication it will be those appearances that will be dwelt upon. However, not only are different appearances reported by different individuals, but the appearances reported by any one individual can be altered by varying either "subjective" or "objective" factors. F. P. Kilpatrick has been investigating these phenomena.

100°. An understanding of the nature of this movement may be obtained from a study of Chart I. In the lower left-hand corner of the chart is a drawing in elevation of the trapezoidal window, the shorter side being designated by the letter A and the longer side by the letter B. In the four rows of figures in the chart the letters A and B and the heavy solid lines show a series of the actual positions of the short and long sides of the trapezoidal window AB as it is rotated in the direction indicated by arrows about a vertical axis through a full revolution, the last figure in the row showing the complete rotation. The letters A' and B' and the light solid lines show the apparent position of the short and long sides of the trapezoidal window. The top row of figures shows by the heavy solid lines marked AB, a series of the actual positions of the window (AB). The second row (II) shows by the light solid lines marked A'B' the apparent localization of the window at each of the positions shown in Row I, the last figure in the row showing the apparent oscillating movement.

By comparing the apparent positions shown in Row II with the actual positions shown in Row I, it can be seen that as the window rotates in a counterclockwise direction, it appears to move in the same direction as it is actually moving, but lags behind, appearing to move more slowly. When the window has rotated 90° (see third figure in Row I), it appears to have rotated only about 50° (see A'B', third figure, Row II). As the window rotates farther than 90°, it ap-

pears very slowly to reverse its direction of rotation (see fourth figures in both Rows I and II). From then on it appears to rotate in a reverse direction to its actual rotation until the window reaches a position normal to the line of sight (see ninth figures in Rows I and II). From then on it appears to move in the direction of the actual rotation until it reaches its starting position (compare first and eleventh figures in both Rows I and II).

The region of the apparent oscillating movement is shown in the last figure, Row II. The short side of the trapezoid appears to move from A' to A' and the long side from B' to B'. No part of the window ever appears to enter into the areas included between A'B' and A'B'. The angle of apparent oscillation with the particular trapezoidal form used is about 100°. The point of actual rotation where the apparent rotation starts to reverse is when the window is normal to the line of sight and thus subtends the largest visual angle.

The apparent speed of movement varies greatly from the actual speed. As the window approaches a position normal to the line of sight, it appears to slow up gradually, come to a dead stop, remain stopped for an appreciable length of time, and then slowly to reverse its direction of movement.

2. *Description of apparent alterations of shape and size of trapezoidal window when observed with one eye from a distance of about 10 feet, eye at the same level as middle of window.* As the trapezoidal window slowly rotates

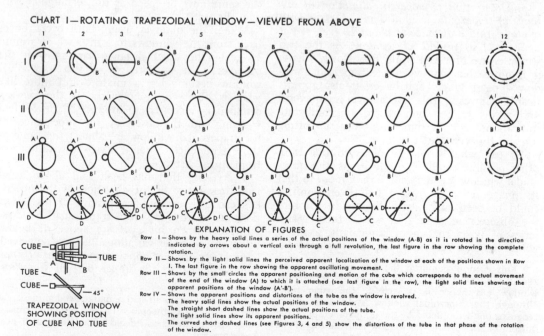

Chart I—Rotating Trapezoidal Window viewed from above.

about a vertical axis, it appears as a rectangular window,[3] but it appears to be continually changing in both shape and size. These alterations are made very apparent by comparing them to the shape and size of the rectangular window just above, which remain constant. This comparison can be best made when the trapezoidal window is positioned on its supporting rod so that it is at an angle of about 38° to the rectangular window above it. When the two windows are turned so the observer's line of sight makes an angle of about 16° to the rectangular window (see Figure 2) with the shorter side of the trapezoidal window A toward the observer, the trapezoidal window appears to be in the same plane and of the same shape and size as the rectangular window, as is shown in Figure 3.

On the other hand, when the two windows are turned so that the trapezoidal window is positioned to subtend a slightly smaller angle, it appears in the same plane as the rectangular window, but it appears much shorter and gives the impression of being smaller, as is shown in Figure 4. And when the two windows are turned so that the trapezoidal window is approximately positioned as shown in the second figure of Row I of the chart, it again appears in much the same plane as the rectangular window, but in this case it appears much longer than the rectangular window and gives the impression of being larger, as is shown in Figure 5. In intermediate positions of rotation the trapezoidal window appears of intermediate shapes and sizes.

3. *Description of apparent alteration of distance of trapezoidal window when observed with one eye from a distance of about 10 feet, eye at same level as middle of window.* As the two windows are observed while they slowly rotate, it is noticeable that when the trapezoidal window appears longer and larger, it also appears nearer. However, this appearance is equivocal and seems to be counteracted by conflicting indications such as those from the supporting rod and the rectangular window.

To test what would be observed free from other possible conflicting indications, the trapezoidal window was set up in a dark room so that its image reflected from a half-silvered mirror could be seen uniocularly directly in front of the observer in a field in which there was a series of posts that were binocularly seen, by which the observer could judge the apparent dis-

tance of the uniocularly seen trapezoidal window. The window was first set so that it appeared longer and larger and then set so that it appeared shorter and smaller. Only preliminary observations were made, but for two observers it appeared nearer when it appeared longer and larger, and farther away when it appeared shorter and smaller, than the rectangular window.

4. *Description of the apparent movement and changes in shape and size of the trapezoidal window when viewed from a distance of about 10 feet with one eye from levels above or below the middle of the trapezoidal window.* Whether viewed from above or below the level of the middle of the trapezoidal window, the window appears to oscillate and change speed and shape and size just as it appears to do when viewed with the eyes at the level of the middle of the window. However, instead of appearing rectangular as it revolves, it appears in trapezium form, the amount of distortion being related to the angular distance of the viewing point above or below. Its vertical axis also appears to oscillate back and forth. And, further, in certain positions of revolution it appears somewhat curved.

5. *Description of the apparent movements and alterations in shape and size of the trapezoidal window when observed with two eyes from a distance of about 10 feet and from greater distances.* If at a near distance of around 10 feet both eyes are used, what is perceived is a variable mixture of the above-described appearances and the appearances of an actual trapezoidal window rotating in the same way and at the same rates of speed as the rectangular window above it.[4]

When the observer, using both eyes, moves back from the windows to a distance of around 15 feet (the exact distance varying with the observer), the appearances of the trapezoidal window become less a mixture and more like what is observed monocularly. If the viewing distance is increased to around 20 or 25 feet (varying with the observer), the appearances of the trapezoidal window are almost the same as those experienced when it is viewed with one eye from a near distance.

Everything that has been said above holds true irrespective of the elevation of the observer's eye or eyes, and irrespective of his lateral position relative to the trapezoidal window. However, when his eyes are above or below, other second-order variations also are perceived.

6. *Description of apparent movement of small cube attached to the upper part of the short*

---

[3] This is more definitely the case when the trapezoidal window is seen alone. When the rectangular window just above it is seen at the same time, although the trapezoidal window is still seen as rectangular, one is bothered by the nonparallelism of the bottom of the rectangular window and the top of the trapezoidal window.

[4] One observer who had a markedly dominant eye and very poor stereoscopic vision got the same appearance with two eyes as he did with one from a near viewing point.

side of the rotating trapezoidal window when observed with one eye from a distance of about 10 feet, eye at same height as middle of window. As the trapezoidal window slowly rotates from its position as shown in Figure 1, Row *I*, of Chart I, the cube which is attached by a wire as shown in the drawing in the lower left-hand corner of the chart, appears to leave its point of attachment and float through the air around the front of the window, returning to its original attached position just before the trapezoidal window reaches its position shown in Figure 11, Row *I*, Chart I. The apparent position of the cube relative to the apparent position of the rotating trapezoidal window is shown by the figures in Row *III* of the chart. Throughout its course, in which it appears to rotate once about its own vertical axis, the cube appears of relatively constant size and appears to be going at a relatively constant rate of speed.

7. *Description of apparent movement and distortion of the tube which is suspended through the lower middle pane of the trapezoidal window, when observed with one eye from a distance of about 10 feet, eye at same height as the middle of the window.* The tube is suspended tipped at an angle of about 45° to the plane of the window, as shown in the drawing in the lower left-hand corner of Chart I. The appearances to be described can be seen with the tube at any inclination to the window, but are possibly more marked when it is at the inclination shown in the drawing.

As the trapezoidal window slowly rotates from its position as shown by the heavy solid line A in Figure 1, Row *IV*, of the chart, the tube shown by the dotted line *CD* appears to swing around with the trapezoidal window until the window starts to reverse its direction of rotation. When this occurs, the tube and the window appear to be rotating in opposite directions, the tube apparently moving clockwise and the window apparently moving counterclockwise. The tube then appears to swing until the left side of the tube comes up against the mullions on the left of the window and the right side of the tube comes up against the mullions on the right of the window. Up to that position the tube appears straight, but from there on it appears to begin to bend (see dotted lines marked *C'D'* in Figure 3, Row *IV*, of chart) and seems to bend more and more (see dotted lines *C'D'* in Figures 4 and 5, Row *IV*, of chart). When the trapezoidal window gets in the position shown in Figure 6, Row *IV* (chart), the tube suddenly snaps straight again and for most observers remains straight during the remaining positions of revolutions shown in Figures 7, 8, and 9, of Row *IV* in Chart I.[5] The rate of movement of the tube also appears to change, as does its apparent length.

If the tube is set at right angles to the plane of the window instead of at an angle of 45°,

[5] There are a number of variations of these appearances.

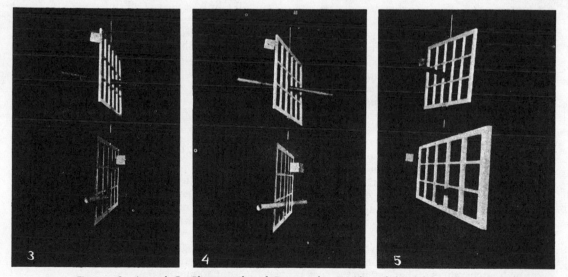

Figures 3, 4, and 5 Photographs of Rectangular Window (left and center) and Trapezoidal Window (right), showing the apparent differences of shape and size of trapezoidal window at different positions of its rotation. When in position shown in Figure 3, it appears approximately the same shape and size as the rectangular window. When in position shown in Figure 4, it appears shorter. When in position shown in Figure 5, it appears longer and larger.

it appears to bend and straighten out through the same sections of its rotation described above, although it starts to bend a little later and does not appear to bend quite so much. If the direction of rotation of the window is reversed, to many observers the tube appears bent in that section of its revolution where it appeared straight when it was revolving in its original direction and straight in that section where it appeared bent.

When both eyes are used at a near distance, variations in the appearances of the cube or tube are observable. These variations are related to variations in the appearances of the window. When both eyes are used at distances of around 12 or 15 feet, this also holds. When both eyes are used at distances of around 20 or 25 feet, about the same appearances are observable as were seen at near distance with one eye.

When the window is looked at with the eye or eyes at a level slightly above or below the middle of the trapezoidal window, appearances similar to those described above are observed, but they become markedly different as the distance of observation above and below is greatly increased.

The observer sees all the above-described appearances when he looks at the trapezoidal window with the appended tube and cube. If he looks at the rectangular window with its tube and cube, the appearances are quite different. The rectangular window appears constant in form, size, and movement; its cube appears at a constant relative position; its tube appears at a constant relative position, shape, and size; and none of these aspects changes when two eyes are used or when point of view changes in direction or in level. Of course, the subjective sense of the positioning of the window and its distance alters with its rotation and with the change of the point of view either in distance or direction or level.

8. *Description of apparent movements and alterations in shape and size of the trapezoidal window and of the cube and tube when viewed from different distances and different directions.* With variation of the distance of observation, the only marked alteration of all of the above-described appearances is in respect to the apparent changes in size of the trapezoidal window. At greater viewing distances the apparent alterations in size of the rotating trapezoidal window are greater.

With variation of the observer's tangential point of view there is no alteration of the above-described appearances. That is, irrespective of the direction from which he looks he will see the same oscillation, changes in shape and size of the trapezoidal window, movement of the small cube, and bending of the tube.

Although a given observer looking at the ro-

tating trapezoidal window from different tangential points of view will perceive certain definite phenomenal happenings (i.e., the oscillating window, the flying cube, and the bending tube), it is important to note that the visual happening he sees from a particular viewpoint at a particular moment he *would not* see at that same moment if he were at another point of view. What he sees can be seen only at one particular moment from one particular point of view.

This also holds if the trapezoidal window is stationary and the observer is looking at it as he walks around it. As he walks around it, he will see all the phenomenal happenings he would see if he stood still and the window rotated. But the visual experiences he sees from one point of view can be seen only from that point of view. No other observer walking around with him can see what he sees at the same moment he sees it. So a number of observers standing around the rotating trapezoidal window at the same distance from its axis will all perceive the same visual happenings occurring, *but no two* of the observers will see the same visual happenings occurring at the same moment.

While it is clear that what each observer sees is determined by his viewpoint both in space and time, there are certain aspects of what each observer sees that are the same from any point of view at all times and for all other observers at other points of view and at other times. For example, the rectangular appearance of the trapezoidal window and the form and size of its small cube remain constant for all observers from all points of view at all times.

When the rectangular window is viewed from different distances and different directions, quite different phenomena occur. Irrespective of the distance or direction from which the rectangular window is viewed, the visual happenings an observer sees from a particular viewpoint at a particular moment he would see at the same moment if he were at another point of view. In other words, he would see a rectangular window of the same shape and size rotating at a constant rate of speed with the small cube in a constant relation to it and a tube of constant shape and length moving at a constant speed at the same moment, irrespective of his point of view. And a number of observers standing around the rotating rectangular window, irrespective of their distance, would perceive the same visual happenings occurring, *and all* observers would see the same visual happenings occurring at the same moment.

This concludes our attempt to communicate to the reader what he would have visually experienced if he himself had witnessed the demonstration. Next we will attempt to explain why one sees what he sees when looking at the rotating trapezoidal window, and why what he sees is so different from what he sees when he looks at the rotating rectangular window just above it. It is the same type of explanation that was formulated to account for the phenomena disclosed by the earlier, simpler demonstrations of the perception of the static aspects of the environment and of motion, and it seems adequately to account for the more complex phenomena described above. We have no illusion, however, that this account is the final word in the matter, but we present it because it seems to us the most intrinsically reasonable one that we can formulate at this time. Our hope is that its presentation will lead others to formulate still more intrinsically reasonable accounts.

Explanations of visual phenomena [6]

A. Explanation of the variations in appearance of the trapezoidal window. The appearances of the trapezoidal window give rise to many questions, among them the following:

1. Why does the trapezoidal window appear rectangular in shape?

2. Why does the rotating trapezoidal window appear to oscillate instead of rotate? Why does the trapezoidal window never appear to be where it actually is?

3. Why does the trapezoidal window, which is moving at a constant rate, appear to be moving at different rates?

4. Why does the trapezoidal window, which is constant in shape, appear of changing shapes?

5. Why does the trapezoidal window, which is constant in size, appear to be of changing size?

6. Why does the trapezoidal window appear rectangular when the eye or eyes are at the level of the middle of the window, but of trapezium form and sometimes curved when the eye or eyes are at other levels?

7. Why, when viewed with both eyes from a distance of around 24 feet (which is well within the distance at which stereoscopic vision is effective), does the trapezoidal window appear essentially the same as it appears with one eye?

It would seem apparent that there is no possibility of accounting for these appearances in causal terms of interactional effects between the objective phenomena and subjective appearances. The so-called "objective factor" that is varied is the trapezoidal shape of a rectangular window,

i.e., making one side of a rectangular window longer and the other shorter. Among the many subjective appearances related to this variation is an alteration of the appearance of length and size. To say that it was caused by change in the trapezoidal form of the "object" in no way helps us to account for the apparent change in length and size. The obscurities that give rise to the above questions can be cleared up only by taking into account more particulars, i.e., other phenomenal processes that play a role in the situation, and understanding the nature of their relationships. This we shall attempt to do.

In what has been said so far, mention has been made of only two aspects of the situation: one, the characteristics of what the observer looks at, i.e., the so-called "objective" revolving trapezoidal window; the other, what the observer visually perceives. It is well known that there are many other phenomenal processes involved in every visual situation, among which is the physiological stimulus pattern that plays the role of relating the "objective" window and its subjective visual awareness.

As an aid in helping the reader understand the role played by the observer's physiological stimulus processes, we will introduce the use of a large artificial eye consisting of a lens corresponding to the dioptric system of the eye and a ground glass marked off in rectangular squares, corresponding to the retina. If this is set up pointing towards the trapezoidal window, the observer can see on the ground glass, stimulus patterns of the same characteristics that exist on his retina when he looks at the trapezoidal window. If this artificial eye is set up at the same level as the middle of the trapezoidal window, he will note as the window revolves that: (a) the image on the ground glass goes through a series of varying trapezoidal forms; (b) the pattern on the ground glass is never rectangular; (c) there is no change in speed or oscillation of the trapezoidal pattern corresponding to the apparent change in speed or oscillation of the trapezoidal window; and (d) there is no change in form or size of the trapezoidal pattern corresponding to the apparent change in form and size of the trapezoidal window.

It is apparent that a knowledge of the characteristics of these stimulus patterns in themselves does not help us in understanding why the observer sees what he does when he looks at the rotating trapezoidal window.

Let us, then, try to see if a knowledge of the characteristics of a stimulus pattern will help us in understanding what we see when we look at the rectangular window. Let us point the artificial eye at the rectangular window and note the characteristics of the images formed on the ground-glass retina by the rectangular window.

[6] The explanations of the significances of the phenomena can at best be only partial explanations. For a more complete explanation, it is necessary to take account of other phenomena which are not disclosed by the demonstration now being considered, such as action, purpose, value, and emergent value-quality, which are beyond the scope of this paper.

It will be noted that these images have the same general characteristics as the images of the trapezoidal window, although the appearances of the rectangular window are different from those of the trapezoidal window, as has been pointed out. It is evident that a knowledge of the characteristics of our stimulus pattern considered in connnection with a knowledge of the object viewed and our perceptual awarenesses alone do not suffice to provide us with an answer to our questions.

Where shall we turn? Apparently a question we can ask gives us a lead, namely: "Why, when we look at the rectangular window, do we see a rectangular window, when the characteristics of its images formed on our retina are trapezoidal?" This question has extra significance because when we look at the trapezoidal window we see it, also, as rectangular, which means that the perceived rectangular form does not come from either the stimulus pattern or the object. If it does not come from the stimulus pattern or the object, whence does it come? This same question has occurred with all our previous demonstrations. In each case the most profitable and reasonable answer lay in bringing into consideration the past experience of the observer, and that consideration appears to be equally reasonable and profitable in this instance.

In his past experience the observer, in carrying out his purposes, has on innumerable occasions had to take into account and act with respect to rectangular forms, e.g., going through doors, locating windows, etc. On almost all such occasions, except in the rare case when his line of sight was normal to the door or window, the image of the rectangular configuration formed on his retina was trapezoidal. He learned to interpret the particularly characterized retinal images that exist when he looks at doors, windows, etc., as rectangular forms. Moreover, he learned to interpret the particular degree of trapezoidal distortion of his retinal images in terms of the positioning of the rectangular form to his particular viewing point. These interpretations do not occur at the conscious level; rather, they are unconscious and may be characterized as *assumptions* as to the probable significance of indications received from the environment. A person's perception thus provides him with an awareness not only of the form of the "thing" he is looking at, i.e., "what it is," but also "where it is" relative to his viewing point.

Let us now take into account past experience in explaining what the observer sees when he is looking at the revolving rectangular window. Suppose the rectangular window is in an edge-on position when it starts to revolve. When it has turned a little, the image formed by its farther side will be shorter than that formed by its nearer side. The retinal image will be trapezoidal, the particular difference in length of its sides being determined by the length of the window and the observer's distance from it. As the window revolves, the lengths of the two sides will become more and more nearly the same until the window is normal to his line of sight, when they will be equal. Then the side which was the far side will become longer and reach its greatest relative length when at its nearest to the observer, i.e., when the window is in an edge-on position. As the window turns farther, the image of the now nearer side will decrease and the image of the farther side increase until the completion of the revolution. The observer interprets these changes in trapezoidal form as changes of position and interprets the continuing changes of position as a rotation of a rectangular window.

It would seem that the above begins to provide a basis for understanding why an observer sees what he does when he looks at the rotating trapezoidal window. Suppose the trapezoidal window starts rotating from the position shown in Figure 1, Row I, Chart I, when its shorter side *A* is farther away and the longer side *B* nearer. When it has turned a little (see Figure 2, Row II, Chart I), the image formed by the farther side *A* will be shorter than that formed by its nearer side *B*. This difference in length is greater than the difference in length of the images of the far and near sides of the rectangular window above it. As it revolves, the image formed by the far side *A* will increase in length and that of the near side *B* decrease. But their relative change will not be as great as that of the images of a rectangular window at the same inclination. So the trapezoidal window will not appear to rotate so far or fast as the rectangular window above it, which is moving at a constant speed. When the trapezoidal window has rotated to a position normal to the line of sight, with the short side *A* to the left (see Figure 3, Row I, Chart I), the image of its side *A* will still be shorter than the image of its side *B*, so it appears tipped back on the left in the position shown in Figure 3, Row II, Chart I. This is as far forward as the short side ever appears to come. With further rotation the vertical dimension of the image of the side *A* will increase in length and that of the side *B* decrease. But the image of the short side *A* of the trapezoidal window can never become longer than that of the long side *B*, and so it can never be seen as nearer. However, this could not explain why the trapezoidal window appears to reverse its direction.

The explanation of the reversing phenomenon is apparently as follows: As the trapezoidal window starts to rotate from the position shown in Figure 3, Row *I*, Chart I, to those shown in Figures 5 and 6, Row *I*, Chart I, the total horizontal angle that the trapezoidal window subtends to the eye decreases. At the beginning of this decrease the trapezoidal window appears tipped back on the left (see Figure 3, Row *II*, Chart I). It has been learned from past experience with rectangular forms that a decrease of the total horizontal angle of our retinal images of a rectangularly perceived form which appears tipped away from us on the left could only take place if the side on the left went farther away. If it came nearer, the total horizontal angle of our retinal images would have to increase. So we interpret this decrease in the total horizontal dimension of our retinal stimulus pattern as a going-away of the left side of the window. That is, the window appears to reverse its direction of rotation, and as the left side of the window keeps coming towards us (see Figures 3 and 4, Row *I*, Chart I), it appears to be going farther away (see Figures 3 and 4, Row *II*, Chart I). A similar apparent reversal is seen to take place when the trapezoidal window has revolved to a position where the short side A is to the right (see Figure 9, Row *I*, Chart I). It is due to these apparent reversals that the trapezoidal window appears to oscillate instead of rotate.

The above considerations seem to furnish a reasonable explanation as to why the rotating trapezoidal window (*a*) appears rectangular in shape, (*b*) appears to oscillate instead of rotate, and (*c*) appears to move at varying rates.[7]

But we have not yet answered the question of why the trapezoidal window appears to change in form and size. A reasonable answer to these questions seems to be based on our making use of variation in the trapezoidal characteristics of our stimulus pattern as indications to positioning of a rectangular configuration. When looking at the rotating rectangular window, the varying trapezoidal stimulus patterns have particular characteristics which give us indications of the position of the window in its rotation. For instance, when looking at the rectangular window tipped at an angle of 45° to our line of sight, the trapezoidal pattern formed on our retina will be the same shape whether the right side or the left side of the window is nearer us, and we will relate the two patterns and rectangular configurations of the same size and shape but at different inclinations.

But when we look at the trapezoidal windows, what happens is quite different. When the trapezoidal window is tipped 45° to our line of sight with the longer side B nearer us (see Figure 2, Row *I*, Chart I), the shape of the trapezoidal image formed on our retina is quite different from that formed when the shorter side A is nearer us (see Figure 8, Row *I*, Chart I). When the longer side B is nearer, there is a greater difference in the relative lengths of the sides of the trapezoid which could only be produced either by a rectangular window of the same height at a nearer distance or by a longer rectangular window at the same distance. When the shorter side A is nearer us, there is a lesser difference in the relative lengths of the sides of the trapezoid, which could only be produced by a rectangular window of the same length at a greater distance or by a shorter rectangular window at the same distance.

Since there are a number of indications that the distance of the window remains constant as it rotates, we translate the difference in the trapezoidal pattern on the retinas into differences in perceived length so that when it is rotating, it appears to be continually changing shape. When the indications of distance are eliminated, as was done in the preliminary experiment noted previously, we see the trapezoidal window as nearer when the longer side B is nearer, and farther away when the shorter side A is nearer. These considerations seem to furnish a reasonable explanation of why the rotating trapezoidal window appears to change shape (question 4) and size (question 5).

We now turn to question 6: Why does the trapezoidal window appear rectangular when the eye or eyes are at the level of the middle of the window, but of trapezium form and sometimes curved when the eye or eyes are at other levels?

The answer to this question is apparently the following: When our eyes are at the level of the middle of the trapezoidal window, the trapezoidal patterns on our retinas are identical with those that could be produced by some rectangular window at some inclination at some distance. When they are above or below, our stimulus patterns for the trapezoidal window are not trapezoids but trapeziums which, although similar to, are different from, the trapezium patterns that exist on our retinas when we look at a rectangular window from above or below.

A conclusive explanation of these appearances will be possible only when by a mathematical analysis (projective geometry) it has been determined just how the two types of trapezium patterns differ. But it seems probable that the trapezium patterns from the trapezoidal window are sufficiently similar to those from the rec-

[7] These alterations of motion related to unaccustomed variations of the trapezoidal characteristic of the stimulus pattern are very similar to phenomena revealed by another of our demonstrations which has to do with the origin and nature of the perception of "radial motion," the movement of objects toward or away from us.

tangular window that we try to translate them into rectangular configurations even to the extent of seeing the window as curved. The apparent forward-and-back tipping of the trapezoidal window about a horizontal axis may be explained on the basis that the trapezium patterns are similar to those that would be produced by a rectangular window tipped about a horizontal axis.[8]

This brings us to the less significant question 7—why the trapezoidal window appears essentially the same when we use two eyes within distances at which stereoscopic vision is effective. The apparent answer is that in this situation we suppress the binocular cues and take account of the uniocular ones because uniocular cues result in perceptions which square better with what we have learned in past experience in dealing with windows. In other words, the uniocular cues have, on the basis of past experience greater prognostic reliability than do the binocular ones. This is confirmed by a number of our other demonstrations. It might also be well to note here that parallax indications of distances, achieved by lateral movement of the head, do give rise to secondary alterations in the appearances of the trapezoidal window. They, however, do not aid one in seeing the trapezoidal window *as* a trapezoid rotating at a constant speed.

B.   Explanation of the appearance of the small cube.[9]   The appearances of the cube give rise to at least the following questions:

1. Why does it appear to rotate in a circular path quite independently of the trapezoidal window to which it is attached?

2. Why does it appear to move at a relatively constant rate when the window to which it is attached oscillates at varying speeds?

3. How is it possible for it to appear sepa-

rated from the trapezoidal window to which it is attached?

To the first question an answer which may come quickly to one's mind is that we see the window move as it does for the reasons given in Chapter II, and we see the small cube rotate in a circle at relatively constant speed because that is how it is actually moving. But this answer is not quite satisfactory because the previous chapter has made it evident that the appearances we see are not determined by what we are looking at but by our interpretation of our stimulus patterns.

Perhaps a better answer for why the small cube appears as it does and seems to move as it does can be derived from the following considerations. In the previous chapter, to understand the appearance and movement of the trapezoidal window it was necessary first to understand that we saw the rectangular window appear and move as it does because we assumed it was rectangular and made use of the varying trapezoidal characteristics of our retinal images as indications of its varying positions. Our perceptions of the movement of the small cube have a similar origin and nature. Due to the characteristics of our retinal image produced by light rays reflected from the small cube, we assume its size and other characteristics. In its rotation as the cube comes towards us, its retinal image increases, and we assume it is coming nearer to us; as it goes away from us, its retinal image becomes smaller, and we assume it is going away. The variations in the sizes of the retinal images and the rate of their movement across our retina, although not uniform or constant in time, are nevertheless so translated, and the cube appears to be moving in a circular path at a relatively constant speed.[10]

Let us now consider the question as to how it is possible for the small cube to appear to separate itself from the trapezoidal window to which it is attached. What has been said above explains why, if the cube were not attached to the window (i.e., if the cube were just above the window), we would see them following separate paths. That the cube does appear to separate itself from the trapezoidal window to which it is most evidently attached can only be explained on the basis that the indications causing the trapezoidal window to appear to move as it does and the cube to move as it does are accepted as definite and unequivocal, and cues indicating otherwise are suppressed.

[8] In the apparatus as constructed, the objective factor that is varied is the trapezoidal form. The phenomena just described make it apparent that different and interesting alterations of perception would be experienced if the window were actually made in a trapezium form. Presumably, if such a form were observed with the eye or eyes at the level of the middle of the window, its appearances would be similar to those experienced when the trapezoidal window is observed with the eye or eyes above or below the level of the window, and more exaggerated appearances would be experienced if such a window were observed from other levels.

[9] The reason for using the small cube and the tube in connection with the rotating trapezoidal window demonstration was to determine if and how the appearance and behavior of objects would appear to be altered when "put together" in different ways with an objective configuration whose form was varied so that its appearance was altered.

[10] Why we see objects move in a circular path at a constant speed was given considerable study prior to the development of the Trapezoidal Window Demonstration. The Circular Motion Demonstration, which was devised as an aid to this study, is described in reference 17.

Various three-dimensional objects were substituted for the cube and were attached in different ways. They all appeared to behave in the same manner. However, two-dimensional objects such as playing cards and small sheets of paper attached to the upper side of the shorter end of the trapezoidal window may or may not appear to move with the window, depending on how they are attached.[11] Apparently the factors involved in these phenomena are of the same nature as those disclosed in our demonstration of Togetherness and Apartness.

C. Explanation of the appearance of the tube.

The appearances of the tube give rise to at least the following questions:

1. Why does it appear to rotate quite independently of the trapezoidal window to which it is attached?

2. Why does it appear to move at varying speeds and at speeds different from that of the trapezoidal window?

3. Why does it appear to bend and change length?

The answer to the first question has already been covered by the explanations as to why the cube appears to rotate in a circular path quite independently of the trapezoidal window to which it is attached.

The answer to the second question appears to be that the tube seems to move at varying speeds (which the cube did not) because it is seen "together" with the window in a way that causes the observer to take account of its motion in relation to the apparent motion of the trapezoidal window.

The answer to the third question involves the necessity of taking into account the phenomenon of overlay. Overlay is one of the numerous indications which we take into account in formulating our presumptions as to the distances of objects. If an object is so positioned that it overlays or cuts off part of another object, we presume that it is nearer and that the other object is farther away. As has been demonstrated, because of its high prognostic reliability, great weight is given this indication relative to the weight given other distance indications such as brightness, size, and parallax. With the rotating trapezoidal window and tube, this phenomenon of overlay comes into play.

As the window rotates we see the left half of the window overlaying the left part of the tube, and therefore in front of the tube, and the right part of the tube overlaying the right half of the window, and therefore in front of the window.

As described, the tube and the window appear to be rotating about the same axis in opposite directions. When their paths cross, the observer has to make an interpretation of the happenings that are occurring to the characteristics of his retinal stimulus pattern. There are various possible interpretations he could make. He might keep the tube straight and whole and the window straight and whole, but then we would have to stop their motion; or he might ignore his overlay indications and see gaps in the mullions of the window to let the tube pass through; or he might see the window bend. If he keeps the window and tube in motion and the window flat and whole, i.e., without gaps in it, he has to see the tube bend.[12] It is this last interpretation that is most commonly made with this particular configuration, and this what most observers see. With this interpretation one also sees the tube increase in length when it bends because presumably only a longer tube could fill the length of space which the apparently bent tube fills.

All of this raises the question as to just why more weight is given to certain indications than to others, or why we insist on holding to certain presumptive aspects and giving up others. Apparently the answer is that we give weight to indications on the basis of their prognostic reliability.

Some preliminary observations were made after replacing the tube with a rectangular box (a cigarette carton) with printing on it. With this setup the appearances changed. The box did not appear to bend as the tube does, or appeared to do so only very slightly; however, the window was still seen in the reverse of its actual position. This apparently means that the overlay indications were given no weight, or the window would be seen in its actual position. This line of investigation should be carried further.

There remains to explain why, when the tube is set at right angles to the plane of the window, it appears bent during a certain portion of its rotation when the window is rotating in one direction, but does not appear bent during the same portion of rotation when the window is rotating in the opposite direction. The only explanation that comes to mind is that we will accept the appearance of bending when it takes place gradually but will not accept seeing a straight tube suddenly bend. Observations have

---

[11] Alterations of appearances related to some variations in method of attachment of objects have been investigated by Kilpatrick.

[12] This phenomenon, i.e., the bending of the tube related to the apparent positionings of the trapezoidal window related to unaccustomed variations of the trapezoidal characteristics of the stimulus pattern, is very similar to another phenomenon made evident by another of our demonstrations, which has to do with the origin and nature of tangential motion, i.e., the movement of objects across our field of view.

been made on this phenomenon, and they should be further checked. But if it is confirmed, it is an important disclosure and should be investigated.

D. Summary. Before going on to consider further questions raised by the trapezoidal window, the material presented will be briefly summarized. The presentation up to now has been an attempt (*a*) to describe to the reader the aspects of his visual experiences that would be altered when observing a rotating window whose trapezoidal form had been varied, and (*b*) to offer what appears to be a reasonable explanation of why these alterations in appearance are experienced. Table 1 may be helpful in making clear just what aspects of the observer's visual perception are not altered (remain constant) and what aspects are altered.

Briefly stated, the explanation as to why the altered aspects appear altered involves the taking into account of the characteristics of the stimulus patterns, which are essentially cryptogrammatic in nature, their translation in terms of the assumptions from past experience, the hypothesis that preceptions are not disclosures but essentially prognostic in nature, i.e., prognostic directives for action from the observer's point of view both in space and time, the weighing of "indications," sense of surety and lack of surety, value judgments.

But it should be realized that such explanations are only partial, for such questions as the following still remain to be answered: What kind of action? Action for what? If these questions are answered by saying: "Carrying out the purposes of the observer," the further questions arise: What kind of purposes? Purposes for what? The answers to these questions are beyond the scope of this paper.

Table 1   Constancy of aspects of visual perception experienced by one observer when looking from one point of view at:

Rectangular window, cube, and tube		Trapezoidal window, cube, and tube from level of window		Trapezoidal window, cube, and tube from above or below level of window	
Constant	Altering	Constant	Altering	Constant	Altering
"Windowness" *		"Windowness"		"Windowness"	
Rectangularity		Rectangularity			Rectangularity
	Inclination		Inclination		Inclination
Size		Size			Size
Shape		Shape			Shape
Motion		Motion			Motion
Direction †		Direction		Direction	
Distance			Distance		Distance

* The word "windowness" is used for the observer's awareness (resulting from his interpretation of certain characteristics of his stimulus pattern) of "something out there" (apart from other "things") of the nature of a window.
† "Direction" refers to the subjective sense of the direction of the window from the observer's egocentric center.

EXPERIENCE AND MOTIVATION

The influence of needs, values, attitudes, emotions, and motivation on perceptual organization has been called the "new look" in perception. Many criticisms have been leveled at the "new look" experiments, but this one seems to have held up.

Points to guide your study

1. Can you think of situations in real life in which perceptual organization might be influenced by motivation?

2. Analysis of variance is a technique for determining whether or not differences in results are probably real or due to chance alone.

36. REINFORCEMENT AND EXTINCTION AS FACTORS IN SIZE ESTIMATION

William W. Lambert, Cornell University, Richard L. Solomon, University of Pennsylvania, and Peter D. Watson, Massachusetts Mental Health Center*

I. Introduction

In recent experiments on the psychology of perceiving, there has been a noticeable tendency to emphasize determinants which might be classed as motivational in character. The work of Sanford (6, 7) involving the relationship between drive states and 'autistic perceiving,' and the extension of this work by Murphy and his collaborators (3, 5, 8), and by McClelland and Atkinson (4), illustrate this trend. More closely related to the present problem is the work of Bruner, Postman, and their collaborators (1, 2) dealing with the 'selection' and 'accentuation' of perceived objects relative to the 'value systems' of an individual. Two of their experiments in particular illustrate the operation of the conceptualized value dimension. Bruner and Postman (2) found that circles of the same diameter, embossed with (1) a high-valued social symbol, and (2) a low-valued social symbol, were judged to be larger than circles embossed with (3) a neutral symbol. This might indicate that 'per-

ceptual accentuation' is a U-shaped function of a value dimension varying from −1 to +1, with a minimum of accentuation at 'neutrality.' Bruner and Goodman (1) have shown that poor children tend to overestimate the size of coins more than rich children do. These experimenters stated: "The reasonable assumption was made that poor children have a greater subjective need for money than rich ones." (1, p. 39) They further asserted that "the greater the value of the coin, the greater is the deviation of *apparent* size from *actual* size." (1, p. 38)

The multitude of influences correlated with being rich or poor makes it difficult to analyze the specific determinants of size overestimation. It was thought that some light could be shed on this problem by experimentally controlling the life history of children with respect to an initially neutral object. Specifically, we wished to associate a relatively neutral poker chip[1] with candy reward and later extinguish this association by removal of reward and to measure the effects of such procedures on the estimated size of the poker chip. Our hypothesis was that 'value,' as defined by changes in apparent size, is a function of both reinforcement and extinction procedures.

II. Subjects and procedure

In the first study, 32 children from the Harvard Nursery School (ages three to five) were divided into 22 experimental subjects and 10 control subjects. In the second study, 22 chil-

* This research was facilitated by the Laboratory of Social Relations, Harvard University. The authors wish to thank Miss Winifred Lydon, Director of the Harvard Veteran's Nursery School, and Major Gertrude Atkinson, of the Salvation Army Nursery School, Boston, for their indispensable help and cooperation in carrying out this study.

W. W. Lambert, R. L. Solomon, and P. D. Watson. Reinforcement and extinction as factors in size estimation. *J. exp. Psychol.*, 1949, **39**, 637–641. Copyright 1949 by the American Psychological Association. Reprinted here with permission from the authors and the American Psychological Association. Footnote 2 omitted.

[1] Only one of our children knew what a poker chip was. It was called a circle in our experiment.

dren of comparable age from a Salvation Army Nursery School provided 15 experimental subjects and 7 control subjects.

The experimental subjects were individually introduced to a token-reward situation where they turned a crank 18 turns in order to receive a white poker chip which, when put into a slot, led to the automatic delivery of a piece of candy. The control subjects were introduced into the same situation, but candy came directly after work, *without* the mediation of a poker chip. In the first study, both groups worked (and were rewarded) once a day for 10 days; in the second study, the subjects worked (and were rewarded) *five* times a day for 10 days.

Size estimates of the white poker chip token were made by the subjects (1) prior to the experiment; (2) after 10 days of reward; (3) after extinction had occurred (11th day); and (4) after reward had been reinstated (12th day).

Measurements were taken with the equipment designed and used by Bruner and Goodman (1). This equipment was composed of a rectangular wooden box (9 x 9 x 18 in.) with a 5-in. square ground-glass screen in the center of the front panel, and a control knob at the lower right-hand corner. At the center of the ground-glass screen the subject was presented with a circular patch of light (16.2 app. ft. cdls.) the diameter of which was under the control of the knob. The light source was a 60-watt incandescent light shining through an iris diaphragm which could be varied (in terms of the visible light patch) from ⅛ to 2 in. As Bruner and Goodman reported: "The circle was not truly round, containing the familiar nine-elliptoid sides found in the Bausch and Lomb iris diaphragm. It was so close, however, that subjects had no difficulty making the subjective equations required of them." (1, p. 37)

The subjects stood in front of the apparatus with the light patch at or slightly below eye level, and about 12 to 18 in. away. The token, pasted on a 5-in. square gray cardboard, was held by the experimenters so that it was parallel to the circular patch. About 7 in. separated the centers of the two objects to be compared.

The judgment problem was presented to the children of both groups as a game. Each child made his estimates alone. Two judgments starting from the open and two starting from the closed position of the iris were obtained from each child at each measurement session; these judgments were made in an order which was counter-balanced for direction of turning of the control knob. The children were not informed of their success in approximating the actual size of the poker chip.

On the 11th day—after 10 days of rewarded trials—extinction was instituted. The children of both groups worked, but no candy was forthcoming. They worked until they met the arbitrary criterion of extinction: three min. during which they did not turn the handle of the work machine. The size estimates were made immediately after the subject had met the extinction criterion.

On the 12th day the subjects were reintroduced to the reward sequence, and the work brought candy to the control group and token plus candy to the experimental group. Size estimates were made immediately after this 12th session.

III. Results

The results for both nursery schools were combined and they are shown graphically in Figure 1. The four size estimation sessions are distributed on the x-axis; the mean estimate of the token size in terms of percent of actual size is shown on the y-axis. The actual size is indicated by the horizontal line parallel to the x-axis. The means for the experimental group are connected by the solid lines, and the means for the control group are connected by the dotted lines. The connecting lines are meant to increase legibility; they do not imply a continuous function of any sort.

It would appear that the control group showed no significant changes with experience. The experimental group, however, showed a rise in the apparent size of the token after ten days of using the token to obtain reward. The estimates dropped to the level of the beginning estimates following the extinction procedure in which the token no longer led to candy reward. The estimates went back in the direction of overestimation when reward was reinstated on the 12th day.

The mean size estimates in arbitrary units of the comparison-stimulus diameter are given in

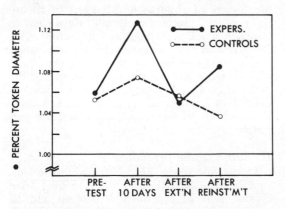

Figure 1　Effects of the experimental conditions upon children's estimates of the diameter of a token when these estimates are taken as percents of the true diameter.

Table 1, together with the corresponding percent of the actual token diameter, for each of the four points in our experiment. The results for our two studies are combined, since there were no appreciable differences between the 10-reinforcement and the 50-reinforcement experiments.

Analyses of variance were performed on the data which are summarized in Table 1. The following differences are of interest: (1) In the experimental group, the estimated size of the token after 10 days of reinforcement was significantly greater than at the pretest. This difference is reliable at the one percent level of confidence. (2) In the experimental group, the size estimates after extinction were significantly smaller than they were after the 10 days of reinforcement. This difference is reliable at the one percent level of confidence. (3) In the experimental group the rise in estimated size following reinstatement of reward is significant at the one percent level of confidence. (4) In the control group, none of the four mean estimates is significantly different from any other. (5) The mean estimates for the experimental and control groups after ten days of reinforcement are significantly different from one another with a reliability between the one and five percent levels of confidence. (6) The mean estimates for the experimental and control groups after reinstatement of reward are not significantly different from one another even though a marked trend seems evident.

IV. Discussion

Several alternative theoretical interpretations for our results could be made. Since experiments are in progress to study further the factors involved, these possibilities will merely be listed at this time. These views are not mutually exclusive, but overlap, as do so many formulations in this field.

1. The estimation changes in the experimental group may be compatible with a generalized pattern of behavior which we could call the 'cookie effect.' That is, the effect may be peculiar to our culture where, for example, a 'bigger cookie is *better* than a little one.' 'Bigness' and 'value,' or 'bigness' and 'goodness,' may be acquired equivalencies for our children, particularly at the ages of the subjects used here. Experiments have been planned which may provide evidence on whether this phenomenon is 'culture bound' or not.

2. These results may provide a measure reflecting some of the secondary reinforcing characteristics taken on by the token during the reinforced trials. These characteristics become lost when reinforcement is not maintained, as during extinction, but are restored when reward is reinstated. This formulation, if further bulwarked with evidence, could serve to integrate perceptual distortion phenomena with learning theory and possibly provide a valuable indirect measure of secondary reinforcement.

3. It is possible that the size enhancement phenomenon can provide us with inferences about perceptual processes as envisioned by Bruner and his collaborators (1, 2). They hypothesize: "The greater the social value of an object, the more will it be susceptible to organization by behavioral determinants." (1, p. 36) In its learning aspects, however, overestimation of size may reflect either 'expectancy' or 'hypothesis' formation (and decay) or it may, as stated above, reflect learned 'needs' which operate in the workings of this conceptualized perceptual process. The actual mechanism which produces overestimation following reinforcement is, however, entirely obscure at the present stage of our research.

In view of the fact that relatively 'neutral' poker chips were used in the experiment, our data cannot be legitimately compared with the coin size data of Bruner and Goodman (1). In addition, our two nursery school groups do not fulfill the criteria of distinct economic class differences. In no sense can we call one group 'rich children' and the other group 'poor children.'

It is interesting to note the possibility that effects such as those discussed here depend on a

---

Table 1   The alteration of size estimation with experience in the experimental situation

	Experimental group			Control group		
	Mean estimated size*	σ_m	Percent actual size	Mean estimated size*	σ_m	Percent actual size
Pretest	66.8	1.2	1.06	66.4	1.5	1.05
After 10 days	70.9	1.1	1.13	67.7	1.2	1.07
After extinction	66.3	1.3	1.05	66.6	1.2	1.06
After reinstatement	68.5	1.8	1.09	65.4	1.4	1.04

* Actual size of poker chip is 63.0 in arbitrary units of diameter. The error of measurement of diameter by experimenter is ±0.2 units.

'difficult' or 'ambiguous' judgment situation. Probably, the more ambiguous the stimulus situation, the more strongly can reinforcement and motivational factors operate in determining size judgments.

4. It is interesting to note that, following extinction procedures, the estimates of the experimental group do not increase above the original level, when the chip was 'neutral.' This could mean that the U-shaped function postulated to relate accentuation and value does not apply here. Or it could mean that extinction removes positive value without producing negative value. Perhaps extinction by punishment is necessary for producing negativity and an increase in size estimates at the negative end of the U-shaped function.

V. Summary

We have described the results of an experiment which was designed to investigate the effects of reinforcement and extinction on size estimation. It was found that the establishment of a token reward sequence results in relative overestimation of the token size. Extinction of the sequence removes this overestimation tendency to a great extent. The results are thought to have relevance for both learning and perception theory.

References

1. Bruner, J. S., and Goodman, C. C. Value and need as organizing factors in perception. *J. abnorm. soc. Psychol.*, 1947, **42**, 33–44.
2. Bruner, J. S., and Postman, L. Symbolic value as an organizing factor in perception. *J. soc. Psychol.*, 1948, **27**, 203–208.
3. Levin, R., Chein, I., and Murphy, G. The relation of the intensity of a need to the amount of perceptual distortion: a preliminary report. *J. Psychol.*, 1942, **13**, 283–293.
4. McClelland, D. C., and Atkinson, J. W. The projective expression of needs: I. The effect of different intensities of hunger drive on perception. *J. Psychol.*, 1948, **25**, 205–222.
5. Proshansky, H., and Murphy, G. The effects of reward and punishment on perception. *J. Psychol.*, 1942, **13**, 295–305.
6. Sanford, R. N. The effect of abstinence from food upon imaginal processes; a preliminary experiment. *J. Psychol.*, 1936, **2**, 129–136.
7. Sanford, R. N. The effect of abstinence from food upon imaginal processes; a further experiment. *J. Psychol.*, 1937, **3**, 145–159.
8. Shafer, R., and Murphy, G. The role of autism in a visual figure-ground relationship. *J. exp. Psychol.*, 1943, **32**, 335–343.

CHAPTER ELEVEN
Vision

S ENSITIVITY OF THE EYE

There are several reasons for including these excerpts. In the first place, they illustrate the concept of absolute threshold and the change from cone to rod function during dark adaptation. This change in function, as shown by the "cone-rod break," was an important piece of evidence used in the duplicity theory, which postulated separate cone and rod functions. In the second place, these excerpts illustrate an ingenious technique for testing animals. This technique gives the animal a "language." It gives him a way of telling us whether or not he can see a light. If he can see it, he pecks key A; if not, he pecks key B.

Points to guide your study

1. Take another sensory phenomenon mentioned in your text and apply this technique to its investigation. *Hint:* This technique can be used with differential thresholds as well as with absolute thresholds.

2. Glossary: mL—This is an abbreviation of millilambert, one-thousandth of a lambert. The lambert is a measure of the luminance of a surface. It is a measure of the physical light energy being reflected from a surface. The measure on the ordinate (vertical axis) of Figure 2 is the $\mu\mu L$, a millionth of a millionth of a lambert. Psychophysics—This refers to the study of the relationship between aspects of the physical stimulus, on the one hand, and experience on the other. For instance, experienced brightness does not follow increases in physical light energy, luminance, in a linear fashion. The determination of the exact function is the job of psychophysics. Photopic—Refers to vision under high illumination (day vision). Scotopic—Refers to vision under low illumination (night vision).

37. DARK ADAPTATION IN THE PIGEON

*Donald S. Blough, Brown University**

Information on sensory thresholds is relevant to research topics that range from discrimination learning to the chemistry of receptive processes. Unfortunately, experiments on many of these topics involve the use of subhuman species from which few precise psychophysical data have as yet been obtained. In improving this situation with respect to visual psychophysics, the choice of the pigeon as a subject is particularly advantageous. The pigeon's vision is good, perhaps comparable to that of man (3, 9, 15); physiological and anatomical studies have been made on its visual apparatus (4, 7, 8, 11); Ferster and

* This research was supported, in part, by Contract N5ori–07663 (Proj. NR140–072) between Harvard University and the Office of Naval Research, directed by Dr. Floyd Ratliff. It represents part of a thesis submitted to the Department of Psychology, Harvard University, in partial fulfillment of the requirements for the Ph.D. degree. The writer is indebted to Dr. Ratliff for his constant interest and helpful advice.

D. S. Blough. Dark adaptation in the pigeon. *J. comp. physiol. Psychol.*, 1956, 49, 425–430. Copyright 1956 by the American Psychological Association. Excerpts reprinted here with permission from the author and the American Psychological Association. Footnote 1 has been changed slightly.

Skinner have outlined (6, 14) attributes that make it an excellent subject for closely controlled behavioral investigation.

This paper reports experiments in which the absolute visual thresholds of pigeons were traced during dark adaptation. The method involves behavior control techniques based on the work of Skinner and his associates (6, 14) and a stimulus control technique similar to Békésy's (1) method of human audiometry. The method, together with the reasons for various training and testing procedures, has been described in some detail elsewhere (2, 10). It has two fundamental features: (a) the stimulus controls the bird's responses as a result of differential reinforcement; (b) the bird's responses control the stimulus through an automatic switching circuit. This reciprocal control process is arranged as follows. The pigeon confronts two response keys and a small lighted stimulus patch. On a random schedule, pecking key A blacks out the stimulus patch; pecking key B raises a food magazine within reach if the patch is dark. Although only a small proportion of pecks on the two keys is reinforced in this way, the bird gradually learns to peck key A when the patch is visible and key B when the patch is dark. The bird's responses control the stimulus through a separate, automatic switching circuit; pecks on key A reduce the luminance of the stimulus patch, while pecks on key B increase the luminance of the patch. As a result, the stimulus is kept oscillating about the bird's absolute threshold. When the luminance rises above threshold, the bird pecks key A, driving the stimulus dimmer again. When the stimulus disappears below threshold, the bird pecks key B and the stimulus gets brighter. A record of the stimulus luminance traces the absolute threshold of the pigeon through time.

Method

Training procedure. The pigeon's basic task was to peck key A when the stimulus patch was visible and key B when the patch was dark. Training proceeded in several stages. When the bird became proficient at one stage, the next was introduced; about fifty training hours were needed before experimental data could be collected. The only light in the adaptation box came from the stimulus patch, except in the earliest stages of training, when a supplementary overhead light was used.

First, the hungry bird (70 per cent to 80 per cent of free-feeding cage weight) was trained to peck the two keys at random by the "response differentiation" technique described by Ferster (6). Next, the stimulus patch was illuminated and the control circuit adjusted so that a peck on key A closed the shutter, blacking out the

patch. After a peck on key A blacked out the patch a peck on key B caused the food magazine to be raised within reach for about 5 sec. After most reinforcements, the shutter opened, and the lighted patch reappeared. Continued darkness followed one reinforcement in five; in this case, a peck on key B brought food a second time.

In the next stage of training, several pecks in a row, rather than a single peck, were required on key A to close the shutter and on key B to obtain food. The number of pecks required varied randomly between one and eight. An interval during which no amount of pecking could close the shutter was introduced after each reinforcement. The duration of this interval varied randomly between 0 and 15 sec., with a mean of 7.5 sec. The longest interval was later increased to 30 sec and the mean to 15 sec.

When training was nearly complete, the luminance of the stimulus patch was put under the control of the bird's responses during the intervals between reinforcements. Each peck on key A reduced the luminance of the patch by .03 log unit, while each peck on key B increased the luminance of the patch by this amount. The pen coupled to the wedge drive recorded these luminance changes continuously. When the patch reappeared following a reinforcement, it always had the same luminance that it had had just before it was blacked out.

Testing procedure. In the last stage of the training just described the procedure was such that absolute thresholds were obtained. When these thresholds became stable from day to day, the collection of experimental data began. At about the same time each day, the bird was carried from its home cage and placed in total darkness in the pre-exposure box. After the

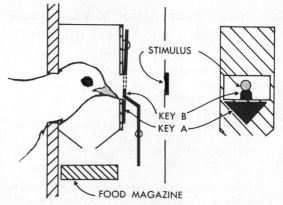

Figure 1 Response chamber of the adaptation box. *Left,* side view, showing relative positions of pigeon, food magazine, response keys, and stimulus patch. *Right,* keys and patch seen from the pigeon's position.

pigeon had been in the dark at least 1 hr., the pre-exposure light was turned on for a pre-determined interval, following which the bird was transferred to the adaptation box. The transfer, done in dim light, took less than 5 sec. The bird usually began to respond within 1 min. after the box was sealed. If it did not peck within 3 min., the bird was returned to its home cage until the next day.

Results

A sample dark-adaptation curve appears in Figure 2. This curve was produced by bird 192 in a single hour, following a 10-min. pre-exposure at 22 mL. The luminance of the stimulus patch is represented on the ordinate; time in dark is on the abscissa. The curve can readily be separated into two continuous segments, joined at a rather sharp "break." These divisions will be referred to as the "first (or 'cone') segment" and the "second (or 'rod') segment." No threshold is shown for 3 min. at the beginning of the adaptation period. This is due to the fact that each run began with the stimulus at a super-threshold luminance (7.2 log $\mu\mu$L); the first responses were all to key A and served only to reduce the luminance to threshold. Consequently, a record of the luminance in this period was a rapidly falling curve that bore no relation to the threshold.

Discussion

A variety of findings (12) relates the first segment of the human adaptation curve to cone function and photopic sensitivity and relates the second segment to rods and scotopic sensitivity. In man, rods far outnumber cones except in or near the fovea, and unless the test stimulus is restricted to the fovea, the second segment char-

acteristically dominates the dark-adaptation picture.

The pigeon possesses a duplex retina with elements grossly similar to their counterparts in the human retina, except for the fact that the pigeon cones contain red, orange, or yellowish oil droplets. Schultze's diagrams (11) of the pigeon retina show up to 20 of these cones for each rod in the temporal retina, while in the nasal region the proportion falls to about two cones to a rod; the fovea is rod-free. This cone dominance in the pigeon retina appears to be expressed in the bird's dark adaptation; a short, low-luminance pre-exposure suffices to produce an identifiable first segment.

Despite the appearance of familiar features in the pigeon data, it would not do to draw the conclusion that differences between pigeon and human dark adaptation are solely a function of the different distributions of elements on the two retinas. Even at the retinal level other important factors may operate. It has been reported (5) that when the retina of the pigeon is exposed to strong light, considerable pigment migration occurs, and the receptor cells change shape and position. These changes seem to proceed in such a way as to reduce the amount of light reaching the receptors in bright light and to increase it in the dark. The pigmentation of the pigeon's retinal cones may also affect the absolute threshold in ways as yet unclear.

References

1. Békésy, G. V. A new audiometer. *Acta Oto-laryngol.*, 1947, **35**, 411–422.
2. Blough, D. S. Method for tracing dark adaptation in the pigeon. *Science*, 1955, **121**, 703-704.
3. Chard, R. D. Visual acuity in the pigeon. *J. exp. Psychol.*, 1939, **24**, 588–608.
4. Chard, R. D., and Grundlach, R. H. The structure of the eye of the homing pigeon. *J. comp. Psychol.*, 1938, **25**, 249–272.
5. Detweiler, S. R. *Vertebrate photoreceptors.* New York: Macmillan, 1943.
6. Ferster, C. B. The use of the free operant in the analysis of behavior. *Psychol. Bull.*, 1953, **50**, 263–274.
7. Graham, C. H., Kemp, E. H., and Riggs, L. A. An analysis of the electrical retinal responses of a color-discriminating eye to light of different wave-lengths. *J. gen. Psychol.*, 1935, **13**, 275–296.
8. Granit, R. The photopic spectrum of the pigeon. *Acta physiol. Scand.*, 1942, **4**, 118–124.
9. Hamilton, W. F., and Coleman, T. B. Trichromatic vision in the pigeon as illustrated by the spectral hue discrimination curve. *J. comp. Psychol.*, 1933, **15**, 183–191.
10. Ratliff, F., and Blough, D. S. Behavioral

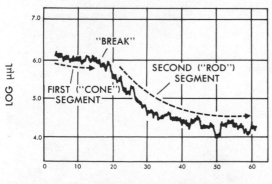

Figure 2 Sample dark-adaptation curve secured from a bird in a single hour. Pre-exposure was 10 min. at 22 mL. The luminance of the stimulus patch, in log micromicrolamberts, is on the ordinate.

studies of visual processes in the pigeon. USN, ONR, Tech. Rep., 1954 (Contract N5 ori–07663, Proj. NR140–072).

11. Schultze, M. Zur Anatomie und Physiologie der Retina. *Arch. f. mikr. Anat.*, 1866, **2**, 175.

12. Sheard, C. Dark adaptation: some physical, physiological, clinical, and aeromedical considerations. *J. opt. Soc. Amer.*, 1944, **34**, 464–508.

13. Skinner, B. F. *The behavior of organisms.* New York: Appleton-Century-Crofts, 1938.

14. Skinner, B. F. Some contributions of an experimental analysis of behavior to psychology as a whole. *Amer. Psychologist*, 1953, **8**, 69–78.

15. Walls, G. L. *The vertebrate eye and its adaptive radiation.* Bloomfield Hills, Mich.: Cranbrook Institute of Science, 1942.

CHAPTER TWELVE

Hearing and lower senses

Ｈow THE EAR WORKS

This article presents evidence for the *place theory* of hearing. Although the details differ, the general statements made here, which are derived from the guinea pig cochlea, may be extended to the human cochlea.

Points to guide your study

1. Pay attention to the experimental method. When the cochlea is stimulated by sound, changes in voltage may be picked up by electrodes on the cochlea. This is the Wever-Bray effect, or the cochlear microphonic. It is an electrical response of the cochlea itself and is not to be confused with auditory nerve impulses. Localization in the cochlea is investigated by this method in this article.

2. Make sure that you can follow the reasoning from the data of Table 1.

3. The results are summarized in Figure 5. Can you give a summary description of this figure in your own words?

38. CONTRIBUTION TO SYMPOSIUM: TONE LOCALIZATION IN THE COCHLEA

*E. A. Culler**

In this symposium on localization I am doubtless expected to report on tests of hearing. Our results in this case were, however, secured by the Wever-Bray technic, not because of any change in my conviction that tests of hearing are always fundamental in otologic work, but simply because in this problem the electric method is more simple and direct.

The question is, what does the cochlea do with the frequencies impressed upon it, in particular those below 1000 cycles? This question has two aspects:

(a) Does each frequency have some kind of focus or resonance point?

(b) If so, where do these various foci reside?

A good many ways of attacking this problem have been used hitherto; most of them, indeed, are represented in our discussion today. Of these

* Communication No. 18 from the Animal Hearing Research, Department of Psychology, University of Illinois. This investigation was maintained with aid from the Research Council of the American Otological Society.

E. A. Culler. Contribution to Symposium: tone localization in the cochlea. *Ann. Otology, Rhinology, and Laryngology,* 1935, **44,** 807–813. Copyright 1935 by the Annals Publishing Co. Reprinted here with permission from the author and the Annals Publishing Co.

may be mentioned: (1) stimulation deafness, in which the lesion is produced by means of intense or protracted acoustic stimulation, and then correlated with associated losses in hearing and in cochlear potentials; (2) introduction of drugs through the round window or through small punctures in the bony wall; (3) mechanical lesions from thrusting a drill into some part of the cochlear spaces; (4) scorching with an electric needle. These methods give excellent service, but they all have one defect in common: the cochlea is obviously not intact or normal after it has been scorched, drilled, drugged or otherwise injured. In puncturing the wall or coagulating the cochlear fluids, we are always beset with the fear that we have changed, in some unknown and unknowable way, the very characteristics of the cochlear system which we are trying to measure. From the laws of hydrodynamics, we know that the behavior of fluid in a closed oscillatory system like the cochlea can be greatly modified by introducing even a tiny hole somewhere in the containing walls. In our laboratory we have sampled almost every one of these localized lesion methods, but have always been troubled with the fear that in so doing we were introducing indeterminate errors into our procedure. We can confirm, what has been so clearly described here today, that some electric response remains even after one or two whole turns have been cut off the apex; but unhappily we have no assurance at all that the locus or pattern of response is even remotely the same after these drastic operations.

In view of these considerations, we decided to work only with the intact mechanism. The bulla was opened in the guinea pig on the ventral side, thus exposing to view the middle ear and cochlea, as shown in Figure 1. As you know, the guinea pig cochlea is particularly suited for experimental work. It has from four to four and one-half turns, and is unusually accessible, projecting from the petrous bone like a thumb. All observations were made on the cochlea as thus exposed; the whole working mechanism, from tympanum through ossicles to cochlea and nerve, being in every respect normal. This is emphasized because it is the distinctive feature of our procedure. A sharp tungsten wire was applied in turn to a number of carefully localized points on the cochlear wall. Figure 2 is an outline drawing of the cochlea, numbered to indicate all the points where the electrode was placed and the response measured. You see one row of points on the mid-ventral aspect directly facing us (Nos. 18 to 24), another row along the lateral side next the tympanum (Nos. 10 to 17), and a third row on the medial aspect, just one-half turn (180°) from the lateral side (Nos. 1 to 8). To illustrate our procedure, assume the animal to be immobile in a holder, with the exposed middle ear dry and warm. The ground electrode is placed on some adjacent muscle, and the active wire electrode (covered with a film of oil to minimize condensation of moisture from the air) is carefully set on point No. 22 (mid-ventral aspect, fourth apical turn). When the sound tube is adjusted and everything rigidly clamped, the tests begin. The following series of twenty tones were regularly used:

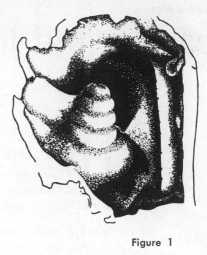

Figure 1

picked up at the electrode; the potential can be read quickly and accurately from the dial, which is far more convenient to use than telephones or bridges. Since very loud sounds introduce harmonics and may even injure the ear, we always work with minimal intensities. I fully agree with Drs. Davis and Lurie that low stimulus intensities must be used in this work for reliable results. A small deflection of the voltmeter (from zero position of the needle up to a given mark) was arbitrarily fixed as the "threshold response" of the cochlea. You will observe that this procedure is directly analogous to methods used in measuring hearing. When you measure a patient's hearing with an audiometer, you reduce the sound intensity until it is just barely loud enough to evoke a response ("yes"). Likewise here we attenuate the sound energy until it is just strong enough to bring the needle up to our threshold mark; we then record in the protocol just how intense was the sound required to give this threshold reading. Having secured the threshold

125	400	1000	3500
150	500	1500	4000
200	600	2000	5000
250	700	2500	6000
300	800	3000	7000

The oscillator is set for 125 cycles. The electric output, before reaching the speaker, passes through an attenuator by means of which the intensity can be reduced in any amount from 1 to 127 decibels. We now feed a weak tone of 125 cycles into the guinea pig's ear. This produces the usual cochlear response, which is picked up by the tungsten electrode on point No. 22 and transmitted through the amplifiers into a so-called "tube voltmeter." As the name indicates, this instrument measures the voltage

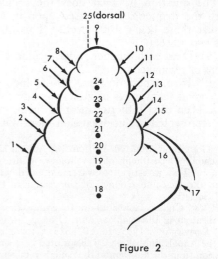

Figure 2

figure at 125 cycles, we proceed to 150, and so on throughout the entire list. We now have the cochlear response to every one of the twenty tones, as registered from point No. 22. To assure ourselves that this list of twenty readings is really dependable, however, we repeat the entire set. If the second reading for each tone is the same within two decibels, the value is accepted as correct; if the second reading differs by more than 2 db, we check the condition of ear and electrode and repeat the series until each pair of readings checks within 2 db. The utmost precaution is needed because a very slight change (e. g., a drop of fluid at the tip of the electrode) alters the readings by 5 or 10 db. To get a double set of readings from each point, we have to take as many as 1,000 readings from the same cochlea.

Having assembled the figures for each point and for all the frequencies, we proceed to analyze them. Where, if anywhere, does each frequency develop the maximal potential? Is there a particular locus where each tone shows the greatest effect? Some of the gross differences are quite obvious. Consider Figure 3. In passing from point 18 on the basal turn up to point 22 on the third turn, we find the high frequencies falling off markedly and the lower tones coming through stronger; the maximal gain being, as you see, near 700 and the low point around 6000 to 7000. This clearly suggests that 6000–7000 must be near the point of departure (No. 18) and 700–800 near the point of arrival (No. 22). Now consider another typical case (Figure 4). We pass through 180° from medial to lateral side of third turn (point 4 to point 14). The low point is 500 and the high point 1000 with a sharp gradient joining the two. This suggests that in going from point 4 to point 14 we are moving away from 500 cycles and toward 1000; in other words, 500 is near point 4 on the medial side and 1000 is near point 14 on the lateral side.

It is thus clear, by gross analysis, that certain frequencies are focalized at certain points; but to make a really accurate map of the cochlea we must resort to more detailed and careful examination of our figures. Suppose we consider point 22 (middle of third turn). It is surrounded by a

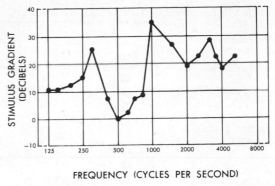

FREQUENCY (CYCLES PER SECOND)

Figure 4

ring of other points, in order: 24, 6, 5, 4, 20, 14, 13, 12. Now if a single frequency is focalized at 22, the magnitude of its electric response ought to decrease if we move away from 22 in any direction whatsoever. Let us see whether any frequency meets this condition. Consider this table (Table 1) of frequencies from 500 to 1000 cycles. We might include all the frequencies, but that would make our table large and confusing. Figure 4 shows us that this point lies somewhere between 500 and 1000; hence the present table will be quite adequate and will serve better to illustrate our analysis. In passing from 22 to 24, the minimal electric potential, as you see, is generated at 700 to 800 (0); from 22 to 6, at 800 (−2); from 22 to 5, again at 800 (−3); from 22 to 4, again at 800 (−7); from 22 to 20, once more at 800 (−2); from 22 to 14, the minimum occurs at 700 (1); from 22 to 13, at 600 and 700 (−2); from 22 to 12 finally, again at 800 (3). Adding the figures for the eight cases, we find that whereas the electric potential at the surrounding points is on the average greater by 3.9 at 500 cycles and by 2.0 at 600 cycles and much greater at 1000 (6.75 units), it is definitely lower at 700 and 800 (−0.62 and −1.00). What does this mean? After careful consideration I can find but one possible meaning in it: that point 22 is located near the focus of 700 and 800 cycles, probably between the two but nearer 800 (say 775). The result is that whenever you move the electrode away from point 22 the response from 700 and 800 lessens, whereas the other potentials are augmented or remain the same.

By using the procedure just described, we have located each of the frequencies shown in Figure 5. The diagram is drawn to four and one-half turns. I am never quite sure, when looking at a guinea pig's cochlea, whether it has four, four and one-quarter or four and one-half turns; but in any event the number lies within that range. Starting from the round window, we find 6000 at the midventral aspect of the basal turn. The

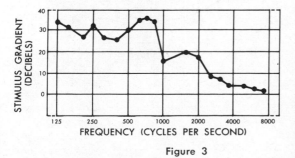

FREQUENCY (CYCLES PER SECOND)

Figure 3

Table 1

Gradient		Frequency				
From	To	500	600	700	800	1000
22	24	4	2	0	0	7
22	6	6	5	0	−2	8
22	5	8	5	−1	−3	10
22	4	3	−2	−6	−7	7
22	20	0	0	−1	−2	2
22	14	3	2	1	3	10
22	13	0	−2	−2	0	1
22	12	7	6	4	3	9
	Sum	31	16	−5	−8	54
	Mean	3.9	2.0	−0.62	−1.0	6.75

first complete turn brings us to about 2800. The second whole turn reaches down to a value between 800 and 1000, say 875; the third turn ends between 250 and 300 (circa 260); the fourth turn finally at the very apex terminates near 75.

No claim is made that this map is wholly accurate; but we are able to say something about the degree of error in our locations. We have, for example, fourteen independent estimates of the focal frequency at point No. 24; how well do these fourteen estimates agree? This is their distribution:

In 2 cases the estimate falls at 125
   2 cases the estimate falls at 150
  7½ cases the estimate falls at 200
  1½ cases the estimate falls at 250
  1 case the estimate falls at 300

The average of these fourteen cases proves to be 195, and the standard error is about 12.7. We can say then with virtual certainty that point 24 falls between 195 plus 25 and 195 minus 25. The greatest possible error in our location is about 10 or 12 per cent.

In reply to the question of this symposium, then, let me state my conclusions in two propositions:

(a) Each frequency within the audible range has its own focus of response within the cochlea, this focus being revealed by the electric potentials which can be shown to be maximal for a single frequency at a given site.

(b) The location of this focal point can be

fixed within a maximal error of 10 or 12 per cent.

So many divergent results, secured by approved methods, have been reported here today that no one can afford to be dogmatic in this complicated problem. I was happy to find myself in substantial agreement with Drs. Davis and Lurie. My results, of course, shed no light on the mechanism by which the electric potential of the cochlea is generated; but they do indicate that each frequency has a focal electric response and that the site of this focal response can be determined.

Figure 5

THE CHEMICAL SENSES

Before reading this selection, make sure you have read about sensation in your text. You will get a lot more out of this if you have.

Points to guide your study

1. What is the doctrine of the "Specific Energies of Nerves"? How does the article bear on this idea?

2. See the notes on the article "Dark Adaptation in the Pigeon" for a discussion of psychophysics. This discussion should help to clarify the phrase "a particular sensory dimension is not isomorphic with a particular physical dimension."

3. Glossary: Modality—Refers to the different types of sensory experience. For instance, visual experience and touch experience are separate modalities. Isomorphism—This literally means "same form." In sensory psychology it usually refers to the relationship between the pattern of activity in the nervous system, on the one hand, and experience on the other. In its crudest form, isomorphism means that the pattern of activity in the nervous system is like that—isomorphic with—which is experienced. Afferent—Refers to input to the central nervous system. This term is to be contrasted with efferent, which refers to nerve impulses flowing from the central nervous system, often to the muscles or glands. Synapse—The region where two nerve fibers come together. The fibers do not actually touch, however. The nerve impulse is transmitted across the gap by a combination of electrical and chemical processes. Molar (M)—The measure of the physical stimulus in most taste studies is in terms of the concentration of dissolved material in the solution which is applied to the taste receptor. The unit of measurement is often the "molar" unit. A molar solution is one in which one molecular weight of substance is dissolved in one liter of the solution. Nociceptor—A receptor which, when stimulated, gives rise to unpleasant experiences. The pain receptors are nociceptors. This term should be contrasted with its opposite, "beneceptor." Temporal—Refers to time. Phenomenology—In psychology this term is usually used to refer to a person's immediate experience. Reify—Refers to the tendency to think about concepts, which are not objects, as if they were actual objects which can be seen, heard, touched, or experienced in some other way. In other words, this is the tendency to make *things* out of *abstractions*.

39. THE AFFERENT CODE FOR SENSORY QUALITY

*Carl Pfaffmann, Brown University**

One of the basic problems in the psychology and physiology of sensation is that of the mechanism by which different sensory qualities are perceived. The classical dictum on this problem was propounded by Johannes Müeller in his doctrine of the Specific Energies of Nerves. Actually Charles Bell had enunciated (Carmichael, 1926) the principle somewhat earlier, but Müeller's version

* Presented as part of the Presidential Address to the Division of Experimental Psychology at the APA Annual Convention, September 3, 1957.

Carl Pfaffmann. The afferent code for sensory quality. *Amer. Psychologist*, 1959, **14**, 226–232. Copyright 1959 by the American Psychological Association. Reprinted here with permission from the author and the American Psychological Association.

is better known. This doctrine made clear that "We are aware of the state of our nerves, not of the external stimulus itself." The eye, however stimulated, gives rise to sensations of light; the ear, to sensations of sound; and the taste buds, to sensations of taste.

The further extension of the doctrine of Specific Nerve Energies to the different sensation qualities within a single modality was made by Helmholtz. According to his place theory of hearing, the perception of a particular pitch was attributed to the activity at a particular region of the basilar membrane of the inner ear, stimulation of the individual nerve fibers at these specific locations gave rise to unique tonal qualities of pitch. *Pitch* depended upon *which* nerve fiber was activated (Boring, 1950). In the less complex modalities, like the cutaneous or gustatory senses, von Frey and his school propounded the view of "modalities within modalities." The cutaneous sense was said to consist of separate modalities: touch, pressure, warm, cold, and pain, each with their specific receptors. The history of research on cutaneous sensitivity is, in large measure, a history of the search for such receptors. In taste the "BIG FOUR" are familiar to all; the qualities, salty, sour, bitter, and sweet, were each mediated by a specific receptor type.

Implicit in these formulations is an isomorphism between receptor structure and phenomenology. Pure sensation as a basic psychological entity was to be reduced to a physiological entity. Psychology (at least a part thereof) was to be "explained" by the underlying physiology, hence, "Physiological Psychology." This formulation, simple and direct, dominated the field of sensory psychology from the beginning with only an occasional and sporadic dissenting voice. The fact that the psychological entities were only postulated and the question of whether they were, in fact, valid were almost forgotten in the search for the "real thing."

Many of the more recent findings in sensory psychology and physiology derive from the application of electrophysiology to the study of sensory processes. The publication of E. D. Adrian's *The Basis of Sensation* in 1928 opened a new era. The invention of the electronic tube, appropriate amplifying circuits, and recording instruments made it possible to study directly the activity of the sense organs and their nerves. Since 1928, the advances in technique and instrumentation have been so dramatic that there is almost no part of the nervous system that cannot be probed by the inquisitive microelectrode. Psychologists have played a significant role in this development. One of their best known early discoveries was that of Wever and Bray (1930), on the cochlea and VIIIth nerve.

This paper will review some experiments with this procedure on another sense, that of taste,

and will discuss their general implications for the theory of afferent coding.[1] It should be emphasized that sensation itself is not being studied. Rather the investigator "taps in" on the "basis of sensation" by recording and amplifying the nerve impulse traffic in the sensory fibers "en route" to the brain.

The sense of taste is particularly well suited to this problem because it consists of well defined differentiated structures, the taste buds, which are capable of mediating quite different sensory qualities, but the array of qualities and dimensions is not too complex for interpretation. The afferent message from receptor to brain can be studied directly in the afferent nerve fibers from the tongue, for the primary sensory nerve fibers from the receptive organs are relatively accessible with no synaptic complexities in the direct line from the receptors except for the junction between sense cell and sensory fiber.

The taste stimulus, like all stimuli, acts first upon a receptor cell. Changes in the receptor cell in turn activate or "trigger" impulses in the nerve fiber. Both the sense cell, as well as the nerve fiber, and in fact all living cells are like tiny batteries with a potential difference across the cell membrane. When stimulated, this membrane is depolarized, and it is this depolarization that can be recorded. Figure 1 schematizes such recording from a single sensory nerve fiber shown in contact with a receptor cell to the left of the

[1] Many of our experiments on taste were supported by a contract with the Office of Naval Research.

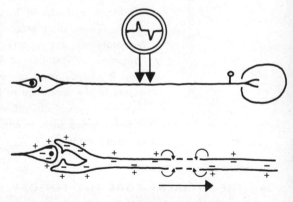

Figure 1   Diagram of electrophysiological recording from a single sensory nerve fiber. Upper diagram shows a single fiber in contact with a single sense cell to the left. A diphasic response on the cathode ray tube is shown as an impulse passes the recording electrodes en route to the central nervous system schematized to the right. The lower figure shows in more detail the positive and negative charges around the cell membranes associated with the passage of the nerve impulse.

figure and entering the central nervous system (CNS) to the right. The recording electrodes on the fiber connect with an appropriate recording device such as a cathode ray oscillograph shown schematically. As the impulse passes the first electrode, there is an upward deflection; as it passes the second electrode, there is a downward deflection. By an appropriate arrangement, a single or monophasic deflection only may be obtained so that at each passage of an impulse there will be a "spike" on the oscillograph tracing. The lower figure shows schematically the electrical activity associated with the passage of a nerve impulse. The message delivered along any single nerve fiber therefore consists of a train of impulses, changes in excitation of the receptor are signaled by changes in the frequency of this train. Thus, changes in strength of solution bathing the tongue change the frequency of impulse discharge per second. In any one fiber, the size of the impulse is nearly constant. The sensory nerve message, therefore, is a digital process.

Figure 2 shows a typical series of oscillograph tracings obtained from a *single* nerve fiber when different concentrations of sodium chloride are applied to the tongue of the rat. The "spikes" signal the passage of each impulse past the recording electrode. With stronger stimuli there is a higher frequency of discharge. Threshold for this fiber lies at approximately 0.003 M. Other fibers will show similar behavior, but may possess higher thresholds, for the tongue contains a population of taste receptors with thresholds of differing value.

This description applies to the impulse in the single sensory nerve fiber. Actually, the sensory nerve is a cable, made up of many different fibers each connected with one or more receptor cells.

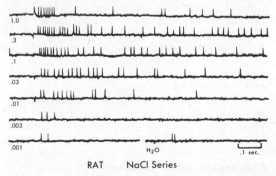

Figure 2 A series of oscillograph tracings obtained from a single taste nerve fiber when different concentrations of salt solution are placed on the tongue. Note that water as well as .001 M NaCl will elicit two impulses. A concentration of .003 M NaCl will elicit three impulses and may be considered as threshold. (Reproduced from the Journal of Neurophysiology.)

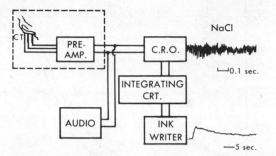

Figure 3 A block diagram of the recording apparatus showing two types of record. The upper trace shows a typical asynchronus, multifiber discharge from a large number of active fibers; the lower trace shows the integrated record of such activity. (Reproduced from the American Journal of Clinical Nutrition.)

The single fiber recordings shown were obtained after the nerve cable had been dissected to a strand containing just one functional unit. Sometimes the same effect is achieved by using microelectrodes.

The nerve fibers subserving taste travel in three nerves from the mouth region: the lingual, glossopharyngeal, and vagus nerves which contain touch, temperature, pressure and pain fibers as well as those concerned with taste. The taste fibers from the anterior tongue branch off from the lingual nerve to form the chorda tympani nerve where it is possible to record almost exclusively from taste nerve fibers. This nerve can be exposed by appropriate surgery in the anesthetized animal and placed on the electrodes leading to the recording apparatus.

A block diagram of the apparatus together with sample records is shown in Figure 3. The integrated record is readily adapted to quantitative treatment by measuring the magnitude of the deflection at each response and so provides a measure of the total activity of all the fibers in the nerve. An index of over-all taste sensitivity can be obtained from such recordings. The curves in Figure 4 are such measures for the cat for quinine, hydrochloric acid, sodium chloride, potassium chloride, and sucrose solutions (Pfaffmann, 1955).

The basic taste stimuli can be arranged in order of thresholds from low to high as follows: quinine, hydrochloric acid, sodium chloride, potassium chloride, and sucrose. In this animal, as in man, quinine is effective in relatively low concentrations. Sugar at the other end of the scale requires relatively high concentrations, and the electrolytes are intermediate. Sugar produces a nerve response of small magnitude compared with that to other stimuli. Differences in response magnitudes are found from one species to another. In the hamster or guinea pig, for ex-

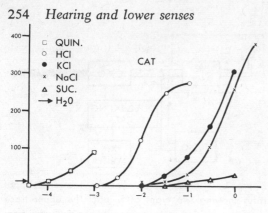

LOG MOLAR CONC.

Figure 4   Curves of taste response in the cat to four different taste stimuli as indicated by the integrated response method. (Reproduced from the Journal of Neurophysiology.)

ample, sugar will elicit a strong discharge, and other species differences with quinine and the salts have been observed (Beidler, Fishman, and Hardiman, 1955; Pfaffmann, 1953). Recently, Carpenter (1956) has correlated certain of these species differences with behavioral data using the preference method.

The representation in Figure 4 does not show that the animal can distinguish one substance from another. Actually an animal like the rat will avoid quinine and acid, but will show a preference for NaCl and sucrose. To find how the animal can discriminate among different chemicals the single fiber analysis is required.

In the early study of the single gustatory fibers in the cat (Pfaffmann, 1941), three different kinds of fiber were found. One was responsive to sodium chloride and acid, another to quinine and acid, and a third to acid alone. Thus, acid stimulated all receptor-neural units found. This established not only that the gustatory endings were differentially sensitive to different chemicals but that the physiological receptor "types" *did not* correspond to the phenomenal categories as reported by man. In view of the more recently demonstrated species difference, this might not appear to be surprising. But, regardless of what the cat "tastes," these findings pointed to an important principle of sensory coding. This is that *the same afferent*

fiber may convey different information depending upon the amount of activity in another parallel fiber. To illustrate, suppose A represents an acid-salt unit and C, an acid sensitive unit, then activity in A only would lead to salty; but activity in that same fiber, A, plus discharge in C would lead to sourness. Recent studies emphasize still another important point, namely, that some stimuli may decrease or inhibit the frequency of sensory discharge. Certain receptors, which can be stimulated by water (as well as other agents), may be inhibited by the application of dilute salt solutions (Liljestrand & Zotterman, 1954). Taste stimuli, therefore, may either increase or decrease, i. e., modulate, the amount of afferent nerve traffic. A diminution in activity may signal, not merely the withdrawal of a particular stimulus, but the application of a different one.

Table 1 taken from a recent paper from Zotterman's laboratory (Cohen, Hagiwara, & Zotterman, 1955) illustrates the afferent code or pattern which may be described for the cat based on a compilation of the "types" so far discovered for that species.

But the use of the term "fiber type" harks back to some of the errors of classical thinking. Types are defined only by the range of stimuli sampled, the wider the range, the more difficult will it be to define pure "types." "Taste types" may turn out to be as varied and individual as "personality types." Figure 5 shows the variety of response patterns of nine single fiber preparations to the following standard test solutions: .03 N HCL, .1 M KCL, .1 M NaCl, .01 M quinine hydrochloride, and 1.0 M sucrose (Pfaffmann, 1955).

The bar graph shows the magnitude of response in each of the single fiber preparations in impulses per second of discharge. The central crosshatched bar graph shows the relative magnitude of response to these same solutions in the integrated response of the whole nerve. It is apparent that the individual fibers do not all have the same pattern. The sum of the activity of all fibers is shown by the crosshatched diagram. Furthermore, fiber types are not immediately apparent in this array.

The fact that the individual receptor cells possess combined sensitivity as salt plus acid, or salt plus sugar, cannot be dismissed as the result of multiple innervation of more than one receptor

Table 1   Fiber type response in the cat*

Stimulus	"Water" fiber	"Salt" fiber	"Acid" fiber	"Quinine" fiber	Sensation evoked
H_2O (0.03M Salt)	+	0	0	0	→ water
NaCl (0.05 M)	0	+	0	0	→ salt
HCL (ph 2.5)	+	+	+	0	→ sour
Quinine	+	0	0	+	→ bitter

* Cf., Cohen, Hagiwara, & Zotterman, 1955.

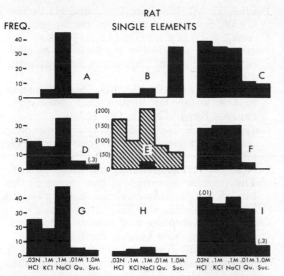

RAT
SINGLE ELEMENTS
FREQ.

Figure 5 The pattern of taste responses in nine different single sensory nerve fibers of the rat. The solid bar graphs give the frequency of response in impulses per second for different taste stimuli (indicated along the abscissa). The crosshatched bar graph shows the relative response of the total nerve (integrated response) to these same solutions. (Reproduced from the Journal of Neurophysiology.)

cell by a single fiber. Kimura (Beidler, 1957; Kimura & Beidler, 1956) has studied the sensitivity patterns of the individual taste cells by inserting micro-pipette electrodes directly into the sense cells themselves. The pattern of sensitivity found in the individual sensory cells is like that already described for the single afferent fiber. Thus, within the individual sense cell there must be different sites which are selectively sensitive to different taste stimuli. These sites on the membrane may be determined by molecular configuration, the shape and size of pores in the membrane, or some such microcellular feature.

One additional principle must be introduced. This is that the relative rather than the absolute amount of activity in any one set of afferent fibers may determine the quality of sensation. Figure 6 shows frequency of discharge as a function of stimulus intensity for two units labelled A and B. Both are stimulated by both stimuli sugar and salt, but it is apparent that A is more sensitive to salt and B to sugar (Pfaffmann, 1955). Once each stimulus intensity exceeds the threshold for a particular receptor unit, the frequency of discharge increases with concentration. Thus the afferent pattern as the code for sensory quality must take account of the changing frequency of discharge with stimulus intensity. The pattern concept may be retained by recognizing that "pattern" is still apparent in the relative

amount of activity of different fibers. In the two-fiber example shown in Figure 6, low concentrations of salt will discharge only A, higher concentrations will discharge both A and B, but activity in A will be greater than that in B. Low concentrations of sugar will activate only B, higher concentrations will activate both B and A, but B will be greater than A. Thus the sensory code might read:

Frequency	Code
A > B	= salty
B > A	= sweet

where A or B may go to zero. It is not only the activity in parallel fibers that is important, it is the *relative amount* of such parallel activity.

Studies of the other senses indicate that these principles are not unique to taste. In the cutaneous senses there is a variety of different endings which overlap two or more of the classical skin modalities (Maruhashi, Mizuguchi, & Tasaki, 1952). For example, some pressure receptors in the cat's tongue are activated by cold (Hensel & Zotterman, 1951), and there are several different pressure, temperature, and nociceptor endings, some serving large or small areas, some adapting slowly, others rapidly to give a variety of temporal as well as spatial "discriminanda." These findings are reminiscent of Nafe's (1934) quantitative theory of feeling, and the recent anatomical studies of Weddell (1955) and his group are of similar import.

In audition, selective sensitivity among the individual primary afferent fibers is very broad. Those fibers arising from the basal turn of the cochlea respond to tones of any audible frequency; those arising in the upper part respond only to a band of low frequency tones (Tasaki, 1954). Further, it has been suggested (Wever, 1949) that the temporal patterning of the dis-

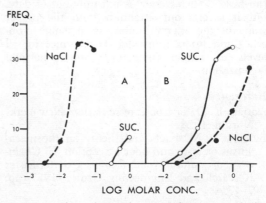

Figure 6 The relation between frequency of discharge and concentration in two fibers both of which are sensitive to sugar and salt. (Reproduced from the Journal of Neurophysiology.)

charge, especially in the low frequencies, provides a basis for pitch discrimination. In vision, Granit (1955) has suggested that different impulse frequencies in the *same* third order neuron from the retina may signal different spectral events at the periphery.

These electrophysiological results should not have been surprising to us. That a particular sensory dimension is not isomorphic with a particular physical dimension is well known. Auditory loudness, functionally dependent upon sound pressure level, is not synonymous with physical intensity. Pitch is not the same as frequency, although the latter is its major determinant (Stevens & Davis, 1938). Visual brightness is not the same as physical luminance. It would, indeed, have been surprising if similar nonidentities had not been found at the physiological level.

And so in attacking Müeller's classic problem with modern techniques, we have found, at least, within the modalities, a solution different from that which was first anticipated. Differential sensitivity rather than specificity, patterned discharges rather than a mosaic of sensitivities is the form of our modern view. Müeller's principle did not answer a problem so much as it posed one. In the answers that I have attempted to suggest, we see, not only the details of the mechanism for which we have searched, but we can discern broader implications for the principles governing the relation between psychology and physiology. Psychology cannot rest content with a pseudophysiology based solely upon phenomenology. So long as the receptor surface was conceived to be a static mosaic where phenomenal qualities were reified (in some instances in the form of specific anatomical structures), sensory psychology and physiology were reduced to the study of how the "little pictures" were transmitted via the sensory nerves to the "sensorium" located presumably somewhere "inside the head." Such a view is not only out of date, but it diverts our attention from the proper study of the afferent influx, its dynamic properties and interactions and its relevance for all levels of neural integration and behavioral organization.

References

Adrian, E. D. *The basis of sensation.* New York: Norton, 1928.

Beidler, L. M. Facts and theory on the mechanism of taste and odor perception. In *Chemistry of natural food flavors.* Quartermaster Research and Engineering Center, 1957, pp. 7–47.

Beidler, L. M., Fishman, I. Y., and Hardiman, C. W. Species differences in taste responses. *Amer. J. Physiol.,* 1955, **181**, 235–239.

Boring, E. G. A *history of experimental psychology.* New York: Appleton-Century-Crofts, 1950.

Carmichael, L. Sir Charles Bell: A contribution to the history of physiological psychology. *Psychol. Rev.,* 1926, **33**, 188–217.

Carpenter, J. A. Species differences in taste preferences. *J. comp. physiol. Psychol.,* 1956, **49**, 139–144.

Cohen, M. J., Hagiwara, S., and Zotterman, Y. The response spectrum of taste fibers in the cat: A single fiber analysis. *Acta. physiol., Scand.,* 1955, **33**, 316–332.

Granit, R. *Receptors and sensory perception.* New Haven: Yale Univer. Press, 1955.

Hensel, H., and Zotterman, Y. The response of mechanoreceptors to thermal stimulation. *J. Physiol.,* 1951, **115**, 16–24.

Kimura, K., and Beidler, L. M. Microelectrode study of taste bud of the rat. *Amer. J. Physiol.,* 1956, **187**, 610.

Liljestrand, G., and Zotterman, Y. The water taste in mammals. *Acta. physiol., Scand.,* 1954, **32**, 291–303.

Maruhashi, J., Mizuguchi, K. and Tasaki, I. Action currents in single afferent nerve fibers elicited by stimulation of the skin of the toad and the cat. *J. Physiol.,* 1952, **117**, 129–151.

Nafe, J. P. The pressure, pain and temperature senses. In C. Murchison (Ed.), *Handbook of general experimental psychology.* Worcester: Clark Univer. Press, 1934, chap. 20.

Pfaffmann, C. Gustatory afferent impulses. *J. cell. comp. Physiol.,* 1941, **17**, 243–258.

Pfaffmann, C. Species differences in taste sensitivity. *Science,* 1953, **117**, 470.

Pfaffmann, C. Gustatory nerve impulses in rat, cat, and rabbit. *J. Neurophysiol.,* 1955, **18**, 429–440.

Stevens, S. S., and Davis, H. *Hearing.* New York: Wiley, 1938.

Tasaki, I. Nerve impulses in individual auditory nerve fibers of guinea pigs. *J. Neurophysiol.,* 1954, **17**, 97–122.

Weddell, G. Somesthesis and the chemical senses. *Ann. Rev. Psychol.,* 1955, **6**, 119–136.

Wever, E. G. *Theory of hearing.* New York: Wiley, 1949.

Wever, E. G., and Bray, C. W. Action currents in the auditory nerve in response to acoustical stimulation. *Proc. Nat. Acad. Sci.,* 1930, **16**, 344–350.

CHAPTER THIRTEEN

Psychological measurement

KINDS OF MEASUREMENT

Some of the basic ideas of sampling and measurement are presented in this selection.

Points to guide your study

1. Make sure that you understand the difference between (a) *population* and *sample;* (b) *descriptive* and *sampling* statistics; (c) *estimate* and *parameter;* (d) *dependent* and *independent* variables; (e) *continuous* and *discrete* variables.

2. The correlations, means, standard deviations, medians, ranges, etc., reported in the articles in this readings book are examples of descriptive statistics, while the statistics yielding *p* values are sampling statistics.

40. STATISTICAL ANALYSIS IN PSYCHOLOGY AND EDUCATION

George A. Ferguson, McGill University*

Basic ideas in statistics

Introduction. The data resulting from any experiment are usually a collection of observations or measurements. The conclusions to be drawn from the experiment cannot be reliably ascertained by simple direct inspection of the data. Classification, summary description, and rules of evidence for the drawing of valid inference are required. Statistics provides the methodology whereby this can be done.

Implicit in any experiment is the presumption that it is possible to argue validly from the particular to the general and that new knowledge can be obtained by the process of inductive inference. The statistician does not assume that such arguments can be made with certainty. On the contrary, he assumes that some degree of uncertainty must attach to all such arguments; that some of the inferences drawn from the data of experiments are wrong. He further assumes that the uncertainty itself is amenable to precise and rigorous treatment, that it is possible to make rigorous statements about the uncertainty which attaches to any particular inference. Thus

* G. A. Ferguson. *Statistical analysis in psychology and education.* New York: McGraw-Hill, 1959. Copyright 1959 by the McGraw-Hill Book Company, Inc. Excerpt reprinted here with permission from the author and the McGraw-Hill Book Company, Inc.

in the uncertain milieu of experimentation he applies a rigorous method.

A knowledge of statistics is an essential part of the training of all students in psychology. There are many reasons for this. *First,* an understanding of the modern literature of psychology requires a knowledge of statistical method and modes of thought. A high proportion of current books and journal articles either report experimental findings in statistical form or present theories or arguments involving statistical concepts. These concepts play an increasing role in our thinking about psychological problems, quite apart from the treatment of data. The student need only consider, for example, the role of statistical concepts in current lines of theorizing in the field of learning to grasp the force of this argument. *Second,* training in psychology at an advanced level requires that the student himself design and conduct experiments. The design of an experiment is inseparable from the statistical treatment of the results. Experiments must be designed to enable the treatment of results in such a way as to permit an adequate test of the hypothesis that led to the conduct of the experiment in the first place. If the design of an experiment is faulty, no amount of statistical manipulation can lead to the drawing of valid inferences. Experimental design and statistical procedures are two sides of the same coin. Thus not only must the advanced student conduct experiments and interpret results, he must plan his experiments in such a way that the interpretation of results can conform to known rules of scientific evidence. *Third*, training in statistics is training in scientific method. Statistical inference is scientific inference, which in turn is inductive inference, the making of general statements from the study of particular cases. These terms are for all practical purposes, and at a certain level of generality, synonymous. Statistics attempts to make induction rigorous. Induction is regarded by some scholars as the only way in which new knowledge comes into the world. While this statement is debatable, the role in modern society of scientific discovery through induction is obviously of the greatest importance. For this reason no serious student of psychology, or any other discipline, can afford not to know something of the rudiments of the scientific approach to problems. Statistical procedures and ideas play an important role in this approach.

The broad role of quantification in psychology. While this book is largely concerned with elementary statistical procedures and ideas, some mention may be made of the broad role of quantitative method in psychology.

The attempt to quantify has a long and distinguished history in experimental psychology, which indeed may be regarded as synonymous with the history of that science itself. Since the experimental work in psychophysics of E. H. Weber and Gustav Fechner in the nineteenth century, determined attempts have been made to develop psychology as an experimental science. The early psychophysicists were concerned with the relationship between the "mind" and the "body" and developed certain mathematical functions which they held to be descriptive of that relationship. While much of their thinking on the mind-body problem has been discarded, their methods and techniques with development and elaboration are still used. Shorn of its philosophical and theoretical encumbrances, the work of the early psychophysicists was reduced in effect to the study of the relationship between measurements, obtained in two different ways, of what were presumed to be the same property. Thus, for example, they studied the relationship between weight, length, and temperature, defined by the responses of human subjects as instruments, and weight, length, and temperature, defined by other measuring instruments, scales, foot rules, and thermometers. A psychophysical law, so called, is a statement of the relationship between measurements obtained by these two methods. Modern psychophysics is concerned to some considerable extent with the scaling of the responses of the human subject as instrument and with the use of the human subject as instrument in dealing with a wide variety of practical problems. It may perhaps be referred to as human instrumentation.

The early psychophysicists invented certain experimental methods and developed statistical procedures for handling the data obtained by these methods. It is of interest to note that one method, the *constant process*, developed by G. E. Müller and F. M. Urban, has recently, with modification, found application in biological-assay work in assessing the potency of hormones, toxicants, and drugs of all types. It is currently known in biology as the *method of probits* (Finney 1944, 1947).

Statistical methods have found extensive application in the psychological testing field and in the study of human ability. Since the time of Binet, who developed the first extensively used test of intelligence and whose thinking was influenced by the early psychophysicists, a comprehensive body of theory and technique has been developed which is primarily statistical in type. This body of theory and technique is concerned with the construction of instruments for measuring human ability, personality characteristics, attitudes, interests, and many other aspects of behavior; with the nature and magnitude of the errors involved in such measurement; with the logical conditions which such measuring instruments must satisfy; with the quantitative prediction of human behavior; and with other related topics.

The use of psychological tests stimulated the development of the techniques of factor analysis, which are used to some extent in contemporary psychology. Problems arise which involve a study of the relationships between sets of variables, sometimes as many as 50 or 60 and perhaps more. Factor analysis attempts to provide a simplified description of these relationships, which facilitates an interpretation and comprehension of the information in the data. Factor analysis has found a number of uses in branches of science other than psychology, including meteorology and agriculture. Some of the problems in factor analysis have not as yet been fully resolved.

Within recent years frequent use has been made of statistical concepts in the construction of models designed to provide some explanation and understanding of observable phenomena. Such models are used in the field of learning. Further, many biological scientists are currently concerned with the construction of models which may possibly bear some correspondence to the functioning of certain aspects of the central nervous system. While these attempts may be premature and their success cannot at this time be evaluated, it is possible that in future the models which will prove helpful in understanding the functioning of the human brain will either implicitly or explicitly involve statistical concepts. In a system comprised of a complex network of nerve fibers, the transmission of impulses can be conceived in probabilistic terms.

While the avenues of quantification mentioned above do not fall within the context of this book, their study demands a knowledge of statistical method and a comprehension of the basic ideas of statistics as a starting point. It would seem that as psychology develops, increasing emphasis will be placed on quantitative procedure and an increasing degree of statistical sophistication will be required of the student.

Statistics as the study of populations. Statistics is a branch of scientific methodology. It deals with the collection, classification, description, and interpretation of data obtained by the conduct of surveys and experiments. Its essential purpose is to describe and draw inferences about the numerical properties of populations. The terms population and numerical property require clarification.

In everyday language the term *population* is used to refer to groups or aggregates of people. We speak, for example, of the population of the United States, or of the state of Texas, or of the city of New York, meaning by this all the people who occupy defined geographical regions at specified times. This, however, is a particular usage of the term population. The statistician employs the term in a more general sense to refer not only to defined groups or aggregates of people, but also to defined groups or aggregates of animals, objects, materials, measurements, or "things" or "happenings" of any kind. Thus the statistician may define, for his particular purposes, populations of laboratory animals, trees, nerve fibers, liquids, soil, manufactured articles, automobile accidents, microorganisms, birds' eggs, insects, or fishes in the sea. On occasion he may deal with a population of measurements. By this is meant an indefinitely large aggregate of measurements which, hypothetically, might be obtained under specified experimental conditions. To illustrate, a series of measurements might be made of the length of a desk. Some or all of these measurements may differ one from another because of the presence of errors of measurement. This series of measurements may be regarded as part of an indefinitely large aggregate or population of measurements which might, hypothetically, be obtained by measuring the length of the desk over and over again an indefinitely large number of times.

The general concept implicit in all these particular uses of the word population is that of group or aggregation. The statistician's concern is with properties which are descriptive of the group or aggregation itself rather than with properties of particular members. Thus measurements may be made of the height and weight of a group of individuals. These measurements may be added together and divided by the number of cases to obtain the mean height and weight. These means describe a property of the group as a whole and are not descriptive of particular individuals. To illustrate further, a child may have an IQ of 90 and belong to a high socioeconomic group. Another child may have an IQ of 120 and belong to a low socioeconomic group. These facts as such about individual children do not directly concern the statistician. If, however, questions are raised about the proportion of children in a particular population or subpopulation with IQ's above or below a specified value, or if more general questions are raised about the relationship between intelligence and socioeconomic level, then these are questions of a statistical nature, and the statistician has techniques which assist their exploration.

The distinction is sometimes made between *finite* and *infinite* populations. The children attending school in the city of Chicago, the inmates of penitentiaries in Ontario, the cards in a deck are examples of finite populations. The members of such a population can presumably be counted, and a finite number obtained. The possible rolls of a die and the possible observations in many scientific experiments are examples of infinite or indefinitely large populations. The number of rolls of a die or the number of scientific observations may, at least theoretically, be increased without any finite limit. In many situations the populations which the statistician proposes to describe are finite, but so large that for all practical purposes they may be regarded as infinite. The 175 million or so people living in the United States constitute a large but finite population. This population is so large that for many types of statistical inference it may be assumed to be infinite. This would not apply to the cards in a deck, which may be thought of as a small finite population of 52 members.

Most populations are comprised of naturally distinguishable members, as is, of course, the case with people, animals, measurements, or the rolls of a die. Some populations are not so comprised, as is the case with liquids, soils, woven fabrics, or, for that matter, human behavior. How is it possible to apply the concept of group or aggregation to populations of this latter type? This may be done by defining the population member arbitrarily as a liter, a cubic centimeter, a square yard, or some such unit. The whole population may be thought to be composed of an aggregate of such members. Likewise, in the study of human behavior, the psychologist frequently concerns himself with arbitrarily defined bits of behavior, although behavior as such may perhaps be regarded as a continuous flow or sequence.

Statistics is concerned with the numerical properties of populations, that is, with properties to which numerals can in some manner be assigned. The logical implications of the term *numerical property* are complex and need not be elaborated here. To illustrate briefly, however, in any population of mental-hospital patients some may be classed as psychoneurotic, others as schizophrenic psychotic, others as psychotic with organic brain disease, and so on. Further, some patients may come from broken homes, while others may have a normal healthy home background. Some may have a history of mental disease in the family, and others may not. We may be said to apply a statistical method when we concern ourselves with how many patients in the population fall within these various classes, that is, how many are psychoneurotic, schizophrenic psychotic, and the like, and how many come from broken homes, how many do not, and so on. Further, the flicker fusion rates of some part or all of the population may be measured and attention directed to the numbers of patients who fall within specified ranges of flicker fusion rate, to mean rates for various classes of patients, and to related problems. The investigation of such problems as these may be said to involve a statistical method. In general, the statistician's concern is with those properties of populations which can be expressed in numerical form.

In summary, statistics is a methodology for the exploration of, and the making of statements about, the properties of groups or aggregates called populations. These statements involve use of numbers. These delimitations of the referent of the word statistics are adequate for the purposes of this book, although quite clearly further delimitations may usefully be made.

Samples and sampling. Many populations are either large but finite or indefinitely large. Consequently, it becomes either impracticable or impossible for the investigator to produce statistics based on all members. If, for example, interest is in investigating the attitudes of adult Canadians toward immigrants, it would obviously be a prohibitively expensive and time-consuming task to measure the attitudes of all adult Canadians and produce statistics based on a study of the complete population. If a population is indefinitely large, it is of course impossible, *ipso facto*, to produce complete population statistics. Under circumstances such as these the investigator draws what is spoken of as a sample. A sample is any subgroup or subaggregate drawn by some appropriate method from a population, the method used in drawing the sample being important. Methods used in drawing samples will be discussed in later chapters of this book. Having drawn his sample, the investigator utilizes appropriate statistical methods to describe its properties. He then proceeds to make statements about the properties of the population from his knowledge of the properties

of the sample; that is, he proceeds to generalize from the sample to the population. To return to the example above, an investigator might draw a sample of 1,000 adult Canadians, the term *adult* being assigned a precise meaning, measure their attitudes toward immigrants using an acceptable technique of measurement, and calculate the required statistics. Questions may then be raised about the attitudes of all adult Canadians from the information obtained from a study of the sample of 1,000.

The fact that inferences can be made about the properties of populations from a knowledge of the properties of samples is basic in research thinking. Such statements are of course subject to error. The magnitude of the error involved in drawing such inferences can, however, in most cases be estimated by appropriate procedures. Where no estimate of error of any kind can be made, generalizations about populations from sample data are worthless.

Information about properties of particular samples, quite apart from any generalizations about the population, is of little intrinsic interest in itself. Consider a case where the investigator's interest is in the relative effects of two types of psychotherapy when applied to patients suffering from a particular mental disorder. He may select two samples of patients, apply one type of treatment to one sample and the other type of treatment to the other sample, and collect data on the relative rates of recovery of patients in the two samples. Clearly, in this case his interest is in finding out whether the one treatment is better or worse than the other when applied to the whole class of patients suffering from the mental disorder in question. He is interested in the sample data only in so far as these data enable him to draw inferences with some acceptable degree of assurance about this general question. His experimental procedures must be designed to enable the drawing of such inferences, otherwise the experiment serves no purpose. On occasion research reports are found where the investigator states that the experimental results obtained should not be generalized beyond the particular sample of individuals who participated in the study. The adoption of this view means that the investigator has missed the essential nature of experimentation. Unless the intention is to generalize from a sample to a population, unless the procedures used are such as to enable such generalizations justifiably to be made, and unless some estimate of error can be obtained, the conduct of experiments is without point.

Statistical procedures used in describing the properties of samples, or of populations where complete population data are available, are referred to by some writers as *descriptive statistics*. If we measure the IQ of the complete population of students in a particular university and compute the mean IQ, that mean is a descriptive statistic because it describes a characteristic of the complete population. If, on the other hand, we measure the IQ of a sample of 100 students and compute the mean IQ for the sample, that mean is also a descriptive statistic.

Statistical procedures used in the drawing of inferences about the properties of populations from sample data are frequently referred to as *sampling statistics*. If, for example, we wish to make a statement about the mean IQ in the complete population of students in a particular university from a knowledge of the mean computed on the sample of 100 and estimate the error involved in this statement, we use procedures from sampling statistics. The application of these procedures provides information about the accuracy of the sample mean as an estimate of the population mean; that is, it indicates the degree of assurance we may place in the inferences we draw from the sample to the population.

While the distinction between descriptive and sampling statistics is a useful one, it may be emphasized that the ultimate object of statistical method is the making of statements about populations. A mean calculated on a sample provides information about the population from which the sample is drawn, although in any particular instance the information may be very inaccurate. The ultimate intent is in all instances to find things out about populations. Most statistical methods, whether referred to as descriptive or sampling methods, are means to this end.

In this section no discussion is advanced on methods of drawing samples or the conditions which these methods must satisfy to allow the drawing of valid inferences from the sample to the population. Further, no precise meaning has been assigned to the term error. These topics will be elaborated at a later stage.

Parameters and estimates. A clear distinction is usually drawn between parameters and estimates. A *parameter* is a property descriptive of the population. The term *estimate* refers to a property of a sample drawn at random from a population. The sample value is presumed to be an estimate of a corresponding population parameter. Suppose, for example, that a sample of 1,000 adult male Canadians of a given age range is drawn from the total population, the height of the members of the sample measured, and a mean value, 68.972 in., obtained. This value is an estimate of the population parameter which would have been obtained had it been possible to measure all the members in the population. Usually parameters or population values are unknown. We estimate them from our sample values. The distinction between parameter and estimate reflects itself in statistical notation.

A widely used convention in notation is to employ Greek letters to represent parameters and Roman letters to represent estimates. Thus the symbol σ, the Greek letter sigma, may be used to represent the standard deviation in the population, the standard deviation being a commonly used measure of variability. The symbol s may be used as an estimate of the parameter σ. This convention in notation is applicable only within broad limits. By and large we shall adhere to this convention in this book, although in certain instances it will be necessary to depart from it.

Variables and their classification. The term *variable* refers to a property whereby the members of a group or set differ one from another. The members of a group may be individuals and may be found to differ in sex, age, eye color, intelligence, auditory acuity, reaction time to a stimulus, attitudes toward a political issue, and in a thousand other ways. Such properties are variables. The term *constant* refers to a property whereby the members of a group do not differ one from another. In a sense a constant is a particular type of variable; it is a variable which does not vary from one member of a group to another or within a particular set of defined conditions.

Labels or numerals may be used to describe the way in which one member of a group is the same as or different from another. With variables like sex, racial origin, religious affiliation, and occupation, labels are employed to identify the members which fall within particular classes. An individual may be classified as male or female; of English, French, or Dutch racial origin; Protestant or Catholic; a shoemaker or a farmer; and so on. The label identifies the class to which the individual belongs. Sex for most practical purposes is a two-valued variable, individuals being either male or female. Occupation, on the other hand, is a multivalued variable. Any particular individual may be assigned to any one of a large number of classes. With variables like height, weight, intelligence, and so on, measuring operations may be employed which enable the assignment of descriptive numerical values. An individual may be 72 in. tall, weigh 190 lb, and have an IQ of 90.

The particular values of a variable are referred to as *variates*, or *variate values*. To illustrate, in considering the height of adult males, height is the variable, whereas the height of any particular individual is a variate, or variate value.

In dealing with variables which bear a functional relationship one to another the distinction may be drawn between *dependent* and *independent* variables. Consider the expression

$$Y = f(X)$$

This expression says that a given variable Y is

some unspecified function of another variable X. The symbol f is used generally to express the fact that a functional relationship exists, although the precise nature of the relationship is not stated. In any particular case the nature of the relationship may be known; that is, we may know precisely what f means. Under these circumstances, for any given value of X a corresponding value of Y can be calculated; that is, given X and a knowledge of the functional relationship, Y can be predicted. It is customary to speak of Y, the predicted variable, as the dependent variable because the prediction of it depends on the value of X and the known functional relationship, whereas X is spoken of as the independent variable. Given an expression of the kind $Y = X^3$ for any given value of X, an exact value of Y can readily be determined. Thus if X is known, Y is also known exactly. Many of the functional relationships found in statistics permit probabilistic and not exact prediction to occur. Such relationships may provide the most probable value of Y for any given value of X, but do not permit the making of perfect predictions.

A distinction may be drawn between *continuous* and *discrete* (or *discontinuous*) variables. A continuous variable may take any value within a defined range of values. The possible values of the variable belong to a continuous series. Between any two values of the variable an indefinitely large number of in-between values may occur. Height, weight, and chronological time are examples of continuous variables. A discontinuous or discrete variable can take specific values only. Size of family is a discontinuous variable. A family may be comprised of 1, 2, 3 or more children, but values between these numbers are not possible. The values obtained in rolling a die are 1, 2, 3, 4, 5, and 6. Values between these numbers are not possible. Although the underlying variable may be continuous, all sets of real data in practice are discontinuous or discrete. Convenience and errors of measurement impose restrictions on the refinement of the measurement employed.

Another classification of variables is possible which is of some importance and is of particular interest to statisticians. This classification is based on differences in the type of information which different operations of classification or measurement yield. To illustrate, consider the following situations. An observer using direct inspection may rank order a group of individuals from the tallest to the shortest according to height. On the other hand, he may use a foot rule and record the height of each individual in the group in feet and inches. These two operations are clearly different, and the nature of the information obtained by applying the two operations is different. The former operation

permits statements of the kind: individual A is taller or shorter than individual B. The latter operation permits statements of how much taller or shorter one individual is than another. Differences along these lines serve as a basis for a classification of variables, the class to which a variable belongs being determined by the nature of the information made available by the measuring operation used to define the variable. Four broad classes of variables may be identified. These are referred to as (1) nominal, (2) ordinal, (3) interval, and (4) ratio variables. This classification is discussed in some detail by Stevens (1951, Chap. 1). A recent and very interesting discussion relevant to this topic is given in Torgerson (1958).

A *nominal variable* is a property of the members of a group defined by an operation which permits the making of statements only of equality or difference. Thus we may state that one member is the *same as* or *different from* another member with respect to the property in question. Statements about the ordering of members, or the equality of differences between members, or the number of times a particular member is greater than or less than another are not possible. To illustrate, individuals may be classified by the color of their eyes. Color is a nominal variable. The statement that an individual with blue eyes is in some sense "greater than" or "less than" an individual with brown eyes is meaningless. Likewise the statement that the difference between blue eyes and brown eyes is equal to the difference between brown eyes and green eyes is meaningless. The only kind of meaningful statement possible with the information available is that the eye color of one individual is the same as or different from the eye color of another. A nominal variable may perhaps be viewed as a primitive type of variable, and the operations whereby the members of a group are classified according to such a variable constitute a primitive form of measurement. In dealing with nominal variables numerals may be assigned to represent classes, but such numerals are labels, and the only purpose they serve is to identify the members within a given class.

An *ordinal variable* is a property defined by an operation which permits the rank ordering of the members of a group; that is, not only are statements of equality and difference possible, but also statements of the kind *greater than* or *less than*. Statements about the equality of differences between members or the number of times one member is greater than or less than another are not possible. If a judge is required to order a group of individuals according to aggressiveness, or cooperativeness, or some other quality, the resulting variable is ordinal in type. Many of the variables used in psychology are ordinal.

A distinction may be made between two types of ordinal variables, those with a natural origin, or "zero" point, and those without a natural origin (Torgerson, 1958). An ordering of pupils on intelligence by a teacher is an ordinal variable without a natural origin. On ordering a set of stimuli according to their pleasantness, the point of transition from unpleasant to pleasant may be taken as a natural origin.

An *interval variable* is a property defined by an operation which permits the making of statements of equality of intervals, in addition to statements of sameness or difference or greater than or less than. Thus we may state that the difference between individuals A and B is equal to the difference between individuals B and C. An interval variable does not have a true zero point, or natural origin, although in many cases a zero point may for convenience be arbitrarily defined. Temperature as measured by a centigrade or Fahrenheit thermometer and calendar time are examples of interval variables.

A *ratio variable* is a property defined by an operation which permits the making of statements of equality of ratios in addition to all the other kinds of statements discussed above. This means that one variate value may be spoken of as double or triple another, and so on. An absolute zero is always implied. The numbers used represent distances from a natural origin. Length, weight, and the numerosity of aggregates are examples of ratio variables. In psychological work variables which conform to the rigorous requirements of ratio variables are not numerous. Scales for measuring loudness, pitch, and other variables have been developed by Stevens and his associates (1957) at Harvard. These appear to satisfy all the conditions of ratio variables.

Some writers distinguish between *quantitative* and *qualitative* variables without being explicit about the nature of this distinction. In the present classificatory system nominal and ordinal variables may be spoken of as qualitative, and interval and ratio variables as quantitative.

Most statistical methods have been developed for the handling of problems involving interval and ratio variables. A method which is appropriate in dealing with one type of variable may not be appropriate with another. In practice, however, we frequently apply procedures appropriate to one type of variable to problems involving other classes of variables. This means that we either discard information which we do in fact possess or assume that we have information which we do not possess. An example of this latter type of situation arises frequently with rank-order data. The members of a group are ordered. Our information consists of relationships greater than or less than, and these are described by a set of ordinal numbers; thus one member is first, another second, and so on. It is a common practice to replace such a set of ordinal numbers by the corresponding set of cardinal numbers, 1, 2, 3, . . . , N, and to proceed then to apply arithmetical operations to these numbers. This means that certain assumptions are made. Information is superimposed on the data which the measuring operation did not yield; that is, for computational purposes we assume we are in possession of information which actually we do not have. In the above instance we are making an assumption about equality of intervals when in fact the measuring operation employed does not yield information of this kind. The assumption is that the difference between the first and second individuals is equal to the difference between the second and third, and so on. In psychological work many variables are either nominal or ordinal. For example, scores on intelligence tests, attitude scales, personality tests, and the like, are in effect ordinal variables. We cannot say, for example, that the difference between an IQ of 80 and an IQ of 90 is in any sense equal to the difference between an IQ of 110 and an IQ of 120. None the less such variables are frequently treated by methods which, from a rigorous logical viewpoint, are appropriate only to interval and ratio variables. The suggestion is not made here that the practice of assuming that we have information we do not have, or the converse practice of discarding information we do in fact have, be discontinued, although a logical puritan might be led to this position. Frequently practical necessity dictates a particular procedure. Nevertheless it is a matter of some importance to know the nature of the information contained in the data. We should be able to distinguish clearly between this and the information either imposed or discarded for the purpose of making some process of calculation possible. In other words, our understanding of precisely what we are doing is enriched by knowing the nature of the assumptions made at each stage in the application of any procedure.

References

Finney, D. J. The application of probit analysis to the results of mental tests. *Psychometrika*, 1944, 9, 31–39.

Finney, D. J. *Probit analysis*. New York: Cambridge University Press, 1947.

Stevens, S. S. (Ed.) *Handbook of experimental psychology*. New York: John Wiley, 1951.

Stevens, S. S. On the psychophysical law. *Psychological Review*, 1957, 64, 153–181.

Torgerson, W. S. *Theory and methods of scaling*. New York: John Wiley, 1958.

CHARACTERISTICS OF "GOOD" PSYCHOLOGICAL TESTS

The most important characteristics of "good" psychological tests are reliability, validity, and standardization. In other words, the consistency with which a test measures something (reliability), whether the test measures what it purports to measure (validity), and whether there is a standard, a normative group, against which to compare scores (standardization) are crucial. These characteristics are illustrated in this article.

The Allport-Vernon-Lindzey *Study of Values* test purports to measure theoretical, economic, aesthetic, social, political, and religious values. This article presents results on a revision of the original test for a special purpose. As measured in two ways, the test-retest and split-half methods, the revision was reliable. The revision also has some validity, as judged by the kinds of magazine articles preferred by persons with different values. The revision has not yet been standardized, however.

A point to guide your study

Can you design a study or experiment in which the Allport-Vernon-Lindzey scale is used?

41. A REVISION OF THE STUDY OF VALUES FOR USE IN MAGAZINE READERSHIP RESEARCH

*Warren C. Engstrom and Mary E. Powers, Curtis Publishing Company**

One of the most important goals in magazine readership research is the development of valid and reliable methods of measuring individuals with respect to whatever psychological attributes we might reasonably assume to be related to the reading of magazines. This goal is based on the assumption that the mental and emotional activity involved is not haphazard or random, but has measurable causes within the individual personality.

Studies which related demographic data to readership represented the first attempts by mass communications researchers to find functional variables of magazine readership. This approach was found to be of limited usefulness as the analysis of readership data progressed from sim-

* The authors are indebted to Herbert C. Ludeke, Manager Development Division, Research Department, The Curtis Publishing Company, for his guidance and support throughout this project.

W. C. Engstrom, and Mary E. Powers. A revision of the study of values for use in magazine readership research. *J. appl. Psychol.*, 1959, **43**, 74–78. Copyright 1959 by the American Psychological Association. Reprinted here with permission from the senior author, for the authors, and the American Psychological Association.

ple studies of item popularity to attempts to understand unique reading patterns. The search for more basic explanations led to the attempt to measure personality factors, which, if they could be found to be discriminators of individuals and groups of individuals with respect to the items they choose to read, could lay the foundation for more adequate explanations of magazine reading behavior.

The Allport-Vernon *Study of Values* was selected as the experimental measurement for this study for the following reasons: (*a*) Its orientation tended to be similar to attitude and opinion studies commonly made of general populations; (*b*) It was not a clinical measurement; its approach to personality measurement was in the area of normal personality; (*c*) Evaluative judgments, as used in the *Study of Values*, appeared to be closely related to the type of behavior involved in magazine reading.

Some historical justification for expecting that the *Study of Values* would be effective in relating magazine reading to values did exist. A. G. Woolbert showed that it was an effective predictor of recall of experimental newspaper items (Cantril & Allport, 1933, p. 265). Other early studies, reported by Cantril and Allport in 1933, demonstrated that general evaluative attitudes influence the activities of everyday life.

The investigators were, of course, aware of the conflicting opinions about the *Study of Values*. The hypothesis was made, however, that this measurement would validly and reliably differentiate groups of individuals with respect to the six values of the test, and that these values would be related to magazine reading.

Revising the study of values

In the form in which it is presently published, the *Study of Values* was found to be considerably above the vocabulary level of noncollege general populations found in national studies of magazine reading. In addition, certain items appeared to be too specialized or of too limited interest to general populations, as they assumed a cultural level far above average. For the purposes of our study, a revision was clearly necessary.

The Curtis revision of the *Study of Values* attempted to reduce the vocabulary and cultural levels to that of readers of mass circulation magazines, while at the same time, to do as little violence as possible to the underlying design and wording of the original test. The investigators were at all times mindful of the necessity of modernizing and simplifying the language of the test without substantially changing its design or thought. It was also found necessary to simplify the original scoring and marking system, and to develop a new type of score sheet for office use. All the revisions were made empirically through the combined experience of the investigators in preparing, testing and analyzing survey questionnaires used with national samples of magazine readers.

The following example will demonstrate the level of the revision:

Item 20, Part I: Original Version (Allport, Vernon, & Lindzey, 1951a)

Which of the following would you consider the more important function of education? (a) its preparation for practical achievement and financial reward; (b) its preparation for participation in community activities and aiding less fortunate persons.

Revised Version

The aim of schools should be: (a) to prepare students to get good jobs; (b) to prepare students for community activities and helping others.

The Curtis revision of the *Study of Values* has been field tested in a variety of situations. Following extensive pretesting within the Curtis Publishing Company, the revision was administered as a house-to-house survey interview with noncollege housewives in a midde-class suburban Philadelphia neighborhood in order to test the feasibility of the revision in a typical field interviewing situation. Results of this field test indicated that the revision was usable under these conditions.

Its most rigorous field test to date was made when it was administered to 300 Ss in a six-city study to test the validity of the revision. Five methods of administering the *Study of Values* were used; the test was conducted both with individuals and with groups, in both office and home situations.

These field testing procedures demonstrated that the Curtis revision of the *Study of Values* is a practical instrument under field conditions, in that all five methods were successful in gaining respondent cooperation and in establishing the understandability of the test items, the scoring and the instructions. The success of the personal interview method, in particular, indicates that the revision can be used on a national sample basis with magazine reader audiences.

Establishing the reliability of the revision

Reliability tests were conducted on two groups of Ss: the Junior Class of the Radnor Senior High School of Wayne, Pennsylvania, and a group of new industrial employees of The Curtis Publishing Company. Both groups met the educational and cultural specifications of the study: no S had received more than a high school education, although the high school group contained many who planned to go on to college. The handicap imposed on the findings through the use of these groups was, of course, recognized at the time of their selection. The groups comprised individuals different in many ways from groups of mass circulation magazine readers found in national studies. If, however, the revision of the *Study of Values* proved to have acceptable reliability for the two experimental groups, it might be argued that the revision would be operating under less difficult conditions among adult readers of national magazines, and could be considered reliable for work with reader audiences.

Both administrations to the high school group were made by the investigators themselves, with a time lapse of four months between the two tests. The time lapse for the industrial group was one month between the two tests, with the administration conducted by members of the Personnel Department of The Curtis Publishing Company. Table 1 shows the test-retest correlations for the two experimental groups.

The repeat reliability coefficients shown in Table 1 were somewhat lower than those reported by Allport, Vernon, and Lindzey for their 1951 revision of the *Studies of Values*. A longer time period, however, was involved for the high school group in this current study than

Table 1 Test-retest product-moment reliability coefficients for the Curtis revision of the Study of Values

Value	Test-retest reliability coefficient	
	Student group * (N = 77)	Industrial group † (N = 58)
Theoretical	.81	.71
Economic	.85	.73
Aesthetic	.87	.77
Social	.79	.80
Political	.80	.86
Religious	.85	.81

* Time lapse between tests: four months.
† Time lapse between tests: one month.

Table 2 Split-half reliability coefficients for the Curtis revision of the Study of Values

Value	Split-half reliability coefficient	
	Student group (N = 77)	Industrial group (N = 58)
Theoretical	.85	.57
Economic	.73	.51
Aesthetic	.70	.66
Social	.48	.58
Political	.54	.47
Religious	.86	.63

Note.—Reliability coefficients of whole test, calculated by applying the Spearman-Brown prophecy formula to the correlation between split halves.

for the groups tested in the 1951 revision study. The mean repeat reliability coefficients were .83 for the high school group and .78 for the Curtis industrial employees, using a z transformation. These mean coefficients may be compared with the mean of .89 for the Allport, Vernon, and Lindzey (1951b) revision.

The student group, as shown in Table 1, had higher test-retest reliability than the industrial employees, despite the fact that the time interval between the two administrations of the revision was four times longer for the student group. These higher reliability coefficients are all the more noteworthy since nonadult, immature Ss would be expected to show less stability on the Allport-Vernon values than the adult, nonstudent group of Curtis employees.

Split-half reliability was tested by dividing the revision into two subscales, the subscales being composed in such a manner that there was ap-

proximately the same number of pairings between the value under study and all remaining values. Table 2 shows the split-half reliability coefficients for the two experimental groups.

The mean reliability coefficient, using a z transformation, was .72 for the group of Radnor High School students and .57 for the group of industrial employees. This compares with a mean reliability coefficient of .82 for the Allport, Vernon, and Lindzey (1951b) revision of the *Study of Values*. Split-half reliability coefficients were lower than the repeat reliability coefficients, as was also true for the Allport, Vernon, and Lindzey (1951b) revision. One possible reason for the lower split-half reliability coefficients is that the *Study of Values* does not contain simple items dealing with only one value; pairings of values take place in every item. Random methods of selecting items for equivalent forms of the test cannot be applied; the investigators had to approximate the pairings of values for the items selected for split-half reliability testing.

The investigators were satisfied that the results of these tests of reliability demonstrated that the Curtis revision was sufficiently reliable to warrant further work with the test, even though it might be argued that the reliability figures would have been somewhat higher if reliability coefficients had been established for groups of adults more similar to those found in national populations of magazine readers.

As far as the discriminative power of the items in the revision was concerned, 96 out of the 120 choices in the test successfully distinguished between Ss whose score indicated that they ranked high on a test value and those ranking low on the value. On the other hand, 24 out of the 120 choices did not distinguish between highs and lows. These 24, however, were evenly distributed among the six values. Analyzing them further, it was found that only one item was totally worthless, in that neither choice was diagnostic. In general, the 24 failures were accepted by the investigators as a limitation of the Curtis revision which did not materially impair its value with respect to the purposes for which it was designed.

Testing the validity of the revision

The hypothesis that the Curtis revision of the *Study of Values* has validity with respect to the relationship between the six values as measured by the revision and expressed interest in reading magazine stories and articles was tested by means of a study conducted on 300 Ss (150 men and 150 women) in six Eastern cities: New York, Trenton, Allentown, Providence, Columbus, and Cincinnati.

The Curtis revision was administered to each S, along with a questionnaire on reading interests containing a list of titles of 35 magazine nonfiction articles and 33 magazine-type short stories. The titles were designed to cover 10 nonfiction and 11 fiction topics, with various themes and appeals within each topic. Interest in reading each of these items was registered by means of a thermometer scaling device, with high and low temperatures indicating high and low interest in reading the items. This thermometer scale had previously been validated as a predictor of reading interest and other behavior. (At the same time, attitudes toward several national magazines were studied by means of semantic differential tests, the results of which are beyond the scope of the present report.) Interviewing for this study was conducted by the Alan C. Russell Marketing Research organization.

Two questions to be answered by this study were, first, whether or not individuals scoring high on a given value differed significantly from those not scoring high on the value with respect to interest shown in story and article titles; and second, if there were differences, how well did reading interests correspond to the values as measured by the test? For the purposes of this analysis, individuals were considered "high" whose score for a value was plus one standard deviation from the mean for the value; individuals were considered to have shown positive interest in a title if they rated it 80 degrees or higher on the thermometer scale. Using these definitions, differences in interest in each story or article title for individuals high in each value were tested for significance.

Results indicated that 29 of the 33 fiction titles and 32 of the 35 nonfiction titles were significantly different in interest among persons scoring high in the six values. Differences significant at the 5 per cent level of confidence or better were then examined against the characterization of the six value types as described by Allport and Vernon in the Manual of Directions for the *Study of Values*, with the following results.

The dominant interest of the "theoretical" person, according to the authors of the *Study of Values*, is the discovery of truth; his interests are described as empirical, critical, and rational; he is seen as an intellectualist, with interests in science (1951b). In the current study, those persons who scored high in the theoretical value indicated a significantly higher interest in reading two of the three articles on science. For the third article, dealing with science in relation to human happiness rather than with "pure" science, they were not significantly higher. They also showed higher interest than others in science fiction. On the other hand they were significantly lower than other people in interest in reading the articles on domestic arts and on religion. They showed lower interest also in fiction themes dealing with romantic or sentimental aspects of love, home, and children. In all, the high theoretical people in this study showed significantly different interest in reading 14 of the 33 stories and 15 of the 35 articles.

The "economic" person as described in the *Study of Values* Manual of Directions is interested in the utilitarian, the tangible, the practical, and "conforms well to the prevailing stereotype of the average American business man." In the present study, those persons scoring high in the economic value indicated significantly higher interest than the noneconomic people in all sports articles, and in fiction dealing with sports and the West. They were significantly less interested than others in articles dealing with the theoretical aspects of a topic, as opposed to the practical, "how-to" aspects, whether the topic was medicine, religion, science, or entertainment. In all, the high economic people showed significantly different interest in reading three of the 33 stories and 12 of the 35 articles.

The "aesthetic" person, as defined by the authors of the *Study of Values*, is one who has a dominant interest in beauty, harmony, symmetry; he need not necessarily be creative, but is highly interested in the artistic. Those scoring high in the aesthetic value in the present test indicated significantly higher interest than nonaesthetic persons in the two articles dealing with aspects of American culture. They showed significantly less interest in reading the magazine-type fiction items included in this study: of the 33 fiction titles, high aesthetic scorers were lower in interest in 23. They also showed less interest in reading the nonfiction items than did nonaesthetic people: of the 35 nonfiction titles, they indicated significantly lower interest in 17.

The "social" person, as described by the test authors in the instruction manual, is one whose highest value is altruistic or philanthropic love of people, and who therefore tends to be sympathetic and unselfish. In the present study, those scoring high in the social value showed significantly higher interest in articles whose theme indicated emphasis on help or service to mankind. They also showed significantly higher interest in articles that centered on the home and family. In fiction their preferences ran to themes of human relationships: romance, home, and children, as well as stories of personal relationships against medical or business settings. They were significantly less interested than other persons in sports, whether fiction or nonfiction. In all, high social scorers differed significantly from others on 17 fiction and 12 nonfiction titles.

The "political" person, according to the test authors, is interested primarily in power, in all competition and struggle, not exclusively in politics. In the present study, those with high political scores expressed higher interest than others in reading articles on politics and on crime that dealt with conflict. They were also significantly higher in interest in competitive sports in both fiction and nonfiction. In addition they expressed preferences for war fiction. They were significantly lower than nonpolitical people in interest in articles on religion and on domestic articles of the home-service variety. In all, they differed significantly from others on four fiction and 11 nonfiction titles.

The "religious" person, as described by Allport and Vernon (1951b), is mystical, and has as his highest value unity, or the relating of himself to the cosmos as a whole. Those scoring high in the religious value in the present study showed significantly higher interest in all the religious articles included in the test. They were also higher than others in interest in articles dealing with some aspect of charity, and with family-service topics. In fiction they were significantly higher in interest for those stories of human relationships that seemed to be concerned with human problems. In all, high religious scorers differed significantly from others on five fiction and 14 nonfiction titles.

In summary, the data showed many areas where there were plausible relationships between the values as defined by the Allport-Vernon *Study of Values* and interest in reading the test items. The value scores were remarkably effective in discriminating among the type of stories and articles of interest to the various value groups. It should be noted that this study of validity was set up as a pilot study prior to a proposed full-scale national sample survey which would be the necessary and final step in establishing the validity of the test with respect to the relationship between the values tested and interest in reading magazines. From the evidence already on hand, however, it seems reasonable to assume that the Curtis revision of the *Study of Values* may be of considerable value to readership researchers in their attempts to understand reading behavior as it pertains to magazines.

Summary

One goal of magazine readership research is to develop measurements of psychological attributes related to readership of magazines. The Allport-Vernon *Study of Values* was chosen for study, and was revised for use with national samples of noncollege, general populations, under the conditions of house-to-house field survey interviewing. The revision was found to fulfill at least the minimum requirements of reliability. A pilot study made on 300 Ss tested the hypothesis that the *Study of Values* has validity with respect to interest in reading magazine fiction and nonfiction. Significant differences were found in reading interest for individuals of different values, and the value scores were effective in discriminating among the types of material chosen for reading by different groups of individuals.

References

Allport, G. W., Vernon, P. E., and Lindzey, G. *Study of values.* (Rev. ed.) Boston: Houghton Mifflin, 1951. (a)

Allport, G. W., Vernon, P. E., and Lindzey, G. *Study of values manual of directions.* (Rev. ed.) Boston: Houghton Mifflin, 1951. (b)

Cantril, H., and Allport, G. W. Recent applications of the study of values. *J. abnorm. soc. Psychol.*, 1933, **28**, 259–273.

CHAPTER FOURTEEN

Intelligence and aptitudes

Extremes of intelligence

A genius is more than a person who gets a high score on an intelligence test. He is more than a person who has an IQ greater than 140. For many psychologists the definition of genius is related to creativity. The chances of being highly creative increase with intelligence, as measured by performance on an intelligence test, but it takes more than a high IQ to be a genius. In other words, "genius is as genius does." Just as not all mentally deficient people (those with IQs less than 70) are feeble-minded (unable to make an adjustment in the world outside an institution), not all highly intelligent persons (with IQs above 140) are geniuses (creative).

Most psychologists would agree that, given a moderately stimulating environment, inheritance plays the largest role in the intelligence test performance (IQ) of an individual. This is a partial answer to the problem of why some people get higher IQ scores than others. The other problem is why some intelligent people are geniuses while others are not. This selection considers the early environment as an especially important factor in the creativity which makes for genius.

A point to guide your study

If you don't know the achievements of some of the people mentioned, look them up in an encyclopedia.

42. THE CHILDHOOD PATTERN OF GENIUS

*Harold G. McCurdy, University of North Carolina**

Genius by any definition is rare. If, following Galton, we make lasting fame one of the requirements, it is very rare indeed, and we are reduced to studying it at a distance through biography. Now, biographies have their limitations; as Havelock Ellis noted, one may search through them in vain for the most ordinary vital statistics. Above all, they cannot be expected to yield information on those details of early life, such as nursing and weaning and toilet training, to which psychoanalysis has attached so much importance. When, therefore, one proposes as I do here to explore the question whether there is some pattern of environmental influences operating on children of genius which might help to account for their later achievement, it should be self-evident that the question is necessarily adjusted to something less than microscopic precision. Not only so, but, because the factor of heredity cannot be controlled, any answer whatsoever must be regarded as partial and tentative and ambiguous. Nevertheless, there may be some profit in asking the question, and insofar as it is directed simply toward the discovery of uniformity of environmental pattern there is no inherent reason why it should not be answerable, provided we do not insist on minute detail.

Table I presents the twenty geniuses into whose childhood this paper will inquire. The selection was partly deliberate, on theoretical grounds, and partly random, as will be explained. In Cox's monumental study of great geniuses (7) the main sample consists of 282 men drawn from the list of 1,000 which was compiled by

* H. G. McCurdy. The Childhood Pattern of Genius. *J. Elisha Mitchell Sci. Society*, 1957, **73**, 448–462. Reprinted here with permission from the author and the Elisha Mitchell Scientific Society.

J. McKeen Cattell on the principle that the amount of space allotted to them in biographical dictionaries could be taken as an objective measure of their true eminence. Though one may certainly quarrel with some of Cattell's results, the sifting process applied by Cox was admirable. She arrived at her smaller list by requiring: one, that the attained eminence should clearly depend upon notable personal achievement; and two, that the biographical material available should be sufficient to permit a reliable estimate of early mental ability. Men born before 1450 were eliminated. The chief task of Cox's investigation was to estimate the intelligence level displayed by these rigorously selected geniuses during childhood and youth. For this purpose the appropriate information was extracted from biographical sources and submitted to the judgment of three raters thoroughly experienced in the use of intelligence tests and the evaluation of IQ from behavior. Their three independent ratings, expressed as IQ's, were combined. Separate estimates were made for two periods of life: from birth to age 17, and from age 17 to age 26. As might be expected, the reliabilities of the estimates increased in proportion to the amount of biographical information, and, in general, the IQ's based on the more adequate material were higher. Consequently, one in search of illumination on the early environment of genius would naturally turn most hopefully to the geniuses in Cox's list who had been assigned the highest

childhood IQ's. This I did. From her list I chose as my preliminary sample the 27 men whose IQ's in childhood had been estimated at 160 or higher. The final sample of 20, as given in Table I, was reached by dropping out those individuals for whom the biographical material in the University of North Carolina Library appeared to be inadequate.[1] As will be observed, the order of listing in the table is from the highest childhood IQ downwards. The reputation of each man is indicated in the column headed "Fame" by his rank number in Cox's sample, as based on Cattell. With respect to fame the sample appears to be a fair cross-section of Cox's larger group; with respect to IQ, as explained, it is highly selected. One sees at a glance that here are individuals who did extraordinary work in science, law, literature, or politics, and who fully deserve to be called geniuses. Their biographies should be relevant to the proposed question.

It should be understood from the outset that Cox did not neglect the problem of environment. Her biographical sketches furnish some very pertinent information, and she states as an important conclusion that, on the whole, youths who achieve eminence have superior advantages in their early days. Though she notes exceptions, she says: "The average opportunity of our young

[1] The seven omitted were Schelling, Haller, Wolsey, Sarpi, Constant, Brougham, Bossuet. In order to retain Leibniz an interlibrary loan was arranged for Guhrauer's biography.

Table I

	Estimated IQ in childhood	Fame (rank in 282)	Birth order	Age at marriage
J. S. Mill (1806–1873)	190	103	1 in 9	45
Leibniz (1646–1717)	185	19	Only	—
Grotius (1583–1645)	185	72	1 in 5	25
Goethe (1749–1832)	185	4	1 in 6	39
Pascal (1623–1662)	180	35	2 in 3	—
Macaulay (1800–1859)	180	53	1 in 9	—
Bentham (1748–1832)	180	181	1 in 2	—
Coleridge (1772–1834)	175	157	10 in 10	23
Voltaire (1694–1778)	170	2	5 in 5	—
Leopardi (1798–1837)	170	280	1 in 5	—
Chatterton (1752–1770)	170	163	3 in 3	—
Niebuhr (1776–1831)	165	135	2 in 2	24
Mirabeau (1749–1791)	165	30	9(?) in 11	22
J. Q. Adams (1767–1848)	165	274	2 in 5	30
Wieland (1733–1813)	160	152	1 in ?	32
Tasso (1544–1595)	160	48	3 in 3	—
Pope (1688–1744)	160	50	Only	—
Pitt (1759–1806)	160	9	2 in 5	—
Musset (1810–1857)	160	261	2 in 2	—
Melanchthon (1497–1560)	160	77	1 in 5	23

geniuses for superior education and for elevating and inspiring social contacts was unusually high." . . . The extraordinary training for leadership received by Pitt the younger, John Quincy Adams, Niebuhr, and the Humboldt brothers; the specialized instruction of Mozart, Weber, and Michelangelo undoubtedly contributed to the rapid progress of these great men among the great" (7, p. 216). The object of the present study is to push forward in the same direction of inquiry, but with more pointed attention to the social relations and their repercussions.

In Table I, one column briefly summarizes facts concerning order of birth. Considerable theoretical importance is sometimes attached to the chronological position of a child in the family. In particular, Galton, who was not prone to overemphasize environment, thought enough of order of birth to pay some heed to it in his investigation of British scientists; and he comments that "the elder sons have, on the whole, decided advantages of nurture over the younger sons. They are more likely to become possessed of independent means, and therefore able to follow the pursuits that have most attraction to their tastes; they are treated more as companions by their parents, and have earlier responsibility, both of which would develop independence of character; probably, also, the first-born child of families not well-to-do in the world would generally have more attention in his infancy, more breathing-space, and better nourishment, than his younger brothers and sisters in their several turns" (13, p. 26). There is an intuitive appeal in the argument, but Galton does not support it by any precise analysis of his data. What may be said about the present sample? First, it must be admitted that there are several ways of stating the facts, depending on whether one includes or excludes half-siblings and siblings who died at an early age. The figures given in the table stand for full siblings and include all births. The half-siblings excluded in the three cases involved (Leibniz, Coleridge, Pope) were children by previous wives of their fathers. The impression produced by inspection is that there may be an excess of only and first children among these twenty geniuses. But an analysis of the probabilities does not favor this view very strongly. The average likelihood of being born in first place in the twenty families works out to about ⅓, and the observed frequencies deviate from the theoretically expected only enough to yield a chi square of 2 in support of the hypothesis; since this corresponds to a confidence level of between .2 and .1 for the one degree of freedom, one is left in doubt. Pascal, Niebuhr, and Adams were first sons. If we estimate in terms of first sons, a total of 13, and adjust the probabilities to the expectation that about half the children in multiple births would be girls,

the chi square is 1.8, again too small to support the hypothesis firmly.

Though the figures do not support a birth order hypothesis, there may nevertheless be something about position in the family which is significant. Let us look at the seven who do not rank as first-born children or first-born sons. Coleridge was born in his father's old age and was his "Benjamin"; Voltaire was so sickly during the first year of his life that there was daily concern over his survival, and his mother, an invalid, was incapable of having any more children; Chatterton was a posthumous child, and the previous boy in the family had died in infancy; Mirabeau was the first son to survive after the death of the first and a succession of girls; Tasso was the only surviving son, his older brother having died before he was born; Pitt was in the interesting position of being able to follow his father in a parliamentary career in the House of Commons, as his older brother could not do because of the inherited title; and Musset, the second of two sons, was younger than the first by a significant span of six years. When we weigh these additional facts, the general notion of some sort of positional effect begins to reassert itself.

One way in which position in the family might favor the development of a child would be by giving it higher attentional value for the parents. Close examination of the biographical data leads to the conclusion that these twenty men of genius, whether because of their position in the family or not, did as children receive a high degree of attention from their parents, as well as from others. In several cases it is clear that the attention exceeded that accorded to their brothers and sisters. Both very decided and very positive parental interest was displayed toward Mill, Leibniz, Grotius, Goethe, Pascal, Macaulay, Bentham, Coleridge, Niebuhr, Adams, Wieland, Pope, Pitt, and Melanchthon. Voltaire and Musset were far from neglected, but the attention bestowed upon them may have lacked some of the intensity of focus notable in the preceding cases. If any of the children suffered comparative neglect or abuse, they would be Leopardi, Chatterton, and Mirabeau. Chatterton had no father from the time of his birth, and the fathers of Leopardi and Mirabeau were lacking in sympathy or worse. On the other hand, Chatterton's mother and sister helped him to learn to read, saw that he went to school, and were good enough to him that the promise he made them when a child to reward them with all kinds of finery when he grew up was fulfilled in the last year of his short life; Leopardi was provided with tutors and had access to his father's rich library; and Mirabeau, cuffed and persecuted as he finally was by his erratic father, was received into the world with an outburst of joy and was always provided for educationally, even though the arrangement may have been savagely disciplinary.

Favorable parental attention may take the two forms of displays of affection and intellectual stimulation. There is strong evidence for both in most of the cases in our list. Remarkable indeed are the educational programs followed by Mill, Goethe, Pascal, Bentham, Niebuhr, Adams, Wieland, Tasso, and Pitt, under the encouragement, guidance, and powerful insistence of their fathers. Yet it is not the educational program itself which requires our notice so much as it is the intimate and constant association with adults which it entails. Not only were these boys often in the company of adults, as genuine companions; they were to a significant extent cut off from the society of other children. The same statement can be made, on the whole, for others in the list whose educations proceeded less directly, or less strenuously under the guidance of fathers.

Warm attachments to children outside the family circle seem to have been rare, and there are several cases of isolation within the family, too. Yet it is within the family that most of the recorded intimacies between these geniuses and other children developed. Goethe, Pascal, Niebuhr, Macaulay, Voltaire, and Mirabeau experienced some intensity of affection for sisters; Musset for his older brother; Macaulay and Voltaire remained attached to their favorite sisters throughout their lives, becoming devoted uncles to their sisters' children; Goethe's and Pascal's affection for their younger sisters approached passion; and Mirabeau speaks of incestuous relations with his.

The reality and nature of the pattern to which I am pointing—the very great dominance of adults in the lives of these children, and their isolation from contemporaries outside the family and, sometimes, within—can be adequately appreciated only through a more detailed statement about each individual.

Mill, under his father's personal and unremitting tutelage, began hard intellectual work before he was three. From very early he was given the responsibility of acting as tutor to his brothers and sisters. This did not increase his affection for them. In fact, he came to share some of his father's own antipathy toward them and toward his mother. He explicitly states in his autobiography that his father kept him apart from other boys. "He was earnestly bent upon my escaping not only the ordinary corrupting influence which boys exercise over boys, but the contagion of vulgar modes of thought and feeling; and for this he was willing that I should pay the price of inferiority in the accomplishments which schoolboys in all countries chiefly cultivate" (21, pp. 24f.) And again: "as I had no boy companions, and the animal need of physical activity was satisfied by walking, my amusements, which were mostly solitary, were in general of a quiet, if not a bookish turn, and gave little stimulus to any other kind even of mental activity than that which was already called forth by my studies" (p. 25).

Leibniz, his mother's only child, lost his father, a prominent university professor, when he was six. He retained two vivid memories of him, both of them expressive of the high esteem in which his father held him. His mother, who died when he was eighteen, devoted the remainder of her life to caring for him. He lived at home, free from "the doubtful liberties, the numerous temptations, the barbarous follies of student life" (18, p. 12). Before he was ten his father's carefully guarded library was opened to him, and he plunged into its treasures eagerly. It was conceivably no small thing to Leibniz that his father had regarded his christening as marked by a symbolic movement which seemed to promise that his son, as he wrote in his domestic chronicle, would continue in a spiritual and burning love for God all his life and do wonderful deeds in honor of the Highest (15, p. 4).

Grotius was close to his father. He signed his early poems Hugeianus, thus joining his own name Hugo with his father's name Janus or Joannes. At eight he reacted to the death of a brother by writing his father consolatory Latin verses. He had competent teachers at home, and entered the University of Leiden at eleven; there he dwelt with a devoutly religious man who impressed him deeply. He was famous in the literary world very early, and received high praise from distinguished men. He sought his father's advice when he chose a wife. One would infer from the limited evidence that his association from early childhood was primarily with adults.

Goethe throughout his childhood was carefully and energetically supervised in his varied studies by his father. He associated frequently with numerous skilled and learned and eminent men in Frankfort, among whom was his grandfather Textor. He enjoyed considerable freedom of movement through the city, in the intervals of his studies, and struck up several acquaintances outside the home among boys and girls; but these were certainly far outweighed by his adult contacts, and by his intimacy with his sister, who had much less freedom than he and who became increasingly embittered by the educational discipline of their father. In his autobiography he notes that he was not on friendly terms with a brother, three years younger, who died in childhood, and scarcely retained any memory of the three subsequent children who also died young. How close he and his sister were may be gauged by these words regarding the after-effects of his love-affair with Gretchen, at about fourteen: "my sister consoled me the more earnestly, because she secretly felt the satisfaction of having gotten rid of a rival; and I, too, could not but feel a quiet, half-delicious pleasure, when she did me the justice to assure me that I was the only one who truly loved, understood, and esteemed her" (14, p. 192).

Pascal was so precious in the eyes of his father, after his mother's death when he was three, that, as the older sister tells us, the father could not bear the thought of leaving his education to others, and accordingly became and remained his only teacher. At eighteen Pascal's health broke down from ceaseless application. He was frequently in the company of the learned men surrounding his father. His primary emotional attachment was to his younger sister, Jacqueline; her religious retirement strongly influenced his own religious development.

Macaulay early became absorbed in books, but his studies were more unobtrusively guided by his father and mother and other relatives than in the cases preceding. He was especially attached to his mother in early childhood, and at home among his brothers and sisters was overflowingly happy and playful. A sister writes: "He hated strangers, and his notion of perfect happiness was to see us all working round him while he read aloud a novel, and then to walk all together on the Common" (30, p. 67). He was reluctant to leave home for school for even a single day, and he was acutely homesick when placed in a boarding school at about twelve; there, though tolerated and even admired by his fellow pupils, he had little to do with them, living almost exclusively among books. The children at home passionately loved him. It should not be overlooked that his father was a deeply religious man of great force of character, energetic in religious and political reform movements of considerable scope.

Bentham's father, ambitious to make a practical lawyer of his first and for nine years his only child, kept him to a rigorous schedule of instruction in everything from dancing and military drill to Greek from a very early age. From seven to twelve he spent the winters at a boarding school, which he did not enjoy; in the vacations at home his schooling, under private tutors, was much more intensive. He was happiest on visits to grandparents in the country, where he could talk to an old gardener or climb up in a tree and read a novel. Too small and weak to win the admiration of his fellows, "he tried to be industrious and honest and noble and dutiful, finding that such a course brought praise from his elders" (10, pp. 20f.). When the death of his warmhearted mother desolated his father and himself, Jeremy "was just turned twelve, and was ready for Oxford, if a frail and under-sized boy of twelve could be said to be ready for anything" (10, p. 22).

Coleridge's father, though unambitious in general and not very attentive to the education of his numerous other children, took special pride in him and endeavored from the beginning to prepare him for the Church. Coleridge was the last of fourteen children (ten by his mother), and the extreme fondness of his parents aroused the hostility of the older boys toward him. They drove him from play and tormented him. On one occasion, when he was eight, he ran away from home after a ferocious combat with the brother whom he had displaced as baby of the family; he was found only after a prolonged search, and he remembered all his life the tears of joy on his father's face and his mother's ecstasy when he was recovered. Death of the father, when he was nine, deprived him of his most valued companion. Shortly afterwards he was sent to a charity school in London. Here he made a few friends, notably Lamb, but he lived a great deal in books and in his own imagination.

Voltaire was born five years after the death in infancy of the next preceding child, and his own life was despaired of daily for the first year. His mother was an invalid; his father was a busy lawyer and does not seem to have concentrated any particular attention on him, beyond desiring that the boy should himself be prepared for the law. His education at home proceeded under the guidance of three distinguished and learned men, particularly the Abbé Chateauneuf, his godfather. The two other surviving children were considerably older than he; the brother he disliked, but he was fond of his seven-years-older sister, and, after his mother's death when he was seven, it was she to whom he was chiefly attached in the family. At ten he was quartered in the best Jesuit school in France by his ambitious and wealthy father; here he made the warmest and most lasting friendships in his life, but they were with the teachers rather than with the boys.

Leopardi, the oldest of five children, remained until he was twenty-four, practically immured, in the house of his father, the Count, in a town which he despised. In Leopardi's own words: "Had no teachers except for the first rudiments, which he learned under tutors kept expressly in the house of his father. But had the use of a rich library collected by his father, a great lover of literature. In this library passed the chief portion of his life, while and as much as permitted by his health, ruined by these studies; which he began independently of teachers, at ten years of age, and continued thenceforth without intermission, making them his sole occupation" (29, p. 2). His closest companion was his brother Carlo, a year younger; but he was reticent even with him. With the other children he liked to produce plays in which the tyrant (his father) was worsted by the hero (himself). At a later age he regarded his home as a prison from which he had to break out.

Chatterton, born three months after his talented father's death, was the second surviving child of his very young mother, who had borne her daughter four or five years earlier before her marriage was legalized. Under their instruction, he learned the alphabet from an old illuminated music manuscript of his father's, which his mother had been about to throw away, and learned how to read from an old blackletter Testament. He had been dismissed from his first school as a dullard. Later, he went to the uninspiring charity school which had been attended by his father. A note on his relations with playmates before he was five speaks of him as "presiding over his playmates as their master and they as his hired servants" (20, p. 22). Already at five he was greedy for fame, and asked that a cup which had been presented to him by a relative should have on it "an angel with a trumpet, '*to blow his name about*,' as he said" (20, p. 23). He did form friendships at school, one in particular; and the death of this boy plunged him into melancholy. But with none of these, or with his sister, was he intimate enough to share the secret of his Rowley poems, those impressive forgeries which seem to have been written under the inspiration and tutelage of the beautiful church of St. Mary Redcliffe rather than any human preceptor.

Niebuhr's father, who had been a military engineer and explorer, took up residence after his marriage at forty in a retired little town and devoted himself to his wife and family of two children. He liked to entertain his own and other children with stories, games, and music; but he concentrated particularly on the instruction of his son, for whom he also provided tutors from about four or five. A cultured neighbor, Boje, who was editor of a literary periodical, took much interest in the boy; and Boje's wife began his instruction in French. Her death when he was ten overwhelmed him with grief and inclined him even more seriously to his studies. Between fourteen and eighteen he spent most of the day in hard work and general reading. When he was sixteen his father, thinking that his attachment to home was excessive and that he was studying too much alone, sent him off to a school in Hamburg in the hope that he would become more sociable; but he was unhappy, and insisted on coming back. From an early age ill health and his mother's anxiety contributed their share to his inclination to solitude.

Mirabeau, the first surviving son of a family of the nobility, was in the beginning his father's pride. Later, after disfigurement by smallpox at three and displacement from the position of only son by the birth of a brother when he was five, he became increasingly the object of his erratic father's dislike. Intense marital discord made him the more hateful because he resembled his mother's side of the house. He was unfavorably compared with the other children, and repeatedly put under severe disciplinarians as tutors. Eventually his father had him imprisoned more than once. In the face of this persecution, helped partly by the affectionate interest of an uncle, Mirabeau succeeded nevertheless in developing an extraordinarily winning manner in speech and personal contacts, even charming his jailers into relaxing their punishments. Whether or not he was inclined to solitude, it was forced on him by his father; much of his learning and literary production took place in prisons or their equivalents. He was highly erotic, and may have had sexual relations with his younger sister; for so he asserts.

Adams regarded even his name, John Quincy, which was his great-grandfather's, as a perpetual admonition to live nobly. The Revolutionary War and the battle of Bunker Hill, which he witnessed, confirmed a serious habit of mind from early childhood. As his father was absent from home a great deal, he was already as a small boy depended upon by his mother as if he were a man. His education commenced at home under a tutor, and continued in Europe in the company of his father and other men notable in the governmental service. It was not until he entered Harvard that he attended a regular school for any length of time. Both his mother and his father tried to keep him from the corrupting influence of other boys, and it is evident from the nature of his life that his chief contacts were with grown men of serious and intellectual character. He read a great deal under the guidance of his father, whom in his earliest letters he obviously wished to please.

Wieland was educated at home under the eyes of his father, a pastor, in somewhat the same severe manner as was Goethe. He studied hard from three years of age. He says of his childhood: "I was deeply in love with solitude and passed whole days and summer nights in the garden, observing and imitating the beauties of nature" (26, p. 19). He was much more attached to books than to people. Prior to age seventeen, says his biographer, "We encounter not a single friend of his own age, only books and those who helped with them!" (26, p. 24). He was sensitive and unsociable when away at school, and when he returned home he lived alone or associated only with older men. His biographer makes no mention of his relations with his several siblings.

Tasso, whose old father was often compelled to be away from home, lived with his young mother and his sister until he was separated from them forever at ten, to join his father at the court of his patron prince. Even while he remained at home he was being strictly educated, first by an old priest, and then in a Jesuit school, which he loved. His mother, of whom he was passionately fond, died two years after he went to join his father. Of his childhood, Boulting says: "The prolonged absences of his father, the tears of his mother, the straitened circumstances and this sudden death were not healthy influences for a sensitive lad, and there was a great deal too much educational pressure put upon him. Bernardo was proud of Torquato's talents and ambitious as to his future. He forced him on and took scudi from a slender purse to pay for special lessons in Greek. But a cousin came to Rome from Bergamo to share in Torquato's studies. No bookworm was this lad, but full of fun and a thorough boy. Nothing could have been luckier" (3, p. 31). A little later he had as his companion in the study of the graces (horsemanship, jousting, etc.) a boy of eight, son of Duke Guidobaldo. Otherwise he seems to have associated primarily with men, often men of great dignity and learning.

Pope, the only child of his mother (there was a half-sister more than nine years older), was from the earliest period a domestic idol, as Stephen says. His father and mother, both forty-six at his birth, and a nurse, concentrated their affection upon him, which must have been all the more intense because he was sickly, and humpbacked like his father. "The religion of the family made their seclusion from the world the more rigid, and by consequence must have strengthened their mutual adhesiveness. Catholics were then harassed by a legislation which would have been condemned by any modern standard as intolerably tyrannical" (28, p. 2). Most of his education was accomplished at home, with some help from a family priest and his father, who corrected his early rhymes. From twelve he threw himself into his studies so passionately that his frail constitution threatened to break down.

Pitt was born at the high peak of his father's career as Prime Minister of England. When the title of Earl of Chatham was conferred on him, this second son, then seven, exclaimed, "I am glad that I am not the eldest son. I want to speak in the House of Commons like papa." Partly because of his feeble health, the boy was brought up at home under the instruction of his father and a tutor. His father concentrated upon developing his oratorical powers. At fourteen he was sent to Cambridge, where he was placed in the care of a sound scholar, who remained his inseparable companion, and practically his only one, for more than two years. He had no social life there. He read with facility such books as Newton's *Principia* and the obscurest of the Greek poets. "Through his whole boyhood, the House of Commons was never out of his thoughts, or out of the thoughts of his instructors" (17, p. 129).

Musset was the second son in a family devoted to literature, "an infant prodigy on whom the intelligence of his brother, six years his elder, did not fail to exercise a stimulating effect. Alfred developed his mind in the constant companionship of Paul much more rapidly than he would have in the company of children his own age" (5, p. 12). He was notable from early childhood for his sensitivity, charm, emotional ardor, dramatic power, and susceptibility to feminine beauty. At a very tender age he was already disappointed in love. He went to school for a short time with his brother, but sickness and the hostility of the other children toward these Bonapartists soon led to their being tutored at home, by a young man who knew how to combine pleasure with instruction.

Melanchthon always remembered the dying injunction of his father: "I have seen many and great changes in the world, but greater ones are yet to follow, in which may God lead and guide you. Fear God, and do right" (25, p. 6). Before this time (his father died when he was eleven) he was, by his father's express wishes, strictly educated, for a while in a local school, and then by a tutor, a conscientious teacher and stern disciplinarian. Afterwards, he came more directly under the influence of the celebrated scholar Reuchlin, who was his relative. It was Reuchlin, impressed by the scholarship of the little boy, who changed his name from Schwartzerd to its Greek equivalent Melanchthon. Of his earlier childhood it is related that he often gathered his schoolfellows around him to discuss what they had been reading and learning; and his grandfather delighted to engage him in learned disputes with traveling scholars, whom he usually confounded.

The brief sketches preceding tend to confirm the rule, I believe, that children of genius are exposed to significantly great amounts of intellectual stimulation by adults and experience very restricted contacts with other children of their age. Nor should we overlook the fact that books themselves, to which these children are so much attached, are representatives of the adult world. This is true in the superficial sense that they are provided by adults and, more significantly, may be drawn from a father's sacred library (one thinks of Leibniz, Leopardi, even Chatterton); it is true in the profounder sense that they are written by adults, and, in the case of most of the reading done by these children, *for* adults. Books extend the boundaries of the adult empire.

There is an effect of this constant intercourse with the adult world which may be especially important in the development of genius. Not only is there an increase of knowledge, which is the usual aim of the instructors; there is also, in many cases, a profound excitement of imagination. Even John Stuart Mill confesses that he did not perfectly understand such grave works as the more difficult dialogues of Plato when he read them in Greek at seven. What, then, happens to such adult material pouring into the child's mind? Mill does not elucidate his own case; but there is evidence in a number of the biographies before me that the dynamic processes of phantasy go to work on it and richly transform both what is understood and what is not.

Much of Goethe's association with other children was simply an occasion for expressing his vivid phantasy life; he entranced them with stories of imaginary adventures. Musset, also, reveled in a world of make-believe based upon the Arabian Nights and similar literature, and bewitched his enemies by the magic power of imagination. These were to become poets. But Bentham, who was no poet, imagined himself growing us as a hero like Fénelon's Telemachus and was stirred to moral fervor by sentimental novels. And two of the practical politicians in the list, Pitt and Niebuhr, may give us some insight into the process. When Pitt was around thirteen or fourteen he had written a tragedy, of which Macaulay has this to say: "This piece is still preserved at Chevening, and is in some respects highly curious. There is no love. The whole plot is political; and it is remarkable that the interest, such as it is, turns on a contest about a regency. On one side is a faithful servant of the Crown, on the other an ambitious and unprincipled conspirator. At length the King, who had been missing, reappears, resumes his power, and rewards the faithful defender of his rights. A reader who should judge only by the internal evidence, would have no hesitation in pronouncing that the play was written by some Pittite poetaster at the time of the rejoicings for the recovery of George the Third in 1789" (17, pp. 68f.). Out of his learning Pitt had constructed a dream prescient of his own future career. And who can say that the actions of a Prime Minister are not as much the expression of a private drama as they are the realistic application of the sciences and the laws? Niebuhr, who became a practical man of business and politics as well as the historian of Rome, writes explicitly about his own childhood experience, in a letter to Jacobi in 1811: "Our great seclusion from the world, in a quiet little provincial town, the prohibition, from our earliest years, to pass beyond the house and garden, accustomed me to gather the materials for the insatiable requirements of my childish fancy, not from life and nature, but from books, engravings, and

conversation. Thus, my imagination laid no hold on the realities around me, but absorbed into her dominions all that I read—and I read without limit and without aim—while the actual world was impenetrable to my gaze; so that I became almost incapable of apprehending anything which had not already been apprehended by another—of forming a mental picture of anything which had not before been shaped into a distinct conception by another. It is true that, in this second-hand world, I was very learned, and could even, at a very early age, pronounce opinions like a grown-up person; but the truth in me and around me was veiled from my eyes—the genuine truth of objective reason. Even when I grew older, and studied antiquity with intense interest, the chief use I made of my knowledge, for a long time, was to give fresh variety and brilliancy to my world of dreams" (4, p. 354).

My point is that phantasy is probably an important aspect of the development of genius, not only in those cases where the chief avenue to fame is through the production of works of imagination in the ordinary sense, but also in those where the adult accomplishment is of a different sort. Instead of becoming proficient in taking and giving the hard knocks of social relations with his contemporaries, the child of genius is thrown back on the resources of his imagination, and through it becomes aware of his own depth, self-conscious in the fullest sense, and essentially independent. There is danger, however, in the intense cultivation of phantasy. If it does not flow over into the ordinary social relations by some channel, if it has to be dammed up as something socially useless, then it threatens life itself. An expression of what I am referring to is given in that powerful scene in the first part of Goethe's *Faust* where the physician-magician, tampering with incantations, raises a spirit of overwhelming presence and quails before him. Something nearer to an outright demonstration is furnished by the life of Chatterton and his suicide.

Before he was eighteen Chatterton was dead by his own hand. If we examine his life, we see that it breaks apart into two distinct regions: an outer shell of schoolboy, apprentice, pretended antiquarian, and writer of brittle satire; and a core—the serious and deeply emotional 15th century poet Rowley, whose connection with himself he never publicly acknowledged. One must not forget that Chatterton's phantasy existence as Rowley has points of contact with his father, the musician schoolteacher who died before his son was born, but who, in a sense, presided over the boy's education through the music manuscript from which he learned his letters and the blackletter Testament in which he learned to read, and who, by his connection and the connection of his family with the magnificent church of St. Mary Redcliffe, which overshadowed the place of Chatterton's birth and was his favorite resort from the brutalities of Bristol, might surely continue to hold converse with the imaginative boy. The Rowley poems furthermore are related to Chatterton's search for a pedigree. In short, through Rowley, Chatterton established relations with the world of the dead; and since he could not admit that he himself was the author of the Rowley poems, but had to pretend to have found them in his role as antiquary, and was thus rejected as an impostor by Walpole, he could not through Rowley establish contact with the world of the living. The surface which he was able to present to the world was hard, brittle, violent, unreal. Yet even in his relations with the world he appeared to be doing the same thing he was doing through the Rowley phantasies, namely, seeking a father to love and protect him. He evidently placed great hopes in Walpole; but he had also tried and been disappointed in the patronage of men of lower caliber in Bristol. Eventually he came to a dead end in London, where he had no friends even of the quality of Bristol's Catcott. Just before he committed suicide he was Rowley once again in the most beautiful of his poems, the *Balade of Charitie*, which sums up his experience of the world and his yearning for a loving father. If it was Rowley who enabled Chatterton to live, it was also Rowley who opened the door of death for him and ushered him out of a world of constant bitter disappointment into a world of kindly and Christian spirits.

Chatterton is a supreme example of the dangers and costs of genius. Having no father or other appreciative adult to link him to the world, he was swallowed up by his imagination. But it is too often overlooked in the textbooks that genius in less tragic cases is generally a costly gift. Superficially an enviable piece of luck, it is actually a fatality which exacts tribute from the possessor. Extreme absorption in very hard work is one of the penalties, and sometimes broken health. Isolation from contemporaries, often increasing with the years, is another. Whether we should include heterosexual difficulties as another, I am not sure, but I have indicated some of the facts in the last column of Table I and wish to consider the matter briefly. Fifty-five percent of our sample did not marry at all. There may be no special significance in this, since according to statistics for the United States (11) the marriage rate for the total population of males above fifteen is only about 60 per cent and may have been lower in earlier times. On the other hand, this group, with the exception of Chatterton, ranges in age from 39 to 84 and should be compared with the higher age groups. According to the 1930 census in the United

States marriage had been entered into by 86 per cent of men in the age range from 35 to 44, and by age 60, which is about the median for our group of geniuses, it had been entered into by about 90 per cent. I will only note further that some delay or reluctance or dissatisfaction attend the marriages of Mill, Goethe, Coleridge, Mirabeau, Wieland, and perhaps Melanchthon, but it would not be desirable here to go into greater detail because of the impossibility of making appropriate comparisons. It may be that for marriages both freely contracted and happily sustained a rate of 3 in 20 is not out of the ordinary, though I should be inclined to say that here too we have an expression of the costliness of genius.

In summary, the present survey of biographical information on a sample of twenty men of genius suggests that the typical developmental pattern includes as important aspects: (1) a high degree of attention focused upon the child by parents and other adults, expressed in intensive educational measures and, usually, abundant love; (2) isolation from other children, especially outside the family; and (3) a rich efflorescence of phantasy, as a reaction of the two preceding conditions. In stating these conclusions I by no means wish to imply that original endowment is an insignificant variable. On the contrary, Galton's strong arguments on behalf of heredity appear to me to be well-founded; and in this particular sample the early promise of these very distinguished men cannot be dissociated from the unusual intellectual qualities evident in their parents and transmitted, one would suppose, genetically as well as socially to their offspring. It is upon a groundwork of inherited ability that I see the pattern operating. Whether the environmental phase of it summarized under (1) and (2) is actually causally important, and to what extent the environmental factors are related to the blossoming out of phantasy, are questions which could be examined experimentally, though obviously any thorough experiment would require both a great deal of money and a certain degree of audacity. It might be remarked that the mass education of our public school system is, in its way, a vast experiment on the effect of reducing all three of the above factors to minimal values, and should, accordingly, tend to suppress the occurrence of genius.

References

1. Adams, C. F. Memoirs of John Quincy Adams. Vol. I. Philadelphia: Lippincott. 1874.
2. Bielschowsky, A. The life of Goethe. Vol. I. New York: Putnam. 1905.
3. Boulting, W. Tasso and his Times. London: Methuen. 1907.

 4. Bunsen, C. C. J., J. Brandis, and J. W. Loebell. The Life and Letters of Barthold George Niebuhr. Vol. I. London: Chapman & Hall. 1852.

 5. Charpentier, J. La Vie Meurtrie de Alfred de Musset. Paris: Piazza. 1928.

 6. Courtney, W. L. Life of John Stuart Mill. London: Walter Scott. 1888.

 7. Cox, C. M. The Early Mental Traits of Three Hundred Geniuses. Stanford University Press. 1926.

 8. Elliot, H. S. R. The Letters of John Stuart Mill. Vol. I. London: Longmans. 1910.

 9. Ellis, H. A Study of British Genius. Boston: Houghton Mifflin. 1926.

10. Everett, C. W. The Education of Jeremy Bentham. New York: Columbia University Press. 1931.

11. Folsom, J. K. The Family and Democratic Society. New York: Wiley. 1943.

12. Galton, F. Hereditary Genius. New York: Appleton. 1871.

13. Galton, F. English Men of Science. New York: Appleton. 1875.

14. Goethe, J. W. von. The Auto-Biography of Goethe. Truth and Poetry: from my own Life. London: Bohn. 1848.

15. Guhrauer, G. E. Gottfried Wilhelm Freiherr von Leibnitz, eine Biographie. Vol. I. Breslau: Hirt. 1842(?).

16. Hanson, L. The Life of S. T. Coleridge: the Early Years. New York: Oxford University Press. 1939.

17. Macaulay, T. B. Life of Pitt. New York: Delisser & Procter. 1859.

18. Merz, J. T. Leibniz. New York: Hacker. 1948.

19. Mesnard, J. Pascal, l'Homme et l'Oeuvre. Paris: Boivin. 1951.

20. Meyerstein, E. H. W. A Life of Thomas Chatterton. London: Ingpen & Grant. 1930.

21. Mill, J. S. Autobiography of John Stuart Mill. New York: Columbia University Press. 1948.

22. Montigny, L. Memoirs of Mirabeau. London: Edward Churton. 1835.

23. Parton, J. Life of Voltaire. Vol. I. Boston: Houghton Mifflin. 1881.

24. Périer, Mme. "Vie de B. Pascal." *In* Pensées de B. Pascal. Paris: Didot. 1854.

25. Richard, J. W. Philip Melanchthon, the Protestant Preceptor of Germany, 1497–1560. New York: Putnam. 1902.

26. Sengle, F. Wieland. Stuttgart: Metzler. 1949.

27. Stanhope, Earl. Life of the Right Honourable William Pitt. Vol. I. London: Murray. 1861.

28. Stephen, L. Alexander Pope. New York: Harper. N.d.

29. Thomson, J. Essays, Dialogues and Thoughts of Giacomo Leopardi. London: Routledge. N.d.

30. Trevelyan, G. O. The Life and Letters of Lord Macaulay. Vol. I. New York: Harper. 1876.

31. Vallentin, A. Mirabeau. New York: Viking. 1948.

32. Vreeland, H. Hugo Grotius, the Father of the Modern Science of International Law. New York: Oxford University Press. 1917.

33. Willert, P. F. Mirabeau. London: Macmillan. 1931.

GROUP DIFFERENCES IN ABILITIES

The study of the difference, if any, which exists between the IQ test performance of Negroes and whites has long been a problem. The correct answer to this problem has many practical implications. Most psychologists, including the authors of this article, accept the fact that the majority of studies show that whites, on the average, score slightly higher than Negroes. Most psychologists, including these authors, do *not* think that this evidence indicates a genetically determined difference in the IQ test performance of Negroes and whites. Rather, most psychologists think that the cultural differences between classes and castes are more than sufficient to explain the small advantage of the whites. In any case, any group difference which exists is quite small in comparison with individual differences.

Points to guide your study

1. What are some of the difficulties encountered in answering the question of IQ-test-performance differences between Negroes and whites?

2. Glossary: FSIQ—Full-scale IQ score (all tests, both performance and verbal subscales included) on the Wechsler Adult Intelligence Scale (WAIS). VIQ—The IQ score on the verbal scale of the WAIS. PIQ—The IQ score on the performance scale of the WAIS. Factor analysis—The attempt to find a few clusters or groupings in a large number of tests or test items. Some concepts of intelligence are in terms of specific factors, instead of general factors. WISC-Wechsler Intelligence Scale for Children.

43. COMPARATIVE PSYCHOLOGICAL STUDIES OF NEGROES AND WHITES IN THE UNITED STATES

Ralph Mason Dreger, Jacksonville University, and
Kent S. Miller, Leon County Health Department, Tallahassee, Florida*

Intellectual functions

Shuey (1958) has reviewed the literature comparing Negro and white intelligences at least as far back as 1913. We shall not endeavor to cover the same ground. In her text are found valuable tabular comparisons of Negroes and whites for various age groups, the armed forces, gifted and retarded, delinquents and criminals, and racial hybrids. (Actually a number of studies reported in the literature are of hybrids even though not recognized as such.) Shuey's bibliography and résumés are a must for serious students, for she has not only gathered together the better known studies, but has ferreted out otherwise obscure and inaccessible articles and theses.

The usefulness of Shuey's otherwise excellent work is limited by what appears to be a polemic attitude. Her book seems to be an attempt to prove a nonegalitarian hypothesis rather than being strictly a review of literature. In this case Shuey does the same rationalizing from an hereditarian standpoint that Klineberg (1944) did in his earlier "review" from an environmental standpoint.

North (1957) likewise surveys the literature and comes to an opposite conclusion from the one Shuey reaches. Whereas the latter concluded that all the evidence points " . . . to the presence of some native differences between Negroes and whites as determined by intelligence tests," North maintains that there is no proof of biological inferiority or that the Negro's potentials for educational and cultural development are more limited than the white person's. North's coverage of the literature is considerably less extensive than Shuey's.

* Prepared with the assistance of a grant from the Human Genetics Fund.
R. M. Dreger and K. S. Miller. Comparative psychological studies of Negroes and whites in the United States. *Psychol. Bull.*, 1960, **57**, 361–402. Copyright 1960 by the American Psychological Association. Excerpts reprinted with permission from the authors and the American Psychological Association.

The following discussion on comparisons of intelligence between the two racial groups endeavors to supplement Shuey's work especially and correct it where it is in patent error.

Children and adolescents

Young children. Aside from the infant studies cited previously, studies of preschool children in which comparisons are made between whites and Negroes are sparse. Shuey (1958) cites only nine altogether and only five reported in 1944 or after. On the whole, young Negro children score lower than whites. But the differences are very much less than in older groups; and in all of the reports in which average IQs are given, Negroes average well within the normal IQ range for whites. Shuey offers several explanations of the discrepancy between the results for preschool and school children, including inadequate sampling of preschool, the relative invalidity and unreliability of tests at younger ages (although some of the lowest Binet standard errors are found in the late preschool years), more verbal and abstract tests in the school years; she also suggests that mental growth curves may not be the same for both races, and that IQs may be less affected by environment in the preschool years.

Special comment is called for with respect to two investigations. Brown (1944) compared Minneapolis kindergarten children on the Binet, Form L, discovering that the Negro mean of 100.8 was significantly lower than the white mean of 107.1. The white children in Occupational Classes VI and VII (Minnesota scale) averaged about the same as Negro children. Shuey takes exception to Brown's conclusion that at "nominally similar" socioeconomic status Negro children are not inferior to whites. Her observation that Brown has small Ns in Levels VI and VII does not constitute an objection from a statistical standpoint. Nevertheless, Brown's conclusion would have been stronger if he had, first, differentiated his Negroes by class without assuming their occupational status and, second, employed an analysis of variance design.

The other study to which special attention must be paid is that of Anastasi and D'Angelo (Anastasi & D'Angelo, 1952; D'Angelo, 1950). Five-year-old children in mixed and unmixed neighborhoods in New York City were administered the Goodenough Draw-a-Man Test and studied for language development in spontaneous conversation recordings. IQs were 101.8 and 101.5 for Negro and white children, respectively. Language development appeared to be somewhat more advanced for white than for colored children. This important study is dismissed by Shuey as permitting no generalizations, because selection of subjects appeared to be biased. The crux of the matter is whether all qualified subjects were utilized or only certain selected ones. Anastasi[1] points out Shuey's error in misjudging the selection procedure, and provides a satisfactory answer to Shuey's objections. With due recognition of the limitations of the Goodenough as a test of intelligence we may yet regard Anastasi and D'Angelo's results as a challenge to nativist theories of intellectual differences between the races.

Older children and adolescents.   Little question need be raised at this time about the results of testing school children. Almost all evidence points to inferior performance of Negroes on tests of either the more traditional variety or those tending to be more "culture-free" or "culture-fair." What Shuey (1958) has done in this respect is not to present startlingly new conclusions, but to marshal data which have been more or less familiar to scholars for many years. Our purpose here, then, is to re-examine some of the data and present material not covered by Shuey, rather than to repeat what Shuey has done with a fair degree of thoroughness.

McGurk's studies.   Evidencing a long time interest (McGurk, 1943) in Negro-white comparisons of intelligence, McGurk (1951, 1953a, 1953b) has received considerable publicity in both scholarly and lay circles because of research which seems to undermine the thesis that cultural factors rather than native endowment factors account for differences between whites and Negroes in intellectual functioning. Two hundred thirteen Negro and 213 white youths were matched for age and curriculum and for social and economic variables by means of a shortened form of Sims' Record Card. McGurk found that even when socioeconomic variables were thus controlled, the mean scores of whites and Negroes differed significantly in the direction usually reported. Also, when the specially de-

[1] Anastasi, Anne. Personal communication, July 19, 1958.

vised test items were separated into "cultural" and "noncultural," the differences were greater on the noncultural questions than on the cultural questions, contrary to environmentalistic indications. Further, as socioeconomic status increased, the differences between Negroes and whites increased rather than decreased, again contrary to expectations from a cultural theory of differences in intelligence.

One point at which McGurk's analysis might be misleading to the statistically untrained has been pointed out by Long (1957). McGurk states that 25% of Negroes overlap whites, from which it might be concluded that only 25% of the specified Negro population have scores in common with the specified white population. Actually, analysis of McGurk's data shows that 91% of the Negroes have scores in common with the whites. Inasmuch as McGurk has addressed himself to the lay public, he should make abundantly clear that "overlap" is used in the technical sense of exceeding (or for an upper distribution, falling below) the mean or median of another group.

McGurk does not claim, though he seems to imply, that the superiority of whites on intelligence tests results from innate factors. In the final analysis the implication may be correct, but research such as McGurk's cannot establish it. Indeed, we do not see how the issue can be resolved by any number of ingenious methods of equating for social and economic variables. The various indices of socioeconomic status already devised or those at present conceivable on the same principles are intended to distinguish social *classes* from one another. How they can be employed to compare individuals in different *castes*, except very roughly, is difficult to see.

In actuality, not only in the South (Dollard, 1949), but North as well (Brown, 1944; Long, 1957) whites and Negroes comprise separate castes; they are not merely representatives of different classes. In the state of Florida where the writers reside there are a number of Negroes whose social and economic statuses exceed those of most white persons. These Negroes, however, cannot yet sit in the same seats on public transportation (in most places), go to the same hotel, restaurant, club, school, church, social events, or even restrooms. Although some of these strictures do not hold in Northern states, attitudes regarding intermarriage and the more personal forms of social intercourse do not appear greatly different from those held in the South. From the Early Childhood Project (Radke, Trager, & Davis, 1949) we learn that in Pennsylvania, from which state McGurk drew part of his sample, children discern within at least the first four or five years of life their social and ethnic roles, with attendant supervaluations or devaluations of self and performance expectations. Interlocked with caste variables are those which influence performance, such as the color of the investigator (Trent, 1954), which in turn may be related to deterioration of intellectual performance under anxiety-provoking conditions (Beier, 1951; Hammer, 1954).

We wish to emphasize that we are not taking sides at this point in the heredity-environment controversy in relation to intellectual differences; we believe both camps (e.g., Canady, 1943, for environmentalists) have mistakenly assumed that if the two racial groups are equated in terms of social class and economic variables that a definitive answer can be found concerning even the *relative* weighting of innate or acquired factors. Involved here are different dimensions (possibly correlated, of course) not merely different quantities along the same scale. Quibbling with Mc-Gurk over minor points of methodology should not obscure the value of the valiant attempt he has made to test hypotheses proposed by the environmentalists. The error lies in the assumptions both he and his opponents make.

Studies on the WISC. Only one investigation (Young & Bright, 1954) is cited by Shuey under WISC studies. Not surprisingly in view of its standardization, the WISC was found inappropriate for testing Southern Negro children from 10 to 13 years of age.

Another more extensive study has come to the writers' attention, that of Caldwell (1954). Four hundred and twenty Negro children were tested ranging from 6 to 12 years of age, with equal numbers of males and females, drawn from towns in five deep South states and randomly selected from school rosters. One examiner tested 342 of the subjects. According to the report, "excellent rapport was obtained," although the means of establishing rapport appear inadequate especially in the light of the conspicuous Southern accent of the chief white examiner. Caldwell's hypothesis that a difference exists between Southern Negro children and the white standardizing group was, as might be expected, borne out. Socioeconomic class influence was probably strong, with 75% of the subjects in the lowest third of SE groupings. Nevertheless, the Full Scale IQ mean of 85.52 is considerably higher than that obtained in the Young and Bright study (mean = 67.74). (Something is wrong with the standard deviations reported on p. 18 of Caldwell's dissertation: SDs ranging from 0.63 to 1.4 sound more like standard errors, but do not seem to jibe with either the WISC Manual's, the data of Young and Bright (1954), or the spread one might expect.) In this investigation the suggestion is also made that cultural bias results from using the WISC, standardized as it was on a white population.

Gifted children. Shuey's review of comparative studies (both directly and by implication) reveals that whites produce a greater proportion of gifted children by far than do Negroes. The percentage reported by Shuey for the latter, about 0.14% or 0.15% is well below the 0.95% for white children testing 140 IQ or above on the Binet or comparable scales. This low proportion among Negroes is only an expression of the general situation, i.e., that the whole curve for Negroes on most intelligence tests is displaced downward. Even taking Jenkins' (1950) figure of 0.3% for the 140 IQ or above places the area under the upper end of the curve below that for whites.

In surveying cases of gifted Negro children, Jenkins at first (1943) maintained that the gifted Negro child has essentially the same characteristics as a comparable white child. But later Jenkins (1950) recognized from more intensive investigation that the most important single fact for any Negro, gifted or not, is his being a Negro. Consequently, the performance he manifests on an intelligence test as well as elsewhere is literally colored by this fact.

That Negro children earn IQs of 160 or above (Jenkins, 1943) or even as high as 200 (Theman & Witty, 1943; Witty & Jenkins, 1935) on tests standardized on whites is a remarkable phenomenon. Anyone who has tested Negro children has probably been impressed with the fact that a Negro child whom the examiner knows to be functioning as a normal, not a retarded child, may receive a score which automatically would classify him in the retarded range if scores only were regarded. Roughly speaking, the Negro child seems to operate in everyday life situations in a way expected of a white child about 10 IQ points above. With the curve of measured Negro intelligence displaced downward it is thus a surprise to find any Negro children scoring among the highest levels on white-standardized tests.

Adults

In addition to Shuey's review (Shuey, 1958), we report here a few other studies from the military services and other special groups for which comparisons have been made. One massive investigation, part of the standardization of the PAT (Tomkins & Miner, 1957), is not mentioned by Shuey, but by all means should be brought to the reader's attention because of the careful selection of representative subjects. The investigator (Miner, 1957) employed a 20-word vocabulary test adapted from the CAVD. The sample of 1500 individuals was chosen from stratified random clusters of blocks or rural areas with quotas on important variables. Whites averaged 11.06, SD 3.41, and Negroes 8.08, SD 2.72, a significant difference.

Armed forces. In the period since 1944 debate over testing of intelligence in both world wars has been carried on. Although it seems to have subsided, it is not so much that the issues have been settled as that the contestants have become exhausted. To Shuey's conclusion, that in both wars whites consistently did better than Negroes on the average, few would take exception. She takes up one by one the reasons advanced by others for the discrepancies and provides reasons on the opposite side which purportedly answer an egalitarian view. The reader will have to study Shuey in order to judge whether the data support her reasoning. Additional discussion of some of the issues involved can be found in a series of articles by Garrett (1945a, 1945b, 1945c, 1947).

Several studies not cited by Shuey are mentioned here (Altus, 1946; Altus & Bell, 1947; Fulk & Harrell, 1952; MacPhee, Wright, & Cummings, 1947), primarily for the sake of completeness inasmuch as they do not differ in their results from others. Fulk and Harrell endeavored to equate groups by the last school grade completed; they compared AGCT scores and discovered that whites were favored at every school grade completed. The authors recognized that equal schooling does not render groups equivalent. Origins of their subjects, a highly important variable, were not controlled. Altus and Bell interpreted their discrepant findings on illiterates as due to cultural factors.

In a survey of "the uneducated" Ginsberg and Bray (1953) cite figures to indicate that the number of Negro illiterates declined from three million to slightly more than one million from 1890 to 1940. In World War II, 391,300 whites and 325,100 Negroes were rejected on the grounds of illiteracy, almost three-fourths of these rejectees being from the Southeast and Southwest.

Ginsberg (1956) draws the conclusion from studies of manpower in the Second World War that there is a great wastage of human potential when one realizes that the absolute numbers of Negroes in the upper classes of the General Classification Test are large, even though percentagewise Negroes have small representation in Classes I and II. The late Walter V. Bingham pointed out the waste of potential of all groups implied by the fact that one-fourth of the truck drivers exceeded one-fourth of the bank executives.

Special civilian groups. A large number of comparisons of college students reviewed by Shuey can be supplemented by only one series of studies by Roberts (1946, 1948, 1950). Northern Negro college students did better on the ACE than did their Southern counterparts. In a longitudinal comparison original differences in academic achievement total scores were erased after four years of college, even though ACE

scores still reflected differences. During the four-year period the subjects made greater gains than those expected by the national norms for a similar period of time.

Comparing Southern Negro and white venereal disease patients, Scarborough (1956) discovered differences on the Wechsler-Bellevue paralleling those of other investigators, but the differences between white and Negro VD patients did not seem to be as great as those between white and Negro controls. Davis (1957) using the same test found no difference between 33 mental patients and 27 controls, though the over-all IQs of 67 and 68 are well below white norms. Also employing the Wechsler, DeStephens (1953) answered his own question, "Are criminals morons?" in the negative when he discovered that 200 white and 100 Negro admissions to an Ohio reformatory yielded the following average scores: FS: W 93.55, N 87.90; V: W 90.13, N 86.70; P: W 98.30, N 91.20. On the basis of the standard deviations reported none of these differences between groups is significant. Findings of Reitzes (1958) on Negro applicants to medical schools yield a different result. Generally it is expected that Negro applicants will rank lower than white applicants on the Medical Colleges Admissions Test. Regional differences appeared among Negro applicants with North and West above border applicants, who in turn ranked higher than Southerners.

Overview of intellectual functions

Several grave issues arise in a review of comparisons of intelligence of whites and Negroes. We shall phrase these and make a few comments on each. It will be obvious that some of the problems apply more generally than to intelligence comparisons, but they are set forth here inasmuch as all of them are related to the foregoing comparisons.

What constitutes a race? For convenience we have assumed that groups belong to the white "race" or Negro "race" as designated by the investigator. Any research, however, which seriously attempts to make comparisons between or among "races" must sooner or later grapple with the problem of this section. Skin color, hair texture, and other physical characteristics have proven illusive as definitive criteria. We cannot settle a question to which anthropologists appear not yet to have given an adequate answer. Nevertheless, psychologists of the future must make explicit the concept of race to which they adhere in order to make clear what populations they are comparing.

Determination of racial composition of groups. Assuming some acceptable definition of race, the investigator needs to determine in each case whether the groups he is comparing actually are differentiated by his criteria. If, for example, he has adopted heredity, the possession of such-and-such a percentage of accepted white or Negro ancestry, as a criterion, the researcher must make certain his groups fall within the limits of the specific heredity he has accepted. One suspects that in a number of cases so-called racial comparisons are being carried out between one group designated as "white" and another designated as "black" which consists of many who are partly or even largely white.

Confusion of class and caste variables. As we have indicated in commenting on McGurk's studies, both hereditarians and environmentalists have fallen into the trap of assuming that if they can get two groups who are equated in socioeconomic terms there can be an *experimentum crucis* which answers the question of what parts heredity and environment play in intelligence differences. Canady (1943a) discussed the great difficulty in equating environments, and Anastasi and Foley (1949) pointed out that formal education and socioeconomic differences were not enough to account for differences in tested abilities of northern and southern Negroes. Actually, we despair of being able to equate groups until caste differences are removed and only class differences remain.

Interaction of examiner and subject variables. In some studies (Trent, 1954) the color of the examiner has been taken into account in assessing results; in others this factor has been ignored. Repeated testing of the same individual, both white and Negro, by both white and Negro examiners would seem to be called for in order to determine the proportion of variance in intelligence test scores attributable to interaction of examiner and subject.

The functional value of intelligence. What kinds of intelligence do white persons need and what do Negro persons need to survive, adjust, and make progress? It is naive to assume that the academic types of intelligence tests which have traditionally been the instruments of comparison compare in reality Negroes and whites in those areas of intelligence which they are called upon to use in "real life" situations. Intelligence test differences between Negroes and whites cannot mean the same as they mean between two groups of whites.

If we assume that intellectual functions develop adaptively and are not entirely determined by heredity, we may suppose that intelligence tests of the usual variety measure in part that which is developed in order to achieve success in a certain culture. A Negro in a white man's world requires a kind of intelligence enabling him to detect from minimal cues how a white man is going to react to a critical situation. Usually his success and sometimes his life depend upon this kind of intelligence, hardly ever upon whether he can define "ethnology." Tests of intelligence tapping the kinds of intellectual functioning called for in achieving success in the actual world men have to face might reveal different results in comparative studies, not only between Negroes and whites, but other groups as well.

Newer concepts of intelligence. Practically no research has been done comparing white and Negro subjects on factors of intellect (Guilford, 1956, 1959; Thurstone, 1938). The only studies of this kind we have found are those by Lee (1951) and Michael (1947). Even studies with performance-type tests, which in a sense go outside of academic intelligence quotient concepts, do not meet the need to reach the many factors revealed in modern factor-analytic research. A world of research is called for to determine how the two groups we are considering compare on the 50 or more factors of intellect. Caution needs to be exercised here in respect to the functional value of even Guilford's many factors. These were derived from tasks set for high-level personnel in the military and might not have anything specifically to do with what a person in a different class and caste needs to do. However, *insofar* as these factors cover the entire range of intellect, comparisons of factors should be much more valid than of gross IQs.

Significance of overlapping distributions. A legitimate question arises in statistics in relation to assigning individuals to one of two (or more) distributions (Horst, 1956). In statistical theory individual scores in a distribution may be regarded as errors departing from a mean (Yule & Kendall, 1949). When two distributions are compared, then, it is assumed that individual scores are only errors of observation from their respective means, which in turn are regarded as estimates of either one true population mean (if the null hypothesis is not rejected) or of two true population means (if the null hypothesis is rejected). In the case of intelligence comparisons the null hypothesis may be stated: the obtained means of these two distributions of intelligence scores differ only by chance, i.e., they are really only estimates of the same true intelligence score population mean. On the whole, investigators have rejected the null hypothesis in comparing Negroes and whites and have concluded that the two means represent two different intelligence population means.

In connection with any one individual, however, especially in the area beyond the mean of either distribution, the question may legitimately be asked: To which *intelligence* mean does he belong—or, from which *intelligence* mean is his score a deviate? It seems to be assumed that because an individual is white or black, his score must therefore be a deviate from a *white* intelligence population mean or a *black* intelligence population mean. But this assumption begs the question. The individual may be a deviate from the *lower* intelligence population mean whether he is white or black, or from the *upper* intelligence population mean whatever his color. The individual who is white but in the very low part of the scale may in truth be a deviant from the upper mean but we cannot know this fact merely because he is white. We could only be relatively sure of this fact if there were no overlap in the absolute sense between the two distributions.

This statistical consideration is a variant of the more general one which suggests that other factors than color (i.e., genetically determined intellectual concomitants of color) decide whether an individual makes a high or low score on an intelligence scale. A statement of the statistical situation focuses attention on the overlap found in virtually every study and what it must signify in relation to any one individual.

Social consequences of research findings. In the introduction to Shuey's book (1958), Garrett discusses the need not to interpret Shuey's conclusion as a basis for differential treatment of the two groups, especially for mistreatment of Negroes. A view strictly limited to scientific conclusions would be, "Here are the results of examination of the data. It is not our responsibility to recommend courses of action." If there should be significant differences between groups which can be shown to arise principally from genetic factors, the practical response of the man on the street (white or Negro) would almost inevitably be to jusify either his treating others as inferiors or to accept his own position of inferiority as natively determined. We are not convinced that genetic differences have been shown; but even if they were so shown, we believe it is incumbent upon the social scientist to set forth the full picture. The wide overlap between white and Negro distributions of scores should be pointed out so that it is evident that within group differences are far greater than between group differences. It should also be shown that ofttimes two groups of white persons differ significantly and probably in some if not all cases, partly because of genetic factors. Social scientists need to be alert to the implications of their findings.

Bibliography

Altus, W. D. The validity of the Terman vocabulary for Army illiterates. *J. consult. Psychol.,* 1946, **10,** 268–276.

Altus, W. D., and Bell, H. M. The validity of a general information test for certain groups of Army illiterates. *J. consult. Psychol.,* 1947, **11,** 120–132.

Anastasi, Anne, and D'Angelo, Rita Y. A comparison of Negro and white preschool children in language development and Goodenough Draw-a-Man I.Q. *J. genet. Psychol.,* 1952, **81,** 147–165.

Anastasi, Anne, and Foley, J. P., Jr. *Differential psychology, individual and group differences in behavior.* (Rev. ed.) New York: Macmillan, 1949.

Beier, E. G. The effect of induced anxiety on flexibility of intellectual functioning. *Psychol. Monogr.,* 1951, **65** (9, Whole No. 326).

Brown, F. An experimental and critical study of the intelligence of Negro and white kindergarten children. *J. genet. Psychol.,* 1944, **65,** 161–175.

Caldwell, M. B. An analysis of responses of a southern urban Negro population to items on the Wechsler Intelligence Scale for Children. Unpublished doctoral dissertation, Penn. State College, 1954.

Canady, H. G. The problem of equating the environment of Negro-white groups for intelligence testing in comparative studies. *J. soc. Psychol.,* 1943, **17,** 3–15.

D'Angelo, Rita Y. A comparison of white and Negro pre-school children in Goodenough I.Q. and language development. Unpublished master's thesis, Fordham University, 1950.

Davis, J. C. The scatter pattern of a southern Negro group on the Wechsler-Bellevue Intelligence Scale. *J. clin. Psychol.,* 1957, **13,** 298–300.

DeStephens, W. P. Are criminals morons? *J. soc. Psychol.,* 1953, **38,** 187–189.

Dollard, J. *Caste and class in a southern town.* (2nd ed.) New York: Harper, 1949.

Fulk, B. E., and Harrell, T. W. Negro-white army test scores and last school grade. *J. appl. Psychol.,* 1952, **36,** 34–35.

Garrett, H. E. Comparison of Negro and white recruits on the Army tests given in 1917–1918. *Amer. J. Psychol.,* 1945, **58,** 480–495. (a)

Garrett, H. E. A note on the intelligence scores of Negroes and whites in 1918. *J. abnorm. soc. Psychol.,* 1945, **40,** 344–346. (b)

Garrett, H. E. Psychological differences as among races. *Science,* 1945, **101,** 16–17. (c)

Garrett, H. E. Negro-white differences in mental ability in the United States *Sci. Mon.,* 1947, **65,** 329–333.

Ginzberg, E. *The Negro potential.* New York: Columbia Univer. Press, 1956.

Ginzberg, E., and Bray, D. W. *The uneducated.* New York: Columbia Univer. Press, 1953.

Guilford, J. P. The structure of intellect. *Psychol. Bull.,* 1956, **53,** 267–293.

Guilford, J. P. Three faces of intellect. *Amer. Psychologist*, 1959, 14, 469–479.

Hammer, E. F. Comparison of the performance of Negro children and adolescents on two tests of intelligence, one an emergency scale. *J. genet. Psychol.*, 1954, 84, 85–93.

Horst, P. Multiple classification by the method of least squares. *J. clin. Psychol.*, 1956, 12, 3–16.

Jenkins, M. D. Case studies of Negro children of Binet IQ 160 and above. *J. Negro Educ.*, 1943, 12, 159–166.

Jenkins, M. D. Intellectually superior Negro youth: Problems and needs. *J. Negro Educ.*, 1950, 19, 322–332.

Klineberg, O. (Ed.), *Characteristics of the American Negro*. New York: Harper, 1944.

Lee, E. S. Negro intelligence and selective migration: A Philadelphia test of the Klineberg hypothesis. *Amer. sociol. Rev.*, 1951, 16, 227–233.

Long, H. H. The relative learning capacity of Negroes and whites. *J. Negro Educ.*, 1957, 26, 121–134.

McGurk, F. C. J. Comparative test scores of Negro and white school children in Richmond, Va. *J. educ. Psychol.*, 1943, 34, 474–484.

McGurk, F. C. J. *Comparison of the performance of Negro and white high school seniors on cultural and non-cultural test questions*. Washington, D. C.: Catholic Univer. Amer. Press, 1951. (Microcard)

McGurk, F. C. J. On white and Negro test performance and socio-economic factors. *J. abnorm. soc. Psychol.*, 1953, 48, 448–450. (a)

McGurk, F. C. J. Socio-economic status and culturally weighted test scores of Negro subjects. *J. appl. Psychol.*, 1953, 37, 276–277. (b)

MacPhee, H. M., Wright, H. F., and Cummings, S. B. The performance of mentally subnormal rural southern Negroes on the verbal scale of the Bellevue Intelligence Examination. *J. soc. Psychol.*, 1947, 25, 217–229.

Michael, W. B. An investigation of the contribution of factors to tests and to their predictive value in two Army Air Force pilot populations. *Amer. Psychologist*, 1947, 2, 417–418. (Abstract)

Miner, J. B. *Intelligence in the United States: A survey—with conclusions for manpower utilization in education and employment*. New York: Springer, 1957.

North, R. D. The intelligence of American Negroes. In M. M. Turmin (Ed.), *Segregation and desegregation: A digest of recent research*. New York: Anti-defamation League of B'nai B'rith, 1957.

Radke, Marian J., Trager, Helen G., and Davis, Hadassah. Social perceptions and attitudes of children. *Genet. psychol. Monogr.*, 1949, 40, 327–447.

Reitzes, D. C. *Negroes and medicine*. Cambridge, Mass.: Harvard Univer. Press, 1958.

Roberts, S. O. Socio-economic status and performance of Negro college women, north and south, on the ACE. *Amer. Psychologist*, 1946, 1, 253. (Abstract)

Roberts, S. O. Socio-economic status and performance on the ACE of Negro freshmen college veterans and non-veterans from the north and the south. *Amer. Psychologist*, 1948, 3, 266. (Abstract)

Roberts, S. O. Socio-economic status and performance over a four-year period on the ACE of Negro college women from the north and south. *Amer. Psychologist*, 1950, 5, 295. (Abstract)

Scarborough, B. B. Some mental characteristics of southern colored and white venereal disease patients as measured by the Wechsler-Bellevue Test. *J. soc. Psychol.*, 1956, 43, 313–321.

Shuey, Audrey M. *The testing of Negro intelligence*. Lynchburg, Va.: Randolph-Macon Women's College, 1958.

Theman, Viola, and Witty, P. Case studies and genetic records of two gifted Negroes. *J. Psychol.*, 1943, 15, 165–181.

Thurstone, L. L. Primary mental abilities. *Psychometr. Monogr.*, 1938, No. 1.

Tomkins, S. S., and Miner, J. B. *The Picture Arrangement Test*. New York: Springer, 1957.

Trent, R. D. The color of the investigator as a variable in experimental research with Negro subjects. *J. soc. Psychol.*, 1954, 40, 281–287.

Witty, P. A., and Jenkins, M. D. The case of "B," a gifted Negro girl. *J. soc. Psychol.*, 1935, 6, 117–124.

Young, Florene M., and Bright, H. A. Results of testing 81 Negro rural juveniles with the Wechsler Intelligence Scale for Children. *J. soc. Psychol.*, 1954, 39, 219–226.

Yule, G. U., and Kendall, M. G. *An introduction to the theory of statistics*. (13th ed.) London: Griffin, 1949.

CHAPTER FIFTEEN

Personality

P**ERSONALITY CHARACTERISTICS**
A rather unusual approach to the measurement and description of two important personality configurations (types) is presented in this article.

Points to guide your study
1. The meaning of p values has been explained in previous introductions.
2. Note that the author is apparently tapping a configuration which has widespread ramifications.

44. PERSONALITY STYLE AND PERCEPTUAL CHOICE

Frank Barron, The Institute of Personality Assessment and Research, University of California, Berkeley*

The experimental investigation to be reported here is part of a comprehensive study of personality functioning in the highly effective, well-integrated American man whose life work is to be in the sciences or professions. The results of this particular subproject, however, are relevant not only to the aims of the larger study, but to the general question of the relationship of perceptual attitude to personality. It is in the context of this latter area of psychological investigation that the findings seem most significant.

History of the research

In 1947 Welsh (8) constructed a test consisting of 200 ruled and freehand line drawings in black on 3-by-5-inch white cards. It was intended as an aid in the detection and diagnosis of psychiatric abnormality. Subjects were asked to indicate for each drawing whether they liked it or did not like it. The test was given to large groups of psychiatric patients as well as to persons who were not then, and had never been, psychiatric patients.

* This study was carried on at the Institute of Personality Assessment and Research, University of California, and was supported financially by the grant of the Rockefeller Foundation to that Institute. The writer owes a special debt of gratitude to the Director of the Institute, Dr. Donald W. MacKinnon, for his unfailing encouragement and generous criticism of this portion of the Institute's program.

Frank Barron. Personality style and perceptual choice. *J. Pers.*, 1952, **20**, 385–401. Copyright 1952 by the Duke University Press. Reprinted here with permission from the author and the Duke University Press.

From a factor analysis of the preferences of these subjects there emerged two factors: an acceptance-rejection factor (expressing the general tendency of the subject either to like or to dislike the figures), and a second, bipolar factor, orthogonal to the first, whose poles, as determined by inspection of the figures, seemed to be simplicity-symmetry and complexity-asymmetry.

Welsh noted that normal subjects who had very high positive scores on this bipolar factor differed markedly in personality style from those who had high negative scores. The consensus of a group of psychologists who were acquainted with the subjects was that the high positives (who preferred simple and symmetrical figures) were extremely conservative and conventional, while the high negatives tended to be dissident, cynical, and somewhat eccentric and deviant.

The possibility suggested itself, however, that the polar opposition evident in the factor was due more to good and poor artistic discrimination than to personality style. Some weight was lent to this view by the fact that the few artists in the normal sample all clustered together at the negative end of the factor. On the other hand, artists have sometimes been known to be dissident, cynical, deviant, and so on. A comparison of the figure preferences of a large sample of artists and nonartists seemed indicated, as a preliminary to the systematic exploration of the possibilities which had suggested themselves.

Accordingly, the set of figures, expanded now to 400 items, was given for sorting, with the same directions, to a sample of 37 artists and art students, and an item analysis was carried out to determine what figures were preferred in a significantly greater frequency by artists, on the one hand, and on the other by people in general. (The latter group consisted of 75 men and 75 women, covering a wide range of age, education, occupation, and geographical location.)

A scale was thus derived (1) consisting of 40 items disliked by artists significantly (p less than .01) more often than by people in general, and 25 items liked by artists significantly (p less than .05) more often. The items disliked by artists proved to be of the simple-symmetrical sort, while the items they liked were complex-asymmetrical. When tested on new groups of artists and nonartists, the scale proved highly effective in differentiating the groups. (This scale will hereafter be referred to as the Barron-Welsh Art Scale.)

It was now clear that artists differed from people in general in liking complex and asymmetrical figures, and in disliking the simple and symmetrical. It remained to be seen whether differences in personality style exist between artists and nonartists, as well as between nonartists who like simple and symmetrical figures as opposed to those who like complex and asymmetrical ones.

The present study

As we pointed out earlier, the present investigation was originally incidental to a study of personal effectiveness in the sciences and professions. A rather unusual sample was drawn for that study; its unique character in some respects restricts the generality of these findings, while at the same time lending them special meaning in other respects.

The sample, in brief, consisted of 40 male university students who were within one year of obtaining their final higher degrees (generally the doctorate) in a variety of departments. Twenty of these forty students had been rated by the faculties of their departments as possessing in high degree such qualities as originality and personal soundness, and were in addition judged to be outstanding in terms of promise and potential success in the fields of their choice. The other 20 students, while they all performed above the minimum required for obtaining the highest degree the department offered, nevertheless were judged, comparatively, to be low in originality, personal soundness, and potential success.

One research hypothesis was that the Highs would prove to differ from the Lows in being better able to discriminate the good from the poor (as judged by experts) in artistic productions. The Barron-Welsh Art Scale of the Welsh Figure Preference test, since it so clearly separated artists from nonartists, strongly recommended itself for partial test of this hypothesis (on the presumption that artists have better taste in such matters than do nonartists). In addition, since the design of the larger investigation called for intensive personality study of the subjects, some light might thereby be shed upon the relationship, if any, between personality style and kinds of figures preferred. The scale was therefore included in the extremely comprehensive battery of tests and techniques being used to study effective functioning.

In this new sample of 40 male graduate students, the scores on the test proved to be distributed bimodally, so much so that there were two distinct groups defined by these figure preferences. When the four middlemost cases of the distribution were excluded, there was an interval of 20 points on the 65-unit scale which was not occupied by any case, 18 cases falling on each side of this interval.

It was evident from an inspection of how scores were arrived at that one of these groups preferred, as did the artists, those figures which were asymmetrical, highly complex, freehand rather than ruled, and rather restless and moving in their general effect. (Several artists, in reacting to them, had described them as "organic.") The other group preferred the symmetrical, relatively simple, and decidedly "balanced" figures.

The symmetrical figures might also be described as "regularly predictable," following some cardinal principle which could be educed at a glance. This is in strong contrast to the asymmetrical figures, which give the impression of being unpredictable, irregular, and a product of the artist's momentary whim.

The 18 subjects who preferred the symmetrical and regularly predictable figures will hereafter be referred to as Group S, and the 18 who preferred the asymmetrical, irregular, and unpredictable figures as Group A.

Comparisons of the groups thus defined will be limited in the present paper to the results of a few fairly clear-cut techniques, involving little specialized psychological knowledge. A later report will deal with group performances on standardized personality tests.

Preferences for paintings

The subjects in this study had been asked to indicate the degree of their liking for each of 105 postcard-size reproductions in color of paintings by a large number of European artists, widely varied both as to time and place of origin, and representing many styles of painting as well as different choices of subject matter. Each painting was to be placed in one of four groups: Like Best of All, Like Much, Like Just Moderately, and Like Least of All. The subjects were asked to place approximately twice as many items in each of the two middle categories as in each of the two extreme ones.

An item was now defined to be a characteristic preference of a group if that item was placed in a given category significantly (.05 level of confidence) more often by that group than by the other. When this sort of analysis was carried out, it was found that no item was "characteristic" of a group in more than one category. It did happen, however, that some items appeared as characteristic of one group in the category "Like Best of All" while appearing as characteristic of the other group in the category "Like Least of All." Such extreme discordances in aesthetic preferences between Groups A and S are of special interest; in the lists below, they are set off from the rest of the paintings in the "Liked Best of All" and "Least of All" categories for the two groups.

Liked best of all by Group S

Veneziano	Portrait of a Young Lady
Botticelli	Virgin and Child
Corot	The Woman with the Pearl
Fra Lippo Lippi	The Adoration
Leonardo da Vinci	John the Baptist
École Française, 16th century	Elizabeth of Austria
Gainsborough	Blue Boy
Raeburn	Boy with a Rabbit
Clouet	Portrait of Francis I
École Française, 16th century	Francis I

Paintings above were "liked least" by Group A

Rembrandt	Portrait of Hendriche Stoffels
Rembrandt	Portrait of Himself in Old Age
Sanzio	Portrait of Balthazar Castiglione
Rembrandt	His Portrait by Himself
Utrillo	A View of Anse
Rembrandt	The Syndics
Gauguin	The Seine at Paris

Discussion. The first thing that strikes the eye about this set of paintings is that it consists largely of portraits. Of seventeen paintings in the group, twelve are portraits, three are religious scenes, and two are landscapes.

Considering how portraits usually get to be painted, one is not surprised to note in addition that the subjects are generally of aristocratic bearing and mien, richly and fashionably clothed. The ladies portrayed are pure and noble—not by character only, but by birth. The gentlemen are clearly persons of substance, accustomed to homage and given to command. (The imperious Francis I is represented twice, the portraits being by different artists.)

The paintings with a religious theme are of the Virgin and Child, the Adoration of the Infant, and Leonardo's St. John the Baptist. The landscapes are tranquil and pleasant ones, somewhat formal and "cultivated."

The dominant note in this set of paintings is one of religion, authority, and aristocracy, personified in the courtly, high-born, and holy personages depicted.

Liked least of all by Group S

Picasso	The bust before the window
Picasso	Still-life by candle-light
Modigliani	The Woman from Burgundy
Gris	The Breakfast
Modigliani	Marcelle
Gris	Woman with a Book
Toulouse-Lautrec	The Clowness
Vuillard	In Bed

Paintings above were "liked best" by Group A

Cézanne	Women bathing
Cézanne	The Black Marble Clock
Léger	Composition in 3 Profiles
Renoir	Woman with the Veil
Cézanne	Onions and Bottle
Lautrec	Jeanne Avril

Discussion. Now, let us examine the paintings which are placed at the opposite pole by Group S.

First, we note that all of the "abstractions" (five in a group of 105) are placed by these subjects in the Like Least of All category. (Four of these same five abstractions are liked "Best" by Group A.) In addition, the Modigliani women (who clearly are not faithful representations of "real" women) are similarly liked "Least" by Group S but "Best" by Group A.

What seems to be expressed here is a strong rejection of the esoteric, the radically experimental, and the "unnatural." (Supernatural themes, however, win approval if naturally represented and peopled by recognizably human beings.)

Rejected along with the unnatural and the radically experimental are ladies of low birth and ignoble pursuits. In this group we find the prostitute painted by Toulouse-Lautrec, the nudes in the Cezanne painting, "Women Bathing," Renoir's "Woman with the Veil" (an impressionistic suggestion of intrigue, assignation, and so on), and Vuillard's young woman "In Bed."

In summary, Group S approves good breeding, religion, and authority, and rejects the daring, the esoteric, the "unnatural," and the frankly sensual.

Liked best of all by Group A

Picasso	The bust before the window
Picasso	Still-life by candle-light

Modigliani	The Woman from Burgundy
Gris	The Breakfast
Modigliani	Marcelle
Gris	Woman with a Book
Toulouse-Lautrec	The Clowness
Vuillard	In Bed

Paintings above were "liked least" by Group S

Renoir	Bathing woman
Van Gogh	The Bridge
Vlaminck	The House with the Weatherboard
Daumier	The Amateur of Etchings
Dunoyer de Segonzac	Staddle
Toulouse-Lautrec	Two Waltzes
Gauguin	Women of Tahiti
Gauguin	And the Gold of Their Bodies
Degas	The Ironers

Discussion. We note immediately that in this set are represented the products of such "modern" art movements as Primitivism, Expressionism, Impressionism, and Cubism. These were revolts against traditional ways in art, expressed in radical experimentation in design, a search for the primitive and the naïve, a rejection of the directly representational in favor of the derivative and the abstract, and a choice of subject matter which affirmed the importance of the commonplace. Here sensuality and the instinctual life receive, to say the least, their due. Like many revolutionary movements, these delighted in being extreme, and one senses at times a certain histrionic and theatrical element accompanying the honest quest for new ways of expressing reality (and new realities to express).

Liked least of all by Group A

Veneziano	Portrait of a Young Lady
Botticelli	Virgin and Child
Fra Lippo Lippi	The Adoration
Corot	The Woman with the Pearl
da Vinci	John the Baptist
École Française, 16th century	Elizabeth of Austria
Gainsborough	Blue Boy
Raeburn	Boy with a Rabbit
Clouet	Portrait of Francis I
École Française	Francis I

Paintings above were "liked best by Group S

da Vinci	The Virgin, Child, and St. Anne
Redon	Flowers
Lucientes	Lady with the Fan
Whistler	Mother
Grunewald	The Annunciation
da Vinci	Portrait of Lucrezia Crivelli

Holbein	Portrait of Ann of Cleves
Watteau	Embarkment for Cythera
Goya y Lucientes	The Manikin
Ingres	The Odalisque
Corot	Landscape
École Française	Francis I
Angelico	The Annunciation

Discussion. It is evident that the members of Group A do not like religious themes in paintings. Of the eight religious scenes in the 105 paintings, six are placed in the Like Least category: Leonardo, Botticelli, Angelico, Grunewald, and Fra Lippo Lippi alike fall before this categorical rejection of the religious.

Further, the members of Group A do not like portraits of lords and ladies. Three different portraits of Francis I are relegated to the "Like Least" category, in company with Lucrezia Crivelli, Ann of Cleves, Elizabeth of Austria, the young aristocrat who served as the model for Blue Boy, and Whistler's Mother. (It is ironic that the eccentric and self-consciously nonconformist Whistler should be remembered to common fame, largely by courtesy of the American commercialization of Mother's Day, for a painting which he intended as an innovation in design, and which he titled "Arrangement in Grey and Black.")

The women in the portraits disliked by Group A have in common that they are rather aloof and distant. Even the odalisque in Ingres' painting is remarkably unsensual in appearance. This is in strong contrast to the women in the paintings liked best by Group A, who are considerably more informal and relaxed, and whose sexual role receives more emphasis.

In summary, Group A approves the modern, the radically experimental, the primitive and the sensual, while disliking what is religious, aristocratic, traditional, and emotionally controlled.

Group differences in self-description

We have seen that the two groups defined by figure preferences show consistently different preferences in paintings as well, and that the two sets of preferences taken together seem to suggest quite different perceptual attitudes bearing on (1) predictability, stability, balance, symmetry, and governance by a simple general principle; and (2) acceptance or rejection of tradition, religion, authority, and sensuality. How do persons with such different attitudes differ in seeing themselves?

A partial answer to this question is provided by an item analysis of the Gough Adjective Check-List, which was used in the study. Each subject had been asked to indicate (by a check mark) what adjectives in the list were, in his opinion, descriptive of himself. There were 279 adjectives in all.

Here are the adjectives which differentiated the groups, listed in the order of their discriminating power:

	Group S	Group A
At the .05 level:	contented	gloomy
	gentle	loud
	conservative	unstable
	unaffected	bitter
	patient	cool
	peaceable	dissatisfied
		pessimistic
		emotional
		irritable
		pleasure-seeking
At the .10 level:	serious	aloof
	individualistic	sarcastic
	stable	spendthrift
	worrying	distractible
	timid	demanding
	thrifty	indifferent
At the .15 level:	dreamy	anxious
	deliberate	opinionated
	moderate	temperamental
	modest	quick
	responsible	
	foresighted	
At the .2 level:	conscientious	

In these self-descriptions, as in the characteristic art preferences, these two groups clearly separate themselves from one another. It seems not too much to say that they hold different views of themselves and of the world. The origins and consequences of such divergent perspectives on self and universe will be explored, necessarily somewhat speculatively, in the concluding section of this paper. Before embarking on that further inquiry, however, we should note immediately that both types, A and S, are represented with about equal frequency among the Highs and the Lows of our sample of graduate students. Neither one nor the other view is significantly related to the total constellation of factors which make for personal effectiveness and success in graduate school. One may be both contented and original, gloomy and personally sound. There is more than one path to personal integrity, and more than one way in which to contribute meaningfully to scientific and professional life.

Relevant work of other psychologists

William James. Although we have come upon these facts largely incidentally while in search of others, it is quite understandable in the light of the facts themselves that they have been anticipated by someone who proceeded more by reason than by experiment. For in his lectures on pragmatism, William James set forth quite clearly the very opposition between "types of mental make-up" which these experimental data have made evident. Consider the respective traits of these two types, as he lists them in "The Present Dilemma in Philosophy" (6):

Rationalistic (going by "principles")	Empiricist (going by "facts")
Intellectualistic	Sensationalistic
Idealistic	Materialistic
Optimistic	Pessimistic
Religious	Irreligious
Free-willist	Fatalistic
Monistic	Pluralistic
Dogmatical	Skeptical

Now compare them with these experimentally found characteristics of Groups S and A:

Group S	*Group A*
In figure preferences: Preferring what is simple, regularly predictable, following some cardinal principle which can be educed at a glance.	In figure preferences: Preferring what is complex, irregular, whimsical.
In art preferences: Preferring themes involving religion, authority, and aristocracy.	In art preferences: Preferring what is radically experimental, sensational, esoteric, primitive, and naïve.
In adjective self-checks: Contented, gentle, conservative, patient, peaceable, etc.	In adjective self-checks: Gloomy, pessimistic, bitter, dissatisfied, emotional, pleasure-seeking, etc.

James set forth these "contrasted mixtures" by way of making more particular his thesis that "the history of philosophy is to a great extent that of a certain clash of human temperaments." He remarks that "nature seems to combine most frequently with intellectualism an idealistic and optimistic tendency. Empiricists on the other hand are not uncommonly materialistic, and their optimism is apt to be decidedly conditional and tremulous. Rationalism is always monistic. It starts from wholes and universals, and makes much of the unity of things. Empiricism starts from the parts, and makes of the whole a collection—is not averse therefore to calling itself pluralistic. Rationalism usually considers itself more religious than empiricism, but there is much to say about this claim; so I merely mention it. It is a true claim when the individual rationalist is what is called a man of feeling, and when the individual empiricist prides himself on being hard-headed. In that case the rationalist will usually also be in favor of what is called free-will, and the empiricist will be a fatalist— I use the terms most popularly current. The rationalist finally will be of dogmatic temper in his affirmations, while the empiricist may be more skeptical and open to discussion." (6, pp. 10f.)

Now it happens that these essays in pragmatism were not known to the present writer at the time this research was carried out. The writer's somewhat similar views, however, led to the inclusion in the research program of an interview with each subject on his philosophy of life, the interview centering generally around the freedom-determinism question and the problem of evil. The results of this interview will be reported in a later paper, and will be discussed both in the context of the types here delineated and in terms of the childhood events which seemed determinative of such basic attitudes towards the world.

Burt and Eysenck. There are two significant lines of experimental investigation in aesthetic choice and personality style which are relevant to the present findings. While both have used primarily the technique of factor analysis, they have been marked by somewhat different approaches to the same subject matter. One point of origin was the search for temperamental factors, while the other was the search for factors present in aesthetic preferences.

The first of these lines of investigation, comprising a series of studies by Cyril Burt and his students, and summarized by him in (2), was centered upon the discovery and description of factors in personality. He distinguished four temperamental types: (1) the unstable extravert; (2) the stable extravert; (3) the unstable introvert; (4) the stable introvert. Tendencies towards these types, when measured by a regression equation or some similar device, prove to be approximately normally distributed; Burt therefore selected the extreme 10 per cent of the distributions as more or less "pure" representatives of the type. In samples thus selected, he found these characteristic aesthetic preferences:

1. The Unstable Extravert likes dramatic and romantic art, and prefers color to form and line in paintings. In music he likes chromatic rather than diatonic harmony, and prefers rhythm to melody. His penchant is for dramatic events, emotionally or even sensationally treated. Pictures in which a human figure is conspicuous are preferred to landscapes, interiors, or still life. The unstable extravert likes vivid colors, strong contrasts, and vigorous and flowing curves. There is strong empathy for "restless movement" in art and architecture.

2. The Stable Extravert differs in emphasizing the cognitive rather than the emotional aspects of external reality. He is strongly representational and practical, and sets more store by solidity and mass than by decoration and flowing curves. He likes historical subject matter, realistically treated.

3. The Unstable Introvert prefers impressionistic art, with emphasis on the supernatural and the mystical—a sort of romanticism, but without the element of adventure in the real world which characterizes the unstable extravert. The unstable introvert prefers landscapes, especially if "mystically" treated, to portraits; he likes the work of such artists as El Greco, Blake, Corot, Durer, Monet, Botticelli, and Rossetti. In literature, his preferences are for Spenser, Shelley, Yeats, Coleridge, De Quincy.

4. The Stable Introvert has a strongly intellectual attitude, and attends to the picture as an object in itself. The chief appeal is in "the significant form." Pattern rather than content is important. Good drawing, clean lines, and chiaroscuro appeal more than colors. There is a strong repugnance for the sentimental and the theatrical. Tranquil landscapes and formal, closed-in scenes are preferred. The stable introvert has little interest in portraiture, except that of Rembrandt and Van Eyck. He prefers unity and repetition to diversity and variegation, likes economy rather than exuberance, and prefers the conventional to the obtrusively original.

While the findings reported by Burt cannot be unequivocally assimilated to the results of the present research, there are certainly many points of contact. In general, Unstable Extraverts would seem to belong to our Group A, while "stable" people, both extraverts and introverts, would probably be classed with Group S. Where the Unstable Introvert would fit is not entirely clear, although the tendency would probably be towards Group A rather than Group S. Indeed, since "stable" is one of the adjectives with which Group S characterizes itself, while Group A describes itself as "unstable," perhaps we can do no better than to take the subjects' own word on the matter, using stability-instability as the most relevant principle of classification.

The second line of investigation, no doubt deriving historically from the first, but conceptually somewhat different, is that carried on by Eysenck. Rather than working from personality factors to their correlates in aesthetic preferences, he began by establishing factors in the latter realm of behavior, and then sought their correlates in personality.

Eysenck demonstrated for a number of stimulus classes (colors, odors, paintings, polygons, poetry, etc.) the existence of a general factor of aesthetic appreciation, and in addition showed that when the influence of this factor is eliminated a secondary, bipolar factor can be found (3, 4, 5). This latter factor, which he named "K," generally has positive and negative saturations in about equal numbers in the populations studied. One of its poles seems to be represented by preference for the simple polygon, the strong, obvious odor, the poem with the obvious rhyming scheme and the definite, unvarying, simple rhythm, and the simple, highly unified picture. At the other pole is preference for the more complex polygon, the more subtle odors, the poem with a less obvious rhythm and a more variable and loose rhyming scheme, and the complex, more diversified picture.

Eysenck's description of this bipolar factor fits quite well the factor found by Welsh in his original study. As a result both of Eysenck's further work and of our own investigations, we now know a great deal more about the relationship of this factor to personality variables. Eysenck himself showed that the K-factor (as measured anew by a "K-test" consisting of 100 pairs of pictures) correlated significantly with both extraversion-introversion and radicalism-conservatism. Subjects who preferred the modern, impressionistic painting were extraverted and radical, while those who preferred the older, more conventional paintings were introverted and conservative. Taken in conjunction with Burt's findings, this would point to the members of Group S as being predominantly stable introverts, while the members of Group A would be best classed as unstable extraverts. There is perhaps little point, however, in attempting to reconcile these different classifications in the absence of data collected specifically to resolve the issue.

Conclusions and discussion

The findings which require explanation, then, are these:

(1) We are dealing with two types of perceptual preferences, one of them being a choice of what is stable, regular, balanced, predictable, clear-cut, traditional, and following some general abstract principle, which in human affairs is personified as authority; the other a choice of what is unstable, asymmetrical, unbalanced, whimsical, rebellious against tradition, and at times seemingly irrational, disordered, and chaotic.

(2) These two types occur with equal frequency in the two classes of subjects defined by ratings as low or high in a constellation of factors making for personal effectiveness.

We suggest that the types of perceptual preference we have observed are related basically to a *choice of what to attend to* in the complex of phenomena which make up the world we experience; for the world *is* both stable and unstable, predictable and unpredictable, ordered and chaotic. To see it predominantly as one or the other is a sort of *perceptual decision;* one may attend to its ordered aspect, to regular sequences of events, to a stable center of the universe (the sun, the church, the state, the home, the parent, God, eternity, etc.) or one may instead attend primarily to the eccentric, the relative, and the arbitrary aspect of the world (the briefness of the individual life, the blind uncaringness of matter, the sometime hypocrisy of authority, accidents of circumstance, the presence of evil, tragic fate, the impossibility of freedom for the only organism capable of conceiving freedom, and so on).

Either of these alternative perceptual decisions may be associated with a high degree of personal effectiveness. It is as though there is an effective and an ineffective aspect of each alternative. Our thinking about these various aspects is as yet based only upon clinical impressions of our subjects, but it is perhaps worth recording while we go on with the business of gathering more objective evidence.

At its best, the decision in favor of order makes for personal stability and balance, a sort of easy-going optimism combined with religious faith, a friendliness towards tradition, custom, and ceremony, and respect for authority without subservience to it. This sort of decision will be made by persons who from an early age had good reason to trust the stability and equilibrium of the world and who derived an inner sense of comfort and balance from their perception of an outer certainty.

At its worst, the decision in favor of order makes for categorical rejection of all that threatens disorder, a fear of anything which might bring disequilibrium. Optimism becomes a matter of policy, religion a prescription and a ritual. Such a decision is associated with stereotyped thinking, rigid and compulsive morality, and hatred of instinctual aggressive and erotic forces which might upset the precariously maintained balance. Equilibrium depends essentially upon exclusion, a kind of perceptual distortion which consists in refusing to see parts of reality which cannot be assimilated to some preconceived system.

The decision in favor of complexity, at its best, makes for originality and creativeness, a greater tolerance for unusual ideas and formulations. The sometimes disordered and unstable world has its counterpart in the person's inner discord, but the crucial ameliorative factor is a constant effort to integrate the inner and outer complexity in a higher-order synthesis. The goal is to achieve the psychological analogue of mathematical elegance: to allow into the perceptual system the greatest possible richness of experience, while yet finding in this complexity some over-all pattern. Such a person is not immobilized by anxiety in the face of great uncertainty, but is at once perturbed and challenged. For such an individual, optimism is impossible, but pessimism is lifted from the personal to the tragic level, resulting not in apathy but in participation in the business of life.

At its worst, such a perceptual attitude leads to grossly disorganized behavior, to a surrender to chaos. It results in nihilism, despair, and disintegration. The personal life itself becomes simply an acting out of the meaninglessness of the universe, a bitter joke directed against its own maker. The individual is overwhelmed by the apparent insolubility of the problem, and finds the disorder of life disgusting and hateful. His essential world-view is thus depreciative and hostile.

We have not hesitated to refer here to perceptual *decision*, to an act of choice on the part of the individual. That is to say, we conceive this as a matter not simply of capacity, but of preference. Such a choice does of course involve perceptual capacity, but beyond capacity it is a matter of orientation towards experience; in a sense, perceptual attitude. In their important theoretical article (in search of the perceiver in perceptual theory) Klein and Schlesinger (7) have emphasized that their empirically found patterns of modes of perceptual response (to which they give the name syndrome) are to be thought of as "*preferred* styles of expression rather than *required* ones" (italics theirs). In search of the perceiver, they came inevitably upon *choice* rather than capacity or necessity as the determiner of observed response.

This very perceptual decision, of course, is itself determined; and it is to the search for the determinants that the next step in this line of research will be devoted.

References

1. Barron, F., and Welsh, G. S. Artistic perception as a possible factor in personality style: its measurement by a figure preference test. (To appear.)
2. Burt, C. The factorial analysis of emotional traits, Parts I and II. *Charact. & Pers.*, 1939, 7, pp. 238–254, 275–299.
3. Eysenck, H. J. The general factor in aesthetic judgments. *Brit. J. Psychol.*, 1940, 31, 94–102.
4. Eysenck, II. J. Some factors in the appreciation of poetry, and their relation to temperamental qualities. *Charact. & Pers.*, 1940–41, 9, 160–167.
5. Eysenck, H. J. "Type" factors in aesthetic judgments. *Brit. J. Psychol.*, 1941, 31, 262–270.
6. James, W. The present dilemma in philosophy, Lecture I in *Pragmatism*, New York: Longmans, Green & Co., 1907.
7. Klein, G., and Schlesinger, H. Where is the perceiver in perceptual theory?, *J. Pers.* 1949, 18, 32–47.
8. Welsh, G. S. A projective figure-preference test for diagnosis of psychopathology: 1. A preliminary investigation. Unpublished Ph.D. thesis, University of Minnesota, 1949.

PERSONALITY MEASUREMENT

The measurement of personality traits is especially important and interesting in experimental studies. In the present experiment, part of a larger monograph consisting of a number of experiments on the personality trait of need for affiliation, the effect of experimentally produced anxiety on *n* affiliation is investigated.

Points to guide your study

1. See the introductions to other readings for the meaning of the *p* values.

2. The experimental investigation of personality traits makes up a large part of the psychologist's study of personality. Can you formulate a testable hypothesis about a personality trait? How would you test this hypothesis?

45. THE PSYCHOLOGY OF AFFILIATION

Stanley Schachter, University of Minnesota[*]

Anxiety and affiliation

One of the consequences of isolation appears to be a psychological state which in its extreme form resembles a full-blown anxiety attack. In many of the autobiographical reports and in the interview protocol of our single subject who demanded his release after only two hours of confinement, there are strong indications of an overwhelming nervousness, of tremendous suffering and pain, and of a general "going-to-pieces." A milder form is illustrated by the two of our five subjects who reported that they had felt jittery, tense, and uneasy. At the other extreme, two subjects went through the experience with complete aplomb and reported no difficulties. The whole range of reactions is represented, and though we have little idea as to the variables which determine whether the reaction to isolation will be equanimity or terror, it is evident that anxiety, in some degree, is a fairly common concomitant of isolation. For a variety of frankly intuitive reasons, it seemed reasonable to expect that if conditions of isolation produce anxiety, conditions of anxiety would lead to the increase of affiliative tendencies. In order to test this proposition the following very simple experiment was constructed.

Experimental procedure

There were two experimental conditions, one of high anxiety and one of low anxiety. Anxiety

* Reprinted from *The psychology of affiliation* by Stanley Schachter with permission from the publishers, Stanford University Press. Copyright 1959 by the Board of Trustees of the Leland Stanford Junior University. The permission of the author has also been obtained.

was manipulated in the following fashion. In the high-anxiety condition, the subjects, all college girls, strangers to one another, entered a room to find facing them a gentleman of serious mien, horn-rimmed glasses, dressed in a white laboratory coat, stethoscope dribbling out of his pocket, behind him an array of formidable electrical junk. After a few preliminaries, the experimenter began:

> Allow me to introduce myself, I am Dr. Gregor Zilstein of the Medical School's Departments of Neurology and Psychiatry. I have asked you all to come today in order to serve as subjects in an experiment concerned with the effects of electrical shock.

Zilstein paused ominously, then continued with a seven- or eight-minute recital of the importance of research in his area, citing electroshock therapy, the increasing number of accidents due to electricity, and so on. He concluded in this vein:

> What we will ask each of you to do is very simple. We would like to give each of you a series of electric shocks. Now, I feel I must be completely honest with you and tell you exactly what you are in for. These shocks will hurt, they will be painful. As you can guess, if, in research of this sort, we're to learn anything at all that will really help humanity, it is necessary that our shocks be intense. What we will do is put an electrode on your hand, hook you into apparatus such as this [Zilstein points to the electrical-looking gadgetry behind him], give you a series of electric shocks, and take various measures such as your pulse rate, blood pressure, and so on.

Again, I do want to be honest with you and tell you that these shocks will be quite painful but, of course, they will do no permanent damage.

In the low-anxiety condition, the setting and costume were precisely the same except that there was no electrical apparatus in the room. After introducing himself, Zilstein proceeded:

I have asked you all to come today in order to serve as subjects in an experiment concerned with the effects of electric shock. I hasten to add, do not let the word "shock" trouble you; I am sure that you will enjoy the experiment.

Then precisely the same recital on the importance of the research, concluding with:

What we will ask each one of you to do is very simple. We would like to give each of you a series of very mild electric shocks. I assure you that what you will feel will not in any way be painful. It will resemble more a tickle or a tingle than anything unpleasant. We will put an electrode on your hand, give you a series of very mild shocks and measure such things as your pulse rate and blood pressure, measures with which I'm sure you are all familiar from visits to your family doctor.

From this point on, the experimental procedures in the two conditions were identical. In order to get a first measurement of the effectiveness of the anxiety manipulation, the experimenter continued:

Before we begin, I'd like to have you tell us how you feel about taking part in this experiment and being shocked. We need this information in order to fully understand your reactions in the shocking apparatus. I ask you therefore to be as honest as possible in answering and describe your feelings as accurately as possible.

He then passed out a sheet headed, "How do you feel about being shocked?" and asked the subjects to check the appropriate point on a five-point scale ranging from "I dislike the idea very much" to "I enjoy the idea very much."[1]

This done, the experimenter continued:

Before we begin with the shocking proper there will be about a ten-minute delay while we get this room in order. We have several pieces of equipment to bring in and get set up. With this many people in the room, this would be very difficult to do, so we will have to ask you to be kind enough to leave the room.

Here is what we will ask you to do for this ten-minute period of waiting. We have on this floor a number of additional rooms, so that each of you, if you would like, can wait alone in your own room. These rooms are comfortable and spacious; they all have armchairs, and there are books and magazines in each room. It did occur to us, however, that some of you might want to wait for these ten minutes together with some of the other girls here. If you would prefer this, of course, just let us know. We'll take one of the empty classrooms on this floor and you can wait together with some of the other girls there.

The experimenter then passed out a sheet on which the subjects could indicate their preference. This sheet read as follows:

Please indicate below whether you prefer waiting your turn to be shocked alone or in the company of others.
_____ I prefer being alone.
_____ I prefer being with others.
_____ I really don't care.

In order to get a measure of the intensity of the subjects' desires to be alone or together, the experimenter continued:

With a group this size and with the number of additional rooms we have, it's not always possible to give each girl exactly what she'd like. So be perfectly honest and let us know how much you'd like to be alone or together with other girls. Let us know just how you feel, and we'll use that information to come as close as possible to putting you into the arrangement of your choice.

The experimenter then passed out the following scale:

I very much prefer being alone	I prefer being alone	I don't care very much	I prefer being together with others	I very much prefer being together with others

To get a final measure of the effectiveness of the anxiety manipulation, the experimenter continued:

It has, of course, occurred to us that some of you may not wish to take part in this experiment. Now, we would find it perfectly understandable if some of you should feel that you do not want to be a subject in an experiment in which you will be shocked. If this is the case just let us know. I'll pass out this sheet on which you may indicate whether or not

---

[1] The reader may well feel that this is hardly the most appropriate scale for measuring degree of anxiety. In experiments to be described in later chapters, precisely the same anxiety manipulation was employed and a scale that more directly tapped the anxiety dimension was added. This scale correlated with the "dislike-enjoy" scale described above with $r = +.76$.

you want to go on. If you do wish to be a subject, check "yes"; if you do not wish to take part, check "no" and you may leave. Of course, if you check "no" we cannot give you credit in your psychology classes for having taken part in this experiment.

After the subjects had marked their sheets, the experiment was over and the experimenter took off his white coat and explained in detail the purpose of the experiments and the reasons for the various deceptions practiced. The cooperation of the subjects was of course enlisted in not talking about the experiment to other students.

In summary, in this experimental set-up, anxiety has been manipulated by varying the fear of being shocked. The affiliative tendency is measured by the subject's preference for "Alone," "Together," or "Don't care" and by the expressed intensity of this preference.

Subjects

The subjects in this study were all girls, students in Introductory Psychology courses at the University of Minnesota. At the beginning of each semester, students in these classes may sign up for a subject pool. More than 90 per cent of the students usually do so, for they receive one additional point on their final examination for each experimental hour they serve. This fact should be kept in mind when considering the proportion of subjects who refused to continue in the experiment.

The experimental sessions were run with groups of five to eight girls at a time, for a total of 32 subjects in the high-anxiety condition and 30 subjects in the low-anxiety condition. A deliberate attempt was made to insure that the subjects did not know one another before coming to the experiment. Despite our best efforts, 16 per cent of the subjects had known one another beforehand. Data for these subjects were discarded, for it seemed clear that previous friendship would thoroughly confound the meaning of a choice of "Together" or "Alone." It should be noted, however, that though in both conditions such girls chose "Together" considerably more often than did girls who had not known one another before the experiment, the between-condition differences were in the same direction for both groups of subjects.

On this same point, an attempt was made to prevent the subjects from talking to one another while waiting for the experiment to begin, for again it was felt that an interesting conversation or a particularly friendly girl might confound the choice of "Together" or "Alone." As each subject entered the experimental room, she was handed a multipaged questionnaire labeled "Biographical Inventory" and asked to begin filling it out. This device worked well and effectively prevented any chatter until all of the subjects had arrived and the experimenter could begin his monologue.

Results

Table 1 presents data permitting evaluation of the effectiveness of the manipulation of anxiety. The column labeled "Anx" presents the mean score, by condition, of responses to the question "How do you feel about being shocked?" The greater the score, the greater the anxiety; a score greater than 3 indicates dislike. Clearly there are large and significant differences between the two conditions.

Table 1   Effectiveness of the anxiety manipulation

	n	Anx	% S's refusing to continue
Hi Anx	32	3.69	18.8
Lo Anx	30	2.48	0
		$t = 5.22$	Exact $p = .03$
		$p* < .001$	

* The probability values reported throughout this volume are all based on two-tailed tests of significance.

The results of the second measure of anxiety, a subject's willingness to continue in the experiment when given the opportunity to drop out, are presented in the column labeled "% S's refusing to continue." This is, perhaps, the best single indicator of the effectiveness of the manipulation, for it is a reality-bound measure. Again it is clear that the manipulation of anxiety has been successful. Some 19 per cent of subjects in the high-anxiety condition refused to continue in the experiment. All subjects in the low-anxiety condition were willing to go through with the experiment.

The effect of anxiety on the affiliative tendency may be noted in Table 2, where, for each condition, the number of subjects choosing "Together," "Alone," or "Don't Care" is tabulated. It is evident that there is a strong positive relationship between anxiety and the index of affiliative tendency, the proportion of subjects choosing the "Together" alternative. Some 63 per cent of subjects in the high-anxiety condition wanted to be together with other subjects while they waited to be shocked. In the low-anxiety condition only 33 per cent of the subjects wished to be together.

The column labeled "Over-all Intensity" in Table 2 presents the mean score for all subjects, in each condition, of responses to the scale designed to measure the intensity of the desire to be alone or together with others. The point "I don't care very much" is scored as zero. The

Table 2 Relationship of anxiety to the affiliative tendency

	No. choosing			Over-all intensity
	Together	Don't care	Alone	
Hi Anx	20	9	3	+.88
Lo Anx	10	18	2	+.35

$$X^2_{Tog \text{ vs } DC + A} = 5.27$$
$$.02 < p < .05$$

$t = 2.83$

$p < .01$

two points in this scale indicating a preference for being together with other subjects are scored as +1 and +2 respectively. The points indicating a preference for being alone are scored as −1 and −2. The mean scores of this scale provide the best over-all index of the magnitude of affiliative desires, for this score combines choice and intensity of choice. Also, this index incorporates the relatively milder preferences of subjects who chose the "Don't Care" alternative, for 30 per cent of these subjects did express some preference on this scale. Again it is clear that affiliative desires increase with anxiety. The mean intensity score for high-anxiety subjects is +.88 and for low-anxiety subjects is +.35.

Expectations, then, are confirmed, but confirmed, in truth, in a blaze of ambiguity, for the several terms of the formulation "anxiety leads to the arousal of affiliative tendencies" are still vague. What is meant by the "affiliative tendency," and precisely why do the subjects choose to be together when anxious? What is meant by "anxiety," and what are the limits of this relationship? What is meant by "leads to," and, historically, just how and why is this relationship established? The remainder of this monograph is devoted to consideration of these questions and to a description of research designed to clarify and elaborate the nature of this relationship.

THEORIES OF PERSONALITY

Psychoanalysis is both theory and therapy. These excerpts are concerned with the theoretical aspects of psychoanalysis. They can give only a sketchy account of the psychoanalytic theories. Many good books, and, unfortunately, some poor books, are available in soft covers. Among the better ones are those by Freud himself. Good summaries, from different points of view, are the following:

G. S. Blum, *Psychoanalytic theories of personality.* McGraw-Hill, 1953.

Charles Brenner, *Elementary textbook of psychoanalysis.* Anchor, 1955.

C. S. Hall, *A primer of Freudian psychology.* Mentor, 1954.

The last two of these are paperbacks.

Notice that there are psychoanalytic theories. The orthodox psychoanalytic school, as founded by Freud, was soon split by the development of the divergent theories of Adler and Jung. More recently, orthodox theory has been reevaluated. Some, for instance, Fenichel and Klein, have tended to reemphasize the orthodox libido theory. Others, for instance, Fromm, Horney, and Sullivan, the so-called neo-Freudians, have put emphasis on the importance of social rather than biological factors in personality development.

Points to guide your study

1. These excerpts will seem a little epigrammatic. A great deal is packed into each paragraph. Therefore, it is especially important for you to read this selection very carefully.

2. A major disadvantage of this method of presenting psychoanalytic theory is that the data on which the theory is based are not presented. This tends to make many of the statements seem quite arbitrary.

3. A point of this book is well-taken. Psychoanalytic theories, while extremely fruitful, lack the rigor characteristic of other scientific theories. The final paragraphs of this selection represent this view quite well.

46. PSYCHOANALYTIC THEORIES OF PERSONALITY

Gerald S. Blum, University of Michigan*

The neonate's personality potential. Orthodox psychoanalytic theory explains mental phenomena as the result of a dynamic interaction between urging forces or instincts within the organism and counterforces set up by the external environment. Instincts, described as psychic representatives of stimuli originating in the soma, already exist for the newborn child. Each instinct has its aim, object, and source. Fenichel classifies instincts generally into the simple physical needs and the sexual urges. The former, such as hunger, breathing, and thirst, are said to be less important for personality development since they require quick satisfaction and thus allow for very little variability among individuals. Sexual urges, conceived in the broadest sense, operate from birth onward so that adult forms of sexuality are continuations of the infantile ones. The energy of the sexual instincts is termed "libido," fixed quantities of which are presumed to be present in the neonate. Jung defines libido more broadly as a primal energy underlying all mental life, not merely the sexual. The neo-Freudians, on the other hand, reject the notions of instinct and libido, though Sullivan does speak of a "power motive."

Freud in his later writings also postulated an innate death instinct to account for aggression and self-destructive urges. However, Fenichel takes issue with this notion and prefers to explain aggression as a mode of response to frustration, growing like the sexual instincts out of a need for tension reduction. Similarly the neo-Freudians offer interpersonal difficulties as a better explanation than the death instinct for aggression and suicide.

Another major element in the personality potential of the neonate is the unconscious, a cornerstone of psychoanalytic theory. Its influence is purported to be far more powerful than that of the conscious mind, for unconscious impulses continually strive in a very active fashion for conscious expression. Processes in the unconscious are timeless and bear little relation to external reality. Incompatible wishes can exist side by side, and there are no considerations of doubt, negation, or uncertainty. The term "id" was added later to designate that portion of the unconscious which functions as a source of instinctual energy, forming a reservoir of libido. Freud's own view on the origin of content in the unconscious is phylogenetic, that is, through some form of racial inheritance. The latter resembles to some extent Jung's formulation of the collective unconscious, a product of the racial inheritance of significant memories or germs of ideas. Transmitted in the collective unconscious are primordial images or archetypes which, according to Jung, become known through the symbolic interpretation of dreams. Examples are the mother and father archetypes, dealing, respectively, with nourishment and strength. In addition to the collective unconscious each individual is said to possess a personal unconscious— forgotten memories which are a consequence, not so much of repression, but of one-sided development. Neo-Freudians accept the principle of unconscious function but criticize Freud's connotation of the unconscious as a place, where, for example, repressed experiences and id forces can combine with each other.

Finally orthodox theory ascribes to the neonate a condition known as "primary narcissism." The infant is unable to differentiate himself from external objects, so that sexual aims are autoerotic and libido is turned inward. Because of the magical gratification of his needs, the infant soon develops a feeling of omnipotence which later in life he may wishfully seek to regain. For Greenacre primary narcissism connotes more than this "oceanic feeling." She considers that narcissism, catalyzed by the birth processes, contains the beginnings of a propulsive drive based on the biological need for survival. An increase in anxiety is said to cause a corresponding defensive increase in narcissism. Fromm quarrels with the fixed-amount-of-libido notion and criticizes Freud's formulation of narcissism on the grounds that a person capable of genuinely loving himself is actually more capable of loving others.

The first year of life. According to orthodox psychoanalytic theory, the newborn child has no awareness of the outside world and can experience only changes in his own tension state. The beginnings of ego functioning appear when he longs for something to be done by the external

* G. S. Blum. *Psychoanalytic theories of personality*. New York: McGraw-Hill, 1953. Copyright 1953 by the McGraw-Hill Book Company, Inc. Excerpts reprinted here with permission from the author and the McGraw-Hill Book Company, Inc. References omitted. Some sections retitled.

world to satisfy his wants. This distinction between self and environment is said to occur in the context of indulgence and deprivation, with some amount of the latter essential for development. Self-esteem, one of the properties of the ego, is first regulated by the supply of nourishment from the outside, a magical source which leads the infant to feel omnipotent. Later there follows a period of passive-receptive mastery, in which he shares in the newly discovered omnipotence of adults and passively induces them to deliver the desired supplies. As the child grows, the earliest forms of pure pleasure seeking are gradually replaced by the reality principle—the ability to substitute future for immediate gratification.

Melanie Klein deviates from orthodox theory by postulating the active functioning of both ego and superego during the first year of life. Her theories are predicated upon the assumption of powerful unconscious fantasies at this time. Sullivan, in the neo-Freudian school, describes the first year as belonging to the prototaxic mode of experience. At first the infant knows only momentary states, with no distinctions of time and place. After a while he perceives or "prehends" the mother, mainly in terms of good and bad.

With respect to psychosexual development, the orthodox theory of infantile sexuality portrays the child as "polymorphous perverse." The beginning expression of the sexual instinct is said to be the act of sucking in the early oral-passive stage. Pleasure from this activity is soon discovered apart from the feeding situation, so that the first aim is autoerotic stimulation of the membranes of the mouth. Later the desire to incorporate persons and things is added. Individuals are looked upon primarily as food or providers of food in terms of these fantasies of incorporation, which are often accompanied by oral fears like the fear of being eaten. The second aspect of the oral stage, commencing with the eruption of teeth, is the sadistic, during which the child seeks to retaliate for frustration by biting.

Klein describes a wide array of sexual and aggressive fantasies in the first year, including oedipal impulses, the desire to incorporate the father's penis, the wish to destroy the mother's body, and so on. For Jung the earliest phase is characterized almost exclusively by nutrition and growth. The link between these nutritive functions and later sexuality is presumed to be rhythmic activity. The neo-Freudians also minimize the erotic element and stress instead cultural and developmental manifestations of orality. Erikson, closer to the orthodox position, adds the concepts of zones and modes, in this case the oral zone and incorporative mode.

In the area of relationships to people, orthodox theory traces a gradual transition from the infant's missing of things which bring satisfaction, to his differentiation of trusted and strange impressions, and finally to his recognition of the mother as a whole object. The notion of ambivalence is introduced in the oral-sadistic stage, at which period he longs for pleasurable union with the mother and yet in times of frustration wishes to attack her. Klein states that the mother probably exists as a whole object from the very beginning, but in vague outline. She tends to emphasize the child's fear of losing the love object. Sullivan concentrates his description of early relationships on the process of empathy—a peculiar nonverbal, emotional communication between parent and child, said to be strongest between the ages of six and twenty-seven months.

Mechanisms used in the first year include introjection, projection, denial, fixation, and regression. Introjection, based on swallowing or taking in food, is aimed first at instinctual satisfaction, later at regaining omnipotence, and still later at destroying the hated object by oral incorporation. Projection, stemming from spitting out the unpleasant, involves the attribution of painful stimuli to the outside world. Denial, also a very primitive mechanism, means the avoidance of unpleasant reality simply by closing one's eyes to it and pretending it does not exist. Fixation and regression refer to the retention of an abnormal number of characteristics of an earlier stage, to which the individual is predisposed to return if difficulties arise. All the preceding mechanisms, as they operate in the first year, are considered forerunners of the later defense mechanisms.

Ages one to three years. In his discussion of ego formation at this age level Fenichel traces the development of active mastery and the handling of anxiety. As a result of both newly acquired control over his motor apparatus and the growth of the function of judgment (reality testing), the young child learns to cope actively with the environment. His ego becomes capable of judging potentially traumatic situations, so that anxiety serves as a protective warning signal. Common sources of anxiety at this time derive from the talion principle—the fear that others may do to him what he fantasies doing to them—and fear over the loss of love and protection. When anxiety-provoking situations have been experienced, the child through a process of belated mastery attempts to reduce tension by reliving the trauma over and over in games and dreams. The acquisition of speech and the advances in thinking contribute heavily to a new feeling of power. Thinking in this period is said to contain many prelogical and symbolic elements. Superego forerunners are also prominent in the form of internalized parental prohibitions.

Sullivan speaks of the parataxic mode, in which experience is undergone as momentary, unconnected organismic states. The earlier prototaxic undifferentiated wholeness is now broken down into parts, but these have no logical relation to one another. Dreams and the transference reaction in psychotherapy are given as illustrations of parataxic distortion. Communication in ages one to three involves the use of autistic language, words having a personal, private meaning. Anxiety is described as a further development of the loss of euphoria and arises from rewards and punishments in the socialization of the child. It serves to make him focus his alertness on performances which bring approval or disapproval, and out of this focusing the self-dynamism is evolved. Three personifications of self gradually emerge: the "good me," "bad me," and "not me."

Psychosexual development in the orthodox system witnesses the anal-sadistic stage. Two trends are distinguished—the earlier expulsive and the later retentive. Expulsiveness is expressed in the physiological pleasure of excretion but can also serve aggressive purposes by defying the parents in their insistence on toilet training. The retentive phase derives from both stimulation of the mucous membrane and the social values placed upon conformity. The neo-Freudians maintain that the emphasis should be placed, not on the pleasure obtained from expelling and retaining feces, but rather on the struggle with parents. Erikson occupies an intermediate position with his stress upon the social modalities of "letting go" and "holding on."

Concomitant relationships, according to orthodox sources, entail ambivalence, bisexuality, sadism, and masochism. Anal ambivalence is said to arise from the contradictory attitude toward feces; bisexuality from the fact that the rectum is an excretory hollow organ; sadism from frustration in the toilet-training situation; and masochism from the erotic stimulation of the buttocks in spankings. Sullivan approaches interpersonal relationships from another angle. He describes the operation of "reflected appraisals," in which the child forms an opinion of himself mainly from the reactions of significant adults to him; and also multiple "me-you patterns," which refer to incongruent attitudes toward others.

Two new mechanisms at these ages include Anna Freud's "denial in word and act," a later counterpart of denial in fantasy, and Sullivan's "consensual validation," a process in which the individual tries to correct his parataxic distortions by evaluating his own thoughts and feelings against those of others.

Ages three to five. At ages three to five the orthodox scene shifts to the phallic stage of psychosexual development. Early in this period urethral preoccupations appear, first in the form of pleasurable autoeroticism and later in association with sadistic fantasies of urinating on others. Interest in the genitals increases, along with masturbation and exhibitionism. The extreme narcissistic value placed upon the penis by boys leads them to fear damage to that organ—castration anxiety—in retaliation for guilt-laden oedipal fantasies. In girls penis envy, arising from observation of differences in male and female genitals, is said to predominate. The lack of a penis is presumably felt as a punishment for some wrongdoing.

Among the neo-Freudians, Thompson questions whether observation of the genitals is sufficient to elicit castration anxiety unless reinforced by parental threats. Horney objects to the notion of primary penis envy in girls. She attributes envy in women to the desire for masculine qualities prized by the culture rather than to sexual experiences in early childhood. In his system Erikson stresses the "intrusive" features of the phallic-locomotor stage, such as aggressiveness, competition, curiosity, and the pleasure of conquest.

Relationships to others revolve around the Oedipus complex, defined as sexual love for the parent of the opposite sex accompanied by hatred for the parent of the same sex. In the case of the boy the transition is relatively simple, for the preoedipal object, the mother, continues to be the preferred parent. The girl, however, has to undergo a complicated switch in her affections from mother to father. The particular form which the Oedipus complex takes is said by Fenichel to be a product of family influence.

Other theorists offer a variety of explanations. Adler emphasizes pampering by the mother and the child's subsequent lust for power over her. Jung considers the Oedipus to be really a possession complex, with the mother seen as the source of protection, nourishment, and love. For Rank it represents an unsuccessful attempt to overcome the birth trauma. He also stresses the importance of the family situation and the child's struggle for individuality. Likewise family attachments are pointed up by Horney, based mainly on two conditions: sexual stimulation by the parents and anxiety aroused by conflict between dependency needs and hostile impulses toward the mother and father. Fromm minimizes the sexual tie and prefers to ascribe the difficulties between father and son to the effects of authoritarian patriarchal society. Sullivan's interpretation is in terms of familiarity and strangeness between parent and child, and Thompson also emphasizes interpersonal relationships beyond the erotic reactions.

In the orthodox framework the heir of the Oedipus complex is the superego. Psychosexual frustrations are said to cause a regression from object choice to identification, so that sexual longing for the object is replaced by an asexual alteration within the ego. The child identifies with his own idealized version of the parents, and being on good or bad terms with his superego becomes as important as being on good or bad terms with the parents previously was. Whereas the ego holds an executive position mediating between id, superego, and outside world, the superego functions center about moral demands and thereby represent the incorporated standards of society.

Rank traces the growth of the superego genetically from inhibited sadism, with the real nucleus being the strict mother as sadistically conceived by the child. Fromm attempts to distinguish authoritarian from humanistic conscience, the relative strengths of which depend upon the individual's experiences. The authoritarian conscience is described as the voice of internalized external authority, corresponding to Freud's superego. In contrast the humanistic is the voice of the person himself, the expression of man's self-interest and integrity.

With respect to mechanisms, Fenichel draws a distinction between successful defenses, which bring a cessation of the blocked impulses, and unsuccessful defenses, which necessitate a continuing repetition of the warding-off process. Included in the former are various types of sublimation, involving the desexualized expression of impulses via an artificial route. Among the latter are the previously discussed mechanisms of denial, projection, introjection, and regression, along with repression, reaction formation, undoing, isolation, and displacement. Sullivan adds his concepts of selective inattention and disassociation; and Fromm offers three mechanisms of escape from the feeling of isolation engendered by our society: sado-masochism, destructiveness, and automaton conformity.

The latency period (age five to prepuberty).
During the latency period, says Anna Freud, the ego becomes much stronger in relation to the outside world. Along with a decline in strength of the instincts, the ego has a new ally, the superego, in its struggle to master impulses. The superego tends to be overly rigid at first but gradually adjusts and grows more pliable. There is said to be a relative drop in infantile sexual interests. Energy for the new activities, interests, and attitudes still derives from the sexual but operates mainly through the mechanisms of partial sublimation and reaction formation. Thompson doubts whether sexual latency even takes place. She maintains that the child, because of his expanded relationships, tends to share his thoughts and actions with those his own age.

Libidinal desires for the parental love object are replaced by sublimated expressions of affection. Hostile reactions seem to drop out and there are beginnings of reaching out toward others in the environment for friendly relations. Sullivan, coining the term "juvenile era," stresses the importance of school experiences and the need to interact with other children in the same age range. One's reputation becomes crucial and fears of ostracism by others are prominent. The introduction of the chum is another characteristic of this period.

Adult character structure. In the orthodox system character is defined as "the ego's habitual modes of adjustment to the external world, the id and the superego, and the characteristic types of combining these modes with one another." It includes in addition to defense mechanisms the positive, organizing functions of the ego. Fenichel classifies character traits into two broad categories: sublimation and reactive. In the former the original instinctual energy is discharged freely as a result of an alteration in aim. The genital character belongs here. In the latter instinctual energy is constantly held in check by countercathexes. The various reactive types are the oral, anal, urethral, and phallic, in which psychosexual fixations predominate.

Among the early deviants, Adler also stresses the importance of early childhood for the molding of character but places his emphasis upon universal feelings of inferiority. The latter are accompanied by a compensatory struggle for power and "masculine protest" behavior. Jung focuses upon four basic psychological functions: thinking, feeling, sensation, and intuition. The conscious aspects of men are said to be thinking and sensation, whereas feeling and intuition are repressed. The opposite is true of women. The four functions are further classified into two general ways of looking at the world, extraverted and introverted. In addition each individual plays a prescribed role in society—the concept of "persona." Rank's characterology hinges upon his theory of will. The average man, the neurotic, and the creative man each correspond to stages in the development of will.

Neo-Freudian theorists like Horney and Fromm discount any causal connections between libidinal manifestations in childhood and later personality traits. Instead they stress the sum total of parent-child interactions in the early environment. Horney distinguishes the compliant type who "moves toward" people; the aggressive type who "moves against"; and the detached who "moves away" from others. Fromm speaks of the "social character," a core common to most members of a social class, on which are superimposed individual variations due to specific parental influences. His typology includes five different orientations: receptive, exploitative, hoarding, marketing, and productive. In applying psychoanalytic principles to the field of anthropology, Kardiner evolved the formulation of "basic personality structure," which refers to the personality configuration shared by the bulk of a society's members as a result of common early experiences. The vehicles through which the specific influences are brought to bear on the growing individual are the institutions, or practices and customs of the society.

A somewhat different approach to character structure is offered by Alexander, who points out the psychological correlates of the physiological life process of intaking, retaining, and elimination. An individual's character is said to reflect the relative participation of these three elementary attitudes in his dealings with other people. Erikson on his part emphasizes the concept of "ego identity," by which a person feels that he belongs to his group and knows where he is going. The development of this feeling arises from an integration of the various identifications experienced in childhood, culminating in late adolescence.

Post-mortem

By rights the last chapter in a book dealing with, in this instance, the eight ages of man should be read softly, accompanied by a few fading strains of organ music. However, our mission in this concluding note is neither to bury nor to praise, but instead to sum up and exhort.

If one may venture a guess as to the reader's (and author's) state of mind upon finishing this effort, the most appropriate word is probably "confused." It seems as though a large number of psychoanalysts through many years of observing patients, discussing cases, and borrowing from their own unconscious ideas have contributed to a massive, vague, yet potent personality theory. Encompassed are many controversial issues and many sharp disagreements. As if this were not enough, we have complicated the picture still further by introducing a curious assortment of bits of evidence. Obviously none of these factors makes for a feeling of closure.

But perhaps some degree of comfort can be gained by looking to the future rather than the past. The scientist typically achieves contentment first by selecting what for him is a meaningful area in which to work; next he sets up hypotheses which he considers to be worth investigating; and finally he puts them to the test. His security and peace of mind derive at least in part from the knowledge that he can apply methods adequate to his task, even though the final answers may be a long way off.

We can reason similarly with respect to psychoanalysis. The importance of its domain has been clearly established. Its assertions continue to enjoy wide application. If these assertions can be viewed, not as indestructible facts, but as hypotheses subject to verification or disproof, we have the makings of a theory. From the preceding pages there is ample justification for the belief that psychoanalytic concepts *can* be put to independent test in settings other than the traditional couch. Herein lies the exhortation. A combined and concerted research approach—through the experimental laboratory, the interview situation, the projective technique, the field study, etc.—holds real promise for the development of a sound theory of personality. With such an approach we can hope to chart, not the "future of an illusion," but the future of a science.

CHAPTER SIXTEEN

Social influences on behavior

SOCIAL GROUPS

The influence of group membership upon behavior is strikingly illustrated in this article. Some of the variables which determine the degree of yielding are even more interesting. The yielding situation provides a model in which the influence of many variables may be explored.

A point to guide your study

Compare the personality descriptions of the yielders and non-yielders with those in the selection by Barron in Chapter 15. Which of Barron's types would you expect to show the greatest amount of yielding?

47. CONFORMITY AND CHARACTER

Richard S. Crutchfield, University of California, Berkeley[*]

During the Spring of 1953, one hundred men visited the Institute of Personality Assessment and Research at the University of California, Berkeley, to participate in an intensive three-day assessment of those qualities related to superior functioning in their profession.

As one of the procedures on the final day of assessment, the men were seated in groups of five in front of an apparatus consisting of five adjacent electrical panels. Each panel had side wings, forming an open cubicle, so that the person, though sitting side by side with his fellow subjects, was unable to see their panels. The experimenter explained that the apparatus was so wired that information could be sent by each man to all the others by closing any of eleven switches at the bottom of his panel. This information would appear on the other panels in the form of signal lights, among five rows of

* Adapted from the address of the retiring president of the Division of Personality and Social Psychology, American Psychological Association, New York City, September 4, 1954. The principal study reported here owes much to the collaboration of Dr. Donald W. MacKinnon, director of the Institute of Personality Assessment and Research, and of his staff. Mr. Donald G. Woodworth has contributed especially to the statistical analysis of data.

R. S. Crutchfield. Conformity and character. *Amer. Psychologist*, 1955, **10**, 191–198. Copyright 1955 by the American Psychological Association. Reprinted here with permission from the author and the American Psychological Association.

eleven lights, each row corresponding to one of the five panels. After a warm up task to acquaint the men with the workings of the apparatus, the actual procedure commenced.

Slides were projected on a wall directly facing the men. Each slide presented a question calling for a judgment by the person. He indicated his choice of one of several multiple-alternative answers by closing the appropriately numbered switch on his panel. Moreover, he responded *in order*, that is, as designated by one of five red lights lettered A, B, C, D, E, on his panel. If he were A, he responded first, if B, second, and so on. The designations, A, B, C, D, and E, were rotated by the experimenter from time to time, thus permitting each person to give his judgments in all the different serial positions. No further explanation about the purpose of this procedure was offered.

It may help to convey the nature of the men's typical experiences by giving an illustrative description of what happens concretely to one of the men. The first slide calls for a simple judgment of which of two geometrical figures is larger in area. Since his red light C is on, he waits for A and B to respond before making his response. And, as he is able to observe on the panel, his own judgment coincides with the judgments of A and B who preceded him, and of D and E who follow him. After judgments on several further slides in position C, he is then shifted to position D for more slides, then to A.

The slides call for various kinds of judgments —lengths of lines, areas of figures, logical completion of number series, vocabulary items, estimates of the opinions of others, expression of his own attitudes on issues, expression of his personal preferences for line drawings, etc. He is not surprised to observe a perfectly sensible relationship between his judgments and those of the other four men. Where clear-cut perceptual or logical judgments are involved, he finds that his judgments are in perfect agreement with those of the other four. Where matters of opinion are involved, and some differences in opinion to be expected, his judgments and those of the other four men are sometimes in agreement and sometimes not.

Eventually the man finds himself for the first time in position E, where he is to respond last. The next slide shows a standard line and five comparison lines, of which he is to pick the one equal in length to the standard. Among the previous slides he has already encountered this kind of perceptual judgment and has found it easy. On looking at this slide it is immediately clear to him that line number 4 is the correct one. But as he waits his turn to respond, he sees light number 5 in row A go on, indicating that that person has judged line number 5 to be correct. And in fairly quick succession light 5 goes on also in rows B, C, and D.

At this point the man is faced with an obvious conflict between his own clear perception and a unanimous contradictory consensus of the other four men. What does he do? Does he rely on the evidence of his own senses and respond independently? Or does he defer to the judgment of the group, complying with their perceptions rather than his own?

We will postpone for a moment the answer as to what he does, and revert to the description of our apparatus.

We have been describing the situation as if seen from the perspective of one of the men. Actually his understanding of the situation is wrong. He has been deceived. For the apparatus is *not* really wired in the way that he was informed. There actually is no connection among the five panels. Instead, they are all wired in an identical manner to a control panel where the experimenter sits behind the men. It is the experimenter who sends all the information which appears on the panels, and the wiring is in parallel in such a way that whatever signals are sent by the experimenter appear simultaneously and identically on all five panels. Moreover, the designations of serial order of responding—A through E—are identical at all times for the five panels, so that at a given moment, for instance, all five men believe themselves to be A, or at another time, E.

As we have just said, the responses actually made by the five men do not affect in any way

the panels of the others. They do get registered individually on one part of the experimenter's control panel. The *latency* of each individual response to one tenth of a second is also recorded by timers on the control panel.

Hence, the situation as we have described it for our one illustrative man is actually the situation simultaneously experienced by all five men. They all commence in position C, and all shift at the same time to position D, and to A, and finally E. They all see the same simulated group judgments.

The entire situation is, in a word, contrived, and contrived so as to expose each individual to a standardized and prearranged series of group judgments. By this means the simulated group judgments can be made to appear sensible and in agreement with the individual, or, at chosen critical points, in conflict with his judgments.

Most of you will recognize at once the basic similarity of our situation to that invented by Asch (2) in his extremely important work of recent years on independence of individual judgment under opposing group pressure. In his method, ten subjects announced aloud and in succession their judgments of the relative length of stimulus lines exposed before the group. The first nine subjects were actually confederates of the experimenter, and gave uniformly false answers at pre-established points, thus placing pressure on the single naïve subject.

For extensive research use, for instance in personality assessment, Asch's technique is handicapped by the severely unfavorable ratio of confederates to true subjects. The present technique, utilizing the electrical network described above, avoids this difficulty. There are no confederates required; all five subjects are tested simultaneously in a thoroughly standardized situation. The experimenter exercises highly flexible control of the simulated group judgments, and of the serial order of responding. Stimulus material to be judged can be varied as widely as desired by use of different slides.

Now at last come back to our man still sitting before his panel, still confronted with the spurious group consensus, still torn between a force toward independent judgment and a force toward conformity to the group. How he is likely to behave in the situation can best be described by summarizing the results for our study of 50 of the 100 men in assessment.

Effects of consensus

All of these men were engaged in a profession in which leadership is one of the salient expected qualifications. Their average age was 34 years. Their educational levels were heterogeneous, but most had had some college training.

Fifty of the men were tested in the procedure as described. Another 40 served as *control* subjects; they simply gave individual judgments of the slides without using the apparatus, and hence without knowledge of the judgments of others. The distribution of judgments of these control subjects on each slide was subsequently used as a baseline for evaluating the amount of group pressure influence on the experimental subjects.

Now as to results. When faced with the dilemma posed by this first critical slide, 15 of the 50 men, or 30 per cent, conformed to the obviously false group consensus. The remaining 70 per cent of the men maintained independence of judgment in face of the contradictory group consensus.

The first critical slide was followed by 20 others, all with the subjects responding in position E. The 20 slides involved a broad sampling of judgmental materials, exploring the question of what would happen to other kinds of perceptions, to matters of factual appraisal and of logic, of opinion and attitude, of personal preference—all under the same conditions of group pressure. Interpolated among them were occasional neutral slides, in which the group consensus was simulated as correct or sensible, in order to help maintain the subjects' acceptance of the genuineness of the apparatus and situation.

The results on several more of the critical slides will give a representative picture of what happens under group pressure. First, take another kind of perceptual judgment. A circle and a star are exposed side by side, the circle being about one third larger in area than the star. The false group consensus is on the *star* as the larger, and 46 per cent of the men express agreement with this false judgment.

On a simple logical judgment of completion of a number series, as found in standard mental tests, 30 per cent of the men conform to an obviously illogical group answer, whereas not a single control subject gives an incorrect answer.

As striking as these influence effects are, they are overshadowed by the even higher degree of influence exhibited on another set of items. These pertain to perceptual, factual, and logical judgments which are designed to maximize the *ambiguity* of the stimulus. There are three such examples: (*a*) two actually equal circles are to be judged for relative size; (*b*) a pair of words are to be judged as either synonyms or antonyms, though actually entirely unrelated in meaning and unfamiliar to all subjects; (*c*) a number series is to be completed which is actually insoluble, that is, for which there is no logically correct completion.

To take the third example, which gives the most pronounced influence effect of all 21 critical items, 79 per cent of the men conform to a spurious group consensus upon an arbitrarily chosen and irrational answer.

Influence effects are found, we see, on both well-structured and poorly-structured stimuli, with markedly greater effects on the latter.

Turning from perceptual and factual judgments to opinions and attitudes, it is clearly evident that here, too, the judgments of many of the men are markedly dependent upon a spurious group consensus which violates their own inner convictions. For example, among control subjects virtually no one expresses disagreement with the statement: "I believe we are made better by the trials and hardships of life." But among the experimental subjects exposed to a group consensus toward disagreement, 31 per cent of the men shift to expressing disagreement.

It can be demonstrated that the conformity behavior is not found solely for attitudes on issues like the foregoing, which may be of rather abstract and remote significance for the person. Among the control sample of men, not a single one expresses agreement with the statement: "I doubt whether I would make a good leader," whereas 37 per cent of the men subjected to group pressure toward agreement succumb to it. Here is an issue relating to appraisal of the self and hence likely to be of some importance to the person, especially in light of the fact already mentioned that one of the salient expected qualifications of men in this particular profession is that of leadership.

The set of 21 critical items ranges from factual to attitudinal, from structured to ambiguous, from impersonal to personal. With only two exceptions, all these items yield significant group pressure influence effects in our sample of 50 men. The very existence of the two exceptional items is in itself an important finding, for it demonstrates that the observed influences are not simply evidence of indiscriminate readiness to conform to group pressure regardless of the specific nature of the judgment involved. The character of the two exceptional items is significant, for they are the two most extremely personal and subjective judgments, namely, those in which the individual is asked which one of two simple line drawings *he prefers*. On these slides there is virtually no effective result of group pressure. Not more than one man of the 50 expresses agreement with the spurious group consensus on the nonpreferred drawing. Such personal preferences, being most isolated from the relevance of group standards, thus seem to be most immune to group pressure.

Individual differences

To what extent do the fifty men differ among themselves in their general degree of conformity to group pressure?

A total "conformity score" is readily obtainable for each individual by counting the number of the 21 critical items on which he exhibits influence to the group pressure. The threshold for influence for each item is arbitrarily fixed on the basis of the distribution of judgments by control subjects on that item.

Considering that we are dealing with a fairly homogeneous sample of limited size, the range of individual differences that we obtain is astonishingly large, covering virtually the entire possible scope of our measure. At the lower extreme, several of the men showed conformity on no more than one or two of the critical items. At the upper extreme, one man was influenced on 17 of the 21 items. The rest of the scores are well distributed between these extremes, with a mean score of about eight items and a tendency for greater concentration of scores toward the lower conformity end.

The reliability of the total score, as a measure of generalized conformity in the situation, is obtained by correlating scores on two matched halves of the items. The correlation is found to be .82, which when corrected for the combined halves gives a reliability estimate for the entire 21-item scale of .90.

To recapitulate, we find large and reliable differences among the 50 men in the amount of conformity behavior exhibited, and there appears to be considerable generality of this conformity behavior with respect to widely varied judgmental materials. Whether such conformity tendencies also generalize to other, quite different behavioral situations is a question for future research.

Relations to personality variables

Assuming that we are, indeed, measuring conformity tendencies which are fundamental in the person, the question is what traits of character distinguish between those men exhibiting much conformity behavior in our test and those exhibiting little conformity. The assessment setting within which these men were studied provides an unusually fertile opportunity to explore this question, in light of the wide range of personality measurements available.

Correlational study of the conformity scores with these other variables of personality provides some picture of the independent and of the conforming person. As contrasted with the high conformist, the independent man shows more intellectual effectiveness, ego strength, leadership ability and maturity of social relations, together with a conspicuous absence of inferiority feelings, rigid and excessive self-control, and authoritarian attitudes.

A few correlations will illustrate. The assessment staff rating on "intellectual competence" correlates −.63 with conformity score, this being the highest relationship of any found. The *Concept Mastery Test*,[1] a measure of superior mental

[1] Used with the kind permission of Dr. Lewis M. Terman.

functioning, correlates −.51 with conformity. An "ego strength" scale, independently derived by Barron (3), correlates −.33, and a staff rating on "leadership ability," −.30 with conformity. Scales of Gough's *California Psychological Inventory* (6), pertaining to such dimensions as "tolerance," "social participation," and "responsibility," range in correlation from −.30 to −.41 with conformity.

And as for some of the positive correlates, the F scale (1), a measure of authoritarian attitudes, correlates +.39 with conformity, and a staff rating on amount of authoritarian behavior manifested in a standard psychodrama situation correlates +.35 with conformity.

The general appraisal of each man by the assessment staff in the form of descriptive Q sorts further enriches this picture. Those men exhibiting extreme independence in the situation as contrasted with those at the high conformity end are described more often in the following terms by the assessment staff, which was entirely ignorant of the actual behavior of the men in the group pressure procedure:

Is an effective leader.
Takes an ascendant role in his relations with others.
Is persuasive; tends to win other people over to his point of view.
Is turned to for advice and reassurance.
Is efficient, capable, able to mobilize resources easily and effectively.
Is active and vigorous.
Is an expressive, ebullient person.
Seeks and enjoys aesthetic and sensuous impressions.
Is natural; free from pretense, unaffected.
Is self-reliant; independent in judgment; able to think for himself.

In sharp contrast to this picture of the independent men is the following description of those high in conformity behavior:

With respect to authority, is submissive, compliant and overly accepting.
Is conforming; tends to do the things that are prescribed.
Has a narrow range of interests.
Overcontrols his impulses; is inhibited; needlessly delays or denies gratification.
Is unable to make decisions without vacillation or delay.
Becomes confused, disorganized, and unadaptive under stress.
Lacks insight into his own motives and behavior.
Is suggestible; overly responsive to other people's evaluations rather than his own.

Further evidence is found in some of the specific items of personality inventories on which the answers of the high and low conformers are significantly different. Here are some illustrative items more frequently answered "True" by the independent subjects than by the conforming subjects:

Sometimes I rather enjoy going against the rules and doing things I'm not supposed to.

I like to fool around with new ideas, even if they turn out later to be a total waste of time.

A person needs to "show off" a little now and then.

At times I have been so entertained by the cleverness of a crook that I have hoped he would get by with it.

It is unusual for me to express strong approval or disapproval of the actions of others.

I am often so annoyed when someone tries to get ahead of me in a line of people that I speak to him about it.

Compared to your own self-respect, the respect of others means very little.

This pattern of expressed attitudes seems to reflect freedom from compulsion about rules, adventurousness (perhaps tinged with exhibitionism), self-assertiveness, and self-respect.

Turning to the opposite side of the picture, here are some illustrative items more frequently answered "True" by the extreme conformists, which reflect a rather rigid, externally sanctioned, and inconsistent, moralistic attitude.

I am in favor of very strict enforcement of all laws, no matter what the consequences.

It is all right to get around the law if you don't actually break it.

Most people are honest chiefly through fear of being caught.

Another set of items reveals a desire for clarity, symmetry, certainty, or, in presently popular phraseology, "an intolerance of ambiguity."

I don't like to work on a problem unless there is a possibility of coming out with a clear-cut and unambiguous answer.

Once I have made up my mind I seldom change it.

Perfect balance is the essence of all good composition.

Other items express conventionality of values:

I always follow the rule: business before pleasure.

The trouble with many people is that they don't take things seriously enough.

I am very careful about my manner of dress.

Anxiety is revealed in numerous items:

I am afraid when I look down from a high place.

I am often bothered by useless thoughts which keep running through my head.

I often think, "I wish I were a child again."

I often feel as though I have done something wrong or wicked.

And, finally, there are various expressions of disturbed, dejected, and distrustful attitudes toward other people:

When I meet a stranger I often think that he is better than I am.

Sometimes I am sure that other people can tell what I am thinking.

I wish that I could get over worrying about things I have said that may have injured other people's feelings.

I commonly wonder what hidden reason another person may have for doing something nice for me.

People pretend to care more about one another than they really do.

Although there is an unmistakable neurotic tone to many of the foregoing statements, one must be chary of inferring that those high on conformity are measurably more neurotic than the others. There does not in fact appear to be any significant correlation of the conformity scores with obvious standard measures of neuroticism as found, for instance, in scales of the Minnesota Multiphasic Personality Inventory. A similar negative finding has been reported by Barron (4) in his study of the personality correlates of independence of judgment in Asch's subjects.

In another area, attitudes concerning parents and children, differences between those high and low on conformity are especially interesting. The extreme conformists describe their parents in highly idealized terms, unrelieved by any semblance of criticism. The independents, on the other hand, offer a more balanced picture of praise and criticism.

Most of the men in the sample are fathers, and it is instructive to see that in their view of child-rearing practices, the conformers are distinctly more "restrictive" in their attitudes, and the independents distinctively more "permissive" (5).

Finally, there appears to be a marked difference in the early home background of the conformists and independents. The high conformers in this sample come almost without exception from stable homes; the independents much more frequently report broken homes and unstable home environments.

Previous theoretical and empirical studies seem to converge, though imperfectly, on a picture of the overconformist as having less ego strength, less ability to tolerate own impulses and to tolerate ambiguity, less ability to accept responsibility, less self-insight, less spontaneity and productive originality, and as having more prejudice and authoritarian attitudes, more idealization of parents, and greater emphasis on external and socially approved values.

All of these elements gain at least some substantiation in the present study of conformity behavior, as objectively measured in our test situation. The decisive influence of intelligence in resisting conformity pressures is perhaps given even fuller weight in the present findings.

Conformity behavior in different populations

Two further studies have been made. The first was with 59 college undergraduates, mostly sophomores. Forty were females, 19 males. An additional 40 students served as control subjects.

Using the same procedures and the same items for judgment, the conformity results for this student sample were highly similar to those already reported for the adult men. Here again extensive group pressure effects are found on almost all items. And here again there are wide individual differences, covering virtually the entire score range.

The male students on the average exhibit just about the same level of conformity as do the adult men. The female students, on the other hand, exhibit significantly *higher* amounts of conformity than the male groups. This greater conformity among females is evident across the entire range of items tested. Interpretation of this sex difference in conformity will require further research.

But before male egos swell overly, let me hasten to report the results of a third study, just completed. Fifty women, all college alumnae in their early forties, were tested in the same group pressure procedure, again as part of a larger assessment setting, and under the auspices of the Mary Conover Mellon Foundation.[2] As in the previous populations, virtually the entire range of individual differences in conformity is exhibited by these women. Some of them show no effect at all; others are influenced on almost all items. But the average conformity score for these 50 women is significantly *lower* than that found in the previous populations.

Thus we find our sample of adult women to be more independent in judgment than our adult men. The interpretation is difficult. The two groups differ in many particulars, other than sex. The women are highly selected for educational and socioeconomic status, are persons active in their community affairs, and would be characterized as relatively stable in personality and free of psychopathology. The adult men in our professional group are less advantageously

[2] The assessment was under the direction of Dr. R. Nevitt Sanford.

selected in all these respects. Differences in intellectual level alone might be sufficient to account for the observed differences in conformity scores.

Psychological processes

Turn now to questions concerning the nature of the psychological processes involved in these expressions of conformity to group pressure. How, for instance, is the situation perceived by the individual? The most striking thing is that almost never do the individuals under this pressure of a false group consensus come to suspect the deception practiced upon them. Of the total of 159 persons already tested in the apparatus, and questioned immediately afterwards, only a small handful expressed doubt of the genuineness of the situation. Of these not more than two or three really seem to have developed this suspicion while in the actual situation.

Yet all the subjects are acutely aware of the sometimes gross discrepancies between their own inner judgments and those expressed by the rest of the group. How do they account for these discrepancies?

Intensive individual questioning of the subjects immediately following the procedure elicits evidence of two quite different tendencies. First, for many persons the discrepancies tend to be resolved through self-blame. They express doubt of their own accuracy of perception or judgment, confessing that they had probably misread or misperceived the slides. Second, for many other persons the main tendency is to blame the rest of the group, expressing doubt that they had perceived or read the slides correctly. This is not a neat dichotomy, of course. Most persons express something of a mixture of these explanations, which is not surprising in view of the fact that some slides may tend to favor one interpretation of the difficulty and other slides the opposite interpretation.

As might be predicted, there is a substantial relationship between conformity score and tendency to self-blame; or, putting it the other way, those who remain relatively independent of the group pressure are more likely to blame the discrepancies on poor judgments by the rest of the group.

But this is by no means a perfect relationship. There are many persons who, though retrospectively expressing doubt of the correctness of the group's judgment, did in fact conform heavily while in the situation. And what is even more striking is that a substantial number of the subjects—between 25 and 30 per cent—freely admit on later questioning that there were times when they responded the way the group did *even when they thought this not the proper answer.* It seems evident, therefore, that along with various forms of cognitive rationalization of the discrepancies, there occurred a considerable amount of what might be called deliberate conforming, that is, choosing to express outward agreement with the group consensus even when believing the group to be wrong.

Another noteworthy effect was the sense of increased psychological distance induced between the person himself and the rest of the group. He felt himself to be queer or different, or felt the group to be quite unlike what he had thought. With this went an arousal of considerable anxiety in most subjects; for some, manifest anxiety was acute.

The existence of these tensions within and between the subjects became dramatically manifest when, shortly after the end of the procedure, the experimenter confessed the deception he had practiced and explained the real situation. There were obvious and audible signs of relaxation and relief, and a shift from an atmosphere of constraint to one of animated discussion.

This is an appropriate point to comment on ethics. No persons when questioned after explanation of the deception expressed feelings that they had been ethically maltreated in the experiment. The most common reaction was a positive one of having engaged in an unusual and significant experience, together with much joking about having been taken in.

Undeniably there are serious ethical issues involved in the experimental use of such deception techniques, especially inasmuch as they appear to penetrate rather deeply into the person. My view is that such deception methods ethically require that great care be taken immediately afterwards to explain the situation fully to the subject.

These remarks on ethics of the method are especially pertinent as we move from study of judgmental materials which are noncontroversial to those which are controversial. In the studies of college students and of mature women, many new critical items were introduced and subjected to the pressure. They were intended to explore more deeply the conformity tendencies in matters of opinion and attitude. And they were so chosen as to pertain to socially important and controversial issues involving civil liberties, political philosophy, crime and punishment, ethical values, and the like.

Here are two salient examples. An expression of agreement or disagreement was called for on the following statement: "Free speech being a privilege rather than a right, it is proper for a society to suspend free speech whenever it feels itself threatened." Among control subjects, only 19 per cent express agreement. But among the experimental subjects confronted with a unanimous group consensus agreeing with the statement, 58 per cent express agreement.

Another item was phrased as follows: "Which one of the following do you feel is the most important problem facing our country today?" And these five alternatives were offered:

Economic recession
Educational facilities
Subversive activities
Mental health
Crime and corruption

Among control subjects, only 12 per cent chose "Subversive activities" as the most important. But when exposed to a spurious group consensus which unanimously selected "Subversive activities" as the most important, 48 per cent of the experimental subjects expressed this same choice.

I think that no one would wish to deny that here we have evidence of the operation of powerful conformity influences in the expression of opinion on matters of critical social controversy.

Reinforcement of conformity

There is one final point upon which I should like to touch briefly. That is the question of whether there are circumstances under which the power of the group to influence the judgments of the individual may be even more greatly reinforced, and if so, how far such power may extend.

One method has been tried as part of the study of college students. With half of the subjects, a further instruction was introduced by the experimenter. They were told that in order to see how well they were doing during the procedure, the experimenter would inform the group immediately after the judgments on each slide what the correct answer was. This was to be done, of course, only for those slides for which there was a correct answer, namely, perceptual judgments, logical solutions, vocabulary, etc. No announcement would be made after slides having to do with opinions and attitudes.

The experimenter here again deceived the subjects, for the answers he announced as correct were deliberately chosen so as to agree with the false group consensus. In short, the external authority of the experimenter was later added on as reinforcement to the group consensus.

The effect of this so-called "correction" method is striking. As the series of judgments goes on, these individuals express greater and greater conformity to the group pressure on slides which are of the same character as those for which earlier in the series the false group consensus was thus reinforced by the false announcement by the experimenter.

But the more critical issue is whether this enhanced power of the group generalizes also to judgments of an entirely unrelated sort, namely, matters of opinion and attitude, rather than of fact. In other words, will the group, through having the rightness of its judgment supported by the experimenter on matters of perception, logic, and the like, thereby come to be regarded by the individual as more right, or more to be complied with, on entirely extraneous matters, such as social issues?

The answer is absolutely clear. The enhanced power of the group does *not* carry over to increase the effective influence on expression of opinions and attitudes. The subjects exposed to this "correction" method do not exhibit greater conformity to group pressure on opinions and attitudes than that found in other subjects.

This crucial finding throws some light on the nature of the psychological processes involved in the conformity situation. For its seems to imply that conformity behavior under such group pressure, rather than being sheerly an indiscriminate and irrational tendency to defer to the authority of the group, has in it important rational elements. There is something of a reasonable differentiation made by the individual in his manner of reliance upon the group. He may be led to accept the superiority of the group judgment on matters where there is an objective frame of reference against which the group can be checked. But he does not, thereby, automatically accept the authority of the group on matters of a less objective sort.

Conclusion

The social psychologist is concerned with the character of conformity, the personologist with conformity of character. Between them they raise many research questions: the comparative incidence of conformity tendencies in various populations; the influence of group structure and the individual's role in the group on the nature and amount of conformity behavior; the effects of reward or punishment for conforming on habits of conformity; the genesis and change of conformity behavior in the individual personality; the determinants of extreme *anticonformity* tendencies.

Contributing to such questions we have what appears to be a powerful new research technique, enabling the study of conformity behavior within a setting which effectively simulates genuine group interaction, yet preserves the essential requirements of objective measurement.

References

1. Adorno, T. W., Frenkel-Brunswik, Else, Levinson, D., and Sanford, R. N. *The authoritarian personality*. New York: Harper, 1950.
2. Asch, S. E. *Social psychology*. New York: Prentice-Hall, 1952.
3. Barron, F. An ego-strength scale which predicts response to psychotherapy. *J. consult. Psychol.*, 1953, 17, 327–333.
4. Barron, F. Some personality correlates of independence of judgment. *J. Pers.*, 1953, 21, 287–297.
5. Block, J. Personality characteristics associated with fathers' attitudes toward child-rearing. *Child Develpm.*, 1955, in press.
6. Gough, H. G. A *preliminary guide for the use and interpretation of the California Psychological Inventory*. Privately distributed by the Institute of Personality Assessment and Research, Univer. of California, Berkeley, 1954. (Mimeo.)

The theory of cognitive dissonance is an important one in contemporary social psychology. The predictions made from this theory sometimes seem completely counter to "common sense." Perhaps this is one of its attractions.

Points to guide your study

1. The *t* tests and *p* values have been explained in previous introductions.

2. Although only a minority of psychological experiments involve misleading the subject, this experiment and several others in this book have contained some slight temporary deception of subjects. How do you feel about the ethics of such deception?

48. THE EFFECT OF SEVERITY OF INITIATION ON LIKING FOR A GROUP

*Elliot Aronson, Harvard University, and Judson Mills, Syracuse University**

It is a frequent observation that persons who go through a great deal of trouble or pain to attain something tend to value it more highly than persons who attain the same thing with a minimum of effort. For example, one would expect persons who travel a great distance to see a motion picture to be more impressed with it than those who see the same picture at a neighborhood theater. By the same token, individuals who go through a severe initiation to gain admission to a club or organization should tend to think more highly of that organization than those who do not go through the severe initiation to gain admission.

Two questions are relevant here: 1. Is this "common observation" valid, that is, does it hold true when tested under controlled conditions? 2. If the observation is valid, how can it be accounted for? The relationship might be simply a result of differences in initial motivation. To take the case of initiations, persons who initially have a strong desire to join a particular club should be more willing to undergo unpleasantness to gain admission to it than persons who are low in initial interest. Therefore, a club that requires a severe initiation for admission should be joined only by those people with a strong desire to become members. On the other hand, a club that does not require a severe initiation

* This research was partially supported by a grant from the National Science Foundation, administered by Leon Festinger. The authors are grateful to Leon Festinger for his help and encouragement during the planning and execution of the study.
Elliot Aronson and Judson Mills. The effect of severity of initiation on liking for a group. *J. abnorm. soc. Psychol.*, 1959, **59**, 177–181. Copyright 1959 by the American Psychological Association. Reprinted here with permission from the authors and the American Psychological Association.

should be joined by some individuals who like it very much, and by others who are relatively uninterested. Because of this self-selection, one would expect persons who are members of clubs with severe initiations to think more highly of their club, on the average, than members of clubs without severe initiations.

But is there something in the initiation itself that might account for this relationship? Is severity of initiation positively related to group preference when motivation for admission is held constant? Such a relationship is strongly implied by Festinger's (1957) theory of cognitive dissonance. The theory of cognitive dissonance predicts this relationship in the following manner. No matter how attractive a group is to a person it is rarely completely positive, i.e., usually there are some aspects of the group that the individual does not like. If he has undergone an unpleasant initiation to gain admission to the group, his cognition that he has gone through an unpleasant experience for the sake of membership is dissonant with his cognition that there are things about the group that he does not like. He can reduce this dissonance in two ways. He can convince himself that the initiation was not very unpleasant, or he can exaggerate the positive characteristics of the group and minimize its negative aspects. With increasing severity of initiation it becomes more and more difficult to believe that the initiation was not very bad. Thus, a person who has gone through a painful initiation to become a member of a group should tend to reduce his dissonance by overestimating the attractiveness of the group. The specific hypothesis tested in the present study is that individuals who undergo an unpleasant initiation to become members of a group increase their liking for the group; that is, they find the group more attractive than do persons who become members without going through a severe initiation.

Method

In designing the experiment it was necessary to have people join groups that were similar in every respect except for the severity of the initiation required for admission—and then to measure each individual's evaluation of the group. It was also necessary to randomize the initial motivation of subjects (Ss) to gain admission to the various groups in order to eliminate systematic effects of differences in motivation. These requirements were met in the following manner: Volunteers were obtained to participate in group discussions. They were assigned randomly to one of three experimental conditions: A *Severe* initiation condition, a *Mild* initiation condition, and a *Control* condition. In the Severe condition, Ss were required to read some embarrassing material before joining the group; in the Mild condition the material they read in order to join the group was not very embarrassing; in the Control condition, Ss were not required to read any material before becoming group members. Each S listened to the same tape recording which was ostensibly an ongoing discussion by the members of the group that he had just joined. Ss then evaluated the discussion.

The Ss were 63 college women. Thirty-three of them volunteered to participate in a series of group discussions on the psychology of sex. The remaining 30, tested at a somewhat later date, were "captive volunteers" from a psychology course who elected to participate in the group discussions on the psychology of sex in preference to several other experiments. Since the results obtained from these two samples were very similar, they were combined in the analysis presented here.

Each S was individually scheduled to "meet with a group." When she arrived at the experimental room, she was told by the experimenter (E) that he was conducting several group discussions on the psychology of sex. E informed her that she was joining a group that had been meeting for several weeks and that she was taking the place of a girl who had to leave the group because of scheduling difficulties. E stated that the discussion had just begun and that she would join the other members of the group after he had explained the nature of the experiment to her. The purpose of the foregoing instructions was to confront S with an ongoing group and thus make plausible the recorded discussion to which she was to be exposed.

E then "explained" the purpose of the experiment. He said that he was interested in investigating the "dynamics of the group discussion process." Sex was chosen as the topic for the groups to discuss in order to provide interesting subject matter so that volunteers for the discussion groups could be obtained without much difficulty. E continued as follows:

But the fact that the discussions are concerned with sex has one major drawback. Although most people are interested in sex, they tend to be a little shy when it comes to discussing it. This is very bad from the point of view of the experiment; if one or two people in a group do not participate as much as they usually do in group discussion because they are embarrassed about sex, the picture we get of the group discussion process is distorted. Therefore, it is extremely important to arrange things so that the members of the discussion group can talk as freely and frankly as possible. We found that the major inhibiting factor in the discussions was the presence of the other people in the room. Somehow, it's easier to talk about embarrassing things if other people aren't staring at you. To get around this, we hit upon an idea which has proved very successful. Each member of the group is placed in a separate room, and the participants communicate through an intercom system using headphones and a microphone. In this way, we've helped people relax, and have succeeded in bringing about an increase in individual participation.

The foregoing explanation set the stage for the tape recording, which could now be presented to the S as a live discussion conducted by three people in separate rooms.

E then mentioned that, in spite of this precaution, occasionally some persons were still too embarrassed to engage in the discussions and had to be asked to withdraw from the discussion group. S was asked if she thought she could discuss sex freely. She invariably answered affirmatively. In the Control condition S was told, at this point, that she would be a member of the group.

In the other two conditions, E went on to say that it was difficult for him to ask people to leave the group once they had become members. Therefore, he had recently decided to screen new people before admitting them to the discussion groups. The screening device was described as an "embarrassment test" which consists of reading aloud some sexually oriented material in the presence of E. S was told that E would make a clinical judgment of her degree of embarrassment, based upon hesitation, blushing, etc. and would determine whether or not she would be capable of participating in the discussion group. He stressed that she was not obligated to take this test, but that she could not become a member unless she did. Only one S declined to take the test. She was excluded from the experiment. It was also emphasized, at this point, that the "embarrassment test" was a recent innovation and that the other members had joined the group before it was required for admission. These instructions were included in order to counteract any tendency to identify more strongly with the group as a result of feelings of having shared a common unpleasant experience. Such a process could conceivably bring about a greater preference for the discussion group on the part of Ss in the Severe condition, introducing ambiguity in the interpretation of the results.

In the Severe condition, the "embarrassment test" consisted of having Ss read aloud, from 3 × 5 cards, 12 obscene words, e.g., fuck, cock, and screw. Ss also read aloud two vivid descriptions of sexual activity from contemporary novels. In the Mild condition, Ss read aloud five words that were related to sex but not obscene, e.g., prostitute, virgin, and petting. In both the Severe and the Mild conditions, after each S finished reading the material, she was told that she had performed satisfactorily and was, therefore, a member of the group and could join the meeting that was now in progress.

It was of the utmost importance to prevent the S from attempting to participate in the discussion, for if she did, she would soon find that no one was responding to her statements and she would probably infer that the discussion was recorded. To insure their silence, all Ss were told that, in preparation for each meeting, the group reads an assignment which serves as the focal point of the discussion; for this meeting, the group read parts of the book, *Sexual Behavior in Animals*. After the S had indicated that she had never read this book, E told her that she would be at a disadvantage and would, consequently, not be able to participate as fully in this discussion as she would had she done the reading. He continued, "Because the presence of a participant who isn't contributing optimally would result in an inaccurate picture of the dynamics of the group discussion process, it would be best if you wouldn't participate at all today, so that we may get an undistorted picture of the dynamics of the other three members of this group. Meanwhile, you can simply listen to the discussion, and get an idea of how the group operates. For the next meeting, you can do the reading and join in the discussion." Ss were invariably more than willing to comply with this suggestion. The above instructions not only prevented S from attempting to participate in the discussion but also served to orient her toward the actual content of discussion.

Under the guise of connecting the S's headphones and microphone, E went into the next room and turned on the tape recorder. He then returned to the experimental room, put on the headphones, picked up the microphone, and pre-tended to break into the discussion which supposedly was in progress. After holding a brief conversation with the "members of the group," he introduced the S to them. Then he handed the headphones to her. The tape was timed so that at the precise moment that S donned her headphones, the "group members" introduced themselves and then continued their discussion.

The use of a tape recording presented all Ss with an identical group experience. The recording was a discussion by three female undergraduates. It was deliberately designed to be as dull and banal as possible in order to maximize the dissonance of the Ss in the Severe condition. The participants spoke dryly and haltingly on secondary sex behavior in the lower animals, "inadvertently" contradicted themselves and one another, mumbled several *non sequiturs*, started sentences that they never finished, hemmed, hawed, and in general conducted one of the most worthless and uninteresting discussions imaginable.

At the conclusion of the recording, E returned and explained that after each meeting every member of the group fills out a questionnaire expressing her reactions to the discussion. The questionnaire asked the S to rate the discussion and the group members on 14 different evaluative scales, e.g., dull–interesting, intelligent–unintelligent, by circling a number from 0 to 15. After completing the questionnaire, S made three additional ratings, orally, in response to questions from E. Nine of the scales concerned the S's reactions to the discussion, while the other eight concerned her reactions to the participants.

At the close of the experiment, E engaged each S in conversation to determine whether or not she was suspicious of the procedure. Only one S entertained definite suspicions; her results were discarded.

Finally, the true nature of the experiment was explained in detail. None of the Ss expressed any resentment or annoyance at having been misled. In fact, the majority were intrigued by the experiment and several returned at the end of the academic quarter to ascertain the results.

Results and discussion

The sum of the ratings for the 17 different scales provides an index of each S's liking for the discussion group. The means and SDs for the three experimental conditions for this measure are presented in Table 1. Means and SDs are also presented in Table 1 separately for the eight scales which tapped the Ss' attitudes toward the discussion and the seven scales which tapped their attitudes toward the participants. The significance of the differences between the means for the different conditions were determined by t tests. The t values and significance levels are presented in Table 2.

Examination of Table 1 shows that Ss in the Severe condition rated both the discussion and the participants higher than did those in the Control and Mild conditions. The over-all difference between the ratings by Ss in the Severe condition and Ss in the Control condition reaches the .01% level of significance. The over-all difference between the ratings by Ss in the Severe initiation condition and Ss in the Mild initiation condition reaches the .05 level.

These differences cannot be explained by differences in initial motivation to become members of the group, since Ss (with varying degrees of motivation) were randomly assigned to the three experimental conditions. The differences in liking for the group must be considered a consequence of the unpleasant experience. The results clearly substantiate the hypothesis: persons who undergo a severe initiation to attain membership in a group increase their liking for the group. This hypothesis follows directly from Festinger's theory of cognitive dissonance. According to the theory, Ss in the Severe initiation condition held the cognition that they had undergone a painful experience to become members of the discussion group. Then they listened

to a dull, banal discussion. Negative cognitions about the discussion which they formed from listening to it were dissonant with the cognition that they had undergone a painful experience to gain membership in this group. The presence of dissonance leads to pressure to reduce it. Ss in this condition could reduce their dissonance either by denying the severity of the initiation or by distorting their cognitions concerning the group discussion in a positive direction. The initiation of the Ss in the Severe condition was apparently too painful for them to deny—hence, they reduced their dissonance by overestimating the attractiveness of the group.

There was no appreciable difference between the ratings made by Ss in the Control condition and those made by Ss in the Mild condition. It would seem that the Mild condition was so devoid of unpleasantness as to constitute little investment in the group. Hence, little dissonance was created. If any dissonance did occur in this situation it would be more realistic for the S to reduce it by minimizing the pain of the initiation, than by distorting her cognitions concerning the discussion. Thus, it is not an initiation per se that leads to increase in liking for a group. The initiation must be severe enough to constitute a genuine investment and to render it difficult to reduce dissonance by playing down the extent of the pain involved.

An examination of Table 1 shows that the rating scales concerning the discussion show greater differences between the conditions than the scales dealing with the evaluations of the participants in the discussion. There are at least two possible explanations for this result: (*a*) It may be easier for people to express negative criticism about an impersonal discussion than about the people involved. Thus, Ss in the Control and Mild conditions may have inflated their ratings of the participants to avoid making negative statements about fellow college students. (*b*) It is possible that Ss in the Severe condition had less need to distort their perception of the participants than of the discussion itself. The dissonance of the Ss in the Severe condition resulted from the actual discussion: they experienced dissonance between going through an unpleasant experience and taking part in worthless uninteresting discussions. The most direct way for them to reduce this dissonance would be to change their perceptions of the discussion in a positive direction. The participants in the discussion were peripheral to the cause of dissonance. If Ss in the Severe condition had less need to distort their perceptions of the participants than their perception of the discussion, their evaluations of the participants could be expected to be closer to the evaluations of the participants made by Ss in the Control and Mild conditions.

Table 1 Means of the sum of ratings for the different experimental conditions

Rating scales	Experimental conditions		
	Control (N = 21)	Mild (N = 21)	Severe (N = 21)
Discussion [9]			
M	80.2	81.8	97.6
SD	13.2	21.0	16.6
Participants [8]			
M	89.9	89.3	97.7
SD	10.9	14.1	13.2
Total [17]			
M	170.1	171.1	195.3
SD	21.6	34.0	31.9

Table 2 Significance levels of the differences between experimental conditions

Rating scales	Differences between conditions		
	Control-severe	Mild-severe	Control-mild
Discussion [9]	$t = 3.66$ $P < .001*$	$t = 2.62$ $P < .02$	$t = .29$ N.S.
Participants [8]	$t = 2.03$ $P < .05$	$t = 1.97$ $P < .10$	$t = .15$ N.S.
Total [17]	$t = 2.92$ $P < .01$	$t = 2.33$ $P < .05$	$t = .49$ N.S.

* The *P* values given are based on both tails of the *t* distribution.

Summary and conclusions

An experiment was conducted to test the hypothesis that persons who undergo an unpleasant initiation to become members of a group increase their liking for the group; that is, they find the group more attractive than do persons who become members without going through a severe initiation. This hypothesis was derived from Festinger's theory of cognitive dissonance.

College women who volunteered to participate in discussion groups were randomly assigned to one of three experimental conditions: A *Severe* initiation condition, a *Mild* initiation condition, and a *Control* condition. In the Severe condition, subjects were required to read some embarrassing material before joining the group; in the Mild condition the material they read in order to join the group was not very embarrassing; in the Control condition, subjects were not required to read any material before becoming group members. Each subject listened to a recording that appeared to be an ongoing discussion being conducted by the group which she had just joined. Afterwards, subjects filled out a questionnaire evaluating the discussion and the participants. The results clearly verified the hypothesis. Subjects who underwent a severe initiation perceived the group as being significantly more attractive than did those who underwent a mild initiation or no initiation. There was no appreciable difference between ratings by subjects who underwent a Mild initiation and those by subjects who underwent no initiation.

References

Festinger, L. A *theory of cognitive dissonance*. Evanston: Row, Peterson, 1957.

Living together in social groups requires a good deal of adjustment or give and take between groups and between members within groups. Bargaining is essential in this adjustment process. For instance, marriage partners bargain with each other, labor union representatives and business representatives bargain with each other, and diplomats bargain with each other. Understanding of the bargaining process is therefore quite important, practical, and useful.

One good way of finding out about the bargaining process is through experiment. In such experiments one sets up a simple model of a "real" social situation and then introduces variables to see how they will affect bargaining behavior in this model situation. In this experiment the influence of threat on bargaining is studied.

Points to guide your study

1. Make sure you understand the model situation and the game which is played. You must grasp this before you can understand the article.

2. Put yourself in the place of Acme or Bolt. Do you think you would behave typically under the three conditions—no threat, unilateral, and bilateral threat—of the experiment?

3. Glossary: Cognitive—Refers to thinking or thought. $P < .01$, etc.— Means that the odds of obtaining a difference as large as the one obtained by chance alone are less than one in a hundred. (See other selections)

49. THE EFFECT OF THREAT UPON INTERPERSONAL BARGAINING

Morton Deutsch and Robert M. Krauss, Bell Telephone Laboratories, Murray Hill, New Jersey[*]

A bargain is defined in Webster's Unabridged Dictionary as "an agreement between parties settling what each shall give and receive in a transaction between them"; it is further specified that a bargain is "an agreement or compact viewed as advantageous or the reverse." When the term "agreement" is broadened to include tacit, informal agreements as well as explicit agreements, it is evident that bargains and the processes involved in arriving at bargains ("bargaining") are pervasive characteristics of social life.

The definition of bargain fits under sociological definitions of the term "social norm." In this light, the experimental study of the bargaining process and of bargaining outcomes provides a means for the laboratory study of the development of certain types of social norms. But unlike many other types of social situations,

* Morton Deutsch and R. M. Krauss. The effect of threat upon interpersonal bargaining. *J. abnorm. soc. Psychol.*, 1960 **61**, 181–189. Copyright 1960 by the American Psychological Association. Reprinted here with permission from the senior author and the American Psychological Association.

bargaining situations have certain distinctive features that make it relevant to consider the conditions that determine whether or not a social norm will develop as well as those that determine the nature of the social norm if it develops. Bargaining situations high-light the possibility that, even where cooperation would be mutually advantageous, shared purposes may not develop, agreement may not be reached, and interaction may be regulated antagonistically rather than normatively.

The essential features of a bargaining situation exist when:

1. Both parties perceive that there is the possibility of reaching an agreement in which each party would be better off, or no worse off, than if no agreement were reached.

2. Both parties perceive that there is more than one such agreement that could be reached.

3. Both parties perceive each other to have conflicting preferences or opposed interests with regard to the different agreements that might be reached.

Everyday examples of bargaining include such situations as: the buyer-seller relationship when the price is not fixed, the husband and wife who want to spend an evening out together but have conflicting preferences about where to go, union-management negotiations, drivers who meet at an intersection when there is no clear right of way, disarmament negotiations.

In terms of our prior conceptualization of co-operation and competition (Deutsch, 1949) bargaining is thus a situation in which the participants have mixed motives toward one another: on the one hand, each has interest in cooperating so that they reach an agreement; on the other hand, they have competitive interests concerning the nature of the agreement they reach. In effect, to reach agreement the cooperative interest of the bargainers must be strong enough to overcome their competitive interests. However, agreement is not only contingent upon the *motivational* balances of cooperative to competitive interests but also upon the situational and *cognitive* factors which facilitate or hinder the recognition or invention of a bargaining agreement that reduces the opposition of interest and enhances the mutuality of interests.[1]

These considerations lead to the formulation of two general, closely related propositions about the likelihood that a bargaining agreement will be reached.

1. Bargainers are more likely to reach an agreement, the stronger are their cooperative interests in comparison with their competitive interests.

2. Bargainers are more likely to reach an agreement, the more resources they have available for recognizing or inventing potential bargaining agreements and for communicating to one another once a potential agreement has been recognized or invented.

From these two basic propositions and additional hypotheses concerning conditions that determine the strengths of the cooperative and competitive interests and the amount of available resources, we believe it is possible to explain the ease or difficulty of arriving at a bargaining agreement. We shall not present a full statement of these hypotheses here but turn instead to a description of an experiment that relates to Proposition 1.

The experiment was concerned with the effect of the availability of threat upon bargaining in a two-person experimental bargaining game.[2] Threat is defined as the expression of an intention to do something detrimental to the interests

of another. Our experiment was guided by two assumptions about threat:

1. If there is a conflict of interest and one person is able to threaten the other, he will tend to use the threat in an attempt to force the other person to yield. This tendency should be stronger, the more irreconcilable the conflict is perceived to be.

2. If a person uses threat in an attempt to intimidate another, the threatened person (if he considers himself to be of equal or superior status) would feel hostility toward the threatener and tend to respond with counterthreat and/or increased resistance to yielding. We qualify this assumption by stating that the tendency to resist should be greater, the greater the perceived probability and magnitude of detriment to the other and the less the perceived probability and magnitude of detriment to the potential resister from the anticipated resistance to yielding.

The second assumption is based upon the view that when resistance is not seen to be suicidal or useless, to allow oneself to be intimidated, particularly by someone who does not have the right to expect deferential behavior, is to suffer a loss of social face and, hence, of self-esteem; and that the culturally defined way of maintaining self-esteem in the face of attempted intimidation is to engage in a contest for supremacy vis-à-vis the power to intimidate or, minimally, to resist intimidation. Thus, in effect, the use of threat (and if it is available to be used, there will be a tendency to use it) should strengthen the competitive interests of the bargainers in relationship to one another by introducing or enhancing the competitive struggle for self-esteem. Hence, from Proposition 1, it follows that the availability of a means of threat should make it more difficult for the bargainers to reach agreement (providing that the threatened person has some means of resisting the threat). The preceding statement is relevant to the comparison of both of our experimental conditions of threat, bilateral and unilateral (described below), with our experimental condition of nonthreat. We hypothesize that a bargaining agreement is more likely to be achieved when neither party can threaten the other, than when one or both parties can threaten the other.

Consider now the situations of bilateral threat and unilateral threat. For several reasons, a situation of bilateral threat is probably less conducive to agreement than is a condition of unilateral threat. First, the sheer likelihood that a threat will be made is greater when two people rather than one have the means of making the threat. Secondly, once a threat is made in the bilateral case it is likely to evoke counterthreat. Withdrawal of threat in the face of counterthreat probably involves more loss of face (for reasons analogous to those discussed in relation to yield-

---

[1] Schelling in a series of stimulating papers on bargaining (1957, 1958) has also stressed the "mixed motive" character of bargaining situations and has analyzed some of the cognitive factors which determine agreements.

[2] The game was conceived and originated by M. Deutsch; R. M. Krauss designed and constructed the apparatus employed in the experiment.

ing to intimidation) than does withdrawal of threat in the face of resistance to threat. Finally, in the unilateral case, although the person without the threat potential can resist and not yield to the threat, his position vis-à-vis the other is not so strong as the position of the threatened person in the bilateral case. In the unilateral case, the threatened person may have a worse outcome than the other whether he resists or yields; while in the bilateral case, the threatened person is sure to have a worse outcome if he yields but he may insure that he does not have a worse outcome if he does not yield.

Method

Procedure. Subjects (Ss) were asked to imagine that they were in charge of a trucking company, carrying merchandise over a road to a destination. For each trip completed they made $.60, minus their operating expenses. Operating expenses were calculated at the rate of one cent per second. So, for example, if it took 37 seconds to complete a particular trip, the player's profit would be $.60 − $.37 or a net profit of $.23 for that particular trip.

Each S was assigned a name, Acme or Bolt. As the "road map" (see Figure 1) indicates, both players start from separate points and go to separate destinations. At one point their paths cross. This is the section of road labeled "one-lane road," which is only one lane wide, so that two trucks, heading in opposite directions, could not pass each other. If one backs up the other can go forward, or both can back up, or both can sit there head-on without moving.

There is another way for each S to reach the destination on the map, labeled the "alternate route." The two players' paths do not cross on this route, but the alternate is 56% longer than the main route. Ss were told that they could expect to lose at least $.10 each time they used the alternate route.

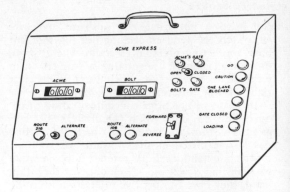

Figure 2   Subject's control panel.

At either end of the one-lane section there is a gate that is under the control of the player to whose starting point it is closest. By closing the gate, one player can prevent the other from traveling over that section of the main route. The use of the gate provides the threat potential in this game. In the bilateral threat potential condition (Two Gates) both players had gates under their control. In a second condition of unilateral threat (One Gate) Acme had control of a gate but Bolt did not. In a third condition (No Gates) neither player controlled a gate.

Ss played the game seated in separate booths placed so that they could not see each other but could see the experimenter (E). Each S had a "control panel" mounted on a 12″ × 18″ × 12″ sloping-front cabinet (see Figure 2). The apparatus consisted essentially of a reversible impulse counter that was pulsed by a recycling timer. When the S wanted to move her truck forward she threw a key that closed a circuit pulsing the "add" coil of the impulse counter mounted on her control panel. As the counter cumulated, S was able to determine her "position" by relating the number on her counter to reference numbers that had been written in on her road map. Similarly, when she wished to reverse, she would throw a switch that activated the "subtract" coil of her counter, thus subtracting from the total on the counter each time the timer cycled.

S's counter was connected in parallel to counters on the other S's panel and on E's panel. Thus each player had two counters on her panel, one representing her own position and the other representing the other player's. Provision was made in construction of the apparatus to permit cutting the other player's counter out of the circuit, so that each S knew only the position of her own truck. This was done in the present experiment. Experiments now in progress are studying the effects of knowledge of the other person's position and other aspects of interpersonal communication upon the bargaining process.

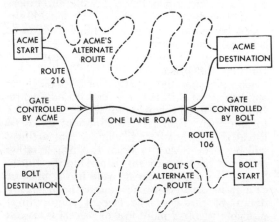

Figure 1   Subject's road map.

The only time one player definitely knew the other player's position was when they had met head-on on the one-way section of road. This was indicated by a traffic light mounted on the panel. When this light was on, neither player could move forward unless the other moved back. The gates were controlled by toggle switches and panel-mounted indicator lights showed, for both Ss, whether each gate was open or closed.

The following "rules of the game" were stated to the Ss:

1. A player who started out on one route and wished to switch to the other route could only do so after first reversing and going back to the start position. Direct transfer from one route to the other was not permitted except at the start position.

2. In the conditions where Ss had gates, they were permitted to close the gates no matter where they were on the main route, so long as they were on the main route (i.e., they were not permitted to close the gate while on the alternate route or after having reached their destinations). However, Ss were permitted to open their gates at any point in the game.

Ss were taken through a number of practice exercises to familiarize them with the game. In the first trial they were made to meet head-on on the one-lane path; Acme was then told to back up until she was just off the one-lane path and Bolt was told to go forward. After Bolt had gone through the one-lane path, Acme was told to go forward. Each continued going forward until each arrived at her destination. The second practice trial was the same as the first except that Bolt rather than Acme backed up after meeting head-on. In the next practice trial, one of the players was made to wait just before the one-way path while the other traversed it and then was allowed to continue. In the next practice trial, one player was made to take the alternate route and the other was made to take the main route. Finally, in the bilateral and unilateral threat conditions the use of the gate was illustrated (by having the player get on the main route, close the gate, and then go back and take the alternate route). The Ss were told explicitly, with emphasis, that they did not have to use the gate. Before each trial in the game the gate or gates were in the open position.

The instructions stressed an individualistic motivational orientation. Ss were told to try to earn as much money for themselves as possible and to have no interest in whether the other player made money or lost money. They were given $4.00 in poker chips to represent their working capital and told that after each trial they would be given "money" if they made a profit or that "money" would be taken from them if they lost (i.e., took more than 60 sec-

onds to complete their trip). The profit or loss of each S was announced so that both Ss could hear the announcement after each trial. Each pair of Ss played a total of 20 trials; on all trials, they started off together. In other words each trial presented a repetition of the same bargaining problem. In cases where Ss lost their working capital before the 20 trials were completed, additional chips were given them. Ss were aware that their monetary winnings and losses were to be imaginary and that no money would change hands as a result of the experiment.

Subjects. Sixteen pairs of Ss were used in each of the three experimental conditions. The Ss were female clerical and supervisory personnel of the New Jersey Bell Telephone Company who volunteered to participate during their working day.[3] Their ages ranged from 20 to 39, with a mean of 26.2. All were naive to the purpose of the experiment. By staggering the arrival times and choosing girls from different locations, we were able to insure that the Ss did not know with whom they were playing.

Data recorded. Several types of data were collected. We obtained a record of the profit or loss of each S on each trial. We also obtained a detailed recording of the actions taken by each S during the course of a trial. For this purpose, we used an Esterline-Angus model AW Operations Recorder which enabled us to obtain a "log" of each move each S made during the game (e.g., whether and when she took the main or alternate route; when she went forward, backward, or remained still; when she closed and opened the gate; when she arrived at her destination).

Results [4]

The best single measure of the difficulty experienced by the bargainers in reaching an agreement is the sum of each pair's profits (or losses) on a given trial. The higher the sum of the payoffs to the two players on a given trial, the less time it took them to arrive at a procedure for sharing the one-lane path of the main route. (It was, of course, possible for one or both of the players to decide to take the alternate route so as to avoid a protracted stalemate during the process of bargaining. This, however, always resulted in at least a $.20 smaller joint payoff if only one player took the alternate route, than an optimally arrived at agreement concerning the use of the one-way path.) Figure 3 presents the medians of the summed payoffs (i.e., Acme's

[3] We are indebted to the New Jersey Bell Telephone Company for their cooperation in providing Ss and facilities for the experiment.
[4] We are indebted to M. J. R. Healy for suggestions concerning the statistical analysis of our data.

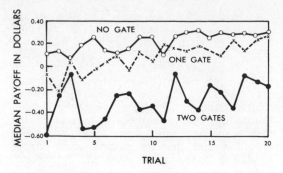

Figure 3 Median joint payoff (Acme + Bolt) over trials.

plus Bolt's) for all pairs in each of the three experimental conditions over the 20 trials.[5] These striking results indicate that agreement was least difficult to arrive at in the no threat condition, was more difficult to arrive at in the unilateral threat condition, and exceedingly difficult or impossible to arrive at in the bilateral threat condition (see also Table 1).

Examination of Figure 3 suggests that learning occurred during the 20 trials: the summed payoffs for pairs of Ss tend to improve as the number of trials increases. This suggestion is confirmed by an analysis of variance of the slopes for the summed payoffs[6] over the 20 trials for each of the 16 pairs in each of the 3 experimental treatments. The results of this analysis indicate that the slopes are significantly greater than zero for the unilateral threat ($p < .01$) and the no threat ($p < .02$) conditions; for the bilateral threat condition, the slope does not reach statistical significance ($.10 < p < .20$). The data indicate that the pairs in the no threat condition started off at a fairly high level but, even so, showed some improvement over the 20 trials; the pairs in the unilateral threat condition started off low and, having considerable opportunity for improvement used their opportunity; the pairs in the bilateral threat condition, on the other hand, did not benefit markedly from repeated trials.

Figure 4 compares Acme's median profit in the three experimental conditions over the 20 trials; while Figure 5 compares Bolt's profit in the three conditions. (In the unilateral threat condition, it was Acme who controlled a gate and Bolt who did not.) Bolt's as well as Acme's outcome is somewhat better in the no threat condition than in the unilateral threat condition; Acme's, as well as Bolt's, outcome is clearly worst in the bilateral threat condition (see Table

[5] Medians are used in graphic presentation of our results because the wide variability of means makes inspection cumbersome.

[6] A logarithmic transformation of the summed payoffs on each trial for each pair was made before computing the slopes for a given pair.

1 also). However, Figure 6 reveals that Acme does somewhat better than Bolt in the unilateral condition. Thus, if threat-potential exists within a bargaining relationship it is better to possess it oneself than to have the other party possess it. However, it is even better for neither party to possess it. Moreover, Figure 5 shows that Bolt is better off not having than having a gate even when Acme has a gate: Bolt tends to do better in the unilateral threat condition than in the bilateral threat condition.

The size of the absolute discrepancy between the payoffs of the players in each pair provides a measure of the confusion or difficulty in predicting what the other player is going to do. Thus, a large absolute discrepancy might indicate that after one player had gone through the one-way path and left it open, the other player continued to wait; or it might indicate that one player continued to wait at a closed gate hoping the other player would open it quickly but the other player did not; etc. Figure 7 indicates that the discrepancy between players in the no threat condition is initially small and remains small for the 20 trials. For the players in both the bilateral and unilateral threat conditions, the discrepancy is initially relatively larger; but it decreases more noticeably in the unilateral threat condition by

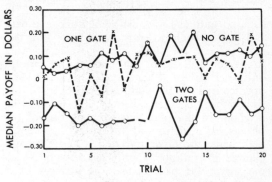

Figure 4 Acme's median payoff.

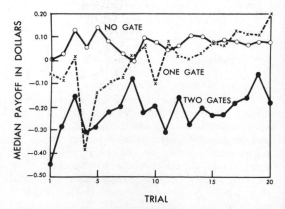

Figure 5 Bolt's median payoff.

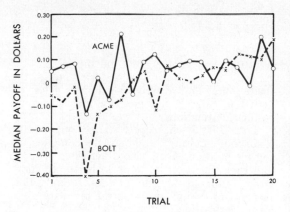

Figure 6 Acme's and Bolt's median payoffs in unilateral threat condition.

the tenth trial and, therefore, is consistently smaller than in the bilateral condition.

By way of concrete illustration, we present a synopsis of the game for one pair in each of three experimental treatments.

No threat condition. *Trial 1.* The players met in the center of the one-way section. After some back-and-forth movement Bolt reversed to the end of the one-way section, allowing Acme to pass through, and then proceeded forward herself.

Trial 2. They again met at the center of the one-way path. This time, after moving back and forth deadlocked for some time, Bolt reversed to "start" and took the alternate route to her destination, thus leaving Acme free to go through on the main route.

Trial 3. The players again met at the center of the one-way path. This time, however, Acme reversed to the beginning of the path, allowing Bolt to go through to her destination. Then Acme was able to proceed forward on the main route.

Trial 5. Both players elected to take the alternate route to their destinations.

Trial 7. Both players took the main route and met in the center. They waited, deadlocked, for a considerable time. Then Acme reversed to the end of the one-way path allowing Bolt to go through, then proceeded through to her destination.

Trials 10–20. Acme and Bolt fall into a pattern of alternating who is to go first on the one-way section. There is no deviation from this pattern.

The only other pattern that emerges in this condition is one in which one player dominates the other. That is, one player consistently goes first on the one-way section and the other player consistently yields.

Unilateral threat condition. *Trial 1.* Both players took the main route and met in the center of it. Acme immediately closed the gate, reversed to "start," and took the alternate route to her destination. Bolt waited for a few seconds,

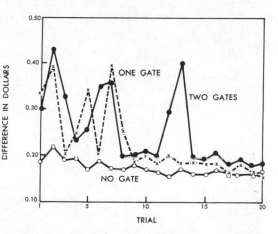

Figure 7 Median absolute differences in payoff.

Table 1 Mean payoffs summated over the twenty trials

	Means			Statistical comparisons: p values*			
Variable	(1) No threat	(2) Unilateral threat	(3) Bilateral threat	Over-all	1 vs 2	1 vs 3	2 vs 3
Summed payoffs (Acme + Bolt)	203.31	−405.88	−875.12	.01	.01	.01	.05
Acme's payoff	122.44	−118.56	−406.56	.01	.10	.01	.05
Bolt's payoff	80.88	−287.31	−468.56	.01	.01	.01	.20
Absolute differences in payoff (A − B)	125.94	294.75	315.25	.05	.05	.01	ns

* Evaluation of the significance of over-all variation between conditions is based on an F test with 2 and 45 df. Comparisons between treatments are based on a two-tailed t test.

at the closed gate, then reversed and took the alternate route.

Trial 2. Both players took the main route and met in the center. After moving back and forth deadlocked for about 15 seconds, Bolt reversed to the beginning of the one-way path, allowed Acme to pass, and then proceeded forward to her destination.

Trial 3. Both players started out on the main route, meeting in the center. After moving back and forth deadlocked for a while, Acme closed her gate, reversed to "start," and took the alternate route. Bolt, meanwhile, waited at the closed gate. When Acme arrived at her destination she opened the gate, and Bolt went through to complete her trip.

Trial 5. Both players took the main route, meeting at the center of the one-way section. Acme immediately closed her gate, reversed, and took the alternate route. Bolt waited at the gate for about 10 seconds, then reversed and took the alternate route to her destination.

Trial 10. Both players took the main route and met in the center. Acme closed her gate, reversed, and took the alternate route. Bolt remained waiting at the closed gate. After Acme arrived at her destination, she opened the gate and Bolt completed her trip.

Trial 15. Acme took the main route to her destination and Bolt took the alternate route.

Trials 17–20. Both players took the main route and met in the center. Bolt waited a few seconds, then reversed to the end of the one-way section allowing Acme to go through. Then Bolt proceeded forward to her destination.

Other typical patterns that developed in this experimental condition included an alternating pattern similar to that described in the no threat condition, a dominating pattern in which Bolt would select the alternate route leaving Acme free to use the main route unobstructed and a pattern in which Acme would close her gate and then take the alternate route, also forcing Bolt to take the alternate route

Bilateral threat condition. *Trial 1.* Acme took the main route and Bolt took the alternate route.

Trial 2. Both players took the main route and met head-on. Bolt closed her gate. Acme waited a few seconds, then closed her gate, reversed to "start," then went forward again to the closed gate. Acme reversed and took the alternate route. Bolt again reversed, then started on the alternate route. Acme opened her gate and Bolt reversed to "start" and went to her destination on the main route.

Trial 3. Acme took the alternate route to her destination. Bolt took the main route and closed her gate before entering the one-way section.

Trial 5. Both players took the main route and met head-on. After about 10 seconds spent backing up and going forward, Acme closed her gate, reversed, and took the alternate route. After waiting a few seconds, Bolt did the same.

Trials 8–10. Both players started out on the main route, immediately closed their gates, reversed to "start," and took the alternate route to their destinations.

Trial 15. Both players started out on the main route and met head-on. After some jockeying for position, Acme closed her gate, reversed, and took the alternate route to her destination. After waiting at the gate for a few seconds, Bolt reversed to "start" and took the alternate route to her destination.

Trials 19–20. Both players started out on the main route, immediately closed their gates, reversed to "start," and took the alternate routes to their destinations.

Other patterns that emerged in the bilateral threat condition included alternating first use of the one-way section, one player's dominating the other on first use of the one-way section, and another dominating pattern in which one player consistently took the main route while the other consistently took the alternate route.

Discussion

From our view of bargaining as a situation in which both cooperative and competitive tendencies are present and acting upon the individual, it is relevant to inquire as to the conditions under which a stable agreement of any form develops. However, implicit in most economic models of bargaining (e.g., Stone, 1958; Zeuthen, 1930) is the assumption that the cooperative interests of the bargainers are sufficiently strong to insure that some form of mutually satisfactory agreement will be reached. For this reason, such models have focused upon the form of the agreement reached by the bargainers. Siegel and Fouraker (1960) report a series of bargaining experiments, quite different in structure from ours, in which only one of many pairs of Ss were unable to reach agreement. Siegel and Fouraker explain this rather startling result as follows:

Apparently the disruptive forces which lead to the rupture of some negotiations were at least partially controlled in our sessions. . . .

Some negotiations collapse when one party becomes incensed at the other, and henceforth strives to maximize his opponent's displeasure rather than his own satisfaction . . . Since it is difficult to transmit insults by means of quantitative bids, such disequilibrating behavior was not induced in the present studies. If subjects were allowed more latitude in their communications and interactions, the possibility of an affront-offense-punitive behavior sequence might be increased (p. 100). (Quoted by permission of McGraw-Hill.)

In our experimental bargaining situation, the availability of threat clearly made it more difficult for bargainers to reach a mutually profitable agreement. These results, we believe, reflect psychological tendencies that are not confined to our bargaining situation: the tendency to use threat (if the means for threatening is available) in an attempt to force the other person to yield, when the other is seen as obstructing one's path; the tendency to respond with counterthreat or increased resistance to attempts at intimidation. How general are these tendencies? What conditions are likely to elicit them? Answers to these questions are necessary before our results can be generalized to other situations.

Dollard, Doob, Miller, Mowrer, and Sears (1939) have cited a variety of evidence to support the view that aggression (i.e., the use of threat) is a common reaction to a person who is seen as the agent of frustration. There seems to be little reason to doubt that the use of threat is a frequent reaction to interpersonal impasses. However, everyday observation indicates that threat does not inevitably occur when there is an interpersonal impasse. We would speculate that it is most likely to occur: when the threatener has no positive interest in the other person's welfare (he is either egocentrically or competitively related to the other); when the threatener believes that the other has no positive interest in his welfare; and when the threatener anticipates either that his threat will be effective or, if ineffective, will not worsen his situation because he expects the worst to happen if he does not use his threat. We suggest that these conditions were operative in our experiment; Ss were either egocentrically or competitively oriented to one another[7] and they felt that they would not be worse off by the use of threat.

Everyday observation suggests that the tendency to respond with counterthreat or increased resistance to attempts at intimidation is also a common occurrence. We believe that introducing threat into a bargaining situation affects the meaning of yielding. Although we have no data to support this interpretation directly, we will attempt to justify it on the basis of some additional assumptions.

Goffman (1955) has pointed out the pervasive significance of "face" in the maintenance of the social order. In this view, self-esteem is a socially

validated system that grows out of the acceptance by others of the claim for deference, prestige, and recognition that a person presents in his behavior toward others. Since the rejection of such a claim would be perceived (by the recipient) as directed against his self-esteem, he must react against it rather than accept it in order to maintain the integrity of his self-esteem system.

One may view the behavior of our Ss as an attempt to make claims upon the other, an attempt to develop a set of shared expectations as to what each was entitled to. Why then did the Ss' reactions differ so markedly as a function of the availability of threat? The explanation lies, we believe, in the cultural interpretation of yielding (to a peer or subordinate) under duress, as compared to giving in without duress. The former, we believe, is perceived as a negatively valued form of behavior, with negative implications for the self-image of the person who so behaves. At least partly, this is so because the locus of causality is perceived to be outside the person's voluntary control. No such evaluation, however, need be placed on the behavior of one who "gives in" in a situation where no threat or duress is a factor. Rather we should expect the culturally defined evaluation of such a person's behavior to be one of "reasonableness" or "maturity," because the source of the individual's behavior is perceived to lie within his own control.

Our discussion so far has suggested that the psychological factors which operate in our experimental bargaining situation are to be found in many real-life bargaining situations. However, it is well to recognize some unique features of our experimental game. First, the bargainers had no opportunity to communicate verbally with one another. Prior research on the role of communication in trust (Deutsch 1958, 1960; Loomis, 1959) suggests that the opportunity for communication would have made reaching an agreement easier for individualistically-oriented bargainers. This same research (Deutsch, 1960) indicates, however, that communication may not be effective between competitively oriented bargainers. This possibility was expressed spontaneously by a number of our Ss in a post-game interview.

Another characteristic of our bargaining game is that the passage of time, without coming to an agreement, is costly to the players. There are, of course, bargaining situations in which lack of agreement may simply preserve the *status quo* without any worsening of the bargainers' respective situations. This is the case in the typical bilateral monopoly case, where the buyer and seller are unable to agree upon a price (e.g., see Siegel & Fouraker, 1960). In other sorts of bargaining situations, however, (e.g., labor-man-

---

[7] A post-experimental questionnaire indicated that, in all three experimental conditions, the Ss were most strongly motivated to win money, next most strongly motivated to do better than the other player, next most motivated to "have fun," and were very little or not at all motivated to help the other player.

agement negotiations during a strike, internation negotiations during an expensive cold war) the passage of time may play an important role. In our experiment, we received the impression that the meaning of time changed as time passed without the bargainers reaching an agreement. Initially, the passage of time seemed to place the players under pressure to come to an agreement before their costs mounted sufficiently to destroy their profit. With the continued passage of time, however, their mounting losses strengthened their resolution not to yield to the other player. They comment: "I've lost so much, I'll be damned if I give in now. At least I'll have the satisfaction of doing better than she does." The mounting losses and continued deadlock seemed to change the game from a mixed motive into a predominantly competitive situation.

It is, of course, hazardous to generalize from a laboratory experiment to the complex problems of the real world. But our experiment and the theoretical ideas underlying it can perhaps serve to emphasize some notions which, otherwise, have an intrinsic plausibility. In brief, these are that there is more safety in cooperative than in competitive coexistence, that it is dangerous for bargainers to have weapons, and that it is possibly even more dangerous for a bargainer to have the capacity to retaliate in kind than not to have this capacity when the other bargainer has a weapon. This last statement assumes that the one who yields has more of his values preserved by accepting the agreement preferred by the other than by extended conflict. Of course, in some bargaining situations in the real world, the loss incurred by yielding may exceed the losses due to extended conflict.

Summary

The nature of bargaining situations was discussed. Two general propositions about the conditions affecting the likelihood of a bargaining agreement were presented. The effects of the availability of threat upon interpersonal bargaining were investigated experimentally in a two-person bargaining game. Three experimental conditions were employed: no threat (neither player could threaten the other), unilateral threat (only one of the players had a means of threat available to her), and bilateral threat (both players could threaten each other). The results indicated that the difficulty in reaching an agreement and the amount of (imaginary) money lost, individually as well as collectively, was greatest in the bilateral and next greatest in the unilateral threat condition. Only in the no threat condition did the players make an overall profit. In the unilateral threat condition, the player with the threat capability did better than the player without the threat capability. However, comparing the bilateral and unilateral threat conditions, the results also indicate that when facing a player who had threat capability one was better off *not* having than having the capacity to retaliate in kind.

References

Deutsch, M. A theory of cooperation and competition. *Hum. Relat.*, 1949, **2**, 129–152.

Deutsch, M. Trust and suspicion. *J. conflict Resolut.*, 1958, **2**, 265–279.

Deutsch, M. The effect of motivational orientation upon trust and suspicion. *Hum. Relat.*, 1960, **13**, 123–140.

Dollard, J., Doob, L. W., Miller, N. E., Mowrer, O. H., and Sears, R. H. *Frustration and aggression.* New Haven: Yale Univer. Press, 1939.

Goffman, E. On face-work. *Psychiatry*, 1955, **18**, 213–231.

Loomis, J. L. Communication, the development of trust and cooperative behavior. *Hum. Relat.*, 1959, **12**, 305–315.

Schelling, T. C. Bargaining, communication and limited war. *J. conflict Resolut.*, 1957, **1**, 19–38.

Schelling, T. C. The strategy of conflict: Prospectus for the reorientation of game theory. *J. conflict Resolut.*, 1958, **2**, 203–264.

Siegel, S., and Fouraker, L. E. *Bargaining and group decision making.* New York: McGraw-Hill, 1960.

Stone, J. J. An experiment in bargain games. *Econometrica*, 1958, **26**, 286–296.

Zeuthen, F. *Problems of monopoly and economic warfare.* London: Routledge, 1930.

This article is concerned with what is sometimes called "person perception." How we respond to another individual depends upon the way we perceive him in terms of certain central aspects. The warmth or coldness of the stimulus person seems to be one such set of aspects.

The social psychologist is interested in this phenomenon because our responses to another individual may depend upon the fact that we perceive that he belongs to a particular social group. We may perceive this group membership directly, or more likely, as in this experiment, we may react to a label which has been placed on the stimulus person.

Points to guide your study

1. Can you think of some labels and situations which would markedly influence responses toward a stimulus person?

2. A biserial correlation may be interpreted in the same way as a product-moment correlation.

3. Glossary: Autochthonous—coming from within (internal as opposed to external).

50. THE WARM-COLD VARIABLE IN FIRST IMPRESSIONS OF PERSONS

*Harold H. Kelley, University of Minnesota**

This experiment is one of several studies of first impressions (3), the purpose of the series being to investigate the stability of early judgments, their determinants, and the relation of such judgments to the behavior of the person making them. In interpreting the data from several non-experimental studies on the stability of first impressions, it proved to be necessary to postulate inner-observer variables which contribute to the impression and which remain relatively constant through time. Also some evidence was obtained which directly demonstrated the existence of these variables and their nature. The present experiment was designed to determine the effects of one kind of inner-observer variable, specifically, *expectations* about the stimulus person which the observer brings to the exposure situation. That prior information or labels attached to a stimulus person make a difference in observers' first impressions is almost too obvious to require demonstration. The expectations resulting from such preinformation may restrict, modify, or accentuate the impressions he will have. The crucial question is: What changes in perception will accompany a given expectation? Studies of stereotyping, for example, that of Katz and Braly (2), indicate that from an ethnic label such as "German" or "Negro," a number of perceptions follow which are culturally determined. The present study finds its main significance in relation to a study by Asch (1) which demonstrates that certain crucial labels can transform the entire impression of the person, leading to attributions which are related to the label on a broad cultural basis or even, perhaps, on an autochthonous basis.

Asch read to his subjects a list of adjectives which purportedly described a particular person. He then asked them to characterize that person. He found that the inclusion in the list of what he called *central* qualities, such as "warm" as opposed to "cold," produced a widespread change in the entire impression. This effect was not adequately explained by the halo effect since it did not extend indiscriminately in a positive or negative direction to all characteristics. Rather, it differentially transformed the other qualities, for example, by changing their relative importance in the total impression. Peripheral qualities (such as "polite" versus "blunt") did not produce effects as strong as those produced by the central qualities.[1]

* The writer acknowledges the constructive advice of Professor Dorwin Cartwright, University of Michigan.

[1] Since the present experiment was carried out, Mensh and Wishner (6) have repeated a number of Asch's experiments because of dissatisfaction with his sex and geographic distribution. Their data substantiate Asch's very closely. Also, Luchins (5) has criticized Asch's experiments for their artificial methodology, repeated some of them, and challenged some of the kinds of interpretations Asch made from his data. Luchins also briefly reports some tantalizing conclusions from a number of studies of first impressions of actual persons.

The present study tested the effects of such central qualities upon the early impressions of *real* persons, the same qualities, "warm" vs. "cold," being used. They were introduced as preinformation about the stimulus person before his actual appearance; so presumably they operated as expectations rather than as part of the stimulus pattern during the exposure period. In addition, information was obtained about the effects of the expectations upon the observers' behavior toward the stimulus person. An earlier study in this series has indicated that the more incompatible the observer initially perceived the stimulus person to be, the less the observer initiated interaction with him thereafter. The second purpose of the present experiment, then, was to provide a better controlled study of this relationship.

No previous studies reported in the literature have dealt with the importance of first impressions for behavior. The most relevant data are found in the sociometric literature, where there are scattered studies of the relation between choices among children having some prior acquaintance and their interaction behavior. For an example, see the study by Newstetter, Feldstein, and Newcomb (8).

Procedure

The experiment was performed in three sections of a psychology course (Economics 70) at the Massachusetts Institute of Technology.[2] The three sections provided 23, 16, and 16 subjects respectively. All 55 subjects were men, most of them in their third college year. In each class the stimulus person (also a male) was completely unknown to the subjects before the experimental period. One person served as stimulus person in two sections, and a second person took this role in the third section. In each case the stimulus person was introduced by the experimenter, who posed as a representative of the course instructors and who gave the following statement:

Your regular instructor is out of town today, and since we of Economics 70 are interested in the general problem of how various classes react to different instructors, we're going to have an instructor today you've never had before, Mr. ———. Then, at the end of the period, I want you to fill out some forms about him. In order to give you some idea of what he's like, we've had a person who knows him write up a little biographical note about him. I'll pass this out to you now and you can read it before he arrives. *Please read these to yourselves and don't talk about this among*

yourselves until the class is over so that he won't get wind of what's going on.

Two kinds of these notes were distributed, the two being identical except that in one the stimulus person was described among other things as being "rather cold" whereas in the other form the phrase "very warm" was substituted. The content of the "rather cold" version is as follows:

Mr. ——— is a graduate student in the Department of Economics and Social Science here at M. I. T. He has had three semesters of teaching experience in psychology at another college. This is his first semester teaching Ec. 70. He is 26 years old, a veteran, and married. People who know him consider him to be a rather cold person, industrious, critical, practical, and determined.

The two types of preinformation were distributed randomly within each of the three classes and in such a manner that the students were not aware that two kinds of information were being given out. The stimulus person then appeared and led the class in a twenty-minute discussion. During this time the experimenter kept a record of how often each student participated in the discussion. Since the discussion was almost totally leader-centered, this participation record indicates the number of times each student initiated verbal interaction with the instructor. After the discussion period, the stimulus person left the room, and the experimenter gave the following instructions:

Now, I'd like to get your impression of Mr. ———. This is not a test of you and can in no way affect your grade in this course. This material will not be identified as belonging to particular persons and will be kept strictly confidential. It will be of most value to us if you are completely honest in your evaluation of Mr. ———. Also, please understand that what you put down will not be used against him or cause him to lose his job or anything like that. This is not a test of him but merely a study of how different classes react to different instructors.

The subjects then wrote free descriptions of the stimulus person and finally rated him on a set of 15 rating scales.

Results and discussion

1. Influence of warm-cold variable on first impressions. The differences in the ratings produced by the warm-cold variable were consistent from one section to another even where different stimulus persons were used. Consequently, the data from the three sections were combined by equating means (the S.D.'s were approximately

[2] Professor Mason Haire, now of the University of California, provided valuable advice and help in executing the experiment.

equal) and the results for the total group are presented in Table 1. Also in this table is presented that part of Asch's data which refers to the qualities included in our rating scales. From this table it is quite clear that those given the "warm" preinformation consistently rated the stimulus person more favorably than did those given the "cold" preinformation. Summarizing the statistically significant differences, the "warm" subjects rated the stimulus person as more considerate of others, more informal, more sociable, more popular, better natured, more humorous, and more humane. These findings are very similar to Asch's for the characteristics common to both studies. He found more frequent attribution to his hypothetical "warm" personalities of sociability, popularity, good naturedness, generosity, humorousness, and humaneness. So these data strongly support his finding that such a central quality as "warmth" can greatly influence the total impression of a personality. This effect is found to be operative in the perception of real persons.

This general favorableness in the perceptions of the "warm" observers as compared with the "cold" ones indicates that something like a halo effect may have been operating in these ratings. Although his data are not completely persuasive on this point, Asch was convinced that such a general effect was *not* operating in his study. Closer inspection of the present data makes it clear that the "warm-cold" effect cannot be explained altogether on the basis of simple halo effect. In Table 1 it is evident that the "warm-cold" variable produced differential effects from one rating scale to another. The size of this effect seems to depend upon the closeness of relation between the specific dimension of any given rating scale and the central quality of "warmth" or "coldness." Even though the rating of intelligence may be influenced by a halo effect, it is not influenced to the same degree to which considerateness is. It seems to make sense to view such strongly influenced items as considerateness, informality, good naturedness, and humaneness as dynamically more closely related to warmth and hence more perceived in terms of this relation than in terms of a general positive or negative feeling toward the stimulus person. If first impressions are normally made in terms of such general dimensions as "warmth" and "coldness," the power they give the observer

Table 1   Comparison of "warm" and "cold" observers in terms of average ratings given stimulus persons

Item	Low end of rating scale	High end of rating scale	Average rating		Level of significance of warm-cold difference	Asch's data: per cent of group assigning quality at low end of our rating scale*	
			Warm, N = 27	Cold, N = 28		Warm	Cold
1	Knows his stuff	Doesn't know his stuff	3.5	4.6			
2	Considerate of others	Self-centered	6.3	9.6	1%		
3 †	Informal	Formal	6.3	9.6	1%		
4 †	Modest	Proud	9.4	10.6			
5	Sociable	Unsociable	5.6	10.4	1%	91	38
6	Self-assured	Uncertain of himself	8.4	9.1			
7	High intelligence	Low intelligence	4.8	5.1			
8	Popular	Unpopular	4.0	7.4	1%	84	28
9 †	Good natured	Irritable	9.4	12.0	5%	94	17
10	Generous	Ungenerous	8.2	9.6		91	08
11	Humorous	Humorless	8.3	11.7	1%	77	13
12	Important	Insignificant	6.5	8.6		88	99
13 †	Humane	Ruthless	8.6	11.0	5%	86	31
14 †	Submissive	Dominant	13.2	14.5			
15	Will go far	Will not get ahead	4.2	5.8			

* Given for all qualities common to Asch's list and this set of rating scales.
† These scales were reversed when presented to the subjects.

in making predictions and specific evaluations about such disparate behavior characteristics as formality and considerateness is considerable (even though these predictions may be incorrect or misleading).

The free report impression data were analyzed for only one of the sections. In general, there were few sizable differences between the "warm" and "cold" observers. The "warm" observers attributed more nervousness, more sincerity, and more industriousness to the stimulus person. Although the frequencies of comparable qualities are very low because of the great variety of descriptions produced by the observers, there is considerable agreement with the rating scale data.

Two important phenomena are illustrated in these free description protocols, the first of them having been noted by Asch. *Firstly*, the characteristics of the stimulus person are interpreted in terms of the precognition of warmth or coldness. For example, a "warm" observer writes about a rather shy and retiring stimulus person as follows: "He makes friends slowly but they are lasting friendships when formed." In another instance, several "cold" observers describe him as being ". . . intolerant: would be angry if you disagree with his views . . ."; while several "warm" observers put the same thing this way: "Unyielding in principle, not easily influenced or swayed from his original attitude." *Secondly*, the preinformation about the stimulus person's warmth or coldness is evaluated and interpreted in the light of the direct behavioral data about him. For example, "He has a slight inferiority complex which leads to his coldness," and "His conscientiousness and industriousness might be mistaken for coldness." Examples of these two phenomena occurred rather infrequently, and there was no way to evaluate the relative strengths of these countertendencies. Certainly some such evaluation is necessary to determine the conditions under which behavior which is contrary to a stereotyped label resists distortion and leads to rejection of the label.

A comparison of the data from the two different stimulus persons is pertinent to the last point in so far as it indicates the interaction between the properties of the stimulus person and the label. The fact that the warm-cold variable generally produced differences in the same direction for the two stimulus persons, even though they are very different in personality, behavior, and mannerisms, indicates the strength of this variable. However, there were some exceptions to this tendency as well as marked differences in the *degree* to which the experimental variable was able to produce differences. For example, stimulus person A typically appears to be anything but lacking in self-esteem and on rating scale 4 he was generally at the "proud" end of the scale. Although the "warm" observers tended to rate him as they did the other stimulus person (i.e., more "modest"), the difference between the "warm" and "cold" means for stimulus person A is very small and not significant as it is for stimulus person B. Similarly, stimulus person B was seen as "unpopular" and "humorless," which agrees with his typical classroom behavior. Again the "warm" observers rated him more favorably on these items, but their ratings were not significantly different from those of the "cold" observers, as was true for the other stimulus person. Thus we see that the strength or compellingness of various qualities of the stimulus person must be reckoned with. The stimulus is not passive to the forces arising from the label but actively resists distortion and may severely limit the degree of influence exerted by the preinformation.[3]

2. Influence of warm-cold variable on interaction with the stimulus person. In the analysis of the frequency with which the various students took part in the discussion led by the stimulus person, a larger proportion of those given the "warm" preinformation participated than of those given the "cold" preinformation. Fifty-six per cent of the "warm" subjects entered the discussion, whereas only 32 per cent of the "cold" subjects did so. Thus the expectation of warmth not only produced more favorable early perceptions of the stimulus person but led to greater initiation of interaction with him. This relation is a low one, significant at between the 5 per cent and 10 per cent level of confidence, but it is in line with the general principle that social perception serves to guide and steer the person's behavior in his social environment.

As would be expected from the foregoing findings, there was also a relation between the favorableness of the impression and whether or not the person participated in the discussion. Although any single item yielded only a small and insignificant relation to participation, when a number are combined the trend becomes clear cut. For example, when we combine the seven items which were influenced to a statistically significant degree by the warm-cold variable, the

---

[3] We must raise an important question here: Would there be a tendency for "warm" observers to distort the perception in the favorable direction regardless of how much the stimulus deviated from the expectation? Future research should test the following hypothesis, which is suggested by Gestalt perception theory (4, pp. 95–98): If the stimulus differs but slightly from the expectation, the perception will tend to be *assimilated* to the expectation; however, if the difference between the stimulus and expectation is too great, the perception will occur by contrast to the expectation and will be distorted in the opposite direction.

total score bears considerable relation to participation, the relationship being significant at well beyond the 1 per cent level. A larger proportion of those having favorable total impressions participated than of those having unfavorable impressions, the biserial correlation between these variables being .34. Although this relation may be interpreted in several ways, it seems most likely that the unfavorable perception led to a curtailment of interaction. Support for this comes from one of the other studies in this series (3). There it was found that those persons having unfavorable impressions of the instructor at the end of the first class meeting tended less often to initiate interactions with him in the succeeding four meetings than did those having favorable first impressions. There was also some tendency in the same study for those persons who interacted least with the instructor to change least in their judgments of him from the first to later impressions.

It will be noted that these relations lend some support to the autistic hostility hypothesis proposed by Newcomb (7). This hypothesis suggests that the possession of an initially hostile attitude toward a person leads to a restriction of communication and contact with him which in turn serves to preserve the hostile attitude by preventing the acquisition of data which could correct it. The present data indicate that a restriction of interaction is associated with unfavorable preinformation and an unfavorable perception. The data from the other study support this result and also indicate the correctness of the second part of the hypothesis, that restricted interaction reduces the likelihood of change in the attitude.

What makes these findings more significant is that they appear in the context of a discussion class where there are numerous *induced* and *own* forces to enter the discussion and to interact with the instructor. It seems likely that the effects predicted by Newcomb's hypothesis would be much more marked in a setting where such forces were not present.

Summary

The warm-cold variable had been found by Asch to produce large differences in the impressions of personality formed from a list of adjectives. In this study the same variable was introduced in the form of expectations about a real person and was found to produce similar differences in first impressions of him in a classroom setting. In addition, the differences in first impressions produced by the different expectations were shown to influence the observers' behavior toward the stimulus person. Those observers given the favorable expectation (who, consequently, had a favorable impression of the stimulus person) tended to interact more with him than did those given the unfavorable expectation.

References

1. Asch, S. E. Forming impressions of personality. *J. abnorm. soc. Psychol.*, 1946, **41**, 258–290.
2. Katz, D., and Braly, K. W. Verbal stereotypes and racial prejudice. In Newcomb, T. M., and Hartley, E. L. (eds.), *Readings in social psychology*. New York: Holt, 1947. Pp. 204–210.
3. Kelly, H. H. First impressions in interpersonal relations. Ph.D. thesis, Massachusetts Institute of Technology, Cambridge, Mass. Sept., 1948.
4. Krech, D., and Crutchfield, R. S. *Theory and problems of social psychology*. New York: McGraw-Hill, 1948.
5. Luchins, A. S. Forming impressions of personality: a critique. *J. abnorm. soc. Psychol.*, 1948, **43**, 318–325.
6. Mensh, I. N., and Wishner, J. Asch on "Forming impressions of personality": further evidence. *J. Personal.*, 1947, **16**, 188–191.
7. Newcomb, T. M. Autistic hostility and social reality. *Hum. Relat.*, 1947, **I**, 69–86.
8. Newstetter, W. I., Feldstein, M. J., and Newcomb, T. M. *Group adjustment: a study in experimental sociology*. Cleveland: Western Reserve University, 1938.

CHAPTER SEVENTEEN

Attitudes, beliefs, and social prejudice

R## RACIAL ATTITUDES AND CONFLICTS

The major point made in this article is that the concept of conformity, rather than several alternative points of view, is the key to understanding attitudes on desegregation.

Points to guide your study

1. At this point, you might want to review some of the experimental studies on conformity mentioned in your text and in this book.

2. What is the evidence against the importance of alternative points of view, e.g., authoritarianism?

3. What is a "latent liberal"? What is some of the evidence supporting this concept?

51. SOCIAL PSYCHOLOGY AND DESEGREGATION RESEARCH

*Thomas F. Pettigrew, Harvard University**

What one hears and what one sees of southern race relations today are sharply divergent. Consider some of the things that occur in interviews with white Southerners.

"As much as my family likes TV," confided a friendly North Carolina farmer, "we always turn the set off when they put them colored people on." But as the two of us were completing the interview, a series of famous Negro entertainers performed on the bright, 21-inch screen in the adjoining room. No one interrupted them.

A rotund banker in Charleston, South Carolina, was equally candid in his remarks: "Son, under no conditions will the white man and the black man ever get together in this state." He

* This paper was given as an invited address at the Annual Meeting of the Southeastern Psychological Association, Atlanta, Georgia, March 31, 1960. The author wishes to express his appreciation to Gordon W. Allport of Harvard University, E. Earl Baughman of the University of North Carolina, and Cooper C. Clements of Emory University for their suggestions.

T. F. Pettigrew. Social psychology and desegregation research. *Amer. Psychologist*, 1961, **16**, 105–112. Copyright 1961 by the American Psychological Association. Reprinted here with permission from the author and the American Psychological Association.

apparently preferred to ignore the government sponsored integration at his city's naval installation, just a short distance from his office.

Another respondent, this time a highly educated Chattanooga businessman, patiently explained to me for over an hour how race relations had not changed at all in his city during the past generation. As I left his office building, I saw a Negro policeman directing downtown traffic. It was the first Negro traffic cop I had ever seen in the South.

The South today is rife with such contradictions; social change has simply been too rapid for many Southerners to recognize it. Such a situation commands the attention of psychologists—particularly those in the South.

There are many other aspects of this sweeping process that should command our professional attention. To name just two, both the pending violence and the stultifying conformity attendant with desegregation are uniquely psychological problems. We might ask, for instance, what leads to violence in some desegregating communities, like Little Rock and Clinton, and not in others, like Norfolk and Winston-Salem? A multiplicity of factors must be relevant and further research is desperately needed to delineate them; but tentative early work seems to indicate that desegregation violence so far has been surprisingly "rational." That is, violence has generally resulted in localities where at least some of the authorities give prior hints that they would gladly return to segregation if disturbances occurred; peaceful integration has generally followed firm and forceful leadership.[1]

Research concerning conformity in the present situation is even more important. Many psychologists know from personal experience how intense the pressures to conform in racial attitudes have become in the present-day South; indeed, it appears that the first amendment guaranteeing free speech is in as much peril as the fourteenth amendment. Those who dare to break consistently this conformity taboo must do so in many parts of the South under the intimidation of slanderous letters and phone calls, burned crosses, and even bomb threats. Moreover, this paper will contend that conformity is the social psychological key to analyzing desegregation.

It is imperative that psychologists study these phenomena for two reasons: first, our psychological insights and methods are needed in understanding and solving this, our nation's primary internal problem; second, this process happening before our eyes offers us a rare opportunity to test in the field the psychological concomitants of cultural stress and social change. Thus I would like in this paper to assess some of the prospects and directions of these potential psychological contributions.

Role of social science in the desegregation process to date

The role of social science, particularly sociology and psychology, in the desegregation process has been much publicized and criticized by southern segregationists.[2] Many of these critics apparently think that sociology is synonymous with socialism and psychology with brainwashing. In any event, their argument that we have been crucially important in the Supreme Court desegregation cases of the fifties is based largely on the reference to seven social science documents in Footnote 11 of the famous 1954 *Brown vs. Board of Education* decision. It would be flattering for us to think that our research has had such a dramatic effect on the course of his-

tory as segregationists claim, but in all truth we do not deserve such high praise.

In making their claim that the 1954 decision was psychological and not legal, the segregationists choose to overlook several things. The 1954 ruling did not come suddenly "out of the blue"; it was a logical continuation of a 44-year Supreme Court trend that began in 1910 when a former private in the Confederate Army, the liberal Edward White, became Chief Justice (Logan, 1956). When compared to this backdrop, our influence on the 1954 ruling was actually of only footnote importance. Furthermore, the language and spirit of the 1896 *Plessy vs. Ferguson*, separate-but-equal decision, so dear to the hearts of segregationists, were as immersed in the jargon and thinking of the social science of that era as the 1954 decision was of our era. Its 1896, Sumnerian argument that laws cannot change "social prejudices" (Allport, 1954, pp. 469–473) and its use of such social Darwinism terms as "racial instincts" and "natural affinities" lacked only a footnote to make it as obviously influenced by the then current social science as the 1954 ruling.

A final reason why we do not deserve the flattering praise of the segregationists is our failure to make substantial contributions to the process since 1954. The lack of penetrating psychological research in this area can be traced directly to three things: the lack of extensive foundation support, conformity pressures applied in many places in the South that deter desegregation research, and the inadequacy of traditional psychological thinking to cope with the present process. Let us discuss each of these matters in turn.

A few years ago Stuart Cook (1957) drew attention to the failure of foundations to support desegregation research; the situation today is only slightly improved. It appears that a combination of foundation fears has produced this situation. One set of fears, as Cook noted, may stem from concern over attacks by southern Congressmen on their tax-free status; the other set may stem from boycotts carried out by some segregationists against products identified with the foundations. In any case, this curtailment of funds is undoubtedly one reason why social scientists have so far left this crucial process relatively unstudied. Recently, however, a few moderate sized grants have been made for work in this area; hopefully, this is the beginning of a reappraisal by foundations of their previous policies. And it is up to us to submit competent research proposals to them to test continually for any change of these policies.

It is difficult to assess just how much damage has been done to desegregation research in the South by segregationist pressures. Probably the number of direct refusals to allow such research

---

[1] Clark (1953) predicted this from early border-state integration, and a variety of field reports have since documented the point in specific instances.

[2] For instance, once-liberal Virginius Dabney (1957, p. 14), editor of the *Richmond Times-Dispatch*, charged that "the violence at Little Rock . . . never would have happened if nine justices had not consulted sociologists and psychologists, instead of lawyers, in 1954, and attempted to legislate through judicial decrees."

by southern institutions outside of the Black Belt has actually been small. More likely, the greatest harm has been rendered indirectly by the stifling atmosphere which prevents us from actually testing the limits of research opportunities. Interested as we may be in the racial realm, we decide to work in a less controversial area. Perhaps it is less a matter of courage than it is of resignation in the face of what are thought to be impossible barriers. If these suspicions are correct, there is real hope for overcoming in part this second obstacle to desegregation research.

In some situations, there should be little resistance. In racially integrated veterans' hospitals, for instance, much needed personality studies comparing Negro and white patients should be possible. In other situations, the amount of resistance to race research may be less than we anticipate. Since Little Rock, many so-called "moderates" in the South, particularly businessmen, have become more interested in the dynamics of desegregation. This is not to say that they are more in favor of racial equality than they were; it is only to suggest that the bad publicity, the closing of schools, and the economic losses suffered by Little Rock have made these influential Southerners more receptive to objective and constructive research on the process. It is for this reason that it is imperative the limits for the southern study of desegregation be tested at this time.

Finally, psychological contributions to desegregation research have been restricted by the inadequacy of traditional thinking in our discipline. More specifically, the relative neglect of situational variables in interracial behavior and a restricted interpretation and use of the attitude concept hinder psychological work in this area.

The importance of the situation for racial interaction has been demonstrated in a wide variety of settings. All-pervasive racial attitudes are often not involved; many individuals seem fully capable of immediate behavioral change as situations change. Thus in Panama there is a divided street, the Canal Zone side of which is racially segregated and the Panamanian side of which is racially integrated. Biesanz and Smith (1951) report that most Panamanians and Americans appear to accommodate without difficulty as they go first on one side of the street and then on the other. Likewise in the coal mining county of McDowell, West Virginia, Minard (1952) relates that the majority of Negro and white miners follow easily a traditional pattern of integration below the ground and almost complete segregation above the ground. The literature abounds with further examples: southern white migrants readily adjusting to integrated situations in the North (Killian, 1949), northern whites approving of

employment and public facility integration but resisting residential integration (Reitzes, 1953), etc. Indeed, at the present time in the South there are many white Southerners who are simultaneously adjusting to bus and public golf course integration and opposing public school integration. Or, as in Nashville, they may have accepted school integration but are opposing lunch counter integration.

This is not to imply that generalized attitudes on race are never invoked. There are some Panamanians and some Americans who act about the same on both sides of the Panamanian street. Minard (1952) estimated about two-fifths of the West Virginian miners he observed behave consistently in either a tolerant or an intolerant fashion both below and above ground. And some whites either approve or disapprove of all desegregation. But these people are easily explained by traditional theory. They probably consist of the extremes in authoritarianism; their attitudes on race are so generalized and so salient that their consistent behavior in racial situations is sometimes in defiance of the prevailing social norms.

On the other hand, the "other directed" individuals who shift their behavior to keep in line with shifting expectations present the real problem for psychologists. Their racial attitudes appear less salient, more specific, and more tied to particular situations. Conformity needs are predominantly important for these people, and we shall return shortly to a further discussion of these conformists.

One complication introduced by a situational analysis is that interracial contact itself frequently leads to the modification of attitudes. A number of studies of racially integrated situations have noted dramatic attitude changes, but in most cases the changes involved specific, situation linked attitudes. For example, white department store employees become more accepting of Negroes in the work situation after equal status, integrated contact but not necessarily more accepting in other situations (Harding & Hogrefe, 1952). And *The American Soldier* studies (Stouffer, Suchman, DeVinney, Star, & Williams, 1949) found that the attitudes of white army personnel toward the Negro as a fighting man improve after equal status, integrated contact in combat, but their attitudes toward the Negro as a social companion do not necessarily change. In other words, experience in a novel situation of equal status leads to acceptance of that specific situation for many persons. Situations, then, not only structure specific racial behavior, but they may change specific attitudes in the process.

One final feature of a situational analysis deserves mention. Typically in psychology we have tested racial attitudes in isolation, apart from conflicting attitudes and values. Yet this is not realistic. As the desegregation process slowly unfolds in such resistant states as Virginia and Georgia, we see clearly that many segregationist Southerners value law and order, public education, and a prosperous economy above their racial views. Once such a situation pits race against other entrenched values, we need to know the public's hierarchy of these values. Thus a rounded situational analysis requires the measures of racial attitudes in the full context of countervalues.[3]

A second and related weakness in our psychological approach is the failure to exploit fully the broad and dynamic implications of the attitude concept. Most social psychological research has dealt with attitudes as if they were serving only an expressive function; but racial attitudes in the South require a more complex treatment.

In their volume, *Opinion and Personality*, Smith, Bruner, and White (1956) urge a more expansive interpretation of attitudes. They note three attitude functions. First, there is the *object appraisal* function; attitudes aid in understanding "reality" as it is defined by the culture. Second, attitudes can play a *social adjustment* role by contributing to the individual's identification with, or differentiation from, various reference groups. Finally, attitudes may reduce anxiety by serving an expressive or *externalization* function.

> Externalization occurs when an individual . . . senses an analogy between a perceived environmental event and some unresolved inner problem . . . [and] adopts an attitude . . . which is a transformed version of his way of dealing with his inner difficulty (pp. 41–44). (Reprinted with permission of John Wiley & Sons, Inc.)

At present the most fashionable psychological theories of prejudice—frustration-aggression, psychoanalytic, and authoritarianism—all deal chiefly with the externalization process. Valuable as these theories have been, this exclusive attention to the expressive component of attitudes has been at the expense of the object appraisal and social adjustment components. Moreover, it is the contention of this paper that these neglected and more socially relevant functions, particularly social adjustment, offer the key to further psychological advances in desegregation research.[4]

[3] A popular treatment of this point has been made by Zinn (1959).

[4] Though this paper emphasizes the social adjustment aspect of southern attitudes toward Negroes, the equally neglected object appraisal function is also of major importance. Most southern whites know only lower class Negroes; consequently their unfavorable stereotype of Negroes serves a definite reality function.

The extent to which this psychological concentration on externalization has influenced the general public was illustrated recently in the popular reaction to the swastika desecrations of Jewish temples. The perpetrators, all agreed, must be juvenile hoodlums, or "sick," or both. In other words, externalization explanations were predominantly offered.[5] Valid though these explanations may be in many cases, is it not also evident that the perpetrators were accurately reflecting the anti-Semitic norms of their subcultures? Thus their acts and the attitudes behind their acts are socially adjusting for these persons, given the circles in which they move.

Much like the public, some sociologists, too, have been understandably misled by our overemphasis on externalization into underestimating the psychological analysis of prejudice. One sociologist (Rose, 1956) categorically concludes:

> There is no evidence that . . . any known source of "prejudice" in the psychological sense is any more prevalent in the South than in the North (p. 174).

Two others (Rabb & Lipset, 1959) maintain firmly:

> the psychological approach, as valuable as it is, does not explain the preponderance of people who engage in prejudiced behavior, but do *not* have special emotional problems (p. 26).

Both of these statements assume, as some psychologists have assumed, that externalization is the only possible psychological explanation of prejudice. These writers employ cultural and situational norms as explanatory concepts for racial prejudice and discrimination, but fail to see that conformity needs are the personality reflections of these norms and offer an equally valid concept on the psychological level. To answer the first assertion, recent evidence indicates that conformity to racial norms, one "known source of prejudice," is "more prevalent in the South than in the North." To answer the second assertion, strong needs to conform to racial norms in a sternly sanctioning South, for instance, are *not* "special emotional problems." Psychology is not just a science of mental illness nor must psychological theories of prejudice be limited to the mentally ill.

Conformity and social adjustment in southern racial attitudes

Evidence of the importance of conformity in southern attitudes on race has been steadily accumulating in recent years. The relevant data come from several different research approaches;

[5] Such explanations also serve for many anti-Semitic observers as an ego-alien defense against guilt.

one of these is the study of anti-Semitism. Roper's (1946, 1947) opinion polls have twice shown the South, together with the Far West, to be one of the least anti-Semitic regions in the United States. Knapp's (1944) study of over 1,000 war rumors from all parts of the country in 1942 lends additional weight to this finding. He noted that anti-Semitic stories constituted 9% of the nation's rumors but only 3% of the South's rumors. By contrast, 8.5% of the southern rumors concerned the Negro as opposed to only 3% for the nation as a whole. Consistent with these data, too, is Prothro's (1952) discovery that two-fifths of his white adult sample in Louisiana was quite favorable in its attitudes toward Jews but at the same time quite unfavorable in its attitudes toward Negroes. But if the externalization function were predominant in southern anti-Negro attitudes, the South should also be highly anti-Semitic. Externalizing bigots do not select out just the Negro; they typically reject all outgroups, even, as Hartley (1946) has demonstrated, out-groups that do not exist.

Further evidence comes from research employing the famous F Scale measure of authoritarianism (Adorno, Frenkel-Brunswik, Levinson, & Sanford, 1950). Several studies, employing both student and adult samples, have reported southern F Scale means that fall well within the range of means of comparable nonsouthern groups (Milton, 1952; Pettigrew, 1959; Smith & Prothro, 1957). Moreover, there is no evidence that the family pattern associated with authoritarianism is any more prevalent in the South than in other parts of the country (Davis, Gardner, & Gardner, 1941; Dollard, 1937). It seems clear, then, that the South's heightened prejudice against the Negro cannot be explained in terms of any regional difference in authoritarianism. This is not to deny, however, the importance of the F Scale in predicting individual differences; it appears to correlate with prejudice in southern samples at approximately the same levels as in northern samples (Pettigrew, 1959).

The third line of evidence relates conformity measures directly to racial attitudes. For lack of a standardized, nonlaboratory measure, one study defined conformity and deviance in terms of the respondents' social characteristics (Pettigrew, 1959). For a southern white sample with age and education held constant, potentially conforming respondents (i.e., females or church attenders) were *more* anti-Negro than their counterparts (i.e., males or nonattenders of church), and potentially deviant respondents (i.e., armed service veterans or political independents) were *less* anti-Negro than their counterparts (i.e., nonveterans or political party identifiers). None of these differences were noted in a comparable northern sample. Furthermore, Southerners living in communities with relatively small percentages of Negroes were less anti-Negro than Southerners living in communities with relatively large percentages of Negroes, though they were *not* less authoritarian. In short, respondents most likely to be conforming to cultural pressures are more prejudiced against Negroes in the South but not in the North. And the percentage of Negroes in the community appears to be a fairly accurate index of the strength of these southern cultural pressures concerning race.

Thus all three types of research agree that conformity to the stern racial norms of southern culture is unusually crucial in the South's heightened hostility toward the Negro.[6] Or, in plain language, it is the path of least resistance in most southern circles to favor white supremacy. When an individual's parents and peers are racially prejudiced, when his limited world accepts racial discrimination as a given of life, when his deviance means certain ostracism, then his anti-Negro attitudes are not so much expressive as they are socially adjusting.

This being the case, it is fortunate that a number of significant laboratory and theoretical advances in the conformity realm have been made recently in our discipline. Solomon Asch's (1951) pioneer research on conformity, followed up by Crutchfield (1955) and others, has provided us with a wealth of laboratory findings, many of them suggestive for desegregation research. And theoretical analyses of conformity have been introduced by Kelman (1958, 1961), Festinger (1953, 1957), and Thibaut and Kelley (1959); these, too, are directly applicable for desegregation research. Indeed, research in southern race relations offers a rare opportunity to test these empirical and theoretical formulations in the field on an issue of maximum salience.

Consider the relevance of one of Asch's (1951) intriguing findings. Asch's standard situation, you will recall, employed seven preinstructed assistants and a genuine subject in a line judgment task. On two-thirds of the judgments, the seven assistants purposely reported aloud an obviously incorrect estimate; thus the subject, seated eighth, faced unanimous pressure to conform by making a similarly incorrect response. On approximately one-third of such judgments, he yielded to the group; like the others, he would estimate a 5-inch line as 4 inches. But when Asch disturbed the unanimity by having one of his seven assistants give the

---

[6] Similar analyses of South African student data indicate that the social adjustment function may also be of unusual importance in the anti-African attitudes of the English in the Union (Pettigrew, 1958, 1960).

correct response, the subjects yielded only a tenth, rather than a third, of the time. Once unanimity no longer existed, even when there was only one supporting colleague, the subject could better withstand the pressure of the majority to conform. To carry through the analogy to today's crisis in the South, obvious 5-inch lines are being widely described as 4 inches. Many Southerners, faced with what appears to be solid unanimity, submit to the distortion. But when even one respected source—a minister, a newspaper editor, even a college professor—conspicuously breaks the unanimity, *perhaps* a dramatic modification is achieved in the private opinions of many conforming Southerners. Only an empirical test can show if such a direct analogy is warranted.

Consider, too, the relevance of recent theoretical distinctions. Kelman (1958, 1961), for example, has clarified the concept of conformity by pointing out that three separate processes are involved: *compliance, identification,* and *internalization.* Compliance exists when an individual accepts influence not because he believes in it, but because he hopes to achieve a favorable reaction from an agent who maintains surveillance over him. Identification exists when an individual accepts influence because he wants to establish or maintain a satisfying relationship with another person or group. The third process, internalization, exists when an individual accepts influence because the content of the behavior itself is satisfying; unlike the other types of conformity, internalized behavior will be performed without the surveillance of the agent or a salient relationship with the agent. It is with this third process that Kelman's ideas overlap with authoritarian theory.

We have all witnessed illustrations of each of these processes in the acceptance by Southerners of the region's racial norms. The "Uncle Tom" Negro is an example of a compliant Southerner; another example is furnished by the white man who treats Negroes as equals only when not under the surveillance of other whites. Identification is best seen in white Southerners whose resistance to racial integration enables them to be a part of what they erroneously imagine to be Confederate tradition. Such identifiers are frequently upwardly mobile people who are still assimilating to urban society; they strive for social status by identifying with the hallowed symbols and shibboleths of the South's past. Southerners who have internalized the white supremacy dictates of the culture are the real racists who use the issue to gain political office, to attract resistance group membership fees, or to meet personality needs. Southerners with such contrasting bases for their racial attitudes should react very differently toward desegregation. For instance, compliant whites can be expected to accept desegregation more readily than those who have internalized segregationist norms.

On the basis of this discussion of conformity, I would like to propose a new concept: *the latent liberal.* This is not to be confused with the cherished southern notion of the "moderate"; the ambiguous term "moderate" is presently used to describe everything from an integrationist who wants to be socially accepted to a racist who wants to be polite. Rather, the latent liberal refers to the Southerner who is neither anti-Semitic nor authoritarian but whose conformity habits and needs cause him to be strongly anti-Negro. Through the processes of compliance and identification, the latent liberal continues to behave in a discriminatory fashion toward Negroes even though such behavior conflicts with his basically tolerant personality. He is at the present time *il*liberal on race, but he has the personality potentiality of becoming liberal once the norms of the culture change. Indeed, as the already unleashed economic, legal, political, and social forces restructure the South's racial norms, the latent liberal's attitudes about Negroes will continue to change. Previously cited research suggests that there are today an abundance of white Southerners who meet this latent liberal description; collectively, they will reflect on the individual level the vast societal changes now taking place in the South.

Some suggested directions for future psychological research on desegregation [7]

We are in serious need of research on the Negro, both in the North and in the South. Most psychological research in this area was conducted during the 1930s and directed at testing racists' claims of Negro inferiority. But the most sweeping advances in American Negro history have been made in the past generation, requiring a fresh new look—particularly at the Negro personality.

Two aspects of this research make it complex and difficult. In the first place, the race of the interviewer is a complicating and not as yet fully understood factor. Further methodological study is needed on this point. Moreover, special problems of control are inherent in this research. Not only are there some relatively unique variables that must be considered (e.g., migration history, differential experience with the white community, etc.), but such simple factors as education are not easy to control. For instance, has the average graduate of a southern rural high school for Negroes received an education equal to the average graduate of such a school for whites? No, in spite of the South's belated efforts to live up to separate-but-equal education,

[7] For other suggestions, see the important analysis of desegregation by Cook (1957).

available school data indicate that the graduates have probably not received equivalent educations. Yet some recent research on Negro personality has been based on the assumption that Negro and white education in the South are equivalent (e.g., Smith & Prothro, 1957).

Fortunately, the Institute for Research in the Social Sciences at the University of North Carolina has embarked on a large study of many of these content and methodological problems. It is to be hoped that their work will stimulate other efforts.

Some of the most valuable psychological data now available on desegregation have been collected by public opinion polls. But typically these data have been gathered without any conceptual framework to guide their coverage and direction.

For example, one of the more interesting poll findings is that a majority of white Southerners realize that racial desegregation of public facilities is inevitable even though about six out of seven strongly oppose the process (Hyman & Sheatsley, 1956). The psychological implications of this result are so extensive that we would like to know more. Do the respondents who oppose desegregation but accept its inevitability have other characteristics of latent liberals? Are these respondents more often found outside of the Black Belt? Typically, we cannot answer such questions from present poll data; we need to build into the desegregation polls broader coverage and more theoretical direction.

The third direction that psychological research in desegregation could usefully take concerns measurement. Save for the partly standardized F Scale, we still lack widely used, standardized field measures of the chief variables in this realm. Such instruments are necessary both for comparability of results and for stimulation of research; witness the invigorating effects on research of the F Scale, the Minnesota Multiphasic Inventory, and the need achievement scoring scheme. Mention of McClelland's need achievement scoring scheme should remind us, too, that projective and other indirect techniques might answer many of these measurement requirements—especially for such sensitive and subtle variables as conformity needs.

Finally, the definitive interdisciplinary case study of desegregation has yet to be started. Properly buttressed by the necessary foundation aid, such a study should involve comparisons before, during, and after desegregation of a wide variety of communities. The interdisciplinary nature of such an undertaking is stressed because desegregation is a peculiarly complex process demanding a broad range of complementary approaches.

Any extensive case project must sample three separate time periods: before a legal ruling or similar happening has alerted the community to imminent desegregation, during the height of the desegregating process, and after several years of accommodation. Without this longitudinal view, desegregation as a dynamic, ongoing process cannot be understood. This time perspective, for instance, would enable us to interpret the fact that an overwhelming majority of Oklahoma whites in a 1954 poll sternly objected to mixed schools, but within a few years has accepted without serious incident integrated education throughout most of the state (Jones, 1957).

A carefully selected range of communities is required to test for differences in the process according to the characteristics of the area. Recent demographic analyses and predictions of the South's school desegregation pattern (Ogburn & Grigg, 1956; Pettigrew, 1957; Pettigrew & Campbell, 1960) could help in making this selection of communities. Comparable data gathered in such a selected variety of locations would allow us to pinpoint precisely the aspects of desegregation unique to, say, a Piedmont city, as opposed to a Black Belt town.

Compare the potential value of such a broad research effort with the limited case studies that have been possible so far. Low budget reports of only one community are the rule; many of them are theses or seminar projects, some remain on the descriptive level, all but a few sample only one time period, and there is almost no comparability of instruments and approach. A comprehensive case project is obviously long overdue.

This has been an appeal for a vigorous empirical look at southern race relations. Despite segregationists' claims to the contrary, social psychological contributions to desegregation research have been relatively meager. There are, however, grounds for hoping that this situation will be partly corrected in the near future—particularly if psychologists get busy.

Foundations appear to be re-evaluating their previous reluctance to support such research. And we can re-evaluate our own resignation in the face of barriers to conduct investigations in this area; the tragedy of Little Rock has had a salutary effect on many influential Southerners in this respect.

Recognition of the importance of the situation in interracial behavior and the full exploitation of the attitude concept can remove inadequacies in the traditional psychological approach to the study of race. In this connection, an extended case for considering conformity as crucial in the Negro attitudes of white Southerners was presented and a new concept—the latent liberal —introduced. One final implication of this latent liberal concept should be mentioned. Some cynics have argued that successful racial desegregation in the South will require an importation of tens of thousands of psychotherapists and therapy for millions of bigoted Southerners. Fortunately for desegregation, psychotherapists, and Southerners, this will not be necessary; a thorough repatterning of southern interracial behavior will be sufficient therapy in itself.

References

Adorno, T. W., Frenkel-Brunswik, Else, Levinson, D. J., and Sanford, N. *The authoritarian personality*. New York: Harper, 1950.

Allport, G. W. *The nature of prejudice*. Cambridge, Mass.: Addison-Wesley, 1954.

Asch, S. E. Effects of group pressure upon the modification and distortion of judgments. In H. Guetzkow (Ed.), *Groups, leadership and men*. Pittsburgh: Carnegie, 1951.

Biesanz, J., and Smith, L. M. Race relations of Panama and the Canal Zone. *Amer. J. Sociol.*, 1951, 57, 7–14.

Clark, K. B. Desegregation: An appraisal of the evidence. *J. soc. Issues*, 1953, 9, 1–76.

Cook, S. W. Desegregation: A psychological analysis. *Amer. Psychologist*, 1957, 12, 1–13.

Crutchfield, R. S. Conformity and character. *Amer. Psychologist*, 1955, 10, 191–198.

Dabney, V. The violence at Little Rock. *Richmond Times-Dispatch*, 1957, 105, September 24, 14.

Davis, A., Gardner, B., and Gardner, Mary. *Deep South*. Chicago: Univer. Chicago Press, 1941.

Dollard, J. *Caste and class in a southern town*. New Haven: Yale Univer. Press, 1937.

Festinger, L. An analysis of compliant behavior. In M. Sherif and M. O. Wilson (Eds.), *Group relations at the crossroads*. New York: Harper, 1953.

Festinger, L. *A theory of cognitive dissonance*. Evanston, Ill.: Row, Peterson, 1957.

Harding, J., and Hogrefe, R. Attitudes of white department store employees toward Negro co-workers. *J. soc. Issues*, 1952, 8, 18–28.

Hartley, E. L. *Problems in prejudice*. New York: King's Crown, 1946.

Hyman, H. H., and Sheatsley, P. B. Attitudes toward desegregation. *Sci. Amer.*, 1956, 195, 35–39.

Jones, E. City limits. In D. Shoemaker (Ed.), *With all deliberate speed*. New York: Harper, 1957.

Kelman, H. C. Compliance, identification, and internalization: Three processes of attitude change. *J. conflict Resolut.*, 1958, 2, 51–60.

Kelman, H. C. *Social influence and personal belief*. New York: Wiley, 1961.

Killian, L. W. Southern white laborers in Chicago's West Side. Unpublished doctoral dissertation, University of Chicago, 1949.

Knapp, R. H. A psychology of rumor. *Publ. opin. Quart.*, 1944, 8, 22–37.

Logan, R. W. The United States Supreme Court and the segregation issue. *Ann. Amer. Acad. Pol. Soc. Sci.*, 1956, 304, 10–16.

Milton, O. Presidential choice and performance on a scale of authoritarianism. *Amer. Psychologist*, 1952, 7, 597–598.

Minard, R. D. Race relations in the Pocahontas coal field. *J. soc. Issues*, 1952, 8, 29–44.

Ogburn, W. F., and Grigg, C. M. Factors related to the Virginia vote on segregation. *Soc. Forces*, 1956, 34, 301–308.

Pettigrew, T. F. Demographic correlates of border-state desegregation. *Amer. sociol. Rev.*, 1957, 22, 683–689.

Pettigrew, T. F. Personality and sociocultural factors in intergroup attitudes: A cross-national comparison. *J. conflict Resolut.*, 1958, 2, 29–42.

Pettigrew, T. F. Regional differences in anti-Negro prejudice. *J. abnorm. soc. Psychol.*, 1959, 59, 28–36.

Pettigrew, T. F. Social distance attitudes of South African students. *Soc. Forces*, 1960, 38, 246–253.

Pettigrew, T. F., and Campbell, E. Q. Faubus and segregation: An analysis of Arkansas voting. *Publ. opin. Quart.*, 1960, 24, 436–447.

Prothro, E. T. Ethnocentrism and anti-Negro attitudes in the deep South. *J. abnorm. soc. Psychol.*, 1952, 47, 105–108.

Rabb, E., and Lipset, S. M. *Prejudice and society*. New York: Anti-Defamation League of B'nai B'rith, 1959.

Reitzes, D. C. The role of organizational structures: Union versus neighborhood in a tension situation. *J. soc. Issues*, 1953, 9, 37–44.

Roper, E. United States anti-Semites. *Fortune*, 1946, 33, 257–260.

Roper, E. United States anti-Semites. *Fortune*, 1947, 36, 5–10.

Rose, A. M. Intergroup relations vs. prejudice: Pertinent theory for the study of social change. *Soc. Probl.*, 1956, 4, 173–176.

Smith, C. U., and Prothro, J. W. Ethnic differences in authoritarian personality. *Soc. Forces*, 1957, 35, 334–338.

Smith, M. B., Bruner, J. S., and White, R. W. *Opinion and personality*. New York: Wiley, 1956.

Stouffer, S. A., Suchman, E. A., DeVinney, L. C., Star, Shirley A., Williams, R. M., Jr. *Studies in social psychology in World War II*. Vol. 1. *The American soldier: Adjustment during army life*. Princeton: Princeton Univer. Press, 1949.

Thibaut, J. W., and Kelley, H. H. *The social psychology of groups*. New York: Wiley, 1959.

Zinn, H. A fate worse than integration. *Harper's*, 1959, 219, August, 53–56.

CHAPTER EIGHTEEN

Vocational adjustment

Engineering for human use

Just as psychology itself has many fields, the field of industrial psychology has many subdivisions. Many industrial psychologists are personnel psychologists, concerned with the placement of people in industry. Personnel psychologists have usually been trained most thoroughly in the area of psychometrics (psychological testing). Another group, the human engineers, applied experimental psychologists, has grown rapidly as the complexity of the devices operated by man has increased. Human engineers are usually trained most thoroughly in experimental psychology. With his knowledge of human sensory and motor capacities, the experimental psychologist is uniquely able to help in design problems of complex equipment.

Points to guide your study

1. What are some of the human-engineering problems which would be involved in the design of an electric stove?

2. What advantages, if any, does a human operator have over an automatic computer-like operator?

52. AUTOMATION, HUMAN ENGINEERING, AND PSYCHOLOGY

Neil D. Warren, University of Southern California*

Ambrose Bierce was once called the wickedest man in San Francisco. This probably has little to do with the fact that he wrote a story about a man who invented a mechanical chess player (1). The inventor played game after game against his invention. So marvelous was the machine, however, that it never lost a game. The inventor tried every legal scheme he knew, but was never able to win. Finally, in desperation, he cheated enough to gain a victory over the machine—which became so incensed over this event that it turned on its inventor and throttled him.

This fable has allegorical significance, if we may believe dire predictions of the machine's triumph over man, which some people have made during recent months. Leading industrial-

* Address of the President of the Western Psychological Association at the meetings of the American Psychological Association in San Francisco, September 3, 1955.

N. D. Warren. Automation, human engineering and psychology. *Amer. Psychologist,* 1956, 11, 531–536. Copyright 1956 by the American Psychological Association. Reprinted here with permission from the author and the American Psychological Association.

ists have found it desirable to attempt to calm fears of the consequences of automation; that is, of automatically controlled industry. Threats of unemployment, overproduction, social dislocations, and so on, have been voiced and debated. The age of automation presents a challenge for the industrial psychologist. At the same time, it clearly presents problems of interest to other areas of psychology besides industrial—social, counseling, and experimental among them. And if the machines become much more human-like, they may require the services of the clinician.

Automation—simply defined as the replacement of man by machine or the use of machines to control machines—is as old as machines themselves. For centuries the machine has been nibbling at the responsibilities—and privileges—of man, with the use of such devices as governors, thermostats, auto-pilots and other servo-controls. Now, with the advent of the continuous-process factory the machine is taking large parts of the areas of human responsibility which remain. To quote Drucker (3):

The Automation Revolution is here, and it is proceeding at high speed. But it will be many years before it permeates the entire economy. Most businesses will not convert to automation overnight but will go at it piecemeal, which will not be easy. . . . But the mental strain will be less. Fewer people will have to "relearn" fewer things; and they will have more time to do it in. While it is a major revolution, automation is therefore not likely to be dramatic; there will be no point when one can say: "This is the year when the American economy went into automation."

But only the speed of automation is uncertain. There can be little doubt that the direction of our progress is toward it. There can be little doubt that it means a tremendous upgrading of the labor force in terms of skill, employment security, standard of living, and opportunity.

How far will this change go? In a previous consideration of this question (9), I was forced to the somewhat reluctant conclusion that there is no limit to the ingenuity of the inventor. It is unjustified complacency to believe that memory, reasoning, and judgment can never be the characteristics of machines—indeed they already exist.

In Volume I of the *American Journal of Psychology*, C. S. Pierce (7) commented that the logical machine is inherently "destitute of all originality, all initiative. It cannot find its own problems." In 1955, I doubt that anyone can be sure that even this is not imminent. Pierce made this further observation: This lack of initiative "however, is no defect in a machine; we do not want it to do its own business, but ours. We no more want an original machine than a housebuilder would want an original journeyman, or an American board of college trustees would hire an original professor." In this comment lies a suggestion of the answer to the question of the ultimate goal of automation. The engineer will go just as far as society will permit. Ultimately society must decide where to call a halt to the development of the machine.

We can expect industry to make use of automatic controls whenever it is economically advantageous to do so. In most industries this will mean considerable, but not complete, automation very soon. In others almost complete automation will be developed rapidly. I recently visited a large factory in which a new unit was being built. In it, I was told, the entire manufacturing process from the carloads of raw materials to the carload of finished product would be continuous and automatic. To some degree this is occurring throughout industry.

I wish to consider two of the many possible implications of this trend for the science and profession of psychology. First, there is increased need for both basic and applied research in the area of problem solving. Second, the application of information about human behavior to the design of man-machine systems is a rapidly expanding field. This is in the area often called human engineering.

Problem solving

Besides the socioeconomic problems which industry must face, automation is causing a rapid shift in emphasis from operation to maintenance. The more complex the machine, the more difficult it is to keep it working properly. If our mechanized society is not to be throttled by its own machines, if it is not to suffer the fate of Bierce's inventor, maintenance must be successful. This will require a shift in manpower from operation. In one factory, which is changing to automatic controls, the ratio of maintenance personnel to operators has been approximately 1 to 5. It is now nearer 1 to 3 and it is expected to reach 1 to 1 in the near future. It is probable that in a completely automatic factory the proportion of maintenance effort would greatly exceed that of operation. In one kind of military equipment, which is extremely complex, it is now estimated that for each hour of operation 40 man-hours of maintenance are required.

What is the relation of this trend to problem solving? The key ability of the mechanic who maintains complex machinery is not skill in repair or replacement of parts, but ability to determine what part is to be repaired or replaced. Anyone can replace a tube in a radio or television set. The skill required to replace other parts is not very great—but it takes something of an expert to determine which tube, capacitor, resistor, or what-not is defective. This skill in diagnosing the cause of a malfunction is like the diagnostic skill of the physician. For very complex machines the problem for the maintenance man is scarcely less difficult than that of the physician. In the machine, the process of diagnosis is called trouble shooting. In certain situations trouble-shooting experts are employed. Their job is diagnosis only and repair is left to other mechanics.

Trouble shooting is a form of problem solving, and the principles which apply to other kinds of problem solving will apply as well to it. The procedures may range from trial-and-error to logic.

It is of interest to note that there has been a considerable increase in study of the problem-solving process in the last five years. As evidence of this, the number of references in the *Psychological Abstracts* dealing with human problem solving has greatly increased on both absolute and relative bases. That this is in part due to a recognition of the importance of the subject for maintenance of machines is indicated by the fact that a considerable amount of the research reported has been sponsored by the Air Force and the Navy. Also, in the 1954 *Abstracts* there appears, for the first time, a number of references specifically to the topic of trouble shooting. These will not be the last, since final answers to the questions of how to select, train, and use trouble-shooting experts are still to be secured. The need becomes greater daily. The production of automobiles, airplanes, home appliances, factory equipment, and so on, of ever-increasing complexity may soon overload our capacity to keep these machines operating.

As one example of research in this area, I may describe briefly a study we have undertaken under contract with the Air Force.[1] The purpose of the project has been to develop a procedure for training mechanics to do a better job of trouble shooting for a highly complex piece of electronic equipment.

The hypotheses were developed that there is a limited number of general principles in logical trouble shooting and that these principles can be learned as abstractions unrelated to any specific device.

The procedure involved recording complete protocols of the diagnostic steps of experts together with their verbalized reasons for each step. This was followed by an analysis of each protocol and a record of each abstracted principle in symbolic form. With an adequate sample of such protocols from a number of different experts, it appeared possible to establish a complete list of principles.

The learnability of such principles is to be tested by the use of a specially devised trainer in which each general principle can be demonstrated with any desired degree of complexity. The first year of effort has verified our first hypothesis: that there are general trouble-shooting principles; and the next year will establish whether or not they can be taught using the trainer and procedures devised for that purpose.

Human engineering

The term "human engineering" is obnoxious to some members of the engineering profession. For that reason I have some reluctance to use it. However, it appears in the *Engineering Index* and is made clear in the *Industrial Arts Index* as well as in many articles and publications, so I believe it is here to stay. However, the *Industrial Arts Index* makes it clear that the term is a designation of a topic—and not of a profession. I think it can be demonstrated that this distinction is a valid one at present although it may not continue to be so.

Broadly defined, human engineering is a phase of engineering which applies knowledge of human factors to design of machines—or of products. It is broader than, and includes, the

fields of engineering psychology, biomechanics, applied experimental psychology, and others.

The first use of the term "human engineering" was as a title for processes of selection and placement of personnel in industry, and of the choice of a vocation for an individual. In industry this was a process of adapting man to the machine. Psychologists have worked in this area for many years.

When machines are relatively simple, selection and training achieve the purpose of supplying adequate operators. As machines become increasingly complex and the demands upon the operator's skill and knowledge become greater, a point is reached where selection and training can no longer meet the needs.

This point has already been reached in some areas. A notable example is that of aviation. The complex pattern of instruments and controls in modern airplanes taxes the capacities of even the most expert airmen. Poorly designed instruments produce errors and confusion. The necessity of integrating the readings of several instruments to determine a single course of action dangerously delays the pilot's responses. The unsatisfactory design and location of controls result in mistakes which may be disastrous.

The solution requires designing the man-machine system in such a way as to take full advantage of man's assets and to avoid imposing on his limitations.

Another term of equal breadth which is intended to cover much of the area defined by human engineering is "ergonomics"—the study of man at work. One author has pointed out that ergonomics "is concerned with the study of human behavior in response to external stress, with particular reference to the stress-strain problems of man at work" (5). Changes in design and in work methods can be expected to result from such study.

It is well to point out that consideration of human factors in design is not new—nor were professional psychologists pioneers in the field. It may be said, in all seriousness, that primitive man was a human engineer when he shaped the handle of his ax or club to fit his hand. Certainly engineering designers have taken the human factor into account to some degree for centuries. Even in the application of the sciences of physiology and psychology to design, engineers have pioneered, as Hatch has pointed out, "ahead of the specialists in those fields."

On the other hand, psychologists have not been entirely unaware of the possible applications of their science to such practical problems. In Volume II of the *American Journal of Psychology*, the first article is by E. C. Sanford, and is entitled "Personal Equation" (8). In it is told the well-known incident which led to research on individual differences in reaction time. It is

---

[1] Contract AF 18(600)–1206.

of interest that on page 652 of the same volume there is a report of a device to take into account human limitations in the observation of sudden phenomena.

Primarily as a result of the pressures of military needs during and following World War II, psychologists and others have become increasingly involved in human engineering. Some psychologists have adopted the title of "human engineer" to describe their own function. Seldom, however, can one individual—or one profession—provide the human factors knowledge required by the designer.

Consider, for example, this list of human factor problems encountered in one aircraft factory. This is a sample. Seventy-two were listed last spring and undoubtedly more have been added:

What is a comfortable finger pressure for knobs?

How much force should be required for a wheel control?

What is the volume occupied by a man?

What are the hourly rates of wash-water use?

What are the angles of vision from a prone position?

How far away can a pilot see another airplane?

What is the weight of the human head and brain?

What should be the height of a "no smoking" sign?

What are the effects of drugs on the human body in flight?

How much work space is required for a bartender in a cocktail lounge? And so on.

Clearly, cooperative effort is called for. As in other areas, the psychologist can serve most effectively as part of a team in which each expert contributes his own special knowledge and skill to the solution of common problems. The trend in industry appears to be in this direction. Although the composition and organization of the team vary widely, there is usually a position for the psychologist.

Brigadier General Don Flickinger, of the Air Force's Research and Development Command, has described a five-man "human factors team" (4). The team captain is a flight surgeon, a specialist in aviation medicine. The other members are an anthropologist, a biophysicist, a physiologist, and a psychologist. The responsibilities of the psychologist include work-space layout, performance criteria, training requirements, component design and mission activities.

Teams of somewhat this make-up have been established in several aircraft factories and there is a trend extending to other industries as well. To consider and to evaluate this trend, it has been proposed that the American Society of Mechanical Engineers establish a working committee (5), including engineers representing industrial engineering, time-and-motion study, machine tool design, plant layout and building design, and health and safety engineering, together with invited specialists in anatomy, physical anthropology, biomechanics, applied physiology, and applied psychology. This is another indication that psychologists will be part of the team approach to design problems.

What can the science and profession of psychology contribute to this important field?

General Flickinger has pointed out that, while there is no lack of interest in or appreciation of human factors, there are three reasons why they have not been fully taken into consideration. First, "lack of fundamental data in the human factors field" in a form usable by the engineers. As regards the first part of this "lack," psychologists can point to the considerable body of fundamental data about human behavior. The experimental psychologists are investigating many specific problems and have formulated a few general principles which are pertinent to the human engineering field. The *Handbook of Human Engineering Data* (6) first published in 1949 by the Tufts College Institute for Applied Experimental Psychology is, in its latest edition, a very imposing volume. Many psychologists stand ready to tell the designer the facts of psychology.

Are these data in a form usable by engineers? Very probably they are not. We are accused of generalities. Industrialists and engineers distrust generalities. The data most frequently are derived from the aseptic conditions of the laboratory and are not "practical." Or, perhaps, we are not able to convey to the practical designer the significance of our findings.

A research engineer for an aircraft factory recently put it this way: When the design engineer realized that he was building aircraft which taxed the limitations of the human, he turned to those specialists, physiologists and psychologists, whom he assumed could tell him what he must do to alleviate these conditions. In all fairness, he admits they probably did, but he couldn't understand a single word of it.

I am reminded of Robert O. Carlson's comment (2) about similar criticism from another applied area. He says,

Of course we . . . recognize that these criticisms are pure nonsense. Ask any (psychologist) and he may point out that such accusations are undoubtedly the manifestation of a fundamentally dichotomous role-status position in which the out-group . . . project their ambivalent affectual status vis-à-vis their significant-other group, . . . in such a manner so that their primordial unconscious aggression stemming from a latent role identification with an authority symbol, perhaps the outgrowth of a suppressed Oedipus complex, takes the form of a semantic-oriented aggressive syndrome against superordinate members of a prestige structure which seems to threaten their affect and basic ego constellation.

Carlson thinks such jargon is on its way out, and perhaps it doesn't exist in the engineering psychology field—but I'm not so sure. Psychologists often seem to find it necessary to express even simple ideas in words of many syllables. At one meeting I listened to a paper in which it was reported that the psychologist working as human engineer had caused to be installed—I quote—"a detachable inclement weather protective device." This, I suspect, bore considerable resemblance to an umbrella.

This problem is being worked on. *The Human Engineering Guide to Equipment Design* being prepared by a joint committee of the military services will be practical, direct, and understandable, even to a nonpsychologist. And if all the textbooks in engineering psychology, and human engineering, which are being written, are as good as their authors are capable of making them, there will soon be no room for the engineers to complain.

General Flickinger's second suggestion is that there is need for "a comprehensive plan for data collection, accumulation, validation, and dissemination to working groups, both scientists and engineers" (4).

There have been many serious attempts to plan research in the human factors area. Anyone who begins trying to apply present knowledge to the man-machine problem will recognize the large, and often crucial areas, in which information is inadequate. Many psychologists have expressed disdain for the applied or "program" research. However, it is here that the opportunity is greatest; and this is the area in which the industrial psychologist can star on the human engineering team. Validation of procedures, evaluation of devices, and establishment of norms are tasks for which he is especially prepared. Moreover, just as industrialists have learned that basic research in the physical sciences is profitable, they will inevitably find it desirable to support basic research in psychology and other biological and social sciences. The Bell Telephone Laboratories has provided an example of this effort for many years.

The third lack is that of "training programs directed toward . . . greater integration of . . . knowledge and skills required by life (scientists) and engineering scientists alike which would prepare them for work in this highly complex field . . ." (4).

What is the situation with regard to courses designed to meet this need? Some part of the

answer can be found in the results of a questionnaire survey of courses in the area of human factors in engineering design. The questionnaire was brief and simple but, even so, the number of responses was amazingly large and seems to indicate a considerable amount of interest in this field. The questions were addressed to 116 departments of industrial or mechanical engineering in the list accredited by the Engineers' Council for Professional Development. We received 104 replies.

Of the 104 answers, 67 indicated that no course in the area of human factors in design was offered.

Sixteen other departments reported that they did not have a course specifically covering the topic but that it was treated in part in other existing courses, such as *Motion and Time Study, Industrial Psychology, Industrial Management, Engineering Design,* etc. It is quite probable that many of the 67 reporting "No course" have similar partial coverage but did not report it since this question was not specifically asked.

The remaining 20 departments have one or more courses in the area. The titles are varied. The following course titles were included: *Human Element in Engineering, Human Factors in Engineering, Human Factors in Equipment Design, Psychological Design Factors, Creative Engineering, Men and Machines, Engineering Psychology, Human Engineering, Methods and Standards, Applied Experimental Psychology, Perceptual and Motor Skills, Psychology of Human Relations, Industrial Psychology, Introduction to Personnel and Industrial Psychology, Personnel and Industrial Efficiency, Industrial Leadership, Personnel Administration, Engineering Administration, Environmental Biotechnology, Machine and Systems Biotechnology.*

In 11 institutions the courses are offered in the Department of Psychology; 5 in Industrial Engineering; 2 in Mechanical Engineering; 1 in Engineering Administration; and 1 in the Department of Engineering.

In one instance the instructor for the course was trained in engineering alone. In ten cases he was trained in psychology only; in eight cases his training was in both engineering and psychology; and at one institution where several courses were offered the reply indicated training in physiology, psychology and mathematics.

At the University of Southern California we offer two courses: *Human Factors in Engineering,* a course in the College of Engineering taught by Dr. Harry Wolbers; and *Human Factors in Aircraft Design,* taught by Dr. William Grings. The latter is part of our program in Aviation Safety.

Virtually all of the students enrolled in these classes were engineers who hoped to find answers to problems they encountered in their daily work. In their comments about the courses, nearly all have expressed the need for more and more "practical" information.

Obviously, a course or two will not make human factors experts of these engineers. Perhaps they help to meet the need expressed by Professor T. F. Hatch, of the American Society of Mechanical Engineers, that engineers "must acquire a deeper understanding of man" which they must "incorporate into their regular thinking and practice" (5).

If the psychologist is to make on effective contribution to the human engineering field he must acquire a deeper understanding of the machine to incorporate into his thinking and practice. Courses in psychology for engineers and in engineering for psychologists are essential, if only to bridge the semantic chasm between the two disciplines.

At a more fundamental level, an interesting trend is developed which academic psychology must note. This is a combination of engineering training, through the undergraduate degree, and of graduate work in psychology through the PhD degree. In this trend or in some modification of it there may develop a truly new professional who may legitimately call himself a human engineer. At the University of Southern California we have already given one PhD with this combination of backgrounds, and there are five other students at various levels of graduate work in the Psychology Department. Other departments are experiencing the same trend. Since job opportunities in this field are great we may expect the pressure to increase. We must give serious consideration to the kind of program.

The Age of Automation confronts not only the industrial psychologist but the entire profession with changes in research and training. It will undoubtedly add to the trend toward an increasing proportion of applied psychologists in the APA. But the experimental psychologist, if he cares, can be assured of the usefulness of his research in the areas of problem solving and learning, of perception, of motor skills, or for that matter of any other aspect of human behavior. Moreover, the experimental psychologist is discovering a fruitful approach to an understanding of human behavior as a result of examination of the behavior of machines.

Let the engineer learn more about man—and the psychologist more about the machine. Together, with other human factor experts, they will help industry to supply all of us products of greater efficiency, comfort and safety. We can expect greater value from the things we look at, manipulate, sit on, ride in, work with, or play with. More and more they will be designed to fit us. More and more they will reflect an acceptance of the statement of the philosopher Protagoras 24 centuries ago that "man is the measure of all things."

References

1. Bierce, A. *Moxon's Master*.
2. Carlson, R. O. How can the social sciences meet the needs of advertisers? *Printer's Ink*, 1953, **242**, 44–56.
3. Drucker, P. F. The promise of automation—America's next twenty years. *Harper's Mag.*, 1955, **210**, 41–47.
4. Flickinger, D. Planning by human factor teams. *J. Aviat. Med.*, 1955, **26**, 2–12.
5. Hatch, T. F. Proposed program in ergonomics. *Mech. Engng.*, 1955, **77**, 394–395.
6. Institute for Applied Experimental Psychology. *Handbook of human engineering data.* Medford, Mass.: Tufts College, 1952.
7. Pierce, C. S. Logical machines. *Amer. J. Psychol.*, 1887, **1**, 165–170.
8. Sanford, E. C. Personal equation. *Amer. J. Psychol.*, 1889, **2**, 3–38.
9. Warren, N. D. Nontransferable functions. *Frontiers of man-controlled flight*. Institute of Transportation and Traffic Engineering, Univ. of California, Los Angeles, 1953.

CHAPTER NINETEEN

Nervous system and internal environment

THE INTERNAL ENVIRONMENT

This article describes both a technique for the investigation of nervous-system functioning—the injection of chemical substances directly into the brain—and a set of findings about one site of action of hormones. Hormones must eventually act upon the nervous or muscular systems if their action is to be reflected in behavior. In this case the site of action seems to be the hypothalamus (the preoptic areas, see your text). This role of the hypothalamus will be considered more fully in the next chapter when drives are discussed.

A point to guide your study

Glossary: Stereotaxic instrument—A device for the accurate location of spots within the skull. It works on a system of coordinates. Maps of animal brains, with coordinates of each structure, are available for reference. Placebo—An inert substance used as a control in pharmacological experiments. Testosterone—A male sex hormone. Notice that it produces maternal behavior, as well as the appropriate sexual behavior, in this experiment.

53. MATERNAL AND SEXUAL BEHAVIOR INDUCED BY INTRACRANIAL CHEMICAL STIMULATION

Alan E. Fisher, University of Pittsburgh*

A technique permitting chemical or electric stimulation, or both, of restricted brain areas in unanesthetized rats, and electroencephalographic (EEG) recording from these areas, has been developed and found to be of value (1).

Implants are prepared as follows. Two Tygon-insulated copper or silver wires (0.1 mm in diameter) are baked along the outside of No. 22 hypodermic tubing extending from 2 to 9 mm below the base of a plastic holder (2). The wires lead from contact points on the holder and terminate at opposite sides of the end of the shaft as a bipolar stimulating-and-recording electrode. The implant shaft is permanently inserted in the brain while the anesthetized rat is held in a

* A. E. Fisher. Maternal and Sexual Behavior Induced by Intracranial Chemical Stimulation. *Science*, 1956, **124**, 228–229. Reprinted here with permission from the author and the American Association for the Advancement of Science.

sterotaxic instrument. Four holes in the base of the holder permit rigid attachment to the skull with jeweler's screws.

Two or more days later, rats are placed in 3- by 3- by 2.5-ft boxes for stimulation testing. A small clip connects the implant to light overhead leads from a 0- to 12-v, 60 cy/sec stimulator, or to an EEG machine. The clip also contains a No. 30 metal cannula that penetrates the implant shaft to the depth of the electrode tips or lower. Seven feet of PE 10 polyethylene tubing (0.024 in. in diameter) leads from the cannula to a microsyringe which can release a minimum of 0.0001 cm³ of solution into the brain. All overhead leads are intertwined and spring-mounted, permitting repeated, controlled stimulation of a freely moving animal. Behavioral tests with a series of external stimulus objects are given before, during, and after chemical stimulation, and placebo solutions and nonhormonal neural excitants are used for control brain injections during initial tests or retests.

The technique is first being used to test whether there are "primary drive centers" under hormonal influence or control (3). Thus far, maternal and sexual behavior have been elicited from separate brain loci in a series of males during stimulation with sodium testosterone sulfate in 0.09-percent saline, and, subject to verification, a mixture of a pure salt of estrone and a suspension of progesterone has induced heat behavior in two females (4). Maternal behavior elicited during chemical stimulation includes nest building and a persistent retrieving and grooming of litters of young. All aspects of mating behavior have been induced or accentuated. Attendant high-drive states are suggested by an exaggerated speed, compulsiveness, and frequency of all overt responses during positive test periods.

Although individual animals respond positively for up to 4 test days, duplication of effect from animal to animal has imposed difficult problems. Of 130 male operates tested with the testosterone salt, five have shown complete maternal response, 14 have shown nesting behavior only, and six have shown exaggerated sexual response. Histological data suggest that locus of immediate action is a critical factor, with slight variation in placement leading to incomplete, confounded, or diffuse drive states, or negative results. Initial findings tentatively implicate the medial preoptic area in maternal behavior and the lateral preoptic area in sexual behavior.

A variety of effects have been noted during testosterone stimulation at adjacent loci. Those seen in five or more cases include respiratory changes, diffuse hyperactivation, long-lasting exploratory-like behavior, repetitive localized muscular response, digging, leaping, and seizures.

The following list includes other significant points of departure from chemical- or electric-stimulation data reported in the literature. Since positive test responses completely transcend control behavioral data, two single cases of possible theoretical significance are also briefly described.

1) Elicited behavior, whether specific or diffuse, commonly continues without decrement for more than 90 minutes following chemical stimulation.

2) An entire hierarchy of related responses can be brought to the threshold of activation, with adequate stimulus objects insuring integrated behavior.

3) A segment of a response hierarchy may occur alone. Excessive nest-building is often seen, and one aspect of the nesting pattern, "pick up paper and push under body," continued rapidly for more than 1 hour in three cases.

4) Specific behavior has occurred in the absence of appropriate external stimuli. One male continuously "retrieved" his tail when stimulated with testosterone and then repeatedly retrieved a female in heat. When pups and paper were supplied, however, the male built a nest and retrieved and groomed the young, neglecting the objects to which he previously reacted.

5) In one case, maternal and sexual drives were activated simultaneously. The testosterone-treated male reacted to stimuli related to each drive and to a degree never shown in control tests. Double activation was most convincingly illustrated when a female (not in heat) and newborn rat pups were presented. The male attempted copulation twice while a pup he was retrieving to a nest was still in his mouth. Shaft placement was adjacent to both areas previously implicated in sexual and maternal response.

All effects have followed injection of minute amounts of solution, containing from 0.003 to 0.05 mg of the testosterone salt. In this connection, it must be emphasized that the possibility remains that causative factors other than hormonal properties may be operating. Thus far, however, control testing with neural excitants, physiological saline, and electric stimulation has failed to produce or perpetuate these complex behavior patterns.

Initial EEG data are promising. Records from six testosterone-treated "maternal" or "nesting" males have shown single spiking lawfully spaced in a normal record rather than the general spiking seen after picrotoxin or metrazol injection. Selective chemical action seems probable. Also, testosterone-induced spiking occurs before, not during, elicited overt behavior. Correlation of EEG changes with brain stimulation and with elicited response presents technical problems but could become a powerful tool.

The early data suggest other implications and further applications.

1) A neurophysiological definition of drive seems within reach. The role of hormones in eliciting behavior should be clarified as well as the organization of neural circuits that mediate or integrate primary drives. Present data favor a "neural center" theory, but control studies are needed.

2) Responses analogous to symptoms of mental dysfunction often occur during chemical stimulation. These include "obsessive-compulsive acts," tics, diffuse excitation, and states of hypo- and hypersensitivity to sensory stimuli. Further work may establish tie-ins between shifts in chemical balance in the central nervous system and certain forms of mental dysfunction.

3) Males having no adult contact with females, young, or paper have responded to chemical stimulation with integrated maternal behavior on the first trial. The data are pertinent to the problem of whether innate, centrally organized

sensory-motor connections exist for complex response systems.

4) Testosterone has ostensibly elicited both sexual and maternal patterns. The findings may reflect multiple properties for the hormone. Limited progesterone-like activity has been proposed for the androgens by Selye, and progesterone has been linked to maternal response.

5) Chemical stimulation has elicited long-lasting, integrated behavior that was free of lapse or interference. The data strongly suggest selective chemical action within the central nervous system. Further work may demonstrate that differential sensitivity to specific physiological change by functionally organized areas of the nervous system is a basic principle of neural function.

In summary, integrated, long-lasting drive states have been induced by direct chemical stimulation of brain loci. Further work with techniques of this type could well lead to breakthroughs in the study of pharmaceutical action, brain organization and function, and the dynamics of behavior.

References and notes

1. I initiated the work as a public health post-doctoral fellow at McGill University with D. O. Hebb as sponsor. Work continues at the University of Wisconsin during the second fellowship year with H. F. Harlow as sponsor.
2. The Lucite holder is identical with that described by J. Olds and P. Milner, *J. comp. physiol. Psychol.* 47, 419 (1954).
3. For example, F. A. Beach, *Psychosomat. Med.* 4, 173 (1942).
4. Hormone salts supplied by Ayerst, McKenna, and Harrison, Ltd., Montreal, Canada.

M ETHODS OF STUDY

Special techniques are needed for the investigation of the correlations between the nervous system and behavior. There are anatomical techniques for the investigation of structure, and there are physiological techniques for the investigation of function. Most of the latter make use of the fact that communication in the nervous system is carried out by a combination of chemical and electrical events.

When using electrophysiological techniques it is possible either to record the electrical activity of the nervous system or to stimulate the system electrically. The electroencephalogram (EEG, "brain-wave" record) is a recording, taken from the scalp, of the complex electrical activity of the brain. Since the voltage changes of the brain are very small, special amplification and recording devices are needed. The EEG is typically recorded with electrodes attached to the scalp. At best, the recordings which are obtained are only roughly related to behavior.

While the relationship between the EEG and normal behavior, personality traits for instance, is not clear, the EEG is a fairly good indicator of some pathological conditions of the nervous system.

In animals it is possible to do more precise work with the recording electrodes on the surface of the cortex of the brain. The recording is then called an electrocorticogram (ECG). Recently such techniques have been used in the investigation of brain events in learning and arousal.

Points to guide your study

1. Be careful to learn the new terms.
2. Why is the EEG a very crude measure of the activity of the brain?

54. PHYSIOLOGICAL PSYCHOLOGY

*Clifford T. Morgan, University of Wisconsin, and
Eliot Stellar, University of Pennsylvania**

Electroencephalogram

This fifty-cent word is too long for most people to use, and it is commonly abbreviated EEG. Some prefer the term "brain waves." Each of these terms refers to the electrical beat, rhythms, or waves that can be recorded when electrodes are placed on the cortex or on the skull and wires are led from them through amplifiers to recording devices. Although investigators had reported electrical changes in the brain for many years, it was not until 1929 that Hans Berger came forth with the first thorough account of these brain rhythms. Since then hundreds of papers have been published on the subject. Today we can only bring out the high lights of the work, making the conclusions that seem most important and most securely founded.

The nature of brain waves

Brain waves are usually recorded on paper by an ink-writing or hot-point pen. The paper moves along at good speed so that one can see waves that occur as rapidly as fifty times a second. For many years it was the custom to look at records of brain waves and describe them much as we might describe different people. One record might be "spindles," another "saw-tooth," and so on. These types are still convenient to use, and we shall come to them in a minute. More recently, however, it has been possible to describe brain waves in terms of the spectrum of frequencies they contain, and it is better to take up this matter before talking about types of records.

Frequency spectra. Waves of any kind can be analyzed into a series of sine waves of stated amplitudes. This is Fourier's theorem, which we took up when we dealt with acoustics. It matters little whether the waves are sound waves, light waves, or electrical waves, the principle is the same. In Figure 1 you can see such an analysis for the waves of the brain (Gibbs). It extends from very slow waves of less than 1 cycle each second to rather fast waves of 50 to 60 cycles per second. There are some peaks at 1 to 2 cycles, 10 to 12 cycles, 20 to 25 cycles and

* C. T. Morgan and Eliot Stellar. *Physiological psychology* (2nd ed.). New York: McGraw-Hill, 1950, pp. 544–547; pp. 550–556. Copyright 1950 by the McGraw-Hill Book Company, Inc. Excerpts reprinted here with permission from the McGraw-Hill Book Company, Inc. Figures re-numbered. References to earlier chapters omitted.

45 to 50 cycles per second. The spectrum of brain waves is not always the same—it may vary considerably from time to time and from one individual to another—but the picture in Figure 1 gives a general idea of what it is like.

Having taken up the spectrum of brain waves, we can now talk more easily about types of records. In Figure 2 you see examples of six types of records often encountered—which is not all of them by any means. Each of these records brings out some special part of the spectrum displayed in Figure 1. Each type of record and each part of the spectrum received a name— sometimes several names—and we can now run down through the different parts of the spectrum indicating their significance.

Alpha waves. The biggest peak in Figure 1 is at 10 to 12 cycles per second. A record of waves consisting mostly of these frequencies is the one on line II of Figure 2. These waves are called *alpha waves*. They have always been thought of as the 'normal' waves of the human adult, for they are typical of normal people when they are awake and relaxed. When these alpha waves are missing in a record or are greatly decreased in number it is usually a sign of something—which we shall talk about a little later. It is hard to draw any sharp line for these alpha waves, and people have not agreed on where to draw it, but waves as low as 8 and as high as 13 are about the boundaries of alpha rhythms.

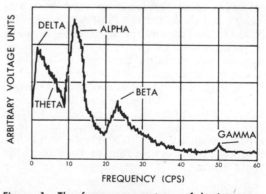

Figure 1 The frequency spectrum of brain waves. There are four peaks, which have been given Greek names: *alpha waves*, 10 cycles per second; *beta waves*, 20 to 25 cycles; *gamma waves*, 40 to 60 cycles; and *delta waves*, 1 to 2 cycles. Waves of 4 to 7 cycles per second, between the delta and alpha waves, are sometimes called *theta waves*.

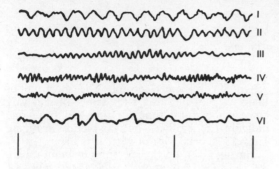

Figure 2 Six types of cerebral action potentials ("brain waves") recorded from the human skull. I, saw-tooth waves, seen commonly in young children and consisting of 4 to 7 cycles per second; II, Berger's alpha waves, usually between 9 and 11 cycles per second and seen in normal adults at rest (but not asleep); III, spindle waves, between 12 and 15 cycles per second and appearing in trains during sleep; IV, rapid rhythms of 20 to 24 cycles per second, only rarely observed; V, Berger's beta waves, 25 to 35 cycles per second, seen in normal waking adults; VI, large random waves of no particular frequency, characteristic of sound sleep. (From L. W. Crafts, T. C. Schneirla, E. E. Robinson, and R. W. Gilbert. Recent experiments in psychology. New York: McGraw-Hill, 1938. P. 195. By permission of the publishers.)

Beta waves. Berger, the great leader in brain-wave research, called all the waves from about 15 cycles per second upward "beta waves." Not too many people have followed this precedent. In fact, most investigators think of beta waves as those at the peak around 20 to 25 cycles in Figure 1 (see also line IV in Figure 2). Frequencies somewhat below that are often called "slow beta waves" and those above it "fast beta waves." In between the beta and the alpha waves are some frequencies between 12 and 15 cycles per second that we frequently see in people during sleep. These appear in trains, as you see them in line III of Figure 2, and are called "spindle waves." In the spectrum of Figure 1, on the right, is a small peak between 40 and 50 cycles. For the sake of a name these sometimes have been called "gamma waves," but they lie within the broad band of beta waves and we know very little about them.

Delta waves. As you can see in the frequency spectrum, a large part of the energy of the spectrum is at the low end below 8 cycles per second. The peak of these slow waves is at 1 to 2 cycles per second. Such slow waves are known as delta waves. We see them appearing irregularly in sleep as in the case of line VI of Figure 2. Custom varies on the naming of the frequencies in between, *i.e.*, those between 3 and 8 cycles per second (Lindsley). Some call all waves below 8 cycles "delta waves." Others have made up the name *theta waves* for bands of 4 to 7 cycles per second (Walter and Walter). Such waves appear under several different circumstances, but are rather common in young children. You see a sample record from a child in line I of Figure 2. Such a record is sometimes called *saw-tooth* waves.

Kappa waves. The alpha, beta, and delta waves have been known from the beginnings of electroencephalography, and research has served only to show us when and where they are to be found. Quite recently, however, a new wave has burst upon our horizon—the "kappa wave" (Kennedy *et al.*). It is rather different and perhaps more significant than the other waves. It has about the same frequency as the alpha wave, *viz.*, 10 per second. Its voltages, however, are much smaller than those for alpha, and it appears under conditions quite different from those for alpha. In Figure 3 is a record of kappa waves appearing in the electrical record of eye movements. The very small waves riding on top of the big ones are the kappa waves.

Correlates of brain waves

We shall now take up a number of factors that have been correlated with brain waves. Whenever we speak of correlation, of course, we have a problem of cause and effect: Which of two correlated variables causes the other, if one does? In this case it is well to avoid the question, because we do not know whether brain waves

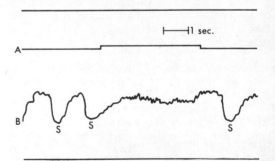

Figure 3 Bursts of kappa waves during reading. The large waves, S, are muscle potentials that come from the eye when it sweeps back from the end of one line to the beginning of the next. The fast small waves superimposed on top of the large slow ones are the kappa waves. (From J. L. Kennedy, R. M. Gottsdanker, J. C. Armington, and F. E. Gray. A new electroencephalogram associated with thinking. P. 527. Science, 1948, 108, 527–529. By permission of the publishers.)

can be the cause of changes in behavior, or vice versa. We shall therefore consider briefly the relationship between brain waves and a number of other factors.

Individual differences.   One of the basic questions about any kind of measure is, How reliable is it? Does a person get the same mark when the measure is used over again? How well does the measure distinguish one person from another? We have the same questions about brain waves. The answers have not been put forth in quantitative terms, but they are fairly clear.

Each individual usually gives a record of brain waves that is fairly characteristic of him, and the trained person comparing many records often can match up records belonging to the same person. Rather extensive studies have been done on twins to see whether the constancy of the brain-wave record is a matter of heredity. In this kind of measure, as in many others, twins are much more alike than are siblings or unrelated persons. We therefore can come to the expected conclusion that both heredity and postnatal life have their parts in the typical record of brain waves.

Age.   Brain waves are not only typically different for different individuals, they are not the same for children as they are for adults. You can see that in Figure 4. At birth there are regular brain waves at about 7 per second in the central regions of the skull. In the occipital region, however, which later is the main source of alpha, there is hardly any rhythm at birth. The waves that appear are rather irregular. After 3 months, however, some regular waves show up in the records. The waves are very slow, *i.e.*, 3 or 4 cycles per second, but they gradually get faster as the child grows older. By 2 years of age, both the occipital and parietal "alpha" waves are about 7 cycles per second, but the parietal rhythm stays a little faster all through the development of the child. Finally, at about nine years of age, both rhythms have come to be about 10 cycles per second, which is the typical adult rhythm.

Sleep and hypnosis.   It has long been known that the brain waves change when we go to sleep. They change in three stages. The first stage is that of drowsiness or drifting. In this stage people who normally have good alpha waves show somewhat smaller ones; others who tend to have a lot of fast waves when awake show somewhat more alpha. In general, the brain waves get slower in this stage and show more waves of about 4 to 6 cycles per second. A second stage is one of dozing and light sleep. In this stage the record of brain waves shows a lot of "spindle" waves, like those in line III of Figure 2. These spindles come in bursts, and

their frequency is about 14 to 16 per second— sometimes called slow beta waves. The third stage is one of deep sleep. It gives us rather large slow waves of ½ to 3 cycles per second, which come rather randomly. The record looks like line VI of Figure 2. If a person is disturbed in a sound sleep by a sudden loud sound, there is a reaction in his brain waves called the K complex (Davis *et al.*). This consists of some slow waves with alpha waves (8 to 14) imposed on top of them.

In passing we may touch upon an old question about the relation of sleep and hypnosis. Although they may sometimes look alike, sleep and hypnosis are basically not the same or even very similar. One way of showing that is with brain waves. Brain waves have been recorded in several experiments with hypnotic trances. They do not change as they do in sleep but remain entirely as they are in normal waking adults (see Lindsley).

Sensory stimulation.   The record of a normal person who is awake and relaxed contains a fair share of alpha waves. These waves, we have just seen, disappear in sleep. They also drop out with almost any kind of sensory stimulation. Visual stimulation is the most effective of all. Simply opening the eyes in a lighted room usually "blocks" the alpha rhythm, although after a time it may return. Turning on a bright light suddenly also "blocks" the alpha rhythm, and the intensity of the light has something to do with the time it takes for the block to occur. The brighter the light, the shorter the blocking time.

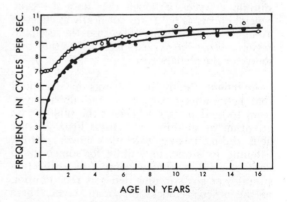

Figure 4   Increase with age in the frequency of the alpha rhythm. The upper curve indicates the frequency from the central region over areas 1, 2, 3, and 4; the lower curve refers to the occipital alpha rhythm. (After J. R. Smith. The frequency growth of the human alpha rhythms during normal infancy and childhood. P. 188. J. Psychol., 1941, 11, 177–198. By permission of the Journal Press.)

If the light stays on for a while there is adaptation and the alpha comes back.

Light can not only block the alpha wave, it can do just about the opposite, viz., drive it. The effect has lately been called "photic driving" (Halstead). If a light is flashed or flickered at a regular rate, instead of the alpha being blocked it sometimes gets bigger. It seems to fall in step or be driven by the flickering light. Moreover, the alpha wave can take on the frequency of the flickering light. Thus a normal alpha can drop down to 5 cycles or up to 15 cycles per second when it is driven by flashes of light.

We may hazard a guess as to why the alpha wave is sometimes blocked and sometimes driven. If alpha waves come from many neurons pulsing in step, a sudden stimulus or a steady stimulus can knock them out of step. Impulses coming from the stimulus are scattered in time, rather than in waves, and thus flatten out the record and "block" the alpha wave. A flickering stimulus, on the other hand, sends impulses into the nervous system in waves. If it is natural for the neurons to pulse together anyway, as they do in brain waves, the flickering stimulus just helps them out, thus making them even bigger.

Other stimuli such as sounds, touch, and pain do about the same thing to alpha waves, at least in their respective areas of the cortex, as does light (Lindsley). Coming on suddenly, they all block the alpha rhythm. After they have been on for a while their effect gets less and the alpha wave may return. When auditory stimuli are repeated at a regular rate, they "drive" the alpha rhythm over the auditory region just as flickering lights "drive" the occipital waves. These other stimuli, however, although they have the same general effects as light, are not nearly as effective as light. Perhaps that is because the occipital region, viz., the visual region, is the best source of the alpha waves.

Attention.   Many investigators have noticed that brain waves, particularly the alpha waves, seem to be depressed whenever the subject pays attention to anything. It matters little whether he is reading, talking, watching a moving picture, listening to music, or waiting for somebody to flash a light or ring a gong. Any distracting stimulus or any stimulus that gets the attention of the observer blocks the brain waves. There is little doubt about this fact. What it means, however, can be argued. Some think that "attention" is a sort of tensing of muscles and increasing of peripheral stimuli and that such stimulation is the major cause of blocking (Knott, Freeman). Others think that mental activity involves a good part of the brain and thus is likely to get in the way of alpha rhythms because they get along best when the brain is doing little but staying awake (Lindsley).

Mental activity.   Whatever attention is, it is not very different from mental activity. It is not surprising, therefore, that both mental activity and work block the alpha waves. Give a man a problem in arithmetic to solve and his alpha usually disappears. Or have him sitting quietly and ask him to tell you what is on his mind when you say "Now." When his brain-wave record shows a block in alpha waves, he will usually admit that he has been having thoughts, visual images, and the like—his mind has been at work—but his record will show fairly regular alpha activity when his mind is a relative blank (Travis).

Mental effort, however, not only blocks the alpha waves, it produces two other kinds of waves. One is fast beta waves. Some have reported waves of 40 to 100 per second or even higher when mental work is going on (Berger). There is the possibility that some of these waves are not brain waves at all but rather muscle potentials; but some waves in the beta range, higher than alpha, are no doubt brain waves and appear during mental effort (Travis).

The other wave that comes out in mental effort is the *kappa wave*. This is a relatively recent discovery (Kennedy et al.). When a subject is given some problems to solve, the kappa wave appears in the record if the electrodes have been put in the right place on the skull. In fact, kappa waves seem to appear only when a person is thinking or making mental effort. As we said, it is about the same frequency as the alpha rhythm, but there are two ways to distinguish it from alpha. One is that it has much less amplitude than the alpha wave, and the second is that it turns up only when the electrodes are in a region of the skull over the temporal lobe just behind the frontal lobe. We should note, incidentally, that kappa waves can be found in only half the subjects. Why this is true, as well as many other questions about kappa activity, is something for future research to tell us.

Emotional reactions.   Research workers have also been trying to find changes in the brain waves that go along with emotions. There are some changes that we can be sure about and others that are a bit doubtful (Lindsley). Certainly emotional reactions, indeed very mild embarrassment or concern, block out the alpha waves. Many investigators have made that clear, and that is what we would expect anyway. Some have found, too, that there are more fast waves (beta) after emotional stimulation than before (Darrow et al.). Others find more slow waves, i.e., delta waves, in emotional states.

Although there is some doubt about these delta waves, they are worth more than a passing thought. Hoagland and his colleagues recorded brain waves from both psychotic and normal people while embarrassing questions were fired at the subjects. The normal people had an increase in delta waves. Schizophrenic patients, however, showed less change than normal people, which is what we might expect. When the questions were repeated, both groups adapted, i.e., their brain waves showed less delta activity.

Unfortunately, however, these results have not been confirmed, and it is possible that the so-called delta waves were not delta waves at all but rather changes in potentials of the skin (Lindsley). We could argue the matter pro and con, but it will not be settled without more research. Like Hoagland, others find some slow waves in people subjected to emotional situations, but they can find them only in the premotor region of the skull (Lindsley and Sassaman). Hoagland got his slow waves best when he recorded from electrodes around the pharynx. He decided, therefore, and with reason, that the slow waves in emotion come from the hypothalamus. Only time will tell.

Personality. A lot of effort has been put to the question of whether brain waves have anything to do with personality. We do not have space here even to mention the names of various studies, let alone give them any detailed description. In some studies it looks as though there is some connection; in others it does not. In general, those studies that use tests to measure traits of personality have had poor luck with any relationship to brain waves. The studies in which more thorough, but more subjective, means of sorting out traits have been used, such as those used in psychoanalysis, have come up with a positive relationship between brain waves and personality (see Lindsley).

To the extent that there is a tie between personality and brain waves, it is what we might expect from what we have already said. Alpha waves are more in view in the passive, reposed individual and less in evidence in active, fidgety people. This ties in with the ways in which alpha waves are blocked. Sensory stimulation, attention, mental effort—all block alpha activity. People whose minds are working every minute should not, therefore, have much alpha activity. Those who stay relaxed, passive, and dependent, with their minds something of a blank, should have a good deal of alpha activity. So goes both the theory and the facts that are sometimes reported. There probably is such a trend, but it is only a trend and a very small one. A really complete, well-controlled, and trustworthy study on this subject is yet to be made.

Brain waves as signs of disorder

This is not the place to go into all the ways in which brain waves can be used in medicine and neurology. Some of them have little to do with physiological psychology. There are, however, three ways in which brain waves have been used as signs of neurological or psychiatric disorder that deserve brief notice.

Brain lesions. If brain waves never do anything else for us, they have earned the effort that has been put into them by their value in locating lesions of the brain. Small lesions are hard to find either with brain-wave methods or with any other, but large gross lesions of the brain often can be found by putting electrodes at many points on the skull and comparing the records of brain waves obtained at each pair of points. In the region of the lesion, especially around its borders, the brain waves are abnormal, and in any one of a variety of ways. There may be isolated fast "spikes," slowing of the alpha waves, "saw-tooth" wave forms (see line I, Figure 2), around 4 to 7 cycles, and very slow delta waves. Any abnormal activity is an occasion for a second look at the region from which they come. In general the slow waves, particularly 1 to 3 cycles per second, are the surest signs of damaged tissue.

Epilepsy. Brain waves can also give signs of epileptic disorders. Everybody who has recorded brain waves in epileptics agrees to that. Investigators have had some trouble, however, in saying just how brain waves can signal such disorder. They vary among themselves in the signs they use. In general, brain waves that are either too fast, too slow, or both are epileptic signs. If the waves are "spike-and-dome," i.e., a series of alternating spikes and slow waves, they are signs of the *petit mal* seizure. This sign usually appears in the frontal and precentral regions when it is present. Brain waves that are very fast and very large, usually coming in bursts, signal *grand mal* attacks—convulsions of the whole body. Another type of epileptic attack, the psychomotor attack, in which a person does things impulsively, goes with large slow waves of 3 to 6 cycles per second (Gibbs and Gibbs).

Using brain waves to diagnose epilepsy is a science and an art of its own. Expert eyes can see signs of epilepsy in a record that looks normal to the novice. We cannot follow all the bypaths of the subject here. The important point is that brain waves do help spot epilepsy. They are not infallible, and there are indeed many normal people who have epileptic brain-wave patterns. The tell-tale waves, however, occur thirty times as often in epileptics as in normal people, and that is extremely helpful.

Psychiatric disorders. One can always hope, and for a while some did, that psychotics may be recognized by their brain waves. They cannot! After studies too numerous to mention, it turns out that brain waves are not very good signs of mental disorder. In schizophrenia there is no consistent relation. It looks as though schizophrenics have more abnormalities of their brain waves than normal people, but not in any one conspicuous way. Their brain waves seem to be a little faster, more irregular, and somewhat weaker in amplitude. Some have reported that *depressed* manic-depressive patients show rather good normal alpha waves but that *manic* manic-depressive patients have abnormal fast alpha mixed with beta and somewhat irregular waves (P. A. Davis).

So far, brain waves are better signs of behavior disorders in children than they are of any other kind of psychiatric disturbance (see Linds-

ley). The vast majority of children who are delinquents and behavior problems show something wrong with their brain waves. Most of them have a great deal of slow activity between 3 and 6 per second, and some also show some kind of damage to their cortices. About that there is little question. The question of cause and effect, however, can be argued. Perhaps it is brain lesions that make children problems and also give them abnormal brain waves. Or perhaps the brain waves are linked with personality traits and emotional disorders that cause their social delinquency.

This article illustrates the use of electrical stimulation as a physiological technique for the investigation of the correlations between brain and behavior. Similar work has been carried out with cats, monkeys, and also with man. The results with cats and monkeys were similar to those with rats. Reports of both pleasant and unpleasant sensations were sometimes obtained from people with electrodes implanted in these regions.

Points to guide your study

1. Can this technique be used for other areas of the brain? What results might you expect for some of these areas?

2. Why does Olds think that his results show that the drive-reduction theory is incorrect?

3. What skills are necessary to do experiments of this kind?

55. SELF-STIMULATION OF THE BRAIN

*James Olds, University of Michigan**

This article reviews experiments which have led to the discovery and analysis of localized systems in the brain where electric stimulation has positive and negative motivational effects. Basically, the experimental animal in these studies is re-

* These studies were aided by a grant from the Foundations Fund for Research in Psychiatry ("Brain Mechanisms and Motivation") to H. W. Magoun and J. Olds, by contract NR 144–102 [Nonr-233 (32)] between the Office of Naval Research, U. S. Department of the Navy, and the University of California, and by a grant from the Carnegie Corporation of New York ("Brain Organization and Behavior") to R. B. Livingston and D. B. Lindsley.

James Olds. Self-stimulation of the brain. *Science*, 1958, **127**, 315–324. Copyright 1958 by the American Association for the Advancement of Science. Excerpts reprinted here by permission from the author and the American Association for the Advancement of Science. Figure 3 (top) slightly changed.

warded or punished by a brain shock. The site of electric stimulation determines the motivational effect.

The studies are important primarily as a beginning step toward filling the large gap which has existed between neurophysiological techniques and an understanding of complex psychological processes. Among other things, they carry the enterprise of brain mapping into the realm of clearly defined motivational functions; this by itself correlates an orderly array of integrative psychological mechanisms with an orderly array of anatomical points in the brain. Furthermore, these studies perform a unification long considered technically impossible between electrophysiological, independent variables and standard, behavioral, dependent variables to produce smooth interaction curves relating the two.

For psychologists, these experiments help to

clarify the basic notions of reward and punishment. Reward and punishment, it is agreed, determine which behaviors will predominate in an organism's repertory and which will be erased from it. Rewarded responses are repeated more frequently than would be expected by chance; punished ones are repeated with less frequency. This is obvious.

Less self-evident is the thesis of the classical theory of reward, according to which reward is interpreted as being the falling phase of the same massive stimulation which at high levels constitutes punishment. This thesis is greatly weakened by the work outlined in this article; however, it has held sway for such a long time in psychology and conditions so many basic attitudes that it will certainly form a foundation stone for the new theories which replace it.

Drive and punishment are synonymous, according to this theory, and a reward is held to be fundamentally nothing more than the reduction of a drive. Physiological conditions which are inimical to survival, such as food deficiencies or tissue damage, cause massive receptor discharge into the central nervous system. This discharge is held to be the drive, and it is held to be reflected in behavioral activation. The latter is a nonselective function of the massive drive stimulation, energizing adaptive and maladaptive responses equally. The drive stimulation, however, also has a selective function by which it combines with other cue stimuli to select those responses which have repaired this particular physiological deficit in the past.

The response actually selected by the combination of drive and cue stimuli is determined entirely by structural cue-response connections whose strength has been determined by prior learning. More specifically, a group of cues actually selects the response which was previously followed by drive reduction in their presence. The drive reduction, on previous occasions, caused a rewarding or positive reinforcing effect which somehow increased the causal connection between these stimuli and this particular response.

The hedonistic view that behavior is pulled forward by pleasure as well as pushed forward by pain is rejected in this classical theory for the more parsimonious notion that pain supplies the push and that learning based on pain reduction supplies the direction.

The work reported in this article clearly shows one implication of the drive-reduction theory to be incorrect, for massive inputs to certain parts of the central nervous system are shown to have rewarding effects. Further, by showing that there are anatomically separate mechanisms for reward and punishment in the brain, it points directly to a physiological basis for the motivational dualism suggested in the hedonistic theory.

In fact, it appears that the area producing rewarding effects, upon electric stimulation, is far larger than the area producing punishment. In one early experiment, 76 electrodes were implanted in the brains of rats in an attempt to get a random sampling of mid-brain and forebrain points. It was found that stimulation at 47 of these points had motivational effects. Stimulation at 36 of these motivational points produced approach behavior—that is, the rats stimulated themselves repeatedly by means of the technique described below; at only 11 points did stimulation produce avoidance behavior (1).

Basic studies

Method. The method of self-stimulation (2) is modeled in part after the chronic implantation technique of W. R. Hess (3) and in part after the box technique of B. F. Skinner (4). The former developed a technique for implanting electrodes permanently in the brain; the technique allows stimulation in the freely behaving animal. The latter worked out a way to measure positive reinforcement—that is, reward—by arranging a situation in which the experimental animal could deliver the reward to itself by a very simple manipulation, and then counting the frequency of the manipulations. Self-stimulation combines these techniques by allowing animals to deliver shocks to specific points in their brains through chronically implanted electrodes.

Figure 1 shows the method used. When the rat stepped on a pedal, a shock was delivered to its brain. The rat never received any other reward for pressing the pedal, and the shock was never turned on except when the rat turned it on itself by stepping on the pedal.

In this box, animals invariably stepped on the pedal about 25 times during the first hour (although there was no rewarding electrical stimulation at all), because the pedal was so placed that it would be pressed when the animal looked out the only opening in the box. After the first hour there were about five responses or less per hour during hours in which no reward was produced. If the pedal-pressing produced a reward, the rate, even for the first hour, rose to 200 or more responses an hour; thus, "reward" was clearly discernible. If the pedal-pressing produced punishment, the rate dropped radically; there were only two or three responses during the total experimental procedure; thus, "punishment" was clearly discernible.

If the electrode was placed in the brain at a point at which maximum self-stimulation is produced, the rat, after its very first electric stimulation, began to search and pursue eagerly. Its response to the first shock was to sniff in all corners of the box and manipulate quickly the objects in its path until it stepped on the pedal

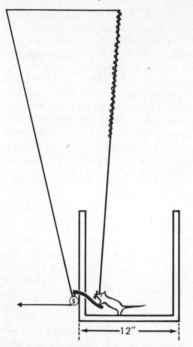

Figure 1   Diagram of apparatus by means of which a rat delivers electric shocks to its own brain. When the rat steps on the pedal, the electric circuit is closed and current is transmitted to its brain by means of implanted electrodes.

a second time. After the rat had pressed the pedal a second or third time, it ceased to wander and began to respond at the rate of one or two pedal-presses per second. These animals learned to press the pedal within a minute or two.

Figure 2 shows, in schematic form, the plastic electrode carrier which was screwed to the skull

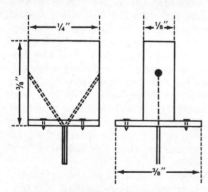

Figure 2   Diagram of plastic electrode carrier, containing a pair of silver electrodes, which is screwed to skull of rat, with wires penetrating deep into the brain, as shown in Figure 3.

and a pair of silver-wire electrodes implanted in the brain through a hole in the skull. The insulated wires, which were 0.01 inch in diameter, stimulated the brain only at their tips. The electrode apparently fired cells up to a distance of at least 0.5 millimeter from its tip. Figure 3 (top) is an x-ray photograph of an electrode in place in the brain of an intact animal; in Figure 3 (bottom) the tip of the electrode track appears as a blackened area on the photomicrograph of a stained brain slice. In these experiments each brain was sectioned and stained after testing; all statements about localization are based

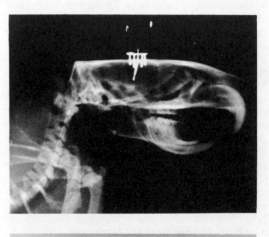

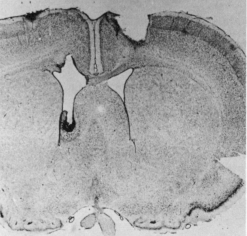

Figure 3   Top, x-ray photograph of an electrode (deepest shaft) in place in the brain of a rat. The four shorter shafts are screws which hold the electrode carrier to the skull. Bottom, photomicrograph of stained brain slice from a rat sacrificed at the end of a series of experiments. The tip of the electrode track appears as darkened area. Wires are insulated along their whole length and stimulate the brain only at the tip.

on examination of this histological material.

The stimulus was a sine-wave shock at 60 cycles per second; the current ranged from 5 to 100 microamperes; the animal received a shock lasting for a maximum of 0.5 second. If the animal held the pedal down for less than 0.5 second, the current went off when it released the pedal. If it held the pedal down for longer than 0.5 second, the current went off automatically and the rat had to release the pedal and press it again to produce another shock.

Locus. Electric stimulation in most parts of the rhinencephalon, and in many parts of the hypothalamus and related structures (see cross-hatching, Figure 4), produced the approach response (1). Stimulation in small areas in the mid-brain and in certain adjacent parts of the thalamus and hypothalamus (see stippling, Figure 4) produced the avoidance response. Such avoidance behavior was first demonstrated in the cat, by Delgado, Roberts, and Miller (5). In the rat, the area in which stimulation produced avoidance behavior was small compared with the area in which it produced approach behavior.

The rate of self-stimulation tended to diminish steadily as the site of stimulation was moved toward the cortex. Rates as high as 7000 per

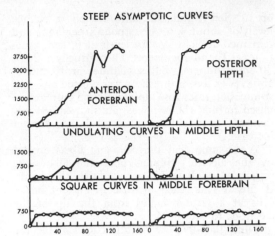

Figure 5   Electric-current functions. The hourly self-stimulation rate (plotted along the ordinate) tends to rise as current (on the abscissa) increases from 0 to 160 microamperes in steps of 10. In the middle hypothalamus the curve shows a temporary decline when the electric field invades an area where electric stimulation has a negative motivational effect. In the middle forebrain there is an abrupt rise to 500 responses an hour and then no further increase, because there is a very small field in which positive motivational effects are obtained, surrounded by a larger neutral area.

hour were achieved when electric stimulation was applied in the region of the interpeduncular nucleus of the tegmentum.

With electrodes placed in the posterior hypothalamus, just in front of the mamillary body, very high rates, in the range of 5000 per hour, occurred frequently. With electrodes placed in the anterior hypothalamus, rates ranged from 400 to 1100 per hour. With electrodes placed farther forward, in the preoptic and telencephalic areas, there was a second series of rates, ranging from quite high ones (about 3000 per hour) for the preoptic area to very low ones (about 200 per hour) for the anterior forebrain. The high rates obtained in the forebrain series were lower than the high ones of the hypothalamic series.

Thus, there was, for the hypothalamus, a decline of response rates as the electrode was moved forward. There was a similar trend for the telencephalic region, and the rates for the whole of the telencephalic region seemed to be lower than those for the whole of the hypothalamic region.

Electric current. Studies in which the level of electric current was varied (see Figure 5) provide some basis for explaining these differences in rate of self-stimulation. The level of the shock was raised from 0 to 150 microamperes by steps

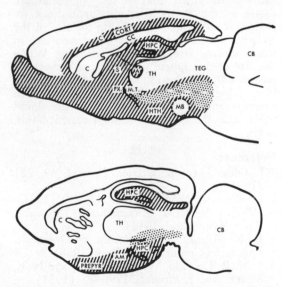

Figure 4   Medial and lateral sagittal sections of the rat brain showing, by cross-hatching, the areas where electric stimulation causes approach behavior and, by stippling, the areas where electric stimulation causes avoidance. A, anterior thalamus; AM, amygdala; C, caudate nucleus; CB, cerebellum; CC, corpus callosum; C CORT, cingulate cortex; FX, fornix; HPC, hippocampus; HTH, hypothalamus; MB, mammillary bodies; MT, mammillothalamic tract; PREPYR, prepyriform cortex; S, septal area; TEG, tegmentum; TH, thalamus.

of 10. Self-stimulation rates started at chance levels of about 4 to 40 responses per hour and remained at these chance levels at 0, and sometimes at 10, microamperes. Then, usually at 20 or 30 microamperes, but sometimes at 10 microamperes or less, a threshold was crossed and self-stimulation rates rose rapidly. As the current was raised further, the response rate showed a steady increase, undulated, or showed no further increase.

We assume that the cells and fibers excited by the electric stimulus obey the all-or-none principle and have relatively similar thresholds. If this is true, each increase in current brings cells at a greater radius from the tip of the electrode to threshold.

Thus, the steep asymptotic curves at the top of Figure 5 indicate that stimulation of several rings of cells around the electrode tip induced the rat to stimulate itself with progressively greater frequency. The undulating curves obtained by stimulation in the middle hypothalamus suggest that stimulation of some rings of cells decreases the rate of self-stimulation; from other evidence it is known (1) that "negative" or "punishing" areas infiltrate into the "reward" system in the part of the middle hypothalamus from which these curves were obtained. The "square" curves obtained for the dorsal septal area show that only one ring of cells around the electrode tip had any motivational function; the rest were neutral. Such "square" functions have always resulted when the electrodes were implanted in or near the diagonal band of Broca; the threshold increased as the distance of the electrode from the diagonal band increased. These data on electric current level permit an important inference to be drawn: the asymptotic self-stimulation rate of an area probably depends on the number of concentric rings of "reward" cells surrounding the tip of the electrode.

The square curves indicate several other important points. Since the full rate occurred at 10 microamperes, when the electrodes were in the diagonal band, it appears that cells outside the diagonal band are neutral (the diagonal band is, thus, the only active site in the septal area). The fact that current up to 150 microamperes does not slow the rate of self-stimulation indicates that the reward units of the diagonal band are affected equally by any current from 10 microamperes (threshold) to 150 microamperes (15 times threshold). Since this function was produced repeatedly by the same rat every day for 8 months, it may be assumed that the current of 15 times threshold did no damage to the nearby cells which produce self-stimulation.

Finally, because electrodes may be placed at varying distances from the diagonal band, it is possible to define the shape and size of the suprathreshold electric field produced by various levels of electric current.

Summary. (i) The areas in which the stimulation produces the approach or rewarding effect occupy a larger proportion of the brain than do the areas in which the avoidance or punishing effect is produced. Therefore, the brain cannot be thought of as tending mainly to produce behaviors which *decrease* its own excitation, for a large portion causes behaviors which *increase* excitation. (ii) There is some sort of orderly arrangement of the rewarding effect in the rhinencephalon and related structures, with the result that response rates tend to decline as stimulation is moved forward toward the cortex; this is true both within structures and from structure to structure. (iii) Finally, by gauging the way in which rates of self-stimulation increase as the strength of the brain-shock increases, it is possible to estimate the size of the sphere, surrounding a point of stimulation, in which electric stimulation is rewarding. When the size of this sphere is large, as in the ventral posterior hypothalamus, the rate of self-stimulation at high current levels is very high. When there is only a narrow ring, as in the dorsal septal area, the rate, even at high current levels, is low.

References

1. J. Olds, *J. comp. physiol. Psychol.* **49**, 281 (1956).
2. J. Olds and P. Milner, *ibid.* **47**, 419 (1954).
3. W. R. Hess, *Das Zwischenhirn* (Schwabe, Basel, Switzerland, 1949).
4. B. F. Skinner, *The Behavior of Organisms* (Appleton-Century, New York, 1938).
5. J. M. R. Delgado, W. W. Roberts, and N. E. Miller, *Am. J. Physiol.*, **179**, 587 (1954).

CHAPTER TWENTY

Physiological basis of behavior

SENSORY MOTOR MECHANISMS

This study was done in the course of operations performed to remove epileptic foci in the cortex. It is more in the tradition of physiology than psychology, but a number of findings of interest to the psychologist have come from this work. For instance, it has been possible to evoke quite complex memories by stimulation of the cerebral cortex in this way.

A point to guide your study

Refer to your text for the location of the structures mentioned. This will provide a good review for you.

56. FURTHER STUDIES OF THE SENSORY AND MOTOR CEREBRAL CORTEX OF MAN

Theodore Rasmussen and Wilder Penfield, McGill University and the Montreal Neurological Institute*

Further analysis of our neurosurgical experience in stimulating the cerebral cortex of man under local anesthesia is made at this time because of the numerous recent physiological contributions to knowledge of the mammalian cortex.

This survey had led us to certain modifications in detail of the sensory sequence as reported by the conscious patient, to minor rearrangements of the motor sequence and to further study of vocalization. Previously unexplained sensory responses from an area just above the fissure of Sylvius become understandable in the light of the discovery of a second somatic sensory area in mammals.

The observations made as a result of electrical stimulation of the sensory and motor cortex at the Montreal Neurological Institute and Royal Victoria Hospital for the period between 1928 and 1936 were previously reported in detail by Penfield and Boldrey (22). Certain aspects of these data were reviewed in conjunction with an analysis of the stimulation records made during the course of 206 further operations on 186 patients during the period from 1936 to 1947. These operations were likewise done by one of

* T. B. Rasmussen and W. G. Penfield. Further studies of the sensory and motor cerebral cortex in man. *Federation Proc.*, 1947, **6**, 452–460. Copyright 1947 by the Federation of American Societies for Experimental Biology. Reprinted here with permission from the authors and the Federation of American Societies for Experimental Biology.

us (W. P.), or were done under his direction. The cortical stimulations were usually done as a preliminary to radical excision of focal epileptogenic lesions. The use of local anesthesia enabled us to study cortical responses which had not been altered by a general anesthetic agent. The subjective response produced by the stimulation was described by the patient, as a rule, with considerable accuracy and frequently with great detail. Frequently the sensory and motor areas could be mapped out throughout most of their extent. In other instances only portions of the central region were available for stimulation.

Description of technique

A brief description of a typical operation will serve to illustrate the conditions under which the data were collected.

G. C., *a boy of 18 years, history of focal seizures since the age of 13 years, starting with sensation in the left side of the body and progressing to clonus of the left arm and leg.*

Following sterilization of the scalp, nupercaine in solutions of 1:1500 and 1:4000 was injected along the line of incision. Sterile towels were then sutured around the operative field and arranged so the patient could be constantly observed by the anesthetist. A right fronto-parietal craniotomy was then done and the dura opened widely, exposing the surface of the hemisphere. The exposed cortex was kept moistened throughout the operation with Ringer's solution, sprayed on with an atomizer. An electroencephalographic exploration of the cortex was next done and the areas of abnormal activity marked by small tickets, bearing letters, which were placed on the brain at the point of origin of the abnormal waves.

The cortex was then stimulated with bipolar electrodes with the points separated about 3 mm. Occasionally a unipolar stimulator has also been used. The current was supplied by a stimulator built by Rahm (25). This apparatus produces a saw-toothed wave with a rising phase lasting a fraction of a millisecond. The frequency and voltage of the stimulation can be accurately controlled and varied independently. The stimulation is ordinarily started with a setting of half a volt and then increased to 1, 1½, 2 or 3 volts as is necessary to produce a response. The maximum voltage used has been 3 volts in the central region and 5 volts elsewhere. Prior to 1945, a thyratron was used which furnished pulses lasting a fraction of a millisecond. The usual frequency employed was 55 to 65 per second. Beginning with a subliminal stimulus, the strength was increased until positive responses were obtained. Because of the short duration of the pulses, considerably higher voltages were used, usually 10 to 30 volts, occasionally up to 60 or 70.

The Rolandic fissure was first outlined, each positive response obtained being marked by a small number which was placed on the brain and indicated the site and order of the positive responses. Any unusual response was verified by repetition before it was accepted. The remainder of the cortex was then explored with the strength of the stimulator current moderately increased, in an effort to reproduce the patient's aura. The details of the electrical exploration were dictated by the surgeon to a stenographer, present in the gallery, who recorded the number of the stimulation, the voltage and frequency used, a description of the response, frequently in the patient's own words, and the time. Life size photographs were taken of the brain with the tickets in place. At the end of the stimulation the surgeon sketched on a life size standard brain chart any gross lesion that was present and entered the numbers at their proper measured distances from the Rolandic, Sylvian and median longitudinal fissures.

Method of analysis

As in the previous analysis any movement or sensation which was part of an epileptiform seizure, however minor, was excluded. In addition, responses which were the result of widespread epileptic facilitation were eliminated (23). After analyzing the sequence of the responses in the record, the points for each individual bodily unit were transferred to full size standard charts of the corresponding hemisphere according to the measured distance on the operative photographs and charts from the Sylvian, Rolandic and median longitudinal fissures. A series of charts was thus compiled, each presenting the points which produced sensation or movement in one part of the body. The points from both hemispheres were then transferred to similar charts of the right hemisphere for purposes of summary.

Special analyses were made of records giving specific information on 1) the banks of the pre- and postcentral gyri within the Rolandic fissure, 2) the medial surface of the hemisphere, 3) bilateral and ipsilateral responses, 4) the question of the sensory representation of the pre- and postaxial surfaces of the extremities, 5) the question of the separation of the cortical representation of the primitive flexor and extensor muscle groups, and 6) a possible second sensory area.

Sensory responses

Cortical areas involved. Sensory responses were elicited primarily from the cortex adjacent to the central fissure. In the face area, 82 per cent of the sensory responses were postcentral and 18 per cent were precentral. In the arm and leg areas, 73 per cent were postcentral and 27 per cent were precentral. The ratio of pre- and postcentral responses varied considerably among the various units of the sensory sequence. Sensation in the eyes and intra-abdominal sensation were located almost exclusively in the precentral gyrus, while sensation in the lips was nearly as completely limited to the postcentral gyrus. The sensory responses for face, arm, leg, foot and toes were divided more equally, 60 per cent postcentral and 40 per cent precentral. The majority of these responses were located adjacent to the fissure, but an appreciable number were situated in the anterior portion of the precentral gyrus or posterior portion of the postcentral gyrus. Rarely were sensory responses encountered at a distance greater than 1 cm. from the central fissure.

The sensory projection area in primates as mapped out under anesthesia by the method of evoked potentials (5) (29) does not extend onto the precentral gyrus and is limited to areas 3, 1 and 2. As mapped out by the method of local strychninization (11) the sensory area seems to extend much more widely both rostrally and caudally from the central fissure.

In 15 operations, the banks of the Rolandic fissure were stimulated after removal of either the pre- or postcentral gyrus. Sensory responses were elicited from the banks of both the pre- and postcentral gyri, somewhat more frequently from the latter. These responses were comparable to those elicited from the surfaces of the gyri and were each located at the expected point in the sensory sequence mapped out by the surface stimulations in that particular patient. The evoked potential studies have also demonstrated the functional similarity of the anterior bank and surface of the postcentral gyrus (29).

We have no instance yet in which a precentral point giving a sensory response has been restimulated following removal of the adjacent portion of the postcentral gyrus and thus have no information yet as to whether this removal results in any change in the response produced. Sensation, however, has been produced several times by stimulation of the bank or surface of the precentral gyrus after such a postcentral removal and the sensation has been similar to that produced throughout the central area. This would indicate that sensation produced by stimulation of the precentral gyrus does not depend upon the presence of collateral fibers to the postcentral gyrus, or upon physical spread of the stimulating current.

Quality of cortical sensation. These near-threshold stimulations from both the precentral and postcentral gyri resulted in sensations described by the patients in the majority of instances as a numbness, tingling, or a feeling of electricity. Less frequently other types of sensation were reported, particularly a sense of movement of a part although no movement could be seen. This occurred somewhat more frequently from the postcentral gyrus than from the precentral gyrus but was elicited from both. A desire to move a part was also occasionally reported, usually from stimulation of the precentral gyrus. A feeling of inability to carry out some movement was also described occasionally, but it is difficult to tell on the basis of the available evidence whether this is primarily a sensory or a motor phenomenon. Its relation to suppressor areas also awaits further study.

The tongue presented the greatest variety of sensory responses. In addition to numbness, tingling or tickling, which comprised the great majority, the following sensations were reported on one or two occasions: a swollen feeling, a feeling as though something were on the tongue, a crawling sensation, a stiff feeling, dry feeling, buzzing feeling, cold, warmth, pain and taste.

Sequence. The familiar classical sensory sequence was repeatedly corroborated, but we would now suggest certain minor changes and additions (Figure 1). There is a representation of head, as a whole, between arm and trunk. This was encountered 14 times, the sensation was referred to the contralateral side of the head in 8 stimulations, to the top of the head in 1, to the ipsilateral side in 1, and was just stated to

be "in the head" in the remaining 4 stimulations. This same representation has been mapped out by the method of evoked potentials in animals by Woolsey and Bard (5) (16) (28) (29) and described as the cortical representation of the second and third cervical segments. Neck sensation may also be definitely placed in the sequence between trunk and arm, and in one case was clearly between trunk and the head representation just described.

The sequence within the face area has been subdivided a little more finely and has been altered in some of its details. Isolated responses of sensation in upper lip alone were consistently located above responses giving sensation in both lips, when both occurred in the same patient. Similarly, sensation in the lower lip was located below sensation in both lips. Taste has been eliminated from the sequence since it occurred only twice among 142 sensory tongue responses. It seems probable that taste is not represented on the easily accessible surface of the hemisphere. Tongue is now placed below teeth, gums and jaw and above throat and roof of mouth, corresponding to its position in the motor sequence. Below throat there is a representation, largely precentral, of intra-abdominal sensation. These sensations differ markedly from those elicited throughout the rest of the central area and were variously described as a "sinking feeling," "nausea," "sick feeling," "choking sensation,"· or "shaking in the heart."

Pre- and postaxial representation. The pre- and postaxial divisions of the upper portions of the extremities, as mapped out by the method of evoked potentials in experimental animals (5) (16) (29) have separate representations in the sensory cortex so that the spinal segments are projected on the sensory cortex in a regular order. There is no evidence in our data on cortical stimulation in man of a corresponding separation, although this has been searched for repeatedly during the past two years. Most patients are able to describe the location of the induced sensation in considerable detail, yet the usual description is "sensation in the whole arm" or "sensation in the whole forearm." Occasionally, sensation in the front or volar aspect of the arm has been reported, but sensory responses of sensation in the radial or ulnar aspect of the upper arm have been extremely rare. There has been no instance in which a sensory arm response has been found between head and trunk, where a postaxial arm response would be expected.

It may be possible that the cortical representation of the postaxial portion of the arm is relatively so small that it has not yet been encountered in a favorable case in which its location relative to head and trunk sensation could be studied. Or the small size of this representation may result in its being "buried" in a trunk or arm response produced by this relatively gross method of sampling the cerebral cortex. Another possibility is that it has escaped detection by being buried in the central fissure.

On the other hand, the explanation may be more fundamental than this. The increasing specialization of function in the sensorimotor cortex may have resulted in an alteration of the original metameric representation of the body in the cortex so that related functional units have become more closely associated, at least such parts of the sensory mechanisms as we are activating with the electrical currents. Thus upper arm and shoulder would be adjacent to upper trunk and head, conforming to the usual pattern mapped out in man by electrical stimulation.

The sequence from face to upper arm, mapped out both by electrical stimulation in man and by the method of evoked potentials in animals (5) (29) (30) is identical (face, thumb, index, middle, ring and little fingers, hand, forearm, upper arm and shoulder). This is a functional subdivision of the arm and suggests that the cortical representation of the arm is complicated by the demands of function so that the metameric pattern of the spinal cord undergoes some rearrangement in the cortex.

In the leg area also we have as yet no evidence to indicate such a separation of the pre- and post-axial limb areas. In the 10 patients in whom sensory responses were elicited from the medial surface of the hemisphere, there was no instance in which leg sensation was produced by stimulation above the foot and toe area (nearer the

gyrus cinculi). The inferior buried border of the paracentral lobule has not yet been successfully stimulated, however, and it may be possible that the lower sacral segments (postaxial leg and genitalia) are represented here, as is the case in the monkey (29).

On the rare occasions when sensation in the genitalia or rectum has been produced, it has been from points somewhat posterior to the foot area, but evidence from stimulation does not yet permit of accurate localization in man. The recent report of erotomania as an expression of epileptic discharge produced by an hemangioma on the medial surface of the hemisphere at the upper end of the Rolandic sulcus (13) adds to the clinical evidence that the genitalia in man are represented in this general vicinity.

There is great variability in the location of the sensory leg area with respect to its extension onto the lateral surface of the hemisphere. Sensation in the foot and toes has been elicited from the lateral surface of the hemisphere near the midline, while at the other extreme the trunk area has been found to extend up to the midline and onto the medial surface of the hemisphere so that in one patient the uppermost stimulation on the medial surface of the hemisphere produced sensation in the lower trunk extending into the leg.

Combined responses. In the majority (70 to 85 per cent) of the stimulations with these near-threshold currents sensation limited to one of the units listed in the sensory sequence was produced. In the remaining stimulations sensation was produced in two or more of these bodily units or movement was produced in addition to the sensation. Detailed examination shows that the great majority of these combined responses involved adjacent units in the sequence. Much more rarely the associated phenomena involved a more distant component of the same primary subdivision of the sequence. Responses involving the face and arm area, or the arm and leg area, were very rarely encountered. The face, arm and leg areas act as units when studied by local strychninization (11). A functional separation between these areas is also indicated by the rarity of cortical stimulations producing sensation in units separated by these boundaries. These responses, occurring among about a thousand sensory responses, are listed below:

Responses involving the face and arm areas. Two stimulations—sensation in mouth and thumb; 1 stimulation—sensation in face and index finger; 1 stimulation—sensation in tongue and index finger; 1 stimulation—sensation in roof of mouth, side of face and fingers; 1 stimulation—sensation in face and ipsilateral side of chest with trembling of lips.

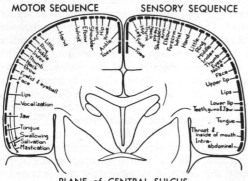

MOTOR SEQUENCE   SENSORY SEQUENCE

PLANE of CENTRAL SULCUS

Figure 1   Diagrammatic representation of the sensory and motor sequences as mapped out by threshold stimulation of the cerebral cortex in man. The length of the bars indicates in a general way the extent of the critical areas devoted to each structure in the average patient. This is subject to considerable variation, however.

Responses involving the arm and leg areas. Three stimulations—sensation in arm and leg; 1 stimulation—sensation in arm and a little in the foot; 1 stimulation—sensation in hand and foot; 1 stimulation—sensation in hand, arm and foot with tremor of arm and foot.

As might be expected from the small size of the trunk area, responses involving the trunk and the arm or leg were relatively more frequent.

Responses involving the trunk and the arm or leg areas. Five stimulations—sensation in arm and trunk; 1 stimulation—sensation in arm, body and foot; 3 stimulations—sensation in back and leg; 1 stimulation—sensation down the entire left side of the body, shoulder to foot; 1 stimulation—sensation down the left side of the body from umbilicus to knee; 1 stimulation—sensation down the left side of the body, into leg with flexion of the knee.

The paucity of these responses is to be contrasted with the combined responses within the principal subdivision of the central area. For example, 20 (14 per cent) of the 142 tongue responses showed associated sensation in neighboring units of the sequence. Similarly 25 (26 per cent) of the 97 thumb responses, 31 (14 per cent) of the 214 hand responses and 30 (30 per cent) of the 100 arm responses were combined responses.

The sensory cortex is thus apparently organized so that various bodily regions are represented in an orderly, constant manner with, however, a variable degree of overlapping so that at any one spot on the sensory cortex there is represented a functional unit pertaining to some region of the body, and possessing a low threshold to electrical stimulation. Into this same area, however, extend functional units related to neighboring portions of the body and exhibiting higher thresholds. This overlap is most marked in the area for the digits of the hand and is least marked at the junctions of the face, arm and leg areas. The degree of this overlap has been well demonstrated by the evoked potential studies in experimental animals (20).

Bilateral and ipsilateral sensory responses. Bilateral and ipsilateral sensory responses occurred only in the face area. The incidence of these responses varied considerably in the different units of the face area, but they occurred in nearly all. Half the sensory eye responses consisted of sensation in both eyes simultaneously; in the other half the sensation involved only the contralateral eye. Eight per cent of the total group of sensory responses in the face area (13 per cent of those in which the lateralization was described) were either clearly bilateral or ipsilateral.

These bilateral and ipsilateral sensory responses were situated in their expected location in the sensory sequence of the individual patient and were frequently adjacent to usual contralateral responses involving the same part. The character of the sensation was also the same as in the ordinary contralateral responses. A discrete cortical area related to the ipsilateral side of the face has not been identified by cortical stimulation in man. On the other hand in experimental evoked potential studies such an area has been outlined for the pig, sheep, rabbit, cat, dog and monkey (34). Adrian found ipsilateral evoked potentials from the face in the goat and sheep and only contralateral responses in the pig, ferret, Shetland pony, cat, dog and monkey (2) (3) (4).

Motor responses

Cortical areas involved. Movements of the various parts of the body were produced primarily from stimulation of the precentral gyrus adjacent to the central fissure and less frequently from stimulation of the adjacent part of the postcentral gyrus. The percentage of responses elicited from the postcentral gyrus varied from unit to unit within the motor sequence. In the case of neck movement, movement of the eyelids, eyeballs and brow, all the points were precentral in location. Mastication, on the other hand, was located mainly in the postcentral gyrus. For the remainder of the face area, 28 per cent of the responses were postcentral, as were 21 per cent of the motor responses of the extremities. In the chimpanzee, also, discrete motor responses have been elicited from the postcentral gyrus as well as from the precentral gyrus (12) (17).

One third of the points for eyeball movement were located adjacent to the central fissure while the remaining two thirds were in the anterior part of the precentral gyrus or in the general vicinity of area 8. The ratio was just reversed for eyelid movement, two thirds of the points being adjacent to the central fissure and one third further anteriorly. Contraversion of the head did not occur as a result of stimulation adjacent to the central fissure and all the points were located in the anterior margin of the precentral gyrus and in the region just anterior, corresponding in general to area 8. Neck movements other than those producing contraversion of the head were localized at the precentral margin of the Rolandic fissure.

While the great majority of the responses in man were located adjacent to the central fissure, occasional points were present in the anterior portion of the precentral gyrus or the posterior portion of the postcentral gyrus, and rarely were situated in the next gyri anteriorly and posteriorly.

Motor responses were elicited in 13 of the 15 operations in which the banks of the Rolandic fissure were stimulated below the outer or superficial surface. These occurred both from stimulation of the pre- and postcentral gyri. As with the sensory responses these motor responses were comparable to those elicited from the outer surfaces of the gyri and were located at the proper site in the motor sequence mapped out by the surface stimulations in each individual patient.

The relative size of the motor face, arm and leg areas varies considerably. The face area may extend to within 4 cm. of the midline, or at the other extreme the face area may be so small that thumb responses are elicited 2 cm. above the fissure of Sylvius.[1] A similar variability exists for the leg area. It may be entirely located on the medial surface of the hemisphere or it may extend well out onto the lateral surface for a distance of 3 cm. Flexion or extension of the ankle was elicited 13 times by stimulation on the lateral surface of the hemisphere and on 2 occasions toe movements were produced here.

Sequence. Only minor changes were made in the motor sequence previously described (Figure 1). Vocalization has now been elicited throughout the lower face area of both the dominant and nondominant hemispheres and does not seem to be sharply localized within this region. It occurs both alone and in association with movement or sensation of units of the lower portion of the face area. Mastication has a separate representation from other jaw movements. It is apparently represented primarily in the postcentral gyrus, in the region of the sensory tongue area and below. The simpler jaw movements, on the other hand, were found to be located primarily in the precentral gyrus and above the motor responses for throat and tongue. Mastication was therefore added to the motor sequence below throat and tongue. Salivation was found in the same region as mastication, in the postcentral gyrus, and was added to the motor sequence here also.

Eyeball movement was inserted into the sequence with eyelid movement, since as stated above, one third of the responses were located in the motor strip adjacent to the central fissure just like motor responses for other units of the body. They were consistently found between face and thumb.

Representation of flexors and extensors. No evidence was found to suggest that the muscles derived from the ventral muscle sheet of the limb bud (the primitive flexors) were separated in their cortical representation from those derived from the dorsal muscle sheet (the primitive extensors) (Woolsey) (28). Flexion and exten-

sion of the same joints were occasionally produced from closely adjacent points. Also no leg movements were produced above foot and toe movements in the motor sequence. It seems likely that the demands of function have brought about an arrangement in the cortex so that agonists and antagonists are closely associated, thus producing the motor sequence classically described for man.

Type of movement produced. Movement of the great toe was rarely produced alone; flexion, extension or separation of all the toes occurred more frequently. Flexion or extension of the ankle, knee or hip occurred both alone and with more widespread movement of the leg.

Motor trunk responses occurred only 4 times, being clearly contralateral in 1 patient and not described in the other 3 in sufficient detail to make clear the lateralization of the response. Neck movements (except head turning) consisted of retraction of the head, contraction of the sternomastoids or trapezius and were represented between fingers and face, as judged by the 12 motor responses that were obtained. It will be recalled, however, that in the sensory sequence neck sensation was placed between arm and trunk along with head sensation.

Contraversion of the head was nearly always associated with conjugate deviation of the eyes to the opposite side. The majority of the points for contraversion of the head were located anterior to the junction between the arm and face areas. This special mechanism is represented separately in the cortex from other neck movements.

The most common response in the arm area was movement of all the fingers together, but flexion or extension of the thumb was fairly frequent and movement of one of the fingers was elicited occasionally. Multiple finger responses were seen only in consecutive digits. Flexion and extension of the wrist and elbow were elicited frequently while shoulder movements occurred somewhat less often. The most common shoulder movements were elevation, inward rotation and flexion.

Flexion responses were in general more frequent than extensor responses. Many combinations were encountered, finger movements occurring most commonly with wrist movements, less commonly with elbow movements, and occurring with shoulder movement only as part of a movement involving the whole arm. Flexion of one joint sometimes occurred with extension of an adjacent joint. A flexion response occasionally occurred immediately adjacent to a point which produced extension of the same joint or joints. When sensation accompanied a motor response it usually involved the same part, but occasionally it occurred in an adjacent structure, i.e., flexion of the elbow with sensation in the hand.

---

[1] Extreme variations may be the result of localized cortical atrophy produced early in life.

The eyeball movements elicited from the anterior portion of the precentral gyrus and further anteriorly consisted almost exclusively of rotation of the eyes to the contralateral side, with an additional upward or downward component in occasional instances. The eyeball movements elicited from the precentral gyrus immediately anterior to the central fissure, on the other hand, exhibited rotation to the ipsilateral side nearly as frequently as rotation to the contralateral side, and, in addition, upward rotation and convergence were occasionally produced. Experimental work has given some indication of localization within the frontal eye fields (10). This literature has been recently summarized by Smith (26).

Our studies show that the most frequent eyelid movement was closure of the eyes. The next most frequent response was twitching or trembling of the eyelids and the least common was opening of the eyes, possibly because the eyes were usually open at the time of the stimulation. Usually the response was bilateral but purely contralateral responses did occur.

Under face movement are included those responses consisting of contraction of the upper and lower facial musculature. A bilateral movement occurred once and an ipsilateral response occurred in a second patient, all the remaining responses being contralateral. Lip movement was the most common of all the sensory or motor responses in the face area (160 stimulations) and they were mainly contralateral (107 stimulations). There were 16 bilateral responses and 2 ipsilateral. Opening of the jaw was the most common jaw movement produced, clonic twitching occurring about half as frequently, while closure of the jaw and pulling of the jaw to the contralateral side occurred still less frequently. In one instance the jaw pulled to the ipsilateral side. Tongue movements were usually retraction, protrusion, or twitching. Doubtless small movements of the tongue frequently escaped detection due to difficulties of observation. Throat movements were either swallowing or gagging. Masticatory or chewing movements were frequently associated with sensation in the tongue, roof of mouth, or throat, but also occurred alone.

These facial motor responses are more discrete than the better organized movements produced by stimulation in the lower animals. The transition as one ascends the animal scale from rat to the higher primates has been described by Walker and Green (27).

Cortical stimulation gives definite evidence of some bilateral representation in the motor face area in man. The relatively slight motor deficit produced by ablation of face area of the precentral gyrus in man suggests that the bilateral representation is more complete than the stimulation data would indicate. Bilateral representation in the face area of the monkey has been studied in detail by Green and Walker (15).

In a recent patient, stimulation (2 volts, 60 cycles per second, bipolar electrodes) at one point in the leg area, immediately anterior to the central fissure, repeatedly produced abduction and extension at the hip in both legs. This may be analogous to the bilateral motor responses of the extremities reported in primates by Bucy and Fulton (7) and by Wyss (35). Aside from this isolated instance, however, there have been no ipsilateral motor responses involving the extremities.

The difficulty in accurately describing in terms of muscular action the movements produced by cortical stimulation in human patients limits the detail with which we can discuss the way in which the motor cortex in man brings about a voluntary movement. More detailed studies of stimulation of the human motor cortex are necessary for correlation with the results of experimental stimulation of the motor cortex in the laboratory. Most of these latter studies have utilized minimal currents (6) (12) (14) (9) (17) (18) (19) (27), but recently maximal subconvulsive currents have been employed (21). The accumulation of careful studies of controlled ablations in man (8) is an important addition.

Second sensory area

The constant presence of second sensory areas in all species of experimental animals thus far studied by the method of evoked potentials (1) (2) (30) (31) (32) makes it probable that such an area is also present in man. A survey of over 350 stimulation records has revealed 8 patients in whom the presence of such an area in man would explain unexpected responses for which there was previously no explanation. Some of these were mentioned briefly, by one of us (W. P.), in the Ferrier Lecture for 1946 (24). These data are presented in this tentative light since we do not feel that sufficient information on this point is available yet for a more positive statement on the presence of such a second area in man.

In all these 8 patients, the responses were elicited from the foot of the sensorimotor strip, just above the fissure of Sylvius (Figure 2). In 3 patients, the area in question was in the precentral gyrus; in 3, it was in the postcentral gyrus; and in 2, it involved both. There were 19 responses in these 8 patients. Fourteen were sensory responses, 2 were motor and sensory, and 3 were motor. The sensory and motor responses were equally distributed as far as lateralization was concerned: 8 were contralateral; 2 were ipsilateral; and in 9, the lateralization was not stated. Thirteen involved the arm, 3 the leg, 2 the arm and leg, and 1 the mouth and arm. The distal

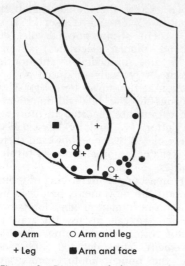

● Arm   ○ Arm and leg

+ Leg   ■ Arm and face

Figure 2   Diagram of the central region of the right hemisphere with summary of stimulations suggesting the presence of a secondary sensory and motor area in man.

portions of the extremities were primarily involved, two thirds of the responses being referred to the hand or foot, one sixth to the digits and the remaining one sixth to the arm or leg. In 6 patients the right hemisphere was stimulated and in 2 the left. The sensations produced were described by the patients in terms similar to those used to describe sensation produced elsewhere throughout the central area.

In view of the presence of motor responses in this area as well as sensory phenomena it is of interest to note that Garol (14) identified a second motor area in the cat in a location that corresponds closely with the second sensory area mapped out by Adrian (1) and Woolsey (31) (34).

Summary

1. As a result of further stimulation studies in man, certain modifications in the sensory sequence are suggested: (a) The head as a whole is represented between trunk and arm. (b) Neck sensation seems to belong between the head representation and trunk. (c) Tongue sensation has been moved to below teeth, gums and jaw, conforming to its location in the motor sequence. (d) Taste has been eliminated from the sequence of the cortical convexity since it occurs very rarely as a result of stimulation here, although somatic sensation in the tongue is the most frequent sensory response in the face area. (e) Intra-abdominal sensation has been added to the lower end of the sequence, below throat. The extent of this representation, which is largely precentral, into the island of Reil has not yet been determined.

2. Sensory responses simultaneously in more than one of the area units of the face region are fairly frequent. The same is true among the units of the upper extremity. It is, however, very rare that overlap occurs between the three major regions—face, upper extremity, lower extremity. This may cast light on the fact demonstrated by Dusser de Barenne and McCulloch (11) that each of these regions may be activated in animals by local application of strychnine without activating the adjacent major region.

3. Stimulation of the banks of the Rolandic fissure has shown that the sensory and motor responses produced there are similar in character and location to those elicited from the superficial surfaces of the pre- and postcentral gyri.

4. In the motor sequence certain minor alterations are also suggested: (a) Salivation and mastication are represented in the lower portion of the motor face area. The latter is predominantly postcentral in location and below tongue, whereas simple jaw movements are predominantly precentral in location and located above tongue. (b) Neck movements are represented between the area for finger movements and the upper margin of the face area.

5. Vocalization may be produced in man from an area between upper face and throat of both the dominant and non-dominant hemispheres, either alone or with movement or sensation in the various structures about or in the mouth.

6. Conjugate eye movements toward the opposite side are produced by stimulation anterior to the precentral gyrus without seeming to be confined to a discrete architectonic area. Eye movements produced from the precentral gyrus may be conjugate to either side or upward, or may be movements of convergence. Eye sensation is produced by stimulation anterior to the central fissure but not posterior.

7. Evidence is presented for the possible existence of a second sensory area for arm and leg in the cortex adjacent to the fissure of Sylvius. It seems likely also that there may exist in the same zone a second representation of movement.

References

1. Adrian, E. D. *J. Physiol.* **98**: 16P–18P, 1940.
2. Adrian, E. D. *J. Physiol.* **100**: 159–191, 1941.
3. Adrian, E. D. *Brain.* **66**: 89–103, 1943.
4. Adrian, E. D. *Brain.* **69**: 1–8, 1946.
5. Bard, P. *Bull. New York Acad. Med.* **14**: 585–607, 1938.
6. Bucy, P. C. *Arch. Neurol. & Psychiat.* **30**: 1205–1225, 1933.
7. Bucy, P. C., and Fulton, J. F. *Brain.* **56**: 318–342, 1933.

8. Bucy, P. C. The Precentral Motor Cortex, Ed. P. C. Bucy, *Illinois Monographs in the Medical Sciences*, vol. 4, Univ. Illinois Press, Chap. 14, 1944.

9. Chang, H., Ruch, T. C., and Ward, A. A., Jr. *J. Neurophysiol.* **10**: 39–56, 1947.

10. Clark, S. L., Ward, J. W., and Dribben, I. S. *J. Comp. Neurol.* **74**: 409–419, 1941.

11. Dusser de Barenne, J. G., and McCulloch, W. S. *J. Neurophysiol.* **1**: 69–85, 1938.

12. Dusser de Barenne, J. G., Garol, H. W., and McCulloch, W. S. *J. Neurophysiol.* **4**: 287–303, 1941.

13. Erickson, T. C. *Arch. Neurol. & Psychiat.* **53**: 226–231, 1945.

14. Garol, H. W. *J. Neuropath. & Exper. Neurol.* **1**: 139–145, 1942.

15. Green, H. D., and Walker, A. E. *J. Neurophysiol.* **1**: 262–280, 1938.

16. Hayes, G. H., and Woolsey, C. N. *Federation Proc.* **3**: 18, 1944.

17. Hines, M. *J. Neurophysiol.* **3**: 443–466, 1940.

18. Hines, M. The Precentral Motor Cortex, Ed. P. C. Bucy, *Illinois Monographs in the Medical Sciences*, vol. 4, Univ. Illinois Press, Chap. 18, 1944.

19. Kennard, M., and McCulloch, W. S. *J. Neurophysiol.* **5**: 231–234, 1942.

20. Marshall, W. H., Woolsey, C. N., and Bard, P. *J. Neurophysiol.* **4**: 1–24, 1941.

21. Murphy, J., and Gellhorn, E. *Arch. Neurol. & Psychiat.* **54**: 256–273, 1945.

22. Penfield, W., and Boldrey, E. *Brain.* **60**: 389–443, 1937.

23. Penfield, W., and Boldrey, E. *Am. J. Psychiat.* **96**: 255–281, 1939.

24. Penfield, W. *Proc. roy. Soc., B,* (in press).

25. Rahm, W. E., and Scarff, J. E. *Arch. Neurol. & Psychiat.* **50**: 183–189, 1943.

26. Smith, W. K. The Precentral Motor Cortex, Ed. P. C. Bucy, *Illinois Monographs in the Medical Sciences*, vol. 4, Univ. Illinois Press, Chap. 12, 1944.

27. Walker, A. E., and Green, H. D. *J. Neurophysiol.* **1**: 152–165, 1938.

28. Woolsey, C. N. *Am. J. Physiol.* **123**: 221–222(p), 1938.

29. Woolsey, C. N., Marshall, W. H., and Bard, P. *Bull. Johns Hopkins Hosp.* **70**: 339–441, 1942.

30. Woolsey, C. N., Marshall, W. H., and Bard, P. *J. Neurophysiol.* **6**: 287–291, 1943.

31. Woolsey, C. N. *Federation Proc.* **2**: 55, 1943.

32. Woolsey, C. N., *Federation Proc.* **3**: 53, 1944.

33. Woolsey, C. N., and Wang, G. H. *Federation Proc.* **4**: 79, 1945.

34. Woolsey, C. N., and Fairman, D. *Surgery.* **19**: 684–701, 1946.

35. Wyss, O. A. M. *J. Neurophysiol.* **1**: 125–126, 1938.

M OTIVATION AND EMOTION

This summary article brings together much of the evidence for the hypothalamus as a motivational center.

When the motor system is considered, the concept of the "final common path" is often used. Many excitatory and inhibitory influences act upon the motor cells in the spinal cord. The transmission of impulses to muscles depends upon what happens in this last link in the chain, "the final common path." Thus, many influences from elsewhere in the nervous system are integrated in this final link. By analogy, although it may be somewhat strained, one may think of the hypothalamus as containing neurons which are "the final common path" for the physiological motives.

The author also criticizes his own theory. Much of this criticism has been

Points to guide your study

1. Figure 1 is a good summary of the theory. Can you summarize this theory of physiological motivation in your own words?
2. Review the chapter on motivation (see your text).

omitted.

57. THE PHYSIOLOGY OF MOTIVATION

Eliot Stellar, University of Pennsylvania*

In the last twenty years motivation has become a central concept in psychology. Indeed, it is fair to say that today it is one of the basic ingredients of most modern theories of learning, personality, and social behavior. There is one stumbling-block in this noteworthy development, however, for the particular conception of motivation which most psychologists employ is based upon the outmoded model implied by Cannon in his classical statement of the local theories of hunger and thirst (23). Cannon's theories were good in their day, but the new facts available on the physiological basis of motivation demand that we abandon the older conceptualizations and follow new theories, not only in the study of motivation itself, but also in the application of motivational concepts to other areas of psychology.

This argument for a new theory of motivation has been made before by Lashley (42) and Morgan (47). But it is more impelling than ever today because so much of the recent evidence is beginning to fit into the general theoretical framework which these men suggested. Both Lashley and Morgan pointed out that the local

* E. Stellar. The Physiology of Motivation. *Psychol. Rev.,* 1954, **61**, 5–22. Copyright 1954 by the American Psychological Association. Excerpts reprinted here with permission from the author and the American Psychological Association. In shortening this article some interesting data have been omitted. The interested reader is referred to the original.

factors proposed by Cannon (e.g., stomach contractions or dryness of the throat) are not necessary conditions for the arousal of motivated behavior. Instead, they offered the more inclusive view that a number of sensory, chemical, and neural factors cooperate in a complicated physiological mechanism that regulates motivation. The crux of their theory was described most recently by Morgan as a *central motive state* (*c.m.s.*) built up in the organism by the combined influences of the sensory, humoral, and neural factors. Presumably, the amount of motivated behavior is determined by the level of the *c.m.s.*

Beach (8, 11), in his extensive work on the specific case of sexual motivation, has amply supported the views of Lashley and Morgan. But the important question still remains: Do other kinds of motivated behavior fit the same general theory? As you will see shortly, a review of the literature makes it clear that they do. As a matter of fact, there is enough evidence today to confirm and extend the views of Lashley, Morgan, and Beach and to propose, in some detail, a more complete physiological theory of motivation.

There are a number of ways to present a theoretical physiological mechanism like the one offered here. Perhaps the best approach is to start with an overview and summarize, in a schematic way, the major factors at work in the mechanism. Then we can fill in the details by reviewing the literature relevant to the operation of each factor. Some advantage is lost by not taking up the literature according to behavioral topics, that is, different kinds of motivation. But the procedure adopted here lets us focus attention directly on the theory itself and permits us to make some very useful comparisons among the various kinds of motivation. Once the theoretical mechanism and the evidence bearing on it are presented, the final step will be to evaluate the theory and show what experiments must be done to check it and extend it.

Theoretical scheme

A schematic diagram of the physiological mechanism believed to be in control of motivated behavior is shown in Figure 1. The basic assumption in this scheme is that *the amount of motivated behavior is a direct function of the amount of activity in certain excitatory centers of the hypothalamus*. The activity of these excitatory centers, in turn, is determined by a large number of factors which can be grouped in four general classes: (*a*) *inhibitory hypothalamic centers* which serve only to depress the activity of the excitatory centers, (*b*) *sensory stimuli* which control hypothalamic activity through the afferent impulses they can set up, (*c*) *the internal environment* which can influence the hypothalamus through its rich vascular supply and the cerebrospinal fluid, and (*d*) *cortical and thalamic centers* which can exert excitatory and inhibitory influences on the hypothalamus.

As can be seen, the present theory holds that the hypothalamus is the seat of Morgan's *c.m.s.* and is the "central nervous mechanism" Lashley claimed was responsible for "drive." Identifying the hypothalamus as the main integrating mechanism in motivation makes the experimental problem we face more specific and more concrete than ever before. But it also makes it more complicated, for the physiological control of the hypothalamus is exceedingly complex. The influence of the internal environment on the hypothalamus is changing continuously according to natural physiological cycles, and of course it may often be changed directly by the chemical and physical consequences of consummatory behavior (see Figure 1). Sensory stimuli may also have varied effects on the hypothalamic mechanism, depending upon their particular pattern, previous stimulation, previous learning, sensory feedback from the consummatory behavior itself, and the influence the internal environment has already exerted on the hypothalamus. Similarly, the influence of the cortex and thalamus will add to the hypothalamic activity already produced by sensory stimuli and the internal environment. Presumably, these cortical and tha-

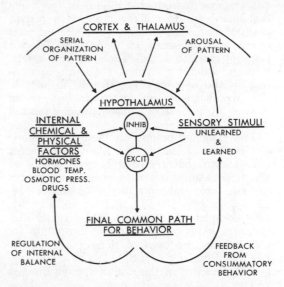

Figure 1   Scheme of the physiological factors contributing to the control of motivated behavior. (See text.)

lamic influences may result directly or indirectly from sensory stimulation, but they may also be controlled partly by the "upward drive" of the hypothalamus itself (43). Then, to complicate the picture even more, there are the inhibitory centers of the hypothalamus which are also controlled by the various internal changes, sensory stimuli, and cortical and thalamic influences. These centers, presumably, depress the activity of the excitatory centers and, therefore, attenuate their output.

Fortunately, this mechanism is not as formidable against experimental attack as it might appear. The basic experimental approach is to isolate the controlling factors in any type of motivation and determine their relative contributions to hypothalamic activity. As you will see, a number of experimental techniques like sensory deprivation, hormone and drug administration, cortical ablation, and the production of subcortical lesions may be used fruitfully to isolate these factors. But that is only half the problem. Obviously, the factors controlling hypothalamic activity and motivation do not operate in isolation. In fact, it is quite clear that their influences interact. Therefore, it becomes an equally important problem to determine the relative contribution of each factor while the others are operating over a wide range of variation.

Experimental evidence

Hypothalamic centers.   Review of the literature on the role of the hypothalamus in motivation brings out three general conclusions.

(*a*) Damage to restricted regions of the hypothalamus leads to striking changes in certain kinds of motivated behavior. (*b*) Different parts of the hypothalamus are critical in different kinds of motivation. (*c*) There are both excitatory and inhibitory centers controlling motivation in the hypothalamus; that is, damage to the hypothalamus can sometimes lead to an increase in motivation and sometimes a marked decrease.

The evidence bearing on these three points can be summarized briefly. Many experiments have shown that restricted bilateral lesions of the hypothalamus will make tremendous changes in basic biological motivations like hunger (16, 22), sleep (49, 50, 53), and sex (6, 18, 20). Less complete evidence strongly suggests that the same kinds of hypothalamic integration are also true in the cases of thirst (61), activity (35), and emotions (5, 62). We have only suggestive evidence in the case of specific hungers (59).

It is clear that there is some kind of localization of function within the hypothalamus although it is not always possible to specify precisely the anatomical nuclei subserving these functions. The centers for hunger are in the region of the ventromedial nucleus which lies in the middle third of the ventral hypothalamus, in the tuberal region (16). (See Figure 2.) Sleep is controlled by centers in the extreme posterior (mammillary bodies) and extreme anterior parts of the hypothalamus (49, 50). The critical region for sexual behavior is in the anterior hypothalamus, between the optic chiasm and the stalk of the pituitary gland (18, 20). The center for activity is not clearly established, but seems to be adjacent with or overlapping the centers for hunger (35). Finally, the centers for emotion are also in the vicinity of the ventromedial nucleus, perhaps somewhat posterior to the hunger centers and overlapping the posterior sleep center (50, 62).

In at least two cases it is clear that there must be both excitatory and inhibitory centers controlling motivated behavior. In the case of hunger, bilateral lesions in the ventromedial nucleus near the midline produce a tremendous amount of overeating (3, 16). Such a center is presumably an inhibitory one since removing it leads directly to an increase in eating behavior. On the other hand, lesions 1½ to 2 millimeters off the midline at the level of the ventromedial nucleus completely eliminate hunger behavior (3, 4). After such lesions animals never eat again, so we can call such centers excitatory centers. Supporting this interpretation is the fact, recently reported, that stimulating these lateral centers in the waking cat through implanted electrodes results in vast overeating (27). The same sort of mechanism turns up in

the case of sleep. In the posterior hypothalamus, in the region of the mammillary bodies, there are excitatory centers or "waking" centers which operate to keep the organism awake (49, 50). When they are removed, the animal becomes somnolent and cannot stay awake. In the anterior hypothalamus, around the preoptic nucleus, there is an inhibitory center (49). When that is removed, the animal is constantly wakeful.

So far, only an excitatory center has been found in the case of sexual behavior. Bilateral lesions anterior to the pituitary stalk eliminate all mating behavior (18, 20), but no lesion of the hypothalamus has ever been reported that resulted in an exaggeration of sexual motivation. What little we know about the center for activity near the ventromedial nucleus suggests that it is also an excitatory center since lesions there produce only inactivity and not hyperactivity (35). In the case of emotions, the picture is not yet clear. Lesions near the ventromedial nucleus make cats highly emotional (62), and therefore this center must be inhibitory. But the lateral regions of the posterior hypothalamus seem to be excitatory, for lesions there make animals placid (50). Furthermore, direct stimulation of these posterior regions produces many of the signs of rage reactions (52).

There is some evidence that sheds light on how the excitatory and inhibitory hypothalamic centers may cooperate in the regulation of motivation. In the clear-cut cases of sleep and hunger it appears that the inhibitory centers operate mainly through their effects on the excitatory centers. At least we know that when both centers are removed simultaneously the effect is indistinguishable from what happens when only the excitatory centers are removed (3, 49). So it is convenient for present theoretical purposes to think of the inhibitory center as one of the factors which influences the level of activity of the excitatory center. In fact, to speculate one step further, it is worth suggesting that the inhibitory centers may constitute the primary neural mechanism regulating the satiation of motivation.

Sensory stimuli. What effects do sensory stimuli have upon the hypothalamus and how important are such stimuli in the control of motivation? Some answer to the first part of this question is given by the schematic outline of hypothalamic connections shown in Figure 2. Clearly the hypothalamus has a rich supply of afferents coming directly or indirectly from all the various sense organs. In fact the diagram is really an understatement of hypothalamic connections because it is an oversimplified and conservative representation. Physiological evidence shows, for example, that there must be connections from the taste receptors via the solitary

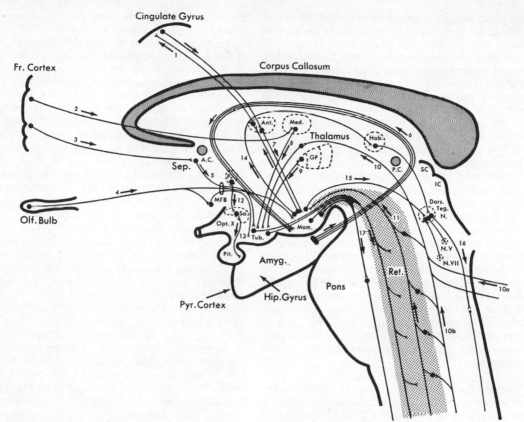

Cingulate Gyrus

Fr. Cortex

Corpus Callosum

Thalamus

Olf. Bulb

Sep.

Amyg.

Pyr. Cortex   Hip. Gyrus

Pons   Ret.

Abbreviations and description of pathways

A.C.	Anterior commissure
Amyg.	Amygdala
Ant.	Anterior thalamic nuclei
Cingulate Gyrus	Cortex of cingulate gyrus
Dors. Teg. N.	Dorsal tegmental nucleus
Fr. Cortex	Cortex of frontal lobe
GP	Globus pallidus
Hab.	Habenular nucleus of thalamus
Hip. Gyrus	Hippocampal gyrus
IC	Inferior colliculus
Mam.	Mammillary nuclei
Med.	Dorsal medial thalamic nucleus
MFB	Medial forebrain bundle
N.V	Motor nucleus, Vth nerve
N.VII	Motor nucleus, VIIth nerve
Olf. Bulb	Olfactory bulb
Opt. X	Optic chiasm
P.C.	Posterior commissure
Pit.	Pituitary gland
Pv.	Paraventricular nucleus
Pyr. Cortex	Pyriform cortex
Ret.	Reticular formation
SC	Superior colliculus
Sep.	Septal nuclei
So.	Supraoptic nucleus
Tub.	Tuber cinereum

Afferents to hypothalamus

1. Corticothalamic fibers
2. Frontothalamic fibers
3. Frontoseptal fibers
4. Olfacto-hypothalamic tract
5. Septo-hypothalamic fibers
6. Fornix
7. Mammillothalamic tract
8. Thalamo-hypothalamic fibers
9. Pallido-hypothalamic fibers
10. Sensory systems ascending to thalamus
    10 a. cranial afferents
    10 b. somatic and visceral afferents
11. Sensory collaterals to hypothalamus
12. Paraventriculo-supraoptic fibers

Efferents from hypothalamus

13. Supraoptic hypophyseal tract
14. Mammillohabenular tract
15. Mammillotegmental tract
16. Dorsal longitudinal fasciculus
17. Descending efferents relaying in brain stem and medulla

Figure 2   Schematic drawing of the hypothalamus and its major neural connections. Adapted from W. R. Ingram's diagram in Gellhorn (30) and D. B. Lindsley's Figure 9 (43).

nucleus of the medulla (36). Also there is evidence of rich connections from the visual system via the lateral geniculate of the thalamus (36). There is no doubt about the fact that the hypothalamus is under very extensive sensory control.

What we know about hunger and thirst suggests that the amount of motivated behavior in

these cases should be a joint function of sensory impulses arising from gastric contractions or dryness of the throat and taste, tactile, and temperature receptors in the mouth. Unfortunately we have no sensory deprivation experiments that are a good test of this point. But all the evidence on the acceptability of foods and fluids of different temperatures, consistencies, and flavoring suggests the joint operation of many stimuli in the control of these types of motivation.

So far, we have mentioned only stimuli which arouse motivation. What stimulus changes could reduce motivation and perhaps lead to satiation? There are three general possibilities: (*a*) a reduction in excitatory stimuli, (*b*) interfering or distracting stimuli that elicit competing behavior, and (*c*) "inhibitory" stimuli. It is easy to find examples of the first two types of stimulus changes and to guess their mechanisms of operation in terms of the present theory. In the case of "inhibitory" stimuli, however, all we have is suggestive evidence. For example, the fact that dogs with esophageal fistulas eat (37) and drink (1, 13) amounts proportional to the severity of deprivation suggests that the stimuli which feed back from consummatory behavior might have a net inhibitory effect on motivation (see Figure 1). Furthermore, some of the experiments on artificially loading the stomach suggest that a full gut may result in stimuli which inhibit further eating (37) or drinking (2, 13) over and above the possibility that there might be no room left in the stomach or that gastric contractions are reduced.

Internal environment. That the internal environment plays an important role in certain kinds of motivated behavior is a well-established fact. Two basic questions must be asked, however, before we can understand much about how the internal environment does its work. What kinds of changes that can occur in the internal environment are the important ones in motivation? How do changes in the internal environment influence the nervous system and, therefore, motivated behavior?

A very similar mechanism seems to be involved in the case of motivated behavior dependent upon the organism's defenses against temperature extremes, (activity, nesting, hoarding, selection of high-calorie diets). We know, for example, that reactions regulating body temperature in the face of heat and cold are integrated in two separate centers in the hypothalamus (15, 51). Lesions in the anterior hypothalamus destroy the ability to lose heat and, therefore, to survive in high temperatures. Posterior hypothalamic lesions, conversely, result in a loss of heat production mechanisms so that the animal succumbs to cold. Furthermore, artificially raising the temperature of the anterior hypothalamus will quickly induce heat loss, suggesting that normally the temperature of the blood may be important in activating the hypothalamic mechanisms (15, 44). Unfortunately our information stops here. There are no direct physiological studies on the role of these temperature-regulating mechanisms in the control of motivated behavior like activity, hoarding, nesting, or food selection. But it seems clear that the temperature of the blood may be one of the kinds of changes in the internal environment that can affect the hypothalamus, and it may be important in motivated behavior.

Ample evidence demonstrates that there are important changes in the internal environment involved in other kinds of motivated behavior. In hunger it has been shown that chemicals like insulin (32, 33, 48) and d-amphetamine (57) influence the rate of eating. It is clear that these chemicals do not operate primarily through their effects on gastric contractions, but it is only by a process of elimination that we can guess that their sites of action are in the hypothalamus. Supporting this possibility is the evidence that there are chemoreceptors in the hypothalamus which are sensitive to variations in blood sugar and important in the regulation of hunger (45). In the case of specific hungers, much evidence shows that food preference and diet selection depend upon changes in the internal environment produced by such things as pregnancy, dietary deficiencies, or disturbances of endocrine glands (54). Furthermore there are some preliminary experimental data, in the case of salt and sugar appetites, to suggest that there are separate regulatory centers in the hypothalamus which are responsive to changes in salt and sugar balance (59). Finally, in the case of thirst we know that a change in osmotic pressure, resulting from cellular dehydration, is the important internal change leading to drinking behavior (31). We know further that in the hypothalamus there are nerve cells, called "osmoreceptors," which are extremely sensitive to minute changes in osmotic pressure (61). But the direct experiment has not been done to check whether or not it is these nerve cells which are mainly responsible for the control of thirst.[1]

It is clear from the foregoing that many types of motivated behavior are dependent upon changes in the internal environment. Several points are worth emphasizing. (*a*) A variety of kinds of changes in the internal environment can play a role in the regulation of motivation: variation in the concentration of certain chemicals, especially hormones, changes in osmotic pressure, and changes in blood temperature. (*b*) The best hypothesis at present is that these internal changes operate by contributing to the

[1] In a recent publication, Anderson of Stockholm has shown that injection of small quantities of hypertonic NaCl directly into restricted regions along the midline of the hypothalamus produces immediate and extensive drinking in water-satiated goats. (B. Anderson. The effect of injections of hypertonic NaCl-solutions into different parts of the hypothalamus of goats. *Acta Physiol. Scand.*, 1953, **28**, 188–201.)

activity of excitatory hypothalamic centers controlling motivation. (c) An equally important but less well-supported hypothesis is that internal changes, normally produced by consummatory behavior, operate in the production of satiation by depressing excitatory centers or arousing inhibitory centers of the hypothalamus.

Cortical and thalamic centers. The case of emotions offers the best example of how the cortex may operate in motivation. According to the early work of Bard and his co-workers on the production of "sham rage" by decortication, it looked as though the entire cortex might normally play an inhibitory role in emotions (5). More recent work, however, shows that cortical control of emotion is more complicated than this. Bard and Mountcastle (7), for example, have found that removal of certain parts of the old cortex (particularly amygdala and transitional cortex of the midline) produced a tremendous increase in rage reactions in cats. On the other hand, removing only new cortex resulted in extremely placid cats. Results of work with monkeys (40) and some very recent experiments with cats disagree somewhat with these findings in showing that similar old cortex removals lead to placidity rather than ferocity. The disagreement is yet to be resolved, but at least it is clear that different parts of the cortex may play different roles in the control of emotion, certain parts being inhibitory and others excitatory.

In the case of sleep, it appears so far that the cortex and thalamus play excitatory roles, perhaps having the effect of maintaining the activity of the waking center in the posterior hypothalamus. Decortication in dogs, for example, results in an inability to postpone sleep and remain awake for very long, or, as Kleitman puts it, a return to polyphasic sleep and waking rhythms (38, 39). Studies of humans, moreover, show that even restricted lesions of the cortex or thalamus alone can result in an inability to stay awake normally (25, 26). But no inhibitory effects of the cortex in sleep have yet been uncovered.

In sexual behavior it has been found that lesions of the new cortex may interfere directly with the arousal of sexual behavior (9, 11). Large lesions are much more effective than small lesions, as you might expect. Furthermore, cortical damage is much more serious in male animals than in females and is much more important in the sexual behavior of primates than it is in the case of lower mammals. On the other hand, in connection with studies of the cortex in emotions, it has been found that lesions of the amygdala and transitional cortex of the midline can lead to heightened sexuality in cats and monkeys (7, 40). So it looks as though the

cortex may exert both excitatory and inhibitory influences in sexual motivation.

Evidence from other types of motivated behavior is only fragmentary, but it fits into the same general picture. In the case of hunger, it has been reported that certain lesions of the frontal lobes will lead to exaggerated eating behavior (41, 55). Hyperactivity may follow similar frontal lobe lesions and is particularly marked after damage to the orbital surface of the frontal lobe (56). The frontal areas may also be involved in what might be called pain avoidance. Clinical studies of man show that lobotomies may be used for the relief of intractable pain (29). The curious thing about these cases is that they still report the same amount of pain after operation but they say that it no longer bothers them. Presumably the frontal cortex normally plays an excitatory role in the motivation to avoid pain.

In all the cases cited so far, the anatomical and physiological evidence available suggests strongly that the main influence of the cortex and thalamus in motivation is mediated by the hypothalamus. But we do not yet have direct proof of this point and need experiments to check it.

Summary and conclusions

A physiological theory of motivated behavior is presented. The basic assumption in this theory is that the amount of motivated behavior is a function of the amount of activity in certain excitatory centers of the hypothalamus. The level of activity of the critical hypothalamic centers, in turn, is governed by the operation of four factors.

1. Inhibitory centers in the hypothalamus directly depress the activity of the excitatory centers and may be responsible for the production of satiation.

2. Sensory stimuli set up afferent impulses which naturally contribute to the excitability of the hypothalamus or come to do so through a process of learning.

3. Changes in the internal environment exert both excitatory and inhibitory effects on the hypothalamus.

4. Cortical and thalamic influences increase and decrease the excitability of hypothalamic centers.

Detailed experimental evidence is brought forward to show how these various factors operate in the management of different kinds of motivated behavior. The over-all scheme is shown diagrammatically in Figure 1.

Out of consideration of this evidence a number of hypotheses are generated to fill in the gaps in experimental knowledge. All these hypotheses are experimentally testable. The ones of major importance can be given here as a summary of what the theory states and a partial list of the experiments it suggests.

1. There are different centers in the hypothalamus responsible for the control of different kinds of basic motivation.

2. In each case of motivation, there is one main excitatory center and one inhibitory center which operates to depress the activity of the excitatory center.

There is already much experimental evidence supporting these two general hypotheses, but it is not certain that they apply fully to all types of basic biological motivation. The hypotheses should be checked further by determining whether changes in all types of motivation can be produced by local hypothalamic lesions and whether both increases and decreases in motivation can always be produced.

3. The activity of hypothalamic centers is, in part, controlled by the excitatory effects of afferent impulses generated by internal and external stimuli.

4. Different stimuli contribute different relative amounts to hypothalamic activity but no one avenue of sensory stimulation is indispensable.

5. It is the sum total of afferent impulses arriving at the hypothalamus that determines the level of excitability and, therefore, the amount of motivation.

The neuroanatomical and neurophysiological evidence shows that the hypothalamus is richly supplied with afferents coming directly and indirectly from all the sense organs (Figure 2). The behavioral evidence, furthermore, strongly suggests that motivation is never controlled, in mammals at least, by one sensory system, but rather is the combination of contributions of several sensory systems. Sensory control and sensory deprivation experiments are needed to check this point in the case of most kinds of biological motivation, particularly hunger, thirst, and specific hungers.

6. A variety of kinds of physical and chemical changes in the internal environment influences the excitability of hypothalamic centers and, therefore, contributes to the control of motivation.

The evidence shows that the hypothalamus is the most richly vascularized region of the central nervous system and is most directly under the influence of the cerebrospinal fluid. Furthermore, it is clear that changes in the internal environment produced by temperature of the blood, osmotic pressure, hormones, and a variety of other chemicals are important in motivation and most likely operate through their influence on the hypothalamus. Direct studies are still needed in many cases, however, to show that the particular change that is important in motivation actually does operate through the hypothalamus and vice versa.

7. The cerebral cortex and thalamus are directly important in the temporal and spatial organization of motivated behavior.

8. Different parts of the cortex and thalamus also operate selectively in the control of motivation by exerting excitatory or inhibitory influences on the hypothalamus.

Tests of these hypotheses can be carried out by total decortication, partial cortical ablations, and local thalamic lesions. It should be especially instructive to see what effects cortical and thalamic lesions have after significant changes in motivation have been produced by hypothalamic lesions.

9. Learning contributes along with other factors to the control of motivation, probably through direct influence on the hypothalamus.

10. The relative contribution of learning should increase in animals higher and higher on the phylogenetic scale.

A whole series of experiments is needed here. Particularly, there should be comparisons of naive and experienced animals to determine the relative effects of sensory deprivation, cortical and thalamic damage, and hypothalamic lesions. Presumably animals that have learned to be aroused to motivated behavior by previously inadequate stimuli should require more sensory deprivation but less cortical and thalamic damage than naive animals before motivation is significantly impaired.

11. The various factors controlling motivation combine their influences at the hypothalamus by the addition of all excitatory influences and the subtraction of all inhibitory influences.

Some experiments have already been done in the study of sexual motivation to show that motivation reduced by the elimination of one factor (cortical lesions) can be restored by increasing the contribution of other factors (hormone therapy). Many combinations of this kind of experiment should be carried out with different kinds of motivated behavior.

A number of the limitations and some of the advantages of the present theoretical approach to the physiology of motivation are discussed.

References

1. Adolph, E. F. The internal environment and behavior. Part III. Water content. *Amer. J. Psychiat.*, 1941, 97, 1365–1373.
2. Adolph, E. F. Thirst and its inhibition in the stomach. *Amer. J. Physiol.*, 1950, **161**, 374–386.
3. Anand, B. K., and Brobeck, J. R. Hypothalamic control of food intake in rats and cats. *Yale J. Biol. Med.*, 1951, 24, 123–140.
4. Anand, B. K., and Brobeck, J. R. Localization of a "feeding center" in the hypothalamus of the rat. *Proc. Soc. exp. Biol. Med.*, 1951, 77, 323–324.

5. Bard, P. Central nervous mechanisms for emotional behavior patterns in animals. *Res. Publ. Ass. nerv. ment. Dis.*, 1939, 19, 190–218.

6. Bard, P. The hypothalamus and sexual behavior. *Res. Publ. Ass. nerv. ment. Dis.*, 1940, 20, 551–579.

7. Bard, P., and Mountcastle, V. B. Some forebrain mechanisms involved in the expression of rage with special reference to the suppression of angry behavior. *Res. Publ. Ass. nerv. ment. Dis.*, 1947, 27, 362-404.

8. Beach, F. A. Analysis of factors involved in the arousal, maintenance and manifestation of sexual excitement in male animals. *Psychosom. Med.*, 1942, 4, 173–198.

9. Beach, F. A. Central nervous mechanisms involved in the reproductive behavior of vertebrates. *Psychol. Bull.*, 1942, 39, 200–206.

10. Beach, F. A. Relative effect of androgen upon the mating behavior of male rats subjected to forebrain injury or castration. *J. exp. Zool.*, 1944, 97, 249–295.

11. Beach, F. A. A review of physiological and psychological studies of sexual behavior in mammals. *Physiol. Rev.*, 1947, 27, 240–307.

12. Beach, F. A. Evolutionary changes in the physiological control of mating behavior in mammals. *Psychol. Rev.*, 1947, 54, 297–315.

13. Bellows, R. T. Time factors in water drinking in dogs. *Amer. J. Physiol.*, 1939, 125, 87–97.

14. Bremer, F. Etude oscillographique des activités sensorielles du cortex cérébral. *C. R. Soc. Biol.*, 1937, 124, 842–846.

15. Brobeck, J. R. Regulation of energy exchange. In J. F. Fulton (Ed.), *A textbook of physiology*. Philadelphia: Saunders, 1950. Pp. 1069–1090.

16. Brobeck, J. R., Tepperman, J., and Long, C. N. H. Experimental hypothalamic hyperphagia in the albino rat. *Yale J. Biol. Med.*, 1943, 15, 831–853.

17. Bromiley, R. B., and Bard, P. A study of the effect of estrin on the responses to genital stimulation shown by decapitate and decerebrate female cats. *Amer. J. Physiol.*, 1940, 129, 318–319.

18. Brookhart, J. M., and Dey, F. L. Reduction of sexual behavior in male guinea pigs by hypothalamic lesions. *Amer. J. Physiol.*, 1941, 133, 551–554.

19. Brookhart, J. M., Dey, F., and Ranson, S. W. Failure of ovarian hormones to cause mating reactions in spayed guinea pigs with hypothalamic lesions. *Proc. Soc. exp. Biol. Med.*, 1940, 44, 61–64.

20. Brookhart, J. M., Dey, F. L., and Ranson, S. W. The abolition of mating behavior by hypothalamic lesions in guinea pigs. *Endocrinology*, 1941, 28, 561–565.

21. Brooks, C. M. The role of the cerebral cortex and of various sense organs in the excitation and execution of mating activity in the rabbit. *Amer. J. Physiol.*, 1937, 120, 544–553.

22. Brooks, C. M. Appetite and obesity. *N. Z. med. J.*, 1947, 46, 243–254.

23. Cannon, W. B. Hunger and thirst. In C. Murchison (Ed.), *A handbook of general experimental psychology*. Worcester, Mass.: Clark Univer. Press, 1934. Pp. 247–263.

24. Craigie, E. H. Measurements of vascularity in some hypothalamic nuclei of the albino rat. *Res. Publ. Ass. nerv. ment. Dis.*, 1940, 20, 310–319.

25. Davison, C., and Demuth, E. L. Disturbances in sleep mechanism: a clinico-pathologic study. I. Lesions at the cortical level. *Arch. Neurol. Psychiat.*, Chicago, 1945, 53, 399–406.

26. Davison, C., and Demuth, E. L. Disturbances in sleep mechanism: a clinico-pathologic study. II. Lesions at the corticodiencephalic level. *Arch. Neurol. Psychiat.*, Chicago, 1945, 54, 241–255.

27. Delgado, J. M. R., and Anand, B. K. Increase of food intake induced by electrical stimulation of the lateral hypothalamus. *Amer. J. Physiol.*, 1953, 172, 162–168.

28. Dempsey, E. W., and Rioch, D. McK. The localization in the brain stem of the oestrous responses of the female guinea pig. *J. Neurophysiol.*, 1939, 2, 9–18.

29. Freeman, W., and Watts, J. W. *Psychosurgery*. (2nd Ed.) Springfield, Ill.: Charles C Thomas, 1950.

30. Gellhorn, E. *Autonomic regulations*. New York: Interscience, 1943.

31. Gilman, A. The relation between blood osmotic pressure, fluid distribution and voluntary water intake. *Amer. J. Physiol.*, 1937, 120, 323-328.

32. Grossman, M. I., Cummins, G. M., and Ivy, A. C. The effect of insulin on food intake after vagotomy and sympathectomy. *Amer. J. Physiol.*, 1947, 149, 100–102.

33. Grossman, M. I., and Stein, I. F. Vagotomy and the hunger producing action of insulin in man. *J. appl. Physiol.*, 1948, 1, 263–269.

34. Harris, L. J., Clay, J., Hargreaves, F. J., and Ward, A. Appetite and choice of diet. The ability of the Vitamin B deficient rat to discriminate between diets containing and lacking the vitamin. *Proc. roy. Soc.*, 1933, 113, 161–190.

35. Hetherington, A. W., and Ranson, S. W. The spontaneous activity and food intake of rats with hypothalamic lesions. *Amer. J. Physiol.*, 1942, 136, 609–617.

36. Ingram, W. R. Nuclear organization and chief connections of the primate hypothalamus. *Res. Publ. Ass. nerv. ment. Dis.*, 1940, 20, 195–244.

37. Janowitz, H. D., and Grossman, M. I. Some factors affecting the food intake of normal dogs and dogs with esophagostomy and gastric fistula. *Amer. J. Physiol.*, 1949, **159**, 143–148.

38. Kleitman, N. *Sleep and wakefulness.* Chicago: Univer. of Chicago Press, 1939.

39. Kleitman, N., and Camille, N. Studies on the physiology of sleep. VI. Behavior of decorticated dogs. *Amer. J. Physiol.*, 1932, **100**, 474–480.

40. Klüver, H., and Bucy, P. C. Preliminary analysis of functions of the temporal lobes in monkeys. *Arch. Neurol. Psychiat., Chicago*, 1939, **42**, 979–1000.

41. Langworthy, O. R., and Richter, C. P. Increased spontaneous activity produced by frontal lobe lesions in cats. *Amer. J. Physiol.*, 1939, **126**, 158–161.

42. Lashley, K. S. Experimental analysis of instinctive behavior. *Psychol. Rev.*, 1938, **45**, 445–471.

43. Lindsley, D. B. Emotion. In S. S. Stevens (Ed.), *Handbook of experimental psychology.* New York: Wiley, 1951. Pp. 473–516.

44. Magoun, H. W., Harrison, F., Brobeck, J. R., and Ranson, S. W. Activation of heat loss mechanisms by local heating of the brain. *J. Neurophysiol.*, 1938, **1**, 101–114.

45. Mayer, J., Vitale, J. J., and Bates, M. W. Mechanism of the regulation of food intake. *Nature, Lond.*, 1951, **167**, 562–563.

46. Miller, N. E., Bailey, C. J., and Stevenson, J. A. F. Decreased "hunger" but increased food intake resulting from hypothalamic lesions. *Science*, 1950, **112**, 256–259.

47. Morgan, C. T. *Physiological psychology.* (1st Ed.) New York: McGraw-Hill, 1943.

48. Morgan, C. T., and Morgan, J. D. Studies in hunger. 1. The effects of insulin upon the rat's rate of eating. *J. genet. Psychol.*, 1940, **56**, 137–147.

49. Nauta, W. J. H. Hypothalamic regulation of sleep in rats; an experimental study. *J. Neurophysiol.*, 1946, 9, 285–316.

50. Ranson, S. W. Somnolence caused by hypothalamic lesions in the monkey. *Arch. Neurol. Psychiat.*, 1939, **41**, 1–23.

51. Ranson, S. W. Regulation of body temperature. *Res. Publ. Ass. nerv. ment. Dis.*, 1940, **20**, 342–399.

52. Ranson, S. W., Kabat, H., and Magoun, H. W. Autonomic responses to electrical stimulation of hypothalamus, preoptic region and septum. *Arch. Neurol. Psychiat., Chicago*, 1935, **33**, 467–477.

53. Ranström, S. *The hypothalamus and sleep regulation.* Uppsala: Almquist and Wiksells, 1947.

54. Richter, C. P. Total self regulatory functions in animals and human beings. *Harvey Lect.*, 1942–43, **38**, 63–103.

55. Richter, C. P., and Hawkes, C. D. Increased spontaneous activity and food intake produced in rats by removal of the frontal poles of the brain. *J. Neurol. Psychiat.*, 1939, **2**, 231–242.

56. Ruch, T. C., and Shenkin, H. A. The relation of area 13 of the orbital surface of the frontal lobe to hyperactivity and hyperphagia in monkeys. *J. Neurophysiol.*, 1943, **6**, 349–360.

57. Sangster, W., Grossman, M. I., and Ivy, A. C. Effect of d-amphetamine on gastric hunger contractions and food intake in the dog. *Amer. J. Physiol.*, 1948, **153**, 259–263.

58. Scott, E. M., and Verney, E. L. Self selection of diet. VI. The nature of appetites for B vitamins. *J. Nutrit.*, 1947, **34**, 471–480.

59. Soulairac, A. La physiologie d'un comportement: L'appétit glucidique et sa régulation neuro-endocrinienne chez les rongeurs. *Bull. Biol.*, 1947, **81**, 1–160.

60. Tinbergen, N. *The study of instinct.* London: Oxford Univer. Press, 1951.

61. Verney, E. B. The antidiuretic hormone and the factors which determine its release. *Proc. roy. Soc., London*, 1947, **135**, 24–106.

62. Wheatley, M. D. The hypothalamus and affective behavior in cats. *Arch. Neurol. Psychiat.*, 1944, **52**, 296–316.

In recent years it has become more and more apparent that the nervous system acts in a unified manner. Thus, it is now an accepted fact, based in part upon evidence similar to that presented here, that there is efferent outflow from the central nervous system to the peripheral sense organs. The afferent input to the central nervous system from most of the receptors is modified by the central nervous system itself. When a system acts in this way to regulate its own activity, the principle of *negative feedback* is said to be in operation. This article illustrates, for auditory reception, this important principle of CNS functioning. (More recent evidence has shown that the effect may be caused by action on the muscles of the middle ear. The efferent outflow may act on these muscles to reduce the effectiveness of the conducting bones. The general feedback principle is still valid, however.)

The article also suggests a possible mechanism for the selection of sensory inputs which may be related to attentive behavior.

Points to guide your study

1. If you have difficulty with your first reading of this article, read it again. It's short. Look up words you don't know.

2. The article illustrates an important technique which is much used in neurophysiology and physiological psychology—the implantation of electrodes for stimulation or recording. This technique was also illustrated in Chapter 19.

A *stereotaxic instrument* is usually used in this implantation process. It is a device for locating certain points inside the skull. One works from a map of the brain on which the various structures are numbered by a series of coordinates. These coordinates are usually in terms of so many millimeters anterior or posterior from a certain point of reference, so many millimeters lateral from the midline, and so many millimeters deep. The animal's head is placed in the stereotaxic instrument, which is then set at the posterior-anterior and lateral map coordinates, and the electrode, in an electrode carrier, is then lowered to the proper depth. Hopefully, the electrode will then be in the structure indicated on the map.

3. Compare the behavioral and CNS records in Figure 1.

58. MODIFICATION OF ELECTRIC ACTIVITY IN COCHLEAR NUCLEUS DURING "ATTENTION" IN UNANESTHETIZED CATS

Raúl Hernández-Peón, University of Mexico, Harald Scherrer, University of British Columbia, and Michel Jouvet, University of Lyon*

Sensory motor mechanisms

Attention involves the selective awareness of certain sensory messages with the simultaneous suppression of others. Our sense organs are activated by a great variety of sensory stimuli, but relatively few evoke conscious sensation at any given moment. It is common experience that there is a pronounced reduction of extraneous sensory awareness when our attention is concentrated on some particular matter. During the attentive state, it seems as though the brain integrates for consciousness only a limited amount of sensory information, specifically, those impulses concerned with the object of attention.

An interference with impulses initiated by

* R. Hernández-Peón, H. Scherrer, and M. Jouvet. Modification of electric activity in cochlear nucleus during "attention" in unanesthetized cats. *Science*, 1956, **123**, 331–332. Copyright 1956 by the American Association for the Advancement of Science. Reprinted here with permission from the senior author, for the authors, and the American Association for the Advancement of Science.

sensory stimuli other than those pertaining to the subject of attention seems to be an obvious possibility. It is clear that this afferent blockade might occur at any point along the classical sensory pathways from receptors to the cortical receiving areas, or else perhaps in the recently disclosed extraclassical sensory paths that traverse the brain-stem reticular system (1).

Recent evidence indicates the existence of central mechanisms that regulate sensory transmission. It has been shown that appropriate stimulation of the brain-stem reticular system will inhibit afferent conduction between the first- and second-order neurons in all three principal somatic paths (2–4). During central anesthesia, the afferent-evoked potentials in the first sensory relays are enhanced. This appears to be due to the release of a tonic descending inhibitory influence that operates during wakefulness and requires the functional integrity of the brain-stem reticular formation.

The possibility that a selective central inhibitory mechanism might operate during attention for filtering sensory impulses was tested by studying (5) afferent transmission in the second- or third-order neurons of the auditory pathway (cochlear nucleus) in unanesthetized, unrestrained cats during experimentally elicited attentive behavior. Bipolar stainless steel electrodes with a total diameter of 0.5 mm were implanted stereotaxically in the dorsal cochlear nucleus through a small hole bored in the skull. The electrode was fixed to the skull with dental cement. A minimum of 1 week elapsed between

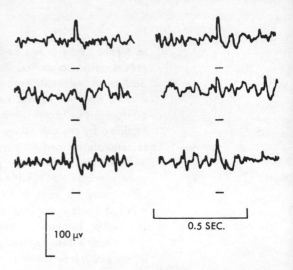

Figure 2   Click responses recorded from the cochlear nucleus of the cat. (Top) cat is relaxed; (middle) cat is attentively sniffing an olfactory stimulus; (bottom) cat is relaxed again. Note the reduced amplitude of the click responses when the animal is sniffing.

the operation and the first electroencephalographic recordings. Electric impulses in the form of short bursts of rectangular waves (0.01 to 0.02 sec) at a frequency of 1000 to 5000 cy/sec were delivered to a loudspeaker near the cats at an intensity comfortable to human observers in the same environment.

Three types of sensory modalities were used to attract the animal's attention: visual, olfactory, and somatic. As is illustrated in Figure 1, during presentation of visual stimuli (two mice in a closed bottle), the auditory responses in the cochlear nucleus were greatly reduced in comparison with the control responses; they were practically abolished as long as the visual stimuli elicited behavioral evidence of attention. When the mice were removed, the auditory responses returned to the same order of magnitude as the initial controls. An olfactory stimulus that attracted the animal's attention produced a similar blocking effect. While the cat was attentively sniffing tubing through which fish odors were being delivered, the auditory potential in the cochlear nucleus was practically absent (Figure 2). After the stimulus had been removed and when the cat appeared to be relaxed once more, the auditorily evoked responses in the cochlear nucleus were of the same magnitude as they had been prior to the olfactory stimulation. Similarly, a nociceptive shock delivered to the forepaw of the cat—a shock that apparently distracted the animal's attention—resulted in marked reduction of auditorily evoked responses in the cochlear nucleus.

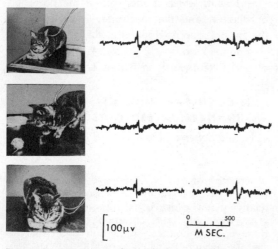

Figure 1   Direct recording of click responses in the cochlear nucleus during three periods: the photographs were taken simultaneously. (Top and bottom) cat is relaxed; the click responses are large. (Middle) While the cat is visually attentive to the mice in the jar, the click responses are diminished in amplitude.

If this sensory inhibition during attentive behavior, as demonstrated in the auditory pathway, occurs in all other sensory paths except the ones concerned with the object of attention, such an inhibitory mechanism might lead to favoring of the attended object by the selective exclusion of incoming signals. It is conceivable not only that such a selective sensory inhibition might operate simultaneously for various sensory modalities, leaving one or more unaffected but that the selectivity could extend to some discriminable aspects of any single modality—for example, to one tone and not to others. This suggestion finds support in the recent demonstration that sensory "habituation" may occur to a particular tone—that is, a slowly developing inhibitory effect on auditorily evoked potentials observed in the cochlear nucleus on prolonged repetition of a given tone, an influence that does not affect other frequencies that are novel to the animal (6). The pathway by which this inhibitory influence acts on incoming auditory impulses remains to be determined, but experiments now in progress have shown that during electric stimulation of the midbrain reticular formation, the auditory potential in the cochlear nucleus is depressed (7).

The present observations suggest that the blocking of afferent impulses in the lower portions of a sensory path may be a mechanism whereby sensory stimuli out of the scope of attention can be markedly reduced while they are still in their trajectory toward higher levels of the central nervous system. This central inhibitory mechanism may, therefore, play an important role in selective exclusion of sensory messages along their passage toward mechanisms of perception and consciousness. In a recent symposium on brain mechanisms and consciousness, Adrian pointed out that "the signals from the sense organs must be treated differently when we attend to them and when we do not, and if we could decide where and how the divergence arises we should be nearer to understanding how the level of consciousness is reached" (8).

References and notes

1. J. D. French, M. Verzeano, H. W. Magoun, Arch. Neurol. Psychiat. 69, 505 (1953).
2. K.-E. Hagbarth and D. I. B. Kerr, J. Neurophysiol. 17, 295 (1954).
3. R. Hernández-Peón and K.-E. Hagbarth, ibid. 18, 44 (1955).
4. H. Scherrer and R. Hernández-Peón, Federation Proc. 14, 132 (1955).
5. This work was aided by grants from the Commonwealth Fund, the National Institute for Neurological Diseases and Blindness of the U.S. Public Health Service, and Eli Lilly and Company. This report is based on a paper presented before the American Physiological Society on 12 Apr. 1955.
6. R. Hernández-Peón and H. Scherrer, Federation Proc. 14, 71 (1955); R. Hernández-Peón, M. Jouvet, H. Scherrer, in preparation.
7. M. Jouvet, E. Berkowitz, R. Hernández-Peón, in preparation.
8. E. D. Adrian, in Brain Mechanisms and Consciousness, J. F. Delafresnaye, Ed. (Blackwell, Oxford, 1954), p. 238.

LEARNING AND THINKING

This selection is an excerpt from a book in which psychological theorists discuss their theories. Each theorist was asked by a committee of the American Psychological Association to fill out an outline pertaining to his theory.

The theory presented here is an attempt to describe the possible states of the brain which correspond to memories and thoughts. The key concepts are those of the *cell assembly* and *phase sequence*. A much fuller account of the theory is to be found in Hebb's book *The Organization of Behavior*. The theory may or may not be a more or less correct account of the actual state of affairs in the brain. However, this way of thinking about the organization of the brain, especially the cerebral cortex, has been quite fruitful. The results in Melzack's article on pain and some of the results in Lilly's article on sensory deprivation may be explained in terms of this theory.

Points to guide your study

1. Apply the concept of the cell assembly to the disturbances of thought mentioned in Lilly's article.

2. Glossary: EMG—the electromyogram—Small electrical potentials which come from a contracting muscle may be recorded. Such potentials may be recorded in the absence of any visible movement. GSR—the galvanic skin response—Small changes in skin conductivity which are controlled by the autonomic nervous system. They may be recorded and used as indicators of emotion or arousal.

3. Note that Hebb maintains that behavior may provide useful hypotheses for neurophysiology. We usually think the other way. We often think that neurophysiology provides the explanation for behavior. In fact, this is not often the case at present.

59. A NEUROPSYCHOLOGICAL THEORY

D. O. Hebb, McGill University*

The key conception is that of the *cell assembly*, a brain process which corresponds to a particular sensory event, or a common aspect of a number of sensory events. This assembly is a closed system in which activity can "reverberate" and thus continue after the sensory event which started it has ceased. Also, one assembly will form connections with others, and it may therefore be made active by one of them in the total absence of the adequate stimulus. In short, the assembly activity is the simplest case of an *image* or an *idea*: a representative process. The formation of connections between assemblies is the mechanism of association.

The way in which the connections are established, between single neurons to form the assembly in the first place, or between neurons connecting one assembly with another, is as follows: If a neuron, A, is near enough to another, B, to have any possibility of firing it, and if it does take part in firing it on one occasion (it often requires two or more neurons working together to trigger the response in another), the probability is increased that when A fires next B will fire as a result. In other words, "synaptic resistance" is decreased, by a microscopic growth at the synapse or some chemical change in one of the two cells. The assembly might be made up of perhaps 25, 50, or 100 neurons, and building it up in the first place would be a very slow proc-

* D. O. Hebb. A neuropsychological theory. In Sigmund Koch (Ed.). *Psychology: a study of a science*, vol. 1. New York: McGraw-Hill, 1959, pp. 622–643. Copyright 1959 by the McGraw-Hill Book Company, Inc. Excerpts reprinted here with permission from the McGraw-Hill Book Company, Inc.

ess, requiring many repetitions of the stimulating conditions. These conditions might be a particular pattern of pressure in a small area of skin, exposure to a particular vowel sound, or an optical contour of a particular slope falling in the central foveal area; or they might be "relational," consisting of a decreased illumination as the eye moves from a lighter to a darker area, or of the common property ("hardness") of a series of tactual stimulations as the infant's hand touches a rattle, a bar of his crib, the milk bottle, and so forth.

It is proposed that these representative activities, each corresponding to some property of environmental stimulation, would form connecting links with each other and with concurrent motor activities, on the basis of the "synaptic resistance" postulate referred to above. Most assemblies would be established during the occurrence of particular motor activities (visual stimulation and eye movements, tactual stimulations and movement of the corresponding part of the body, auditory stimulation and vocalization); each would therefore establish neural connections with, and tend to produce, its own motor activity. However, actual muscle contraction would often not occur, because some other assembly activity occurring at the same time might inhibit the motor path, or simultaneously active assemblies might have motor effects that were physically incompatible with each other (e.g., flexing and extending a limb at the same time). Overt movements would result whenever such inhibition or conflict was absent.

The *phase sequence* is a temporally integrated series of assembly activities; it amounts to one current in the stream of thought. Each assembly activity in the series might be aroused (1) sensorily, (2) by excitation from other assemblies, or (3) in both ways. It is assumed that the last, (3), is what usually happens in an organized flow of behavior. Each assembly must establish connections with a number of other assemblies, at different times; which of these others it will arouse on any specific occasion will depend on what other activity, and especially what sensory activity, is going on at that moment. Assembly A tends to excite B, C, and D; sensory activity tends to excite D only, so A is followed by D. At each point in time, behavior would thus be steered both sensorily and centrally, jointly controlled by the present sensory input and the immediately prior central activity.

The possibility—or the inevitability, on the assumptions already made—that two or more phase sequences may run concurrently opens up the possibility that one may conflict with the other, in the sense that they may produce incoordinated behavior, motor components belonging to one sequence perhaps alternating randomly with those belonging to the other; or if one is inhibitory of the other, all motor outflow might be nullified. This, it is assumed, is what happens in gross emotional disturbances. The later development (since the theory was first published) of knowledge of the brain-stem arousal system on the whole fits in here rather well. Higher levels of arousal would increase the probability of incompatible assembly actions, or "conflicting" phase sequences in this sense, and hence contribute to the incoordinations of strong emotion [5].

A closely related possibility is that the occurrence of two phase sequences simultaneously, which have never occurred with just that timing before, will produce new combinations of motor components that have adaptive value. This is considered to be insight behavior, and the new combination of assemblies at that moment means seeing the situation in a new way.

Set, in this scheme, is the influence of the preexistent central activity on the next link in the phase-sequence chain. The animal is presented with a stimulus situation that can arouse different central activities, each meaning a different motor response; which will occur is in part determined by excitation from assemblies already active. The significance of the theory, as I see it, is principally in trying to get these central processes out of the bushes where we can look at them. Everyone knows that set and expectancy and the stimulus trace exist. How are we to learn more about these ideational or mediating processes, and the limits on their role in behavior, except by forming hypotheses (as explicit as we can reasonably make them) and then seeing what implications they have for behavior, and whether these implications are borne out in experiment? By all means, if you will, call these central events mediating processes instead of ideas or cell assemblies, but let us get busy and investigate them.

Variables dealt with, and level of analysis. It is clear that this theorizing is at several levels. The hypothesis about synaptic change is a very "molecular" one indeed. Each neuron might have up to a thousand such contacts with other neurons. The cell assembly might comprise something of the order of a hundred neurons. The perception of a simple object, or the "idea" or "image" of such an object, is supposed to consist of the activity of a number of assemblies, corresponding to its various properties, occurring within a time period of a second or so. A phase sequence, or series of assembly activities, would comprise a large number of assemblies.

Much of the theorizing is at the very molar level of assuming the existence of the phase sequence, with properties defined in rather general terms and no reference to constituent cellular activities. That is, the theory might be divided roughly in two parts. The main part, as far as actually dealing with behavior is concerned, assumes the existence of ideational elements renamed with a physiological reference (cell assemblies) and a stream of thought, also renamed (phase sequence). A logically separate part of the theory attempts to show how the ideational element would come about, on the basis of existing anatomical and physiological knowledge. This is the molecular aspect of the theorizing; the main part is molar.

Similarly the variables dealt with are at different levels. The *independent variables* are: sensory excitations, at varying levels of complexity of patterning, temporal as well as spatial; direct neural stimulations; content of blood stream and plasma, stimulating neural cells or modifying their excitability; and the structural and functional properties of the nervous system, controlled by using animals of different heredities, animals suffering from disease, or animals subjected to surgical injury.

The *intervening variables* are: unobserved functioning of sense organs, nervous system or effectors (e.g., gut movements, or changes of skeletal-muscle tension producing no overt change of posture), and activity of glands of internal secretion. In short, unobserved processes inside the skin which, one supposes, mediate the observed response.

Here particularly, it is important to be clear that different levels are involved, and one may get very far from what is reasonably considered to be a "hypothetical construct"—i.e., something potentially observable. For this and other reasons (see below), a "phase sequence" or "emotional disturbance" or a "conceptual activity" is a psychological construct, too complex to be directly examined; ten thousand electrodes, with simultaneous recordings, might be too few for the purpose—even if we knew where to place them.

The *dependent variables* are observed muscular and glandular activities, treated again at different levels of complexity. Also, such things as the EEG, EMG, and GSR may be dependent variables, but according to the context as well as the level of analysis, they may at other times be independent or intervening variables. The EEG, for example, would be an independent variable if one were to study intelligence in epileptics during subclinical attacks, comparing test performance in the subject when the EEG was abnormal and when it was not. At a low molecular level, an independent variable might be the punctate, momentary stimulation of a specific receptor group, and the dependent variable a single integrated movement of a limb or an eyeball. More frequently, however, discourse is at the level of making the sight of a particular object the independent variable and the dependent variable a movement of the whole animal toward or away from it. "The sight of an object" can be made more molecular, reduced hypothetically to a series of stimulations and responses in rapid sequence as the animal looks at the object. But only one such reduction would be possible at a time; in practice one could not deal with a maze run (e.g.) at this level, and would have to deal with such larger segments of behavior in more molar terms. More and less molar accounts of behavior are related in that one is prepared at any point to (hypothetically) make a reduction from the higher to the lower level, considering one of the higher items at a time.

It was said above that a phase sequence is a psychological construct, not a physiological one. The statement, which applies also to the cell assembly, needs explanation. Not only are these hypothetical processes too complex to be recorded physiologically; they also relate primarily to the behavior of the whole intact animal, and exist as constructs whose necessity is found only in the attempt to explain such behavior. It is the evidence of behavior that led Pavlov and Hull to the stimulus trace, not physiology; the physiological evidence, by itself, and for traces with time period of 10 to 15 secs, almost rules this out. It is behavior alone that justifies the conception of expectancy. When behavior indicates the existence of such forms of ideation or mediating process, we reconsider the evidence of anatomy and physiology and, with hindsight, see how the constructs may, conceivably, be made compatible with what we know of brain function; but this does not change the fact that they originated as *behavioral* constructs, nor the fact

that the knowledge we have of their properties is still derived mostly from behavior.

This becomes very clear indeed when one tries to translate them into physiological terms, as I did. I started with the preconception that ideation existed; the difficulty was to see what brain process could have the properties that ideation implies, in relation to behavior. The assembly did not follow logically from the neurological evidence; on the contrary, its specifications put a heavy strain on the evidence, and only the known existence of delayed response, expectancies, imagery, and so forth made the argument even remotely plausible.

What I mean by a psychological as opposed to a physiological construct, therefore, is that its referents are primarily in the behavior of the intact animal. One may name it, and hypothetically describe it, in physiological terms; but this is in the effort to maintain communication between different levels or universes of discourse. My theory is not an attempt to substitute physiology for psychology. No theory of the behavior of the whole animal could be, because in such a theory one is trying to deal with the functioning of the whole brain and nervous system, as influenced moment by moment by the whole internal environment, and the kind of construct one must work with ("learning capacity," "anxiety," "intelligence") takes one at times completely out of the universe of physiological method and its concentration on the functioning of part systems rather than of the whole body over extended periods of time.

Initial evidential grounds of the system. It has always seemed to me that learning is the crucial question in psychological theory. Even in talking about the innate or instinctive, one is concerned in a sense with delimiting the role of learning. But as has been said, all lines of thought about learning and memory seemed nullified by the facts of perception. It seemed certain to me that this hurdle would have to be crossed first.

This was not what happened. Without meaning to, I bypassed the strategically important perception. The solution found was one that married ideation and learning, and gave perception the second-rate status of a concubine. That is to say, the main structure of the theory was such as to provide for the acquisition (learning) of ideational processes, and for their part in subsequent modifications of behavior. Only then did I turn to the question of the equivalence of stimuli—the great stumbling block for learning theory—and the rather implausible treatment of this question was largely dictated by the direction the theory had already taken. When they were reexamined in detail, however, the facts of perception were not as clearly opposed to this line of speculation as I had thought—

some of them seemed instead clearly to support it—and so, as other facts began to fit together, it began to be possible to take all this seriously.

Constructing the theory was at first playing a little game, not a very serious undertaking. The idea about attention and set as being the selective action of some sort of self-maintaining (reverberatory?) process in the brain seemed a neat one, but unreal, because of failing to provide for sensory and cortical equipotentiality. But it had interesting possibilities when I went further, so a mechanism was worked out by which a "cell assembly" (though at that time it was referred to as a "lattice") might develop, in accord with what I knew about the anatomy and physiology of the visual system.

Here a check was encountered. The assembly would take a considerable time to develop, which implies that some of the most important aspects of perception and of learning would be delayed for an equally long time. The game was finished at this point—it seemed—because the implication was contrary to fact. Before giving it up, however, I cast around in an attempt to see how an experiment might be devised to test the question again, in the light of these new ideas, and then recalled vaguely the evidence compiled by von Senden [15] from all the cases of congenitally blind persons given their sight after they were old enough to report what they saw. I looked his monograph up again; what he reported, in short, was that the patient could not perceive patterns as normal persons do until he had been exposed to the visual world for a period of months, that there was no stimulus equivalence in this period, and that visual memory for patterns was almost at a zero level. Subsequently, if the patient kept on trying, these capacities showed a sharp rate of improvement, all about the same time. This evidence of course was very exciting; it fitted closely into the conception of a first period of slow development of assemblies and a subsequent period of normal performance (or nearly so) after the assemblies had reached an adequate level of functioning. At this point, then, I began to take the game seriously.

Almost at once, however, another difficulty arose. As the functioning of assemblies was thought of, it would have to occur in a perceptual environment in which most of the stimulus combinations were familiar; otherwise cells would fire chaotically and organized sequences of assembly action ("phase sequences") could not occur. Thus behavior would be random and uncoordinated in a strange environment, since an orderly progression of muscular movements would depend on an orderly sequence of brain events. Clearly—it seemed again—the idea that unfamiliar stimulus combinations would disorganize behavior was contrary to fact.

Now it happened that my serious research in the preceding months had dealt with the emotional sensitivity of the chimpanzees at the Yerkes Laboratories of Primate Biology, Orange Park, Florida. I had, as a matter of fact, just completed a paper reporting data for which I could find no rationale but which seemed too significant not to publish. When the idea occurred to me to identify chaotic assembly activity with emotion and when this, in a general way, made sense of a lot of facts about emotion that had made no sense before, I felt sure at last that I was in business as a theorist. If perception happened to get manhandled in making it accord with the rest of the theory, so much the worse for perception as the key determinant. But in fact, when I now went back over the perceptual evidence that had seemed so decisive before and looked at it from the new theoretical point of view, there were obviously large holes in it.

These incidents, in each of which a necessary implication first seemed a fatal flaw and then, when the behavioral evidence was looked at from the new point of view, became instead an asset, extending the scope of the theory, gave me confidence that the line pursued was sound. It also seemed quite clear that "physiologizing," if one physiologized on the right lines, could be broadening instead of narrowing, and could stimulate purely behavioral research as well as research employing physiological methods. The research in this laboratory on the adult's perception of printed words [12, 13, 17], for example, or the child's perception of inverted pictures [18], arose from the considerations just dealt with, as well as the larger program studying restrictions of the early environment and the development of intellectual and motivational processes [9, 4, 2, 11, 14]. Certain other physiological considerations were at the bottom of the study of restriction of the later environment [1, 3, 5]. It is also relevant to point out that the reevaluation of man's emotionality as a factor in his social behavior by Dr. Thompson and me [6] was specifically initiated by trying to see whether the implications of the physiologizing about emotion, referred to above, were (as they seemed) contrary to the facts of adult human behavior.

References

1. Bexton, W. H., Heron, W., and Scott, T. H. Effects of decreased variation in the sensory environment. *Canad. J. Psychol.*, 1954, **8**, 70–76.
2. Clarke, R. S., Heron, W., Fetherstonhaugh, M. L., Forgays, D. G., and Hebb, D. O. Individual differences in dogs: preliminary report on the effects of early experience. *Canad. J. Psychol.*, 1951, **5**, 150–156.

3. Doane, B. K. Changes in visual function with perceptual isolation. Unpublished doctoral dissertation, McGill Univer., 1955.

4. Forgays, D. G., and Forgays, Janet. The nature of the effect of free-environmental experience in the rat. *J. comp. physiol. Psychol.*, 1952, **45**, 322-328.

5. Hebb, D. O. Drives and the CNS (conceptual nervous system). *Psychol. Rev.*, 1955, **62**, 243-254.

6. Hebb, D. O., and Thompson, W. R. The social significance of animal studies. In G. Lindzey (Ed.), *Handbook of social psychology*. Cambridge, Mass.: Addison-Wesley, 1954.

7. Heron, W. Perception as a function of retinal locus. *Amer. J. Psychol.*, 1957, 70, 38-48.

8. Hunton, Vera. The perception of inverted pictures by children. *J. genet. Psychol.*, 1955, 86, 281-288.

9. Hymovitch, B. The effects of experiential variations in problem-solving in the rat. *J. comp. physiol. Psychol.*, 1952, **45**, 313-321.

10. Mahut, Helen. Breed differences in the dog's emotional behavior. In press.

11. Melzack, R. The genesis of emotional behavior. *J. comp. physiol. Psychol.*, 1954, **47**, 166-168.

12. Mishkin, M., and Forgays, D. C. Word recognition as a function of retinal locus. *J. exp. Psychol.*, 1952, **43**, 43-48.

13. Orbach, J. Retinal locus as a factor in the recognition of visually perceived words. *Amer. J. Psychol.*, 1952, **65**, 555-562.

14. Thompson, W. R., and Heron, W. The effects of restricting early experience on the problem-solving capacity of dogs. *Canad. J. Psychol.*, 1954, 8, 17-31.

15. Von Senden, M. *Raum-und Gestalt Auffassung bei Operierten Blinogeborenen. Vor und nach der Operation.* Leipzig: Barth, 1932.

Most of the cortex in man and the higher primates does not seem to have obvious sensory or motor functions. These are the "association" areas of the older terminology. A great deal of effort has been expended to determine the functions of these areas. In part, it has been found that they are responsible for rather subtle aspects of behavior. For instance, according to some, damage to the frontal lobes involves loss of the ability to perform delayed-response tasks and a lowering of general emotionality. The posterior association areas in the parietal, temporal and occipital lobes are said by some to involve the integration and organization of sensory input.

The authors of this article, in a number of short experiments, demonstrate this difference between frontal and posterior areas very nicely. This is also a good example of the use of ablation methods in the investigation of the correlation between brain and behavior.

Points to guide your study

1. How can the results of the present study be used against Lashley's argument of equipotentiality in cortical functioning?

2. Can you interpret the data from the experiments on facilitation of the delayed-response task. (experiments 4 to 7)?

60. ANALYSIS OF FRONTAL AND POSTERIOR ASSOCIATION SYNDROMES IN BRAIN-DAMAGED MONKEYS

*H. F. Harlow, University of Wisconsin, R. T. Davis, University of South Dakota, P. H. Settlage, and D. R. Meyer, Ohio State University**

This report summarizes a program of experiments on the behavior of brain-damaged monkeys. The ablations of the animals comprise extensive destruction of one hemisphere combined with decortication of either the contralateral prefrontal or parieto-temporo-preoccipital regions.

* This research was supported in part by the Research Committee of the Graduate School from funds supplied by the Wisconsin Alumni Research Foundation.

All the tasks investigated were varieties of delayed-response and discrimination problems. The studies were designed to further the analysis of the differential effects of anterior and posterior lesions upon performance in the two situations and to discover procedures that might enable monkeys with prefrontal lesions to perform efficiently on delayed-response tests.

It has already been shown that the monkeys with the additional frontal destruction have difficulty with delayed-response problems (10), whereas the animals with the additional posterior ablation are less efficient than normal controls in the solution of discrimination problems (13). Furthermore, the monkeys of the first group have very little trouble with discrimination problems (10), in keeping with earlier findings (4). To complete a picture of differential frontal and posterior syndromes, it is necessary to demonstrate that monkeys with posterior lesions are capable of delayed response. Jacobsen (4) believed that posterior lesions did not affect delayed response, but his position was questioned by Lashley (5), who found that some monkeys with ablations of the prestriate cortex could not perform delayed reactions. Lashley concluded that the delayed-response problem provides no basis for distinction between the functions of the anterior and posterior association areas. His conclusion has not, however, been confirmed by Meyer, Harlow, and Ades (9) or by Blum, Chow, and Pribram (1) except for the finding by the latter investigators that one monkey with isolated bilateral destruction of the tip of the temporal lobe could not be trained to solve delayed-response problems. Thus, the question is far from settled.

Experiments are described which demonstrate that massive posterior ablations which produce a lasting decrement in discrimination learning do not necessarily impair delayed response. It should be noted that this datum is useful from the standpoint of control for sensory loss, because demonstration of the adequacy of the visual system for the delayed-response situation is a very effective way to combat the interpretive difficulties that are born of the interruption or probable interruption of parts of the optic radiation.

The second phase of the investigation concerns the effects of variations in the over-all level of success upon the delayed-response performance of the prefrontal ablation monkeys. In no observations of animals with anterior lesions has this

H. F. Harlow, R. T. Davis, P. H. Settlage, and D. R. Meyer. Analysis of frontal and posterior association syndromes in brain-damaged monkeys. *J. comp. physiol. Psychol.*, 1952, **45**, 419–429. Copyright 1952 by the American Psychological Association. Reprinted here with permission from the authors and the American Psychological Association.

laboratory been able to confirm the reports of emotional flattening and indifference to failure that were instrumental in the initiation of the technique of prefrontal lobotomy. Instead, the behavioral changes have been in the opposite direction. Recently, Lichtenstein (6) has reported similar increased emotional lability in lobotomized dogs. The possibility that emotional lability might be a significant variable in the delayed-response situation was first explored by Campbell and Harlow (2), who found that delay limits for some monkeys were increased if trials with minimum delay were included in the test series. Another technique for maintenance of nonspecific success was explored by Meyer, Harlow, and Settlage (10), but the expected facilitation was not forthcoming. Four experiments have been designed to re-evaluate the findings of Campbell and Harlow and to explore the effects of interpolated discrimination learning upon delayed-response performance.

Further experiments are concerned with theoretical interpretations of delayed-response deficit. One viewpoint maintains that the animals are capable of making the relevant association, but for varying reasons they are unable to retain it for the requisite interval of time. Jacobsen's (4) "loss of immediate memory" and Malmo's (7) "increased susceptibility to retroactive inhibition" are examples of this class of hypothesis. The contrasting assumption is that the monkeys have difficulty because they fail to learn enough to solve the problem during the critical trial-setting period that precedes the interval of delay. Finan (3), Campbell and Harlow (2), Wade (12), Lashley (5), Pribram (11), and Meyer, Harlow, and Settlage (10) have all espoused varieties of this notion. Interest also centers in the manipulations that make differential acquisition possible. A study suggested by each of these approaches completes the experimental program.

Method

Subjects and apparatus. A group of 12 rhesus monkeys, all with very extensive and almost identical test experience, participated in this investigation. There were 4 normal controls and 8 operated animals with severe unilateral lesions combined with destruction of the contralateral-anterior or contralateral-posterior association areas. Idealized diagrams of the brains are shown in Figure 1. In keeping with other published reports of studies with this sample, the three groups are designated the Normal, the Frontal, and the Posterior. The period between operation and the initial test reported in this paper exceeded 4 mo. for both operated groups. The reported test program was completed in approximately 15 mo. The chronological order in which the experiments were carried out was as follows: Experiment 4, 1, 2, 5, 6, 7, 8, 3, 9, and 10.

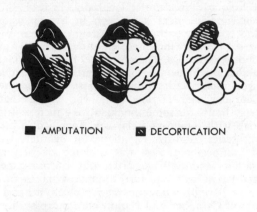

■ AMPUTATION   ◪ DECORTICATION

■ AMPUTATION   ◪ DECORTICATION

Figure 1A Extensive unilateral ablation combined with contralateral prefrontal ablation.
Figure 1B Extensive unilateral ablation combined with contralateral posterior ablation.

The basic item of equipment was the Wisconsin General Test Apparatus (2), which consists of a restraining cage, an adjacent table, and a superstructure that supports opaque and one-way vision screens. Mounted on the table is a rolling tray in which there are two small food wells spaced 12 in. apart. The task for the monkey in all problems is to displace one of two small stimulus objects (e.g., tobacco tin, rubber heel) placed over these food wells, and the animal is rewarded with a raisin or peanut for each correct choice.

General procedure. In each delayed-response trial the experimenter shows a piece of food to the monkey, drops it into one of the food wells, then simultaneously covers both wells with identical stimulus-objects. After a delay the tray is pushed to within reach of the monkey, and a single choice is permitted. Neither screen is used. Unless otherwise specified, the delay interval is 5 sec.

Each discrimination-learning problem employs, for a series of trials, a different pair of dissimilar stimulus-objects chosen from the laboratory's large collection of randomly paired and ordered

sets. On a given trial, the opaque screen of the apparatus is lowered and a piece of food is placed in the predetermined correct one of the two food wells on the test tray. Then, the predetermined correct stimulus-object is placed over this food well, and simultaneously, the predetermined incorrect object is placed over the other food well. The one-way vision screen in front of the experimenter is lowered, the opaque screen is raised, and the monkey is permitted to make a single choice.

The four animals in each of the three groups had been previously matched to form four groups of three animals, and in every experiment a single experimenter always conducted the tests on a matched Normal, Frontal, and Posterior monkey.

Specific procedures and results

Experiment 1. Estimates of performance of the three groups in a straightforward, direct-method delayed-response situation were obtained in this experiment. There were 12 daily sessions, 36 trials per day, with the delay interval constant at 5 sec. The position of the reward was arranged so that the effects of shifts after varying numbers of trials could be ascertained, but this proved not to be a relevant variable.

Scores for individual animals are given in Table 1. Although the Normal animals averaged less than 1 per cent errors and the Posteriors about 6 per cent, the mean for the Frontal subjects was almost 37 per cent. One Frontal animal made only 18 per cent errors, but the rest scored 40 per cent or greater. The differences between the means of all three groups are statistically significant at or beyond the .05 level as tested by the Mann-Whitney procedure (8), the method used for all the group statistical analyses reported in this paper.

Inasmuch as Meyer, Harlow, and Settlage (10) found that the present Frontal group suffered a complete loss of delayed response immediately after operation for removal of the

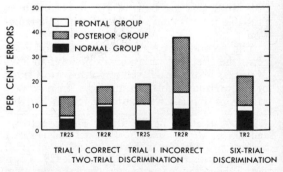

Figure 2 Mean per cent errors on Trial 2 of discrimination problems (Experiment 2).

Table 1   Per cent errors with 5-sec. delays (Experiment 1)

Normal group		Frontal group		Posterior group	
Subject	% errors	Subject	% errors	Subject	% errors
127	0.2	114	45.0	117	10.0
128	0.4	120	40.0	122	10.0
129	0.0	126	18.0	123	0.9
130	1.1	131	43.0	125	2.5
M	0.4	M	36.5	M	5.8

second prefrontal area, the obtained scores suggest a partial recovery. Nevertheless, the Normal animals improved even more, which points to the operation of some other factor. Comparable scores for the Posterior group are not available from the earlier study, for at that time the animals were still unilateral preparations. The data of the present study, however, show unequivocally that the subjects are still quite capable of delayed-response performance after the additional ablation of the posterior areas.

Experiment 2. Two different types of discrimination problem were presented: (a) a standard six-trial and (b) a two-trial type analogous to Finan's (3) prefeeding delayed-response technique. For half the two-trial problems the initial choice of the monkey was rewarded regardless of the object chosen. In the remainder, the initial choice was inevitably wrong because neither food well was baited. In the first condition the object chosen on Trial 1 was rewarded on Trial 2, and in the second condition the object not chosen on Trial 1 was rewarded on Trial 2. The positions of the objects were so arranged that half the time the reward shifted position and half the time it did not. Each day for ten days the animals were given 16 such problems together with 4 standard six-trial discrimination problems.

The results for Trial 2 responses are summarized in Figure 2. This time, the Frontal group is almost the equal of the Normal, but the performance of the Posterior monkeys is quite inferior. They make more than twice as many errors as the Frontals in the ordinary six-trial problems and, under the least favorable two-trial condition, average 37 per cent errors. The differences between the Posterior group and each of the other groups on Trial 2 of the two-trial condition are significant at the .02 confidence level.

Experiment 3. The preceding data confirm the association of delayed-response and discrimination deficits with frontal and posterior lesions, respectively. A further instructive experi-

ment is one which combines the two problems so that the monkey has alternative bases for solution. Nine problems were presented each day for 12 days. Three of these were similar to the two-trial discrimination problems of Experiment 2, but the second trial added a delayed-response technique. The objects were displaced in full view of the animal, the appropriate food well was baited, and the objects were replaced. The monkey was permitted to choose after a delay of 5 sec. In the other six problems two or four discrimination trials preceded the combination trial.

The results are compared in Figure 3 with performance on the six-trial discrimination problems of Experiment 2. The Posterior group is clearly inferior to the Frontal on the ordinary discrimination problems, but clearly superior when the delayed response is possible. Posterior performance on the combination trials does not change as a function of the number of previous discrimination trials; this group's mean performance closely approximates the score obtained in Experiment 1.

An examination of the Frontal data shows that the added delayed-response cue does not improve performance. More significant is the fact that the efficiency was not reduced, for this indicates that the delayed-response technique per se is not

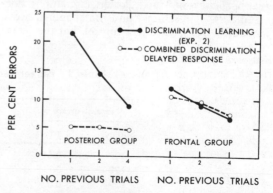

Figure 3 Performance of frontal and posterior monkeys on discrimination and combined discrimination—delayed-response trials (Experiment 3).

disruptive. This evidence may be interpreted as further support for the hypothesis that the emotional reactivity of the Frontal animals in the delayed-response situation is a response to failure.

Experiment 4. The first study in this series on the possible role of nonspecific success was set up to keep the Frontal monkeys test-active during the time that the Posterior group was recovering from the second operation. The procedure was patterned after that of Campbell and Harlow (2), and was designed to ascertain whether or not there is a functional relationship between the number of interpolated 0-sec. delayed-response trials and the level of performance on 5-sec. delays. Sequences were devised such that the tests were preceded by 1, 2, 4, or 8 0-sec. delay trials. Each day for five days 16 test trials were given. The trend obtained was unreliable and in a direction contrary to hypothesis: 31 per cent errors after 1 interpolation, 34 per cent after 2, and 39 per cent after 4 or 8. A repetition of this experiment with all three groups, ten days' testing, and 10-sec. delays gave no indication that increasing the number of interpolated 0-sec. delay trials in any way improved the performance of the Frontal animals on 10-sec. delays.

Experiment 5. The problem of facilitation by maintenance of success was continued with four sets of problems presented to the monkeys each day for ten days. Each set consisted of a four-trial discrimination problem, four 0-sec. delayed-response trials, and four 5-sec. delayed-response trials. The results are presented in Table 2.

Here, delayed-response performance of the Frontal group can only be described as phenomenal. All Frontal animals made scores far better than chance, and two of the four monkeys made less than 10 per cent errors. The difference between the Normal and Frontal animals is significant at the .05 level; the difference between the Frontal and Posterior groups is not significant. The score of no Frontal animal overlapped that of its Normal control, but the score

of one Frontal animal was superior to that of its matched Posterior. This is the only case in any of the delayed-response studies in which any Frontal animal equaled or exceeded its matched Normal or Posterior.

Experiment 6. Because the facilitation of performance that was obtained with the preceding technique far exceeded expectations, it was decided to concentrate on the interpolated discrimination problems as a procedure for supporting delayed-response performance. Each day for 24 days 12, 5-sec. delayed-response trials and 24 discrimination problems were presented to the monkeys. The problems appeared in four different orders, with two-trial and four-trial discrimination problems alternating with blocks of two or four delayed-response trials. Six-trial discrimination problems were used to complete the daily run on short sequences.

No evidence whatever of the facilitating effect found in Experiment 5 was obtained in Experiment 6. Over-all performance of the Frontal monkeys was 41.0 per cent errors contrasted with the 12.3 per cent errors of Experiment 5 and comparable to the 36.5 per cent errors in Experiment 1. There were no demonstrable systematic variations in performance from arrangement to arrangement. The performance of the Frontal monkeys on discrimination problems was also significantly less efficient than would be expected from the level achieved in Experiment 2. Rechecks of the data of Experiments 5 and 6 failed to reveal any clue to explain the discrepancy. The relative efficiency of all the subjects within the three groups was highly consistent even though the absolute error scores for all animals were greatly increased.

Experiment 7. Because of the discrepancy between the negative results of Experiments 4 and 6 and the positive findings of Experiment 5, the latter experiment was repeated 4 mo. later. The design was duplicated in every detail, but the facilitation of delayed-response performance by the Frontal group did not occur. The mean

Table 2   Per cent errors with 5-sec. delays on facilitated delayed-response test (Experiment 5)

Normal group		Frontal group		Posterior group	
Subject	% errors	Subject	% errors	Subject	% errors
127	0.6	114	3.7	117	7.5
128	3.7	120	6.9	122	5.0
129	0.0	126	18.1	123	2.9
130	0.0	131	20.6	125	5.6
M	1.1	M	12.3	M	5.2

score of the Frontal group for the second attempt was 33 per cent errors instead of the previously obtained 12 per cent. Another repetition four additional months later gave substantially the same results, the Frontal monkeys averaging 30 per cent errors. It should be pointed out, however, that two of the Frontal animals always made scores significantly better than chance at the .001 confidence level, one monkey never making more than 18 per cent errors and the other 26 per cent errors on any of the three identical experiments.

Experiment 8. In order to estimate any long-range changes in performance, 8 mo. after the completion of Experiment 1 a repetition of Experiment 1 was done by presenting 24 5-sec. delayed-response trials per day for 5 days instead of 36 trials per day for 12 days as in the earlier study. The results (Table 3) closely approximate those of Experiment 1 (Table 1), indicating no essential change in any group. The differences between the Frontal group and both the Normal and Posterior groups were significant at the .02 level.

Experiment 9. In keeping with the proposal of Meyer, Harlow, and Settlage (10) that monkeys with prefrontal ablations have difficulty with direct-method delayed response because they cannot react differentially during changes in the over-all level of stimulation, an attempt was made to facilitate Frontal performance with a variation in the trial-setting procedure. On each of 20 trials per day for 10 days the experimenter baited the appropriate food well, paused motionless for 10 sec., placed the stimulus-objects over the food wells, paused for another 5 sec., then permitted the animal to choose. The hoped-for momentary change in hyperactivity, which according to Wade (12) and Pribram (11) always precedes correct responses, was not elicited. The primary effect of this procedure was to increase the group variability of the Frontals, although the scores of both Normal and Posterior monkeys were somewhat improved. The Frontal group made 34 per cent errors, the Normal

group 2 per cent errors, and the Posterior group 4 per cent errors. The differences between the Frontal group and both the Normal and Posterior groups were significant at the .02 level.

Experiment 10. A final experiment grew from the observation that Frontal animals are quiet during the time that the test tray is in motion. It seemed possible that the closest approach to the Malmo (7) condition that can be arranged in the direct-method situation is one in which the problem is set at a considerable distance and the test tray is kept in slow and uniform motion during the entire delay period. The apparatus was modified to increase the distance of movement of the test tray from its usual 12 in. up to 20 in. The correct food well was baited and the stimulus-objects were placed with the apparatus in retracted position; then the tray was advanced at a rate of 4 in./sec. Under these conditions the mean performance for the Frontal group was 31 per cent errors, which is little or no better than their performance on most other delayed-response experiments reported in this paper. The differences between the Frontal group and each of the other groups were significant at the .02 level.

Discussion

Most of the implications of these ten experiments are already apparent. On the positive side, the differential effects of anterior and posterior lesions on delayed-response and discrimination learning are confirmed. The data support the original contention of Jacobsen (4) that the deficit in delayed response is characteristic of prefrontal ablations. The findings are not in accord with Lashley's (5) contention that similar impairment can be produced by extensive destruction of preoccipital cortex. Further, this sparing of function demonstrates that the concurrent deficits in discrimination learning with posterior lesions cannot be attributed primarily to interference with the visual input system.

The remainder of the experiments yield essentially negative results. None of the procedures for manipulation of nonspecific success produces

Table 3   Per cent errors with 5-sec. delays (Experiment 8)

Normal group		Frontal group		Posterior group	
Subject	% errors	Subject	% errors	Subject	% errors
127	3.0	114	22.5	117	15.8
128	1.6	120	18.3	122	3.3
129	1.6	126	50.0	123	0.0
130	0.8	131	45.0	125	3.3
M	1.8	M	34.0	M	5.6

significant facilitation, nor do the modifications of procedure studied consistently improve the performance of the prefrontal preparations. These data question the generality of the results obtained by Campbell and Harlow (2) with interspersed limited-delay trials, and do not support the hypothesis advanced by Meyer, Harlow, and Settlage (10) concerning the nature of delayed-response deficit in the prefrontal monkey.

The striking findings of these investigations are the severity of deficit on delayed-response performance that is produced by prefrontal lesions, the persistence of this deficit over a long period of time, and the failure to obtain any indication of improvement in delayed-response performance by the Frontal monkeys as a function of intensive training. Also obtained are confirmation and further substantiation, in monkeys with extensive bilateral frontal-area lesions, of a syndrome involving vast impairment of performance on delayed-response tests and little or no impairment on discrimination tests, and, in monkeys with extensive bilateral lesions in posterior associative areas, a syndrome involving serious impairment on discrimination-test performance and little or no impairment on delayed responses. The demonstration of differential and complementary frontal and posterior syndromes categorically refutes the assumption that associative cortex is equipotential.

Summary and conclusions

Four normal monkeys, four with bilateral frontal lesions, and four with bilateral posterior lesions, were studied in a series of 10 different experiments involving varieties of delayed-response and discrimination problems.

No delayed-response procedure was found that enabled the Frontal monkeys to perform consistently at a high level of efficiency, but performance of these animals on all discrimination tests was excellent. The Posterior monkeys, on the contrary, always showed inefficient performance on all tests of discrimination learning but efficient performance on all tests of delayed response.

In spite of the poor performance by Frontal animals on the delayed-response tests and the poor performance by the Posterior monkeys on discrimination tests, it should be emphasized that these lesions do not entirely eliminate such functions inasmuch as performance, at least by individual members of the operative groups, is always significantly better than chance.

The demonstration of differential and complementary frontal and posterior syndromes categorically refutes the hypothesis that associative cortex is equipotential.

References

1. Blum, Josephine S., Chow, K. L., and Pribram, K. H. A behavioral analysis of the organization of the parieto-temporo-preoccipital cortex. *J. comp. Neurol.*, 1950, **93**, 53–100.
2. Campbell, R. J., and Harlow, H. F. Problem solution by monkeys following bilateral removal of the prefrontal areas. V. Spatial delayed reactions. *J. exp. Psychol.*, 1945, **35**, 110–126.
3. Finan, J. L. Delayed response with pre-delay reenforcement in monkeys after the removal of the frontal lobes. *Amer. J. Psychol.*, 1942, **55**, 202–214.
4. Jacobsen, C. F. Studies of cerebral function in primates. *Comp. Psychol. Monogr.*, 1936, **13**, No. 63.
5. Lashley, K. S. The mechanism of vision XVIII. Effects of destroying the visual "associative areas" of the monkey. *Genet. Psychol. Monogr.*, 1948, **37**, 107–166.
6. Lichtenstein, P. E. Studies of anxiety: II The effects of lobotomy on a feeding inhibition in dogs. *J. comp. physiol. Psychol.* 1950, **43**, 419–427.
7. Malmo, R. B. Interference factors in delayed response in monkeys after removal of the frontal lobes. *J. Neurophysiol.*, 1942, **5**, 295–308.
8. Mann, H. B., and Whitney, D. R. On a test of whether one of two random variables is stochastically larger than the other. *Ann. math. Statist.*, 1947, **18**, 50–55.
9. Meyer, D. R., Harlow, H. F., and Ades, H. W. Retention of delayed responses and proficiency in oddity problems by monkeys with preoccipital ablations. *Amer. J. Psychol.*, 1951, **64**, 391–396.
10. Meyer, D. R., Harlow, H. F., and Settlage, P. H. A survey of delayed response performance by normal and brain-damaged monkeys. *J. comp. physiol. Psychol.*, 1951, **44**, 17–25.
11. Pribram, K. H. Some physical and pharmacological factors affecting delayed response performance of baboons following frontal lobotomy. *J. Neurophysiol.*, 1950, **13**, 373–382.
12. Wade, Marjorie. The effect of sedatives upon delayed response in monkeys following removal of the prefrontal lobes. *J. Neurophysiol.*, 1947, **10**, 57–61.
13. Warren, J. M., and Harlow, H. F. Learned discrimination performance by monkeys after prolonged postoperative recovery from large cortical lesions. *J. comp. physiol. Psychol.* 1952, **45**, 119–126.